D1025316

THE LABEL

THE LABEL

THE STORY OF
COLUMBIA RECORDS

CL 1515
NONBREAKABLE

SIDE I
XLP 7750

Gary Marmorstein

"360 SOUND" STEREO "360 SOUND"

© "COLUMBIA" MARCAS 🚶 REG. PRINTED IN U.S.A.

Thunder's Mouth Press
New York

THE LABEL
The Story of Columbia Records

Copyright © 2007 by Gary Marmorstein

Published by
Thunder's Mouth Press
An Imprint of Avalon Publishing Group, Inc.
245 West 17th Street, 11th Floor
New York, NY 10011

AVALON
publishing group incorporated

First Printing March 2007

Library of Congress Cataloging-in-Publication Data is available.

ISBN-13: 978-1-56025-707-3
ISBN-10: 1-56025-707-5

9 8 7 6 5 4 3 2 1

Interior book design by Bettina Wilhelm

Printed in the United States of America
Distributed by Publishers Group West

To Leslie and Darius

CONTENTS

LINER NOTES:

One Boy's Columbia Records

In the spring of 1963, our mother informed my brother Dan and me, ages eight and ten respectively, that we would be moving from New Jersey to Southern California at the end of summer. We'd suspected this was coming. Months earlier she'd left us with her parents while she and her second husband had gone west to investigate job possibilities. To ease our sense of abandonment, she'd allowed us to join the Columbia Record Club. Now, with the cross-country move imminent, we were permitted one last summer at camp in the Berkshires.

That summer one of our few nighttime camp outings was to the Pittsfield High School gymnasium to hear Joan Baez. My counselor professed a celestial love for Baez because she sang like a meadowlark, was already at the forefront of public social protest, and was undeniably beautiful. We sat in the gym's bleachers. Most of the counselors, like mine, sighed with admiration as Baez warbled her way through several folk anthems. I was unmoved, maybe because there didn't seem to be anything particularly personal about her songs. About halfway through the show, though, she brought on a scrawny young guy named Bob Dylan, whose second album, Baez announced, was about to be released by Columbia Records. Accompanying himself on guitar, Dylan sang "A Hard Rain's A-Gonna Fall" alone and "Blowin' in the Wind" with Baez, who clearly adored him. Her adoration rankled the camp counselors, for they were all about his age and wanted Baez to notice them, not this adenoidal kid with the curly hair. *I been out in front of a dozen dead oceans* was a line from "Hard Rain" and, attuned as I'd been to songs by Lerner & Loewe and Rodgers & Hammerstein, it was like nothing I'd heard before. After he'd sung his two songs, Dylan gave a little wave to the enthralled audience, then lost his footing going down the proscenium stairs and barely managed to steady himself on the iron banister, prompting howls of derision from the counselors.

Walking out into the humid Berkshires night, however, the counselors were silent, uneasily so, and I wondered if they were feeling something close to what I was feeling: Bob Dylan was dangerous. At ten I hadn't read yet Rimbaud, whose visionary poetry was said to have inspired Dylan; hadn't gotten stoned; considered myself "liberal" largely because my grandparents had been FDR Democrats who had also voted twice for Adlai Stevenson and for John F. Kennedy; and got to Greenwich Village, Dylan's neighborhood, only whenever my father, long divorced from my mother and living in the East Thirties, escorted me down there as though we were entering a foreign country. But Dylan's sensibility—the deceptively simple melodies, the Old Testament imagery, the simmering fury, personal as well as political—was shocking to me, and to practically everyone, young and old, I think, who heard him.

Around the time Dan and I were dragged kicking and screaming to Southern California, the '62 album *Bob Dylan* began to travel with us. Dylan's expression on the cover, somewhere between a smirk and a sneer, dared you to slide the LP out and listen. (The photographer was Don Hunstein, who has surely shot more Columbia covers than any other photographer.) In the coming decade we would await each new Dylan record as though it might change our lives. And in the forty years since that last summer in the Berkshires, this particular brother and I have each lived on different continents, in various dwellings, and worked for countless employers. But in all that time Dylan, excepting one brief fling with Asylum Records, has had only one working home: Columbia Records.

• • •

In the overlapping epochs of the 78-rpm platter, the 33-rpm vinyl disk, the cassette tape, and the compact disk, Columbia Records seemed to be everywhere. That ubiquitousness was true for no other record label, including the better capitalized RCA Victor. By definition a record label has an astonishing degree of power: with one signature on a contract, it can change in an instant the fortunes of a recording artist; and by distributing that artist's material to the world it provides a permanent record—a sound print that, for better or worse, becomes part of the culture. Decade by decade, Columbia launched the careers of our most seminal recording artists and deposited their sound prints onto the permanent record.

It did so by keeping its ears open not just in its corporate offices but in the most remote places. It's worth remembering that the American Record Company, Columbia's parent company before William S. Paley bought it in 1938 and restored the label's old name, cosponsored a motor trip through the Deep South by the writer-producer John Hammond. Accompanied by his new acquaintance Goddard Lieberson, the Eastman School of Music refugee who had no special love for jazz and blues but appreciated every kind of music, Hammond found the blind harmonica player Sonny Terry in North Carolina, signed Mitchell's Christian Singers for an upcoming concert at Carnegie Hall, and brought Big Bill Broonzy back to New York. Hammond and Lieberson were only two in Columbia's long line of legendary producers and A&R men— George Avakian, Teo Macero, and Mitch Miller among them—with extraordinary musical sensibilities. In the parlance of 1938 jazzmen, these cats had ears.

Musically, Columbia frequently found itself flat on its back, clueless, left behind. But part of its strength was its ability to pick itself up, dust itself off, and readjust according to the times. To stick with Hammond for the moment, in 1939 Hammond declined to record Billie Holiday singing Abel Meeropol's unique "Strange Fruit," insisting that the song made Holiday too studied and didn't allow her to swing. Although Columbia owned the masters to most of the recordings Holiday had made on Brunswick and Vocalion and could re-release those, she wouldn't record again for the label until the 1950s—and Hammond himself would be employed elsewhere for much of that period. Meanwhile the label, through the work of Avakian and others, had amassed a jazz catalog nonpareil. Two decades into CBS's ownership of the label, Joan Baez spurned a contract with Columbia because, given the hard sell in the company's Seventh Avenue offices, she found Hammond to be a patronizing blowhard, and signed instead with Vanguard, the premiere folk label of the era. (Hammond's one-sentence version of the episode: "I passed on Joan Baez, whom I had heard at the Newport Folk Festival, because she was asking a great deal of money while still a relatively unknown artist.")[1] Hammond, realizing he had blown a unique opportunity to cash in on the folk explosion, redoubled his efforts to find a young new artist. That was how Bob Dylan, the shambling kid I first heard in the summer of '63, landed at the label.

• • •

As I remember it, I first saw the ad for the Columbia Record Club in *The Reporter*, a left-leaning fortnightly that my grandparents subscribed to, whose advertisers included the usual mail-order promos (Book-of-the-Month Club, the Seven Arts Book Society, etc.). The Columbia Record Club offered five records for a total of $3.98 plus shipping costs. Send No Money, the promo assured, in the USA's buy-now-pay-later tradition. The club's address was in Terre Haute, Indiana. I pictured a football field–sized warehouse in the middle of the country sending the Columbia product out in all directions, spokes of a postal wheel. (That wasn't far from the truth, it turned out. Columbia was already pressing LPs in a factory nearby, making distribution that much more efficient. Its main rival, RCA Victor, was doing the same thing from Indianapolis. Both companies, however, maintained corporate headquarters and recording studios in midtown Manhattan.) To keep my end of the bargain, I agreed to purchase five more Columbia records, at the club's retail price, in the ensuing twelve months.

After intense discussions with my brother, those first five for $3.98

were selected. In each case there were extramusical considerations. I chose a Ray Conniff album because, as with most Conniff and Percy Faith albums on the label, its cover model quickened my pre-adolescent blood. (What is glamour to a ten-year-old? The concept changes according to the era he grows up in, doesn't it?) We went for *Time Out*, by the Dave Brubeck Quartet, partly because the Neil Fujita cover painting was the most arresting of all album covers, mostly because our father had a whole Brubeck collection in his studio apartment, so we knew what we were getting into. In fact our father owned hundreds of jazz records, a disproportionate number of them—Benny Goodman, Erroll Garner, recent Miles Davis, Duke Ellington, Charles Mingus—on Columbia. Visiting us in New Jersey once, our father stood on the front porch of our grandparents' house and pointed out a black man in the passenger seat of a white car as long as a yacht as it drove by. "There goes Monk," he said, the one name being at once mysterious and sufficient. Thelonious Monk was then commuting frequently between a house around the corner owned by Nica de Koenigswarter (we knew of her as the Baroness Rothschild) and the West 63rd Street apartment he shared with his wife Nellie and their children. Our father's record collection included plenty of Monk, though all of it was on Riverside or Prestige.

We chose the original cast recording of *West Side Story* because, though we knew the score almost note for note, we didn't own it. We were already staging mock rumbles, tossing butter knives back and forth between our hands, like George Chakiris in the movie version. Our fourth and fifth records, distributed by Columbia's major subsidiary Epic, were each made by the actor George Maharis. *Portrait in Music* and *George Maharis Sings!* were recorded in 1962 in an attempt to flood the market with the notion that Maharis was a legitimate singer. Maharis had been playing the often-hotheaded drifter Buzz Murdock on the CBS television series *Route 66* since 1960. My brother thought he was cool.

●　　●　　●

So we waited for the records to arrive. There were already, to be sure, many records in our grandparents' house, most of them 10" and 12" 78s. These had been filed in a large green box called the Regina Record Index, with slots for exactly one hundred records. Printed on the underside of the lid were one hundred rows for annotations on each record. A lot of the 78s were cracked, rendering them unplayable.

This was, as I saw it, the primary problem with those heavy, shellac-covered 78s. In 1962 the long-playing record (the LP) was more than a decade old but, as with so many new technologies, had taken a while to take hold, particularly for older listeners like my grandparents. My favorite episode of *The Honeymooners*, then in reruns on WPIX (Channel 11) in New York, was "The $99,000 Answer," written by Leonard Stern and Sydney Zelinka. In that episode Ralph Kramden (Jackie Gleason) bones up on the subject of popular music for his upcoming appearance on a quiz show. Offering his musical services, Ed Norton (Art Carney) moves a piano into the Kramdens' Brooklyn apartment, and together they go through much of the Tin Pan Alley catalog using sheet music interpreted by Norton's primitive piano playing. I regarded Kramden and Norton's study method as hopelessly inefficient because I could play dozens of songs from various LPs in a single evening simply by putting the records on the turntable. In 1956, however, when "The $99,000 Answer" was first broadcast, a piano was still a household fixture, not yet so widely displaced by the cool hearth of television, and playing songs from sheet music was probably no less efficient than carrying heavy stacks of 78s and going through each one.

Still, that Regina Record box contained some real beauties. There were plenty of Victors and Deccas, a few Capitols, and the odd Dot or Musicraft. The predominant label, however—red for the popular stuff, green for the Masterworks releases—was Columbia. And no Columbia artist in that box was more extensively represented than Frank Sinatra.

●　●　●

At my grandparents' house the Columbia 78s that got played all the time included Sinatra's "You Go to My Head." That record suggested an adult world—cocktails and love affairs and a nocturnal Manhattan—far out of my reach. At ten I didn't understand how startling Sinatra was when he'd made this record and so many others for Columbia, beginning in 1939, when he was singing with Harry James. If Bing Crosby was "the first hip white" singer, Sinatra was the first who seemed to believe every-thing he was singing, regarding the lyric as sacred. Sinatra's sincerity, coupled with his unerring sense of rhythm, turned even the most banal standard (one of them was "I Don't Know Why," the B side of "You Go to My Head") into something approaching the power of gospel.[2] In the wake of Sinatra's spectacular December 1942 run at the Paramount The-ater, Columbia had had the good sense to sign him as a solo artist and set him loose on what would become the Great American Songbook.

Sinatra was a presence at my grandparents' not just because of the Columbia records but because he'd bought a house for his parents behind the one my grandparents moved into in 1946. A great-uncle and -aunt knew him from Hoboken and from early radio days. On July 22 of that year my grandfather wrote to my mother, who was then away at the Berkshires camp I would attend eighteen years later:

I am sure you are having a wonderful time this summer, but you missed a great thrill last week. Nobody was home but [housekeeper extraordi-naire] Jessie one day when Frankie Sinatra walked in looking for Herb and Midge. If you had been there you would have had him all to your-self. As it was, when he gave Jessie his name, I am sure that she did not believe him. Anyway, he was stopping at Toots Shor's. . . .

By 1963, of course, Sinatra had been gone from Columbia for a decade. But because of all those red-labeled 78s in the house, he remained one of three high-profile artists I associated with Columbia. One of the other two was Mitch Miller—first a studio musician for CBS radio, later the label's dominant A&R man and a producer alternately admired and feared among recording artists. As a bandleader he had enjoyed eleven consecutive gold albums, all released by Columbia. *Sing Along with Mitch*, carried on NBC each week, put him front and center conducting a male chorus singing antique American songs while the lyrics rolled across the bottom of the screen to encourage sing-alongs. Even in the year before the Beatles appeared on *Ed Sullivan* and bent the course of popular music for the next half century, these songs were doddering. NBC carried *Sing Along with Mitch* through September 1964, but by then I had spurned the show as hopelessly dated.

By contrast, Leonard Bernstein, the other Columbia personality who was a TV fixture in the years up to and including 1963, never seemed dated. I knew about Bernstein from *West Side Story*, and from his *Young People's Concerts* in which he conducted the New York Philharmonic, the concerts broadcast on CBS beginning in 1958. On television Bernstein was no less glamorous than a movie star, "a lean, lanky genius with big hair" (Deborah Solomon's description in a *New York Times* jeremiad against Lincoln Center) "who removed the fussiness from classical music and brought out the bright, rousing rhythms."[3] For two decades Bernstein was the Columbia Masterworks tentpole, the figure that supported its prestigious catalog from dead center. On February 4, 1957, Bernstein's likeness had adorned the cover of *Time*. It was an era when symphony conductors could still be seen as heroic.

•　　•　　•

Finally those first five Columbia Records Club albums arrived by mail. The Ray Conniff was almost immediately consigned to the bottom of the pile, not because I was tired of looking at the cover model but because Conniff's anodyne, chorus-heavy arrangements reduced every track to the same mush. The two George Maharis albums, meanwhile, were recorded at a strange time in American culture. The junction where various kinds of popular music crisscrossed was bearing increasingly heavy traffic from rock 'n' roll; radio stations that programmed mostly Broadway and standards—what was termed MOR or middle-of-the-road—were overtaken by increasingly aggressive channels aimed squarely at the young (including me), who were seen as consistent, if capricious, consumers. The Broadway songs I had grown up on, so many of them first heard on the Columbia label, were now consigned to niche stations. "We could no longer duplicate the sales successes of *South Pacific, My Fair Lady,* or *Camelot,*" Clive Davis wrote of that period. "The most popular radio stations didn't play their songs. . . . It was as if Columbia had collected a vast vault of gold and then the country disavowed the gold standard."[4] Mitch Miller loathed rock 'n' roll and wouldn't touch it; Goddard Lieberson, though receptive to most music, had clearly marked out his territory, which was classical and Broadway, dominating those fields since the late forties. In 1963, just months before the British Invasion, rock music was little more than a footnote in the Columbia catalog. In keeping with Columbia's pattern, it would take a while before that was rectified.

As for Maharis, from *Route 66*'s Buzz Murdock I think my brother in particular expected something grittier and a bit insolent, though I didn't know those words then. Maharis and costar Martin Milner were the closest things in mainstream media to Jack Kerouac and Neal Cassady. What a letdown, then, to hear this TV idol's singing evoke not so much being on the road as reclining on a couch in Queens.

Route 66 was canceled by CBS before the fall 1964 season, and Maharis never did quite emerge as a singing star. Of the other Columbia Record Club albums, Brubeck's *Time Out* was played incessantly; on "Take Five" I'd advance the tone-arm to hear Joe Morello's drum solo in that eccentric 5/4 time. And the original cast recording of *West Side Story* is still with me, scratches and pops, monaural sound and all, the slightly mildew-warped cardboard cover with Larry Kert reaching joyously for Carol Lawrence's hand, the photographic frame unable to contain the Romeo and Juliet–like lovers.

• • •

My mother and stepfather finally found a new address. We all moved into a house in Redondo Beach, California. I pined for Manhattan, for evenings with my father in his "studio," and for the East in general. In the Redondo Beach garage my stepfather kept a German-made Grundig table radio—clear tone, elegantly lighted dial, a beautiful piece of furniture—that was usually dialed to the Bill Baliance show on KFWB ("Channel 98!") night after night. Talk radio, like the wood shop he set up in the garage, relaxed him; Bob Dylan's chiding whine did not.

●   ●   ●

As a sop to my discontent in the land of surfing, aircraft factories, and drive-through hamburger stands, my mother brought a Garrard stereo turntable into the house. The thing wasn't pretty, but, plugged into a cheap Electrovoice receiver, good god, what sound! Toward the end of my yearlong commitment, the Record Club offered its *Magic of Stereo* Limited Edition boxed set. There, in hypnotic stereophonic sound, on five LPs, were longtime members of the Columbia gang: Andre Kostelanetz, Percy Faith, Bobby Hackett, Tony Bennett, Miles Davis, Dave Brubeck, Duke Ellington, and André Previn. There were curiosities, like Flatt & Scruggs doing "The Legend of the Johnson Boys" (a revelation!) and, singing that godawful Lionel Bart song "As Long as He Needs Me," Anita Bryant, who was not yet notorious for her intractable antigay stance. Then there were Columbia artists, like trombonist J. J. Johnson and pianist Ray Bryant, whom I wouldn't learn to appreciate for several more years. What other record label had a roster like this? The back of the box advertised three Columbia-manufactured phonographs on which to play these discs. For those not ready to switch from hi-fi to stereo, there was the Solid State Monaural "Drop-a-Matic" Portable record changer; the starter stereo was the Deluxe Stereophonic Solid State Packaged Component Sound System; and for the more comfortable record listener, the company was offering the Deluxe Self-Contained Stereophonic High Fidelity Console with AM/FM Stereo. (All these caps and quotation marks appeared in the ad.)

So sue me, I went stereo-crazy. Tommy Bee, a popular DJ with a soporific baritone on the Los Angeles jazz station KBCA, would play the

Miles Davis–Gil Evans rendition of Brubeck's "The Duke" (in honor of Ellington) beneath his between-song patter; I craved that recording, from *Miles Ahead*, perhaps because I associated it with peaceful sleep, and the Record Club soon provided it. Leonard Bernstein's and the New York Philharmonic's stereo version of Copland's *Third Symphony* was so vibrant that I listened to it before I went to school, when I came home, and before I went to bed. I ordered my second Dylan record, *The Freewheelin' Bob Dylan*, and there was Dylan and his then-girlfriend Suze Rotolo on the cover, Dylan wearing that little fake-suede jacket, the photograph (Don Hunstein again) taken on Great Jones Street. *My Fair Lady*, which had been originally recorded in mono only a few months before Columbia began to release stereo albums in late '56, was now available in stereo, so that record entered the household all over again. Its Hirschfeld cover—Eliza Doolittle revealed to be a puppet controlled by Professor Henry Higgins who, in turn, is only a puppet controlled by George Bernard Shaw—was an image that felt almost preverbal to some of us. And, as if to reconnect with the beloved neighborhood I'd been untimely ripped from, I ordered *Monk's Dream*, Thelonious Monk's first Columbia record. Monk's recording sessions had been made at Columbia's 30th Street studio, housed in what had been a church, in late October to early November 1962, but hadn't been released until 1963—and then, in keeping with the Record Club's rule of not offering a record until six months after its release, was finally available by mail that summer. *Monk's Dream* was conveyed in a jagged musical language I lacked the vocabulary for. But the album required that I come back to it time and again.

• • •

That was the autumn of 1963. Too shy to make friends easily in an alien land, I relied for companionship on the phonograph and on the records that regularly arrived from the Record Club. A four-record album of the original cast recording of *Who's Afraid of Virginia Woolf?*, produced by Goddard Lieberson, arrived at the house. Furtively opening the package as though it were contraband, I got to listen to the furious, profanity-laden play twice through before my mother, mortified, confiscated it. As a corrective, one evening in early October she sat us in front of the television to watch *The Judy Garland Show*, and there was Garland countersinging "Get Happy" to a knockout rendition of "Happy Days Are Here Again" by the 21-year-old sensation Barbra Streisand. A copy of *The Second Barbra Streisand Album* soon found its way to the Redondo Beach house. Columbia recorded Streisand as well as Edward Albee, Thelonious Monk as well as Percy Faith, Louis Armstrong as well as Edward R. Murrow. After a while my unhappiness in Southern California dissipated, less because the place had become more congenial than because my truer home was the magical, aural world I was immersed in, a landscape of the ear and mind, most of it constructed by Columbia Records. I hadn't known that at the time, of course. "Few companies," the producer John Hammond wrote about Columbia, "have swung so dramatically between preeminence and extinction."[5] I hadn't known that, either.

Then came the assassination that (in Don DeLillo's phrase) broke the back of the American century. Mystified and frightened, I retreated even deeper into those Columbia records, having no idea that the label I claimed as mine was older than the century.

SIDE A
Some Pre-CBS History

1

My Mother Was a Phonograph

On the morning of January 23, 1908, a day before a blizzard crippled the New York metropolitan area with ten and a quarter inches of snow, Edward D. Easton, the longtime president of the Columbia Phonograph Company, began his weekday commute to the city as he usually did, by boarding the Susquehanna & Western line at Hackensack, New Jersey. He would ride the train to the connecting ferry in Jersey City, which would then take him across the Hudson River to downtown Manhattan. At 52, Easton lived in Arcola, New Jersey, the Bergen County town where he was raised. (Arcola has long since been folded into Paramus.) With his Columbia colleague and neighbor William Morse, Easton climbed aboard the 8:42 express. As the train rounded the bend at Bogota, Easton moved ahead of Morse and into the smoker car—and vanished. Morse had the train stopped. Stepping back along the line a conductor, Morse, and several other men found Easton lying unconscious between the tracks. They carried the Columbia Phonograph president back to the baggage car and the train backed its way into Hackensack. A physician there diagnosed Easton as having suffered an attack of vertigo. Easton was taken to Hackensack Hospital, where he was to begin an eight-month-long convalescence. In those first weeks he had no recollection of stepping off the train and didn't recognize his family members.[1]

Whether Easton ever really recovered—not from what appeared to be a suicide attempt but from the circumstances that led to it—is debatable. After twenty years Columbia's graphophone hadn't made the in-roads into stenography that Easton had hoped; professional stenographers and secretaries were still taking dictation rather than using graphophones. An October 1907 financial panic—"the trouble in New York," the *Times* called it—less than three months before the train incident had packed a wallop.[2] A run on the Knickerbocker Trust and on the Trust Company of America, two of New York's largest banks, was the result of several factors, including enormous payouts made for the 1906 San Francisco earthquake. Easton had had to order drastic cuts, laying off hundreds of employees in New York, Washington, and other branches. "A deep melancholy settled over father," Easton's daughter Mary said. "He could not smile. He would hardly speak in the long evenings at home. He would sit for hours staring into space."[3]

Born in Gloucester, Massachusetts, Edward Denison Easton was raised in Arcola and went to school in Paterson. In Bergen County he worked for a while as a reporter, then became a stenographer, combining the two fields into a lucrative kind of semijournalism. In his midtwenties he moved to Washington, D.C., where he covered the 1881–82 trial of Charles Guiteau, the assassin of President James Garfield. Some accounts have Easton selling the Guiteau story for as much as $25,000. The following year he and only one other stenographer covered every session of the Star Route trials—government officials had been charged with conspiracy to defraud the United States in its contracts for mail routes—commanding the kind of fees now paid for, say, rare celebrity photographs. Easton married a second time at 27 and put himself through Georgetown Law School. Nearing completion of his law studies, he became intrigued by the phonograph, particularly in the possibility that it could render stenography, his own handsomely profitable profession, obsolete.

The story of Columbia Records then begins with Edward Easton. Almost.

● ● ●

In 1881, while Easton was dominating the exclusively male world of stenography, Alexander Graham Bell set up a new laboratory in

Washington, D.C., to promote research relating to acoustics.[4] Bell had recently won the $10,000 Volta prize from the French government for his invention of the telephone, and he wasn't about to fritter it away. Joining him at the lab were his cousin Chichester Bell, a chemical engineer, and Charles Sumner Tainter, a scientist and instrument maker steeped in the reproduction of sound. One of their goals was to improve upon Edison's forsaken tinfoil phonograph. They referred to this improvement as the graphophone, an obvious inversion of the word *phonograph*. Alexander Graham Bell, tirelessly defending his telephone patents and now deeply immersed in research involving deaf-mute communication, gradually left the bulk of the Volta Graphophone work to his cousin and to Tainter. After four years of experimentation, Bell-Tainter developed a wax-coated cardboard disk on which sound vibrations could be engraved vertically in narrow grooves, and a hand crank instrument with a loosely mounted reproducing needle that was easily guided by the record. You listened through stethoscope tubes. Bell and Tainter applied for a patent on June 27, 1885. Before the end of that year, they'd discarded the disk as inadequate and substituted a wax cylinder, or "phonogram." Bell-Tainter deposited with the Smithsonian Institute in Washington a phonogram, sealed in a metal box, on which had been recorded passages from *Hamlet*. Quotations such as "There are more things in heaven and earth, Horatio, than are dreamed of in our philosophies" were followed by the identification, "I am a graphophone and my mother was a phonograph." The speaker was unidentified, but it was believed to be Alexander Graham Bell. (When the box was opened fifty-six years later and the cylinder played, every word was heard distinctly.)[5]

Bell-Tainter was issued a series of patents on May 4, 1886. Because of manufacturing restrictions in the city, the Volta Graphophone Company was organized in Alexandria, West Virginia, with executive offices on G Street in Washington, D.C. Batteries operated the graphophone, its grooves distinguishing it from Edison's phonograph. The record industry executive and historian Charles Schicke contrasted the two talking machines this way: "The rigid metal stylus of Edison's phonograph made vertical indentations on the tinfoil phonogram as it traced the groovings of the brass cylinder. The graphophone, on the other hand, featured a loosely mounted stylus that cut hill-and-dale grooves directly into the wax-coated cardboard. The playback stylus of the graphophone rode smoothly in the grooves, rather than in the herky-jerky manner of the phonograph. This so-called floating stylus did much to improve the quality of playback sound."[6]

Bell-Tainter sent two agents to visit Edison and propose a partnership. Edison said no, probably because he'd been burned by an earlier capital venture involving the electric light. But the proposal sent him back to work on the phonograph, the invention that had lain untouched for a while. Edison soon found a method of employing the foot treadle, much like the sewing machine had, to propel the phonograph's two-and-a-half-volt DC motor at a constant speed.[7]

* * *

As the capital's most prominent stenographer, and now with a law degree on his résumé, Edward D. Easton had made a considerable fortune for a young man. One of the original stockholders in Volta Graphophone, he now poured some of that fortune into the American Graphophone Company, which was organized in June 1887. Colonel James G. Payne became the company's first president, Easton its general manager. Easton was still a partner in the stenographic firm Johns & Easton, but spent most of his time at American Graphophone. The new company purchased the Bell-Tainter patents to the graphophone as an office dictating machine—the impetus for Easton's interest in the first place—and set up shop next to Volta on G Street.

It was time to make graphophones in volume. For $4,500 a year, American Graphophone leased one wing of an enormous factory complex—essentially the remains of the bankrupt Howe Sewing Machine Company—in Bridgeport, Connecticut.[8] Like the even larger Remington Arms plant just up the road, the factory's buildings were conveniently located near a major railroad line, facilitating deliveries, and not far from the Pequonnock River. By 1890 Bridgeport had a population of 44,000, making it the second-largest city in Connecticut, with a large supply of cheap labor.[9] It was in this already-old Bridgeport complex, as Allen Koenigsberg wrote, "that the first treadle Graphophones were sold, their upper chasses converted to electric and springboard operation."[10]

The talking machines that came out of Bridgeport were meant for just that—for talking, for dictation. Easton, Payne, and their partners saw their home city of Washington, with its innumerable government offices, as a major source of talking-machine clients. Although Edison, sorting through his groaning workbench in Essex County, New Jersey, continued to view the graphophone as an unwanted stepchild, he too saw his phonograph as a tool for the school and the office. If that view now seems to us almost Puritanical, folding a Protestant work ethic into the most dynamic of inventions, it came naturally to these men. Listening to either the phonograph or the graphophone was an auscultative activity—that is, as in the use of a stethoscope, listening through tubes was required to make a diagnosis. It was serious business.

*   *   *

A German immigrant named Emile Berliner had a different idea. Born in Hanover in 1851, Berliner spent years shuttling between Washington, D.C., and New York and absorbing what he could from Bell's experiments with the telephone.[11] In 1887 Berliner introduced his "Gramophone," which featured the first flat disk record. The disk was produced by photo-engraving in metal a plate-glass disk coated with lampblack; sound vibrations were traced laterally on the disk and fixed in place with varnish. The instrument was operated by a hand crank. Berliner applied for a patent on September 26, 1887; the patent was granted four years later. Long before Edison, even before Easton, Berliner saw the Gramophone as a medium of home entertainment.

Years later, Berliner would focus on developing the microphone. Before the microphone's widespread use in the 1920s, however, the method of recording was crude yet surprisingly effective. In his book on the industry giant EMI, Peter Martland gave a succinct description of how a recording was made in the decades before the microphone . . .

> simply by reversing the mechanical process of an old-fashioned horn gramophone. The sound vibrations in the air were collected and "funneled" via a conical horn on to a diaphragm. This activated the recording stylus to produce a direct analogue of the sound in the wavy groove of a revolving disc or cylinder. The earliest gramophone recording-machines were hand-powered but, by 1898, electric power was used and, later, a more reliable falling-weight mechanism.[12]

Even before 1887 some fine recordings were made by funneling them through that conical horn. But it would be another couple of years—and then only after a business flameout that shriveled a tycoon into a Willy Loman—before the company that would become Columbia Records got into the music business.

●　　●　　●

First came the split. In February 1888, acquiring exclusive sales rights from the American Graphophone Company, Edward Easton and some new partners set up another company, essentially a selling agent, to promote the graphophone as a business machine. The company was incorporated on January 22, 1889, in West Virginia. The sales territory—Virginia, Delaware, and the District of Columbia— was small but potentially lucrative. Easton and partners named the new company Columbia Phonograph, for its home city, and took offices at 627 E NW.[13]

Daringly, Columbia began to record music within six months of its incorporation.[14] There was a new demand for music cylinders, due largely to the ingenuity of Louis Glass, manager of the Pacific Phonographic Company in San Francisco. Glass made practical dropping a nickel into a slot to hear a brief recording. (The idea was given full flower with the advent of the jukebox.) A year and a half after Columbia came into existence, Glass sold his cylinder-machine patents to Felix Gottschalk, who started the Automatic Phonograph Company, the most ubiquitous and musically ravenous of the machine makers. "As the number of pay locations increased," Charlie Schicke wrote of the years 1890–92, "so did the demand for 'entertainment' cylinders."[15]

In the months leading up to the incorporation of Columbia Phonograph, American Graphophone and Edison were going at each other through their lawyers. That tough buzzard Colonel Payne and his partners at American accused Edison, who'd returned to work with a vengeance on the phonograph, of infringing on the copyrighted Bell-Tainter patents. The legal contest was averted when Jesse H. Lippincott stepped in with a proposition composed of millions of dollars and priceless hubris.[16]

Lippincott had built Rochester (Pennsylvania) Tumbler into a major glassware manufacturer. He'd also helped organize the Bridgewater Gas Company, which served the Pittsburgh area and happened to save Rochester Tumbler a bundle in utility costs. (No monopolist worth the epithet would have done otherwise.) As a young man Lippincott had fought in the Civil War; whether his stint as a soldier instilled in him a taste for battle, or whether he always had it, isn't clear. But he couldn't stop building, amassing, rebuilding. In 1885 he moved to Manhattan, kept a suite at the old Waldorf-Astoria (later the site of the Empire State Building), took a large apartment on West 59th Street (what is now Central Park South), joined the Fifth Avenue Baptist Church, and began to investigate the talking-machine industry. By 1888 he'd sold his stake in Rochester Tumbler, reportedly for a million dollars, but appears to have retained executive titles—first president, then treasurer. The New York press often referred to him as "The Pittsburgh Millionaire." Lippincott imagined a talking-machine empire structured along the lines of Bell Telephone. The telephone behemoth was young but already fabulously successful. Lippincott figured he was ready to build a company of that magnitude.

So he set out to make deals with Edison and Payne. In an agreement dated June 28, 1888, Edison sold Lippincott his talking-machine patents and exclusive sales rights for $750,000, though he reserved manufacturing rights. (The sum going to Edison was actually $500,000; a complex financial arrangement with Edison's former staff inventor Ezra Gilliland would cost Lippincott another $250,000 and keep him going to court for the remainder of his life.)[17] Edison continued to manufacture under his two linked companies, Edison Phonograph Works and Edison Speaking Phonograph. On July 14, 1888, Lippincott formed the North American Phonograph Company as a national sales agency, based in West Orange, New Jersey, a short ride from Edison's headquarters. (A Manhattan office was rented at 32 Park Place.) Lippincott was to pay Edison in installments. The idea behind the enterprise was something called "states' rights"—territorial companies (or "states") would lease out the machines, which were too expensive for most local companies to buy, at an annual rental of $40 each. Half of this sum was to be retained by the territorial company, half paid to parent company North American. Toward this end Lippincott collected $1,080,000 from the local companies. This was his attempt to emulate the sales policies of Bell Telephone, dividing the nation into geographic territories and licensing exclusive exploitation rights to the machines to local companies in each area. Within a year thirty-three companies were licensed.

Having lured Edison into a partnership, Lippincott went to work on American Graphophone. Colonel Payne didn't trust Edison, but he didn't even know Lippincott, and he remained wary. Payne declined to sell Lippincott the Bell-Tainter patents and insisted, much as Edison had, that American Graphophone retain manufacturing rights to its own instrument. Payne grudgingly agreed to sell national sales rights for $200,000, but only to Lippincott himself—a deal with yet another new company was undesirable to American—and only after Lippincott guaranteed that he would buy thousands of machines every year. Lippincott wrote a check. And there was one American Graphophone territory that Lippincott couldn't take for his own: the sales territory encompassing the District of Columbia, Delaware, and Virginia and already franchised to Edward D. Easton and his partners at Columbia Phonograph.[18] Columbia was licensed by, but did not answer to,

North American. The new association with North American also gave Columbia sales rights to the Edison Phonograph in its territory.

· · ·

Trouble between Lippincott and Edison was apparent from the get-go. The local companies that comprised North American tended to be displeased with the quality of musical recording that Edison had supplied, as stipulated by the contract. As early as February 1890, Edison was fed up:

> I have read the correspondence from various Phonograph Companies, addressed to the North American Phonograph Co., and referred by them to yourselves, complaining of the quality of musical records furnished by my Laboratory. In response to your inquiries regarding these complaints I beg to say that I have permitted musical records to be made here purely as a matter of accommodation to the North American people. . . .[19]

Edison had always resented the perceived preference for musical rather than spoken word recordings, as though music somehow demeaned his invention. (At the sunset of his career thirty years later, even Edison could no longer deny that his distaste for popular music, and for jazz in particular, had badly damaged his Phonograph operations.)

Edison's irritation was a chronic thing and rarely surprised anyone. Lippincott, however, wasn't used to feeling thwarted in his business ventures. The public, shunning the appliances, was seen as "fickle," having wearied of another "fad."[20]

Not everyone blamed the public. Edison's longtime secretary Alfred Tate, who became a director of North American to keep the two companies executively linked, recalled dining with Lippincott at the capacious Cafe Savarin, in the Equitable Building on lower Broadway. There Tate told his lunch companion that he thought he'd made a mistake in using Bell Telephone as a model to exploit the phonograph: telephone subscribers didn't pay specifically for the instruments they leased but for the service rendered. "I suggested that the sewing machine industry," Tate recalled, "in which machines were sold for cash and on the installment plan, seemed better adapted to the nature of the phonograph industry."[21] Lippincott heard Tate out but stuck with his plan.

Easton, meanwhile, was still a major shareholder in the American Graphophone Company, eventually becoming a director. In March 1890 American's board commissioned him to visit North American's branches ("the local companies") to see how the public was responding to the talking machine, whether the phonograph or the graphophone. Visiting thirty-one branches and traveling as far west as Portland, Oregon, and as far south as Florida, Easton came away with the impression that the dealers wished to sell just one machine, making it easier on both the dealers and the consumers.[22]

The trip also convinced Easton that consumers were interested in music—the very thing Edison regarded as cheapening his invention.

●　●　●

Lippincott's attempt to control sales and distribution of all talking-machine sales wasn't working. For one thing, the graphophone was being outperformed by the phonograph, which didn't threaten the livelihood of stenographers—an honorable, lucrative, and then an almost exclusively male profession—and could be serviced much more easily. (This is essentially what Easton had seen during his March 1890 tour.) For another, Edison Phonograph and American Graphophone—already uneasy partners, step-siblings answering to Lippincott—were still trying to come to terms with each other's productivity. As part of one 1890 agreement between them, production at the old Howe factory in Bridgeport was slowed down and American Graphophone stockholders would receive 3 percent quarterly dividends, primarily so that Edison could control production volume from his New Jersey plant. That agreement was called off six months later when James Payne got American Graphophone's Bridgeport operations up and running again.[23]

None of these developments helped Lippincott. North American's branches often stiffed the parent company on the machines they'd leased. Implementing Tate's advice to sell instead of rent the talking machines also failed to bail out North American. Threats of litigation were everywhere, but Lippincott, who had been in shaky health since the death of his wife Mary Richardson, in 1886, was too ill to go to court.[24] In the fall of 1890 the former glass magnate turned would-be phonograph monopolist went into what the papers called "a despondent paralysis." He'd had a stroke.

That winter North American, headquartered in a loft in Jersey City, sent out instructions to its sales branches that suggested defeat was already in the air. "Phonograph Companies desiring to return machines not in use, upon which they do no not wish to have rentals charged, as per contract from January 1st, 1891, will ship phonographs to the Edison Phonograph Works, Orange, N.J. and phonograph-graphophones to the American Graphophone Company, Bridgeport, Conn., carefully packed and complete in every particular."[25]

By May 1891 North American had collapsed. Lippincott personally had over a hundred creditors knocking. Among them was his own former company Rochester Tumbler, which wanted a staggering $167,000 paid back.[26]

Easton, surveying this dismal landscape, made an aggressive move. Alfred Tate outlined the situation, as it stood on December 9, 1891, to his craggy old boss:

Mr Easton of the Columbia Phonograph Company called to see me yesterday. You are probably aware that he is one of the Directors of the Graphophone Company. He told me that the Graphophone people were going to operate their [Bridgeport] factory and put their machines on the market, and I saw a letter in [North American's legal advisor] Bush's office to-day from the Columbia Phonograph Company signed by Mr Easton as President, asking the authority of the North American Phonograph Company to sell graphophones. They of course will not obtain this authority, which will perhaps result in a new wheel being formed within the many wheels which are now revolving.

> Mr Easton stated that Mr Lippincott owed the Graphophone people a large amount of money. I could not ascertain the exact amount, but from his general conversation I would judge that it is somewhere around $100,000 or $150,000. . . .[27]

The sum reflected Lippincott's colossal failure, whether through a lack of vision, overambitiousness, or several economic factors at once, and it also indicated how thorny the still-young recording industry had become. Less than three years after Easton and Columbia consolidated their power in the wake of North American's insolvency, Lippincott was dead at 51. His *Times* obit said "excessive work" had paralyzed him. A subsequent *Times* piece about North American's receivership said that Lippincott "became insane when he lost all his money."[28]

● ● ● ●

Easton and his Columbia colleagues knew they had to pounce if they were to capitalize on North American's collapse. Edison was no longer in possession of his own phonograph patents, and American Graphophone, though hardly profitable, still controlled the Bell-Tainter patents. Easton and his lawyers (that durable Columbia theme) manipulated some stock and, with a little Wall Street razzle-dazzle, soon had control of both Columbia and American Graphophone, in effect rendering them two divisions of the same company. The reorganization was executed on May 1, 1893, with Easton as president. In rather loose divisions, American Graphophone would be the company's development and manufacturing arm, while Columbia Phonograph would handle distribution and sales.[29]

During this reorganization period, Columbia benefited mightily from the services of two young men. One of them, Thomas Hood MacDonald, came directly out of the North American debacle. A California native, MacDonald had joined the merchant marine at 18. Seafaring stories about him, surely told by him stateside, make him out to be a character out of Conrad. Whether these stories were apocryphal or not, MacDonald subsequently went to work for the Eastern Pennsylvania Phonograph

Company, one of the territories served by Lippincott. That connection led to a job with Columbia Phonograph, beginning probably in 1891. Installed as manager of the twelve-man factory in Bridgeport, MacDonald became a champion of his workers, eventually winning them a nine-hour workday, and a demon inventor in his own right. Only Edison was granted more phonograph patents. Eventually, MacDonald made the graphophone a viable home appliance by coming up with the spring-driven motor in the mid-1890s, and made Columbia's first disk-playing machine, the fingerwound "Toy" Graphophone, in 1899.

The other figure who bridged North American and Columbia in the coming years was Frank Dorian. Born and educated in Washington, D.C., and, like Easton, trained as a stenographer, Dorian joined the new Columbia Phonograph Company in 1889, when he was only 19, as Easton's personal secretary. Soon he was given the title general manager. As Easton and Columbia sifted through the ruins of North American, it was Dorian who saw the graphophone as a machine with universal appeal *as entertainment*. Eventually Dorian, under Easton's aegis, would go to Europe to effectively market the graphophone and Columbia's recorded cylinders. Dorian was so close to Easton that he named one of his sons after him. After Easton's attempted suicide, Dorian would return to the States to be near his old boss and take over sales of Columbia's Dictaphone.[30]

As the American-Columbia combine geared up, Emile Berliner continued to improve his Gramophone. He came up with a metal master disk that could produce duplicate copies, made of hard rubber, with a groove that vibrated the needle laterally by means of modulation in the walls of the groove. Between 1893 and 1895 Berliner promoted this new development of the gramophone, which was scheduled to be sold for home use.[31]

The new duplicable disk accentuated a sexual contradiction in the whole enterprise of recording. Up through the first decade of the twentieth century a preponderant number of recordings were made by men, whose lower voices were said to reproduce better, more audibly. Yet that very reproductiveness could be viewed as female. Although the spindle, tone arm, and needle of the post-cylinder phonograph are phallic, as Evan Eisenberg pointed out in *The Recording Angel*, the new disk itself was round and concentric, with more than a vague similarity to the female breast.[32] The disk's surface, when penetrated, produced sound—musical or not, pleasurable or not. And, just as Jesse Lippincott had emulated the sales practices of "Ma" Bell, with her children scattered around the country, so the talking machine's purpose was to bring far-flung sounds up close—the maternal desire to have all the kids in touch. In the recording process, the final apparatus was the machine's horn, whose flared shape made it appear more receptacle than phallus.

Emile Berliner probably didn't waste time contemplating such grandiose sexual metaphors. For the next few years he and Columbia's MacDonald would trade phonograph developments like dueling inventors. MacDonald's spring-driven motor graphophone, retailing for $75, coupled with a new stamping process that enabled mass duplication of wax cylinders, kept Columbia in the game. As Easton and his protégé Frank Dorian had envisioned, the talking machine—whether female or male, gramophone or graphophone—entered the home as a form of popular entertainment.

•   •   •

Easton, by now persuaded that Americans would buy records if they contained music, oversaw his company's acquisition and development of its first musical artists. From 1889 to 1895, Columbia promoted recording artists like Eddie Giguere, "the well known yodeler of the Washington Police Patrol," and John Y. Atlee, a whistler who clerked at the Treasury Department.[33] Whistling was cheap to record and reproduced with less interference.

Columbia's pool of artists came mostly from right there in the District; it didn't yet pay to send for a musician or storyteller from too far away. Len Spencer, a white baritone who specialized in minstrelsy, first went to work for Columbia in 1889. A local boy, born in 1867, Spencer was a descendant of Platt Rogers Spencer, whose florid cursive style was probably America's most popular script in the last decades of the nineteenth century.[34] Len Spencer was also a godson of James Garfield. Although he took a long hiatus from Columbia to work for the rival New Jersey Phonograph, Spencer proved invaluable to the label as an inventive monologist and because he could organize cover versions of other artists' hits quickly.

In the middle of the 1890s, Victor Emerson, Columbia's "superintendent of records," made several recordings with black singer George Washington Johnson, who was born a slave in the South and whose recording of "Whistling Coon" had supplied him with his nickname. It was Emerson's idea that whites would buy the record just to hear a black man make fun of himself: *I've seen in my time some very funny folks / But the funniest of all I know / Is a colored individual as sure as you're alive / He's black as any crow* . . .[35] "Whistling Coon" and "The Laughing Song" were two of the songs that helped make Johnson the first black American recording star. When Johnson was indicted in 1899 for beating his common-law wife to death in the basement of her apartment on West 41st Street in Manhattan, Columbia paid for his legal representation. The Times pointed out that one of the twelve jurors chosen was "colored," and that "The 'Whistling Coon' [meaning Johnson] seems to have suffered little from confinement and suspense. He spends much of his time in jail in whistling for his own and other prisoners' diversion. He manages to keep from bursting into music in the courtroom by keeping his mouth firmly shut."[36] Apart from the casual racism in such a report, the shame was that Johnson came through beautifully on records. "His notes are as perfect as those of a flute," the Times had reported upon his arraignment.[37] Johnson was acquitted—the prosecution had a weak case, and the New York Police Department of the era was notoriously antiblack, rendering its charges and testimony suspect—and resumed his career.[38] Eventually he lost recording work to whites who covered his songs— not quite Little Richard being outsold by Pat Boone, but close.

As for Victor Emerson, then in his thirties, he had come to Columbia from another phonograph company bearing no musical training but a congeniality attractive to his recording artists. His brother Clyde was for a while Columbia's technical director when its studios were on 28th Street and Broadway.[39] Victor Emerson was around for another fifteen years, departing Columbia under what Tim Brooks called "somewhat clouded circumstances," perhaps having to do with his exploiting Columbia's patents in the interests of the Little Wonder children's label, in which he had an interest.[40] After that he started Emerson Phonograph, which thrived as a relatively cheap-disk label for more than a decade.

In the fall of 1890, Columbia first recorded the U.S. Marine Band, also based in Washington and dedicated largely to the compositions of John Philip Sousa. Sousa's marches "The High School Cadets" and "Corcoran Cadets" quickly found their way onto Columbia's cylinders.[41] Sousa, trained as a violinist and enamored of Gilbert & Sullivan, and the Marine Band went back a long way: Sousa's father, Antonio, was a trombonist in the band and, to keep the boy out of the circus, enlisted him as an apprentice. Two years after the Marine Band's first recording for Columbia, there were over two hundred different cylinders of its music released, comprising an enormous body of work.

Columbia, raking in profits from its Marine Band recordings, soon decided it had to be where the entertainment was. In 1897 it moved its headquarters to Manhattan, specifically to the Tribune Building at 154 Nassau Street. In the next few years the label set up branches in Chicago, Philadelphia, St. Louis, Baltimore, Washington, Buffalo, and San Francisco, as well as in Paris, Berlin, and London. The move also brought Edward Easton back to the New York area. He was father to several children who were now being raised in bucolic surroundings in Bergen County, where he'd grown up. Because he was president of a major phonograph company, his comings and goings were reported in society columns along with those of the Vanderbilts and the Astors.[42]

2

Litigation vs. Innovation

Columbia Phonograph was in the music business to stay. Music played on talking machines was no longer considered novel. All this Columbia music was still on cylinders, though. Meanwhile, Easton tried to figure out a way around the obstacle of Emile Berliner's disk patents. By 1897 Berliner's hand-powered Gramophone already seemed antiquated when compared with the spring-driven motor, first made practical by Columbia's MacDonald—featured on its Eagle gramophone, cheap but eminently playable—so Berliner's company went for its own spring-wound motor. After a Camden, New Jersey, machinist named Eldridge Johnson devised the actual mechanism, he was awarded a contract to produce gramophones for the Berliner Gramophone Company. Johnson had compared the sound produced by the Berliner disk to "a partially educated parrot with a sore throat and a cold in the head."[1] In the process of making new gramophones he also developed a superior disk using a shellac compound as a substitute for hard rubber. Sown by Johnson's mechanical green thumb, advances in both the player and the disk would bloom into what would become Victor, Columbia's primary—and sometimes its only—rival throughout the twentieth century.

To continue to finance Johnson's work in Camden and keep his own concern afloat, Emile Berliner sent to London his young staffer William Barry Owen, who sold European rights to the gramophone for £15,000, resulting in the 1897 organization of the Gramophone Company Ltd. as the English affiliate of the Berliner Company.

After that the industry's major players took off the gloves. Easton hired Philip Mauro, then in his late thirties, as Columbia Records's general attorney. Mauro had a Washington practice with patent expert Anthony Pollak, and he proved to be an effective legal linesman, running interference for Columbia through the court system over several crucial issues.

One of Mauro's more aggressive maneuvers involved Berliner's former employee Joseph Jones. It was said that Jones had betrayed Berliner by developing both a phonograph and an electroplated wax disk under his former boss's aegis and then taking the secrets with him. This was probably true, but it was a full decade after that before Jones went into partnership with Albert Armstrong to form Standard Talking Machine. Jones had the know-how, Armstrong the cash. Standard Talking produced a dual-horn player, the Double Bell Wonder, and made 7" disks that played at 80 rpm. "At that speed," John Hammond remembered, "they offered a minute and thirty seconds of music. They retailed for fifty cents."[2] Berliner, citing patent infringement, sued to enjoin Standard from manufacturing these disks—after all, Jones didn't have a patent yet—and it would be another year before Jones and Armstrong were up and running again, this time with American Graphophone as partners. The disks that came out of this partnership bore the label American Talking Machine Disk, but technically they were the first disks (as opposed to cylinders) that Columbia had a hand in distributing.

By dint of its hand-in-glove relationship with American, Columbia was now keen to produce lateral-cut disks on a large scale. While they waited for Philip Mauro to push through Jones's patents, the company partnered with the Burt Company of Millburn, New Jersey, whose main product was poker chips, to form the Globe Record Company. Out of Globe came the 7" disks labeled Climax, but they were distributed by Columbia, which still had to keep a low profile.[3]

Despite its brief legal victory, Berliner went out of business. Early in 1898 Eldridge Johnson organized his own company in Camden, New Jersey, under the name Consolidated Talking Machine Company. The consolidation was literal: to hurdle the patent conflicts that had beset the industry throughout the previous decade, Johnson persuaded Berliner to combine many of his patents with his own.

* * *

Widening its scope, American Graphophone organized the Columbia Graphophone Company Ltd. in London in 1899 as its English branch. Trademarks used by this English branch throughout Europe and other countries in the Eastern Hemisphere were registered in such countries in the name of and owned by the American Graphophone Company.[4] In the next quarter century Columbia Graphophone Ltd. would take on roles in Columbia Records's history—as savior of and rival to—that nobody could have anticipated at the time.

Back in New York, Easton was all puffed up. Would-be rivals were clearing out, leaving the American-Columbia combine with an open field. As American Graphophone's president, Easton was quoted in the March 15, 1900, Report to Stockholders:

> Our fundamental patents have stood every test, and are admitted to have created and to control the present art. Very many new patents have been taken out by the Company, not only in this country but in the principal countries of the world where there are patent laws; and it is believed that in this respect we are constantly growing stronger. Patents of recent date have been granted which are essential to the best operation of the modern talking machine. The management, however, relies so much upon perfect, experienced and devoted organization, that the question of patents does not have great relative importance.[5]

If the view of Columbia Records was that it had relied heavily on winning patent judgments in court, Easton himself promoted it. Edison had "the better machines, Bell and Tainter the better lawyers," Marc Kirkeby wrote of the period when Easton was beginning to immerse himself in the business of recording.[6] "Columbia entered the disc business through the back door, relying less on innovation than litigation," Sherman and

Nauck wrote in *Note the Notes*, their illustrated history of the label.[7] In the last five years of the nineteenth century, Columbia managed to marshal its record company cousins against both Edison and Berliner, the two great minds (and threats) of the industry, by promoting companies' "rights." Due to Columbia's litigiousness, and to a legal rebellion led by Berliner's former sales chief Frank Seamon, Berliner was enjoined from conducting business in America in 1900.[8] Eldridge Johnson and his new Consolidated, built in 1899 on some of Berliner's leftovers, stepped into the breach by putting his gramophone on the market, along with his new wax disks.[9]

The following year Columbia was awarded the Grand Prix at the Paris Exposition for scientific achievement—specifically for a three-horned graphophone—in the field of recording. The field of candidates was still relatively narrow. But Columbia would exploit the 1900 Paris award, then the 1904 award won in St. Louis, over and over again—on its labels as well as in its print advertising. It supplied Columbia with a built-in blurb, like a book winning a Pulitzer Prize or a Newbury Medal.

Despite all the glitches the graphophone still had to work out, it remained a thing of wonder. "The music was playing in the house. It was one of them graphophones," Cash says in Faulkner's *As I Lay Dying*. People had gotten used to the idea of playing music on demand, at any hour of the day, even repeating the same piece over and over, on the cylinder or on the new disk, if they so desired. Now they were also listening to nuances of fidelity. "It was natural as a music band," says Cash.[10]

On December 10, 1901, Columbia swelled with its greatest legal coup: Mauro's long-awaited court victory granting Joseph Jones the wax disk patent, at last enabling Columbia to openly sell disks with its name on them. Anticipating the victory, Columbia would normally have publicized it everywhere, but not this time. In the fall of 1901 there were a couple of brief squibs about it, but not much else.[11] It was as though Columbia were already trying to minimize the sinister motives that critics would impute to the company for decades.

Not that Columbia could afford to be retiring. The Victor Talking

Machine Company was organized on October 3, 1901, by Eldridge Johnson, who combined Berliner's old gramophone patents with his own. Victor was an outgrowth of Consolidated, but there was something more threatening about this new company—maybe because Johnson had been angered by all the legal turmoil he'd been put through. At his Camden plant Johnson increased production more than threefold—he aimed to make 1,500 gramophones a week—by keeping it operating twenty-fours a day.[12] While Edward Easton was away from New York, Johnson bought the Globe Record Company, which felt abandoned by Columbia in the wake of the granting of the Joseph Jones patents. Now owning the Climax records put out by Globe, Johnson had the masters shipped to Philadelphia, where the labels were embossed with the letters VTM (for Victor Talking Machine). It took a while for Easton to realize what had hit him. Mauro and the lawyers were hauled in again. This appeared to be precisely what Johnson had wanted. Columbia finally agreed to buy back Globe for the $10,000 that Johnson had paid for it, in exchange for dropping all legal actions against Victor. In addition, Columbia bought the Burt Company outright so that it would control subsidiaries like Globe. Through most of 1902 Burt pressed Victor's disks as well as Columbia's, suggesting that Columbia, as Burt's new owner, had the last laugh. But Victor soon made other arrangements. Columbia closed Burt's Millburn plant and folded its operations into American Graphophone's Bridgeport facility.[13]

Johnson's left hook arrived, as a knockout punch often does, seemingly from out of nowhere. Actually it came from London, and in the deceptively benign form of a painting by Francis Barraud. In the original painting a terrier, who would come to be called Nipper, sits cocking its head at a cylinder phonograph. William Barry Owen, of the London Gramophone Company (now allied with Victor's English arm), expressed interest in the painting but wanted a disk gramophone painted over the phonograph. Barraud complied.[14] Owen bought the new version for £100 and shipped it to Camden, New Jersey, as a gift to Johnson and Berliner.[15] Victor soon had its His Master's Voice logo, one of the most distinctive trademarks in twentieth-century life and one that

Columbia never came close to matching. In a few years Columbia would settle on its Note the Notes logo, which would prove to be an effective design, off and on, for the thirty years before CBS bought the label.

●　　●　　●

By 1902 disks were the sound conduit of choice. Cylinders became something of a loss leader, cheaply priced—usually less than half the price of a disk—and said to sound tinny compared with the better disks. Columbia's cylinders sold for a quarter and Edison's for thirty-five cents, while Victor's cheapest 10" single-sided disk sold for $1. With Columbia now openly competing in the disk market, a price war was inevitable.

Columbia's Grand Opera series, begun in 1903, was considered a class act—10" disks priced at an exorbitant $2 each but well worth it. The series included the Czech contralto Ernestine Schumann-Heink, Italian baritone Antonio Scotti, and French baritone Charles Gilbert. Within weeks, however, Victor introduced its Red Seal line. The combination of that distinguished red label and the Nipper logo eventually crushed the Grand Opera series. After Victor won the contract to record the Metropolitan Opera stars, including Caruso and Chaliapin, Columbia threw in the opera towel. This was a costly mistake, for it ceded the entire field to Victor. (In opera, Columbia wouldn't become competitive again until long after Masterworks was established, and then only intermittently.)

Henry Burr (né Harry McClaskey) didn't have the voice of an opera singer, but he had the physique and then some. Burr's name didn't appear on a disk until 1904, though he was surely recording before then. He had been a boy soprano in St. Stephen, New Brunswick, and been encouraged to go to New York to study voice. By the time he was 20, Burr was a member of the Columbia Male Quartet. Its repertoire consisted of familiar pieces like "Let Me Call You Sweetheart" and "Whispering." Despite an enormous output over the next 35 years, Burr might have been forgotten today, but his career was representative of so many singers of the era. He recorded often and simultaneously for Victor and under various names (including his birth name), as much to avoid flooding the market with Henry Burr records as to protect his respective contracts.[16]

Columbia often had to accept such arrangements if it wanted to stay competitive with Victor. The label resorted to a certain international scrappiness, courting and recording artists all across Europe. The result was a more ethnically diverse artist roster—and consumer base—than Victor's, which didn't need it at the time. Realizing it was number two, Columbia tried harder. In 1904 Columbia announced the opening of a record-making laboratory in Mexico—its first international venture outside Europe—though it would be years before that lab produced more Latin records than New York did.[17]

* * *

In 1906 Victor introduced its "Victrola," with its internal horn and record-storage space. Victrolas ranged in price from $22 to $100; at any price they were a hit, and brought Columbia's graphophone sales almost to a standstill. In addition, Victor was running away with the disk business while Edison, forever retooling, was now capturing the lion's share of the cylinder business.[18] Columbia would continue to make cylinders for the next five years, but it did so halfheartedly.

Victor had another asset, though it was ambivalent about this one. John Philip Sousa had a contract with Victor but was decidedly no fan of recording. He reckoned the quality poor and a live audience superfluous, even detrimental, to the recording process; the effect was the antithesis of the sidewalk enthusiasm and dazzle of his marches. Yet those early Marine Band recordings had clicked with the public and had only encouraged Columbia to record more. The high volume of recording did nothing to placate Sousa. When he departed the Marine Band to form his own—he would first move over to Emile Berliner's U.S. Gramophone Company, then still based in Washington—he was succeeded as leader by Francesco Fanciulli, who kept the Marine Band at Columbia until 1899.[19] When Columbia published its first catalog in 1902, Sousa's "The Stars and Stripes Forever" was the first disk listed.

In 1906 Sousa blared his virulent opposition to phonographs when he published "The Menace of Mechanical Music" in the September edition of *Appleton's Magazine*.[20] This is where he coined the term "canned music." Sousa meant that the music was, in effect, stored for profit by the record companies, without asking its composers' consent and without paying them. The following year, after the term had rushed into the lexicon—and took on a musically pejorative meaning as well—the *Times* published a balanced, unsigned editorial about the issue:

> Canned music, the term is Mr Sousa's invention and an admirably expressive one, has been abused a great deal and made needlessly offensive. But all who have seriously thought about the self-playing piano and the improved phonograph know that they are effective instruments in the spread of culture. Appreciation of the best music is largely growing through their influence.
>
> The sensitive virtuoso condemns them, and in so doing places himself with the mechanic who condemns modern machinery. As a matter of fact, they are helping to greatly increase the virtuoso's audience, for they are musically educating the multitude. Their manufacturers should not be permitted to do so, however, at the expense of the composers.[21]

Sousa saw the phonograph as ultimately ripping off earnings that belonged to him and his fellow composers, who didn't yet have an organized way of collecting those earnings. A music publisher like Edward Marks, however, saw the record as the best way to plug a song, its sheet music then sold to amateur and professional musicians alike. (A descendant issue would erupt a hundred years later over the distribution of recordings over the Internet.)

Sousa went from Columbia to Victor. The great Bert Williams went from Victor to Columbia. Williams and his partner George Walker had been making records since 1901, when they were already Broadway stars. "Williams and Walker, the inimitable pair whose negro songs and antics made such a hit two years ago in this city, have been engaged . . . to appear on next Sunday evening in a grand darky jubilee," trumpeted the Times in October 1898.[22] Williams & Walker introduced the cakewalk to the American public, took the traditional minstrel show and stood it on its head. In the first decade of the twentieth century, they appeared in three all-black musical comedies on Broadway and recorded for Victor for the first five years, both separately and together.[23] They weren't happy at Victor, and the jump to Columbia, then the only other recording company of consequence, was natural. In July 1906 Columbia listed Williams's "Nobody" in its catalog with the advertisement: *The Ethiopian baritone, Bert Williams, sings his big hit, "Nobody" . . . in an extremely funny way, the haunting melody being supported by the trombone and orchestra.*[24]

* * *

Bert Williams was born in the British West Indies in 1874. His parents supplied a deeply beguiling racial mix: Frederick Williams's father had been a plantation owner, probably of Scandinavian descent, and his mother three-quarters Spanish and one-quarter African; Julia Monceur was a quadroon. Bert and his parents moved from Nassau to Manhattan (West 26th Street, in the shadows of what was then considered Tin Pan Alley), back to Nassau, then to Florida and Southern California; Bert graduated from high school in Riverside. The family's financial situation prohibited him from attending Stanford, as he'd hoped, so he went into show business. It was probably in the San Francisco Bay Area that Williams first encountered George Walker, a year older than he and a native of Lawrence, Kansas.

To get bookings from reluctant theater managers, Williams and Walker billed themselves as "The Two Real Coons." One evening in Detroit, "just for a lark," Williams blacked up—the ritual of white performers who'd appeared in blackface, using burnt cork, since the Civil War—and went onstage to sing "Oh, I Don't Know, You're Not So Warm." The reception was wildly enthusiastic, and Williams knew he'd created a character he could play onstage with confidence.

Williams & Walker had begun their act in the West and, with an ill-advised stop in the South and one or two inhospitable towns in the

Midwest, gradually took it east. An invitation to appear in Victor Herbert's *The Gold Bug* got them to New York in 1896. The show closed faster than a camera shutter, but the Two Real Coons were still in their early twenties and ready for action. That came with publicity for the cakewalk, the new dance craze, of which Williams & Walker became the prime exponents. (Variations on the cakewalk would appear throughout the next century, culminating in Michael Jackson's stage and video act during his years with CBS Records.) Like teams that came before (Weber & Fields) and after (Hope & Crosby, Martin & Lewis), Williams and Walker took on specific stage personalities that, when one was struck against the other, produced a spark, sometimes a flame. Walker was the smooth urban operator to Williams's trusting rube. They danced and joked and sang, with Williams occasionally playing rather simple, heavy-fingered piano accompaniment, their songs captured on record, beginning in 1901, by the fledgling Victor label and five years later by Columbia. The Victor recordings were crudely made, and, according to Allen Debus and Richard Martin in their Williams annotations, Walker was particularly unhappy with the process. (Ironically, by 1902 Victor had improved its process but didn't record Williams and Walker again.) By 1905 the Two Real Coons had been dropped from Victor's catalog—a very early example of cut-outs based on a lack of foresight. Their 1906 show *Abysinnia* reaffirmed their stage stardom—if you remove some of the subtler African vs. American Negro aspects, its plot could be a model for practically every Hope-Crosby *Road* picture—and got them a contract with Columbia. That April, Walker sang on "Pretty Desdamona" (from *Abysinnia*), and it would be his last recording before illness kept him out of the recording studio (though not yet off the stage) and eventually killed him. The Williams–Alex Rogers number "Nobody," also from *Abysinnia*, would become Williams's signature song, done in at least two versions. Other Columbia titles, all of songs that had to come in at barely more than two minutes for recording purposes, reveal Williams's hearty humor: "I'm Tired of Eating in the Restaurants," "All In, Out and Down," "Here It Comes Again," and "I've Such a Funny Feeling When I Look at You." A few Williams and Walker songs like "The Right Church and the Wrong Pew" went unrecorded by the team but became numbers for other Columbia artists.

The center of their appeal lay in the way Williams subverted the idea of the blackfaced comic. In his introduction to a revised edition of James Weldon Johnson's *Black Manhattan*, Allan H. Spear addressed this subversion:

> In the nineteenth century, the only commercially successful Negro songwriters and performers had been those who tailored their work to the demands of white stereotypes. They had operated within the minstrel tradition, playing the role of the irresponsible but lovable "darky" that white audiences expected of them. By the turn of the century, however, the best of the black vaudevillians began to rebel against such blatant pandering to white tastes and attempted to create a more three-dimensional portrait of Negro life. . . . Yet, at the same time, such artists as Will Marion Cook, Bob Cole and the Johnson brothers also came to recognize the richness of Negro folk culture as a source for an honest and vital art.[25]

George Walker said it another way in a 1906 essay for *The Theatre Magazine*: "Black-faced white comedians used to make themselves look as ridiculous as they could when portraying a 'darky' character. . . . The one fatal result of this to the colored performers was that they imitated the white performers in their make-up as 'darkies.' Nothing seemed more absurd than to see a colored man making himself ridiculous in order to portray himself."[26] Williams's genius, Walker went on, was to play "darky" in a natural rather than exaggerated way, his naturalness commenting slyly on decades of minstrel tradition even as he sang and danced.

Williams wasn't the first important black artist recorded by Columbia; the first was surely George Washington Johnson, "The Whistling Coon." But Williams's recordings—perhaps because they were made in the lateral disk era, perhaps because they stemmed from intellectually deeper roots—lay the foundation for the black recording artist in the twentieth century. The black race that was, if by national law only, supposed to be equal to the white race still had no voice—not in business or politics, and barely in education. Black artists, whether as singers or instrumentalists, had a voice when they recorded, however; the dynamics of phonography placed them on equal footing with white artists. Bert Williams had a voice, suffused with humor and earned wisdom, that still matters a century later.

There was another unique element captured on Columbia disks in Williams's performances and recordings. Some commentators have called it melancholy; it also has to do with a more prosaic loneliness. Williams was often the only black person in the theater, a phenomenon he was all too aware of when he looked out over the footlights at the paying customers. "However, he understands," the novelist Caryl Phillips wrote of Williams as he prepares to leave the Ziegfeld stage after nine years,

> that in this theater there will always be motion and unrest in these cones of light, and even after he is gone from this place there will remain some form of silent activity that will always mirror the disquieted movement of his heart with particles leaping first one way, and then the next, invisible to these people's eyes, yet dancing just above their heads.[27]

That disquieted movement can be heard on the old Columbia recordings.

• • •

One of Williams's recordings of "Nobody" was distributed on Columbia's Marconi label. Guglielmo Marconi, the young but already famous inventor of wireless telegraphy, had come to America at the end of the nineteenth century to install antennae on Cape Cod and in Nova Scotia. In 1899 American Marconi Wireless Telegraph Company was incorporated in New Jersey.[28] Columbia directors, referring to Marconi as their "consulting physicist," took him to Bridgeport to show him around and perhaps to inspire him. Whether Marconi did some honest work for the company or was merely lending his celebrity to a new campaign isn't clear, but records soon appeared on the market bearing his name and likeness. In July 1906 American Graphophone announced its first laminated disk records, the Columbia-Marconi Velvet-Tone records—thin, flexible, with a paper core and a plastic surface, pressed by American Graphophone from standard stampers at a slightly higher price.[29] Columbia had high hopes for an "unbreakable" record. Just before Marconi sailed back to Europe in September, Edward Easton threw him a lavish dinner at the Waldorf-Astoria.[30] But the Marconi record ultimately failed because a special gold-plated needle, good for no more than twelve plays, was required. The Marconi Velvet-Tones had one fabulous cultural trope, though: in the first series, Marconi's image is on the label showing his receding hairline; in a subsequent series, the inventor appears to have a full head of hair.[31]

●   ●   ●

In February 1906 Columbia created a department devoted exclusively to the manufacture and sales of its graphophone, separating them from the business of recording musical and spoken-word artists. Essentially, the new department was about dictation. The label began an in-house sales publication called *Graphonotes*. "Its literary model will be [Hearst editor] Arthur Brisbane rather than Henry James," declared the first edition, in April 1907. "In making this selection it is not influenced by the fact that Brisbane dictates all his editorials, while James still writes with a pen, vintage of '66."[32] The publication contracted with the author-humorist Elbert Hubbard to provide editorial material each month. Meanwhile *Graphonotes* did its bit in rousing the sales force:

> You heard of Theodore Roosevelt. He is apt to "want what he wants when he wants it." . . .
>
> So the Graphophone was called in.
>
> Reporters dictating their notes [about a case involving the Inter-State Commerce Commission] to a Graphophone got all the testimony to TR within thirty minutes.[33]

Graphonotes claimed that Columbia's Graphophone "cut the stenographic payroll in two," and that New Jersey Governor E. C. Stokes had his office equipped with commercial graphophones. The same edition then endorsed William M. Johnson of Hackensack—and a friend of Easton's—as the next governor of New Jersey.[34] (Johnson subsequently withdrew his name from the Republican primary race.)

Although it was Easton (along with Frank Dorian) who had pushed Columbia to record music in the first place, he couldn't let go of a vision of the graphophone as the premiere dictation machine. By winter 1907 he and Mauro were also devising ways to keep the peace with Victor, now the other dominant recording company. Edison had turned his attention to other matters. To bolster protection of their respective patents, Columbia pooled theirs with Victor's on June 3, 1907, locking up the legal right to manufacture the lateral-cut disk.

But the alliance wasn't enough to calm Easton, especially after the panic of October 1907. The firings that followed at Columbia sent him into a deep psychic well. Then came the train episode of January 1908, forcing Easton into a convalescence that took him away from the office for several months.

●　●　●

The Easton era wasn't over, though other men assumed day-to-day control of the company. The mood was dark. Paul Cromelin, then 37 and one of only three Columbia vice presidents in the decades before that corporate title was devalued, took over legal and patent matters and, as president of the American Musical Copyright League, protected Columbia's right to reproduce music.[35] Cromelin was also instrumental in bringing some of the more illustrious singing stars to the label, notably the soprano Lillian Nordica (née Lillian Norton) from Maine, whose stage name reflected her identification with Wagnerian roles.

By the time Easton was back at work, there was more than one reason to celebrate. Columbia brought out a new double-sided record for its popular line in 10" and 12" formats. The disks were heavy, laminated, inflexible, and shellacked—but they were a hit for a while. "Advertised as Double-Disc records," Sherman and Nauck wrote, "these new offerings were aggressively priced at 65 cents in the 10" size and $1.00 for the 12" size. An attractive new label appeared on the double-faced disks, sporting a large pair of musical notes in the upper center, partially fulfilling a long-time need for a logo to match Victor's popular 'Nipper.'"[36] Tim Brooks reproduced a 1908 ad, titled "Evolution of a Trade-mark," that showed a violinist in five tortured poses, squeaking out various note combinations, until he looks pleased with his "tandem note" sound in the sixth.[37] Columbia's Note the Notes logo never did, in fact, challenge the His Master's Voice logo, but it was distinguished enough to be associated with the label, on and off, until long after CBS took ownership.

With the Double-Discs being marketed to even working-class listeners, Columbia had all those cylinders on its hands. The label dumped a lot of these into Sears stores nationwide at eighteen cents a pop. "Standard size wax cylinder records," went the come-on, "that can be used on any graphophone, phonograph or other style of talking machine using the regular standard size wax cylinder records." Among the categories being offered were Vocal Solos in German, Negro Shouts, Records by the Vienna Orchestra, and Uncle John Weatherby's Laughing Stories.[38]

Edison, meanwhile, had a similar marketing connection to Montgomery Ward.[39] His opera cylinders sold for seventy-five cents, but their two-minute playing time—half that of some disks—now seemed woefully inadequate. Columbia would continue to make cylinders until 1912; Edison, clinging to the format of his earliest experiments in sound, never stopped making them until he retired in 1929, days after the stock market crash.

●　　●　　●

Despite the popularity of its double-sided disks, Columbia was still relying heavily on its London operation. On the heels of the American layoffs that had caused such despair for Easton, London let some of its staff go. In 1909 Frank Dorian left his post as Columbia's European general manager to return to America and again be at Easton's elbow. Officially, Dorian took over as sales director of Columbia's Dictaphone division; unofficially, he was Easton's chief advisor. Succeeding Dorian in London, John Cromelin (apparently no relation to Paul) halted cylinder production in England. In November 1909, Cromelin hired an American named Louis Sterling as British sales manager.[40] Sterling was then 30. Over the next 30 years Sterling, operating almost exclusively out of London, would be Columbia's White Knight, then one of its most formidable competitors, and finally a distant benefactor.

Louis Saul Sterling was born in 1879 on New York's Lower East Side, raised there on Orchard Street, and, while working as a newsboy, attended the Hebrew Technical Institute on Stuyvesant Street.[41] (Hebrew Technical was established in 1884, initially on Crosby Street, as a progressive manual arts high school for scientifically inclined sons of European immigrants.) In 1903, Sterling went to England in a cattleboat. The night he arrived he blew every penny he had, the equivalent of about $30, and was forced to spend the night in a London jail cell. When King George VI, knighting Sterling in 1937, asked him where he'd stayed on arrival, the new lord replied, "I was a guest of your grandfather, Sir."[42]

Within a year of his arrival Sterling impressed William Barry Owen, who hired him at the London Gramophone Company. Sterling quickly learned the record business and soon started his own company, Rena Records (probably named for his mother). Using Columbia's pressing plant for inexpensive Rena disks, Sterling got to know Cromelin and the staff there. Working his way up the English Columbia ladder, Sterling would sign Thomas Beecham, among other critical artists. When American collapsed in the early 1920s, Sterling would pick up the company and dust it off, showing there was silk beneath it.

●   ●   ●

But that was well into Columbia's future. In 1906 Victor had introduced the Victrola, its internal horn and built-in record storage an immediate hit. Columbia never quite countered, though the Victrola was enough of a triumph to push Columbia toward its double-sided disks. It wasn't until 1911 that Columbia offered the Grafanola, an obvious variation on the name Victrola, using an inside horn and adjustable front louvers. The Grafanola was never quite as fashionable as the Victrola, which was fast becoming a generic brand name, like Kleenex and Coke, and the name was a little silly. But the machines were handsome. A singularly beautiful advertisement from the era depicts the great Pavlowa dancing to Columbia records played on a Columbia Grafanola. "I use your Grafanola and dance records in my rehearsals with complete satisfaction," goes the world-famous ballerina's testimonial.[43]

With the introduction of the Grafanola, Columbia stepped up its classical recording. On March 14, 1911, the diminutive Mary Garden recorded selections from La Traviata.[44] Pianist Josef Hofmann, who gave recitals that included Rachmaninoff as well as Beethoven, stayed with the label for a while. Pablo Casals, the supreme cellist on record, began his long recording career in 1911 and was at Columbia by 1915; half a century later he would still be associated with the label. Violinist Eugene Ysaye, into middle age and already renowned throughout Europe, was signed in 1913. Within a few months Austrian conductor Felix Weingartner made his first recordings with the Columbia Symphony Orchestra; eventually Weingartner would conduct the first Masterworks album as well.

Columbia's pop roster boasted the white team of Collins & Harlan, whose 1911 version of Irving Berlin's "Alexander's Ragtime Band" took off like a rocket. Before partnering with Byron Harlan to form one of the more profitable duos of the acoustic era, Arthur Collins was a Philadelphia bookkeeper who had begun to record as early as 1898.[45] For Edison's National Phonograph, Collins recorded sides characteristically titled "Every Night I See That Nigger Standing Round," "Happy Days in Dixie," and "All Coons Look Alike to Me." Collins preferred the label "King of Ragtime Songs" to "coon singer." Collins recorded Bert Williams's signature song "Nobody" even before Williams could.

The concept of the coon song had been around since Reconstruction, when, as the American music expert Sigmund Spaeth put it, "American popular music became more and more distinctive. The Negro atmosphere increased in popularity and to it were added songs in other dialects, particularly Irish and German."[46]

"Most of the coon songs in the '90s were written by white composers (and mainly of Irish extraction)," wrote Douglas Gilbert.[47] If the coon song was on its face racist, it was also, in a deeper way, a testament to the way Negro music and dialect were being co-opted—and waiting for Negroes to subvert and remake the form.

3

Foxtrotting In and Out of War

In the autumn of 1911, Easton, who still had a nose for lucrative opportunities, proposed that Edison's National Phonograph Company merge with Columbia. Edison's president, Frank L. Dyer, outlined the proposal to his boss:

> Before Mr [Paul] Cromelin left [Columbia] he told me that he had been approached by Mr [George] Lyle, General Manager of the Columbia Phonograph Co., with the request that he try to interest us in some plan by which there could be a consolidation of the two interests, whereby very great savings in manufacture as well as administration could be secured.

Among the points in the proposal: that Edison would replace Columbia as the exclusive selling agent for American Graphophone; that the talking machines would bear Edison's name, exclusively if he desired; and that manufacturing would gradually shift from Bridgeport to Orange, New Jersey. "Naturally, the first question I asked," Dyer wrote to Edison, "was why, if you people are doing so well, are you willing to turn your business into our hands? Mr Easton said that their books are open to examination by any chartered accountants we may select, and they will show that last year their net earnings were $519,002.52 and that this year they are running much higher and would probably exceed $750,000. He said there was never a time when such a plan was less a necessity." On the other hand, Easton told Dyer that "personally he was anxious to get out of the business, that his old friends and associates in the business had most of them died and that he did not feel the interest that he once did."[1] Easton's proposal prompted Edison and Dyer to discuss two related problems: the unhealthy state of Edison's business and Victor's growing dominance over both companies. (In 1910 Victor's profits were *ten times* that of Columbia's.) Dyer articulated one possible objection to a merger that called up old antagonisms:

> In the next place, there is a feeling that has always existed against the Columbia Co. and Mr Easton personally as being unscrupulous and unreliable. This seems to be almost a tradition within our company. I know that Mr [Eldridge] Johnson entertains the same feeling. Undoubtedly the Columbia people have done many things that were extremely sharp and resourceful, but they have always managed to justify them when the effort has been made to stop the practices. Many of the men who have worked with Mr Easton for years speak in highest terms of him. Mr Cromelin, for example, has told me that Mr Easton has always been most considerate of him and that he regards him most highly. Whatever may be said of the Columbia Company or Mr Easton, can they possibly be any worse than some of our friends in the moving picture business?[2]

Edison rejected the proposal. Columbia would have to go up against big, bad Victor without Edison's know-how or his globally recognized name.

• • •

In the first month of 1913 Columbia Phonograph was reorganized and incorporated in West Virginia under the name Columbia Graphophone Company.[3] As a major recording entity, American Graphophone was gradually receding from its corporate sibling and its name would soon be spun out of the family altogether.

Americans were also spinning. Records could be played quickly, cheaply, and repeatedly, which helped give rise to the dance craze. In turn, record sales leaped as never before. Everyone followed the shows and schedules of the married dancers Irene and Vernon Castle, who were based on Long Island but danced all across Europe. At the end of 1913 the Castles opened their Castle House, on East 46th Street; the clientele, arriving by carriage and limousine "to enjoy modern dancing every afternoon from 4 to 6:30," paid to dance with the Castles, who had engaged at least two orchestras to play for them in separate parts of the town house.[4] Dancers of lower social station didn't have even one orchestra, but if they had access to a Victrola or Grafanola, they were in business. Columbia's all-around orchestra leader Charles Prince, then in his midforties, turned out foxtrot records with several studio orchestras. Initially a piano accompanist for Columbia with limited musical resources but a can-do professionalism, Prince was (not to put too fine a point on it) probably then at the peak of his musicianship. In the years just before World War I he conducted so many small dance orchestras for Columbia that he practically lived in its studios, frequently acting as straight man for the label's comedians.[5]

Two of the label's comedians were Weber & Fields, who repeated their "Mike and Meyer" stage characters at Columbia's studios and whose recordings would sell well into the 1930s. Lew Fields, father of the lyricist Dorothy Fields (she would become an indispensable contributor to Columbia's post-LP success in Broadway musical recordings), gave Vernon Castle, an emaciated Englishman who wanted to be a magician, his first stage opportunity as a dancer. Only a few years after Castle met and married Irene Foote, of New Rochelle, he had joined the Royal Flying Corps and gone to war.[6] In Irene Castle's My Husband, published soon after Vernon was killed in a flying accident at a Fort Worth air base, there's a scene in which Vernon writes from France to Irene in Manhasset: "There is a gramophone here playing all of the Watch Your Step music [by Irving Berlin; the Castles were the original stars] and it makes me so homesick."[7] The gramophone was His Master's Voice, but the show had been recorded at the behest of Louis Sterling.[8]

The label's most profitable comedy artist of the period was probably Joe Hayman, whose 1914 record Cohen on the Telephone proved particularly popular in Great Britain, where the American Hayman had settled after the turn of the century. Raised on the Lower East Side and graduated from City College, Hayman wrote most of his material and appeared frequently on stage with his wife under the name Hayman & Franklin. Decades before Shelley Berman and Bob Newhart used the telephone as a prop in their comedy acts, *Cohen on the Telephone* turned out to be only one of Hayman's many telephonic "misadventures."[9] Hayman eventually decamped for Victor, but through the war he was still putting the series out on Columbia with entries like *Cohen Telephones from Brighton* ("the first time Cohen uses a coin-in-the-slot telephone—and he strikes a rich streak of trouble") and *Cohen Telephones the Health Department*, written for Hayman by the humorist Montague Glass. "Are you dere?" was the Cohen catchphrase, delivered in an affectionate Yiddish accent. "Vot number do I vant? Vell, vot numbers have you got?" As conceived by Hayman, the character was originally named Schleima Cohen, anglicized to Sam after the boy had escaped from Novogeorgievski, a military camp in Poland that "sheltered an army of 60,000 troops in those days, ninety-nine per cent of whom were anti-Semites."[10] In the biography Hayman worked up for his character, Sam Cohen labored in an East End sweatshop until he'd saved enough money for passage to America, landing at Castle Garden at age 14 but never quite shedding his Polish-Yiddish accent. The Cohen series sent up the accent, of course, as well as the headaches involved in communicating on the telephone. Though the records might have been marketed to Jewish listeners, some of them sold in the millions and exposed an Eastern European immigrant idiom to listeners who had never—not willingly, anyway—met a Jew.

•　　•　　•

In the years leading up to America's entry into World War I, Columbia could still boast Bert Williams. "You're on the Right Road but You're Going the Wrong Way" and "I Was Certainly Going Some" extended his insouciant wit captured on record. But Williams wasn't the only important black artist on the label. In 1915 alone the great W. C. Handy was paid $3,827 in royalties by Columbia—an extraordinary income for the era. Most of this was from recordings of his "Yellow Dog Blues," "The Girl You Never Met," and "Memphis Blues," which had been originally composed as an election campaign song. Handy's on-off association with Columbia would lead, nearly four decades later, to what may be the high-water mark of Columbia's jazz catalog, *Louis Armstrong Plays W. C. Handy*. Meanwhile Handy continued to record whenever he was invited to. In 1918 Columbia sent him a contract in Memphis to bring 12 musicians to New York to make 12 records. Handy picked up several musicians in Chicago, then they all raced along the platform to catch the New York Central express. The sight of them—well-dressed Negroes about to board the train not as porters but as passengers—caused a stir. "My God," exclaimed a portly dowager with several chins. "A gang of niggers!"[11] Handy and his men went on to New York to fulfill the recording assignment. Columbia promoted the resulting 12 sides by proclaiming "Handy Week" throughout the United States.

The Fisk Jubilee Singers, the black quartet out of Fisk University, first recorded in the 1890s and became a Columbia staple in 1915. This group was a full generation past the original Jubilee Singers, and the acclaim it received had as much to do with the group's reputation from prerecording days.

Even in the recording industry, however, the Lord giveth and taketh away. Interest in gospel had grown partly due to recordings and partly to the late nineteenth-century expansion of singing in American colleges. But now Fisk and other Negro liberal arts colleges found their endowments being peeled away—for their own good, it was argued. The historian David Levering Lewis wrote, "The first chairman of the Rockefeller-based General Education Board had argued the necessity of protecting the Afro-American from 'so-called higher education' so that he 'should not be educated beyond his environment.' Booker Washington had concurred, regretting that in the past 'men have tried to use, with these simple people just freed from slavery and with no past, no inherited traditions of learning, the same methods of education which they have used in New England.'"[12] So grants to Atlanta, Fisk, and Lincoln were sharply cut by several foundations, including the mighty

Carnegie, and by the General Education Board. This had the effect of further marginalizing the colleges serving the second generation born out of slavery and reducing their musical programs to silence.

A few years earlier Columbia had recorded the Standard Quartette, the Chicago-based black group that garnered an enormous audience through its rose-colored, misty-eyed traveling show *South before the War*, which romanticized slavery as a time of happy-go-lucky songfests and the Negro knowing his place.[13] In the coming postelectrical years it would take the tough, criminally musical Louis Armstrong and Bessie Smith, among several others, to burn through those misty anachronisms by recording for Columbia and its subsidiaries.

●   ●   ●

In 1915 Columbia began to make records in Chicago, home base for some of Armstrong's greatest recordings to come. But back in New York's Central Valley, Edward Easton was fading. At 59 he'd left the metropolitan area one last time to die in a sanitarium 60 miles from Columbia headquarters, leaving four daughters and a son and an estate estimated at $1 million. That son, Mortimer, served on the board of directors but never carried much authority in the brief time he was there. As Tim Brooks remarked, the founder's era was over.[14]

In late summer through early fall of 1915, Columbia's plant in Bridgeport went through labor turmoil that was felt nationwide. Representatives of the AFL had arrived in Bridgeport to organize workers at Remington Arms and Ammunition, housed down the block from Columbia Phonograph, on Barnum Avenue. (The street was named for the showman P. T. Barnum, who was descended from a long line of Connecticut Barnums and elected mayor of Bridgeport in 1875.) Seeking eight-hour days, workers began to stay out, and the strikes spread like alley fires. Bridgeport was a town of factory workers, of women and men who could only dream each day of leisure. Columbia employees, already enjoying a nine-hour day, walked out in concert with their city's trade union brethren: Remington, long one of Connecticut's

major employers; Bryant Electric Company; Connecticut Electric Manufacturing; Salts Textile; Crawford Laundry; and Canfield Rubber—these
were only six among fourteen companies that had been struck.[15] Maureen Howard published Bridgeport Bus half a century later, but her vision
of the "city on the banks of the exhausted Naugatuck" reflected those
even darker earlier decades when she wrote, "There is a line of rust
along the shore that smells of rubber—the gardens, if I may be allowed,
of factories, and then the hills with all the streets of brown houses
coming up toward me and towards my street of superior brown
houses."[16] Columbia closed the Bridgeport plant for two weeks. Tim
Brooks has speculated that Columbia's new president, Philip T. Dodge,
who had previously run International Paper and Mergenthaler Linotype,
might have instituted practices that caused the plant's workers to
bridle.[17] (Dodge's link to Columbia probably had been made years earlier through Andrew Devine, another prominent reporter-stenographer
who was one of the original investors in American Graphophone and
had remained a director there and at Mergenthaler.)[18] At Remington
and other Bridgeport-based factories the eight-hour day was declared
won, but many of the strikers weren't rehired.

●   ●   ●

There was political activity among Columbia's artists, too. The English
contralto Clara Butt, who'd made several recordings for the label—
sometimes with Thomas Beecham—campaigned in Britain for
"women's right to work" as the war expanded in Europe.[19] Mme. Butt
(later Dame Clara) sang war songs as well. Columbia, meanwhile, was
recording not only for the German market but, up through April 1917
when the United States entered the war, specifically for the widows of
German soldiers.[20]

Within weeks the label did an about-face by destroying its catalog of
German artists and composers in what John Hammed called "a fit of
patriotism."[21] The order to do so might have come from Philip Dodge,
who had been bumped up to Columbia chairman, or from the label's

new president, Francis Whitten, who had trained in the navy as an engineer. Disks of Bach, Beethoven, Brahms, and Wagner were smashed. The music critic Olin Downes published *The Lure of Music*, "depicting the human side of great composers" in the Columbia Graphophone catalog. Beneath the book's table of contents Downes declared, "Composers representative of Germany have been omitted from this volume." Although the book was published by Harper & Brothers, Downes was probably advanced money by Columbia, whose dealers eventually carried the book for a high-priced $1.50. Downes acknowledged "indebtedness to the Columbia Graphophone Company" for use of its records and record "laboratory."[22] (Later in 1917 Harper and Columbia would collaborate on the publication of its Bubble Books children's series to coincide with Columbia's distribution of its Little Wonder series of disks.)[23]

The expulsion of the Germans occurred right around the time American Graphophone, as the parent company, was dissolved. The rechristened Columbia Graphophone Manufacturing Company was incorporated in Delaware on December 13, 1917. This had been a long time coming, but industry conditions during the war—a shortage of materials for one, necessitating the reclaiming and recycling of old records, and the lapsing of Columbia's and Victor's lateral-cut disk patents, which meant that any old company could make lateral-cut records—accelerated the dissolution. The corporate father ceased to exist. American's assets were assigned to Columbia, and most of its executives found positions in this reorganization, which was now headquartered in the Woolworth Building at 233 Broadway in Manhattan.[24] The Dictaphone Company became a separate division of Columbia Graphophone.

Columbia was pushing the Grafanola, but times were tough. "A Columbia Record is like that old story—two sides to it—only *both* sides of a Columbia Record are good," proclaimed the in-house sales publication the *Peptimist*. "This is our point. When selling Grafanolas or talking Grafanolas, say 'Grafanola.' Don't talk about 'this machine' or 'that model'; cut the words 'machine' and 'instrument' out of your vocabulary. Put in the word 'Grafanola.'"[25] (It could sound like a double-talking Berlitz lesson.) Columbia published *The Grafanola in the Class Room* to try to interest schools in ordering them in lots. One model was the Pushmobile—basically a graphophone on two wheels and two stationary legs, your choice of oak or mahogany. The booklet included Music Appreciation suggestions and a come-on for Columbia's Measures of Musical Talent series, which would teach the listener a sense of pitch, intensity, time, consonance, and tonal memory.[26]

Although Columbia had jettisoned its German music during the war, it expanded its Eastern European catalog, particularly records made by and for immigrant Jews. This wasn't peculiar to Columbia—most of the larger labels, including Edison, had built Jewish or Rumanian catalog, going back to Fred Gaisberg's field recordings for the Gramophone Company at the turn of the century—but Columbia was headquartered closest to the Lower East Side, and this proved crucial because, during the war, Yiddish recordings made in Eastern Europe were hard to get. Through its A&R man David Nodiff, Columbia was in touch with the Jewish street. In 1917 Nodiff brought in composer-fiddler-bandleader Abe Schwartz, who would oversee Columbia's Jewish division for many years. Schwartz made just about every kind of music, from klezmer to large ensemble secular recordings, and was so consumed by recording that, in 1920, he yanked his painfully reluctant 12-year-old daughter Sylvia into playing piano on one of his sessions—a session that started her own recording career.[27] Columbia recorded more than its share of cantors, including David Roitman and Josef Rosenblatt, who was sometimes called "The Jewish Caruso."[28]

* * *

Despite a slight depression toward the end of the war, Columbia in the post-Easton era appeared to be holding its own. By late 1917 Columbia had record plants in London, Toronto, and Brazil as well. The Bridgeport plant, which now housed hundreds of workers, was spread over eleven and a half acres; the main building was three stories high and measured 410 by 80 feet.[29] The notion of *record collecting*, of *owning* music because you bought disks that contained the music, was displacing the amassing of sheet music, just as the player (Grafanola, Victrola, etc.) was displacing pianos in living rooms all across Europe and the Americas. The July 1918, *Peptimist* reported that piano dealer Howard Farwell & Company, of St. Paul, Minnesota, was "erecting 10 record booths in space formerly occupied by pianos." That same month, just a couple of summers before radio would begin its long dominance of mass media, Columbia introduced its Nation's Forum series—recordings of political leaders addressing issues they were associated with. The series was inaugurated with General John J. Pershing on one side, former ambassador to Germany James W. Gerard on the other. "At American Headquarters in France," went the ad copy for Pershing's side, "this grim, iron-gray man spoke with crisp, soldierly brevity, into the horn of a recording instrument a message to the mothers, wives, fathers, children of the men who are fighting there with him on the shell-torn fields of France." Gerard—"the man the Kaiser couldn't bluff; known to millions for his fearless Americanism, his splendid action in the face of an emergency—in his own ringing voice, tells what true loyalty is." The Nation's Forum disks were intended to deliver news, but Columbia was also getting at the miracle of recording when the ad copy promised, "To hear them, long years after the war, will bring again to your heart the surge and thrill of these wonderful days."[30] The records had their own Nation's Forum logo, though design and colors changed according to the recording. When Eamon De Valera came to the United States to raise money for Sinn Fein and recorded three sides, the label used was an Irish green and gold.[31]

Although Columbia continued to release its standard popular fare, from Henry Burr to the ubiquitous Irving Kaufman, its war-inflected records sold even better. On December 21, 1918, Nora Bayes (née Dora Goldberg) had a hit with the brand-new "How You Gonna Keep 'Em Down on the Farm?," written in response to the new worldliness of American soldiers. Prince's Band sold hundreds of thousands of copies of the 10" "Columbia, the Gem of the Ocean" backed with "Hail Columbia"—a paean to the nation, of course, rather than the label Prince worked for, but great publicity nevertheless. There were also several versions of Schubert's *Marche Militaire*. It paid to be patriotic.

• • •

With the Great War over and sales looking pretty strong, Columbia could afford to sign artists to both its popular and pre-Masterworks classical divisions. In 1919 it brought in the soprano Rosa Ponselle. Ponselle's coach and accompanist Romano (Nino) Romani was a studio conductor for Columbia Graphophone, and it behooved him to have the soprano, then singing at the Met, signed to the label instead of the more prestigious Victor. Ponselle would have preferred Victor, mostly because she had made her Metropolitan debut in *La Forza del Destino* opposite Caruso, the Red Seal label's greatest star. She speculated that her manager William Thorner took a payoff to steer her to Columbia.[32] (If so, the under-the-table practice went back to the beginnings of vaudeville and would continue, in one form or another, throughout the twentieth century.) Between late 1918 and 1923, Ponselle recorded nearly 50 acoustic sides for Columbia before moving at last to Victor in 1925. Her career is notable not only because her memoirs allow us a peek behind the curtain of the Metropolitan Opera but also because as a child she came out of vaudeville, not classical singing. The girl from Meriden, Connecticut, had made it to the Met and a Columbia recording career with a gorgeous but largely untrained voice.

Columbia also corralled the dynamic young Russian violinist Toscha Seidel. Having moved to New York by the time he was a teenager, Seidel played often in the East Coast's best concert halls and was available to Columbia to make records whenever he was in town.

In 1919 Columbia also signed the bandleader Ted Lewis (né Friedman). Lewis's music could be located somewhere between steerage and the captain's ballroom—less overtly Jewish than Abe Schwartz but looser than Sam Lanin. Columbia, acknowledging Lewis's popularity, and perhaps feeding his ego just enough to keep him satisfied, gave him his own special label—a crude drawing of the bandleader raising his hat—to adorn all his records.[33]

After popularizing "After You've Gone" at Victor, the actress-singer Marion Harris wanted to record W. C. Handy's "St. Louis Blues." Many record buyers who heard Harris's Victor recordings assumed she was black; in fact she was a blond Midwesterner. Whatever the color of her skin, Victor was queasy about the blues, and it was this, according to Handy's memoir, that prompted her to jump to Columbia. There she recorded "St. Louis Blues" as well as Handy's "Beale Street Blues" and "Memphis Blues." (In many of her Columbia recordings she's backed by Charles Prince, who rarely sounded equipped to deal with anything remotely jazz-inflected.) Two years and many recordings later, Harris moved over to Brunswick, where she remained for the rest of the decade. After some Hollywood movie work, many appearances on Broadway, and a long residence in England, she barely escaped the London Blitz alive, only to die at 48 in a midtown Manhattan hotel in a fire she probably inadvertently started with a cigarette.

Columbia had two great Jewish belters in Al Jolson and Sophie Tucker, each owning voices large enough to be heard in the crudest acoustical recordings. When Tucker made her first recording—for Edison, in 1910, when she was 26—she was scheduled to be paid $1,000 for ten sides. "When I heard the playback I turned to the boys and let out a yell. 'My God, I sound like a foghorn.' I was terrible." Dismayed, Tucker made only two of the negotiated ten, for $200.[34] During the next decade, of course, she learned how to sing on record. Jolson had first recorded for Columbia in 1913, backed by (who else?) Charles Prince. Jolie's version of Gershwin's "Swanee," which he had insisted on interpolating into the show Sinbad after hearing Gershwin play it at a party, sold a lot of records for Columbia in 1920.

●　●　●

In the summer of 1919, another monthlong strike halted work at the Bridgeport plant. After Columbia management threatened to close the plant and move its operations, the strikers returned to work under unchanged conditions. "On the other hand," the Times reported, "the company agrees to take back all the strikers without prejudice, the adjustment of wages in the controversy to be through shop committees and not through union representatives."[35]

The company was losing its sense of humor. So was the nation. On October 28, 1919, Woodrow Wilson vetoed the Volstead Act, the enforcement arm of Prohibition, but the veto was overridden and on January 16, 1920, Prohibition became the law of the land. Music publishing had always been dominated by scrappy, aggressive men, but that didn't mean they were necessarily unlawful. Prohibition threw open the recording industry's door to a more openly criminal element, particularly when it came to the dusky netherworld where recordings meet live performances. "Prohibition led to smuggling and bootlegging," wrote the music business historian Hazel Meyer, "and the men who engaged in these lucrative enterprises became powerful in the entertainment world. The underworld liked consorting familiarly with show business personalities. The bootlegging set were big spenders, and night club proprietors were far from reluctant to take their money. Also, several of the tough but fun-loving types thought it would be nice to own their own clubs where they could not only reap all the profits, but also stand as boss-men to the entertainers who worked there."[36]

Columbia withstood Prohibition's criminal element but couldn't quite stave off the depression that followed the postwar boom. Radio was seen as the prime culprit. In 1920 KDKA Pittsburgh was the first radio station licensed for broadcasting. Two years later there were 200 licensed stations. Records still sold well for a while, but radio was seen as an overpowering presence and, offering plenty of live music as well as the spoken word (news, drama), supposedly made most recordings superfluous. With Prohibition the so-called Jazz Age had begun, the speakeasy and live jazz affianced in a long engagement, but Columbia didn't quite know what to do with it. Okeh Phonograph, which started in New York in 1915 as the American distributor for the Lindstrom chain of European record companies, became the premiere blues label. Black Swan, founded by W. C. Handy's former publishing partner Harry Pace and also based in New York, proved to be the most daring for black music in general. Okeh and Black Swan, along with a few other small labels, gave rise to something new: the reproduction of a jazz *performance* so that other players could study an improvised solo over and over. The twenties decade was probably the first in which some jazz musicians schooled themselves entirely by listening to records.

•   •   •

While no one was looking, Columbia Graphophone had come under the control of DuPont. As early as 1919, brokerage listings folded Columbia's stock into DuPont's.[37] Subsequent hits like Jolson's "Avalon," "April Showers," and "Toot, Toot, Tootsie! (Goo'Bye)" couldn't keep the company profitable. DuPont wasn't equipped to handle the downturn that accompanied the rise of radio—by the end of 1922 there were said to be 3 million radios in American homes—and Columbia teetered on the edge of bankruptcy.

The stage was set for Louis Sterling to inspect what was left. Sterling loved books as well as numbers—in fact he looked a little like a Semitic, merrier version of H. L. Mencken—and, after twenty years working in every capacity in the record industry, knew the business inside out. The deal he negotiated was complicated and not pretty, but it would ultimately resuscitate Columbia. On November 16, 1922, Sterling bought Columbia Graphophone Company Ltd. of England, Columbia's longtime British arm, for $500,000, including ownership of trademark registrations in the European countries and other countries in the Eastern Hemisphere. (For international use, that trademark wouldn't revert to American Columbia until Sony purchased the company 65 years later.) Sterling, ardent reader and budding bibliophile that he was, knew that what has come to be called phonography—the business of writing on sound—had, after some 30 years, so invaded the culture as to be felt everywhere, radio's recent apparent conquest notwithstanding. That same year James Joyce would publish *Ulysses*, with its many references to gramophones and recorded music. There was Bella Cohen's gramophone, for one, but the novel also contained upward of 300 *yeses*, uttered by Molly Bloom and others, the dizzying number said to reflect the phenomenon of "needle-stick," repetition in new fiction and poetry that was inspired by the way a phonograph needle skips or remains stuck on a disk. (The scholar John M. Picker gives Conrad's "The horror! The horror!" and Eliot's "Do I dare? Do I dare?" as examples.)[38]

Five months after the sale of its English branch to Sterling, who had made it profitable in the first place, Columbia, needing much more cash to keep the wolf away, unloaded the Dictaphone Company to investment bankers Richard Swartwout and Paul Appenzellar for a cool million.[39] But the million came too late. On October 15, 1923, Columbia Graphophone fell into receivership.

4

Acoustic Prohibition to Electric Depression

While the bankruptcy court sorted out Columbia Graphophone's affairs, Louis Sterling consolidated his holdings. Encouraged by Thomas Lamont of J. P. Morgan, a major Graphophone shareholder, Sterling was already considering the possibility of merging Columbia Graphophone Ltd. with the Gramophone Company, now known as HMV for His Master's Voice.[1] The merger wouldn't come to fruition for several years. But the very idea suggested that Sterling was hardly terrified of radio; where other men saw death throes, Sterling saw birth pangs. Back in New York, Columbia Graphophone's assets were purchased by a creditors' committee and transferred to the Columbia Phonograph Company, Inc., organized in the State of New York on February 27, 1924. Stock of the Columbia Phonograph Company, Inc. was distributed to creditors of the bankrupt company.[2]

Not that Columbia recording had gone dormant. In fact Felix Weingartner recorded the Brahms First Symphony in what became the first official Masterworks recording. Also in her first years with the label was the young singer Bessie Smith, whose recordings would bridge the acoustic and electric, blues and jazz, her overwhelming influence felt long after she was dead.

Meanwhile the Columbia name appeared to be up for grabs, to be affixed to any old shop. In Manhattan alone there were more than three dozen concerns that carried the name. A Poverty Row movie company called C.B.C., which made pictures in Los Angeles but was incorporated in New York, had been named for its partners, Jack Cohn, Joe Brandt, and Harry Cohn. As it became more successful, it needed to turn away from its reputation for cheapness, reflected by its sobriquet Corned Beef and Cabbage. On January 10, 1924, C.B.C. became Columbia Pictures, with no affiliation to the record label, though many cultural observers thought otherwise.[3] That affiliation would in fact be realized, though not for another 65 years.

By 1924 any company involved in the reproduction of sound ignored radio at its own peril. As the smoke cleared around the reorganized Columbia, Alfred H. Grebe, owner of the Grebe Radio Manufacturing Company, proposed that Columbia invest with him in a radio station. Grebe's factory, on Van Wyck Boulevard on Long Island, turned out hundreds of thousands of radios each year. Columbia, wading warily into the terrifying crosscurrents of wireless entertainment, became a stockholder of Grebe's Atlantic Broadcasting Company, which owned one station, WAHG (Grebe's initials) in Richmond Hill (Grebe's birthplace on the Island). Eventually Grebe operated station WBOQ (borough of Queens), which also became part of the WABC network. [4]

Radio was like a healthy infant: insatiable, impossible to ignore, and depriving those around it from slumber. While Columbia and other phonograph companies tried to figure out how to handle the medium, Bell Labs, under the supervision of Joseph Maxfield, had been experimenting with electrical recording. To use Charlie Schicke's necessarily simple explanation: "The three basic acoustical recording components—recording horn, diaphragm and cutting stylus—were replaced by a condenser microphone, a vacuum tube amplifier and an electromagnetically controlled cutting stylus."[5] The stylus (needle) was actuated not by sound waves but by electrical impulses; you could capture highs and lows that had been out of bounds with the acoustic method. After five years of experimentation, Bell Labs was ready to license the new system through Western Electric.

There was a catch: Western Electric was offering the system, for a $50,000 advance payment and a percentage of recording royalties, only to American companies. (This effectively excluded the all-powerful French company Pathé, which had established New York offices after

World War I, from participating immediately.) Columbia took a look and knew the possibilities, but it was still cash-poor, if not broke.

But not for long. Louis Sterling, who now owned Columbia Graphophone Ltd., came to the United States and, buying Columbia Phonograph— that is, the old American company that had just sold its English affiliate to him—for $2.5 million, also bought into Western Electric's new system. Sterling and his partners now owned Columbia, with Sterling acting as its managing director, and also owned rights (among other American companies) to the electrical process.

It's tempting to overdramatize the development and say that electric reproduction replaced acoustic overnight; it's more accurate to say electric *supplanted* acoustic, because acoustic hung on for a while, particularly among the cheaper labels. Columbia would begin its durable Harmony budget line in 1925 to distribute the acoustic recordings it had in its vault.[6] Several years later it would still occasionally record using the acoustic method—usually when there was a contract issue to skirt.

On February 26, 1925, Columbia became the first American company to obtain the Western Electric rights to the electrical recording process, two months ahead of Victor. Sterling's reorganization officially took effect on June 17, 1925, under the name Columbia Phonograph Company. Offices were in Manhattan at 1819 Broadway and 121 West 20th Street (essentially the new and old loci of Tin Pan Alley). Sterling became chairman of the board.[7] H. L. Willson was president; F. J. Ames secretary; H. C. Cox, an alumnus of American Graphophone, was treasurer and soon to replace Willson.[8]

Western Electric's wasn't the only new electrical recording process: General Electric, also based in Bridgeport, collaborated with the old billiard- and bowling-ball manufacturer Brunswick and came up with a process driven by photoelectric cell. The system turned out to be less practical than Western Electric's, but it would be modified for motion picture recording. Brunswick had begun its own record division, too, overseen by Ted Wallerstein, a former college athlete turned oil worker who came from a prominent Philadelphia family. In another fifteen years, wary of heart trouble and no longer so young,

Wallerstein would become the first Columbia Records president under CBS ownership.[9]

Radio was new, of course—and free. Despite the new electrical recording process and noticeably improved fidelity, phonograph records sat in shops, piled high and gathering dust. According to Robert Sobel's history of RCA, "Industry-wide phonograph sales evaporated, going from 2.2 million in 1919 to 596,000 in 1922, and purchases of records declined almost as dramatically."[10] The news now seemed to be about radio waves and broadcasting.

Yet, curiously, it was radio, which had seemed so capable of crushing the record business once and for all, that became its chief benefactor. Recording artists whose names and voices had been known by the public were now regarded, thanks in part to the immediacy of live broadcasts, as *personalities*—as women and men you felt you knew—which, in turn, only enhanced their recording careers. As far as the hardware went, if you can't beat 'em, join 'em. By 1928 Columbia, Victor, and Brunswick were all selling radio-phonograph combinations. (The radios were manufactured elsewhere and merely introduced as an added attraction to the basic phonograph instrument.) Columbia went into business with Kolster Radio, selling a no-frills portable phonograph for $50, while its top-of-the-line Columbia-Kolster Viva-Tonal—walnut cabinet, mahogany overlay, gold-plated parts, satin finish—went for $475.[11] Who could afford $475? For some passionate record buyers, it was half a year's salary. Undeniably, though, the status signaled by owning such a piece of furniture, whether or not music was coming out of it, could help a phonograph company turn a profit, even if the profit had to be shared with a radio manufacturer.

•   •   •

Louis Sterling left the day-to-day management of his new subsidiary American Columbia in the capable hands of Harry Cox, who had become president of the label, and went back to England. There he would continue to build an extraordinary roster of artists, including

Fred Astaire making his earliest recordings, tapping alongside George Gershwin's piano-playing, and Thomas Beecham conducting his dreamy interpretations of Delius.[12] In New York, Columbia's new electrical process, coupled with exposure offered by radio, was making recording stars out of unlikely candidates. One of them was Art Gillham, "The Whispering Pianist," a radio performer who sent telegrams to several labels offering his services. "The only companies that responded to the telegrams were Pathé, then Okeh, then Columbia," Gillham recalled in 1957, "so I made records." Gillham appears to have been the first Columbia artist to be recorded with the new Western Electric process (February 1925). Gillham was recorded frequently by Frank Walker. Today Walker is remembered largely as the man who brought Bessie Smith into the studio in 1923, when he was in charge of popular recording for Columbia.

Walker had first heard Smith sing in Selma, Alabama, in 1917. So when Clarence Williams, the peripatetic piano player who was paid as a consultant to Okeh, spoke about having heard Smith recently, Walker was eager to have her record. "Go down there and find her," Walker instructed Williams, "and bring her back."[13]

•   •   •

Smith was born in Chattanooga on April 15, 1894, daughter of a part-time Baptist preacher who died while she was an infant.[14] Raised primarily by her older sister, she left Chattanooga at 18 to go on the road with the Moses Stokes Troupe. Ma Rainey was a member of that troupe, and it's fair to say that Smith drank in Rainey's singing style. Smith's first husband died, leaving her widowed in Philadelphia. In 1922 or so, Smith sang for Fred Hager, who had so successfully recorded Mamie Smith for Okeh. Hager found Bessie Smith "too black," her voice "too rough."

So it was up to Frank Walker and Clarence Williams to bring Smith in to Columbia. In New York Walker took Smith under his wing and arranged for her to record with some of the best players available. Beginning in February 1923, accompanied by Clarence Williams on piano,

Smith recorded mostly at the label's Columbus Circle studio. In April she recorded "Baby, Won't You Please Come Home" and "Tain't Nobody's Biz-ness If I Do," both sides becoming instant classics. In those last two years of standard acoustic recording, Smith's voice sounds as though it came with its own pre-amp. "Down Hearted Blues," released in 1924, sold a million disks. Smith's Columbia contract stipulated that she'd make a minimum of 12 sides per year, but by December 1925 she'd made 100 sides. On many of these she was accompanied on piano by Fletcher Henderson, who was still in the early stages of a brilliant if recessive music career—he had been an Atlanta University graduate in chemistry and then a song demonstrator for Pace & Handy in Harlem—much of it to be captured later on Columbia.[15] Louis Armstrong, that sun about to burst into an all-enveloping warmth, was also on hand for some sessions.

Meanwhile, Frank Walker turned his administrative responsibilities over to Eddie King in order to manage Smith himself.[16] Smith relied on Walker, trusted him. On tour in the summer of 1926, she heard that Walker's young son John was seriously ill. Smith, according to Paul Oliver, "promptly suspended the rest of her tour, presenting herself to a surprised Mrs Walker at her Long Island home, and insisted on acting as servant, maid, and nurse until the two-year-old child was out of danger three weeks later."[17]

Walker was tough on Smith and had little compunction about canceling a recording session if she was drunk. He also advised her to stop frittering away her earnings, maybe even buy a house in Philadelphia. In the winter of 1928, Smith dismissed Walker as her manager and put her finances in the hands of husband Jackie Gee, the former night watchman who apparently gave as good as he got from her—and maybe worse. Walker continued to supervise her recordings through 1931, however, and those sides are ripe with Smith's rich singing and accompaniment by such seasoned musicians as stride pianist James P. Johnson and cornetist Ed Allen.

In the first years of electrical recording, Columbia had another great black singing star, though one who consciously moved away from the roots she shared with Bessie Smith. Decades before she settled, lucratively but uncomfortably, into playing mammy roles, Ethel Waters was a slinky singer who recorded some of Columbia's more thrilling records of the era. As a child she was shuttled by her family between Camden, New Jersey, and Philadelphia—two key cities in phonographic history—and grew into the sobriquet Sweet Mama Stringbean. Waters's sexiness was apparent even in her voice. Her earliest recordings were made for the Cardinal Company, and then for Black Swan. In Harlem she earned a reputation as a fine singer, then went to Atlantic City, where she caught the ear (and presumably the eye) of Bert Williams. Williams told her, "Young lady, you have the makings of a great artist." Sophie Tucker, then known as a "coon shouter," paid Waters to sing privately for her so Tucker could study her delivery.[18] Right around the time Columbia went into business with Western Electric, Waters discovered the repertoire that would become the foundation of the Great American Songbook. Her style turned more cabaret than jazz, with emotional depths that only occasionally glanced back at the raunchy material she'd discarded. In 1925 she began to make records for Columbia at $250 apiece, or $125 per side—not close to Jolson's or Tucker's fees (Tucker was getting $1,500 a week at the Paradise Room, on Columbus Circle), but not bad either.[19] Tucker clung to her old-fashioned bluesy innuendo and, influenced or not by Waters, recorded two powerhouse hits, "Some of These Days" (1926) and "My Yiddishe Momma" (1928; English on one side, Yiddish on the other) for Columbia. Waters, in the shank of her own Columbia evening, wrote, "But I still wanted no part of the white time."[20]

Neither Waters nor any other black artist could sing at the Club Frivolity, on Broadway near 52nd Street. (The routine integration of nightlife in midtown Manhattan was still more than a decade away.) That's where Ben Selvin was playing one night when Harry Cox, by then president of the new Columbia Broadcasting System, and Frank Walker came in to ask him if he'd consider becoming music liaison between Columbia Broadcasting and Columbia Phonograph—only 21 hours a week, leaving him plenty of time for his bandleading. Selvin, whose 1919 Victor recording of "Dardanella" was said to be the first million-selling pop record, was making plenty of dough by recording for several labels at once and, like Abe Schwartz, under several different names. Cox and Walker met Selvin's price. Selvin was soon backing Waters and would come to regard her as his favorite recording artist. "A doll," is how Selvin described her a half century later.[21] The peak of Waters's recording work at Columbia might have come in 1929 with "Am I Blue?" By the time she left the label she had recorded nearly 200 sides. Those Columbia sides comprise a wise, love-affirming middle ground, the musical station connecting her saucier hedonist years at Black Swan and the publicly religious years—first as a devout Catholic, then a tireless spokesperson for Billy Graham—after she had retired from recording and acting.[22]

. . .

In his first year as broadcasting-recording liaison, Ben Selvin handed a $76,000 check for royalties on four records to the team of Moran and Mack.[23] Released in 1927, Columbia's *Two Black Crows, Parts I & II* spun right out of the stores, selling more than a million copies. Two white men whose act was invariably in blackface, Moran and Mack were viewed by some progressive souls as anachronisms.

They were not. Initially, nobody at the label but Sterling believed Columbia could make a dime with the duo. Both natives of Kansas, though they hadn't met there, Moran and Mack ran into each other on the road now and then, and finally appeared individually in a 1917 Broadway show called *Over the Top*. After that they were a team, managed by Alexander Pantages (founder of the vaudeville theater chain), assembling gags and bits of business through several shows—George White's *Scandals*, Ziegfeld's *Follies*, and others—until they became something of an institution.[24] It's not known whether Sterling first heard them in London, where the team played fourteen consecutive weeks, or in New York, where Sterling spent considerable time once he'd assumed control of American Columbia. One thing is certain, though: Moran and Mack made Sterling laugh like nobody else.

In 1928 Charles Mack published *Two Black Crows in the A.E.F.* It's one of the earlier attempts at parlaying success in one medium (in this case, recording) into another (publishing). Mack again recounts the adventures of the "two black crows" from Tennessee, Amos and Willie, as they volunteer for a colored regiment during World War I. They are so nicknamed by local farmers, whose cornfields are often picked clean by the two hungry men. As in Moran and Mack's recordings, the characters' exchanges are coated in minstrelsy but also dipped in the sly wit that black performers (notably Bert Williams) often employed to subvert the tradition. That is, although Moran and Mack were white, they knew how to use irony and mordancy within the "coon" sketch framework. Willie: "Well, I put my name down for de draft but it don't bother me none. Dey cain't make me fight lessen I want to." Amos: "Dey cain't make you fight. But dey can take you where de fighting is and you can use your own judgment!"[25] Mack's book is dedicated to "My Good Friends, The Makers, Distributors and Users of the Columbia Phonograph Records, Whose Interest and Encouragement Have Meant so Much to The Two Black Crows."

* * *

Okeh Records had been established in New York City in 1915 by Felix Kahn, a former member of the Carl Lindstrom chain of European record companies, including the Odeon and Parlophone labels. Three years later Okeh was bought by the Otto Heinemann Phonograph Supply Company, which changed its name in 1921 to General Phonograph. The offices were in midtown Manhattan, the factories in Putnam, Connecticut. On October 23, 1926, Columbia gobbled up Okeh, which would arguably remain the most distinctive of the few subsidiary labels to come. Part of Columbia's deal was its acquisition of Odeon's and Parlophone's European catalogs. Columbia also grabbed General Phonograph's recording studios in Union Square.

Okeh, taking a cue from the all-Negro Black Swan label, quickly expanded its race records catalog and also included country, hillbilly, and Western music. Much of the credit for this should go to Thomas G. Rockwell, a former Columbia Records salesman in Hollywood who became Okeh's general manager in Chicago before he was twenty-five. Through the reverse lens of politically correct revisionism, Tommy Rockwell is often viewed as a white man who exploited black recording artists. But he did much to promote Louis Armstrong in the years when Armstrong was stepping in and out of roles as sideman—to singers Bessie Smith and Sippie Wallace, to name only two—and as leader. After Rockwell was brought to New York to run Okeh's operation there—the executive offices were on 45th Street, the recording studio at 11 Union Square—Armstrong followed to record with him.[26]

Like John Lomax before him and John Hammond after him, Tommy Rockwell traveled through the South to hear what was startling if not necessarily "authentic," recording his way through the hills of West Virginia and Tennessee. On a scouting trip in 1928, Rockwell was led to Mississippi John Hurt, then in his midthirties and playing guitar with a fullness that suggested two musicians at once. Rockwell recorded Hurt in Memphis, then later that year in New York. The Depression swept aside Hurt's career for the next 35 years, but Rockwell's employer, Okeh, by then a subsidiary of Columbia, retained all those masters. (Not that it kept Hurt fed.)

As for Armstrong's career, his gifts could no longer be contained solely as a sideman. The early Okeh recordings under his own name poured out inventive new music with every breath. In July 1929 he would record Fats Waller and Andy Razaf's "What Did I Do to Be So Black and Blue?" The title would find its way into Ralph Ellison's *Invisible Man*, the narrator imagining hearing five recordings of the song at the same time, five phonographs all playing Louis on Okeh, because "Louis made poetry out of being invisible."[27]

● ● ●

With the jazzy, more exotic Okeh now in its belly, Columbia reported a solid fiscal year ending February 28, 1927, with net earnings of

$270,214, compared with an $875,311 loss the previous year.[28] Sophie
Tucker's "Some of These Days," recorded during the year in Chicago
with Ted Lewis and His Orchestra, was on its way to selling a million
records. Sterling continued the Masterworks series with at least nine
major conductors: Weingartner, Beecham, Dr. Karl Muck, Bruno Walter,
Willem Mengelberg, Ernest Ansermet, Sir Henry Wood, Sir Hamilton
Harty, and Walter Damrosch. Composers conducting their own works
included Igor Stravinsky, Dame Ethel Smyth, Gustav Holst, and Alexander
Glazunov.[29]

Another development made 1926 particularly interesting at
Columbia. In an in-house history prepared in 1962 for Clive Davis,
then Columbia's general counsel, the stage is set for the arrival of a
Great Young Man: "In 1926 a pioneer in the field of radio appeared
on the scene, an enterprising young man by the name of WILLIAM S.
PALEY, with an idea for expanding the scope of radio by creating a
network system for nationwide broadcasts."[30] Would that it were so
simple.

Paley had been a reluctant convert to the power of radio, and then
mostly through its advertising influence. In his midtwenties and hardly
the dynamic dandy he would turn himself into, Paley was being
groomed to run Congress Cigar, his father Sam's Philadelphia-based
company. Up until 1927, when radio stations all over the land were
failing from a lack of programming and a surfeit of dead air time, Paley
had barely thought about the young medium. But he was intrigued by
its possibilities after Sam bought advertising time for Congress Cigar
and the ads appeared to pay off handsomely. While young Bill Paley was
intoxicated by the glitter of high society—as a Jew he was excluded
from many of its portals—and champing at the bit to relocate to New
York, there was another company coming together that would pull in
the Paleys.[31] The story has been told many times before, but it's worth
reviewing for a moment because its repercussions would be felt at
Columbia Records for the next 60 years.

●　　●　　●

Arthur Judson, a former violinist who managed the Philadelphia Orchestra through his firm Judson Concert Management, and paving machinery salesman George Coats persuaded Major Andrew White, a popular announcer on station WJZ, to form a new radio network. Initially Paramount-Famous-Lasky—in effect Paramount Pictures—was to be involved; then it dropped out. With the intention of pitting its new network against NBC's dominant Red Network—which would also soon come under RCA's control—the Judson-Coats-White partnership offered its services to RCA's chief David Sarnoff. Sarnoff, citing their inability to obtain the necessary phone lines for their network, waved them out.

Columbia Phonograph stepped into the breach, at least in part because talks were already underway between Victor Talking Machine and RCA, threatening to form an unbeatable colossus. (In December 1926 Eldridge Johnson had sold his interest in Victor to the linked investment banking firms of Speyer & Co. and J. W. Seligman & Co. for just under $40 million.)[32] Judson-Coats-White, partnered with New York music publisher Francis Marsh and Philadelphia music angel Edward Ervin, and backed by Columbia, organized a new network called United Independent Broadcasters. With offices high in the Paramount Building, United Independent would be overseen by the newly created Columbia Phonograph Broadcasting System—the name was a proviso of its investment—with Harry Cox sidling over as president. There was a vague notion of promoting Columbia records and phonographs, just as there'd been an earlier determination, when Paramount-Famous-Lasky was involved, to exploit first-run Paramount movies. Major White, who'd been a reporter for the New York Herald and founded the radio monthly The Wireless Age in 1913, was in charge of the new system's technical affairs, Judson of procuring the talent. WOR–New York was its flagship station.[33] The new network, regarding itself as equal to NBC's Red Network, had the temerity to ask an advertising rate of $5,000 an hour—the same as the established NBC and 20 times the average rate of smaller stations.[34] The joke was that UIB had no programming yet, it could offer only promises and Judson's and White's concert and show business connections.

One of the stations that signed on with UIB was WCAU, in Philadel-phia, owned by Ike Levy, an attorney, and his brother Leon, a dentist. Leon Levy had married Sam Paley's daughter Blanche, but it was Ike who'd persuaded Sam to match his $50,000 to rescue the new network when it was shown to be out of its league against big, bad RCA. Sam Paley got his son involved. Soon Bill Paley had moved to New York, taken a crash course in the new medium, and, having bought himself a new wardrobe to present himself as older, was actively running United Inde-pendent Broadcasters and its parent, the Columbia Phonograph Broad-casting System. After a two-week delay to avoid Labor Day travel, the first UIB broadcast was the opera *The King's Henchman* by Deems Taylor and Edna St. Vincent Millay, on September 18, 1927. Staged at WOR's studios with a high percentage of the cast recruited from the Metropolitan Opera production that premiered earlier in the year, the broadcast went over 74 UIB stations.[35] Grebe's old Atlantic Broadcasting System was still in the Columbia family; Paley took charge of that, dropped the word "Phonograph" from the parent name and, on January 3, 1929, reorgan-ized and incorporated under the name Columbia Broadcasting System. Perceiving that his radio audience wanted programming considerably lower-brow than Judson's mostly classical clientele, Paley would soon shed Judson and break away from the record company that had origi-nally supplied the name for the network.

Paley kept close to his side the young attorney Ralph Colin, of the downtown firm Rosenberg, Goldmark, Colin & Kaye, because he'd been impressed by the way he'd represented Judson. In 1921 Colin had joined the Jewish law firm Rosenberg & Ball. (Managing partner James N. Rosenberg lectured widely for free speech and against anti-Semitism.) By 1927 the firm had changed to Goldmark, Bennitt & Colin, and in 1930 again to Rosenberg, Goldmark & Colin. Over the next half century the firm would only slightly alter its partnerships and move uptown. After World War II Rosenberg would be replaced on the masthead by Samuel Rosenman, who had been a judge on the Supreme Court of the State of New York before writing speeches for FDR and serving as spe-cial counsel to Truman.[36] Colin would remain Paley's attorney until a notorious disagreement involving the Museum of Modern Art caused a rift that never healed. Sidney Kaye, who presided over the birth of BMI in 1939, would be intimately involved with Columbia Records's legal affairs through the Lieberson era. The law firm would also send to Columbia several attorneys, including Clive Davis and Walter Yetnikoff, the label's last two presidents under CBS ownership.

Columbia's in-house history portrays Paley as the brains behind the whole conception of a new radio network; Arthur Judson goes unmentioned. Maybe that's the prerogative of a history written by a media giant's legal department. In another decade Paley would appear again at Columbia's doorstep, cash in hand, and acquire the label that had given his company a name in the first place.

*   *   *

American Columbia's reliance on Columbia Graphophone Ltd. for its musical product was apparent in its 1928 catalog and put the company on the defensive: "Note: Many of the records in the succeeding pages devoted to the Columbia Fine-Art Series of Musical Masterworks were recorded in Great Britain by Columbia Graphophone Company, Ltd., matrices being imported into this country by Columbia Phonograph Company, Inc. All such records listed here are manufactured in America."[37] Sterling, well counseled by his friends at J. P. Morgan, was still wheeling and dealing. For Columbia he bought Compagnie Generale des Machines Parlantes Pathé Frères, more commonly known as Pathé.[38] So powerful was Pathé in France and its colonies that people who owned no other modern conveniences would often have a phonograph on which to play the label's records. (For many years Pathé was also France's most important film studio.) The 1931 French comedy À Nous la Liberté was said to be lampooning its phonograph empire, depicted as illustrative of modern life's mechanization.[39] Columbia's acquisition of Pathé opened the label to the French popular singers who flourished between the two world wars: Lucienne Boyer, whose 1930 recording of "Parlez-moi d'amour" became a romantic anthem that has never been surpassed in Europe, and, later, Edith Piaf, Jean Sablon, and Charles Trenet.[40]

Sometimes it seemed as though any Columbia recording that mattered was made in Sterling's backyard, in London or somewhere in Europe. Not quite. By early 1929 American radio stations were not only recovering but also proliferating. The terror that radio first inspired among record companies was real—in fact there had been a tremendous downturn in record sales for the first two or three years of broadcasting—but, as usual, Columbia and the other labels eventually adapted and began to exploit it. Records and radio shared a revolutionary development, the microphone, that made recording as well as broadcasting more intimate. The microphone was creating new musical artists—most of them popular singers, some instrumentalists who came through more distinctively through electrical recording—who employed a more directly emotional appeal.

So the peripatetic banjoist Harry Reser could now be heard with remarkable clarity on many of the label's recordings. Ben Selvin's various bands, including the Cavaliers and the Knickerbockers, sounded as close as the pantry door. Electricity made even the Lanins, Sam and Howard, listenable, each leading orchestras that handled the hits of the day, much as Charles Prince had done at Columbia in the first two decades of the century. (By 1930 their younger brother Lester would begin a career as society bandleader and subsequently record for Columbia's midcentury subsidiary Epic.) Louis Sterling knew how electrical recording would enhance the sound of these musicians. Had he also known that the microphone would deliver such intimacy and greater opportunities for imitation?

Columbia's singer Johnny Marvin, who would later make himself indispensable to Gene Autry's career, had been around since the acoustic era, and now, singing into an electric mike, he was accused of imitating Cliff Edwards. Ruth Etting's relationship with the label went back to 1926. Her rendition of Rodgers & Hart's "Ten Cents a Dance" was justly popular, and her career, molded by manager-husband Moe Snyder, would be dramatically documented 30 years later in *Love Me or Leave Me*.

But she was aghast when she first heard Columbia singer Annette Han-shaw sounding so much like her. Will Osborne was said to be modeling himself on Rudy Vallee, the Yalie whose megaphone crooning was widely parodied. Vallee, flinty even then, talked about suing Osborne. Instead Osborne sued Vallee in New York's Supreme Court, asking $500,000 damages from Vallee for asserting in his book *Vagabond Dreams Come True* that he'd "instructed" Osborne on how to croon. "I do not question the right of the defendant, Vallee, to imitate me," Osborne said, explaining his March 1930 lawsuit, "but when my imitators invade my legal rights by printing a false libel to the effect that I am the imitator, the law should come to my aid and enforce my legal rights."[41] Vallee was with Victor at the time, but he too would hop over to Columbia in 1932. There he got what Ted Lewis had gotten a dozen years earlier—his likeness right on the label—but for Vallee it was just an ectoplasmic tracing of the head. (Vallee would maintain a relationship with Columbia, off and on, until he stopped singing in the fifties.)

The microphone enabled second-tier singers to sound passable coming out of a phonograph speaker. Movie-star handsome Buddy Rogers recorded often with Ben Selvin. Irving Kaufman, who made records for practically everybody, had recorded off and on for Columbia since World War I and, like Ben Selvin, under several names. Guy Lombardo recorded for the label with various singers at the microphone.

Then there was the great Jimmy Durante. Born to entertain and widely regarded as a more than competent piano player long before his movie and television stardom, Durante could put over a comic number, with the help of his partners Lou Clayton and Eddie Jackson, in his sleep. Not that he ever seemed to sleep. "The one really great low comedian of recent years,"[42] Edward Marks called Durante. The vaudeville act Clayton, Jackson & Durante had come together in 1918 at Durante's nightclub. Clayton had been a professional dancer until a streetcar accident immobilized him; Jackson had worked in a Tenth Avenue box factory—and that was one of the better jobs.[43] Few Columbia recordings from 1929 are as immediate—or, for that matter, as pleasurable—as Clayton, Jackson & Durante's "Can Broadway Do without Me?"[44]

Subsequently, Durante would record mostly on Decca. Columbia was lucky to have him for a while.

When it came to mastering the microphone, no singer proved to be more natural than Bing Crosby. In late 1929 Crosby came to the label to sing for Paul Whiteman, the highest-paid bandleader in the land, whose potato-head visage squinted from the orange-and-green Columbia Viva-Tonal label as it spun. Commentators have said that Whiteman's two-and-a-half-year stay at Columbia didn't amount to much. While there, though, he frequently used the great cornetist-composer Bix Beiderbecke. (Each had already recorded for Columbia-owned labels, including Okeh.) Ferde Grofe was Whiteman's sometime pianist and tireless arranger in those years. Whiteman was back at Victor by late 1930, though not before recording Gershwin's *Concerto in F*, which Columbia issued on three disks in one (heavy) album. His greatest Columbia accomplishment may have been getting Crosby more recognition. You can hear it in the ease with which he puts across "I'm a Dreamer, Aren't We All?" from the movie *Sunny Side Up*.

Through Crosby the microphone altered, once and for all, the current of musical seduction: instead of projecting to the recording horn, the artist—the singer in particular—became the object of the microphone's pursuit. It *picked up* the artist. Crosby developed a cool demeanor that allowed his voice to be picked up without making him sound either passive or feminine.

●　　●　　●

It was some year, 1929—for Columbia, for the entire record industry, for America. It was the year that the American Record Corporation was incorporated in the State of Delaware (July 25) as a subsidiary of the Consolidated Film Industries, Inc. Prior to its reorganization, the American Record Corporation had operated as the Scranton Button Works, founded in 1885 to manufacture buttons and electrical insulators, and had pressed records on a contract basis for the Columbia companies and for the five-and-dime trade. In order to obtain the assets of two small record companies, Cameo and Regal, the American Record Corporation purchased both of those companies for the sum of $1 each—an apparent mugging until you realize the price included the companies' liabilities.[45] (To return to the theme of incestuousness in the record business, Regal was an offshoot of Emerson, which had been founded by Victor Emerson, one of Columbia's earliest A&R men.) Both companies were then dissolved into ARC. Pathé-Perfect, an American stepchild of Pathé in France, also went the way of all flesh.

Just as Warners had wanted a piece of the record business to buttress its new talkies, buying and briefly holding onto Brunswick, Paramount was still interested in a recording company, too. Louis Sterling sailed to New York to reopen talks. But the two companies never got together.[46] It's likely that the October stock market crash put the final kibosh on it.

The crash certainly put Edison out of business. He'd been unwell since that summer anyway. Loathing jazz, which was the popular music of the day, the old man knew he'd mishandled the record boom by being so obstinate. Celebrating his eighty-second birthday earlier in the year, Edison gave Time a quote: "I am not acquainted with anyone who is happy."[47] Would an openness to jazz have made him happy? Or does one have to be capable of happiness to be open to jazz?

Whatever the answer, the Depression deepened, proving catastrophic for almost every corner of society—first as an emergency, then as an extended period of mass deprivation. At such times, the general wisdom goes, entertainment fares better than other areas because even deprived people need it. That was demonstrably true for the movies—apart from the brief downturn after the novelty of the talkies wore off, the numbers proved it—but less so for records. Warners, meanwhile, had backed away from its soundtrack recording on disk and was looking for a new way to shore up its Vitaphone process. Toward that end it bought the Brunswick Phonograph & Record Company from Brunswick-Balke-Collender, including its engineering arm, the United Research Corporation, and rights to the name Brunswick. But Warners was really a movie company, not a record company, with little or no interest in the record business per se. Herman Starr, one of the more influential directors of Warners's movie arm First National, considered himself a radio man and thought the record business was much too thorny. Holding onto the United Research technical properties involved, Warners consigned the record company to producing transcriptions for radio stations on 16" disks.

American Record soon snapped up Brunswick Phonograph from Warners. On December 3, 1931, American purchased the offices, equipment, artist contracts, and other assets of that business, but were merely licensed the right to use the name "Brunswick" and Brunswick masters recorded prior to that date. The license and certain other assets retained by Warners were held in the radio division of the company, which was renamed Brunswick Radio Corporation. The recording director of ARC's new subsidiary was Jack Kapp, who had begun his career as a teenage shipping clerk at Columbia's Chicago branch.[48]

• • •

Maybe Herman Starr was right: records weren't the business to bet on. Industry sales in 1930 had dropped from a high of over 100 million disks per year to about 10 million. Radio and the Depression had knocked the industry to the canvas, despite some ingenious innovations in hardware. The 1931 Victor catalog boasted, "Victor records have reached a point in development as to make it reasonable to assume that it will never be necessary to remake records dated from 1931 onward, because of any possible future progress in recording." Victor also manufactured a long-playing 33 1/3–rpm record. Introduced on September 17, 1931, the record was pressed in a flexible plastic, had double the grooves per inch of a conventional 78-rpm record, and played up to 14 minutes per side; but it was lacking in durability and tonal quality. Edward Wallerstein, who had come over from Brunswick, was Victor's recording director at the time and was asked to resolve the issue. With the heavy pickups then in use and the unreliable steel needles, further experimentation seemed impractical. After the extravagant advertising claims that Victor made in the introduction of this record, an apology was in order. With the announcement, "Long playing records were first presented by Victor, not as a complete achievement, but more accurately, as an experiment in public reaction," Victor scratched the project.[49]

Wallerstein pushed for the Duo, Jr., a phonograph that got by without its own tubes or speaker because it was designed to be jacked into radio sets. The idea, according to Wallerstein's son-in-law Charlie Schicke, was to "convert radio listeners into record collectors."[50] Although the Duo, Jr. had only a brief commercial life, Wallerstein's idea would be adapted in later years under his auspices at Columbia.

Columbia remained mired in its own troubles. Even in the popular field, a high proportion of its recordings were coming from Europe. British light classics were now more available than the jazz Columbia had sold on its own label and on Okeh. The situation turned bleak when Columbia felt it could no longer keep Bessie Smith. Some commentators have found racist motives in this—a conspiratorial muting of blues recordings—but in fact the industry as a whole was barely solvent.[51]

But Smith wasn't quite finished.

●　　●　　●

In March 1931, Louis Sterling of the Columbia Graphophone Company Ltd. and Alfred Clark of HMV Gramophone Company Ltd. announced that the two English companies had merged, forming Electric & Musical Industries Ltd. otherwise known as EMI.[52] Their announcement included the insistence that the companies would continue to compete, but without making duplicate recordings. This was tricky because 57 percent of Gramophone was owned by Victor (they'd shared the His Master's Voice logo since the beginning of the century), and Victor in turn was owned by the behemoth RCA. American Columbia and Victor were still rivals, even if Victor almost invariably wound up on top. It's one thing to justify a merger that creates more jobs and more salable product; it's another to own the two dominant record labels, one of which was likely to beat up the other year in and year out. Sterling knew this wasn't workable. By the end of the year, the newly formed EMI had unloaded American Columbia to Grigsby-Grunow, the Chicago-based manufacturer of Majestic radios and refrigerators.[53]

Grigsby-Grunow was ill-equipped to handle a phonograph company, particularly in the jaws of the Depression and at such a geographic remove. There was some feeling that the radio manufacturer wanted a record company among its holdings as a hedge against RCA, which it had been suing in U.S. District Court in a licensing dispute. The old Columbia Graphophone days, when it was seen as a clever though weaker rival to Victor, were practically forgotten. Edward Easton was dead. Frank Dorian was alive but no longer active. John Philip Sousa was around, still railing at the older canned music of phonograph records and the newer kind from radio, but wanted nothing to do with Columbia, his maiden label. The only major survivor of the label's turn-of-the-century heyday, when it could boast of its World's Fair prizes and its aggressive introduction to double-sided disks, was the patent attorney Philip Mauro, who at 70 was still a prominent, practicing Washington attorney. But Mauro was less interested now in recording industry advancements than in Armageddon, turning out evangelical books and pamphlets whose preoccupation was the Second Coming. For years Mauro had been ripe for divine revelation: his law partner had drowned in the shipwreck of the *LaBourgogne* en route to France in 1898; and then, reimagining that horror up close, he was sailing the Mediterranean aboard the *Carpathia* in 1912 when its voyage was detoured to pick up passengers of the *Titanic*.[54] A long slumbering interest in Scripture had been awakened the following year, he wrote, by reading Martin Anstey's *The Romance of Bible Chronology*.[55] Mauro began to compose his own books in which recordings and the law were subsets of Scripture. In *The Hope of Israel? What Is It?*, Mauro reminded his readers that Paul's "hope of Israel" wasn't for an earthly Jewish state but as a ramp to the Apocalypse.[56] Billing the author as "of the Bar of the U.S. Supreme Court," Mauro's *Of Things Which Must Soon Come to Pass* was a "commentary on the Book of Revelation."[57] The Paris Expo and electroplated records seemed to be far from Mauro's mind.

5

Cheap but Often Unforgettable

"In 1932 Columbia Records was selling about one hundred thousand units a year," according to John Hammond, "hardly as much as a single hit record sells today. Labels included Columbia Masterworks for classical music, Columbia for popular records, and Okeh for country music and anything by and for the Negro." Harmony, the discount label born after electric recording had made acoustic recording obsolete, was slapped onto records pressed for the five-and-dime stores.[1]

This is when Hammond, a 21-year-old Vanderbilt heir, entered the recording business. After meeting him in 1932 in Kentucky, where they'd both gone as members of the Delegation for Independent Miners' Relief Committee, Edmund Wilson described Hammond as "like somebody who had modeled himself on Proust, then received an injection of Communism."[2] Even jazz fans and surviving colleagues who are fed up with Hammond's frequent self-importance acknowledge that he was unique in the music business—a wealthy young white man who enjoyed every privilege imaginable yet chose to stick his neck out, politically and socially, to champion music made mostly by men and women who were unwelcome in the circles he was born to.

Hammond was born in December 1910, the only son of John Henry Hammond, a Wall Street attorney, and Emily Sloane. Emily's father was William Douglas Sloane, of the venerable furniture store, her grandfather William H. Vanderbilt of the fortune first made by Commodore Vanderbilt. For a wedding present in 1899, Sloane had bought his daughter and new son-in-law a town house at 9 East 91st Street in Manhattan.

Upon John Jr.'s birth, the butler met John Sr. at the front door as he returned from work, and said, "There's a gentleman to see you, sir." Writing about his childhood some sixty-five years later, Hammond remembered that his father, who could have paid for a different car and driver for each day of the week, preferred commuting by subway because he thought it immunized him from disease.[3] Initially religion played a large role in Hammond's life. Brought up a Christian Scientist, he had every intention of becoming a minister. Hearing one of his sisters sing Sissle & Blake's "I'm Just Wild about Harry," however, Hammond put his ambitions for the ministry on hold and began to collect records, the hotter the better.

Then came viola lessons in Harlem, prep school at Hotchkiss, and an increasing fascination with black dance music. Though the lanky, crew-cutted Hammond didn't dance, he appeared so frequently in front of the Alhambra and the Savoy Ballroom that the bouncers called him by name—a desirable station for any patron of nightlife.[4] (It's easy to forget that Upper Fifth Avenue is geographically much closer to Harlem than, say, the once-swinging joints on 52nd Street.) Buoyed by a $12,000-a-year trust fund and his father's reluctant blessing, Hammond dropped out of Yale after a year and a half to collect records and write about them for various publications. In New York he came to know many of the men who made the music he admired.

"The jazz I liked best was played by Negroes," Hammond wrote in his 1977 memoir *John Hammond on Record.* "My two best friends, Edgar Siskin and Artie Bernstein, were Jews. . . . The fact that the best jazz players barely made a living, were barred from all well-paying jobs in radio and in most night clubs, enraged me. . . . To bring recognition to the Negro's supremacy in jazz was the most effective and constructive form of social protest I could think of."[5]

Hammond's first recordings as a producer were made in 1931, when he was 20, for American Columbia. He had admired Columbia above all other labels largely because of Bessie Smith's records, and went to Frank Walker, who had recorded Smith, to see if he could arrange to record the Harlem-based pianist Garland Wilson. To get into the studio in the first place, Hammond had agreed to pay the $125 studio recording costs himself and buy 150 copies of the recordings. Columbia was in such financial trouble that it eagerly took his money. Wilson's playing was less impressive than Hammond had remembered. They recorded 12" sides of "St. James Infirmary" and "When Your Lover Has Gone." For Hammond the best thing that came out of the session was learning about studio equipment. When Hammond presented Garland Wilson with a Movado wristwatch to supplement the parsimonious union recording scale, the gay Wilson clearly regarded it as a token of romantic affection. "Look what John gave me," Wilson boasted to his friends. Hammond wrote, "It took me a while to live that down."[6]

Hammond's lifelong inclination toward playing the impresario might have been genetically encoded. His maternal grandmother Mrs. Henry White—after being widowed, she had married the U.S. ambassador to France—was known for the musicales she sponsored after World War I.[7] Hammond became a jazz showman of sorts in spring 1932, weeks after he'd first stepped into a recording studio. A friend from the Mt. Kisco Golf & Country Club asked him if he could bring a band to a party at the club. Hammond, who played golf there and enjoyed a pretty low handicap, complied. Arriving in Westchester in two cars, with a lubricating bottle of gin for each car, Hammond brought a motley crew of musicians: Fats Waller (piano), Zutty Singleton (drums), Frankie Newton (trumpet), Benny Carter (alto sax), Artie Bernstein (bass), Eddie Condon (guitar), and Pee Wee Russell (clarinet). "Four Negroes and a Jew," Jack Kahn labeled the first five of the seven men on the list in his 1939 New Yorker profile of Hammond. That those four Negroes and a Jew wouldn't be welcome as members at the club apparently didn't faze Hammond. (All seven would become internationally renowned jazz musicians.) It took a while for the Westchester socialites to respond to the complicated but hard-swinging music; then they seemed hooked. Everyone, including Hammond, might have had an easier time relaxing if Hammond's father hadn't been the club's president.[8]

Turning 21, Hammond collected part of his inheritance. Without much familial fuss he moved out of the East 91st Street house and into a two-room walk-up on Sullivan Street, in the heart of the Village. Investigating several Harlem churches, including storefront tabernacles, he finally switched his church membership from the Madison Avenue Presbyterian to the Church of the Master, on Morningside Avenue.[9] He had his name stricken from the Social Register.

Hammond's credentials as an ardent integrationist were already in place when he went south to Alabama to cover the Scottsboro Case for the *Nation*. The indictments, convictions, and sentences—death in some cases, 99-year prison terms in others—of nine black youths, accused of raping two white girls in a passing freight car, were among the most shameful displays of American jurisprudence gone berserk. Before Hammond was finished with the story—a story that wouldn't be resolved for three decades—Hammond would also write about it for the *New Republic* and the *Brooklyn Eagle*. His reports were passionate but sober. That these young black men were being railroaded was beyond question by many northerners. Eventually, even Hammond's father, as representative of blueblood capitalism as could be found, made clear his abhorrence of the case and contributed to the Scottsboro Defense Fund.[10] (In 1937 charges against five of the nine were dropped; by 1951 three were paroled—one of the accusing girls had recanted her testimony about being raped, which made their parole status seem like an insult anyway—and one had fled to Michigan, which declined to extradite him.)

* * *

Partnered with lyricist Edward Eliscu ("More Than You Know," "Flying Down to Rio") and Alhambra Theatre owner Milton Gosdorfer, Hammond presented Fletcher Henderson at the Public, at Second Avenue and 4th Street, a neighborhood where German immigrants had given way to the Irish, who then moved away as the Jews moved in and the Yiddish theater thrived for a while. Two weeks into the run the Public caught fire, and Hammond was out some ten grand.[11]

Ben Selvin, who'd recorded hundreds of sides for the label by then, introduced Hammond to Columbia president Herman Ward and promotion head Harry Kruse. Columbia was then at one of the lowest points in its four-decade history, having lost Sterling's protection and now barely hanging on under Grisgsby-Grunow. Selvin thought Hammond could make jazz records in New York for the healthier English market, Sterling's English Columbia-Parlophone in particular. That's how Hammond ended up at Columbia's studios just south of Union Square (55 Fifth Avenue, between 12th and 13th Streets), recording three sides with Fletcher Henderson: "Underneath the Harlem Moon," "Honeysuckle Rose," and "New King Porter Stomp." W. C. Handy's daughter Katherine sang on part of that session.[12] Hammond became the American correspondent for *Melody Maker* and, again for English Columbia, recorded Benny Goodman's first band, Fletcher's brother Horace Henderson, Coleman Hawkins, Bud Freeman, and the trumpeter Bunny Berigan.

Having gotten his feet wet in the booth, Hammond went to Philadelphia to implore Bessie Smith, who hadn't recorded in two years, to come to New York and record for Okeh. Smith, then working as a hostess at the Wander Inn, was wary—no one seemed to want to listen to the blues in the heart of the Depression—but agreed to have husband-wife team Socks Wilson and Coot Grant write some novelty tunes for her.[13] One of these turned out to be "Gimme a Pigfoot." To play behind Smith, Hammond brought in an all-star aggregation that included Jack Teagarden on trombone, Chu Berry on tenor sax, even Benny Goodman (on "Pigfoot" only, and then you have to strain to hear him). It was an extraordinary valedictory session for Smith, who lived another four years. Details of her death—the result of an auto accident and an apparently long wait for medical care—would pass through the dim, peeling halls of American apocrypha, narrated to underscore just about any point the storyteller wanted to make.

•　•　•

Who wasn't pleased by the 1933 repeal of Prohibition? Most record companies certainly were. Americans had never stopped drinking, of course, but they were again drinking legally and doing a lot of it while records played automatically in the background. The jukebox had found its proper home, the legitimate bar.

The automatic record changer, first developed by Indiana native Homer Capehart, had been put on in the market in 1927 by Victor. The changer wasn't perfect; like the complex, ultimately mindless machines in Chaplin's *Modern Times*, the Capehart often broke the records as it turned them over. (Breakage was the price you paid for convenience.) Squeezed out of his own company, Capehart went to work for the organ manufacturer Wurlitzer, which began making jukeboxes—Seeburg, Rock-Ola. The jukebox supplied the jazzy atmosphere found in such volume in speakeasies, but at considerably lower cost than live bands. And it went through a lot of records, not just because of breakage but because, unlike the 1890s when the nickel slot cylinder machines were still novel, the public was used to a wide selection of songs on the radio. By 1934 some 25,000 jukeboxes had been sold. By the end of the thirties, there would be ten times that many in operation.[14]

American Record was one of the beneficiaries of the jukebox boom. Its product was cheap—Vocalion and Melotone disks cost 35 cents apiece, Brunswick's twice that price—and revolved around pop music. (Not everyone loved the jukebox. Bunny Berigan, who would become part of the American Record family by dint of his brief association with Raymond Scott and his own Vocalion recordings, carped, "There's no reason in the world why some stupid son-of-a-bitch with a nickel should have the right to impose his tastes on a roomful of people."[15] Between 1933 and 1935 those stupid sons-of-bitches, for better or worse, probably kept American Record solvent.)

Not that any of this helped Columbia. Under Grigsby-Grunow's Depression-flattened ownership, pop recording had been cut back to practically nothing; classical disks continued to come mostly from Europe. Although Grigsby-Grunow settled its suit against RCA, it went into receivership in November 1933.[16] In April 1934, on the verge of bankruptcy, Grigsby-Grunow placed the Columbia Phonograph Company on the block.

•   •   •

How Columbia ended up in the hands of Herbert Yates is a matter of some dispute. John Hammond wrote that Yates, who owned American Record as well as several film concerns, and the Welsh stockbroker-entrepreneur E. R. Lewis, owner of English Decca, had agreed to buy Columbia on a 50-50 basis.[17] Columbia's in-house history recorded the story as Lewis having negotiated to buy Columbia, which would become his record company's American branch, from Grigsby-Grunow for $75,000, before setting sail from England on the 29th of June. Apparently incommunicado on the ocean, Lewis landed in New York on July 6 only to be told by friends on the dock that the American Record Corporation had stolen Columbia earlier that day for $70,500—less than his own bid.[18] (In his biography of Bing Crosby, Gary Giddins has Lewis returning to Southampton believing his deal was in place.)[19]

In any case, Yates hadn't become wealthy by refraining from ruthlessness. Born in Syracuse and raised in Brooklyn, Yates made a fortune rising in the ranks of the American Tobacco Company and then set his sights on the movies. His Consolidated Film Industries owned ARC and would soon own Republic Pictures, the old Poverty Row studio in Hollywood that specialized in Westerns and serials. Consolidated Film also controlled smaller studios like Mascot and Monogram. As John Hammond remembered it, Yates, like Adolph Zukor and the Warners before him, wanted a record company to provide sound production for his movies. Columbia, though quiet through the Grigsby-Grunow years (hence the bargain price), still had a brand name and had been successful enough in the past to be desirable.

E. R. Lewis, wiping the egg off his face, stayed in New York to see what he could salvage from this transatlantic fiasco. Through Jack Kapp, Lewis learned that Warners would be willing to unload the pieces of Brunswick, including a Michigan factory, that it hadn't sold or leased to

American Record. Lewis, Kapp, and two executives from American Columbia organized American Decca on August 4, 1934. Much of the equipment from the Michigan factory was shipped back to New York. "The first products [Decca] released were among the worst ever pressed by an American record company," Hammond wrote. But Decca had three things going for it: the ravenous jukebox; Jack Kapp's slashing of prices, so that the new label's popular records were available to just about everyone; and, most important of all, Kapp's pied-piper ability to lure Brunswick stars to Decca, so that its roster quickly welcomed the Dorseys, Fletcher Henderson, Guy Lombardo, the Mills Brothers, and "the first hip white man in America," Bing Crosby.[20] In fact Kapp had had an escape clause written into all of his Brunswick artist contracts, to the effect that, in the event Kapp should cease to be employed by Brunswick, the artist had the right to terminate his or her own contract.

For a while everyone was a little scared of Decca, and with good reason. The lineup of artists, with Crosby batting cleanup, intimidated even powerhouse Victor. E. R. Lewis, hardened to antagonism within the industry, got fed up with the larger labels' attempts to thwart Decca's relatively small operation. On February 26, 1935, Decca brought suit in New York State Supreme Court against several of them, including American Record Corporation, charging they had conspired to maintain a monopoly.[21]

Decca was modest but distinctively shaped by one man, Kapp. American Record splintered in a dozen directions because its owner was so cheap. Recalling the nineteenth-century railroad barons, Yates had no patience with the concept of a closed shop—Consolidated Film would be defiant in the face of a walkout of its Fort Lee, New Jersey, plant when the CIO tried to organize it—and bristled at the suggestion that his new Bridgeport factory be unionized.[22] Yates appears to have been so ruthless, so tin-eared about the record business, that he too was excised from Columbia's history when it was written in-house in 1962. Even as the industry was rebounding from its worst years since the October 1929 crash, record-plant conditions remained awful, and Yates was responsible for a lot of it.

•   •   •

Though John Hammond had become a seasoned producer and was always a keen talent scout, he continued to write critically about the phonograph business. Beginning on March 3, 1936, Hammond authored a column for Eric Bernay's *New Masses*, using the pseudonym Henry Johnson so he could write freely about some of the men he often worked with. The charade would prove transparent—almost everybody in the jazz world and many in the classical world knew that Johnson and Hammond were the same man—and Hammond reverted to signing his own name fourteen months later. In the meantime Henry Johnson's clear, unadorned style got the job done.

One of his best muckraking pieces was about working conditions in the record industry in general and at Columbia's Bridgeport plant in particular. "Factory conditions are of necessity oppressive because of the tremendous heat, the distasteful smell of the hot shellac composition, and the constant tension of the workers—tension caused by the necessity for the absolutely correct placing on the press of the master plates, the correct labeling, taking the record from the press at precisely the right temperature, and the avoidance of breakage."[23] Pointing out that, by and large, Columbia had put out the best-pressed disks for decades, Hammond declared that this all changed in 1934, when American Record Corporation bought Columbia Records. ARC had been pressing records on its various labels—Brunswick, Vocalion, Melotone—at its Scranton factory until the Columbia deal, when it transferred operations to Columbia's Bridgeport factory and promptly laid off the old, worker-friendly management. In the recording industry RCA Victor had already been unionized by United Electrical & Radio Workers of the CIO, subsequently producing a superior product (not least because its workers were laboring under better conditions); and, connected to the industry and right there in Bridgeport, General Electric workers had also gone with UERW. Hammond deplored Columbia's current conditions, with its suffocating, overheated atmosphere and absurdly low wages—Bridgeport pressmen averaged $16 a week, low even for the typical post-Depression factory worker—and revealed that the factory had been cited numerous times by the Connecticut Labor Board for violations.

Hammond was also utzing Herbert Yates, whom he did not name in the piece but who fought every attempt to organize his employees. Columbia's president at the time, Dick Altschuler, challenged Hammond to tour the Bridgeport plant with him to correct that impression. Hammond's allegations turned out to be accurate, prompting Columbia to raise wages, install air-conditioning, and sign a CIO closed-shop contract—apparently the first in Connecticut.[24]

• • •

Never mind Herb Yates; Columbia's 1962 in-house history mentioned American Record, its parent company for half a decade, only once. Reviewing American Record's output of the era, it might seem undistinguished. But this is deceptive. Columbia continued to import European classical recordings, usually through Sterling (who maintained an arm's-length distance). Otherwise there wasn't much—a few holdovers from the twenties, like Ruth Etting and Cliff Edwards, and a few society bands. Even the ubiquitous Ben Selvin had departed. Meanwhile American Record's aggregate catalog was messy and cheap. But it couldn't be dismissed.

ARC, though the transplanted Englishman Art Satherley and other scouts, was very much in the country business. If Gid Tanner and Riley Puckett were the first important Southern country artists to record for Columbia (1924), Patsy Montana, whose 1935 "I Want to Be a Cowboy's Sweetheart" eventually sold a million copies, was the first important *female* country artist at American Record. Born Rubye Blevins in Arkansas, Montana was a powerful yodeler who modeled her singing on Jimmie Rodgers's. Appearing regularly on WLS (World's Largest Store, referring to Sears) in Chicago, she began to record on ARC. It's startling to hear her now and realize that, by the time of that first hit, she was only 21. A few years later she would appear with ARC's major male country star, Gene Autry, in *Colorado Sunset*.

Recording years before Patsy Montana did, Autry would turn into a one-man entertainment industry—records, movies, television, Major

League Baseball—and no artist would prove more essential to either American Record or Columbia Records. Autry was an Oklahoma boy working for his father-in-law when he began to record. In Chicago as early as September 1927 he was sent to Tommy Rockwell at Okeh. After that he became a peripatetic cowboy singer, recording for one label, then another. By 1929 Autry was recording songs for Victor, then he'd turn around and within a week record the same songs for Columbia's subsidiary Velvetone. Columbia's engineer at the time was Clyde Emerson, brother of the label's erstwhile recording supervisor (also named Victor), and his method of getting around Victor's "exclusive" contract with Autry was ingenious: Victor owned Autry's electronic rights so, to avoid paying royalties, Clyde went back to the acoustic method, placing one horn for Autry to sing in and one on a chair in front of his guitar.[25] Velvetone's sales manager was Ted Collins, who later managed Kate Smith (despite generations of "God Bless America" parodies, another major Columbia artist). Sears, Kresge's, and other stores each distributed their own labels under ARC's umbrella. The Sears label, Conqueror, led to Autry's singing on the *National Barn Dance* on WLS in 1932. Four years later Autry, still recording for ARC under Yates's ownership, began to make cowboy pictures at Republic, a studio rebuilt out of four—Mascot, Republic, Monogram, and Liberty—that Yates had controlled under his Consolidated Film Industries.[26]

* * *

American Record owned Vocalion, which, along with Okeh, put out some fine jazz and blues recordings that would eventually glow in Columbia's vault. Among Vocalion's artists in the midthirties was the witty violinist-singer Stuff Smith, the trumpeter Henry "Red" Allen, and the one-armed trumpeter Wingy Manone. Surely one of Vocalion's greatest blues artists was Leroy Carr, the Nashville-born piano player. Despite his Southern roots and years spent working in and around Indianapolis, Carr now seems almost cosmopolitan—big-city blues infused with urban rhythms—and in fact recorded primarily in Chicago, St.

Louis, and New York City between 1932 and 1936.[27] Alcohol killed him at 30. His recordings were among the gems purchased by CBS when it bought American Record a few years later.

A great many blues lovers and musicians listened to Carr while he was alive, and one of them was Robert Johnson. If American Record had accomplished nothing else in the four-plus years it had control of Columbia, it could still boast of recording this mysterious Mississippian. As with so many legends, Johnson's story has been embellished over time. How he got to record for Vocalion is due to the foresight of several men. Vocalion's chief talent scout appears to have been Jimmy Long, who brought several Southern black singers into the recording studio, but Long doesn't figure in Johnson's story.

H. C. Speir, a white man who ran a music store in Jackson, also served as a local music scout. Speir had brought Son House, among others, into his recording studio. By 1936 Speir was a veteran blues producer, but he was frustrated with his recent batting average with ARC—less than .250 for the artists Speir wanted the company to sign. So when the young Robert Johnson came into the music store to play for him, Speir figured there wasn't much he could do and passed him onto Ernie Oertle, a traveling salesman who moonlighted as one of ARC's men in the South.

Johnson was young—24 or 25, probably—dark-skinned, confident despite his youth. His blues songs tended to be elaborate reworkings of some familiar numbers, fired with biblical imagery and what Peter Guralnick has referred to as Johnson's "iron chords." "Terraplane Blues" was already at the center of his slim repertoire. His "Kind-Hearted Woman" sounded as though he'd found a way to transpose Leroy Carr's piano to guitar.

Oertle hadn't heard anyone quite like Johnson and invited him to accompany him to San Antonio to record. Unable to contain his excitement, Johnson went to see his sister Carrie and told her he was going to Texas to make records. In November 1936 Oertle took Johnson several hundred miles to San Antonio.[28] Three decades later people along the route remembered the day a white man and a guitar-toting black man passed through together. Forbidden by law to share accommodations with a black man, Oertle often had to find a place where Johnson could sleep.

Arriving in San Antonio, Oertle took Johnson to the Gunter Hotel. Art Satherley had been passing through Texas—first San Antonio, later Dallas and Fort Worth—making several recordings. With Satherley was Don Law who, like Satherly, would become vital to Columbia's interests in Nashville. Law remembered Johnson as taller than average, looking even younger than his years, and painfully shy. Asked to sit in on guitar with the Mexican musicians whom Law was recording those same days, Johnson could play only with his back to them. In three days during the week of November 23, 1936, Johnson recorded 16 sides. Thirteen were issued quickly by Vocalion.

The Vocalion records sold well in the South and Southwest—some 5,000 disks scattered about the land. Several of them eventually found their way into the hands of John Hammond. What made Johnson so compelling? While he was alive there was that extraordinary guitar-playing, slide and otherwise, and the pared-down lyrics that suggested the singer was beholden to Satan. But Johnson's playing and singing were as tightly bound as a serpent and a branch—"a single incandescent instrument," Pete Welding called it—and his songs kept him on the run, whether from hellhounds or women.[29] Johnson's devil references, which turned the Mississippi Delta into an all-shadows Hades as if in a dream, had less to do with blasphemy than the sheer absence of religion. At 17, Johnson had married a 15-year-old who died giving birth—the baby died, too—and few experiences make a once-devout survivor so deeply question who has the upper hand, God or Satan. The blues historian Paul Oliver wrote, "To the church member, the blues were 'devil songs' and Robert Johnson, a singer who walked hand-in-hand with the devil in life, sardonically greeted him as a friend."[30]

Six months later, in Dallas, Johnson made a second set of recordings. The engineer this time was Vin Liebler, who would remain with ARC and then Columbia deep into the CBS years. Liebler had earned his engineering degree at Pratt, in Brooklyn, and was recording for Brunswick by 1928. After a brief stint with Warners, he returned to Brunswick, which by then was part of the ARC combine. Out of the Dallas session came "Hell Hound on My Trail," in which Satan is knocking on the singer's door, and "Me and the Devil Blues." It's pointless to argue that ARC didn't know what it had in Johnson; of course it did. But Vocalion was by design a small jazz and blues label and wasn't widely promoted. That Johnson captured the imaginations of so many listeners so quickly is no longer a surprise. In his *New Masses* phonograph column, John Hammond wrote that "Johnson makes Leadbelly sound like an accomplished poseur."[31] (This was a quarter-century before the recordings, released on LP by Columbia, galvanized rock musicians to not only imitate Johnson but to attack the songs themselves, from "Love in Vain" and "Cross Road Blues" to "Rambling on My Mind.")

Hammond wanted to present Johnson at his "From Spirituals to Swing" concert at Carnegie Hall and asked Don Law about him. Law passed the word to Ernie Oertle, who went looking for Johnson.

But Johnson was already dead. The uncertainty about how and why only further promoted the notion that the devil had come to collect on Johnson's debt, which was to be able to make such powerful music. One plausible story is that Johnson had been messing with the wife of a country dance host in Three Forks, Mississippi. In a simmering rage the host gave Johnson a glass of spiked whiskey. Johnson held on for a few days but then succumbed to the poison (whatever it was) and was quickly buried in an unmarked grave in a churchyard near Morgan City.[32] In the end, though, it was only one of many possible scenarios. Other accounts have him stabbed to death, some say by an angry woman, some insisting that voodoo was involved. It all sounds like too much until we remember that Johnson's own songs ignited such dark imagery.

Hammond, learning of Johnson's death, eulogized him in the December 13, 1938, issue of *New Masses*. Ten days later the publication was the chief sponsor of Hammond's Carnegie Hall concert, which was now billed as "An Evening of American Negro Music." As Guralnick has pointed out, the fundamental tension in Johnson's career is that it inverted the arc of an "authentic" blues singer, a man or woman whose life is traceable but who never got a chance to record; by contrast, the facts of Johnson's life are sketchy at best, but we have the indelible documentation of the recordings. There are 29 of them. When Columbia released them on LP in the early sixties, they served up a blues revival that proved abundant enough to feed rock 'n' roll for decades.

•   •   •

John Hammond did get to record another shockingly gifted Vocalion performer, and one whose recordings would be at the center of Columbia's jazz catalog for the rest of the century. Billie Holiday's story is familiar from countless books and a few films, but the incandescent recordings keep reilluminating the Great American Songbook, the standard repertoire that she helped to popularize in the first place. Holiday managed the rare feat of swinging while communicating with breathtaking intimacy, particularly with the rapport she enjoyed with musicians like pianist Teddy Wilson, trumpeter Buck Clayton, and, the greatest of all, tenor saxophonist Lester Young.

Although Hammond's ear as a scout and producer has been acclaimed for decades, there were other men in the American Record family who did important work for Columbia and various labels. Tommy Rockwell, in sympathy with musicians even when he couldn't pay them enough, became general manager of American Record after Yates bought Rockwell's two previous employers, Okeh and Brunswick.[33] Morty Palitz was a facile pianist who could also play fiddle and got into the business largely by being Dick Altschuler's nephew.[34] Palitz collaborated occasionally with the brilliant, eccentric composer Alec Wilder, who had come to Manhattan from the Eastman School of Music in Rochester to find work. (Wilder and Palitz wrote "While We're Young" together.) The writer George T. Simon credited Palitz and John Hammond with allowing Columbia's big band recordings a looser atmosphere. "Decca and Victor seemed more conservative," Simon wrote, "Columbia more daring," because Palitz and Hammond sympathized with the leaders and musicians and were willing to "experiment and approach recording sessions from the long-range rather than from the quick buck point of view." Nearly a decade before Mitch Miller and Bob Fine created the "echo" at Mercury Records, then re-created it at Columbia, Palitz recorded with an echo at Brunswick's studio by placing a speaker and a mike in the men's room.[35]

When it came to business practices, though, Palitz and Hammond were pikers. No other producer exemplified the head-spinning combination of exploitativeness and street smarts the way Irving Mills did. He was a character out of an earlier era, when the wits of a song plugger or publisher counted for a lot more than musicianship.

* * *

Irving Mills, born and bred on the Lower East Side, started the publishing firm Mills Music in 1919 with his brother Jack.[36] With no musical education to speak of, Mills lent his name, and occasionally his untrained voice, to several bands that recorded for Columbia in the 1920s like the Blue Ribbon Band and then, in 1930, the Hotsie-Totsie Gang, which at one time or another included the Dorsey brothers, Benny Goodman, Joe Venuti, Eddie Lang, Matty Melnick, Mannie Klein, and Bix Beiderbecke. Later that decade, Mills went to work for Brunswick; when Warners divested itself of the company, its offices at 799 Seventh Avenue went to American Record, which was headquartered around the block on Broadway.

Meanwhile, Mills was engaged in a practice that harked back to Tin Pan Alley's earliest days, when a music publisher bought a song for a pittance, cut himself in for the royalties, and cut the composer out. Through Mills Music, Mills was among the worst offenders of this practice. John Hammond, writing as Henry Johnson for the July 1936 *New Masses*, published "Sold—for Less Than a Song," which gently but firmly took Mills apart: "Mills's method is as ingenious as it is unfair to the author and composer: he usually buys the tune outright for a small sum, attaches his own name as co-author, instructs his bands (Duke Ellington, Cab Calloway, Blue Rhythm, etc., etc.) to record it for the various companies (Columbia, Brunswick, Melotone) with which he is affiliated, and collects sums ranging from one to two cents per record as royalty, *all of which he pockets* [italics Hammond's]. Hundreds of dollars are often collected from phonograph royalties alone, because the sale of this music is even wider in Europe than in America; but the composer is deprived of any share of it."[37] As a particularly egregious example, Hammond referred to Mills's exploitation of Benny Carter's song "Blues in My Heart": Carter received a $25 payment from Mills, who went on to collect thousands.

This had been a courageous piece to write, even under his nom de plume, because Hammond had previously worked for Mills as associate editor of Mills's magazine *Melody News*. (Like other music men whose literacy had been picked up in bits of scrap, Mills fractured the language. When Hammond first met Mills face to face, he noted the blank walls of the office. "You know what we're going to put there?" said the self-made impresario, waving a cigar. "Muriels!" Soon murals depicting Harlem scenes covered the walls.)[38]

Nine months after attacking Mills in print, Hammond was claiming that Mills had changed his practices and was getting better contracts for the dance bands he employed. Mills might have had to clean up his act anyway. Under the imprimatur Master Records—named, one presumes, for the process of making disks rather than as a paean to Adolf Hitler—organized on February 13, 1937, Mills's mandate was to "furnish artists and supervise recordings made and issued by that company, pursuant to a three-year employment agreement."[39] Master Records became a subsidiary of the American Record Corporation almost precisely halfway through its ownership of Columbia Records. In effect Mills became ARC's major liaison to the preswing bands he'd come up with, the writers whose music he'd played fast and loose with. Duke Ellington was in and out of the stable, as he would be for the nearly 40 years remaining to him. The young composer Harry Warnow had changed his name to Raymond Scott, and he would take his bands and his Rube Goldberg–like compositions from Mills's Master right over to Columbia. Scott and his Quintette made about 30 sides for Brunswick, Master, and Columbia. Meanwhile Mills's official responsibilities for the parent company proved to be a headache because the small labels that ARC had swallowed had contractual obligations they hadn't bothered to fulfill. Yes, ARC had a sales manager and plenty of legal help, but there was too much to keep track of.

Mills went to London and met with Louis Sterling, who was irritated that ARC's labels weren't supplying him with recordings he'd already paid for. At 58 Sterling had just been knighted. Sir Louis and his wife had made their Regent's Park home a gathering place for artists, bankers, and men of letters, their Sunday-afternoon soirees now a cultural institution. "Jolly luncheon at Louis Sterling's" goes one entry in James Agate's *The Later Ego*, the critic's journal of the 1930s. And another: "Lunch at Louis Sterling's. Beecham with an eye more rolling and mischievous than ever."[40] By then Sterling was the most beloved record executive in the world. As he and Mills sat in a dining room at the Savoy Hotel, though, Sterling wanted to know why the hell American Record wasn't honoring its contracts. Mills said, "I've got an idea for you, Louis. Why don't I make the records for you and, instead of you paying a royalty to American, who now owns the master, you own the master and have American owe it to you?" "Well," Mills recalled nearly 40 years later, "he looked at me and he stuck out his hand and we shook hands, and for the next twenty years I recorded for Louis Sterling."[41]

Well, sort of. In a couple more years Mills would move to the West Coast and watch his publishing garden bloom in the desert. Sterling, losing an edge to HMV director Alfred Clark, resigned altogether from EMI, the musical juggernaut he'd built through the 1930s. He had just given away £100,000 to EMI employees on his sixtieth birthday, and it wasn't the first time he'd made such a gesture.[42] Although he retained a large interest in the British music publisher Chappell, he wouldn't work again in the record industry—not officially, anyway. In 1956 he would turn his library over to the University of London. "I have made most of my money in London," he said at the time. "I think it fitting that my books should be used for relaxation and knowledge by coming generations."[43]

● ● ●

As music became "hotter," as swing became the dominant popular music of the late thirties, American Record's potpourri of small labels could claim a respectable lineup of hot artists. A famous *Life* spread from the summer of 1938 lists thirty "Good Hot Records." More than a third of the recordings were made or owned by ARC, and they're worth listing here because, with one or two exceptions, they're still considered classics: Louis Armstrong's "West End Blues" (Okeh); Mildred Bailey's "Long about Midnight" (Vocalion); Bunny Berigan's "I Can't Get Started" (Brunswick); Fletcher Henderson's "Money Blues" (Columbia); Joe Marsala's "Hot String Beans" (Vocalion); Red Norvo's "Blues in E Flat" (Columbia); King Oliver's "Dipper Mouth Blues" (Okeh); Artie Shaw's "Nightmare" (Brunswick); Stuff Smith's "You're a Viper" (Vocalion); Maxine Sullivan's "Loch Lomond" (Okeh); and Slim & Slam's "Flat Foot Floogie" (Vocalion).[44]

If Herbert Yates had had any feeling for the record business, he would have put money in the Bridgeport factory and pressed the best disks available—as good as Columbia's had been in the early years under Sterling's stewardship. But Yates had become a Hollywood mogul, delighting in reading his name in Hedda Hopper's column, and barely paid attention to his New York–based phonograph concern. Through 1938, American Record was running a distant third to Victor and Decca, selling 7 million disks to Victor's 13 million and Decca's 12 million.[45]

So this Broadway combine of cheap record labels, including the pitifully shrunken Columbia, was ripe for the plucking when William S. Paley, the flashy Philadelphian who had purloined the label's name more than a decade earlier and since built the Columbia Broadcasting System into NBC's only real rival in radio, came shopping for a record label. Like so many stories about the groundbreaking of a colossus, this one is a matter of some dispute. The most popular version of the story is that Ike Levy bemoaned to his neighbor Ted Wallerstein how his beloved Philadelphia Orchestra, then conducted by the lady-killing and weirdly accented Leopold Stokowski, was being treated by Victor. Ike Levy was on the Philadelphia Orchestra's board of directors, and the orchestra itself was about to receive a gift—namely Eugene Ormandy, its new conductor. The way to turn that gift into an annuity was to enable the orchestra to record for a label that appreciated it. RCA Victor had other first-rate orchestras (Toscanini's at the top) that took priority. Wallerstein, still managing Victor but forced to slow down because of heart problems, told Levy that he ought to get his brother's brother-in-law Paley to buy a record company so he could give the Philadelphia Orchestra the care it required.[46] Another version is that Wallerstein himself tried in 1938 to raise money to buy Columbia from American Record; Paley, always intrigued by other men's business interests and even turned on by competition, decided to make a bid himself.[47]

Whatever the sequence of events leading to the purchase, Paley's $700,000 check—ten times the price paid by Consolidated Film four years earlier—bought for CBS the American Record Corporation, including its three prime subsidiaries: the Columbia Phonograph Company, Inc.; the Brunswick Record Corporation; and Master Records, which Irving Mills had been playing like a personal slot machine.[48] Taking the deal another step, the two existing subsidiary companies of the Columbia Phonograph Company, Inc.—the Columbia Phonograph & Radio Company and the Okeh Radio & Record Corporation—were both soon dissolved (Columbia on September 21, 1938, and Okeh on December 15, 1938), and the assets of both companies assigned to Columbia Phonograph Company, Inc. The talk on Wall Street and Madison Avenue was that Paley had been taken for a ride. If the price had been three times as much, however, Paley would still have gotten a helluva deal.

SIDE B
The CBS Years

6
Sign 'Em Up

On January 1, 1939, William Paley's purchase of the American Record Corporation became final. Three days later CBS announced the appointment of Edward (Ted) Wallerstein as president; Frank White, treasurer; C. C. Boydston, assistant treasurer; and Ralph F. Colin, secretary.[1] White would remain with the company for a decade. Colin would maintain a close relationship to Paley, sometimes as CBS chief counsel, for another three decades.

Until spring, the label was still known as the American Record Corporation; the ingenious notion of renaming the entire record company Columbia, which had given its name to United Independent Broadcasters back in 1928, hadn't yet been put into practice. In April 1939 CBS cut its financial ties to early United Independent partner Ike Levy. It also bought the East Fifty-second Street Corporation, which would serve as one of the label's primary recording studios.[2]

CBS moved its new corporate child from offices at 57th and Broadway into the seven-story 799 Seventh Avenue, at 52nd Street, where Brunswick had been headquartered. Before packing up his various operations and heading to California, Irving Mills was still on the second floor. Irving Berlin kept a piano and a desk at the music publisher Robbins, which was also housed there. American Record leased the top floors—the sixth for offices, the seventh for studios. For a while American Record's attorney Lee Eastman (né Leopold Epstein) stayed on; Eastman's future son-in-law Paul McCartney hadn't yet entered the world. On May 22, 1939, American Record was finally reorganized and incorporated in the State of Delaware under the name Columbia Recording Corporation. For years to come it would be known as CRC.

Wallerstein, who had already run Brunswick and RCA Victor and proved to be (in John Hammond's words) "the greatest record salesman of his day," began to make the staff his own.[3] He maintained some independence from CBS's Madison Avenue headquarters by keeping an office at the Bridgeport plant, at 1473 Barnum Avenue. The three-story building housed offices on the bottom floor—sales manager Paul Southard, a strong executive held over from ARC, was also based there—the metal masters on the second, and, on the third, a Graphophone museum, Columbia's modest tribute to its own history. ARC's former president Dick Altschuler, who had challenged John Hammond three years earlier about Hammond's condemnation of the Bridgeport factory's working conditions, didn't join the new company but remained instead with Yates's Consolidated Film in various capacities.

For the New York office Wallerstein hired John Hammond as associate director of popular recording. As Hammond remembered it, Wallerstein was counting on him to persuade Benny Goodman to return to Columbia, for whom he'd made his first records in 1933, after years at RCA. "[Wallerstein] also wanted Basie as well as other artists whose careers I had had something to do with, realizing that the largest market for records was among teenagers and college students, groups the American Record Company, Columbia's former owners, had not been able to reach with any success."[4] When CBS took ownership of Columbia, the label's only black band belonged to the already-regal Duke Ellington, who had first recorded for Columbia under Irving Mills's aegis back in 1932. One of Hammond's first recordings for the CBS-owned Columbia was of singer Josh White, whose *Chain Gang* album of 78s included, among other singers, Bayard Rustin, future head of the NAACP.

Hammond answered to Manie Sacks, a relative of the Levy brothers and a former MCA talent executive, who had an easy rapport with many pop artists, especially singers. Sacks commuted to Seventh Avenue from his home in Philadelphia, occasionally bunking at Hampshire House when he needed to stay in town. Joe Higgins, who had started in the business in 1909 and had worked under Wallerstein in Camden, New Jersey, had more recently been with American Record and was asked to stay in the pop division because of his close ties to music publishers. Morty Palitz stayed on, largely to teach Manie Sacks the technical side of record-making; but Sacks couldn't get the hang of it, or wasn't all that interested, and Palitz soon bolted for Decca.[5] Moses Smith, who had written extensively and knowledgably about classical music for the *Boston Globe*, was asked to oversee Masterworks. In September 1939, on Hammond's recommendation, 28-year-old Goddard Lieberson was hired to assist Smith.

For the manufacturing unit in Bridgeport, Wallerstein brought Jim Hunter over from RCA. Earlier in the thirties, when Wallerstein tried to put a long-playing record on the market, Hunter had developed VictorLac, a vinyl compound that made for lighter disks. (The 1932–33 experiment at RCA failed largely because the pickups were still too heavy.) Wallerstein put a lot of faith in Hunter. He also continued to think about developing a long-playing record. The 799 building had more room than American Record's old quarters, so work proceeded quietly there and in Bridgeport. Besides Hunter's, among the minds at work on the project were the ARC recording chief Vin Liebler, the ace microphone man Bill Savory, who would soon be married to Benny Goodman's beloved former vocalist Helen Ward, and Ike Rodman, who had been the chief engineer at Muzak Transcription Company. "The first thing Rodman did in January of 1939," Hammond wrote more than thirty years later, "was to make use of sixteen-inch acetate discs recorded at the speed of 33 and 1/3 rpm for safeties on everything recorded by Columbia, Okeh, Vocalion and Harmony. There were 15 minutes of acetates to a side."[6] This was so that it could be more immediately transferred to microgroove when the time was right. Before World War II put the project on hold, Wallerstein persuaded General Electric's young engineer Bill Bachman to come over to its Bridgeport neighbor Columbia. Bachman, despite scant references in the media, would prove to be essential to the project.

Wallerstein had an effective way of delegating. At this point, however,

Columbia was a relatively small operation—a dozen people or so outside the Bridgeport factory. Of all of them, the most crucial was Wallerstein himself. Cordial and somewhat aloof, he didn't publicize his own accomplishments. Without him, however, it's likely that Columbia would have limped along as it had in the thirties.

•   •   •

Wallerstein was born in 1891 in Kansas City, Missouri, but his parents, David and Nellie, had been based in and around Philadelphia most of their lives. Ted Wallerstein graduated from Germantown Academy and then majored in economics at Haverford College (Quaker, like Germantown), where he quarterbacked the varsity football team. David Wallerstein practiced corporate law, but when John Reed was charged with "incitement to seditious remarks" and assault and battery in early 1919, Wallerstein represented him for nothing.[7] (Reed and his lover Louise Bryant stayed with the Wallersteins for a brief period that winter.) At the time Ted Wallerstein, who'd served in the army as a lieutenant during the First World War without ever leaving the States, was working in the oil fields of Oklahoma. He claimed to have played semi-pro football, too, and that one of his opponents was Jim Thorpe.[8] Whether or not the oil fields somehow led to Wallerstein's first recording company position is unclear, but by the time he was 30 he found himself managing the East Coast music division at Brunswick. Living in Greenwich Village he met Helen Ault. In 1927 they married and began a family—eventually two sons and a daughter. Under Warners's aegis, Wallerstein was promoted to sales manager of the Brunswick Record Corporation. After Victor became part of the RCA family, he was invited to oversee its operations. It was imperative that the Wallersteins be closer to RCA Victor's headquarters in Camden, so they moved to New Jersey, where Wallerstein's immersion in sports—golf, baseball, fly-fishing—was more readily indulged.

Wallerstein's musicianship was limited to boyhood piano lessons (which he skipped in favor of gymnastics and boxing), but the appreciation of music stayed with him. When he was living in the Village he would get into the Metropolitan Opera by volunteering as an onstage extra. Before he'd moved to Victor he had much of the classical repertoire, symphonic as well as operatic, in his head.

* * *

Apart from Wallerstein, Columbia now had another advantage over other labels: for its laminated disks, Columbia used a plastic that was technically superior to that used by Victor and Decca, providing a smoother surface. The plastic also proved to be sturdier, standing up to the punishment meted by the automatic record changer and the jukebox. With more than 250,000 Seeburg and Wurlitzer jukeboxes in circulation, the sturdiness was imperative.

Columbia needed that slight edge because hostilities in Europe, predating America's declaration of war on Germany by at least two years, had halted recording there as well as the exportation of classical masters. Like Victor and Decca, Columbia now had to sign its own roster instead of depending on the product sent from England. Although Columbia's disks were at once stronger and cheaper to produce than the other labels'—its coarse center filler and laminated process required less shellac for each disk—it had to scramble because there was no more virgin shellac arriving from India. Scrap shellac was no longer the material of the tiny record operation, but a necessity for any label to survive. Old records were sold back to Columbia at two cents a pound. In the depths of the shellac shortage, bootleggers would back up trucks to the loading dock at 1473 Barnum to take what they could.[9] Milt Goldstein, one of Columbia's earliest and best salesmen, said that factory employees would pilfer records and hide them under their coats as they clocked out; after a while Columbia positioned a man outside with a baseball bat to hit them just hard enough to break the records and discourage the thefts.

* * *

Meanwhile there was the essential business of putting out records. While the Masterworks roster was being rebuilt, Columbia cast its old pop product onto the waters to see what bit. Since early in the ARC days, Columbia had had Kay Kyser, Eddy Duchin, and Gene Autry. Kyser was a clowning, appealing bandleader with a fondness for musical jokes but a narrowly defined sense of swing. Kyser's "Three Little Fishes," featuring the trumpeter who called himself Ish Kabibble (real name: Merwin Brogue), sold a million disks. So did Cab Calloway's "Jumpin' Jive"— Calloway's most successful record ever. Eddy Duchin kept rolling out his florid piano albums, collections of Gershwin and the like. Duchin was a society favorite, though jazz cognoscenti didn't take him seriously. Harry James had a hit with "Ciribiribin," Grace Moore's trademark melody. Al Goodman, who had been far better known to the public than the unrelated Benny Goodman until 1936, recorded just about everything that wasn't nailed down. Gene Autry's "That Silver Haired Daddy of Mine," written with his father-in-law Jimmy Long, was given a tremendous boost past Autry's earlier recordings because he was now a movie star.[10] At this point the talkies were less than a dozen years old; the concept of a movie star promoting his recordings, or a recording star promoting his pictures, was still a marketing live-wire. Kyser, whose showmanship far outweighed his musicianship—though good musicians flowed bracingly through his bands—scored again with "Playmates," shared with Sully Mason and His Playmates, and "Ferry-Boat Serenade."

In its first year under CBS, Columbia got by on some of these hits. The record that really took off, though, came almost from out of nowhere. "Oh Johnny, Oh Johnny, Oh!" was recorded August 20, 1939, sung by Wee Bonnie Baker with Orrin Tucker and His Orchestra. The song had been popular during World War I—recorded, in fact, by the team of Howard Kopp and Frank Banta on Columbia. The Tucker-Baker version has a benign whininess that bores right through your head and sold, astonishingly, half a million copies. (Sixty-five years after Stan Kavan shipped thousands of "Oh Johnny" disks from the Bridgeport factory in 1940, he could still tick off its catalog number, 35228.)[11] "Oh Johnny" is backed by Tucker himself singing Irving Berlin's "How Many Times," and it's quite good. The disk made the new Columbia competitive in the pop field.

Still, RCA Victor, with a decade's head start and plenty of money, had the bigger, badder catalog. The big bands were locked up by Glenn Miller and Tommy Dorsey. Perry Como was RCA's top crooner. And RCA Victor boasted the most dominant musical personality of all, Arturo Toscanini, whose NBC Symphony was surely the most listened-to orchestra in the nation.

Columbia didn't have a Toscanini. Not yet, anyway. Its most prominent conductor was probably still Sir Thomas Beecham, who was contractually tied to English Columbia but had been distributed by American Columbia back in the midtwenties. It also had the conductors Erich Leinsdorf and Fritz Reiner, the pianist Walter Gieseking, and the Hungarian violinist Joseph Szigeti, who had been recording since almost the beginning of the century and more recently recorded by Hammond.[12] A classical string man since boyhood himself, Hammond was at least partly responsible for grabbing the Budapest String Quartet, maybe the sturdiest chamber group in the world at the time, although by then with no more connection to anything Hungarian. (The quartet, even as it changed personnel over the years, remained fundamentally Russian.) In the thirties Budapest had recorded extensively with His Master's Voice (HMV), but the war made recording in London unfeasible, so HMV sent the Quartet to its American-based affiliate Victor. But Victor had all the string quartets from HMV it could market. Besides, the Budapest players must have resented it when Elizabeth Sprague Coolidge, financial angel to classical music, sponsored the Coolidge Quartet's Beethoven cycle on Victor, effectively crowding them out.[13]

If Masterworks could be said to have had a tentpole at the time, it was probably Bruno Walter. Age 64 in 1940, Walter was born Bruno Schlesinger in Berlin, won acclaim as Mahler's greatest conducting protégé, and fled Germany—along with scores of other Jewish musicians—when Hitler came to power in 1933. Walter's recordings for Columbia, both in those first CBS-owned years and much later, when his sensitivity as a conductor of Beethoven and Mahler could be heard in every chord, would help make it the premiere classical label.

•   •   •

In August 1940 Ted Wallerstein slashed classical prices in half: a Columbia classical record was now $1, a popular record 50 cents, an Okeh down to 35 cents.[14] The competition had little choice but to follow suit. Wallerstein's gutsy price-cutting was made possible in part by Joe Higgins, who'd worked tirelessly to persuade music publishers to reduce their royalty from two cents per side to one and a half cents.

Wallerstein also knew that RCA's classical lineup was too fat. Andre Kostelanetz hadn't been given much attention there, and had had only slightly more support at Brunswick. Wallerstein, who'd signed Koste-lanetz to Victor in the first place, now brought him to Columbia and gave him what amounted to carte blanche. (Recording for Columbia, Kostelanetz wouldn't go over budget for nearly 20 years.) On three different albums Columbia debuted the mezzo-soprano Suzanne Sten, the Metropolitan tenor John Carter, and then the recording career of opera and film star Gitta Alpar with six 10" sides comprising an album called *A Musicale of Continental Song*. Alpar, daughter of a Hungarian rabbi, was as much about glamour as about opera. Wallerstein wanted Moses Smith to build a stronger opera catalog for Masterworks, and Smith complied. German soprano Lotte Lehman, the lovely Brazilian soprano Bidu Sayao, the Polish tenor Jan Kiepura, the Belgian tenor and Wagnerian specialist Rene Maison, the Met's basso buffo Salvatore Baccaloni, and Robert Weede, who would gain a wider fan base the following decade with Columbia's original cast recording of *The Most Happy Fella*: all these singers were signed to the label between late 1940 and early '41.[15] Columbia began to record Mahler—no other label has been so closely associated with his music—when Mitropoulos and the Minneapolis Symphony Orchestra recorded the First Symphony. This was due in large part to Moe Smith's tireless work. (Smith was subsequently awarded the Mahler Medal of the Bruckner Society "in appreciation of his efforts to create a greater interest in and appreciation of Mahler's music").[16] Wallerstein signed the New York Philharmonic-Symphony, which was already under contract to CBS Radio. That orchestra could be heard on what would be a benchmark 1940 recording of Igor Stravinsky's *Le Sacre du Printemps*, with the composer conducting.

Vocalion was slipped into the sleeve of Okeh. As its parent company once more, Columbia enjoyed its first hit on that old label with "San Antonio Rose," by Bob Wills and His Texas Playboys. Meanwhile, the jazz catalog was being rebuilt. As directed, Hammond brought back to the label Benny Goodman, who had probably done more than any other big band leader to turn jazz into a popular genre. Hammond also got Count Basie to leave Decca.

Hammond had first heard Basie around 1933 in New York, when Basie worked as Benny Moten's second pianist and was playing (for him) a lot of notes. Three years later in Chicago, half-frozen in the driver's seat of his parked Hudson in the icy early-morning hours, Hammond turned the dial on his 12-tube Motorola car radio. "The local stations had gone off the air and the only music I could find was at the top of the dial, 1550 kilocycles, where I picked up W9XBY, an experimental station in Kansas City. The nightly broadcast by the Count Basie band from the Reno Club was just beginning. I couldn't believe my ears."[17] Basie had evidently matured since Hammond had last heard him, paring away all those notes for the economical style he would become known for. That economy allowed greater freedom for his players, especially the tenor saxophonist Lester Young. Starting that winter of 1936, Hammond considered Basie and Goodman to be the two giant bandleaders.

At first Basie was placed on the Okeh roster, either because someone had decided the Basie band would sell more records that way, or, more likely, that Duke Ellington didn't want to compete with Basie on Columbia. (In fact, once Basie moved over to the more prestigious Columbia, Ellington returned to Victor in 1940.)[18] The superb Golden Gate Quartet, whom Hammond had brought from Charlotte, North Carolina, for his second "From Spirituals to Swing" concert on Christmas Eve 1939, was placed on Okeh.[19] A few years later, with some personnel changes, they recorded their first album of 78s for Columbia, honing their jubilee style to a brilliant sheen.[20] Columbia signed Sister Rosetta Tharpe, the magnificent Arkansas gospel singer ("This Train," "Rock

Me," etc.) who accompanied herself first on acoustic guitar, then electric, before returning to pure gospel without accompaniment.[21]

Another recent Hammond discovery would soar on Columbia and flame out all too quickly. Annoyed by the gimmicky quality of electric guitars, which were often played for their Hawaiian-sounding effects, Hammond heard from pianist Mary Lou Williams about a kid named Charlie Christian who played the electric guitar like an acoustic. Hammond first heard Charlie Christian at the Ritz Cafe in Oklahoma City in July 1939; the kid was 18 and had come up recently from Texas. Salaries for the musicians were $2.50 a night. In the teeth of critical insistence that Christian was a primitive talent, Ralph Ellison pointed out that Christian, who went to school with Ellison's younger brother, had been admired for his playing since the first grade, and in fact was playing the light classics on guitar as a boy.[22] Hammond, who knew better than such patronizing critics, got Benny Goodman's radio show *Camel Caravan* to use its $300 guest budget to fly Charlie to the West Coast to play with Goodman on August 10 at the label's studios on Western Avenue, where Goodman was making his first recordings for CBS-owned Columbia. Goodman was initially unimpressed. Hammond and his old friend Artie Bernstein, Goodman's bassist, were determined to force Goodman to hear Charlie once more. They arranged for Charlie to sit in on Goodman's Los Angeles nightclub gig at the Victor Hugo on Beverly Drive. On the bandstand with Goodman, Christian comported himself beautifully. But Goodman still seemed to be fighting it. It was Christian's playing on "Rose Room," suddenly called out by Goodman as a way to throw the young guitarist off his stride, that finally convinced the bandleader. Fletcher Henderson and Lionel Hampton, the two black members of Goodman's otherwise white band, tried to persuade him that the public would never accept a third black member.

Charlie Christian's playing with the entire Goodman band swings effortlessly, and the smaller-scaled Goodman Sextet records of 1941 on Columbia are among the supreme jazz recordings.[23] But the Christian epoch didn't last long. Apparently walking around for years with tuberculosis, Christian was finally too sick to play and was admitted to

Seaview Sanitarium on Staten Island. John Hammond suggested that Christian's health was improving until an unnamed musician friend sneaked in some marijuana and a woman less than two weeks before he died in 1942, at 23.[24]

Meanwhile, in March 1941, Hammond had been married to the Irish-Canadian Jemy McBride, the ceremony performed by Hammond's old friend Rabbi Edgar Siskin, in Siskin's New Haven apartment. Both Hammond and McBride had been raised Christian Scientists, but Hammond had long since stopped believing, and his annual trust fund income permitted him to thumb his nose, when he felt the need, at just about anyone he wanted to. "I'm glad Edgar is marrying you," Hammond's mother, Emily Vanderbilt Sloane, told him. "I hope he says a prayer, even if it's in Hebrew."[25] The wedding excluded the parents of both bride and groom. In his memoir Hammond names three or four guests, including Goodman. His close friend Cecelia Ager, an entertainment writer and wife of the songwriter Milton Ager, was in attendance. So was a Yale senior who discovered only at the wedding that an aborted blind date he'd had in Springfield, Ohio, two years earlier happened to be with the bride.[26] The Yalie was a relatively new hire at Columbia named George Avakian.

• • •

Avakian's name was known among jazz aficionados while he was still in college because he'd been writing about these blazing recordings for some time—since high school at Horace Mann, in fact, in Morningside Heights. He listened and wrote like a seasoned scholar. His work caught the attention of John Hammond, who was a decade older but knew an expert when he read one.

George Avakian was born in Russia in 1919 and came to New York's East Side at age 4. The family lived on 76th Street, just off Lexington Avenue. Avakian's parents spoke very little English, which might have spurred him to investigate English literature deeper than he otherwise might have. At an early age he fell in love with the New York Public

Library and with Arthur Conan Doyle's Sherlock Holmes series. Avakian listened avidly to the radio and was soon as keen on jazz as he was on reading.[27] Early on he preferred Benny Goodman to the popular singers Bing Crosby and Russ Columbo. In 1935, when he was sixteen, he got hooked on the NBC radio show *Let's Dance*, broadcast every Saturday night. *Let's Dance* featured bands led by Kel Murray and Xavier Cugat, but it was Benny Goodman's band that really tugged at Avakian's ear. A summer 1935 tour finally made Goodman a star. At the Palomar Ballroom in Los Angeles, Goodman, pulling some old Fletcher Henderson arrangements from the drawer, so excited the crowd that the band relaxed and swung more than ever.

It took Goodman a year to return to his home base in New York City. In the fall of 1936, Avakian, then the editor of Horace Mann's school newspaper, went to the Hotel Pennsylvania to interview Goodman in his two-room suite there. Avakian wrote up the results. Even before he arrived at Yale the following year, Avakian was setting down his thoughts on jazz recordings. At 17 he was elected senior class president, but he still had a lot to learn and he knew it. Meeting Lester Koenig, the older brother of Avakian's Horace Mann classmate Julian (and later to become a prominent writer-producer in Hollywood), Avakian discovered that his own opinion of Louis Armstrong—"a flashy trumpet, and he sings kind of funny"—was, to put it gently, misinformed. Once Avakian really listened to Armstrong's out-of-print Brunswick and Okeh records, he was hooked. Koenig also turned him on to two recent French publications, Charles Delauney's *Hot Discography* and Hughes Panassie's *Le Jazz Hot*. Avakian sent an $8 money order to a Paris address and, fluent in French, had no trouble devouring the information from both books.

With the fervor of the new collector, Avakian had to have the records so lavishly praised by these Frenchmen. His fellow jazz collectors, he learned, had organized the United Hot Clubs of America, which put out the earliest jazz reissues. On a Saturday in September 1937, the Yale freshman ducked into David Dean Smith's record shop in New Haven to see what they had in the way of UHCA reissues. "In those days," Avakian remembered, "they had listening booths. You could take a record, play it, and take it back to the counter and then you'd either buy it or say, 'No, thank you.' In an adjoining booth there was another student listening to an Ellington record and I was listening to the latest Goodman record. His name was Jerry King. 'Have you been to Marshall Stearns's house yet?' asked King."

Stearns had a byline in *Tempo*, one of the few jazz magazines going, while studying for his doctorate in English at Yale. Every Friday night he held an open house, playing 78s that he shelved in an enormous closet and answering questions about them. Along with King, Avakian became a regular at these jazz soirees. Stearns had Avakian and King catalog each new record with a Dennison label (red-striped, just enough space for minimal annotation). Stearns's closet library held for Avakian the musical foundation that would support his future career as a producer of records, jazz and otherwise. As a child he had had rudimentary piano lessons but never learned to read music—and yet it didn't matter. Avakian, lover of jazz and literature—and, by the way, of most things French—was so attuned to harmonic nuance and swing that he didn't need to sight-read to know how the music was made.

Typing madly in his rooms at Jonathan Edwards, his residential college at Yale, Avakian published a piece in *Tempo* on the battle of the bands, Ellington vs. Basie. Even though *Tempo* spelled his name wrong, the article won him attention in jazz circles far beyond Horace Mann. Avakian wrote to Decca to propose three albums of jazz reissues, each covering a different territory and idiom: New Orleans, Kansas City, Chicago. In the summer of 1939, Decca told him to proceed. The results were put together by the 20-year-old Avakian, though his name appeared nowhere on them.

During a cross-country car trip with Marshall Stearns that summer, Avakian stopped in Springfield, Ohio, to get together with his pal Bob Sun, son of the vaudeville impresario Gus Sun. A blind date was arranged with a local college student, who never showed up because she was delayed by the requirements of her dramatics society. The student turned out to be Jemy McBride, though Avakian wouldn't know this until he attended John Hammond's wedding a couple of years later.

Hammond had met the kid in Manhattan where they were both hanging around Goodman and had invited him once or twice to his Sullivan Street apartment to listen to records; since then he had kept up with Avakian's published articles. Now, in 1940, entrusted with finding jazz that could be profitable, Hammond told Wallerstein about Avakian. A classical guy through and through, Wallerstein was wary of jazz in general and of older jazz in particular. But Wallerstein was also aware of swing's popularity, and of the August 1938 *Life* magazine article that had generated so much talk. Half the artists mentioned in the article—Armstrong, Bix, and Mildred Bailey, to name just three—had made masters that Columbia now owned. Could these be reissued? Hammond said to him, "There's a young man at Yale, only twenty-five miles or so from Bridgeport, and you ought to call him. He can do this better than I can."

Wallerstein called. After an interview, he offered Avakian $25 a week to research old masters at the Bridgeport factory. Avakian was in his third year at Yale and figured he could manage it. With help from Herb Greenspon, who'd first worked in the Bridgeport facility in 1935 as a shipping clerk for ARC, and Greenspon's young assistant Jimmy Sparling, an avid swing fan, Avakian scoured the second-floor stacks of masters. This became the basis for Columbia's Hot Jazz Classics series.[28]

The real find came in March 1940: a cache of unreleased Armstrong masters, recorded in Chicago some ten years earlier. Avakian had pressings made in the factory and took them to the Apollo in Harlem, where Armstrong was appearing. Avakian was directed across the street to the Braddock Bar and Grill where he found Louis having lunch. Armstrong, who always kept a portable phonograph in his dressing room, cordially took Avakian back to the Apollo and together they listened to each record. "Hey, that's great!" he said, though he didn't remember the circumstances of the recordings. Avakian, still in his junior year in college, got permission from Armstrong to release the recordings on Columbia.

The Hot Five and Hot Sevens were primarily recording bands—that is, they barely existed as musical aggregations away from the studio microphone. Most of the recordings were made between November 1925 and November 1931. Avakian's annotations on these records served as models of the form, at once erudite and conversational, as though he were shooting the breeze with a friend who was listening to the records with him, jumping up every few minutes to change the disk. Some writers possessed Avakian's deep musical and literary knowledge; others wrote with a similar, deceptively casual style; but no one else managed to combine the two the way he did.

There were, in fact, two major note-writing models for Avakian: one of them was Warren Scholl, by day a stockbroker who composed the booklet that accompanied Victor's 1936 *Bix Beiderbecke Memorial Album*; the other was Hammond, who annotated the eight-song *Bessie Smith Memorial Album* on Columbia.

Avakian followed up the Armstrong with reissues of Duke Ellington and Bessie Smith. Hammond had taken credit on the Armstrong, though he'd had no hand in that seminal reissue, and he'd rewritten Avakian's notes on Ellington to criticize the Duke for his persistence in composing longer pieces. (Hammond's notes so quietly infuriated Ellington that the two men never again went beyond a polite formality.)[29] Although Avakian didn't answer to Hammond—that was an impression that the much written-about Hammond would foster about several jazz producers over the years—he was philosophical about the credits. Graduating from Yale with a BA in English, Avakian was a full-fledged record producer now, and a profitable one at that.

Then he was drafted.

7

Battlegrounds

Avakian went into the army, eventually logging four and a half years in the service, most of them in the South Pacific. As America went to war in the aftermath of the Pearl Harbor attack, Columbia got its pop footing with several hits. Horace Heidt, a holdover from American Record and regarded as a society bandleader along the lines of Lester Lanin, had taken his lumps from Hammond in the press; after Hammond was assigned to record him, Heidt, still smarting from the criticism, threw him out of the studio.[1] Horace Heidt and His Musical Kings promptly sold hundreds of thousands of copies of "Deep in the Heart of Texas," a record that Hammond would have repudiated anyway. Harry James did all right with the old McCarthy-Monaco "You Made Me Love You." The songwriter and bandleader Ray Noble, British but based in New York and Hollywood after 1935, put Snooky Lanson in front of the microphone and made "By the Light of the Silvery Moon." And then Kate Smith, the dancer turned portly singer and radio star, recorded "Rose O'Day." Smith's version of "God Bless America" ascended to anthem status when the war effort demanded it. These were all newly recorded versions of old songs that brought Columbia closer to the pop numbers put up by RCA and Decca.

The world war took over. Before another war—hardly as lethal or as global but effectively interning the recording industry—began, Columbia did its part. In early '42 the label released "Wabash Cannon Ball," recorded by Roy Acuff and His Smoky Mountain Boys. Acuff, the aspiring Major League Baseball player turned music publisher (Acuff-Rose), would remain a music dynamo for decades to come. In song after song Harry James's horn sounded to be coming from some sort of cumulus memory cloud, billowing down hits like Berlin's "Easter Parade" and the Cahn-Styne "I've Heard That Song Before." Spectacularly though not surprisingly, Benny Goodman landed on the charts with his new singer Peggy Lee and "Why Don't You Do Right?" Lee was the most recent in the line of Goodman's female singers—Helen Ward in front, with Martha Tilton, Helen Forrest, and Liza Morrow right behind—her masticating, sandy-voiced style all her own.

It was also the period when Goodman and his old producer Hammond became related by marriage: after her divorce from George Arthur Victor Duckworth, MP, Lady Duckworth (née Alice Hammond, one of John's four sisters) married Goodman in Las Vegas. Describing Alice Hammond as a "very striking lady," George Simon wrote, "Whereas John would aggravate musicians by sitting up close to them and seemingly concentrating more on his newspaper than on their music, his sister would create the same reaction by sitting right by the bandstand and either knitting or playing gin rummy."[2] Announcing the Duckworth-Goodman wedding, the *Times* referred to Hammond as "an ardent swing fan."[3]

The war itself began to be addressed in Kay Kyser's version of Frank Loesser's "Praise the Lord and Pass the Ammunition." Columbia did well with that one, as well as a grab bag of other Kyser recordings. The war was addressed, too, if ever so secretly, in the Bridgeport factory. When the day's work was done, the lights turned out and everyone else home for supper, Ted Wallerstein and Jim Hunter went back inside to make records. There might have even been music on them; Andre Kostelanetz speculated that Wallerstein was an agent for the Office of Strategic Services (OSS) and used his recording of "Clair de Lune" to send coded messages to prisoners of war.[4] Using the bastardized composition that included scrap shellac, Wallerstein and Hunter pressed maps of various parts of Europe, presumably provided by stateside army representatives, between the disks' laminated layers.[5] The disks were meant to be broken, of course—a patriotic reversal of the manufacturing process.

It was just as well. Five months after Pearl Harbor, the U.S. government proclaimed shellac vital to national defense.[6] The War Production Board was limiting record manufacturers to no more than 30 percent of their 1941 use of shellac. For a while everything would be made of scrap.

•   •   •

As the war in Europe and the Pacific began to inform every facet of American life, there was a second battlefront that affected musicians, radio networks, and record labels. On its face it seemed to have been triggered by the licensing wars between the two major music fee-collecting organizations. The American Society of Composers, Authors and Publishers, more commonly known as ASCAP, had been around since the First World War and was formed to address payment injustices going back to John Philip Sousa's canned-music grievances and earlier, to the beginning of recorded sound. After a quarter century, as radio became an accepted part of everyday life, the National Association of Broadcasters had decried the "song monopoly" that ASCAP held on American music.[7] So the broadcasters' association created Broadcast Music, Inc., also known as BMI, to compete with ASCAP. The legal muscle behind BMI was the expert copyright attorney Sidney Kaye, a partner in Rosenman, Goldmark, Colin & Kaye, which maintained close ties to CBS and Columbia Records. The general wisdom was that ASCAP had a lock on the works that comprised the Great American Songbook (Rodgers & Hart, Rodgers & Hammerstein, Porter, Berlin, Kern, and others) while BMI licensed "Jeannie with the Light Brown Hair," "Turkey in the Straw," and a lot of contemporary doggerel.

Jobs had also been cut back on radio. Radio stars appeared live in prime time (as a regular media tool, recording tape was still several years away), when production costs could be justified; programming for the rest of the day consisted of talk, news, or daytime dramas. If music was called for, that was often played by a disk jockey. As disk jockeys—say, Al Jarvis on the West Coast, Martin Block on the East Coast—became known as on-air personalities, their popularity often supplanted that of most musicians.

Disk jockeys. ASCAP. BMI. Jukeboxes. The American Federation of Musicians (AFM) said, Hey, what about us? Thirty-five years after "canned music" gained notoriety in print, the phrase had taken on new significance. On August 1, 1942, AFM president James C. Petrillo called for a musicians' ban on recording. The strike meant no orchestrations, no vocal or instrumental backing. It meant 180,000 musicians across the country were forbidden by their union to record. Elmer Davis, the director of the Office of War Information, appealed to Petrillo to rescind the walkout order. Petrillo swatted away the appeal like an insect.

Petrillo, the son of a sewer worker, was a trumpeter. He became president of the Chicago musicians' local in 1922, when he was 30. Said to be the highest-paid union leader in history, with a team of bodyguards and "the biggest damn desk I could find in Marshall Field's," Petrillo provided good copy that often cited his preference for imported beer, his abusive language, and his germ phobia.[8] When he became president of the national organization, he moved his head-quarters to midtown Manhattan and bethroned himself like an emperor. (His middle name, after all, was Caesar.) His declaration of war against the recording companies was aimed specifically at the making of recorded music to the detriment of those who made live music (i.e., Petrillo's constituents).

Through the Associated Press, Ted Wallerstein released a statement describing Petrillo's action as "unreasonable and unfair" and stating that "the American public will be deprived of enjoying great artists and fine music. In a period when the spirit and morale of our nation needs music, Mr Petrillo's edict seems particularly ill-considered and ill-timed."[9]

The strike was on. Columbia, RCA, and Decca reconsidered their release schedules and also saw new value in reissues. At the end of 1942, Howard Taubman published a survey of the upcoming year in the recording industry; the survey focused on the shellac shortage and referred to the ban only as an afterthought. Close to 130 million records were sold in 1941, and only the government's 1942 freeze on shellac stockpiling prevented that figure from being topped. If 1943 were to prove disappointing, Taubman suggested, it would be due to the shortage. "The representatives of the three major companies . . . do not expect to be able to produce new disks as fast as the consumers ask for them, any more than they were able to do so in 1942. . . . The backlog of orders is tremendous, possibly the largest in the history of the record industry."[10]

One year earlier songwriter Johnny Mercer, movie executive (and occasional lyricist) Buddy DeSylva, and record store proprietor Glenn Wallichs had formed Capitol Records, in Hollywood. Capitol was not yet the major player it would become later in the forties and especially through the fifties, but the other companies were watching it closely. Given its location and the achievements and persuasiveness of its founders, it had easy access to West Coast–based artists. The three New York–based majors took every opportunity, including the shellac shortage, to pick at the new label.

"Gossip has it," reported the *Times*, "that Capitol recordings is [sic] employing a formula that eliminates shellac. It can be told, however, that rival companies have purchased Capitol disks, melted them down and tried to discover the nature of the substitute. They report sadly that such records as they have obtained have had shellac in them, but they are quick to add that this is no evidence that there are not some Capitol records without shellac."[11]

As in any crisis, the ban made for some remarkable developments. One of them was the V-Disc, instituted by the War Department. Determined to provide music and recordings "for the boys" in the face of the AFM ban, the V-Disc essentially got the War Department into the business of making records, inducing artists to work for free and shipping the results overseas. Another was the increase in spoken word recordings, the sessions requiring no musicians. The most renowned of these was probably Columbia's recording of *Othello*, with its own singing artist Paul Robeson in the title role, Uta Hagen as Desdemona, and José Ferrer as Iago. The AFM couldn't touch the recording because there were no musicians. Curiously, too, there were exceptions to the ban, like harmonica players—hence the push to the Columbia career of the virtuoso Larry Adler. Ever-reliable Art Satherley had noticed a song called "Truck Drivin' Blues," surely one of the first important truck-driving songs, and signed its writer-singer, Ted Daffan, to Okeh. Soon Okeh released Daffan's "Born to Lose," tailor-made for the jukebox and, more than a decade later, for Ray Charles.[12] Either the AFM didn't cover Satherley's territory or Okeh released it under the New York radar. Okeh also sent out hundreds of thousands of copies of "Pistol Packin' Mama" (Lay that pistol down, Ma) by Al Dexter and his Pistol Packin' Troopers.

● ● ●

Despite the AFM strike, Columbia signed two contracts that would shore up its catalog for many years. In the summer of 1942, the 26-year-old Frank Sinatra finally gave in to Manie Sacks's entreaties to go it alone as an artist. Sinatra's boss, Tommy Dorsey, whose band Sinatra joined after his brief tenure with Harry James—and, critically, whose trombone-playing remained a deep influence on Sinatra's singing—couldn't record because of the ban anyway. At first blush there was no bad blood between employer and employee. Sacks, who looked like a slightly jowlier Sinatra (with a touch of tap dancer George Murphy thrown in), persuaded William Paley to make use of their new acquisition by putting him on CBS radio shows. That got Sinatra's voice out to millions who hadn't heard him. Then came the star-making engagement at New York's Paramount Theater, where he was held for eight weeks, every show sold out. Columbia rode that wave by reissuing Harry James's version of "All or Nothing at All," with the Sinatra vocal that got him invited to Dorsey's band in the first place. On its initial release the record had done nothing; now it quickly sold a million copies, with Columbia pressing more day and night. Sinatra, beginning to feel his own worth, finally bridled at the whopping 43 1/3 percent of gross earnings he had agreed to pay Dorsey and Dorsey's business manager, Leonard Vannerson.[13]

Although Columbia still hadn't made a record with Sinatra under his new contract, it loaned him $25,000 to help pay off Dorsey and Vannerson. The label knew what it had in Sinatra—and in Sacks, who had escorted The Voice onto its roster and who became one of his closest cronies. When Sinatra was mobbed by adoring fans, his near-doppelganger

Sacks was, too. Nobody at Columbia, least of all Sacks, objected. In January 1944 Sinatra and New York Philharmonic conductor Artur Rodzinski duked it out on page one of the *New York Sun* over whether jazz contributed to juvenile delinquency. The conductor said yes, the singer said no. Rodzinski couldn't understand why teenagers went so wild over Sinatra and saw no need for "swing" when there was so much beautiful classical music available to them. Boogie-woogie, to Rodzinski, bred bad behavior. "I don't know exactly what the causes of juvenile delinquency are," an eminently reasonable Sinatra told the Associated Press, "but I don't think any one can prove that popular music is one of them."[14] The page one dustup might have been cooked up by Sinatra's publicist George Evans, but in any case it generated only more anticipation for all those Columbia disks waiting to be recorded.

The second critical signing came in May 1943 when, at long last, the Philadelphia Orchestra joined the label. Eugene Ormandy was now the director, Harl McDonald the general manager. It would be another sixteen months before the orchestra would record again, in Philadelphia— Beethoven's Seventh Symphony, Brahms's Fourth Symphony, and Richard Strauss's *Death and Transfiguration* were recorded in that premiere session—but Wallerstein had landed the orchestra that prompted CBS's purchase of the record label in the first place.[15]

On furlough in 1944, George Avakian poked his head into his hometown. The jazz critic Charles Edward Smith had been assigned by Moses Asch to record W. C. Handy's daughter Katherine, with the great Harlem pianist James P. Johnson accompanying her. (Asch had no respect for the Petrillo ban.) Smith, lacking experience in a recording studio, asked Avakian to help on the date. Avakian wasn't enthusiastic about the results—Asch's operation folded before they could be released—but the session made him familiar with Handy's rather obscure "Chantez-Les Bas" ("Sing 'Em Low"), which he'd resurrect a decade later when he produced *Louis Armstrong Plays W. C. Handy* for Columbia.[16]

The recording war ended on Armistice Day 1944 when Columbia and RCA, the last holdouts, signed contracts specifying royalties payable to a trust fund set up by the AFM on every record sold. A year earlier Decca had come to more favorable terms with the union, agreeing to throw open its books to the union at any time and supply the serial number of each record made; in exchange, Decca could, in the event of another strike, lock in the artists it had under contract. By trying to wait out the strike, RCA and Columbia were penalized by having this last provision excluded from their capitulating agreements with the AFM.

In fact Wallerstein and Jim Murray, RCA Victor's general manager, had tried to negotiate through Washington. Petrillo's office was right on Lexington Avenue, only a few blocks east from those of the two men, but he wouldn't see them until they were ready to cave. In March 1944 Wallerstein sent a telegram to Fred M. Vinson, director of the Office of Economic Stabilization, to see if he could rouse the Roosevelt administration into action. It took a while to respond, but that October FDR himself petitioned Petrillo to allow his members to go back into the recording studio. Petrillo held fast. Union leaders have been known to be corrupt, but few have stirred their power with the potent mixture of smugness and sanctimony that Petrillo did. Comparing Columbia and RCA Victor to "the slave owners of the civil war days," Petrillo warned that his union "will not hesitate to break off relations with these companies and leave them to die by their own nefarious schemes."

If there was a joke in all this, it was that the financial concessions the AFM yanked from the major companies wouldn't go directly to (presumably underpaid) recording musicians but to a fund whose use and distribution were yet to be decided. It was estimated that payments into the fund would be close to $4 million a year. The ban, meanwhile, had ceased the normal flow of recording—of music new and old—for twenty-eight months. Wallerstein was publicly bitter, though some of the bitterness may have been for political effect: "The economic pressures on us are such that we can wait no longer and must now either sign or go out of business. We are finally accepting because of the Government's unwillingness or incapacity to enforce its orders."[17]

• • • •

At the beginning of 1945, Columbia purchased a munitions factory in Kings Mills, Ohio, 25 miles northeast of Cincinnati. The War Production Board had limited civilian arms manufacturing since January 1942, rendering Remington's Kings Mills facility idle.[18] CBS overhauled it for record production to supplement facilities in Bridgeport. The purchase remains shrouded in mystery, and there are no references to it in CBS's various histories. According to John Hammond, William Paley arranged, over Wallerstein's objections, to acquire the Remington plant at Kings Mills, with 3 million square feet of space, for $250,000 as war surplus.[19] That November, with the war over, Wallerstein went to Europe to reestablish European distribution as the market was revived. On his way home Wallerstein got stuck in a storm in Lisbon, leaving Goddard Lieberson briefly in charge in New York—a taste of things to come.[20] Lieberson had moved into the directorship of Masterworks after Moses Smith resigned. It would be another decade before Lieberson had Wallerstein's title.

America's boom years—financial, industrial, procreational—had begun. The GI Bill helped swell college enrollment. Columbia Records pressed more and more disks in its factories in Bridgeport and Kings Mills, Ohio, with one to be built any day now in Pitman, New Jersey. In 1946 the label held its first annual national sales convention, not far from Kings Mills, at the Gibson Hotel in Cincinnati.

And what sales! Gene Autry's recording career still hadn't peaked. Dinah Shore was probably the label's biggest female pop artist, though she would gradually be overtaken by a pert blond singer named Doris Day. As service men and women headed home, the railroad rhythms of "Sentimental Journey" seemed to be accompanying them. The record was made by the West Coast–based bandleader Les Brown, but it was Day's vocal that probably made the song a hit. Day's daisy voice was deceptive, a slightly bitter taste buried deep in the nectary. She would remain with Columbia throughout her long recording career—a career only enhanced by the movie stardom she achieved in the fifties.

Like Les Brown, Woody Herman was also LA-based. Herman's

Columbia version of David Raksin's "Laura" became the first hit record of that perennially haunting movie theme. From Columbia France came Tino Rossi, whose European hits—"Reginella" and "Vieni Vieni" among them—sold nicely in the States. Perennial favorite Harry James made "I Can't Begin to Tell You" with a singer called Ruth Haag, who was in fact James's wife, Twentieth Century Fox movie star Betty Grable. (The nom de disque, deemed necessary because Fox discouraged its stars from recording for companies it wasn't affiliated with, joined Grable's birth first name and the maiden name of James's mother.) The revelation among James's admirers was that Grable could sing so well.[21]

There was Kostelanetz, of course, and his wife Lily Pons, together and individually promoted by the label. The incomparable Victor Borge was already recording his distinctive acrostic of classical piano and wordplay. Frankie Carle was about to release "Oh! What It Seemed to Be," an enormous seller. Cab Calloway and Eddy Duchin were still on hand. The label prized Kate Smith, though she was, by many accounts, a holy terror to work with. Danny Kaye, the consummate tummeler who happened to be an unerringly rhythmic singer, skittered back and forth to Decca. Charles Trenet sailed from France now and then to make appearances at U.S. record stores. Spade Cooley, like Autry, got a lot of airplay on jukeboxes across the land; his "Shame on You" was a major 1946 record.[22] Columbia began an American Folk Music and Blues Division that included Autry, Roy Acuff, Al Dexter, Bill Monroe, and Johnny Bond.[23] Their sales proved to be essential to the label. One Acuff record alone could finance a season's Masterworks recordings of Zino Francescatti, Gregor Piatigorsky, Rudolf Serkin, and the label's new, dizzyingly gifted young violinist Isaac Stern, put together.

The Golden Gate Quartet and the Charioteers, two of the supreme gospel groups in the land, each survived through personnel changes. Harry James was still around. Elliot Lawrence led one of the more admired postwar big bands and, feeling the big band market drying up around him, would eventually turn his arranging talents to Broadway. Frank Sinatra was only the most visible illustration of the new phenomenon of the singer, rather than the bandleader, as star.

• • •

Sinatra, squired around by Manie Sacks whenever he was back on the East Coast, remained the label's premiere male singer. In New York to record for Columbia, he would hold court at Patsy's, the Italian joint where he had his own booth near the front, behind the glass entryway where you could see him as you walked in, and he frequently answered the pay phone himself.[24] (Not that he was being helpful; the calls were usually for him.) In the three years following the end of the Petrillo ban and the war, Sinatra commenced the first phase of his astonishingly intimate rapport with listeners. This opening round of classic recordings included "You Go to My Head," "These Foolish Things," "Try a Little Tenderness," and "(I Don't Stand) A Ghost of a Chance."[25]

Columbia Records put so much faith in The Voice's ability to sell records that the company once let him conduct music he felt passionate about, even though he could barely read a lead sheet. The music was by Eastman graduate Alec Wilder, who had come to New York to compose for a living. Tall, chain-smoking, and increasingly acerbic when fueled by alcohol, Wilder ran interference for Sinatra backstage during the famous Paramount Theater run, blocking bobbysoxers and would-be hangers-on from the singer. While the AFM recording ban was still in force, the CBS Orchestra performed six of Wilder's airs for radio broadcast. Wilder, humble and a bit nervous, presented the air-check acetates to Sinatra. Despite frequently boorish, thuggish behavior even then, Sinatra possessed fine musical instincts and knew what he had. When the AFM ban was lifted, Columbia allowed Sinatra to make *Frank Sinatra Conducts the Music of Alec Wilder*. These octets—they sound something like Delius passing through a Gil Evans sensibility—are jazz chamber music of a very high order. Although he held the baton, Sinatra didn't get in the way. It was a stroke of marketing genius and won Wilder listeners who otherwise wouldn't have paid attention.[26]

Some people didn't think the marketing was so wonderful. The novelist Dorothy Baker (*Young Man with a Horn*) was evidently irritated when she wrote to Goddard Lieberson:

I find, partisan as I am (see above), that the composer's billing makes me sort of sore. I can see the point, of course—the company wants to sell records, so it does a stunt, obviously in the interests of the composer, but quite a lot too obviously working in different directions. Sinatra's name will sell the album (maybe), and it will also add a dimension to the reputation of Mr Sinatra. But where does Mr Wilder really come in? I suppose I could take it easier if on the edge of the album you could really see any word but SINATRA. . . . [27]

One of Sinatra's major proponents, Martin Block, the disk jockey behind WNEW's *Make Believe Ballroom*, became the "proprietor" of the *Columbia Record Shop*—actually a half-hour radio program that played only Columbia records and went out to 325 stations. Although Sinatra was now a movie star, he remained openly grateful for the support he got from his label—for a while longer, anyway.

Columbia employees who'd gone to war began to return home. At the same time the label was turning into a media company where experienced business executives wanted to be. When the artist Jim Flora left his position as advertising manager to go to RCA, Albert Earl took over. Ken McAllister ran merchandising. Jeff Wilson was second in the sales division to Paul Southard and also managed sales training. One of Wilson's trainees was Stan Kavan, who had begun in the shipping department while he was still in high school at Hartford High, before the war. Growing to well over six feet, Kavan became an Air Corps cadet, then flew several bombing missions in Italy. When he returned in '45, Columbia granted him a local record distributorship, which he maintained over the next four years. When he finally visited the Columbia offices at 799 Seventh Avenue, he ran into George Dale, the label's chief liner-note writer, and recognized him as his Air Corps paymaster.[28]

One guy who didn't come back from Europe right away was Herb Greenspon, who had been with American Record since 1936 and knew the Bridgeport plant from the inside. Serving under Colonel Richard Ranger, the magnetic-tape whiz of the Signal Corps, Greenspon remained in Germany to head up the recording of the Nuremberg trials.[29] He would eventually return to Bridgeport and become director of manufacturing and technical operations.

*   *   *

Home from the Pacific in 1946 and just before getting his old Columbia job back, George Avakian, several pounds lighter but fuller than ever with jazz knowledge and recording savvy, went to Town Hall to hear pianist Maro Ajemian and pianist-composer Alan Hovhaness in concert.[30] Maro had been a highly regarded piano student at Juilliard in the early forties, and this was only her second recital. Avakian had been aware of Maro and her younger sister Anahid since they were children; their families, each prominent in the Armenian-American community in New York, had known each other slightly. Knocked out by Maro's playing at Town Hall on that April night in 1946, Avakian was waiting backstage to congratulate her when he got a look at the grown-up Anahid, a Juilliard-educated violinist of considerable skill and recent winner of the Naumberg Award. (Few female violinists of the period would record so extensively as Anahid Ajemian.) As a preadolescent, Avakian's younger brother Aram had been smitten with Anahid. Now, Avakian wrote, "The moment I laid eyes on Anahid after the concert, Aram was a dead duck." Avakian joined the Ajemian sisters for dinner, along with the composer John Cage, Merce Cunningham, and the pianist William Masselos. By the time dinner was over, Avakian knew he'd met the girl he wanted to marry.

A month earlier Avakian had telephoned Ted Wallerstein to ask if his offer to bring him into Columbia full-time after the service still stood. Wallerstein had said yes, though not before asking Avakian if he had his father's permission. (Avakian was about to turn 27, but Wallerstein knew that his father was expecting him to join the family rug business.) When it was time to report back to 799 Seventh Avenue, Avakian, self-aware and cautious, wondered about the possibility of a conflict with Hammond's responsibilities. Hammond, Avakian knew, had returned from the army a couple of months earlier and was certain to be signing up his most cherished players for the label. To Avakian's astonishment Wallerstein declared, "John Hammond will never again work for Columbia as long as I'm president!" Avakian didn't probe—you didn't do that to the austere, private Wallerstein—but thought his ire might have been roused by Hammond's penchant for sticking his name on records he had nothing to do with, in particular the last seven of the prewar Hot Jazz Classics. "Later," Avakian said, "I found out that a much bigger reason was that John had also started working *sub rosa* for Ben [Selvin] right after Wallerstein brought him back." Hammond was in fact recording his old friend Mildred Bailey, a longtime favorite, for Majestic. "I never inquired further, but quickly found myself very welcome as the new pop A&R guy. John had not made many friends at Columbia."[31]

Although Hammond admitted he'd been recording for Ben Selvin at Majestic, he wrote that Wallerstein was already furious at him because, after he too came back from the war, he took a seat on the editorial board of Keynote Records at the invitation of his former sponsor Eric Bernay.[32] In Wallerstein's mind, ya went home with the guy what brung ya. Hammond would be away from Columbia Records for another 13 years.

His "discovery" Billie Holiday would be away almost as long. There had been an understandable break between them in 1939, when Hammond famously declined to record "Strange Fruit," insisting its sensationalism and lack of swing would turn her into a chanteuse rather than a jazz singer. "Strange Fruit" was subtly political, angry, and, maybe most important to Hammond, didn't swing—except of course in the imagery of its livid lyric about the lynching of Negroes. While Hammond was in the army, Holiday had stopped recording because of the Petrillo ban; later she would be either recording for Decca or in jail. Although they apparently remained cordial whenever they ran into each other, there was always a beast hunched between them in the room: Hammond told a correspondent that Billie had been sexually involved with the female cousin of Hammond's Yale roommate and, fearing the possibility of blackmail because of her involvement with Jimmy and

Clark Monroe, blew the whistle on the affair. [33] (Jimmy Monroe and Billie Holiday eloped in 1941 and, through drug addiction and some very lean, violent times, stayed married until 1950. Clark Monroe owned the Uptown House on 134th Street, which, along with Minton's Playhouse, was one of Harlem's incubating stations of bebop.) By 1946 Holiday was inactive as a recording artist and Hammond was *persona non grata* at Columbia.

· · ·

The offices at 799 Seventh Avenue expanded. The switchboard now handled hundreds of phone calls a day. (The widespread presumption was that operators Anne Fox and Verne Reynolds were listening in whenever they felt like it and knew the secrets of every CRC employee.) A trainee program was instituted, a kind of company GI Bill, in which young men coming out of the service could be put to work. Entering the program in 1946, Roy Friedman trained first in electroplating—part of Jim Hunter's manufacturing division—under chief chemist Leo Kosowsky in Bridgeport. Soon Friedman was sent to 799, which, astonishingly, housed anywhere from 15 to 20 high-speed plating tanks, right there in a midtown office building.[34] For a while Friedman oversaw the complicated electroplating process, which included coding of the masters in New York. Because lacquer itself is nonconductive, the masters had to be sputtered with gold. Part of a gold sheet would vaporize on the surface of the master and coat the lacquer. Columbia bought its gold sheets— each 24 pure karats, worth several thousand dollars apiece—from Connecticut bullion dealers Handy & Harmon. When a sheet became worn out at the edges, Handy & Harmon would weigh the difference and credit Columbia toward the next new one. The *mother* and the *stamper* were the next record-making generations after the *master*, and, down the line, everything was tested for sound quality and degradation in Bridgeport. After several years of making what seemed to be an inferior product, Columbia was again releasing disks of high sound quality.

Now with electroplating, advertising, merchandising, art, and sales departments all moving at top speed, Columbia reconsidered how to get its product out to the public. An in-house study, signed by Paul Southard, reported that only 29 percent of American households contained a record player, but 300 million records had been sold the previous year.[35] There was a listening audience out there, but still too few machines to play the records on. Meanwhile Columbia tried the first of several promotional tie-ins with Revlon. In the summer of 1947 the company opened a West Hollywood record plant near the corner of Robertson and Beverly Boulevards. The locale would make western U.S. shipping considerably less expensive.

Columbia stepped up its radio programming. *Masterworks of Music* showcased the classical line and ran nearly 55 minutes each week. Fred Robbins, the popular DJ of *Robbins Nest*, took over the *Columbia Record Shop* from Martin Block. Arthur Godfrey's "Too Fat Polka," backed by "For Me and My Gal," was one of the best-selling records of 1947.[36] Records by Dorothy Shay, the "Park Avenue Hillbilly," landed on the charts.[37] George Avakian, encouraged by Wallerstein to go into the "icebox" of old masters to see what could be released, found an old Les Brown recording of Irving Berlin's "I've Got My Love to Keep Me Warm." Disappointingly, Brown's singer Doris Day, who had since become a star in her own right, didn't sing on it; but Avakian released it anyway as a 78. The record sold spectacularly, and Avakian's star rose a few more light years.

With record sales almost doubled between 1945 and 1946, Columbia was pulling closer to RCA Victor. As a reward, Wallerstein was elected a director of CBS. At the end of March 1947, the Columbia Recording Corporation was reorganized under the name Columbia Records, Inc., subsidiary of Columbia Broadcasting System, Inc.

* * *

Magnetic recording tape was first used in 1947 for recording radio programs in advance of the broadcasts. (Bing Crosby has often been credited as the first radio personality to insist on taping his shows, freeing his time for the links and the racetrack.) Soon recording studios began to routinely use tape; within a year, the old method of direct recording on wax or acetate blanks was almost completely superseded. Tape could be played back for immediate audition and lent itself to editing— erasing distortions, deleting and adding segments, and splicing together for perfect continuity.

During the war CBS executive Adrian Murphy had seen a German Magnetophon tape recorder in Luxembourg. He shipped one back to CBS. It was a revelation to everyone there. EMI and Ampex each came out with similar machines. By mid-1947, Columbia Records was using these to edit and was quickly phasing out direct disk cutting, which was less accurate as well as cumbersome. Because the Ampex outperformed the EMI model, that became the standard for Columbia.[38]

As 1947 ended, Ted Wallerstein was elevated to Columbia's chairman of the board, and longtime treasurer Frank White was promoted to the presidency.[39] The double shift got a lot of press but would prove short-lived. In classical music circles around the same time, erstwhile Masterworks director Moses Smith was getting some attention as the author of a book about Serge Koussevitsky, the Russian conductor whose tenure leading the Boston Symphony Orchestra and building of the Berkshire Festival at Tanglewood was a natural for a biography.[40] As he had as a critic at the *Boston Globe*, Smith proved to be at once analytical and easy to read. He also infuriated his subject by not gushing at every turn. The conductor sued Smith and his publisher, Allen, Towne & Heath, for half a million dollars, charging that the book depicted him as "brutal to the musicians in my orchestra, incompetent as an instructor of conducting and a poseur, deficient in musical education and training."[41] Koussevitsky lost the suit. It was a minor victory for Smith, though. The articulate writer who had reignited Masterworks under CBS had been all but overshadowed by his former assistant, Goddard Lieberson.

8

Bedroom, Boardroom

"John Hammond told me that once Goddard came in as Smith's assistant, Moe's days were numbered," George Avakian remembered. "I never asked just what happened, but Hammond, who was a friend of Smith's, was pretty bitter."[1] It was Hammond who had recommended Lieberson for a job in the first place, in 1939. But Hammond could afford to stay off the corporate track and stick to scouting and recording. Lieberson had bigger plans. Those plans would place him in New York's most exclusive social circles, clear the way for a climb up the CBS corporate ladder, and make him wealthy. He would socialize with the Western world's finest musicians, as well as society and showbiz types, from Igor Stravinsky to Groucho Marx. A musician himself, he possessed a deep love of literature and the quickest wit in the land. In addition to a gleeful, continually punning deployment of English, he could string together a few sentences in four languages—French, German, Japanese, and, later in life, Italian—and, when the joke called for it, a smattering of Yiddish. As a boss, he knew how to delegate; he left his people alone to do their jobs.

Many record buyers first became aware of Lieberson through Columbia's original cast recordings of musical comedies. *Produced for Records by Goddard Lieberson* was his standard credit. Growing up in Nebraska with those cast albums, Dick Cavett dreamed of calling himself Goddard Lieberson Cavett, a name that would denote exquisite taste in all things. One day in the late 1960s, Cavett, by then a national television personality, received a phone call from his friend Groucho Marx. "Do you want to have dinner with a man named Goddard Lieberson?" asked Groucho. Barely containing his excitement, Cavett said yes. "All right," Groucho said, "I'll see if I can find one."[2]

There was, in fact, only one. To borrow the lyric from the hit song "One"—from *A Chorus Line*, Lieberson's final Broadway recording project—the man was a singular sensation. For nearly 40 years, when it came to Columbia Records, he was the one.

•   •   •

Goddard Lieberson was born in 1911 in Hanley, Staffordshire, the youngest (by ten years) of five children of Rachel and Abraham Lieberson. Abraham, Russian-born, was the owner of the first rubber-heel factory in England and also manufactured shakos, the military headdresses adorned with metal plates and plumes, for the British guards.[3] At seven Lieberson joined his family in a move to Canada, then, after a brief stay in Northern California, to Seattle. From 1921 to 1925 Lieberson attended North Queen Anne School. The relatively comfortable life the family had enjoyed in England, with servants tending to their needs, rapidly descended into less-familiar strife during the pre-Depression years in Seattle. Rachel, who had never had to prepare meals before, cooked chicken legs to feed the brood. When Lieberson contracted diphtheria and was confined to the house, one of his brothers taught him some rudimentary piano. By the time he was at Ballard High School, Lieberson was playing popular music for his friends. In the spring of 1929, just before Lieberson graduated from high school, a University of Washington professor named George McKay was impressed by one of Lieberson's compositions and arranged for him to get a scholarship there.

The University of Washington's Pro Musica was playing a program of Lieberson's works when the Viennese composer Ernest Toch gave him a card of recommendation—several, in fact, in case he lost the one.[4] Lieberson knew whom to cultivate. In January 1932, still at Washington, Lieberson wrote to the Chicago Musical College to inquire about scholarships. Chicago's director, Rudolph Ganz, replied with some discouragement and suggested Lieberson apply to Juilliard, the Curtis Institute in Philadelphia, "or directly to Howard Hanson, Director of the Eastman School in Rochester, New York."[5] Lieberson wrote to Hanson and soon received an acceptance by mail. (In the interim the school's founder, George Eastman, committed suicide, leaving behind the note, "My work is done. Why wait?")[6] Lieberson, in the words of his *Esquire* profiler Martin Mayer, "was rocketed off" to the East Coast to study further.

He made his mark quickly. "I was a Rochester boy," his Eastman classmate Mitch Miller told Mayer, "so I knew all the professors from a long time before. But that never cut any ice. Lieberson came out of the West, into my class, and before he'd been at school three months the professors there were taking him out to dinner."[7]

Lieberson made it worth their while. His professors could hear his musical gifts, and he was already great company, his banter rife with literary as well as musical references. At 16 he had set James Joyce's poem "Alone" to music then wrote to Joyce to tell him so. (That time there was no response.) At 21 he began a correspondence with the writer-composer James Weldon Johnson, first plying him with rare pipe tobacco, then, months later, requesting permission to set parts of Johnson's *God's Trombone* to music. Johnson, teaching at Fisk, in Nashville, apparently agreed to let Lieberson do what he wanted and gave him the address of his friend Carl Van Vechten, Teutonic champion of all things black, in New York.

Lieberson wrote to Van Vechten and asked if he could set one of the scenes in his novel *Nigger Heaven* to music. Van Vechten invited him to New York. Lieberson, though decidedly not black, was tall, young, and handsome—qualities that the married but homosexual Van Vechten didn't mind. At his apartment on West 55th Street, Van Vechten greeted Lieberson warmly and photographed him. "Carlo," as Van Vechten liked to be called, was then 52 and not immune to the Eastman student's immense charm. While in New York, Lieberson stayed at an apartment leased by Lehman Engel, a young composer who would become one of Lieberson's closest friends.[8] In October 1932, Van Vechten gave

Lieberson permission to use *Nigger Heaven*, but warned him that the title, though meant ironically, had offended many people.

• • •

Lieberson admired gospel and blues, though he may not have had a real musical feel for them. It appears he didn't do anything with *Nigger Heaven*—not by that title, anyway—but at Eastman in January 1934 he arranged "Sometimes I Feel Like a Motherless Child" for a classmate to sing in concert. While still composing, he stepped up his critical writing. He worked as an editor of the *International Encyclopedia of Music and Musicians* and wrote for the *Rochester Evening Journal* and *Musical America*. For the 1935–36 school year, Lieberson was hired as a music teacher at the exclusive Harley Country Day School, in Rochester, at an annual salary of $600. He did not hide the fact that he hadn't taken a degree from either Eastman or the University of Washington.[9]

Harley was founded in 1917 by a woman named Harriet Bentley (Har-ley) and was already considered posh.[10] Lieberson was responsible for the entire school's chorus, and for music history and musical composition for the Upper School. There was a new music room—ivory walls, red tables and chairs, a piano, radio, and victrola—to work in. The *Rochester Democrat & Chronicle* quoted the new music teacher: "Harley's aim is to develop taste and feeling rather than give pupils mere information, so that intelligent understanding and criticism will grow out of an honest delight in music." At 24 Lieberson was already prepared to shape the sensibilities of others—in this case children who were wide open to learning. Lieberson directed his students in a Chinese playlet with music and in the processional interludes and recessional of the Christmas pageant, and played for them, apparently over and over, parts of *The Nutcracker Suite*.[11] (The Tchaikovsky would remain an essential work for him long after he arrived at Columbia Records.) Students recalled that Lieberson related easily to both girls and boys, played baseball with the boys at recess, and owned a convertible that he sometimes used to ferry students to lunch in nearby Pittsford.[12] Teaching gave him time off to write and travel. Lieberson composed music to lyrics written by Harley's Upper School dramatics teacher Mildred Waterman. In November 1935 he went to New York to hear several of his pieces played. "Cradle Song" (part of a series of faux English lullabies), "Gramaphone [sic], 1912," and "Eight Negro Sermons in Verse, by James Weldon Johnson" were included in a WPA-sponsored program right after Thanksgiving of that year.[13] This was part of the Composers' Forum-Laboratory, founded and directed by Ashley Pettis, and after each performance listeners were invited to grill the composers. It was good public exposure and, in a time when the dialogue was often about the place of unionism and socialism in the arts, led to some heated exchanges. Lieberson was almost a contradiction in terms, an elitist composer who espoused inclusiveness.

His String Quartet dates from 1937. Just over 15 minutes long, the piece was recorded in 1938 by the Galimir Quartet and released many years later by Columbia on LP.[14] The recording is well done, energetic, and confident. As a composer, though, you could die of encouragement. Before rock 'n' roll, what 24-year-olds made livings as composers? Writing furiously, Lieberson was sending articles to New York Times music critic Olin Downes, Columbia's longtime friend, who praised his writing but didn't take anything for publication.

While teaching at Harley, Lieberson met a beautiful hometown girl, Margaret Rosenberg.[15] Margaret was a member of the prominent Jewish family who had founded the Fashion Park line of men's clothing in Rochester in the nineteenth century, a line that later amalgamated with Weber & Heilbroner.[16] Everyone knew the Rosenbergs. Margaret, known to friends and family as Peggy, had been Phi Beta Kappa at Smith. She and Lieberson fell in love, their courtship observed by his Harley students, and married.

• • •

It's not clear whether the Liebersons moved to Manhattan together. In the late thirties they did travel extensively, mostly, if not exclusively, on

Peggy's dime. By 1939 Lieberson, either with her or alone, had settled in New York. Like other non-native New Yorkers who alight on the city and sprinkle it with the silvery dust of their artistic vitality, making it theirs—Cole Porter comes to mind—Lieberson appears to have had little choice but to do so. "My career was always thought to be that of a composer," Lieberson wrote to his Seattle friend Margaret Callahan many years later. "I came to New York with not quite that in mind because one doesn't have to come to New York to become a composer. I guess I came to New York to see what the hell was going on."[17]

Modern Music was the magazine of the League of Composers, and its various departments were authored by some of the best: Edwin Denby covered dance; Aaron Copland reviewed records and published music; George Antheil wrote about film music; Paul Bowles turned up works from Latin America; Colin McPhee and Elliot Carter covered the New York premieres; Virgil Thomson served as theater and opera critic; and Lieberson wrote about radio.[18]

And spoke on the radio. His good friend Morton Gould, whose politics mirrored Lieberson's, was two years younger but was already getting musical work throughout the city; one of his new jobs was to orchestrate and conduct on WOR. Gould got Lieberson signed on as commentator. Apart from his British birth, the job might have helped Lieberson keep from being drafted.[19]

During a 1938 meeting at the MacDowell Club about pending federal legislation to create a bureau of fine arts, Lieberson found himself vociferously disagreeing with just about everybody, getting heckled in the process, and apparently enjoying it. Lieberson, representing the American Composers Alliance, had no patience with Walter Damrosch's swipe at the Musicians Union, nor with the opinion of Scott Williams, president of the National Society of Mural Painters, who had declared that art was "aristocratic" rather than "democratic." Lieberson claimed to be speaking for "hundreds of thousands," and, when challenged to name the organizations he represented, was heckled that the organizations weren't "artistic."[20] The young leftist composer couldn't win. In fact Lieberson was a joiner, perhaps to make career contacts but also because he felt it was incumbent upon him to support his fellow composers. Later in 1938 he was elected vice president of the Society of Professional Musicians, which was formed to "promote American compositions."[21]

Around this time Lieberson's old Eastman schoolmate Alec Wilder, already ensconced at the Algonquin with the cigarettes, liquor, and reams of staff paper that would sustain him for the rest of his life, introduced him to John Hammond. The same age, Lieberson and Hammond got on well. Lieberson overflowed with punning wit, while Hammond was the proud owner of a hornlike, highly appreciative laugh. (Not necessarily, however, a strong sense of humor. When Wilder gave his song "Who Can I Turn To?" to Mildred Bailey, Hammond advised him to change the title to "Whom Can I Turn To?" Wilder then asked Hammond if he'd seen the new musical *Better Foot Forward*. The joke was lost on Hammond.)[22] Hammond invited Lieberson along on one of his talent-scouting trips to the South. Lieberson proved to be excellent company and came back to New York telling some of the colorful stories—Blind Boy Fuller's attempt to shoot his wife, for instance, by standing in the middle of a room and taking intermittent shots while rotating slowly—that Hammond later wrote up for publication. When Hammond presented some of the talent he'd found in his Carnegie Hall concert "From Spirituals to Swing," Lieberson served as his stage manager.

"Backstage was absolute hell," Lieberson recalled. "Those who were on didn't want to get off, and those who were off didn't want to get on."[23]

* * *

The contacts he made those first years in New York would prove invaluable. In March 1939 he wrote a bitter letter to *Modern Music* editor Minna Lederman, resigning because she had rejected a piece of his. Lederman ought to replace him, he wrote, with "a retired colonel or a member of the Union Club" who'd have the leisure to listen to the daytime programs she wanted reviewed.[24] Lieberson threw caution to the winds. He had left Eastman without taking a degree—in fact he never did receive

a baccalaureate—but had written, composed, and socialized his way
into position. John Hammond was offering to introduce him to Ted
Wallerstein. At the same time Lieberson was considering a position with
a music publisher. Morton Gould advised him to go with the publisher,
which he considered steadier employment than the more volatile record
business. Lieberson thought Gould a brilliant friend but went with the
recording company.[25] In the autumn of 1939, he was assigned to Masterworks as assistant to Moe Smith, the Masterworks director whom
Wallerstein had hired away from the *Boston Globe*.

Everyone knew Lieberson was talented, witty, and plugged-in—a
good man to have in the classical division. Immediately he began to
solicit works to record—writing to composers like Henry Cowell and
Ernest Toch (whom he'd so impressed while in college). Within a matter
of months Toch and Walter Piston were making records of their own
works for Columbia.

Lieberson's marriage, though, had unraveled. The prevailing view was
that Lieberson had outgrown Peggy and was trolling for someone who'd
be considered a greater catch in the world of the arts. As these painful
divisions often are, it was surely more complicated than that. The Liebersons began to spend an increasing amount of time apart—Peggy
retreating to Rochester, Goddard to a farm he'd bought near Rhinebeck,
in Dutchess County, and spending parts of one or two summers in Bucks
County, Pennsylvania, with Alec Wilder and Morty Palitz. There Wilder
dashed off bawdy musicals, which his friends performed with exuber-
ance. One of them, the 1941 production of a Wilder sketch called "The
Best Laid Plans," is unabashedly lewd.[26] In the fall of 1942, Lieberson
leased an apartment at 150 West 55th Street.[27] Now living in the heart
of midtown and close to 799 Seventh Avenue, he was delighted with the
social position he found himself in.

Sunday, at Andre Kostelanetz' and Lily Pons' home, I met—I don't know
if you can stand it, so prepare yourself—I met—GRETA GARBO! You will
want to know that her feet are not big, that she has very charming
speech, is curiously (for a movie star) intelligent, and she has the chest

of a small boy, which I know because she went in swimming only in her man's-type linen shorts. . . . I went swimming, too, but in the most embarrassing bathing suit of this century, a little number which Andre brought back from Hawaii—very Pago-Pago and very large for me, with the result that everybody looked at me as though I were a dirty French postcard—which I was.[28]

Lieberson was making it a point to know everyone worth knowing. Even when the *Times* misidentified him and Erich Leinsdorf as "opera singers" who'd presented Eleanor Roosevelt with a recording in a birthday tribute to FDR, the implication was that Lieberson was connected.[29]

*   *   *

It took four years for Lieberson to replace Moses Smith. Ted Wallerstein knew what he had in Lieberson, and the two men, despite an age difference of twenty years, respected each other. (It helped that they were stationed in separate towns—Wallerstein mostly in Bridgeport, Lieberson exclusively in Manhattan. When Wallerstein needed a Manhattan pad for the night, Lieberson's West 55th Street door was open to him.) The 1943 promotion to director of Masterworks fit Lieberson like a bespoke suit. Curiously, for a man so ambitious, Lieberson wasn't a workaholic—not at the office, anyway, for much of the requirements of his job were blended into an active social life. In the next two years Lieberson moved, discreetly and without much interference, toward an affair with the renowned ballet dancer Vera Zorina.

Zorina's fame in the late 1930s and early '40s glowed with the wattage of a rock star. She was beautiful, articulate, and, as dancers go, voluptuous in a way that her first husband, George Balanchine, would subsequently all but banish from the ballet corps. If her ripe physique went out of fashion in the dance world, her beauty never did.

Zorina was born Eva Brigitta Hartwig in 1917 in Berlin, of a Norwegian mother and German father, both professional singers. Known as

Brigitta as a child and in later private life as an adult, she was only 14 when she appeared in Max Reinhardt's productions of *A Midsummer Night's Dream* and *Tales of Hoffman*. At 17 she was invited to join the Ballets Russes de Monte Carlo; its director, Leonide Massine, in Russian tradition, changed her name to the Russian-sounding Vera Zorina. Massine cast her in several of his ballets and took her as his mistress in a ménage à trois with his wife, Eugenia Delarova. Zorina's resounding success in the London production of Rodgers & Hart's *On Your Toes*, choreographed by Balanchine, and then a sparkling Broadway appearance in the same team's *I Married an Angel*, had everybody talking about her. Reviewing *Married*, Brooks Atkinson, who wasn't inclined toward extravagant praise, wrote, "Vera Zorina, trained in the ballet, can act the part of the angel with some of the plastic grace of other-worldliness and she can dance like a goddess. Young, beautiful and accomplished, she is something of a treasure on our stage."[30] Balanchine, who had unhitched his American Ballet company from the Metropolitan Opera, worked on *Married*, too, keeping him close to her. It's no wonder Hollywood was intrigued. "Although Balanchine was considered the genius behind much of Ms Zorina's success onstage and screen in the 1930s and 1940s, she was better known to the general public in 1938," wrote Anna Kisselgoff in Zorina's *Times* obituary.[31] Working in Hollywood, she appeared in *The Goldwyn Follies* and several other films, a few of them without Balanchine's participation, and danced in the underrated (and too little seen) film version of *On Your Toes*, where she holds the screen less with technique than with a warm glow beneath her skin. Zorina's employment by Goldwyn, as well as her marriage to Balanchine, beginning in 1939, "embodied an experiment that integrated high art into popular culture," Kisselgoff wrote. "Ms Zorina's films, in which she often played a dancer, did much to introduce audiences to ballet as an art form, one that was witty and contemporary."[32]

Zorina was a star, though not necessarily a movie star. Men of achievement sighed for her. It's not surprising to come across her mentioned in one of Fitzgerald's Pat Hobby stories. A studio executive sends for Pat Hobby to rewrite a project called *Ballet Shoes*. "We think we can borrow Zorina, so we want to hurry things up—do a shooting script instead of just a treatment."[33] As late as the mid-1950s Lieberson, sending over a phonograph for Samuel Goldwyn to use at his Park Avenue hotel, introduced himself through her fame: "We met several times, but I suppose the best way I can identify myself to you is to tell you that my wife is Vera Zorina."[34]

* * *

In New York, Zorina and Balanchine attended a party for the conductor Efrem Kurtz, a Columbia Masterworks artist. Lieberson was there (whether stag or with Peggy isn't clear) and, as Zorina remembered it, "constantly turned around toward us and made funny remarks, which I thought was rather rude to his own dinner companions."[35] A year or so later, Zorina was staying at the Beverly Wilshire in Los Angeles when she ran into Lieberson. Each of them was still married. Lieberson was divorced first; Zorina's divorce wouldn't come through until she was pregnant by Lieberson.

"As George had begun my musical education," Zorina wrote, "so Goddard began to educate me—period. I read and read. I became aware of how little I knew about everything, how narrow my life had been, how much I wanted to know."[36] What Zorina saw in Lieberson is clear: wit, erudition, a debonair handsomeness, executive responsibility and accomplishment, perhaps even talent. What Lieberson saw in Zorina, her beauty a given, might be more complicated. For a Seattle boy whose closest sibling in age was a decade older, who read and wrote poetry and composed on the piano at an early age, Zorina represented a high level of conquest. For years he'd been drawn to the ballet world, and Zorina, even if more a great presence than a great dancer, was a supernova in that world. (In one of the stranger ironies of New York's incestuous high culture life, Lieberson maintained an avuncular relationship with the adolescent ballerina Tanaquil LeClercq, encouraging her to ride her horse on his Dutchess County farm and sending her records as early as 1943, for her fourteenth birthday. Zorina was Balanchine's third wife; LeClercq would become his fifth.)

Zorina's marriage was far more public than Lieberson's, so it was necessary to keep a low profile. During the first Petrillo ban, Lieberson recorded *Othello* with its Broadway stars, Paul Robeson, Uta Hagen, and José Ferrer. (Offstage there was a messy triangle. Hagen, married at the time to Ferrer, had an affair with Robeson. Iago doesn't always come out the winner.) In September 1944 Ferrer wrote to his new friend Lieberson: "Are you coaching Zorina in her new part? The Essex House should make an excellent rehearsal hall."[37]

At the office, meanwhile, Lieberson consoled, cajoled, and entertained— all to keep his Masterworks artists happy. "I wouldn't ever think of writing to disturb your sun bath, except that I have a little check for you," he wrote to Kostelanetz, who was vacationing in Florida. "I thought that you would want to know about it. The amount (it says here) is exactly $40,485.35. Oscar Levant will probably claim that by rights the thirty-five cents is his. If there is any chance of his sueing [sic] you, I think you ought to give it to him. There was an income tax of $10,050.84—naturally I have kept that, figuring that nobody would even know the difference."[38] When fellow Eastman alumnus David Diamond, who addressed him as "Godebski," needed a loan, Lieberson reached into his pocket.[39] Lieberson sent pianist Rudolf Serkin a royalty check accompanied by the note, "Here is another Utrillo!"[40] Doing a favor for Alec Wilder—an often thankless task, given Wilder's penchant for turning on people—Lieberson wrote to Arthur Freed's office at MGM hoping to interest Freed in a musical Wilder had written with frequent collaborator Bill Engvick.[41] Letter writing alone could take up a whole day's work, never mind recording sessions and garden variety hand-holding when artists appeared in the office. Once in a while Lieberson had a correspondent who gave as good as he got. Garson Kanin proposed that Lieberson record his wife, Ruth Gordon, reading from Lucretia Hale's *The Peterkin Papers*, a proposal Lieberson accepted. Kanin and Lieberson, their friendship cemented, possessed almost interchangeably witty sensibilities. "Dear Goddard," Kanin wrote to him at the beginning of 1943, "I love this letter already. It gives me the illusion that I'm writing to Paulette."[42]

Lieberson kept up his political activity. Much of this concerned Soviet-U.S. relations—a charged issue for anticommunist, self-styled "patriots" even during the war. Observers close to Lieberson at the time have suggested that Lieberson was deeply influenced by the politics of the Revuers (Betty Comden, Adolph Green, Judy Holliday, John Frank, and Alvin Hammer), with whom he spent time in the Catskills. Even if this is true, Lieberson's politics were probably fully formed long before America entered the war. Lieberson was proud to promote the Congress Celebrating American-Soviet Friendship, along with his good friend Morton Gould and conductor Serge Koussevitsky and the Musicians Committee, in autumn 1943. His determination that the communist experiment could coexist with the American brand of capitalism was genuine. In November 1945 he wired a request of the first secretary of the Embassy of the Union of Soviet Socialist Republics in Washington to intercede in what would prove to be a cultural if not musical milestone:

BENNY GOODMAN AUTHORIZED ME OFFER PROKOFIEFF THREE-THOUSAND DOLLARS PIECE FOR CLARINET AND ORCHESTRA, EIGHT TO FIFTEEN MINUTES. WILL YOU EXPLAIN IMPORTANCE OF SUCH A COMMISSION BY GOODMAN. GREETINGS.[43]

Running Masterworks, Lieberson leaned heavily on the frighteningly capable Greta Rauch, whose German—the first language of many of the Masterworks conductors—was better than Lieberson's. When the singer Lotte Lehman left the label in a fury in 1945, for instance, Rauch translated Lehman's angry, vernacular-filled letter. Paul Turner had been at Eastman with Lieberson and may have known at least as much about contemporary classical music. Around campus Turner was valued for his mechanical as well as musical talent, in particular the time he took apart a motorcycle, too big to fit through the door, in one dorm room and reassembled it in another.[44] Turner preceded Lieberson to New York City but followed him to Columbia Records. Married, Turner was sometimes known as the Very Rev. Tyler Turner, prefect of the Orthodox-Catholic

College for Liturgical Study, Provincial-Order of Saint Basil, St. Clement's Chapel, at 210 East 58th Street. While Lieberson was busy wining and dining the likes of Eugene Ormandy, the moonlighting priest did the gritty work of negotiating with the Philadelphia Orchestra's manager Harl McDonald.

"This is a madhouse since the [Petrillo] ban was lifted," Lieberson wrote to his psychiatrist friend Dr. Gregory Zilboorg, joking that he'd probably see him next as a patient.[45] During the frenzy of artists' new and renewed negotiations, conducted at 799 Seventh Avenue and in various Manhattan hotel rooms and restaurants, Abraham Lieberson died in California. Lieberson was broken up about it. After his father's funeral, Lieberson would keep his family at a greater remove. He would continue to support his mother, installed in an apartment in Los Angeles, but often couldn't see her when he had business there. He corresponded with his brothers Gershon, a tailor, and Maurice, a tobacco and liquor wholesaler, but didn't see them either.

Awaiting Zorina's divorce from Balanchine, the Lieberson-Zorina romance became more public. One afternoon in the autumn of 1945, while Zorina was appearing on Broadway as Ariel in *The Tempest*, Lieberson received a note from Cheryl Crawford, *The Tempest*'s producer: "Dear Goddard, We just asked Briggita [sic] to a party at my apartment, 400 E. 52 on Nov. 11th at five. I hope you can come and bring her. Please let me know. Yours in Bedroom C."[46] Crawford's ostensibly flirtatious closing was really a reference to a not-yet-published novel. Somehow, among the countless hours of recording accomplished musicians, composing correspondence, plunging into Manhattan nightlife, and courting the world-famous Zorina, Lieberson had found time to write a fictional confection called 3 *for Bedroom C*.

•   •   •

Bedroom C is in Pullman train car 409, traveling west from Chicago to Pasadena. Dr. Oliphant Thrumm, 42, is a chemistry professor at Harvard who finds himself in the same bedroom car as movie star Ann Haven and her young daughter Barbara. "That Miss Haven was the object of innumerable celluloid sexual fantasies was something that would never have occurred to him. He thought she was quite beautiful, in, perhaps, a Restoration period way, but he suspected, too, that she would turn out to be quite stupid."[47]

Miss Haven is anything but. She is taking her daughter to California to see the child's father, whom she divorced after scoring her first hit on the stage. The passive Thrumm learns some of this from Pullman porter Fred Johnson, a voracious reader (of Milton, no less) who provides Ann's backstory. The comedy—part Wodehouse, part *Ball of Fire*, maybe even inspired by some madcap moments from Preston Sturges's movies—proceeds from there.

But the wit—at least the kind of flashing, wicked wit that later made the author such an electric presence—is hard to find. One consistent problem is protagonist Thrumm, an academic with a collection of aesthetic preferences rather than a personality. Botticelli and Sir Joshua Reynolds are all right with him. Thrumm, we learn, whistles a bit of Handel's *Acis and Galatea*, and there's no real narrative reason for it except to display the author's appreciation of music. The fastidious Thrumm wonders if movies and nightclubs are good for lovemaking because they destroy your ethics, and lovemaking is better without emotional responsibilities. "And maybe it's no use having read Shelley and Keats," Thrumm reflects, "if the object of your love hasn't read them. That would be like broadcasting to someone who doesn't have a receiving set."[48] Preparing to meet the sandman, Thrumm recites Shakespeare's "If music be the food of love, play on" in the train's clackety-clack rhythm. The author's attempt to dazzle with his erudition turns his hero into a bore.

Long before the book was readied for publication in early 1947, Lieberson had spent a lot of time in Los Angeles and was on familiar terms with its lunacies, some of them finding their way into the novel. Ann Haven's agent Johnny Pizer wears monogrammed Sulka shirts, Countess Mara ties, and accessories from Tiffany—and still manages to look like a shlub. There's something absolutely right that Ann Haven, "object of innumerable celluloid sexual fantasies," was in an earlier life Ann Voscevic, a marathon dancer affecting a mascaraed Joan Crawford look. (Lieberson knew that celebrities, like war-era disks, are often constructed from scrap material.) The book's most entertaining creation is the self-regarding, autodidact actor Ray White, who may also serve as authorial self-deprecation. Ann Haven can't stand Ray's pretentiousness: after she dismisses him, he rifles through the foreign-phrase section of his mind and comes up with *odio profanum vulgus et arceo*; in the book's lone footnote, the phrase is translated as *I hate the profane rabble and keep them far from me.*

But the comedy has no bite; there's no spark in the characters' reactions to each other—everything happens all too easily. The two leads are immediately, mutually enchanted, and the reader is asked to encourage them into deeper intimacy. As soon as her daughter falls asleep, Ann Haven the movie star kisses Harvard professor Thrumm—then kisses him again. It's a young man's comic novel—clever, its protagonists thoroughly attractive, its satiric targets all too obvious.

One throwaway moment in *3 for Bedroom C* provides a glint of Lieberson's personal willfulness. A dowager named Mrs. Hawthorne boasts about having persuaded her daughter to name her two boys Peter and Jonathan. They would be the names of Lieberson's own two sons.

*   *   *

In fact Peter Lieberson, born in October 1946, arrived three months before the book's publication and six months after Lieberson and Zorina married. Zorina's divorce from Balanchine had come through only a few weeks earlier. The wedding was held at Ted Wallerstein's house in Westport, Connecticut.[49] Peter was born while his parents had rooms at the Ritz Tower, on 57th and Park. By the end of the year the Liebersons had bought a brownstone at 247 East 61st Street, between Second and Third Avenues. Its location made for a not unpleasant amble crosstown to the office.

Earlier in 1946 Lieberson had been made vice president of Columbia

Recording Corporation. The promotion pleased his friends, who remained as playfully impertinent as ever. Morton Gould was trying to negotiate a more favorable contract for himself when he wrote, "If you do not see fit to meet these demands, then my counter-proposal is to turn over the Columbia Recording Company to me and you can be assured how grateful I would be for such a gesture on your part. If not, just lend me five bucks."[50] As 1947 came around, Lieberson had a wife, a son, a published novel, a handsome East Side residence, and an impressive corporate title and salary. Just below Wallerstein, Lieberson was on the same executive level as Manie Sacks, who oversaw the popular side of the label. Sacks, whose signing of Frank Sinatra was still considered a major coup for CBS, and whose negotiations with Broadway producers had made it attractive for them to record for Columbia, could rightly expect to be in line to run the label. So could Lieberson. The difference was that Sacks was about gin rummy and the pizza at Patsy's, and felt as comfortable at the Metropolitan Opera House as Nathan Detroit at a cotillion; Lieberson, by contrast, could go either way, trading profane insults with writers and musicians and then donning black tie for dinner at Elsa Maxwell's.

*   *   *

3 for *Bedroom C* was favorably reviewed in the *Times* by Nancy Ladd, who described Thrumm's train as "Hollywood bound" and might well have been describing the novel itself.[51] Inevitably, there was movie interest. Years before he turned into the commodore of blockbuster disaster pictures, Irwin Allen toiled as an agent at the Orsatti Agency in Hollywood. On June 6, 1947, months after the novel was published by Doubleday, Lieberson authorized Irwin Allen to peddle the project for ninety days. Allen kept him posted. Lieberson was disappointed when Melvyn Douglas, his dream actor for Oliphant Thrumm, passed on the project. Lieberson suggested Bob Hope. Claire Trevor agreed to play Ann Haven, with Fred MacMurray thinking about Thrumm.[52] Eventually the project went to producer Milton Bren, who was contractually obligated to let

Lieberson have a crack at adapting his own novel. Lieberson was proud that he took only three weeks to write the screenplay.[53] His draft didn't turn out well (screenwriting can seem so elementary until you try it), so Bren engaged Corey Ford to rewrite.[54] Around this time, Lieberson began to seek treatment for "herring spots," or, in more everyday language, ulcers. Whether this was a reaction to the Hollywood development of his novel or a response to matters closer to home, or neither, is anybody's guess. (A few years later Lieberson's friend Betty MacDonald, the author of The Egg and I, wrote to him wondering if he still suffered from colitis, which suggests that internal problems were nothing new.)

At the end of 1947 Wallerstein had been kicked upstairs to Columbia's chairmanship, to be replaced as president by longtime treasurer Frank White; then, after hardly more than a year, White left to run Mutual Broadcasting and Wallerstein was back in. Through that unnerving period Lieberson's ambitiousness was no surprise to anyone at the label. "Lieberson had been a mousy guy," said art director Alex Steinweiss, who would lock horns with him in the coming years. "As time went on, he sharpened his daggers."[55]

It took several years for 3 for Bedroom C to make its way to the screen—a not extraordinary length of time when measured by the Hollywood clock. In the summer of 1951, Gloria Swanson's participation was announced. Sunset Boulevard wouldn't be Swanson's only film work "of her latterday career," said Publishers' Weekly.[56]

Once Swanson was on board, Three for Bedroom C was filmed quickly. (The movie title spelled out the first word.) Bren directed, with Fred Clark—a far cry from Fred MacMurray and Melvyn Douglas—in the role of Professor Thrumm. By most accounts the picture was a train wreck, and a personal embarrassment to Lieberson. In an October 1952 letter to an old Seattle friend, Lieberson wrote, "Mary dear: The only thing wrong with the movie of Three for Bedroom C was the casting: Gloria Swanson was not the right age for the actress—that should have been played by Gigi Perreau [she played the little girl] or whatever her name is. On the other hand, Gloria should have played the child. . . . In all, it was about the most horrifying movie experience I have had in years and would have been even if I had not written the book, on which it was ostensibly based."[57] Twenty-six years later, when CBS paid tribute to Lieberson in memoriam, Charles Kuralt said that Lieberson and Swanson "never forgave each other" for the experience.[58] Nobody winced at the phrase: Lieberson had been cavorting with film stars since he was a young man. He married one.

*   *   *

Peggy Rosenberg had receded from Lieberson's life, but she'd hardly withered and died. In June 1948 she married Abram Spanel, the chairman of International Latex Corporation. The Delaware-based corporation would eventually become Playtex. Spanel, born in Russia and raised mostly in Paris, had become a U.S. citizen by 1914 and founded International Latex in 1932. In early 1947 Spanel went to Rochester to see about manufacturing a new girdle, and it was there he met Peggy.[59] Spanel was already notorious for buying space in prominent newspapers to air his political views. Those views, largely espousing peace and the halting of nuclear proliferation, as well as ardent support for the new State of Israel, rankled some of the nation's more conservative columnists. One of those columnists, Westbrook Pegler, saw himself as not just rooting out Communists but knocking down giants, and Spanel was a giant, a dynamic industrialist with more than a thousand patents to his name. Pegler accused Spanel of demagoguery—surely a charge that could apply to the accuser—and insinuated that Spanel posed a greater threat to American security for having been born in Russia. But in a startling turnabout in the fall of 1949, Pegler, reeling from the threat of lawsuits, published a 98-word apology in the New York Journal-American for implying that Spanel was "a communist or fellow traveler."[60]

Peggy Rosenberg saw Spanel through these crises and grounded him in a way she couldn't Lieberson. Proudly pacifist in her own right, she became the locus of a circle of Princeton physicists and antiwar activists in a time when, staring into McCarthy's dripping jaws, it was considered foolhardy to admit either antiwar or leftist leanings. The Spanels lived in a kind of academic splendor on the old Moses Taylor Pine estate, where they entertained friends like Robert Oppenheimer and Leo Szilard. Theirs was a social, high-achieving life, no less so than the Liebersons'. But neither Peggy nor Spanel was ever mentioned in interviews Lieberson gave. His need to excise her from his biography might have had less to do with considerations for Brigitta than a need to distance himself from political views that he and Peggy had once so openly shared. Abe Spanel was his own boss; Goddard Lieberson still answered to Bill Paley and Frank Stanton, who in turn were dependent on government approval to keep operating their huge network, which now included television.

●　●　●

The political dance gave Lieberson more ulcers. But perhaps they were worth it. In the autumn of 1949, Lieberson received another promotion, this time to executive vice president of Columbia Records. Columbia Records general counsel Chuck Seaton, who'd succeeded Lee Eastman in the position, celebrated with heroic quatrains:

> Each time a Masterworks I play
> On standard or L/P
> My mind goes back a long long way
> To days of CRC.

> We were the daring little group
> A challenge to Red Seal.
> They tried to get us in the soup—
> Or crush us under heel.

> The tempus fugits—mores change
> And Victor's on the fade.
> With G/L as exe vice-pres.
> New records will be made![61]

The general feeling was that Lieberson's promotion was in recognition for his passionate advocacy of recording contemporary composers, the core of Masterworks' Modern Music Series. Sometimes Lieberson had had to defend this advocacy even to composers who benefited from it. Responding to an angry letter from Igor Stravinsky, Lieberson wrote, "We have no intention of suppressing your unreleased recordings; quite the contrary, since they represent a large investment on which we have had no return whatsoever. You put this on the basis of my not being willing to produce important works of the contemporary musical output and so I must say to you something which I have never said before: that is, that in giving a picture of the contemporary output, we cannot limit ourselves exclusively to Stravinsky and we have been issuing in the last years recordings of music by Alban Berg, Milhaud, Villa-Lobos, Charles Ives, David Diamond, Bela Bartok, Menotti, Copland, and many others, too numerous to mention."[62]

Recording contemporary composers wasn't profitable, of course. We'd like to imagine that, in the pre–rock 'n' roll era, classical music was beloved by a greater percentage of the population. But the image is illusory. It's true that classical record sales accounted for a larger portion of all sales prior to 1956—but that's only because few rock 'n' roll recordings had been made, and almost none by the major labels. Lieberson, as he championed even the most difficult work of, say, Schoenberg, Carl Ruggles, and Charles Ives, never wavered in his mission to make the music available to record buyers.

It's not likely, though, that Lieberson's 1949 executive promotion was based only on recording for the elite few. Instead his appointment as vice president in charge of all of Artists & Repertoire was made by Wallerstein because Lieberson dealt with both, the artists and the repertoire, with Franklinesque diplomacy. Mollifying Artur Rodzinski, who was miffed that Columbia wasn't doing more to promote his new post as director of the Chicago Symphony in spring 1947, Lieberson wrote that Rodzinski received the largest royalties of any symphonic conductor on the list. "I must tell you something, dear Artur, unemotionally, since this is business: we are on the road to becoming the greatest recording company in the world, which may seem to you as immodest a statement as can be made. However, I can say it because it has nothing to do with my ego since when it happens it will be primarily the result of Mr Wallerstein's brains, not mine."[63] The closing touch of crediting the boss was brilliant. "Dear Leopold," Lieberson wrote to Stokowski in June 1949, "I will be glad to discuss with you any time the question of composers' and publishers' royalties. Particularly, if the discussion doesn't lead to our paying anything."[64] Wallerstein appreciated Lieberson's wit as well as his handling of music and musicians. But he was also grateful for his boundless support for the long-playing record, a development that changed Columbia Records in particular and the recording industry in general practically overnight.

9

Creation of the LP

From Radio City in Manhattan—only two crosstown blocks away but, in many ways, another world altogether—RCA chairman David Sarnoff arrived promptly in the paneled CBS boardroom, followed by a retinue of engineers. The RCA men took chairs on one side of the boardroom table, with the cigar-smoking General Sarnoff seated at the center, while the CBS executives, including at least two from Columbia Records, sat across the table. This April 1948 meeting wasn't only a summit of the two most influential radio networks, but also of the two most powerful men in the recording industry: Sarnoff and his longtime rival, CBS chairman William S. Paley, who had decided it was finally time to demonstrate his company's revolutionary new development.

"I must admit I felt nervous," Peter Goldmark, CBS's resident inventor, wrote of the meeting. "Years of arduous work had gone into this moment, and here in a sense was the Day of Judgment."[1]

That meeting, Sarnoff and his RCA engineering staff naturally assumed, was about some CBS development in color TV. CBS had already taken it on the chin when RCA's color television preempted the so-called "color wheel" that Goldmark had worked on at CBS Labs. It had been one of Paley's few business humiliations up to that point. No, what the CBS and Columbia Records execs wanted to show Sarnoff was something they had developed in absolute secrecy: the long-playing record—up to 22 minutes of music without changing or flipping the disk.

"The pop album made its way through the 20th century by staying adaptable," Jon Pareles wrote in the New York Times in July 2003, "transforming itself from analog grooves to digital bits."[2] No adaptation was more startling, however, or proved to be more sublime than the long-playing record.

• • •

Peter Goldmark liked to say he'd been directing the top-secret project since its prewar inception. Escaping Hitler in 1933, Goldmark had sailed to New York with $150 borrowed from his family, to offer his services as a scientist. Although he economized by eating at Horn & Hardart, where you could pull a meatloaf out of the automat window for a nickel, he soon ran out of money because every company he wrote to turned down his initial request for an interview. Finally he was summoned to 485 Madison Avenue by Paul Kesten, a CBS vice president, who had been impressed by an article about television design that Goldmark had just published. On January 1, 1936, Goldmark became a CBS employee, earning $100 a week. CBS's ownership of Columbia Records was still three years into the future.

At the time, Ted Wallerstein was running RCA Victor, the record division of the Radio Corporation of America. In a 90-minute audio interview he gave in 1969, Wallerstein remembered that RCA had begun to process 33 1/3-rpm recordings as early as 1931.[3] RCA's chief engineer, Jim Hunter, pressed these on Victorlac, the company's version of Vinylite, the plastic compound that had come into widespread use in the late twenties.

These records clocked in at about seven minutes. On the promotional disk Victor Artists' Party, on the A side, Victor comedian-singer Frank Crumit introduces the new format. "We've always felt a little bit cramped for elbow room, so to speak," Crumit says in his nasal Yankee twang. "In other words, we could get just so much on a record, and then we simply had to stop. But here's something new that the RCA Victor people have developed—a long-playing record that can hold an entire vaudeville act, or even a symphony, plus a wonderful new instrument to play it on."[4] Crumit sings his signature song, "The Gay Caballero," followed by a chorus of "And Then He Took up Golf." "It's a grand and glorious feeling when you don't have to worry how long the record is," Crumit says. Arden & Ohman play "The Wedding of the Painted Dolls," and house orchestra leader Nathaniel Shilkret rolls through a minute of Ellington's "Daydream." On the B side, Shilkret conducts the orchestra through bits of familiar classical pieces. The 33 1/3 recordings that the *Victor Artists' Party* was meant to introduce were a daring idea, but they proved to be no good for commercial use: after just a few playings the heavy styluses would cut right through them. Wallerstein, vigilantly protective of his company's reputation, kept them off the market.

Suffering a heart attack in his midforties, Wallerstein was forced to slow down. From 1933 on, RCA had cut back on its recording anyway—shellac was becoming increasingly difficult to ship from India, turning the company instead toward the marketing of its $6 phonograph, manufactured in Camden—and Wallerstein felt his authority at the company wane. He claimed to have been the one, while still with RCA Victor, to persuade Bill Paley to purchase the old American Record Corporation for $700,000 in late 1938—but then half a dozen men had made the same claim. Wallerstein moved from RCA to the renamed Columbia Records as its new president in January 1939. Among his immediate mandates was to develop a long-playing record. So began the joint project between CBS and its new subsidiary Columbia Records.

* * *

A decade after his arrival at the company, Goldmark was CBS's go-to guy for technological advancement—or, at the very least, its scientist figurehead. An ardent music lover, Goldmark couldn't bear to listen to the inferior fidelity of the 78-rpm disk.

"My initial interest in the LP arose out of my sincere hatred of the phonograph. All my life I had what we engineers call zero response to the phonograph, because it seemed to violate what I thought the quality of music should be."[5] The man appeared to be on a mission.

If only it had been so simple. Regarding RCA's triumph with color TV, George Avakian remembered, "Paley was so anxious to save face that he did something even Wallerstein couldn't do anything about. He insisted that virtually all the credit for LP go to Goldmark, so that his defeat on color TV wouldn't be compounded."[6]

Goldmark burnished his own legend in his memoir, *Maverick Inventor*, escorting the reader through his thought processes during the LP's earliest stages of development. He figured, he wrote, that the duration of the recording was determined by the record diameter, rpm, and the number of grooves per inch in which the needle operates. Using an everyday ruler, he counted 80 grooves to the inch in the Brahms Concerto. How many grooves constituted a long-playing record, one that satisfied the public's idea of hearing an uninterrupted piece?

Goldmark absorbed every facet of recording that he could, then went to see Ted Wallerstein, "an assertive fellow, full of self-importance," in Goldmark's estimation. Wallerstein listened to the scientist for three minutes, put an arm around his shoulders, and suggested that he drop the entire project.

"Go back to television," Wallerstein said. RCA, Wallerstein pointed out, had toyed with the 33 1/3 record for the consumer back in the thirties and gotten nowhere.

"That was his final word to me on the matter," Goldmark wrote.[7]

●　●　●

In Goldmark's telling, Wallerstein's patronizing attitude toward him redoubled his determination to come up with a solution. Goldmark discovered that several manufacturers had huge investments in pressing shellac records; using new, lightweight material in the disk itself would run counter to those investments. Vinylite, then being used primarily to make garden hose, was unbreakable and light but cost twice as much as shellac, rendering it too expensive for any ambitious purpose such as recording a classical symphony, which then required five or six records.

"On the other hand," Goldmark reasoned, "if you could put an entire symphony on one vinyl record, you not only could afford to make vinyl records, you could make a handsome profit on a product that would eventually be less expensive to the music-lover."[8]

Goldmark went to Paul Kesten, who had hired him in the first place, and told him his idea, as well as Wallerstein's brusque dismissal of it. A precise, fastidious man who had made his mark early as a Madison Avenue copywriter, Kesten shared William Paley's studied sartorial elegance and was known to have some influence with the boss, though they didn't socialize. Kesten listened patiently to the enthusiastic, though frustrated, CBS scientist. Goldmark went on and on about a "systems approach," a management term derived from World War II military operations that looks at a complex operation as a whole. In a flush of hubris, Goldmark proposed to change a number of elements of the recording process—the amplifier, the material of the disk, the shape of the groove, the cartridge, the stylus, the microphones, the turntable drive—"and, I remotely hoped," he wrote, "the musical taste of the nation."

"How much?" asked the weary Kesten.

"At least a hundred thousand," Goldmark replied, fearing the worst.

"You've got it," Kesten said, apparently confident that Paley wouldn't go into cardiac arrest when he heard the figure.[9]

*   *   *

So, shrouded in secrecy, Goldmark and a team of engineers went to work on the tenth floor of 485 Madison. Years later Goldmark and Wallerstein, who had little affection for each other, would disagree on who the crucial players were. But both of them singled out Bill Bachman, a former General Electric engineer already known by most of the team because GE headquarters had been housed not far from the Columbia Records pressing plant in Bridgeport, Connecticut. And both credited Belgian-born Rene Snepvangers, who was known for his sensitivity to sound.

Wallerstein, apprised of the newly funded research and development he had counseled against, began to breathe all over the scientists. The team's first experimental 33 1/3 disk ran seven to eight minutes.

"That's not a long-playing record," Wallerstein chided. He said the same thing when they came up with ten to 12 minutes per side. Wallerstein wanted 17 minutes per side, the approximate running time of Beethoven's *Eroica*, to make it worthwhile.

His demands weren't arbitrary. Wallerstein oversaw Columbia's entire artist list, which now included the New York Philharmonic, the Philadelphia Orchestra, the Chicago Symphony, and the Cleveland Orchestra—four of the greatest orchestras in the nation. Columbia's popular division could continue to release 78-rpm recordings by Sinatra, Eddy Duchin, and Benny Goodman without too much concern for playing time; but for Columbia Masterworks, which housed the label's classical lineup, the longer disk could provide a much-needed shot of adrenaline.

"I recall that we gave Wallerstein a rendition of Tchaikovsky's Violin Concerto on one of our first demonstration records," Goldmark wrote, "I can still see the two turntables in action side by side, with the sapphire stylus carving its canyons into the soft body of the lacquer of the LP master, each canyon implanted with the Russian composer's wonderful music. . . . We had to do it a number of times because small variations in cutting would change the pitch, and we knew Wallerstein had ears like a bat. Every time the pitch changed, he'd yell."[10]

In the meantime Adrian Murphy, an army combat veteran who had recently replaced Paul Kesten at CBS, acted as liaison with the engineers. Whenever the scientists came up with something they deemed progress, Murphy would report to Paley, whose enthusiasm would mount, especially at the prospect of having something that Sarnoff and RCA didn't. At that point the chief executives' rivalry went back 20 years, since the days when United Independent Broadcasters introduced Paley to the business of radio.

But Wallerstein, ever cautious about the long-playing record, repeatedly threw cold water on Paley's enthusiasm.

"Eighteen minutes?" said Wallerstein. "Sorry, that's still not a long-playing record." Initially, Wallerstein had wanted 17 minutes; now 18 wasn't enough.

"Well, what the hell is a long-playing record?" said Paley, unaccustomed to being denied.

Wallerstein, to the alternating despair and grudging admiration of Goldmark, stood firm. With Rene Snepvangers by his side, Goldmark (again, in the Goldmark version) went back to the drawing board to capture nuances that Wallerstein wanted to hear, not the fuzz that the records had produced.

"Rene suggested we fire pistol shots, record them, and then compare the actual shot sounds with the recordings. A pistol shot is a sort of sonic boom, or train of shockwaves with a pulse of its own. I agreed. So he brought in a gun to the studio one day and fired it into a heavy mattress; the noise was sharp. At the same time we made a record. Then we listened to the two sounds. The recorded shot sounded like a baked potato falling on the floor."[11]

New York City may be the only metropolis where two trained engineers could fire bullets into a mattress and nobody would blink.

Frustrated, the team disassembled all the components that went into the recording. A process of elimination suggested they needed a new microphone, so they turned to a German-made condenser mike that eliminated phase distortion. This time the pistol shot sounded authentic.

Wallerstein still questioned how Goldmark's team could sustain the pitch of an orchestra when several recordings had to be made and then spliced together. So Goldmark made a kind of electronic computer to keep the pitch of each session consistent.

Hearing the computer's first product, the Brahms Fourth, Wallerstein pounced. "You lost a bar!"

"The man was inhuman," Goldmark wrote. (John Hammond insisted it was Goddard Lieberson, not Wallerstein, who detected the lost bar.)[12]

Whoever noticed the lost bar was correct: the machine had missed. So a precise cueing system was developed, while Bill Bachman perfected the "hot stylus"—capable of picking up the most sensitive sound waves in the grooves, but light enough to keep the vinyl undamaged. Goldmark's team subsequently managed to get 22 $\frac{1}{2}$ minutes of high-fidelity music on a side. For music listeners acclimated to changing a disk every three or four minutes, this was an astounding achievement.

By late summer 1947 the long-playing record appeared to be marketable, though not yet perfect. Earlier that year George Avakian had been designated director of popular albums—a rather narrow purview because this meant *albums of 78s*. But in the fall Wallerstein stepped into Avakian's office and shut the door behind him. "We're hoping to have a long-playing record very soon," he told Avakian. "You can't tell anyone, not even your fiancée."[13] Wallerstein still wanted to iron out some kinks, particularly those involving separate tracks on a side—multiple songs that could be geared to the pop market.

But Paley, whose investment in the project had risen to $250,000, was ready to move. "Let's get it on the market," he decreed, aiming for a mid-1948 introduction.

* * *

This was brave of Paley, if also a touch reckless. For one thing, although a long-playing record was seen as desirable, there had hardly been a clarion call for change. In 1947 more than $200 million worth of records were sold—a high point, until the first of several postwar recessions kicked in.[14] Dealers feared that a long-playing record would appeal only to classical music buyers; for pop music listeners, the 78 worked fine, thank you. It was pointed out that not a single person outside Columbia Records and CBS Labs had the capability of playing a long-playing record. There were no machines.

Columbia Records claimed to lack the resources to manufacture a new line of phonographs—a prototype, yes, perhaps even a dozen sets, but the market called for *tens of thousands* of new turntables capable of playing 33s. CBS executives finally jobbed it out exclusively to Philco because CBS wanted its advertising.

Or so went the company line. According to John Hammond, it was more complicated and carried a touch of the sinister. In 1945 CBS had bought the Remington Arms plant at King's Mills, Ohio, for only $250,000. Philco, apprised of the deal, "blackmailed" (Hammond's word) CBS into forcing it to abandon the manufacture of its own player.[15] Whether or not there was something crooked about the deal, you can hear Wallerstein's tamped-down frustration when he told interviewer Ward Bostford, "Although several were willing, Philco was chosen to make the first models. I was a little unhappy about this because I felt that that all of the manufacturers should be making a player of some sort; the more players that got on the market, the more records could be sold. . . . Our engineering group showed [Philco] how. In fact all of the basic technology came from Columbia Records."[16] After the Remington acquisition, Wallerstein and Paley—or Wallerstein and CBS president Frank Stanton, at any rate—were never again on the same page.

"Philco did a good job in developing the player," said Goldmark. Critical to its success was Bachman's new lightweight pickup, less than four grams, as opposed to the old 78-rpm pickup that weighed three and a half ounces—by comparison, a veritable bowling ball.

Several commentators who were present at the time have suggested that Goldmark, who contractually received credit for every invention that came out of his lab, took far more than his share for the creation of the LP. Yes, they say, Goldmark was nominally the supervisor. But it was Bill Bachman's contribution that made the thing viable. "Let's put it this way," George Avakian said: "no Bachman, no LP."[17] In fact John Hammond maintained that Bachman had developed the lightweight pickup while he was still at General Electric and brought it with him to Columbia Records.[18] Rene Snepvangers's experiments in sound, according to many of these same people, also went a long way toward smoothing out the Vinylite fidelity. Snepvangers and engineer Howard Chinn had worked hard on the microgroove hills and dales, using 200 grooves per disk inch, and on the disk's variable margin. Goldmark, they say, was less a scientist than a brilliant salesman with a powerful publicist.[19]

• • •

While Philco made the new phonograph attachments, Columbia had to make the records—each and every one in absolute secrecy. The project was given the code name "Roulette." Bachman inspected every batch of records that came out of the Bridgeport factory and used an especially brassy passage in Duke Ellington's *Liberian Suite* to test the tracking of the lightweight pickup arm.[20] Around the office Goddard Lieberson, who knew the long-playing record would be a boon to the Masterworks division he ran, cracked that the label would soon develop an even longer-playing record that held a year's worth of music "with two weeks of silence, blank grooves, for vacations." When Manie Sacks got a call from a magazine editor who'd heard about something cooking at Columbia, Wallerstein and his men threw reporters off the scent by announcing a new line of Vinylite 78s. All the secrecy produced tremendous anxiety. But no one who was in on it denied that introducing the long-playing record—and to a public that wasn't clamoring for it—was an extraordinary leap of faith. "What was most amazing about this thing," Ken McAllister, in charge of advertising and promotion, told the writer Martin Mayer, "was that we went into it strictly on judgment. You'd never try to market a bar of soap the way we tried to revolutionize the record business."[21]

Wallerstein wanted 100 long-playing titles to be marketed by spring 1948. Most of these would be edited from 16" lacquered masters, some of which had already been released on 78 rpm. Meanwhile, the invaluable acetate process, developed by Ike Rodman years earlier, had to be protected. Rodman, long gone from the company and relocated to Cambridge, Massachusetts, applied for and received a patent for a "phonograph recording and reproducing system" and reassigned the rights to the Columbia Recording Corporation.[22]

Howard Scott, a young pianist from Eastman and the Institute of Musical Arts (later the Juilliard), who'd coincidentally grown up in Bridgeport, had been hired on July 5, 1946, as a Masterworks trainee. "Bill Bachman went down to see Goddard Lieberson and said he needed someone who could read a score," Scott said. "So Lieberson sent me up to engineering with Bachman, but at my request I was still on Goddard's payroll so that he could keep an eye on what was going on."[23] Under Bachman's supervision, Scott was the music coordinator in making the first hundred transfers to long-playing. Paul Gordon was the splicing engineer; Art Buckner handled the cutting of the 16" spliced lacquers; Bill Savory then cut the long-playing masters.[24] They were a sonic Tinker to Evers to Chance infield. This was done primarily in the sixth-floor control room of 799 Seventh Avenue. Scott and Gordon started out with two huge belt-driven turntables connected by a photoelectric cell, but the turntable motors couldn't stay in synch for longer than four minutes. The two men devised a clock method of splicing—marking the master disk with a red arrow, then turning the turntable clockwise, measuring the number of musical splice points, starting the audio and counting each revolution of the red arrow. It worked fine. So did Scott's "snap" cue—Scott snapping his fingers on tape to identify each splice point.[25] "The splices were, I think, as good as anything one can do today in tape," Goldmark wrote, generously crediting Scott.[26]

Wallerstein was breathing down the necks of Bachman and his assistant Lou Perrota, demanding progress reports. The pressure, in turn, was on Scott as he transferred piece after piece, many of them having been laid down on 78s in brief, frequently overlapping bits. Between September and November 1947, the Scott-Gordon-Buckner-Savory team had completed the transfer of some 30 titles to long-playing disk. Then word came upstairs that the records were no good: it was a technical rather than musical problem; the groove masters had been improperly cut.[27]

So, in January 1948, the team started over. Despite the extra time pressure—maybe *because* of the extra time pressure—they were quicker now. One of Scott's many responsibilities was to listen to test pressings as they came down from Bridgeport. ("I was a very busy camper," said Scott, whose name on those early job sheets was his birth name, Howard Shapiro.)[28] One pressing was by Eugene Ormandy and the Philadelphia Orchestra, recorded at the Academy of Music, of *Scheherazade*. Scott found the tone rather dry, so he decided to use something called a reverbatron, which was part of the regular radio equipment at CBS facilities at 485 Madison. Scott's engineer hitched his playback setup to the reverbatron and, running an old CBS tape that had presumably been erased, created a delay to add some body to the Philadelphia's sound. He didn't realize till much later that the tape still contained the faint sound of a barking dog—the remnants of a Rin Tin Tin radio program. "See, Howard was so overworked," Peter Munves said, "he didn't always have time to listen all the way through."[29] Once Scott did listen, he heard the dog behind Jacob Krachmalnick's reprised violin solo. "I decided on the spot to let it go to production because I wanted to see if any of the record critics would pick it up," Scott said.[30]

●　●　●

So came the fateful day in April 1948. CBS president Frank Stanton greeted David Sarnoff and his RCA engineers as they arrived at the CBS boardroom.[31] Then, with Paley and the Columbia Records team observing, Stanton used two different turntables to demonstrate the long-playing record versus the old 78 disk. The actual audio material played that day has been lost to memory, but the effect, according to Goldmark, "was electrifying, as we knew it would be. I never saw eight engineers look so much like carbon copies of tight-lipped gloom."[32]

Stanton remembered how upset Sarnoff was. "I can't believe little Columbia Graphophone invented this without my knowing it," Sarnoff whined, trying to belittle the achievement by employing the company's nineteenth-century name.[33]

Wallerstein's memory was that Sarnoff looked down his side of the table at his RCA engineers, pulled the cigar from his mouth and said, "You sonsabitches got caught with your pants down again!"[34]

When the atmospshere calmed, Paley offered to discuss a licensing arrangement with Sarnoff. This was really what Paley had been going for all along—to cash in on the long-playing technology by making other companies, RCA in particular, pay for it. (Wallerstein claimed that it was Goldmark who planted the idea in the boss's head.) Sarnoff graciously congratulated Paley and said he would consider his offer to share the technology. But there was no reason to do so because there was nothing patentable; the long-playing record had been developed using only tools at hand.

• • •

After that meeting, events gathered momentum. During the spring of 1948, CBS held an internal contest to name the new long-playing format. Every suggestion, according to Goldmark, was rejected. "I guess the LP isn't going to have a name after all," Goldmark muttered to Frank Stanton. "*What* did you say?" said the startled Stanton. "I repeated my statement," wrote Goldmark, "and that's how LP got its name."

Well, maybe. Wallerstein also claimed to have come up with the term "LP." Whatever the truth, "LP" was the one thing that CBS could—and did—copyright. Record buyers would come to refer to the LP the way they referred to Coke or the Victrola—brand names that subsumed the products they were named for. By the late fifties Columbia Records' office typewriters had been retooled to have an "LP" trademark key.[35] (Remaining mystery: which key was removed to make room for it?)

Columbia Records introduced the LP at a Waldorf press conference on June 21, 1948, the longest day of the year. It was the longest disk with acceptable fidelity ever played. In front of some forty reporters, executives stacked a wobbly skyscraper of 78s alongside a squat pile of 33s, which was said to contain the same amount of music.

In Atlantic City exactly one week later, sales director Paul Southard gave a speech about the new LP to Columbia's distributors. Cued by Howard Scott, Southard timed his speech to run the length of one whole side of *The Nutcracker Suite*, Lieberson's perennial favorite piece to play for students and nonmusicians alike. Southard's remarks came to a close, the last chords of "Waltz of the Flowers" came up forte, and the lightweight stylus floated off the disk. The room went up for grabs.[36]

The July 1948 cover of the in-house *Promotion News* showed the LP as though it had been shot off like fireworks. "At last!" trumpeted the accompanying article. "Up to 45 minutes of music on one unbreakable

Columbia record!" Goldmark got the credit and was lauded as the "Father of the LP" in *Newsweek*; Bachman was mentioned in passing. *Life* published a photograph showing Goldmark cradling an armful of 33s, the musical equivalent of the eight-foot tower of 78s stacked next to him.[37]

• • •

Musical revolution was in the air. That revolution wasn't just about the amount of information, musical or otherwise, that could fit onto a single disk. The microgroove LP immediately opened up other artistic and marketing avenues, like cover art and extensive liner notes. The format was larger but also lighter, easier to store, easier to handle, and—the thing that would subsequently make the Columbia Record Club viable—easier to mail. To simplify its releases and ease the pressure on the art department, Columbia instituted its "Tombstone" covers, the records' credits encased in the outlines of a gothic headstone.

The earliest 12" LPs were all classical or Broadway. The first 12" LP was Beethoven's Violin Concerto, with Nathan Milstein soloing and Bruno Walter conducting the Philharmonic Symphony of New York, assigned the catalog number ML 4001. The first pop LP was *The Voice of Frank Sinatra*, extending the Sinatra series that had begun in 1945. Pop LPs were still 10", though also in the microgroove format. In 78-rpm format the traditional pop album rarely contained more than four disks (that was already a lot of weight), with a single song on each side. For the LP, that translated into an acceptable eight songs, which fit perfectly on the 10" disk. It would be another couple of years before Stan Kavan, always savvy about merchandising, suggested that Columbia release 12" pop albums.

Eventually the label released the Philadelphia Orchestra *Scheherazade*, barking dog and all, as ML 4089—the eighty-ninth long-playing Columbia record to be released. "How many critics do you think picked up the barking?" said Scott. "Correctimundo! None!"[38]

• • •

Through those early months of LP transfers, George Avakian had been busy starting a family of his own. In the spring of 1948 he and Anahid Ajemian married at Riverside Church, on the Upper West Side of Manhattan. Composer Alan Hovhaness, who had been the organist for the St. James Armenian Church in Watertown, Massachusetts, played the organ at the wedding. After the honeymoon, reinstalled in his office at 799, Avakian's position as director of pop albums now took on greater import. Because Avakian spoke French and German and had maintained especially close ties to Paris through his brother Aram, Wallerstein also named him director of international recordings. (In those early LP days there was an "—F" in the catalog number to denote a foreign recording.)

Avakian got a call from Frank Yankovic, an Ohio-based barkeep and polka bandleader who had enough songs to make an album. Built around his hit single "Just Because," Yankovic's album became an immediate hit on 10" LP.[39] Serendipitously—and maybe with a dash of subtle self-marketing—Yankovic was proclaimed America's Polka King by winning a Milwaukee polka contest.

Masterworks, stronger than ever under Lieberson's stewardship and the division most likely to benefit from the LP, went through some changes. Charles O'Connell, who had been a house conductor and an important A&R man at Victor, where Wallerstein had valued him, had arrived with some fanfare at Columbia in 1946 and was assigned immediately to the pianist–Ives scholar John Kirkpatrick, as well as a handful of the label's opera singers.[40] But now O'Connell began to miss recording sessions due to a fondness for the bottle. He published *The Other Side of the Record*, a memoir recounting his experiences at Victor and slamming several artists, notably Kostelanetz and Lily Pons. More than once O'Connell referred to Kostelanetz as "shrewd"—which, in each context, came off as more contemptuous than complimentary—-and to "the Pons-Kostelanetz combination," insinuating that the couple wielded power far beyond their musical gifts.[41] Despite two respectful mentions of "Mr Edward Wallerstein," the memoir was handled at 799 with tongs. Wallerstein, furious at what he regarded as public disloyalty, replaced O'Connell with Dick Gilbert.[42] Chain-smoking and even edgier than O'Connell, Gilbert took charge of the Budapest String Quartet and many of the division's pianists, while Lieberson assumed responsibility for most of O'Connell's artists. Two important Masterworks entities, the Mormon Tabernacle Choir and Richard Tucker, began long associations with the division.

Inevitably it came time to slow the flow of reissues from the 16" lacquers and make new recordings for LP. But where would all this new recording be done? For years Columbia had been using Liederkranz Hall, the old German beer hall on East 58th Street, for many of its full-scale recordings, particularly those by the tireless Kostelanetz. In warmer weather the studio—one hundred feet long and thirty feet wide, with thirty-foot-high ceilings—provided a magnificent sound; in winter, however, the hall had to go unheated because tape picked up the clanking and hissing of radiators that had been installed at the beginning of the century. (The taped result could sound like a John Cage piece.) In early 1949 Bachman, Vin Liebler, and Howard Scott went hunting for a new studio. They found a Greek Orthodox church at 207 East 30th Street. The front part of the church housed radio station WLIB.[43] For the next thirty years the 30th Street studio—even larger than Liederkranz, with plenty of room to store mono tape machines and microphones and space for a walled-off control booth—would be crucial to Columbia's ascension in the record industry.

●   ●   ●

Since its release of the 78-rpm album of Oklahoma! in 1943, Decca had virtually owned the territory. Now Columbia was getting into the Broadway area. On LP an original cast recording almost perfectly miniaturized the experience of seeing a musical in a theater: Side A equals Act One; turning the record over is an intermission; and Side B equals Act Two.

At the beginning of 1949, Cole Porter's Kiss Me, Kate was released by Columbia almost simultaneously on 78s and on LP.[44] The album of 78s—"conventional records," Columbia was calling them—sold for $7;

the LP, containing as much music, sold for $4.85.[45] The original cast recordings series was given the prefix OL to distinguish it from Masterworks's ML. *Finian's Rainbow*, though it premiered on Broadway nearly two years before *Kate*, came next.[46] This recording, made late in the musical's run, wasn't of the entire original cast, but it was close enough to be deemed true to the Broadway production. In 1949 *South Pacific*, the first Rodgers & Hammerstein on Columbia, was released in a 78 album, but it was the 33 1/3 version—cheaper than the 78s as well as lighter and more durable—that became the most ubiquitous LP of the era.[47] Practically every household that owned a long-playing phonograph had a copy of *South Pacific*. The album's success put Columbia in the original cast recording business for keeps. Ezio Pinza, reveling in fame beyond the opera crowd, prepared to move from RCA to Columbia as a solo artist. Mary Martin would be with the label, off and on, throughout the next decade, culminating in the original cast recording of *The Sound of Music*.

South Pacific was one of two LPs to popularize the format nationally. The other was surely Edward R. Murrow's *I Can Hear It Now*, which covered world news events from the 1930s and '40s and, like *Kiss Me, Kate*, had been originally pressed on 78s and released in the winter of 1948, with the already-developed LP waiting in the wings. CBS radio producer Fred Friendly had been reading Frederick Lewis Allen's *Only Yesterday*, an "informal history" of the 1920s, and conceived of a similar but more recent aural history. Friendly presented the idea to Murrow over lunch. (It was the beginning of their long broadcasting partnership.) Murrow went for it. As head of Masterworks, Lieberson agreed to make the record and pay $1,000 advance to the guys because the second Petrillo strike had just been called and there'd be no music to record anyway. Friendly culled some five hundred hours' worth of recordings and wrote a connecting narrative for Murrow.[48] The LP version of *I Can Hear It Now* was like listening to an entire radio program without interruption.

•   •   •

Spurned by RCA but realizing it had to bring other recording companies to the new format, Columbia pressed LPs for smaller classical labels, notably Vox, Cetra-Soria, and Concert Hall. It pushed for English-based EMI to adopt the long-playing disk. But EMI declined because it had contracts with RCA as well as with Columbia. Consequently, the second major label to release 33-rpm discs was English Decca.[49] Capitol and Mercury soon followed. Between March and June 1949, Columbia's sales chief Paul Southard offered "Double Return Privileges," an inducement to dealers to return old 78s and stock new LPs.[50] There were record dealers out there who still didn't know what a long-playing record was, never mind the initials LP.

Like a petulant child, RCA made a show of ignoring the long-playing record and kept up work on a project it referred to as "Madame X." This was the not quite 7" 45-rpm record. It could easily hold five minutes of music per side, but Victor, fearing distortion toward the end, kept those first 45-rpm recordings to under four minutes. Classical selections could only be excerpted, of course; the format was best for popular music that stayed under the four-minute mark. The decision to record at 45 rpm was based on calculations made more than 30 years earlier by J. P. Maxfield at Bell Labs, not on the more amusing notion that an RCA executive spitefully subtracted 33 from 78 and—bingo!—came up with 45.[51] Victor made the light little record even more attractive by designing a mechanism that took only three seconds to drop the next record onto the turntable for playing. The efficiency of this mechanism went a long way toward making the 45 the dominant singles format for the next twenty years. The format proved to be fine for a jukebox, which could hold many more 45s than 78s; for classical music or the extended jazz solo, however, it was virtually useless.

•   •   •

The competitive sniping between Columbia and RCA only got louder. Wallerstein said that Columbia was "unable to fathom the purpose of records revolving at forty-five revolutions per minute." RCA shot back that Columbia demonstrated the long-playing record to its executives only sixty days before it was being routinely manufactured.[52] Sixty days? RCA hadn't known the half of it. At a meeting of dealers and distributors at the New Yorker Hotel on Eighth Avenue, Wallerstein and Joe Elliot of RCA took questions about the future of records. Wallerstein, who had resumed the Columbia presidency after Frank White jumped over to Mutual Broadcasting, had all the answers.[53] It was as though Elliot's bosses had muzzled him.

Rumors caromed from midtown Manhattan to Bridgeport, across the country to Hollywood, and back again to RCA's labs in New Jersey. In December 1949 Wallerstein issued a denial that Columbia Records would manufacture 45s.

Naturally, the record-buying public was confused. In turn this confounded both Columbia and RCA, which had seen a pronounced slump in sales toward the end of 1948. Neil Harrison, editor of the trade publication *Record Retailing*, said sales for jukebox records were way down. Wallerstein quantified the slump as 35 percent of the industry's previous year's sales.[54] One obvious problem was that record buyers now had to shell out $29.95 for the new Philco radio attachment. Certain that the new 33 1/3 format would catch on, Magnavox took after Philco in manufacturing its own line of two-speed phonographs that played shellac at 78 and Vinylite at 33 1/3. Music critics hailed the sound of Vinylite, which, in test after test, sounded no worse than the heavier disks and often appreciably better. "You may be sure," Howard Taubman wrote in the *Times*, "that Columbia's competitors will be bestirring themselves to come up with something as useful."[55] Within a year, Wallerstein arranged with Philco to drop the attachment price to $9.95, the cost to manufacture it. Columbia wanted to get back to selling records, not hardware.

*   *   *

Still, RCA took longer than practically every other major label to adopt the new long-playing record. Immediately after George Marek, formerly the music editor of *Good Housekeeping*, agreed to take over as director of RCA Victor, he implored Sarnoff to reconsider his stance against the LP. "So what's wrong with the 45?" said the chairman. Marek's response was crisp. "It's no good for classical music because every few minutes you have to stop it. Look at it this way. You're in bed with your best friend's wife, and every five or six minutes the door opens and the husband is standing there."[56]

Marek's may not have been the argument that clinched the switch. According to Rene Snepvangers, RCA finally caved when Arturo Toscanini, its premiere classical artist, heard Bruno Walter conducting the New York Philharmonic on a Columbia LP and resented that his rival's performance went uninterrupted while a Victor version would have entailed several interruptions to change disks.[57]

On January 3, 1950, RCA Victor announced that it would begin to issue long-playing records as a "step toward standardization."[58] Wallerstein wished rival RCA good luck. Although RCA had taken a huge hit in its powerful classical department—enough of a hit to cause Columbia Masterworks to boast of its profits—Columbia knew this standardization would be better for the industry as a whole. At the end of the previous year RCA had tipped its hand by showing its new radio-phonograph combinations that played all three speeds. Grabbing the olive branch—or maybe just pretending one was being offered—Wallerstein stopped deriding 45s and said his company would be glad to make them "if the public wanted them." In August 1950, Columbia released its first 45s.

But Columbia remained the LP label. In Cambridge, Massachusetts, record shop proprietor Bill Schwann started his *Schwann Catalog of LP's*, with 674 entries and Columbia predominating.[59] Avakian produced Arthur Godfrey's *TV Calendar Show*, which included Julius LaRosa and Lu Ann Simms, and it became the first pop LP smash, selling steadily through 1955.

• • •

The LP wasn't universally swooned over. That you could put it on the turntable and sit back for ten to 22 minutes was considered undesirable by consumers who equated active listening with record-changing. The notion of background music wasn't novel—it's what bands had long supplied at restaurants and night clubs—but the LP now offered it at home. While one side of a record played you could eat an entire meal or sit through the sound of a jackhammer tearing up your sidewalk. The longer format gave new meaning to Muzak, the extant transcription company whose name would become a generic designation for what in some circles was considered anti-music. Eighteen months after the LP was introduced, the Lombardo-Loeb hit exhorted listeners to "Get Out Those Old Records," as if to rescue 78s from antiquity.

And there was a purely musical dissatisfaction with the LP, particularly when it came to jazz. Some critics had reckoned the two- or three-minute time limit of the 78 as the proper framework for a band to say what it had to say. The poet Philip Larkin, who wrote frequently about jazz, couldn't abide the longer format because it smashed his dearly held concept of the music. In the 1930s, when Larkin was an adolescent, jazz was a fugitive pleasure, popular without being respectable. Larkin associated the halcyon days of his youth with winding the gramophone and listening to 78s by Louis Armstrong. To Larkin, a single shellacked side was a gem, not these vinyl platters that played interminably. "When the long-playing record was introduced," Larkin wrote, "I was suspicious of it: it seemed a package deal, forcing you to buy bad tracks along with good at an unwantedly high price. (The dubbing or remastering of 78s as LPs, too, was regarded as a damaging practice.)"[60]

Nevertheless, the LP was hailed not only by the majority of consumers but by the music-makers, the musicians, and their producers for. the way it captured sound. The LP created a demand for still higher fidelity—Hi-Fi, in industry lingo—a path that would lead to the same company's introduction of stereo in the late fifties and the development of the compact disc in the early eighties.

•   •   •

Peter Goldmark remained at CBS Labs for another twenty-one years, retiring when he reached his sixty-fifth birthday. CBS had offered him a ten-year contract at a healthy $75,000 a year, but no office space in its Stamford facility and no project to work on. Goldmark declined to be an inventor without portfolio. To some observers it confirmed that he was really more salesman than scientist, not averse to taking credit for other men's achievements. Just before Goldmark's 1973 memoir, Maverick Inventor, came out, John Hammond wrote to Ben Bauer, the new head of CBS Labs: "Perhaps we can have lunch once Mr Goldmark's fantasies are finally published."[61]

Bill Bachman remained with Columbia Records for the rest of his career. In 1955 he was named director of engineering research and development.[62] For years he consulted on all matters concerning sound. While New York City's Lincoln Center was still in the planning stages, Bachman was asked for his opinion regarding acoustics. "Many halls which are satisfactory for performances are not good for recording," Bachman memoed Goddard Lieberson. "The Philadelphia Academy of Music is a good example. On the other hand, those which are good for recording apparently are also good for concerts. The more reverberant large halls are usually preferable." Bachman rated Orchestra Hall in Chicago as the best for recording, with Symphony Hall in Boston as second best. "The good halls generally have simple rectangular shapes, wood floors and paneling, with plaster walls and ceilings. The poor ones use much acoustic tile, rock wool, and complex diffusing surfaces. . . ."[63] An avid sailor, Bachman often got out in the sunshine on Long Island Sound, blissfully out from the long public shadow cast by Goldmark. He spent his last days at a retirement community near Wilmington, Delaware. George Avakian found him there, still unfazed by his relative anonymity. "Oh, it doesn't matter," Bachman said to Avakian. "I know what I did."[64]

Perhaps Goldmark knew, too. During the CBS years, he had shuttled between Manhattan and Connecticut with the services of a car and driver.[65] Not in his retirement, though. On a December morning in 1977 Goldmark was changing lanes on the Hutchison River Parkway, in Westchester, when his car caught the bumper of another car. The next day his Times obituary referred to him as the "Scientist Who Invented the LP Disk."[66]

10

Midcentury

As the 1940s faded at Columbia Records, it wasn't all about the LP. Doris Day, undeniably a movie star even in her debut in the 1948 *Romance on the High Seas*, had a hit single with "It's Magic," written expressly for her by Jule Styne and Sammy Cahn to sing in the picture. Frank Yankovic's "Blue Skirt Waltz" twirled its way into gold. Kay Kyser, still doing his clowning bandleader thing at the label, recorded "The Woody Woodpecker Song," which would become a children's anthem for the next decade. George Morgan's "Candy Kisses" sweetened the Columbia coffer. And then riding back with four back-to-back hits was American Record's reliable cowboy, Gene Autry. After Autry sold a tower of "Here Comes Santa Claus" disks in 1947, children's division head Hecky Krasnow paired Autry with Johnny Marks's "Rudolph the Red-Nosed Reindeer." Autry's version of "Peter Cottontail" was almost as successful in 1949. Lightning struck a fourth time in 1950 with "Frosty the Snow Man." By then Autry had his own TV series, which provided nationwide publicity for anything he recorded. In a rare visit to the East Coast, Autry appeared at the Bridgeport factory to thank Columbia's employees, singling out Goddard Lieberman.[1]

Lieberson must have been amused. In 1950, though, at the dawn of the decade of Columbia's bionic growth spurt, Lieberson didn't always have a lot to smile about. Manie Sacks, livid that he now had to answer to Lieberson as executive vice president, had departed in a huff, "trailing clouds of brimstone," in Martin Mayer's memorable phrase, and gone over to RCA Victor.[2] Lieberson was forced to cool his heels while Wallerstein, in his second term as president, quietly battled the brass (mostly Dr. Stanton) at 485 Madison Avenue. Once again Lieberson was contending with ulcers. On December 12, 1950, he wrote to Cole Porter from Lenox Hill Hospital describing his condition. Still in his hospital bed ten days later, he opened that evening's *Journal-American* to stare in disbelief at "CBS Disc Exec Wrote for Reds," by Howard Rushmore:

> Employees of Columbia Broadcasting System's record subsidiary, Columbia Records, escape the loyalty pledge demanded of all CBS officials and workers.
>
> Under this policy, Goddard Lieberson, executive vice president of Columbia Records, one of the nation's biggest musical enterprises, will not have to state:
>
> That in 1938 he wrote a poem, "Invitation from Lady Astor," which appeared in "New Masses," a Communist Party organ.
>
> That his name appeared as sponsor or affiliate of five organizations named as Communist fronts by Congress and the Attorney General. . . .[3]

The article went on to list several of the organizations Lieberson had belonged to in the thirties, including that highly subversive group, the American Composers Alliance. The surprise wasn't that this acid was being splashed from inside the notoriously Communist-baiting *Journal-American*, but that Lieberson—already a member of Manhattan's cultural elite, a director of the powerful Columbia Broadcasting System, and now laid up in a hospital bed—would be vulnerable to the mention of a poem he'd published 12 years earlier. From his bed Lieberson dictated a response to the editor denying both Communist membership and sympathy; the memberships named in the article, he wrote, were during the war and all about music. In addition, his poem attacking the Cliveden Set was "not pro-Communist, but anti-Nazi."[4]

Mostly forgotten today, the Cliveden Set was a group of "high-born and influential persons," Malcolm Muggeridge wrote, "a mysterious entity whose activities, directed towards promoting an Anglo-German understanding, and perhaps towards emulating Nazi methods in England, needed to be, and often were, exposed."[5] That had been Lieberson's aim in publishing "Invitation from Lady Astor," which contains his renowned wit, in this instance as sharp as a bayonet:

> O, jump the hedges, skip the fen,
> And weekend here at Cliveden,
> I'm sure you'll like the guinea hen
> At Cliveden, at Cliveden.
>
> We'll talk of oil and guns and stuff,
> And loans to Hitler on the cuff—
> You see? It'll be so terribly gay,
> Trumping the Duce with an Austrian trey.
>
> Everything will be done in style,
> Neat, brown-shirted, with a "heil."
>
> You know the games that we can play:
> "Double cross" and "Czech away,"
> All the things you like to do,
> Even "France—I love you."
>
> There'll be no talk of territories;
> Let Hitler take the Russian quarries!
> We may even put the seal
> On just that kind of deal.
>
> It's going to be so pleasant, dear,
> Goebbels promised Rothermere
> That we don't ever, ever hear
> A single tiny bit of news

About the torture of the Jews.
(I think he's got some silent screws.)

You see, I made it doubly clear,
At Cliveden, we need atmosphere.
So won't you come and share a bun
With Lord and Lady Lothian?

Now Neville dear, please don't say no.
Joachim's all set to go.
But we needn't stop at Rippentrop
Now Halifax is Adolf's beau.

You'll come? Oh, Neville, you're a dear!
I really didn't have much fear,
Because I know that you're the kind
That has a (retro) active mind.

White tie, of course.[6]

Lieberson's communist affiliations were a matter of conjecture. Howard Scott believed that Lieberson came under openly communist influences in the Catskills, specifically at Grossinger's, where he spent summers with members of the Revuers—Betty Comden, Adolph Green, and Judy Holliday.[7] In October 1953 Groucho Marx, who was incapable of authoring more than three lines that lacked a joke, wrote to Lieberson's secretary Dinorah Press to decline, even with the inducement of a Columbia "360" phonograph, to appear in a Columbia Records Life magazine ad because he was then under personal contract to NBC. Groucho added, "When you see your boss, Goddard (who is probably crawling under the Iron Curtain at the moment), give him my love."[8]

Lieberson worked hard to hide his disappointment when Frank Stanton brought in Jim Conkling from Capitol Records, in Los Angeles, where he'd spent the postwar years overseeing Artists & Repertoire, and named him president of Columbia. Conkling had a reputation as a smart deal maker and was well liked throughout the industry. He'd attended Dartmouth, where he played cornet in a band that included Paul Weston on piano, and served in the navy. A practicing Mormon, blocky and blond, Conkling was married to Donna King, one of the singing King Sisters.

•   •   •

Conkling and Lieberson were practically the same age. When Lieberson privately asked why he didn't get the job, Stanton suggested that, good as he was with artists, he needed business experience.[9] It was a curious assessment of a man who'd spent the previous decade in almost daily contact with Masterworks artists about contracts, royalties, concerts, and recording sessions. Despite his dismay, Lieberson remained loyal to Columbia and forward-thinking in every aspect of the company. As early as 1951, according to Martin Mayer's profile of him, he was promoting the idea of a record club. "Clubs are the way to reach the mass market for books or records," Lieberson wrote in a memo that year; "the book publishers let the club business go to outsiders, leaving out both the publishers and the dealers, and we'd be fools to do the same."[10] Though he was never a hardware man, Lieberson pushed through Columbia's "360" phonograph, the so-called full-frequency table model, sometimes referred to as "high fidelity in a hatbox," that came with twin speakers (though still in monaural sound). In the building he was known as the Mayor of Paramount Pharmacy, the drugstore on the ground floor, where gossip profane and meaningless was exchanged every hour. Everybody knew Goddard and Goddard knew everybody.

But it was during that limbo period in 1950—that ulcerous time when Ted Wallerstein was still president but had ceded a lot of the staff-building to him—that Lieberson made a decision that would shape Columbia Records for the entire decade and beyond. He hired the oboist turned record producer Mitchell William Miller.

•   •   •

Mitch Miller was the third child of Russian-Jewish immigrants from Keneshyn, near Bialystock, which was then part of Russia.[11] His father, who had served in the czar's army in the Russian-Japanese war, didn't want to fight anymore so he set sail for the *goldeneh medina* in 1904. A year later he sent for his wife and their infant daughter, one of Mitch's two older sisters. They moved to Rochester, New York, where they had relatives. When Mitch arrived on July 4, 1911, he would become the middle child of five (with two younger brothers to come).

His father, a Eugene Debs Socialist, worked as a toolmaker, his mother a seamstress. One day his father brought home a wind-up phonograph, and they listened to Chaliapin in *Boris Godounow*: $5 for a fat one-sided 78 disk, four and a half minutes of music (surely a Victor Red Seal record). In 1917, when Mitch was 6, the Rochester department store Edwards was dumping its Chickering square pianos to make room for the more fashionable new grands and uprights; his parents took one with inlaid mother-of-pearl and paid $14 to have the piano trucked home. Mitch took lessons from a Mrs. Gottlieb. He skipped two grades. Before George Eastman established the Eastman School in 1923, he gave money for the first public music education in America; the schools provided music instruction on Saturday mornings. By the time Mitch was instructed to choose an instrument, the oboe was the only one available through the program. Mitch wasn't aware he needed a reed for it. Since each reed cost two bucks, his father taught him how to make his own.

Rochester had a strong Jewish community at the time, and much of that community, like Miller's father, considered itself Socialist. Miller attended Sunday school at the Socialist Labor Lyceum. While still in high school, he was summoned to play oboe for the Syracuse Symphony, some 80 miles away, after its oboist committed suicide. Soon he became the second oboist for the Rochester Philharmonic and was making over $100 a week—serious dough for a pre-Depression teenager. At the Eastman School his woodwind style deepened and his social contacts expanded. His schoolmates included Goddard Lieberson, only a few months older, and Alec Wilder, who was several years older than the others in that crowd.

Wilder was already composing beautiful songs. Miller, despite his relative youth, was a father figure to him. When Wilder fell ill, Miller took him his mother's chicken soup.[12] In one of the letters he says he "never mailed," Wilder wrote to a former schoolmate that the schoolmate and a couple of friends "and Mitch in the Eastman School quite literally saved my sanity and possibly my life. I had never known such dedicated and compassionate people existed."[13]

Miller graduated from Eastman in 1932. Nearly two years later he went to New York City hoping to meet violinist-conductor David Mannes, the father of his Rochester friend Leopold and director of the Mannes School of Music. Eventually Miller got a job with Charles Previn, André's first cousin once removed. This led to his playing oboe for Alexander Smallens in the traveling version of *Porgy and Bess*. Alec Wilder, arriving after Miller had made several contacts, was lucky to have Miller as his unofficial agent. "His approach to the rough world of business," Wilder said of his younger friend, "with all its violence and corruption, was much more realistic than mine and naturally was a great help to me. He was my sponsor and spokesman."[14] Meanwhile Miller had begun to play oboe regularly for CBS radio—for the CBS Symphony as well as on CBS's *Swing Club*, a Saturday-night jazz program. He would play every Kostelanetz show for 18 years—well into the decade when he was running pop A&R for Columbia. "Kostelanetz was a whiz in the recording studio," Miller said. "He made effects no one had ever heard of."

Soon Alec Wilder came to New York, too. Wilder recalled, "Mitch Miller managed to con some pathetic fellow who knows nothing about popular music but wanted to conduct into believing that I was the perfect person to do the arrangements for his new show."[15] The show was probably the *Ford Hour*, Sunday nights on CBS, for which Wilder made swing arrangements of Debussy and Ravel.

"Benny Goodman was in the morning band at CBS," Miller recalled for Stephen Paley. "It had Artie Shaw, Phil Lang, Buddy Rich, Jerry Colonna—and they were the morning jazz band. The guy who used to shine the shoes at CBS, an Italian guy, said to Benny, 'You take away the clarinet you got a-nothin' to say.' Benny used to play Nielsen. I had never even heard of Nielsen.

"Remember, there was no tape, no record of performances, so we had to do it all live. That's why when we did *War of the Worlds* we just thought it was a joke."

In the late thirties and early forties, Miller was spread all over New York, at the radio stations and in the recording studios. He claimed that Stravinsky composed the *Dumbarton Oaks Concerto* for him and Sasha Schneider (of the Budapest String Quartet) in 1938. He encouraged Wilder to write several airs for a CBS-BBC wartime exchange. The completed octets were performed live on CBS and the music sent to the BBC, which sent back some Benjamin Britten pieces in return. If Miller's career had stopped there, after he'd promoted Wilder's music, he would have already made a significant contribution to American music.

But Miller had a lot more ground to cover. He was held in such high regard around town that musicians alerted each other when he was part of a program. In June 1945 Bernard Herrmann told Lieberson to listen that week to *Invitation to Music*, which would include the American premiere of Vaughn-Williams's Oboe Concerto, with Mitch as soloist.[16]

● ● ●

When Sinatra recorded "Try a Little Tenderness" for Columbia in 1945, Miller played oboe on the session. Manie Sacks came in from the booth and said the take was too long for jukebox. Miller said, "It's a great record. What's the difference?" and Sinatra echoed, "Yeah, what's the difference?" After that humiliation, Sacks banned Miller from the studio—at least until he was needed again.[17]

All those studio sessions gave Miller a sense of what worked in the recording process. "See, in the days before tape," he told Martin Bookspan in 1978, "so many good performances were lost because they didn't have the right balance, they weren't ready to take it. They'd say, 'Let's rehearse.' Well, why rehearse, you know, if the guys are good enough and you're ready? 'Let's do one for a playback'—that was a famous saying. I said, 'Why do it for a playback? Do it for a recording.'"

John Hammond had taken over Keynote and, admiring Miller's sonic sensibilities, hired him to supervise classical recordings. Keynote was soon subsumed by Mercury Records. There, Miller produced the Fine Arts recording of Schubert's *Death and the Maiden*. With the engineer Bob Fine, Miller made his own echo chamber—the effect that he would deploy to such profit (and scathing criticism) at Columbia. David Oistrakh had done the Khatchaturian Violin Concerto, the "metal mothers on 78s and it was the driest sound you ever heard." Miller had previously asked Fine to put a "halo" around a singer's voice. "He put a speaker in a toilet and hung a microphone there," Miller remembered. "Then he took the main signal and shot it through that and he kept the original main signal through the other line. Then he brought back the reverberation from the toilet and mixed it with the original voice, just enough to put the halo around. Now, everybody sounds great in the bathroom. The toilet was the first echo chamber." Using the same principle, Fine and Miller enlivened the Khatchaturian.

Miller moved over to popular records, replacing A&R man Jimmy Hilliard in October 1947.[18] The second Petrillo strike had halted a lot of recording (though not all; many musicians didn't take this second one seriously), so it was a while before Miller could go back into the studio for Mercury. He moonlighted as musical director at Golden Records, the venerable children's label, which had been conceived by Golden Books editor Georges Duplaix. (Golden Books was a subsidiary of Simon & Schuster.) Many Golden Records recordings didn't require AFM musicians. As the strike wore on and Miller had to channel all his energies to Mercury, his Golden Records job went to Jay Blackton, who had conducted *Oklahoma!* and *Annie Get Your Gun*, among many other musicals, on Broadway.[19]

In late 1948, with the strike still officially on, Miller took singer Frankie Laine, who had preceded him at Mercury, into a Newark studio to record six jazz sides with Cootie Williams.[20] The sessions bonded Miller and Laine. In April 1949 the second strike was just a bad memory, and Miller gave Laine the song "That Lucky Old Sun," which he described as "a combination of 'Old Man River' and 'Black and Blue.'" It became Laine's signature song. In September Miller persuaded the reluctant Laine to record "Mule Train," dubbing the famous whip sound in later.[21] In a matter of weeks the recording sold over a million dollars' worth of disks. At the same time, Miller was recording Patti Page and the very young Vic Damone, who had ushered at the Paramount Theater only six months before winning an Arthur Godfrey Talent Scout contest. With Page, Miller claimed to have made the first multiple-track recording in 1949 on "Money, Marbles and Chalk." Miller also supervised some Sarah Vaughan sessions before her husband, George Treadwell, took control of her career.

At Mercury the pressure to produce hits was tacit but intense. The writer Gene Lees described the stress involved:

> The culture was undergoing a change whose nature was not yet obvious; in retrospect it seems to have come about with bewildering speed. The three major radio networks, CBS, NBC, and Mutual, were slowly closing down as these corporations hastened to set up their television operations, which were immensely more profitable. Cut off from high-quality network programming from New York, Los Angeles, and Chicago, the affiliated stations turned more and more to records and began a scramble for ratings that placed a premium on repetition and a short "play list" and sought the lowest common denominator of public musical taste.[22]

"John [Hammond] gave me my first opportunity [in A&R]," Miller told Stephen Paley. "Lieberson got me the Columbia job. Lieberson said, 'Here's your budget. Do what you can within the budget.' And he never second-guessed me. And neither did Jim Conkling." Lieberson and Conkling told Miller not to raid artists from other companies, but to go out and recruit his own.[23] Miller answered to Lieberson through the presidencies of Wallerstein, Conkling, and Lieberson. The first man was austere, sometimes even severe, his knowledge of records beyond reproach; the second was affable, open-handed, and artist-friendly; the third, for all the imputations of Machiavellianism, was like no one else in the business.

"People don't realize what a guiding genius [Lieberson] was," Miller said. "He was like a great parent. It's not what he did that mattered; what he did was plenty. It's what he didn't do. He never second-guessed you, he backed you up; he encouraged you to experiment, because if you're not going to shoot for something big, you'll never make something big. You can always imitate. The sales department would say, 'Ooh, Capitol has a record like this, let's copy it,' and he'd say, 'No, why waste an artist and come in second best? We'll make our own.' And they would lose some immediate sale, but they would gain a much greater sale later and this was nothing but straight common sense."[24]

•   •   •

Miller's first record for Columbia was a duet by two artists who routinely recorded for the label: Arthur Godfrey and Mary Martin singing "Go to Sleep, Go to Sleep, Go to Sleep." Although it charted as high as number 28 in May 1950, the record was soon banned because the couple was implicitly in bed together. (On television and in the movies, married couples still occupied separate twin beds.) Frankie Laine's Mercury contract was up in March 1951, and he soon landed alongside Mitch. They made a formidable combination. Laine had another hit with "Jezebel," recorded "Do Not Forsake Me," the *High Noon* theme (Tex Ritter had sung it on the soundtrack), and then what became his biggest hit of all, "I Believe," with Paul Weston, Columbia's man in Los Angeles.[25] When Laine sang "I Believe" on *Ed Sullivan* in 1953, the performance reached millions of listeners, coast to coast, in a matter of hours. Could you plug a song more effectively?

Miller liked to pair Laine's virile baritone with lighter voices—Jo Stafford, Doris Day, the preadolescent Jimmy Boyd. During long recording sessions at 30th Street, Laine remembered, Miller would spring for sandwiches at Trinacria, the Near Eastern importer around the corner, at Third Avenue and 29th Street.[26]

The now-dominant television audience forced radio to change or become extinct. By 1956, when Elvis Presley became a star and Laine recorded "Moonlight Gambler" at Mitch Miller's behest, most dramatic

shows had vanished from radio. This made the disk jockey more authoritative than ever, but it also forced white-owned radio stations—that is,
some 99 percent of all stations—to expand their playlists to include jazz
and R&B records, or to contract the playlists according to the new Todd
Storz–Gordon McLendon Top Forty programming. Miller didn't care for
either option. Even if he'd decided to join 'em by recording rock 'n' roll,
he didn't have the rock 'n' roll talent. As Laine pointed out, "It certainly
wasn't in Tony Bennett's or Rosemary Clooney's ballpark. Jo Stafford had
that pure, liquid-silver voice which wouldn't have worked. Johnny [sic]
Ray might have been more readily accepted by the rockers if he hadn't
become popular before the rock era, because he was doing similar
things with music in the early fifties. Guy Mitchell sounded too country.
That left me."[27]

In fact Laine's career became more international, not more rock 'n'
roll. With Miller increasingly occupied by other artists' recordings, Laine
began to record under Irving Townsend's supervision. "His style as a
producer was very different from Mitch's," Laine wrote. "Rather than
constantly suggest material, he went along with whatever the artist
wanted to do. He felt that performers were more inclined to give their
best when involved with a pet project."[28]

•   •   •

Vic Damone took detours to Hollywood and into the army, but eventually he too would come to Columbia. At Miller's suggestion Patti Page
stayed at Mercury, where she'd reign as pop queen and not have to compete with the likes of Dinah Shore and the young, vibrantly pretty Ken-
tuckian Rosemary Clooney. By Miller's lights, Shore was tired—a good
singer who hadn't generated any real hits. More to his liking was Doris
Day, whose swelling movie stardom was just about the best publicity a
recording artist could ask for.

In the movies Doris Day's persona as a professional virgin worked in
part because it was a safe lie, particularly in the comedies she made with
Rock Hudson beginning in 1959. Her ripeness was impossible to

conceal, which is what made her characters' chastity entertaining. (A more blatantly "virginal" actress of the era would have generated too much anxiety for the comedies to bear.) In Day's recordings for Columbia, behind all the sunshine the voice harbored something dark and plangent. You can listen a hundred times to Alec Wilder's "Give Me Time," for instance, Day's phrasing as pleasant as daybreak in a Disney cartoon, only to sense that she may be reminding a lover that she's still married. The Rodgers & Hart songs she covers in Love Me or Leave Me, the biopic of longtime Columbia artist Ruth Etting, can't approach Ella Fitzgerald's renditions for Verve a couple of years later, but they leave a sting.[29]

On the opposite end of the publicity spectrum from Day was the retiring, nectar-voiced Jo Stafford. Married to Paul Weston, who usually made her arrangements and backed her, Stafford recorded "You Belong to Me" and "Jambalaya" at Miller's behest. Unlike many A&R men based in New York or Los Angeles, Miller didn't deride country music but valued it highly. "A great song is a great song!" he was fond of saying. Jerry Wexler had turned Miller on to Hank Williams, whose "Cold Cold Heart" was begging (in Miller's ears) to be recorded in a noncountry setting. The singer he finally pushed it on was as noncountry as they came.

* * *

"In three seconds I can tell a talent," Mitch Miller said. "I signed Tony Bennett before I ever met him. I heard a demo record he did." The demo was Bennett's version of "Boulevard of Broken Dreams." Miller signed him at Columbia in April 1950. Bennett wasn't yet 25, but he'd been on the music scene for years.

Anthony Benedetto ("blessed one") was born in Long Island City on August 3, 1926. There was a lot of music in the house, particularly Bing Crosby. Tony's brother Johnny, three years older, was chosen to perform in the Met's children's choir and was thereafter referred to as the Little Caruso. Growing up in Astoria, Queens, Bennett was close to the musical Katzes, Fred and Abe. Fred, Tony's original friend, played piano and cello and became an important figure on the jazz scene in New York. But it was Abe, first trumpet at the Metropolitan Opera, who taught Tony how to breathe. (Tommy Dorsey and Frank Sinatra, half a generation older than Katz and Bennett, had a similar teacher-pupil relationship for a while.) Tony's closest friend of all, Jack Wilson, was a poet; together they hung out with aspiring writer Abby Mann (Mann would write several acclaimed screenplays for the filmmaker Stanley Kramer), each of them daydreaming of living one day on Central Park South.[30] Wilson managed Tony through his first years of singing.

But Fred Katz was handled by the well-connected Ray Muscarella. Tony, still using the name Benedetto, jumped over to Muscarella, causing a break with Jack Wilson. In the spring of 1949, Tony made his first record for Leslie Records, a small label that recorded mostly baseball players, owned by Sy Leslie. (John Hammond told people he first heard Tony sing in 1949, at Ebbets Field.[31] The engagement might have been connected to his recording for Leslie.) Jazz writer George Simon produced the record. Under the name Joe Bari, Tony recorded two sides for Decca at its 57th Street studios. It was during this period that Tony recorded the "Boulevard" demo that got Mitch Miller interested. Bob Hope had advised Tony to shorten his name, so Benedetto became Bennett. Mitch Miller went out of his way to promote Bennett and Rosemary Clooney, whose careers kept swirling around each other. Marty Manning rearranged "Boulevard of Broken Dreams," and Bennett—and Columbia Records—had a hit.

Inevitably, there was a lull. In every season artists are cut from the roster; by early 1951, Bennett was already an underperforming artist in trouble.

Mitch Miller had recently brought Percy Faith to the label. A Toronto native, Faith was born in 1908, probably with the surname Weinstein, though it's not clear whether he changed his name or his family did.[32] A piano prodigy, Faith played behind silent movies until a fire injured his hands and snuffed out the possibility of a concert career. That got him arranging, first for hotel orchestras, then for the CBC. Eventually he worked his way to NBC and took American citizenship in 1945. During those busy radio years, Faith and Miller got to know each other well. If Miller was a master satyr, Faith was his prize pupil.[33] In the city's intimidating sound studios young female singers often felt the need for direction; Miller and Faith gave it. When Miller became head of pop A&R in 1950, he brought Faith to the label. Few music men would prove so versatile to any record label.

Faith was especially good at arranging for strings, and at supporting the singers he wrote for. Preparing to record "Because of You," Faith, aware that Bennett liked to emphasize the drama in his songs, told him to relax this time and use his natural voice all the way through.[34] Bennett relaxed. "Because of You" reached number one on the *Billboard* charts in June 1951 and held on for ten weeks.

That's when Miller dangled Hank Williams's "Cold Cold Heart" before his new star. Bennett resisted at first because it was country—and Bennett, no matter how you sliced it, wasn't country. "Tony Bennett said, 'I don't want to sing that cowboy music. I said, 'Listen to the lyrics.'"[35] Before Miller had heard Bernie Wayne audition his new song "Blue Velvet" all the way through, he interrupted and said, "How about Tony Bennett?" "Don't you want to hear the rest of the song?" asked Wayne, and Miller replied, "Quit while you're ahead."[36] Bennett's "Blue Velvet" went gold more than a decade before Bobby Vinton's—both versions in the Columbia Records family.

Bennett chafed under Miller's authority and often stood up to him. When he first heard "Rags to Riches" in 1953, he hated it. "Mitch laid down the law," Bennett recalled.[37] The song doesn't sound like the distinctive work of Richard Adler and Jerry Ross, whose *The Pajama Game* would be a breakout Columbia Broadway album the following year, but it is. Once again Percy Faith came to the rescue by providing a double tango in the instrumental break. "Rags to Riches" helped define an era, particularly in New York. (It was absolutely right for the *Goodfellas* soundtrack.) Columbia was always pushing its artists to try material from the Broadway shows it was recording. In the autumn of 1953 Bennett agreed to record "Stranger in Paradise" though *Kismet*, the show that included it, hadn't yet opened, let alone been recorded by Lieberson.[38]

With Miller guiding him through his Columbia sessions and strong arrangers writing for him—in addition to Faith and Manning, Neal Hefti, Gil Evans, Don Costa, and Ray Conniff were all around in those early years—Bennett was a dependable hit maker, even when he sang over the top. *Dedicated to You* was really a collection of hit singles. The first concept LP was *Cloud 7*, followed by *Tony!* Of male singers who began to record only after the advent of the LP, Bennett became the most essential to the label.

• • •

The field was wide open since Frank Sinatra had walked away in 1953. Mitch Miller was widely blamed for Sinatra's defection to Capitol. The word, particularly on the West Coast, was that Miller had kept Sinatra away from the songs he was right for and instead forced him to sing novelty songs. The number that everyone pointed to was "Mama Don't Bark," with the big blonde known as Dagmar, who had known Sinatra in the forties and was earning laughs and a ton of money on the new TV show *Broadway Open House*. Miller said to Stephen Paley, "I thought, We can't sell a good one, so let's try a novelty." In fact Sinatra had had serious troubles, personal and professional, for some time. His marriage to Ava Gardner had imploded, he'd lost his television contract, and, during one humiliating run at the Copa, his voice gave out altogether.

"Stop and think for a second," Miller said. "Who tells Sinatra what to do? Who *ever* told Sinatra what to do? You can't get somebody into the studio and have him sing a song he doesn't want to. You must remember, Sinatra took out a loan [from Columbia]—a quarter of a million dollars—to pay back income taxes, and Wallerstein said to me, 'Make that money back, please!'

"Sinatra alienated everybody. When Manie Sacks left and Sinatra's contract was up, why didn't Manie take him to Victor? Sinatra pleaded with Ava Gardner to get him the *From Here to Eternity* job. This may be pop psychology. He got stomped to death in the movie, and in the public mind he did his penance there."

It's no wonder Miller was defensive on the subject. We want our musical artists to grow, not shrink, and we tend to blame others—parents, managers, hangers-on, producers—if their gifts come to sound diminished. No popular singer was greater than Frank Sinatra, and no artist fell so far from such a great height. It is, in fact, peculiarly American to fail so spectacularly, with media ears and eyes in attendance and schadenfreude beating in so many hearts. If Sinatra's collapse hadn't been so complete, if all those gorgeous Columbia recordings of the 1940s hadn't devolved into the unsalable doggerel of the early '50s, would we have had the supreme Capitol recordings of 1954 and beyond? Perhaps Sinatra only had to meet Nelson Riddle to get back on his feet. Just as likely, though, he had to have his talent and his dignity robbed before he could recover them and move beyond them. Mitch Miller wasn't the culprit. The first half of Sinatra's Columbia years are still thrilling and extraordinarily evocative of the era; the troubled second half was necessary to transform Sinatra into the swingiest, most sympathetic interpreter of popular song America has ever had.

• • •

Percy Faith, like Miller, made his own records while arranging for Columbia's popular singers. His adaptation of Alfven's "Swedish Rhapsody" and his version of Georges Auric's "The Song from Moulin Rouge" (English lyrics by Alec Wilder's frequent lyricist Bill Engvick; vocal by Felicia Sanders) were huge Columbia sellers in the 1953–1954 season. Shortly after Miller brought him to the label in 1950, Faith was sitting in his office and—a musician after Miller's own heart—was deriding rock 'n' roll as simple-minded. On a dare, Faith wrote a song with Carl Sigman using only three chords in "My Heart Cries for You," an adaptation of an ancient melody. Miller hated rock 'n' roll but thought the parody worked. He intended to have Sinatra record it. "When Sinatra came in with Hank Sanicola at the airport," Miller said, "I met him at the plane. I had a chorus hired, a studio, it was a Monday night. There was a kid named Al Cernik. He'd been sleeping in the office at King

Records, but he had a kind of nice voice. He said, 'I'll rescue the session' and did just those two songs, 'My Heart Cries for You' and 'The Roving Kind.' Those were the two Sinatra wouldn't do." Miller conducted. Cernik changed his name to Guy Mitchell, using his conductor-mentor's first name. Mitchell would never be in Sinatra's or Bennett's league, or even Vic Damone's, but he did well enough for Columbia through the middle of the decade.

With most artists, Miller was usually the controlling personality—clearly the boss, if not also a musical Svengali. But occasionally he handled an artist whose sensibility was already carved in ivory. One of them was the dimpled, pouf-haired, florid pianist who went by the single name Liberace.

• • •

In the late 1940s Los Angeles airwaves were becoming crowded with new VHF stations like KLAC, channel 13. KLAC first aired *The Liberace Show* on February 3, 1952. One of the program's sponsors was Citizen's National Trust & Savings Bank. On one of those early shows, Liberace announced that anyone who opened a new account with a minimum of $10 would receive a free recording of his. The following morning the bank opened to a line of customers going halfway round the block; the bankers mistook it for a run on the bank until they remembered Liberace's TV offer.[39] Paul Weston read about the bank incident in the *Los Angeles Times*. Liberace's manager Seymour Heller suggested to Weston that he tune in to KLAC one day at noon to catch his client. Weston wondered why a guy playing piano for 15 minutes on daytime TV should interest Columbia Records. "At the start of every broadcast," Heller told Weston, "he lights a candelabra on the piano top, talks to the listeners between songs, tells them how happy he is that they tuned in, asks them to tune in again tomorrow and blows them a kiss." "So?" said Weston. "So, since he started broadcasting a few weeks ago," Heller explained, "the bank that sponsors him says they've had about a thousand little old tennis-shoe ladies come in to transfer their savings accounts from other banks."[40] Weston met Liberace at a charity telethon and, though Weston played a mean piano himself, was impressed. He phoned George Avakian in New York and told him he wanted to sign a pianist who used only his surname. After negotiating with Heller, Columbia signed him and let him do his thing.

At first Liberace's arrangements were made by his brother. Then Weston recorded him in Los Angeles: *Liberace by Candlelight, Liberace at the Piano,* and *An Evening with Liberace* sold $400,000 worth of albums by mid-1954.[41] Mitch Miller produced Liberace's version of "September Song," which outsold all his previous records.

Besides Liberace, Seymour Heller managed the Hi-Lo's, perhaps the most pleasing pop male vocal group among many of the era. The Los Angeles–based Hi-Lo's consisted of four men, harmonically guided by Gene Puerling, so named for the range of their voices as well as their respective statures, from the 5' 5" Clark Burroughs to the 6' 2" Bob Strasen. There was also the label's not-uncommon career incestuous-ness: Hi-Lo member Bob Morse (not the actor Robert Morse) sang occasionally on Rosemary Clooney's television show; Clooney's hus-band José Ferrer wrote the liner notes for the Hi-Lo's first Columbia album *Suddenly It's the Hi-Lo's* in 1954.[42] One way or another everybody wanted to be connected to Rosie Clooney. For a while at Columbia Records, everybody was.

●　●　●

Like Sinatra, Clooney was already at Columbia when Miller arrived. She'd signed her Columbia contract as a solo artist on May 24, 1949, the morning after her twenty-first birthday, at the behest of Miller's prede-cessor, Manie Sacks, though she'd sung with her sister Betty in Tony Pastor's band. The sisters had first recorded for Columbia, with Pastor's band, a couple of years earlier at the CBS studio in Hollywood. Clooney photographed beautifully and, following the lead of her idol, Bing Crosby, already knew how to use the intimacy of a microphone, even if she hadn't yet fully developed the mistake-free rhythm that would become her trademark. Mitch Miller took over. He claimed to have loved her recording of "Grievin' for You" before he'd come to Columbia. He paired her with Sinatra for "Peachtree Street," a duet that Clooney declared was "dead on arrival" in 1950.[43]

Goddard Lieberson was enchanted with her. Though Columbia wouldn't get to make the original cast recording of *Guys and Dolls*, he put in a word, evidently backed by recordings, for Clooney. "You are right, she is very good," Frank Loesser replied. "That is, she is very good on those records . . . which doesn't have much to do with how good she could be in a theatre singing to the people in the dollar-ten seats. . . . Mostly what I like about Clooney so far is her versatility. I imagine she is a good impersonator. Good promotion phrase for you: 'Who's Clooney now?' You can have this free. She is also very pretty."[44]

Mitch Miller conducted behind Clooney when she recorded "Beautiful Brown Eyes" in January 1951. The record sold over 400,000 copies. Somehow, in the days before instant digital communication, Miller got hold of radio vocalist Kay Armen's newly recorded version of "Come On-a My House" and ordered Clooney to sing it. The song had been written during a cross-country drive by the Armenian-American cousins William Saroyan (the Pulitzer Prize–winning playwright) and Ross Bagdasarian (later known as David Seville, producer-songwriter of Alvin & the Chipmunks). Clooney expressed great reservations about recording such willful nonsense. But her fiancé José Ferrer connected the lyric to a play by Christopher Marlowe, quoting the lines "No, thou shalt go with me unto my house and I have an orchard that hath store of plums, brown almonds, services, ripe figs, and dates." If "Come On-a My House" has any similarity to Marlowe, though, it's probably to his poem "The Passionate Shepherd to His Love" ("Come live with me and be my love"). In any case, Clooney was mollified and recorded "Come On-a My House" on June 6, 1951. Within a week or so, everybody was happy.

Clooney scored again and again. "This Ole House," written by Stuart Hamblen, the West Coast radio personality who had renamed Rubye Blevins "Patsy Montana" and had begun writing sacred songs after his conversion to Christianity, was a hit.[45] Clooney's version of Walter

Gross's "Tenderly" followed more than a dozen others, but she earned—and deserved—the hit record. In the meantime Sinatra had departed, instituting legal action against Miller, claiming he was forced to sing songs controlled by BMI because CBS had a sizable stake in it. The litigation affected Clooney enormously, not just because she admired both men but because she'd been cared for—chaperoned, almost—by Sinatra and Manie Sacks when she first got to Columbia.

Making movies, Clooney spent more time rooted to Beverly Hills. She married the Puerto Rican–born Princeton graduate José Ferrer, a member of the extended Columbia family since his 1944 recording of Othello with first wife Uta Hagen. When Clooney became pregnant with her first child, Miller flew to Los Angeles to record her; out of those sessions came "Hey, There!," a number from The Pajama Game that he had already recorded with Johnnie Ray, and "Mambo Italiano." The Clooney numbers were among the best-selling records of 1954.

But Clooney was worn out by Miller's intrusiveness, particularly regarding her work in Hollywood in general and her marriage to Ferrer in particular. Playing his own version of Iago, Miller reminded Clooney that Ferrer's first marriage had ended in scandal. At the beginning of 1955, the Saturday Evening Post published a profile of Clooney in which Miller made no secret of his qualms regarding her career. Her films stank, he said, and she was going to be ruined "out there" in Hollywood. "She married this José Ferrer, and suddenly she's with the books. She's got culture and she's got him."[46] Clooney, fed up with Miller's control, declined to record again in New York. When she made an album with Duke Ellington, it was an early instance of long-distance recording: Clooney never went east and Ellington never went west; instead Billy Strayhorn, a bespectacled Hermes, flew back and forth bearing lead sheets, orchestral and vocal tracks, and the album got done without the two name artists being in the same room. Lieberson, his promotion to company president hardly dimming his charm, tried to smooth things over for her. Recording "How About You?" with the Hi-Lo's in February 1957, Clooney inserted Lieberson's name into the exalted slot originally occupied by Franklin Roosevelt: it was now Goddard Lieberson's looks, not FDR's, that gave her a thrill.[47] Clooney remained with the label another two years, but without Miller's guidance and the career-building, however invasive, he had supplied.

• • •

Miller could be a despotic master, shaping the voices and careers of young singers. But he also sensed what would communicate with an audience. When a song called "Let Me Go, Devil" was brought to him by the music publisher Hill & Range, Miller thought it wasn't quite right—a too-personal, too-plaintive cry from a songwriter trying to shake booze.[48] (The original songwriter was said to be female, but Ben Weisman, who wrote over 50 songs recorded by Elvis Presley and also composed "The Night Has a Thousand Eyes," is credited.) When the song came back to him as "Let Me Go, Lover"—just a few revised lyrics transforming it into a love song—Miller went to work. He had it recorded by 18-year-old Jersey girl Joan Weber. Miller, always looking for strong marketing, persuaded the *Studio One* people to use the song in an upcoming live teleplay. *Studio One* had been rehearsing a play based on a short story called "Who's Been Sitting in My Chair?" about a popular disk jockey who finds himself in danger. Joan Weber's recording was inserted into the teleplay, which was retitled "Let Me Go, Lover," and broadcast on November 15, 1954.

It's a curious project in which nothing quite fits together, musically or dramatically. The DJ, Johnny Baer, has a show called *Midnight to Dawn Record Shop* on WTVK, in Los Angeles. (A minor mistake: call letters west of the Mississippi have always begun with K.) When Baer arrives at his apartment at dawn he realizes someone has been there; the intruder has placed a disk of "Let Me Go, Lover" on Baer's home phonograph. Baer's landlady tells him it's "an old record." Another tenant tells him there was a murder in the apartment complex six months earlier, that the killer has just escaped from prison, and that the killer's girlfriend lived in Baer's apartment. Gulp. When Baer plays Weber's recording on his show, it's a 78, although it's already six years past the advent of the LP.

(Of course Weber hadn't made an LP yet. But it's possible that Columbia didn't want to show a 45, which had been developed by RCA.) Baer also announces Weber's name. As the clock ticks and we wait for the inevitable return of the escaped convict, Baer has to put up with an irritated police inspector, who also refers to "Let Me Go, Lover" as "an old song—hardly played anymore." When the play is finished, Weber's record plays once more.[49]

The "Let Me Go, Lover" episode, directed by future movie director Franklin Schaffner, appears to have been the first time a pop record was used on television as source music—played on a phonograph as part of the action. To include dialogue suggesting that it's an old record is probably no more than an attempt at verisimilitude. It was the most up-to-date live plug imaginable—selling the song to an audience of millions. In any case the record's inclusion in the play worked wonders. The day after the broadcast 185,000 copies of Weber's 45 were ordered; 12 days later 700,000 copies had been sold.[50] Weber's career ended shortly after that. Pregnant, she was dropped by Columbia and never had another hit. Hearing her now, she does sound like Teresa Brewer, who subsequently scored with the same song, and, weirdly, a lot like Miller's earlier discovery, Johnnie Ray.

Weber was one of several Miller discoveries. He could savage young singers but also salvage their careers. Meanwhile Mitch had a publicist and appeared frequently in magazine ads, making him probably the first A&R man well known to the public. He had a great many fans at Columbia Records, partly because he made so much money for the label, partly because he was articulate, deeply educated, and left-wing among a group of largely like-minded men and women. One of the women observing him was Deborah Ishlon, head of publicity for the label and soon to consolidate her power by running its Creative Services department. At the end of the decade Ishlon would be named the label's first female vice president. Long before then, however, she began watching Miller closely—and taking notes.

11

Changing Horses in Midstream

Debbie Ishlon was in love with Goddard Lieberson. That is, she worshipped him, would do anything for him, though there's no evidence that they were more than colleagues. Ishlon, who never married, had a more pronounced taste for jazz than Lieberson did, but she absorbed his taste in classical music and promoted the Masterworks catalog with enormous enthusiasm.

She was even fond of the beautiful but sometimes forbidding Mrs. Lieberson. Vera Zorina was recording for Columbia at least as early as 1952, when she spoke the title role of Honegger's *Jeanne d'Arc Au Bucher* (*Joan of Arc at the Stake*), a two-LP set with Ormandy and the Philadelphia Orchestra.[1] Lieberson, who rarely left New York for a recording session, supported his wife by taking the train to Philadelphia and looking over Howard Scott's shoulder as Scott supervised the recording session.

Still inexhaustible in his shaping of Masterworks even as broader vice-presidential duties called, Lieberson had to make staff changes. Dick Gilbert, who had taken over from Charlie O'Connell as a director at the end of the previous decade, was seen to lack diplomacy.[2] Howard Scott had been moved out of editing and remastering (all those acetates!) to help out with the artists. But Scott was on the brash side and his wicked sense of humor was perceived, despite Lieberson's own *méchant* wit, as lacking sobriety. So Lieberson had Scott straddle A&R and engineering and replaced Gilbert with David Oppenheim, the first clarinetist with the New York Symphony Orchestra.

Oppenheim looked like a clarinet, if clarinets can be described as tall, dark, and lean. Like so many other Columbia men, Oppenheim had attended Eastman. He was 34 and had been playing professionally all his adult life. Since January 1948 he'd been married to the actress Judy Holliday (née Tuvim), who'd become a star on Broadway the previous year playing Billie Dawn in Garson Kanin's *Born Yesterday*. Holliday—along with her fellow Revuers Betty Comden, Adolph Green, John Frank, and Alvin Hammer—was already a close friend of Lieberson's. Back in the American Record days, Holliday's father worked briefly for Irving Mills. So Oppenheim was already part of the Columbia family when he joined the label as director of Masterworks. The young Leonard Bernstein had composed a clarinet concerto specifically for him. Howard Scott, though passed over to run Masterworks, worked easily with him.

The Oppenheims lived in a floor-through apartment on Waverly Place, all the way across the country from the (then unrelated) Columbia Pictures lot where she'd filmed the movie version of *Born Yesterday*. Though he had extensive A&R responsibilities, Oppenheim continued to play professionally, notably with the Budapest String Quartet. From Columbia's pop division, Mitch Miller still played on other artists' sessions and recorded his own albums—and always with Lieberson's blessing—but Oppenheim went a step further: he often played *concerts* with the Budapest.[3]

The Budapest had remained the premiere string quartet in the nation, possibly in the world. It had gone through changes over the 30-odd years since its founding in 1921 by three Hungarians and a Dutchman. By the time the Budapest had become one of the major recording entities at Masterworks, the personnel shifts had turned it into a largely Russian quartet, with each musician multilingual but not one speaking Hungarian. With the Petrillo ban, violinist Alexander (Sasha) Schneider had moved on to pursue an independent career. Sasha was replaced by Odessa native Edgar Ortenberg, who joined Schneider's brother Mischa (cello), Joseph Roisman (violin), and Boris Kroyt (viola), the only one among them who had ever even been to Budapest. It was widely agreed that Ortenberg's participation caused a falling off in the Budapest's performances—Ortenberg himself decried the group's lack of rehearsal time—and was replaced after several years by another Russian, Jac Gorodetzky. By far the youngest of the ensemble, Gorodetzky brought a technical polish to the Budapest. But he suffered from para-lyzing stage fright and concomitant terrors. Sasha returned with increasing frequency to substitute for the incapacitated Gorodetzky—not that the group's fans minded; the brothers were playing together again!—and, after a complete breakdown in 1955, Gorodetzky took an overdose of sleeping pills in a Washington hotel room.[4]

Meanwhile Howard Scott was all over the place. He'd fly to Cleveland to record Szell and the Cleveland Orchestra at Severance Hall, then hop over to Louisville for another recording of the adventurous Louisville Orchestra, under the baton of Robert Whitney. The Louisville had begun commissioning musical works in 1948, and Columbia released two albums before the Rockefeller Foundation gave the orchestra a $400,000 grant, enabling it to commission still more works and release albums of serious music on its own label. Still, it needed Columbia's production expertise (Scott) and recording equipment. Lieberson liked the arrangement because all that contemporary music, from Carlos Chavez to Villa-Lobos, was being recorded.[5]

Columbia continued to release recordings made earlier and else-where. In one of its most important acquisitions, it got hold of a few hours of recordings made in the late forties for English Columbia by the Rumanian pianist Dinu Lipatti. Dead by the end of 1950, at 33, Lipatti had an extraordinary touch, with an almost quivering sensitivity to Bach.[6]

* * *

No matter how magnificent the Masterworks music could be, it still had to be sold to the public. In February 1953 a young force of nature walked into the Columbia offices and, for better and sometimes worse, changed the way classical records were marketed. The force was the 25-year-old hypomanic Peter Munves, a Syracuse University graduate who had come relatively late to classical music. Columbia's market dominance from the fifties through the early seventies was due, in large part, to Munves's pinwheeling ideas. "If only two out of ten of Peter's ideas were any good, that was enough," said Joseph Dash, who became his boss at Masterworks many years later.[7] Nobody could sell the unsalable like Munves.

I grew up in Cedarhurst, Long Island—the Five Towns. My mother played the piano, and she used to have her friends come over. We had a six-foot Steinway, and they'd play the symphonies, piano four hands. So that's where I first heard the symphonies of Brahms and Schumann and Mozart, on the piano. So when I heard them in the orchestra I felt that I knew them.

I had a delayed reaction to music because as a kid I could take or leave classical music. I liked all the bridge music and the theme music that was played—"Heigh-o, Silver," *The Lone Ranger.* That was my introduction to Rossini and Wagner and Liszt. *Les Preludes and Ride of Valkyries* and all that. But for the finest stuff, the real good stuff, my mother had a few records in the house and I didn't give a damn whether I played them or not.

But I went to Syracuse University and had an operation for an undescended testicle, the right testicle. That must have been the musical one. As soon as that came down my interest in music blossomed.

I was recuperating, walking stooped over like an old man because the cord there had to lengthen gradually. You exercise so you can stand up straight; otherwise you're walking like an ape. So what did I do? They gave me some Mozart symphonies and the Rachmaninoff Second Concerto. That was when I was about eighteen. At Syracuse they have a Carnegie Foundation library. Carnegie in the thirties sent out libraries of records to colleges—maybe about eighteen hundred colleges throughout North America and they had one of these collections. And they had added to it, too. So I'd go to the music room where we went to listen and do our homework. I got more and more musical and we got tired of hearing the Brahms First Symphony and the Beethoven Fifth because they were warhorses and they were coming out of our ears. So, to empty the room,

Harley School Faculty, Winter 1936. Goddard Lieberson is standing in the back row, third from right. His frequent musical collaborator, Mildred Waterman, is in the second row, second from right. *Courtesy of Anne Townsend, Harley School.*

Cover of Columbia Records catalog, 1928.
Courtesy of the author.

Cover of Columbia Records catalog, 1944. The cover painting
is almost surely by Alex Steinweiss. *Courtesy of the author.*

Manie Sacks and Frank Sinatra at CBS Radio, late 1940s. *Photo by Fred Plaut. Courtesy
of Frederick and Rose Plaut Papers, Irving S. Gilmore Music Library, Yale University.*

Columbia Records convention during introduction of the new long-playing record, Atlantic City, June 28, 1948. From front row middle, left to right: Howard Scott cueing the playing of *The Nutcracker Suite* excerpts; Manie Sacks holding program notes; Frank White (briefly the label's president); and Peter Goldmark, right leg crossed over the left. *Courtesy of Stan Kavan.*

Goddard Lieberson and Brigitta Lieberson (Vera Zorina) at home, late 1940s. *Photo by Fred Plaut. Courtesy of Fred Plaut Papers, Yale.*

Lawrence Winters (Porgy), Camilla Williams (Bess), and Lehman Engel (conductor) at the 1951 recording session of *Porgy and Bess*. Photo by Fred Plaut. *Courtesy of Fred Plaut Papers, Yale.*

Gene Autry and Columbia employees, including Stan Kavan at right, Bridgeport, Connecticut, 1950. *Courtesy of Stan Kavan.*

George Avakian, Louis Armstrong, and Piet Beishuizen (publicist
for Philips Phonogram), following recording of *Ambassador Satch*,
Paris, 1955. *Courtesy of George Avakian.*

Edith Piaf, George Avakian. *Photo by Fred Plaut.*
Courtsey of Fred Plaut Papers, Yale.

Mahalia Jackson. Photo by Fred Plaut. *Courtesy of Fred Plaut Papers, Yale.*

Debbie Ishlon, 1955. *Courtesy of the author's collection.*

Mitch Miller. *Courtesy of the author.*

Benny Goodman and Leonard Bernstein. *Photo by Fred Plaut. Courtesy of Fred Plaut Papers, Yale.*

Percy Faith, Eileen Farrell, and Irving Townsend. *Courtesy of Jeremy Townsend.*

Left to right: Andre Kostelanetz, Noel Coward, Lily Pons, and Goddard Lieberson, 1951.
Photo by Fred Plaut. Courtesy of Fred Plaut Papers, Yale.

one of the wise guys—maybe it was me—put on a Bach cello suite by Casals. You should have seen the exodus, this one instrument going on and on! This was about 1948, '49. Within two years I ran through the whole classical repertoire, except for opera. The only opera I knew was Mozart but I didn't know Verdi or Puccini. Those I learned later.

So I discovered all this music and I started working at record stores in Syracuse, and then when I came home on the holidays in New York I started working for stores that sold secondhand 78s. The LP has just arrived, '48, and that, of course, revolutionized the business.

But listen, everything is who you know. My father wanted me to go into the printing business. So I was closing out the outside thirty-two pages of *Aviation Week* up in Albany, which was a very lonely job because I worked till three or four in the morning at a press near Troy. I was a young bachelor then. I used to go to all the music festivals and everything. But I wasn't happy. I wanted to go into the music business, so I gravitated back to New York and started working at record stores again.[8]

In 1951 Uncle Sam called. Munves's testicle had been fixed, so he couldn't get out of service on that pretext. He was sent to Fort Devens, about thirty miles north of Boston, where he was called Mozart because he was reading the Mozart letters at the time, and he was sometimes called Pajamas because he was the only man there who slept in pajamas. Within two months his bad feet got him out of further service. Declining to return to his father's profession, Munves got a job writing for the Long Branch (New Jersey) *Daily Record*. But he had the itch to go to Europe, so he sold his Chevy coupe, a present from his parents, for $750, and bought himself a round-trip boat ticket for $95. He attended the Casals Festivals in Perpignan and saw remote trucks leased by Philips there to make the recording. Columbia was already in negotiations with Philips to become its transatlantic partner.

"My father was in trouble after the war," Munves said, "because he only had letterpress, which was very good but very expensive. All the type had to be set in lead and then carefully placed in these forms and locked up. It took hours and hours. My father had a staff of maybe thirty-five men who worked on locking up the flatbeds—they called them flatbed presses and some of them were handfed, some were sheetfed. He was starting to lose business in the forties because after the war people wanted to use offset. The halftones were much cheaper to produce.

"One of my father's partners was a lovely guy named Vic Friedman and he was crazy about music. He asked me to try and get him a recording of the Schubert B-flat Trio on LP. He said, 'Look, Al'—my father's name was Alexander—'Peter's not gonna be a printer, but he likes music. I know the art director Bill Cowan at CBS.'"

Munves went to 485 Madison and met with Cowan. Impressed by Munves's knowledge, Cowan sent him to 799 Seventh Avenue. The first person who interviewed him was Irving Townsend. "God, he was so nervous, his cup of coffee was shaking," Munves recalled. Townsend considered Munves's background and sent him to see Paul Wexler, who'd succeeded Paul Southard as head of sales. (Southard was then running Times Columbia, the distributorship that would be part of the enormous distribution change, from independent to wholly owned by Columbia, under Hal Cook and Jack Loetz.) Wexler hired Munves as a marketing writer for Masterworks. At the time Doug Duer was in charge of the division's marketing; but Duer hated to write. Wexler told Munves what was expected of him. "You have to write up the releases and you have to get them out to the salesmen. You have to tell them why we made the record, how it competes, where they should put it in the stores and how to sell it." Munves wrote—and wrote. Wexler said to him, "The salesmen aren't reading what you write because you're too loquacious. Tell you what, for two weeks you go out in the field with the salesmen." Munves presented himself to Boston regional sales manager Joe Broderick and went around to all the dealers. He got to know the label's veteran classical salesmen Lou Weinstein and Milt Goldstein. Convinced that honesty was the best policy, Munves would tell a dealer if a record couldn't be sold because, frankly, it stank. Consequently, the dealers trusted him whenever he expressed enthusiasm. "Then I came back from the field," Munves said, "and I invented bullet points. Bang! Bang! Bang! It worked like a charm; I was in like Flynn."

• • •

In 1953, the year that Munves joined Columbia Records and was learning how to sell the Masterworks line, the label ended its partnership with EMI and began a long alliance with Philips Electrical. Since EMI had risen out of the old Columbia Gramophone Ltd. and the recording empire built by Louis Sterling, it had seemed like a decent fit through the forties. But the advent of the LP had wedged the two media giants apart—EMI was late in accepting the new format—and Columbia was ready for a new partner. Philips had become the largest electronics firm in the world. Its origins went back to the 1890s, in the Netherlands, where the young mechanical engineer Gerard Leonard Frederik Philips had begun to mass-produce incandescent lightbulbs.[9] Philips remained headquartered in the Netherlands but maintained important recording branches in Paris and London. EMI kept the Columbia logo in Europe, but CBS's Columbia Records was only too happy to get into bed with Philips. For its part, Philips found Columbia Records attractive because two of its recording stars, Frank Sinatra and Doris Day, were movie stars whose pictures did well in Europe.[10] The producer Didier Deutsch recalled that, during his boyhood in France, the most popular Columbia Records stars were Doris Day, Frankie Laine, and, for a while, Johnnie Ray.[11] The exports worked in reverse as well, mostly through Paris-based music director Georges Meyerstein. In the coming years Yves Montand and Juliette Greco would appear on Columbia's label in the States and sell very well.

Thomas Beecham left the label in December 1955, having made hundreds of recordings for Columbia since World War I but no longer able to protect his beloved Royal Philharmonic Orchestra and its other conductors, or to be assured of English distribution after Columbia switched to Philips.[12] But the pianist Robert Casadesus, who was spending less time in his native France and more time in his American home base at Princeton, was still a major Masterworks artist. Lieberson used to joke that everyone adored Casadesus even if no one could pronounce his name. "Get your caskadoo tickets here," Lieberson barked in mock sales mode.[13] Rudolf Serkin, widely believed to be the greatest Beethoven interpreter among pianists, had been with the label since shortly after CBS's purchase of it, and was recording with several orchestras, notably the Philadelphia. After all these years the Philadelphia's *Scheherazade* was still the catalog's best-selling album.

Bruno Walter was recording cycles of Mahler and Bruckner. Columbia, believing that Walter's exacting rehearsal style was compelling, released two albums of Walter rehearsing the New York Philharmonic Symphony-Orchestra in several of the later Mozart symphonies. Columbia recorded the Nobel Prize–winning French missionary-physician Albert Schweitzer, then pushing 80, playing organ in what seemed like a novelty item, except that Schweitzer had been recording Bach organ pieces since the midthirties (for Victor) and was deeply involved in the marketing of his records.

One of the label's other organists, E. Power Biggs, would travel with his own tape recorder and returned from Westminster Abbey in 1954 with a tape he'd made of Bach's *Toccata & Fugue in D Minor.*[14] Zino Francescatti, whose parents were violinists and who'd made his debut when he was all of five, had a best seller with Mendelssohn's *Concerto in E Minor for Violin.* In the States the Francescattis spent most of their time in the Berkshires in the house they called Fiddletop. They eventually sold the house to Eugene Ormandy. Howard Scott remembered going there for weekends of Scrabble played with only French words.[15]

Columbia had Anna Russell, the "International Concert Comedienne," who sounded a bit like Bea Lillie if Lillie had been a musicologist. Born in Ontario in 1911, Claudia Anna Russell-Brown had studied at London's Royal College of Music and trained as a pianist, singer, and arranger. When she discovered that she could make audiences laugh, she began to develop her uproarious analyses of Wagner, Gilbert & Sullivan operettas and contemporary singers.[16] In *A Square Talk on Popular Music*, she decried the transformation of classics like the Tchaikovsky B Flat Concerto into "Tonight We Love" and the Rachmaninoff Concerto No. 2 into "Full Moon and Empty Arms." The audience, responding to her opinionated dottiness, adored her. Treasuring her recordings, Columbia promoted her with the marketing power it put behind its musical funnymen Danny Kaye and Victor Borge.

As a composer and conductor quite apart from his Broadway shows, Richard Rodgers was brought into the catalog. Where the recordings of other "serious" composers rarely made a profit, Rodgers almost never failed to make money—due, of course, to his name recognition and the adoration of all those shows, particularly the more recent ones written with Oscar Hammerstein. The Philharmonic-Symphony Society persuaded him to conduct an evening of his waltzes at Carnegie Hall (November 15, 1954). With the addition of a few other pieces, like "Slaughter on Tenth Avenue," Columbia Records had an album.[17] Implicitly, the label was giving Rodgers the respect it gave to Schoenberg, Bartok, and Stravinsky.

The Norman Luboff Choir had been with Columbia for several years, even singing behind Frankie Laine earlier in the decade. Its *Songs of the West* was a straight-faced treatment of so-called cowboy songs; one of them, "Streets of Laredo," became popular as a single. *Songs of the West* was recorded on the boot heels of the stunning attention given to *The Confederacy*, the first entry in the series that Lieberson called Columbia Legacy. The idea was to combine recordings with the printed word—booklets if not whole books—and it was originally a one-man operation, based largely on Lieberson's enthusiasms of the moment. In this case Lieberson had immersed himself in the Civil War. He'd attracted the participation of Richard Bales, assistant to the director of the National Gallery and an able conductor. The result was probably more literary than musical. In the fall 1955 edition of the *Columbia Retailer*, distributed to its sales force and record stores across the land, an Atlanta dealer is recorded as saying, "Ah can sell a copy of *The Confederacy* to a customer who don't even own a phonograph!"[18] That was all too true. Nevertheless, out of *The Confederacy* album came Bales's re-creation of "Yellow Rose of Texas," which had been known during the Civil War as "The Gallant Hood of Texas," named for Confederate general John B. Hood. (Hood was the losing commanding officer when Sherman took Atlanta for the Union.) The year after the Legacy version, Mitch Miller picked up on the old song and recorded it with his orchestra. As one of his protégés, Johnnie Ray, put it, Mitch "eschewed the A&R ritual, lunches at Lindy's, Toots Shor and the Plaza Oak Room, preferring to work through lunch while raiding a small refrigerator stocked with cheeses and health foods." Miller needed those extra hours to make his own records.[19]

• • •

In the winter of 1954, 799 Seventh Avenue had an expensive facelift, parts of its exterior and the lobby redone in French Rouge dark marble and Italian light marble.[20] Columbia's current promotional tie-in was with the Bell & Howell tape recorder, which was then overseen by Charles Percy before he became the U.S. senator from Illinois. A publicity campaign was mounted by George Avakian and A&R man Gene Becker to herald the return of dance bands in America, but this was mostly a way to promote Les & Larry Elgart, the Connecticut brothers whose band was fine but never came close to matching bands led by Basie, Ellington, and Goodman. Through the summer of 1954 Columbia's top-selling records belonged to Clooney ("Hey There!" and "This Ole House"), the Four Lads ("Skokiaan" and "Why Should I Love You"), Doris Day ("Anyone Can Fall in Love" and "If I Give My Heart to You"), Jo Stafford ("Nearer My Love to Me" and "The Temple of an Under-standing Heart"), and Liberace ("Polonaise" and Liebestraum").

Lieberson was spending a lot of time investigating the possibilities of a record club. He was in touch with Doubleday editor Ken McCormick about mail-order books, and talking almost daily to Les Wunderman, who handled the advertising for the Book-of-the-Month Club. Jim Conkling was still the number one man. He'd signed many pop artists, par-ticularly those he'd known on the West Coast, and relied on his old Dartmouth classmate Paul Weston to be his ears out there. He made a critical hire when he brought Hal Cook, who'd been with him at Capitol, to be the new head of sales, replacing Paul Wexler. In the three years he was at Columbia, Cook would terminate the independent dis-tributors system and institute the system of wholly owned distribution branches, giving Columbia more control (and, subsequently, more headaches). Conkling oversaw the introduction of the 12" pop record at the urging of merchandising manager Stan Kavan—previously, only classical LPs were 12"—and presided over the emergence of rack jobbing, which changed how records were sold in drug and department stores. If Conkling ran the show, however, Lieberson was the showman, the guy who craved the spotlight and controlled the microphone. He wasn't called the Mayor of the Paramount Pharmacy for nothing. On the *Columbia Retailer* record in the fall of 1955, Lieberson cracks jokes, schmoozes with his A&R men, and pronounces various pieces of music "Terrific!" or "Sensational!" Then, as if summoning a meek accountant to the lectern, he calls on Conkling to "summarize our new price structure." Conkling was the nuts-and-bolts guy, Lieberson the architect.

In the late spring of 1955 Lieberson went to Las Vegas on what was for him a dream task: to supervise the recording of Noel Coward's nightclub act at the Desert Inn, with Peter Matz accompanying Coward on piano. In one of those showbiz moments that have passed into legend, Lieberson introduced Coward to the city's chief of police. (As far as we know, no song came out of the meeting.) During the editing process of the album, Lieberson sent Coward a telegram:

DO YOU THINK WE SHOULD DROP CARMEN MIRANDA LINE IN VIEW OF HER DEATH TWO DAYS AGO (?) CAN SPLICE FROM WORD MOON TO BEGUINE MUST KNOW AT ONCE RSVP LOVE GODDARD.[21]

The album contained only a handful of Coward's own songs, but it was so aggressively marketed that it won him a new generation of fans.

Through late 1955 and into 1956, both Lieberson and Conkling could be proud of the hits that kept coming. They weren't in the uncharted stratosphere of RCA Victor's Presley records that would come later in the year, but they held their own—the old guard, led by Miller and Faith, taking a stand against rock 'n' roll. The Four Lads, classmates from the Cathedral Choir School in Toronto, scored back-to-back-to-back with "Moments to Remember," "No, Not Much," and "Standing on the Corner." Johnnie Ray, who spent his rookie year on the Okeh label before being called up to the big show at Columbia, crossed the plate with "Just Walking in the Rain." The former Al Cernik charted again with "Singing the Blues." That consummate pro, Vic Damone, who'd been guided by Miller at Mercury but detoured to Hollywood and then into the army, now appeared at Columbia's refurbished doorstep. Owner of "the best pipes in the business," according to Sinatra, Damone was welcomed with open arms. Cruelly underrated by critics who should have known better, Damone was seen as a pretty boy who crooned vacuously. In fact Damone's *voice* was pretty, yet never less than masculine and full of feeling. Just weeks before *My Fair Lady* changed Columbia's fortunes through Lieberson's astute judgment, Mitch Miller gave Damone "On the Street Where You Live" to record. "Everything falls on the strong beat," Miller said. "In the show they're changing the scenery—it's just a guy singing to a house. So Percy makes the arrangement, and it just can't seem to get off the ground. But Percy was so fabulous. I suggested we take the 'Oh, that towering feeling' as the introduction. In five minutes, Percy remade the arrangement." Damone's record was one of the biggest hits of the season. Before the decade was out, Damone, born Vittorio Farinola in 1928, would sell hundreds of thousands of copies of "An Affair to Remember" and "Gigi," their undeniable prettiness only confirming for detractors that Damone lacked Sinatra's gravitas. (Then again, who didn't?)

In Hitchcock's remake of his own *The Man Who Knew Too Much*, Doris Day sang the Livingston & Evans song "Whatever Will Be, Will Be." It was a lovely moment in the film, its carousel lilt serving as counterpoint to the tense climax. Did anyone at Columbia predict the record would become Day's sixth million-seller? Saroyan's lyric for "Come On-a My House" was said by José Ferrer to be inspired by Marlowe. Perhaps. Much closer to Marlowe is "Que Sera Sera," the alternate title to "Whatever Will Be, Will Be." ("Che Sara Sara / What will be, shall be"—*Dr. Faustus* I.i.) These antecedents matter only to lyric detectives, however. Even if we resist, our ears pull in "Whatever Will Be, Will Be" like magnets.

A former golf pro named Don Cherry had a hit with "Band of Gold."

The arranger was Ray Conniff, a Massachusetts native who'd been around for a while. As far back as 1940, George Avakian had run into him at the old Forest Hotel, a musicians' den of iniquity, on 49th Street off Eighth Avenue. Conniff was holed up in a room trying to write arrangements because he knew that's where the future work could be found. Sure enough, Conniff spent much of the forties arranging for Artie Shaw and Harry James. A decade-long wrestling match with the bottle sidelined him. Through Mitch Miller's auspices, Conniff went back to work as a Columbia Records staff arranger. In 1955, working on "Band of Gold," Conniff used an arrangement in which voices doubled the brass lines. The song was a hit. Within another 18 months, Conniff would begin to make records under his own name and write arrangements for a young San Franciscan whose first Columbia album had tanked. Conniff would record and release one top-selling album after another, and so would the San Franciscan, Johnny Mathis. By the time Mathis had stopped recording for Columbia, only Presley and Sinatra had sold more albums.

* * *

Despite a deep catalog that held Louis Armstrong, Bessie Smith, Billie Holiday, some Bix Beiderbecke, and some of the best recordings of Basie, Ellington, and Goodman, Columbia's latest brand of jazz wasn't yet distinctive. In the early fifties John Hammond was working largely as a freelance writer before going to work for Seymour Solomon at Vanguard Records. George Avakian was already overset with responsibilities as director of pop albums (which included jazz) and international recordings. Irving Townsend, whom Avakian had brought over from the advertising department, was still writing ad copy and unsigned liner notes and hadn't yet been let loose in the recording studio. Avakian was politely resisting Miles Davis's entreaties to sign him to the label because he knew Davis hadn't yet kicked junk. (Among the more romantic myths promulgated by jazz fans is the notion that heroin enables a musician to play better. The record producer is naturally wary of such fiction because he's responsible for every minute and every dollar spent on a recording session.) The great Belgian harmonica player–guitarist Toots Thielemans would come to the label in 1955 and make some fine recordings that didn't go anywhere. The nearly unclassifiable Erroll Garner was on Columbia, though his unique piano-playing—rolling, joyfully percussive, and as shadowless as reveille—often sounded overmiked. That's the way Garner and his fiercely protective manager, Martha Glaser, liked it, however. The Oklahoma native Lee Wiley, incapable of singing a false note, recorded all too briefly for the label. Sarah Vaughan had recently come and gone, recording many sides for Columbia—briefly under the direction of Hugo Winterhalter, later with Paul Weston or Percy Faith leading the way—but placing her career in the hands of her husband, George Treadwell, whose musical ideas for her rarely matched Avakian's. Les & Larry Elgart were in residence but, pleasing as their big band material could be, wasn't causing any listeners to lose sleep.

When it came to the *sound* of jazz, the long-playing record wasn't being properly exploited by the major labels. Through 1953 independent labels like Clef (precursor to Verve), Contemporary, Discovery, Prestige, Riverside, and, the most influential of them all, Blue Note, were releasing sometimes-startling jazz records that rang with clarity. But Columbia was barely using the extended format for high-fidelity jazz.

Everything changed the following year, and for several reasons. One was the Columbia arrival of Dave Brubeck. As a boy growing up outside the San Francisco Bay Area, Dave, the youngest of three sons, wanted to be a cattleman like his dad Pete.[22] His mother, Bessie, was a piano teacher, which was essentially how Dave learned to play. The family moved to the Sierra Nevadas where Pete became the manager of a 45,000-acre cattle ranch. (Did those panoramic vistas inform Brubeck's later compositions?) At the College of the Pacific, Brubeck started in veterinary medicine but then switched to music. He couldn't read it, though he could write it, and in order to graduate he had to promise never to take a job teaching it. That was easy—he didn't want to teach anyway. At graduate school at Mills College he came under the influence of Darius Milhaud. Around this time he met Paul Desmond, who was playing alto sax in a local octet. Brubeck formed a trio with Cal Tjader and Ron Crotty. Another version of the band included Desmond, and then came the falling out that left the Brubeck and his wife, Iola, bitter for a while. Desmond had stolen the band away from Brubeck.

By 1951 Brubeck and Desmond were back together, even if the wounds hadn't quite healed. Released by the Bay Area–based Fantasy, owned by Max and Sol Weiss, the albums they made weren't quite like anything else—at once highly percussive and often beautiful, particularly with Desmond stirring his dry-martini tone into most numbers. Some critics derided them as West Coast Jazz—code for all-white musicians. (Bassist Gene Wright eventually joined the group, making it only three-quarters white.) "Crow Jim," the reverse-discriminatory notion that only blacks can play jazz, raised its head. East Coast critics liked to say that Brubeck didn't know how to swing. "Any jackass can swing," was Brubeck's frequent retort.

The Fantasy records were loose and dreamy. But Brubeck had been confused by Fantasy's deliberately obfuscating contract terms, which gave him only a half-interest in his own masters.[23] By early 1954 Brubeck needed a record company with more money and more clout. Avakian, learning Brubeck was available, said, "What do you want for a contract?" Brubeck said, "I need $6,000 to pay off the mortgage on the family ranch in California and if I can get an advance of $6,000 against the usual 5% royalty that will be fine." Avakian got him what he asked for.[24] For the next three years Avakian would produce Brubeck's recordings. Later in '54 Brubeck made the cover of Time—only the second time for a jazz musician, following Louis Armstrong's cover appearance on February 21, 1949. Though Brubeck would remain based in the San Francisco Bay Area for the rest of the decade, he and the quartet spent an increasing amount of time in and around the Columbia studios in New York. He was fortunate to have nearby two women who handled some of the essentials of his career: his wife, the former Iola Whitlock, who would write with him while raising four sons; and Debbie Ishlon, whose publicity for him and for the label paid enormous career dividends, including the Time cover.

What Brubeck didn't have was a manager. As it turned out, though, his next-door neighbor Mort Lewis was the best possible candidate. Lewis, originally from Minneapolis, had come out of the army and worked as a road manager for Stan Kenton. One night in 1950, after Kenton played in San Francisco with his forty-three-piece "Innovations in Modern Music" orchestra, Lewis was invited along to hear "this great piano player," Dave Brubeck.[25] It proved to be one of those revelatory music nights. Lewis soon became Brubeck's tenant and next-door neighbor in Montclair, a few miles east of Berkeley. For Lewis, who by then had split off from Kenton, each conversation with Brubeck was an education in the vicissitudes of a recording career. "Dave would tell you that he was Mort Lewis's first manager," Lewis said with a laugh. After the *Time* issue appeared, Brubeck asked Lewis to officially manage him. Lewis already knew Columbia president Jim Conkling from Kenton's days at Capitol, where Conkling had been head of A&R. It was a good fit.

●　●　●

Just before Brubeck signed with the label, Conkling asked Avakian what he'd most like to record. "W. C. Handy," Avakian said. And who would interpret Handy's music? The old man himself was alive but had stopped playing decades earlier. That Avakian would name Louis Armstrong shouldn't have surprised anyone, least of all Conkling. Avakian hadn't worked with Armstrong since his exhumation, from the vault in Bridgeport, of Okeh's 13 unissued Armstrong sides—six Hot Fives and Sevens, plus half a dozen others—that became the foundation of the Columbia Record Corporation's jazz catalog.[26] Avakian hadn't actually recorded those sides (his age wasn't yet in double figures when they were made) but he had rescued them, annotated them, and released them, and had since become the label's premier jazz producer. The problem now was that Armstrong had been with Decca throughout the late forties and early fifties. His manager Joe Glaser, who practiced a brand of tough love long before the term was in vogue, arranged a release for Armstrong to record. Avakian had several Handy songs in mind, most of them less well known than "St. Louis Blues," including "Chantez-les Bas," which Avakian first heard while he was on furlough and helping the critic Charles Edward Smith record W. C. Handy's daughter Katherine. Because Armstrong was staying in Chicago, Avakian arranged the sessions there in mid-July 1954. Armstrong's frequent singing partner was Velma Middleton, as vivacious as Armstrong and sometimes even bawdier. A few weeks later the blind Handy, sitting in a studio at 799 Seventh Avenue, heard the tapes of the Chicago sessions and his sightless eyes filled with wonder. There would never be, he knew, a greater interpreter of his music than Armstrong.

The album *Louis Armstrong Sings W. C. Handy* ranks as one of the supreme achievements in recorded jazz. Avakian, then all of 35, named the album as his epitaph. It kicked off a mini-Armstrong revival. The following May, Avakian went into the studio in New York with much the same ensemble as in Chicago and emerged with *Satch Plays Fats*, a tribute to Waller, who'd recorded briefly for Columbia in 1931. In December of that year and January of 1956, Armstrong, recording in Milan, Amsterdam, and Hollywood, went back to his own catalog to record *Ambassador Satch*, a title that Avakian had had in his head for a while. The album cover showed Louis at his most dapper in a morning coat, holding a stylish valise, his trumpet, and his ever-present handkerchief. On a suggestion from Philips publicist Piet Beishuizen, the morning coat was borrowed from Dr. Willem Schuitema, the president of Philips, who happened to be in Paris while Armstrong was and, despite measuring half a foot taller and thirty pounds heavier, was only too happy to lend his formal clothes to the most ambassadorial of jazzmen. During preparations for *Ambassador Satch* the seed of a fourth album was planted when Avakian was waiting in the rain for train at the Gare du Nord in Paris and ran into Edward R. Murrow. After Avakian told Murrow about the latest Armstrong recording, Murrow and Fred Friendly began to film Armstrong's tour of Europe and his return to New York. Despite some synch problems, the results became two separate broadcasts, produced almost a year apart, of Murrow's *See It Now* on CBS, as well as the 1957 album *Satchmo the Great*.[27]

The Armstrong-Handy album, which Avakian shaped from the control booth without ever losing the musicians' complete participation, got him immersed again in the jazz he grew up with. So he made albums with Buck Clayton, with Eddie Condon, and put together the first I Like Jazz! sampler, which in 1955 sold for 98 cents. It offered recordings by some of the usual Columbia suspects like Armstrong, Benny Goodman, Duke, Lady Day, Turk Murphy, Eddie Condon, and Brubeck, but it also included lesser-known artists like Wally Rose and Phil Napoleon. What made it special, though—and this was part of Avakian's touch as both producer and collector—was that none of the recordings had yet appeared on LP and several had never been released in any form. In later years the long-playing sampler would become a dump for second-rate recordings of various artists, but I Like Jazz! was a first-rate compilation, issued with great care and, given Debbie Ishlon's enthusiastic promotion, with an eye toward building on the expanding jazz audience of the fifties.[28]

After the first Newport Jazz Festival in 1954, Avakian pushed for Columbia to consider recording its artists at the next one. The Jazz Festival was initially bankrolled by Louis and Elaine Lorillard, of the cigarette fortune, and the pianist-impresario George Wein became its musical director. Lieberson appreciated jazz but wasn't passionate about it; sales chief Hal Cook persuaded Lieberson that getting involved in the festival was a good idea. In 1955 Harold Schonberg, reviewing that summer's Newport performances, knocked Erroll Garner's playing as "not good" and not even jazz.[29] (After a subsequent dust-up involving Glenn Gould, whose technique he abhorred, Schonberg was perceived as being hostile to Columbia artists. The Times would keep Schonberg as its chief music critic but turn to John S. Wilson as its full-time jazz critic.) For Avakian, the eureka moment was hearing Miles Davis solo on "'Round Midnight," his decision made there to sign Davis if he still wanted to be signed. The following summer Wein made an agreement with Irving Townsend about making recordings of the 1956 festival. "Our arrangement seemed like a good deal," Wein wrote. "For each artist recorded, the record company has to pay us an amount equal to that of the artist's performance fee. As it turned out, it was a terrible deal, because the record company got exclusive rights and all the royalties."[30] Out of that festival came the Columbia albums *Louis Armstrong and Eddie Condon at Newport*, *Dave Brubeck & J. J. Johnson-Kai Winding at Newport*, *Duke Ellington & Buck Clayton All-Stars at Newport* (two volumes), and *Ellington at Newport*.

This last album, which gave Ellington a career transfusion, was his best-selling LP up to that time and remains a project of enormous dispute. Wein and others insisted that half of Ellington's "Newport Suite," composed by Ellington for the band's appearance, was recorded several days after his appearance at the festival, along with a reworking of other tracks. But a bit of digging into the album's provenance yields information that runs counter to claims made by the reissue producer in rather self-aggrandizing notes on the Sony compact disc. The primary musical contention concerned Paul Gonsalves's legendary saxophone solo on "Diminuendo in Blue," 27 choruses' worth of dizzying improvisation that provided a bridge to "Crescendo in Blue" and wasn't captured by Columbia because Gonsalves was playing into the wrong mike. Fortunately, Voice of America had also recorded the concert, making the solo available many years later to Columbia. But there was nothing sinister or deceptive about the re-recordings done a couple of days after the festival— *at Ellington's behest*. Commentators have made it sound as though the despotic record company forced Ellington into the studio to patch pieces that were flubbed, but this was Ellington's decision entirely. A recording session for July 9 had already been booked by Columbia, at Ellington's request, in case there were mistakes. Avakian said to Ellington, "But what if people ask, 'How come I don't hear on the record the obvious wrong notes I heard at the concert?' and Ellington replied, 'Ask them if they'd rather buy a record with mistakes or a performance without mistakes?'" Billy Strayhorn listened to what he could get of Gonsalves's earliest choruses and made a meticulous transcription during the morning studio session. And engineer Ad Theroux had tried to pull the Gonsalves solo into proper balance with adjustments on the control board; but, once Ellington heard the results in the booth, he knew these wouldn't quite work. Ellington didn't lose his temper and order the band to pack up; pro that he was, he completed the studio session to fill out what was needed. When the album was released on three LP sides, one of the jackets contained a photograph of Count Basie's drummer, Jo Jones, because Jones, sitting in the pit in front of the grandstand, egged on Gonsalves and the Ellington band by slapping out an infectious backbeat with a newspaper. The Jones photograph has infuriated purists (including the reissue producer) who go to some pains to remind listeners that Jones didn't, of course, play with the Ellington band; but it was Ellington himself, in his autobiography, Music Is My Mistress, who credited Jones with inspiring Gonsalves and the band into "the rhythmic groove of the century."[31] There was no "phony applause" on the three LP sides of Ellington at Newport, as the reissue producer claims, just applause recorded at the festival that was edited later. When Ellington appeared at Newport on July 7, 1956, he was hardly "excited by the prospect of a cover story at long last in Time magazine"; in fact he had no way of knowing about the story, which was arranged only in midsummer after Debbie Ishlon and George Avakian approached Time's managing editor Henry Anatole Grunwald about doing a piece on Ellington. (The cover story appeared on August 20, 1956.) The 1956 Newport Jazz Festival is a fascinating case because so much of its music ended up on Columbia disk. Still, like Harold Bloom's theory of poets needing to devour their artistic fathers as they make their own poetry, it's dispiriting to see younger jazz scholars make extravagant revisionist claims that have scant relation to what actually took place.

The following year George Wein's nose was again out of joint when the documentary Jazz on a Summer's Day, made by the photographer Bert Stern with Aram Avakian, was released with nary a mention of Wein, though George Avakian is listed in the closing credits as "Musical Director." Columbia, in Wein's view, had muscled its way into the Newport Jazz Festival, and though it proved to be an excellent recording venue for the label's jazz stars, it rankled Wein, whose dedication to the festival was beyond question.

•   •   •

As if Avakian weren't busy enough, there was the 1956 trip to San Francisco where he'd gone to hear the athlete turned singer Johnny Mathis. Mathis had been invited by pianist Vince Guaraldi to sit in at Ann's Four Forty Club, at 440 Broadway in San Francisco, a nightclub with a largely homosexual clientele. Mathis's manager, Helen Noga, who owned the Blackhawk jazz club with her husband, asked George Avakian to come down and hear Mathis at the Four Forty. Mathis had been a track-and-field star, reputed to have high-jumped 6' 5 1/2" in one track meet—only 2 3/4" short of the 1952 Olympic record.[32] When Avakian heard him that night, he didn't sound quite like anybody else.

But that's not how he came off on his first record. The problem with Johnny Mathis, according to Mitch Miller, was that the arrangements and selections of standards (Cole Porter's "Easy to Love," for one) made him sound like too many other singers. "Johnny Mathis's first album just didn't work," Miller said. "This record didn't sell at all. His manager, Helen Noga, literally cried in my office! So I said I will do one session with Johnny. I see qualities in his voice, but I have to find songs to fit those qualities. Ray Conniff showed up."[33] Miller put Conniff to work on the new Johnny Mathis; out came "Wonderful Wonderful" and "It's Not for Me to Say," with Dick Hyman's kite-tail piano rippling in the breeze. Miller knew that Conniff, sober, could arrange entire albums of this stuff.

And Conniff did. Out they came, album after Columbia album, using that same formula. It was background music that could be offensive for being so professionally inoffensive. And it *was* professional; every number boasted factory-inspected arrangements—never a voice or a trombone out of place, never a shock to the ear. In one episode of the TV series *Seinfeld*, George Costanza (Jason Alexander) is trying to impress a young woman by pretending that his parents' apartment is his own; she asks if the Ray Conniff records on the shelf are his. It wasn't that Conniff was so old-fashioned, but that his Columbia recordings appealed to people who otherwise didn't listen much to music.

Beyond the easy-listening sameness of the Conniff recordings, which were particularly popular with Columbia Record Club subscribers, there were those album covers—invariably featuring a beautiful white model, either alone or surrounded by men. This wasn't unusual; Percy Faith's covers were given a similar gauzy high-fashion treatment. But after a while Conniff had more artwork input than most Columbia artists because, by 1960 or so, he and Mathis were the most consistent pop sellers on the label. In later years Conniff would use his second wife, Vera, on his covers.[34]

Meanwhile, by the winter of 1957, the success of Johnny Mathis's albums was almost a sure thing—a phenomenon in the business, considering that his first commendable semi-jazz album was ignored. Stan Kavan and Mitch Miller were looking for a way to get the youth market, which had traditionally been for singles, interested in albums. Mathis's popularity with both adults and kids (who bought his singles) was the launching pad for the "Greatest Hits" concept. *Johnny's Greatest Hits* was released in 1958; *More Johnny's Greatest Hits* followed.[35] The concept would eventually be applied to recording artists who didn't even know they'd had hits.

●   ●   ●

In the middle of the 1950s Columbia was getting fat like a king, with few signs of ill health. Masterworks, still directed by David Oppenheim and injected with a certain robust whimsy by the producer Howard Scott, was holding its own, at least as far as classical divisions went. George Avakian and the producers he'd brought in to help—Cal Lampley and Irving Townsend, with Bob Prince and Teo Macero soon to arrive— were building the strongest jazz catalog in the business. And Mitch Miller, with the musical assistance of Faith and Conniff and other arranger-leaders, had already turned Columbia's popular division into a hit-making juggernaut.

Even before he had advised CBS to back *My Fair Lady*, an artistic tip of pari-mutuel proportions, Lieberson had made the original cast recording his personal property. And he continued to refine his method of executive flattery, whether in the music world or beyond. He could be respectful and formal when necessary, although, when familiar enough with his correspondent, he preferred irreverence spiced with a dash of Jewishness. In a late-summer 1955 wire to the concert impresario Sol Hurok, Lieberson wrote:

DEAR SOL I HAVE TRIED TO REACH YOU ALL WEEK BECAUSE I LEAVE TODAY FOR SALZBURG BUT YOU ARE SUCH A MESHUGENER THAT WHEN I GOT BACK FROM CALIFORNIA YOU WENT THERE (.) I HAVE ASKED DAVID OPPENHEIM WHOM YOU WILL ENJOY MEETING BECAUSE I THINK YOU SHOULD KNOW SOME GENTILES TO PHONE YOU AND KEEP PHONING UNTIL HE REACHES YOU TO DISCUSS THE ISAAC STERN MATTER WHICH I AM SURE WE CAN BRING TO A SATISFACTORY CONCLUSION I WILL BE BACK SEPTEMBER 19TH AND WILL TAKE YOU TO DINNER IF YOU BRING THE BALLET GIRLS LOVE AND KISSES [SIGNED] GODDARD LIEBERSON, A SOL HUROK PRODUCTION.[36]

Flattery and jokes kept artists and their patrons in line—even a Sol Hurok.

More immediately on Lieberson's mind was the establishment at last of the Columbia Record Club. In August 1955 *Variety* carried a four-page spread about the new club; every month after that, in almost every major national magazine, the club advertised its new mail-order offerings. Both Conkling and Lieberson had had a lot to do with this, but Hal Cook's sales research proved critical at the last minute. Before the LP was developed the club wouldn't have been feasible because the mailings would cause too much breakage. Norman Adler, a Rosenman Colin attorney, was named the Record Club's first president. Headquarters were set up on West 47th, close enough to 799 Seventh Avenue to arrange an in-person conference in a matter of minutes but still separate from Columbia's offices. Les Wunderman, executive vice president of the Maxwell Sackheim Company, handled the advertising because he was so well-versed in the mail-order business. (Maxwell Sackheim had been writing mail-order ads since 1905 and was instrumental in launching the Book-of-the-Month Club in 1926.)[37] In the earliest months Lieberson selected most of the Record Club's offerings; when more pressing responsibilities made this impractical, a series of A&R directors came aboard. For its distribution center, Columbia chose Terre Haute, Indiana, where LPs were already being pressed, because the Midwestern location facilitated shipping to all parts of the country. Initially, the record industry was dubious because the idea of a record club encroached on the traditional methods of distribution by retailers and rack jobbers. Hal Cook's team reassured them that the Record Club, with its long advertising reach, would complement their business rather than detract from it. To protect retailers' interests, the Record Club wouldn't offer any Columbia recording until at least six months after its commercial release. And the club would be servicing potential record buyers in rural areas where there were no retail record stores, perhaps getting them interested in buying still more records when they became available.[38] At once diplomatic and aggressive in its introduction of the club, Columbia signed up more than 125,000 members in the first year of its existence.

If there was a Columbia division not performing up to expectations, it was probably the children's division, which was moving away from its in-house recordings featuring the likes of Percy Faith and Rosemary Clooney and was beginning to exploit television themes. Columbia had enjoyed a substantial hit with "The Ballad of Davy Crockett," so it released music and songs from *Walt Disney's Magic Kingdom, The Adventures of Rin Tin Tin,* and *Captain Kangaroo,* with the pacifying Bob Keeshan hosting as the Captain. (*Captain Kangaroo* went network in October 1955 and would remain a children's television institution for the next 30 years. Its theme song "Puffin' Billy" was a railroad ditty extracted from the Chappell library.) For years Columbia had placed a premium on children's recordings by Burl Ives ("Big Rock Candy Mountain,"), even if he was sometimes released on its Harmony budget label. But in 1955 Ives's acting career, which went back to the 1930s, took off with his appearance on Broadway as Big Daddy in *Cat on a Hot Tin Roof.* After that, his manager and wife, Helen Ives, always a nerve-pinching negotiator, made so many contractual demands that Ives spent the rest of his recording career at other labels, mostly at Decca. Hecky Krasnow, who had detoured Gene Autry toward kids and gold records with "Rudolph the Red-Nosed Reindeer" and "Peter Cottontail," had moved on. (In one of the more curious career shifts in the music business, Krasnow would soon produce Nina Simone's records, which were anything but childlike.) Krasnow was succeeded by Arthur Shimkin, who'd steered Golden Books and Records through profitable times. But the children's division had stalled, perhaps because the TV themes it now promoted could be heard at least weekly if not daily on television. Until *Sesame Street* came along a dozen years later, Columbia's last original children's successes were probably records by Rosemary Rice, the young actress who'd played Katrin, the daughter through whose eyes we see the Norwegian-American family, in *I Remember Mama*.[39]

●　●　●

In the spring of 1956 Columbia Records listened closely as the New York Philharmonic went through a cymbal-crashing, on the final day of its 114th season, that shook the music world. Music critic Howard Taubman wrote a piece in the Sunday *Times* titled "The Philharmonic—What's Wrong with It and Why."[40] Taubman attacked the Philharmonic's programming, charged the orchestra as being second-rate, and, while praising Dimitri Mitropoulos's ability to communicate intensity when conducting Berg, Schoenberg, or Richard Strauss, decried his lack of subtlety for more romantic pieces and his inability to lead as musical director. Mitropoulos had led the Philharmonic since 1951 and was considered an important Masterworks artist. The Taubman piece jackhammered right through the Philharmonic board and broke ground for the ascension of Leonard Bernstein as the first American-born conductor of a major American orchestra. By 1956 Bernstein had already been associated with Columbia Records for several years, and, besides the recent original cast recording of *Candide*, Columbia had kept him close at hand, first through David Oppenheim, then through Lieberson.

In June 1956 Lieberson ascended another step—several steps, actually, because everything seemed to be happening at once, and they built on one another. His determination to have Columbia Records own most if not all of the musical *My Fair Lady* would enrich the label and make him seem wiser than ever. Martin Mayer, who had been reporting on the recording industry for the *New York Times*, wrote an admiring profile of Lieberson for *Esquire*. The profile was published right after Lieberson was named president.

Jim Conkling had wanted out for a while. His wife Donna King didn't care for the East Coast, not even the relatively sylvan Bronxville, and both Conklings were observant Mormons who felt out of place in New York. In 1951 Frank Stanton had brought Conkling in over Lieberson because Conkling was a management guy, while Lieberson, as Stanton saw it at the time, had worked entirely on the creative end and didn't yet know the ropes. During the next five years Columbia Records began to dominate the industry, and Stanton focused on Conkling as his own probable successor. But this would mean bringing Conkling over to the television network—a position of far greater power and as close to Paley and Stanton as anyone could get. Twenty-four hours after Stanton offered Conkling the position that network head Jack Van Volkenburg was vacating, Conkling told him he was resigning altogether. Stanton was stunned.[41]

Just as *Esquire* was set to publish the profile of Columbia vice president Lieberson, making him sound as though he were already president, Stanton offered him the job in name. Conkling officially resigned on June 1, 1956, and CBS put out a press release on June 4, citing "personal and business reasons in order to relocate to California, where he will establish independent production activities."[42] That summer the Conklings returned to Los Angeles. A year and a half later, Conkling took over the struggling Warners record operation and, with the critical help of two Columbia refugees, began to turn it around.

Back in New York, Lieberson polished his own profile by shedding his assistant, Dinorah Press. Capable and loyal, Press was especially friendly with the Schneiders, Sasha and Mischa, and adored classical music in general and Lieberson in particular. Among Columbia producers, though, there was a feeling that Press simply knew too much about Lieberson. She had to go. After that, Lieberson took on a series of assistants, some of them as devoted as Press but none of them permitted anywhere near his psyche.

Lieberson's charm was immense, though, and Press remained loyal to him. She went to Angel Records and continued to write to him now and then. "Goddard would fire you," Howard Scott said, "and as you backed out of his office you'd thank him."[43]

The Liebersons' East 61st Street house was often referred to as a townhouse, as if its description as a brownstone were too inelegant for a family of such social station. In the same inflated manner Liebersons' Japanese houseman, Kusumi, was often described as a gourmet chef. A native of a Japanese fishing village, he taught himself how to cook basic American food as it was requested. During the week Kusumi lived upstairs in a room next to Peter Lieberson and performed most of the duties of a butler; on weekends he went home to his wife, Tomi, who lived in one of the outer boroughs.[44] Lieberson's friends imputed to Kusumi an intimate knowledge of his employer. That might have been true. A butler in one of the most storied neighborhoods in the world, Kusumi was certainly a talisman of Lieberson's ascension in New York culture as well as at Columbia Records. Kusumi could prepare breakfast for the Lieberson boys before they went off to school, then begin cooking for that evening's dinner party of musicians and actors. "The Lunts! How marvelous!" mimics Holden Caulfield in *The Catcher in the Rye*, and although he's sending up the cultural pretensions of his friend Sally, he might as well have been imitating Lieberson, who actually knew the Lunts and wrote to them like a son affectionately checking in with his parents.[45]

12
Catching Up to Victor

More than most labels, Columbia Records appreciated humor on record. Victor Borge was a Danish delight, at home in the English language as he was in his music-filled brain, as vast as the Masterworks catalog. Red Buttons was on the label with "The Ho Ho Song" and other special material. Art Carney, then appearing as sewer worker Ed Norton in *The Honeymooners*, made a few records under the supervision of Columbia producer Gene Becker; "Song of the Sewer," another testament to the marketing power of television, sold hundreds of thousand of copies. Carney and Buttons were both known as second bananas and, though Carney had sung briefly with Horace Heidt's orchestra, they were funnymen first and last.

On the other hand, Columbia's West Coast A&R man Paul Weston had been a musician all his life. In a 1955 edition of the *Columbia Retailer*, Weston says he's made a special trip East, and we hear him arriving on a horse. He hadn't been invited to participate in an earlier jam session, he says, because of professional jealousy on the part of Percy Face. Of course Weston means *Faith*. He plays a cauliflower-ear rendition of "Stardust," one discordant passage after another, and you can't help wondering what the gag is.[1] In fact it was an act he'd cooked up with his wife, Jo Stafford, when they entertained at parties in Hollywood. Stafford played the part of housewife Darlene Edwards, who had sacrificed a singing career for marriage but still sang now and then, accompanied by her husband, both of them musically inept. Avakian heard Weston's playing as the husband and, persuading him to prepare enough songs in that manner to fill an LP, dubbed him Jonathan Edwards. At the time Kapp Records had launched the career of the florid pianist Roger Williams to compete with Columbia's Liberace. "Roger Williams was also the name of a Revolutionary era New England preacher, who with his followers founded the state of Rhode Island," Avakian wrote. "Jonathan Edwards was another clerical leader (in Connecticut) of the time, and my residential college at Yale was named after him." Darlene and Jonathan Edwards made at least four albums, all of them selling fairly well as party items. There would have been nothing funny about them, of course, if Stafford hadn't been one of the most gorgeously in-control singers to come out of the war years. When you hear her as Darlene Edwards singing sharp on "Autumn in New York," you hesitate for a moment because it's subtly rather than overtly awful.[2]

Lieberson was supportive of almost any kind of pop recording material, even stuff that wasn't to his taste, as long as it sold enough to help pay for Masterworks. Even though he didn't care for rock 'n' roll, he could defend it persuasively. Sammy Davis Jr., probably inveigled into a movement led by Clare Boothe Luce, who was vociferous in her loathing of the movie *The Blackboard Jungle* and its rock 'n' roll soundtrack, tried to enlist Lieberson's support to forge a committee decrying the music. "My second reservation is that a 'powerhouse' committee made up of all of the top names in the music industry," Lieberson replied to Davis, "to fight juvenile delinquency somehow conveys the idea of a tacit admission that music, and pop music in particular, is connected with juvenile delinquency. I emphatically do not believe this to be the case. Perhaps it is true that juvenile delinquents do like certain types of pop music extant, but I do not believe that music can contribute to juvenile delinquency. Anyone who has a scientific interest in the subject knows that the origins are much deeper and are rooted in the psychological, sociological, and economic foundations of the family unit. Therefore, a song entitled 'Don't Be a Juvenile Delinquent' is not going to stop juvenile delinquency any more than a song entitled 'Don't Have Cancer' is going to prevent cancer."[3] Lieberson's stance was so close to that of Frank Sinatra's a decade earlier, when Sinatra was duking it out with Artur Rodzinski, you might conclude it had been conceived by the same publicist.

Columbia was only marginally involved with rock 'n' roll anyway. Mitch Miller was still seen as the warder at the gates, refusing to permit any three-chord nonsense from slipping through. Roy Hamilton's records on Epic were heard by many as rock 'n' roll, but there wasn't much more than that. At an April 1957 CBS stockholders' meeting, a songwriter named Gloria Parker, who held one share of CBS stock, demanded that the company divest itself of its 9 percent interest in BMI because it promoted "this rock 'n' roll junk which is creating juvenile delinquency." People who hated rock 'n' roll really, really hated it, but perhaps none more so than those composers and lyricists who, trained in Tin Pan Alley song construction, couldn't sell their work. Meanwhile Lieberson, who was about to receive an honorary doctorate in music from Temple University, felt it was incumbent on him to defend all kinds of music. And so he did.[4]

* * *

Lieberson probably wouldn't have gone to hear Miles Davis on his own. But once Avakian finally signed Davis to Columbia, Lieberson appreciated him. 'Round About Midnight, displaying Davis as hipster nonpareil, came first. For the next Davis album, Avakian wanted either Gunther Schuller or Gil Evans to write arrangements for a big band behind Miles. Evans was hired. The result, recorded on three nonconsecutive days in May 1957 at 30th Street, was Miles Ahead—Miles Davis plus nineteen musicians, all playing to Evans's beautiful charts. (One of the numbers was Dave Brubeck's "The Duke," composed in honor of you know who in 1955 while Brubeck was listening to the windshield wipers as he drove his son to nursery school in the rain.) The embarrassing joke about Miles Ahead was Columbia's initial marketing plan, featuring a white fashion model on a sailboat, with a little boy in the background. Miles screamed bloody murder. "I told 'em to take it off," he told an English jazz magazine many years later. "There's some sad things happen, man."[5] *Milestones*, with Miles's then current quintet, roared out the following year. Having heard the title track or Red Garland's blocky-happy rendition of "Billy Boy," who can forget them? *Porgy and Bess* resumed the collaboration with Gil Evans. Columbia producer Calvin Lampley, who had been first hired by Howard Scott to edit tape and then brought into A&R by Avakian, conceived the project and put it together, but Davis liked to tell journalists that he thought of it because his future wife Frances Taylor was then appearing in the *Porgy and Bess* revival at City Center (1957).[6] The absurdly beautiful *Sketches of Spain* was the third Davis-Evans collaboration and, despite the impressionistic title, maybe the most thematically cohesive. The centerpiece of the album was the excerpt from *Conciertio de Aranjuez*, the Rodrigo composition that's been a guitarist's dream since it was first published. Hearing the Columbia record after it went on sale, Rodrigo, through his Paris publisher, threatened legal action because he was offended by the jazz treatment of his composition. Teo Macero wrote to the publisher suggesting Rodrigo hold off on legal action until his first royalty check arrived. Columbia never heard from Rodrigo or his representatives again.[7]

By then George Avakian was gone, leaving the full-time chore of caretaking Miles Davis to others.

• • •

At a mere 38, George Avakian was among the most veteran of jazz record producers, even if jazz occupied only part of his Columbia time. By 1957 he'd been at it for two decades. His ears rarely failed him. His manner was polite, low-key, and modest. Goddard Lieberson could navigate his way through at least four languages—but so could Avakian. There had been a touch of condescension in May 1952 when Lieberson, responding to Doubleday editor Ken McCormick's inquiry about commissioning a biography of Bessie Smith, wrote back, "I think a book on Bessie Smith might be very worthwhile. The reason I thought I'd call you about the figures [regarding sales of the albums] was that I had in mind to recommend to you a boy who works for us here, who is a great expert on Bessie Smith. Indeed, one of the few around. His name is George Avakian. If you want to know more about him, please phone me."[8] The "boy" was then 33 years, two months, and four days old.

For the most part, though, Lieberson left Avakian alone because his recordings yielded profits. Avakian's international duties still took up a lot of time. Meanwhile the new LP made it easier to create a buzz around international stars. To suggest two obvious reasons: placing several songs instead of just two on a single disk gave American listeners time to absorb the work of that artist who, more likely than not, was getting only limited radio play; and the album format accommodated extensive notes, so an American listener could learn about, say, Columbia's long-time artist Charles Trenet.

The LP also arrived in a postwar period in which Europe was more familiar than ever to Americans. Airlines like TWA and Pan Am scheduled more flights to Paris, London, and Rome. Hollywood movies were just entering their international phase, a brief era when tax breaks made filming in Europe more feasible. Avakian remained closely linked to his beloved Paris through his younger brother Aram, a photographer, film editor, and future director. Aram, known to his friends as Al, had also gotten his degree at Yale and decided to do graduate work in French literature when he got out of the navy. Through the G.I. Bill of Rights he studied at the Sorbonne and fell in with a bunch of Americans, some of them connected to the upstart *Paris Review*.

"Al would write to me about what was happening there," Avakian remembered, "and [drummer] Kenny Clarke had just gone there and he would say, 'Send me some records from the States; we can't get them here. Send me duplicates because I can trade them here for something else.' In those days 78s still brought good money on the black market. He was always reluctant to take money from Mom and Dad and he tried to support himself.

"Inez Cavanaugh, the pop singer, opened a restaurant called Chez Inez on the Left Bank, and Al took a job there as a waiter. In walks Doris Duke and Porfirio Rubirosa, who was of course a fascist s.o.b. So Al made sure to spill soup all over Rubirosa. That made him a hero in the circles he was in."[9]

Al introduced George to the music of Edith Piaf. In early 1950 Avakian made the famous recording of Edith Piaf singing her own lyrics to "La Vie en Rose." The tune was by the Spanish-born Louis Louiguy and had been recorded two years earlier on Columbia by Buddy Clark, whose Anglicized version (Mack David's lyrics) was called "You're Too Dangerous, Cherie." Piaf's version had such a dreamy, wistful tone that many listeners assumed it to be a World War I chanson. It proved so popular, and so quickly, that Radio City Music Hall incorporated it into a live stage show called "Going Places" for two weeks in March; the places were London, Paris, Dublin, and Vienna, and the Paris set displayed a giant record onstage while "La Vie en Rose" played.[10] Avakian also recorded Piaf singing "Autumn Leaves" in English (Johnny Mercer's loose translation of Jacques Prevert), in New York.

Also in New York Avakian recorded the expatriate English journalist Alistair Cooke. Playing sixteen jazz-inflected songs on piano, Cooke wove a commentary between the LP's tunes. *An Evening with Alistair Cooke*, its album cover drawn by the journalist, was released by Columbia in 1954. Cooke became, in the words of his biographer Nick Clarke, "perhaps the only man in history to hold, at the same time, a White House press pass and membership of Local 802."[11]

Georges Meyerstein was the recording honcho at Columbia's European partner Philips. During a meeting of the international divisions in Chicago, Avakian said he wanted to make a record that covered three different places—Paris, Rome, and Spain, with London waiting in the wings as the fourth. Avakian's idea was that three Columbia music directors—Percy Faith, Andre Kostelanetz, and Paul Weston—would each make an album; it was just a question of divvying up the geography and the music to go with it. Avakian was particularly determined to call the Paris album *I Love Paris*, after the Cole Porter song from *Can-Can*. Meyerstein mentioned the 21-year-old Michel Legrand as a candidate for the assignment. Avakian was skeptical that a young French composer-arranger could compete in the American marketplace with Columbia's big guns. But Meyerstein persuaded Avakian to listen to tapes of Legrand. Once he did, Avakian knew the kid could do it. After the album was almost put together, Avakian turned to the new art director, Neil Fujita, and said, "How can we express Paris without the usual Eiffel Tower and all that?" Fred Plaut, apprised of the dilemma, told Avakian that he'd taken a photograph that might work. The result is one of the great unsigned covers of all time—a Cartier-Bresson–like shot of a French pumpkin vendor wearing a beret, a smock, Coke-bottle spectacles, and an enigmatic smile. Al Avakian wrote the liner notes for the American release. (The French album was released with a different cover and Legrand listed as "Big Mike" because, as the son of the popular French bandleader Raymond Legrand, he was determined to avoid accusations of nepotism.)[12]

Jim Conkling supported Avakian's international recording because it usually made money. After becoming president, Lieberson did, too, though often with tighter budget constraints because there was ever more pressure from CBS. One key project involved Lotte Lenya. In 1956 Lenya and second husband George Davis were working on a recording of the Brecht-Weill *Mahagonny*, one in a series of recordings of the Kurt Weill canon, in Hamburg, under Philips supervision. (Lenya had been Weill's widow.) In New York Lieberson was aghast at the expense reports and summoned Avakian, who was coproducing the recording with Davis. "I've been looking at these bills that Lenya and George Davis have run up. We should drop this project. It's never going to pay." For several reasons Avakian tried to talk Lieberson out of killing the recording; the best reason was that the tapes coming back from Hamburg sounded terrific. Still, Lieberson balked, and left it to Avakian to wield the ax. A few hours later the art director Neil Fujita found Avakian holding his head in his hands. "What's the matter, George?" said Fujita. Avakian explained the crisis at hand. Fujita, a great fan of Lenya's, told him not to worry and asked Avakian to see him in his office that afternoon. When Avakian appeared, Fujita showed him a layout he'd centered on Lieberson holding a pen and proclaiming the importance of the Weill series. Once Lieberson, never reticent about being photographed as Columbia Records's executive leader, saw the flattering layout he allowed the Lenya-Davis project to proceed. Eventually the Brecht scholar Eric Bentley wrote to Lieberson to congratulate him and Columbia on the new *Mahagonny*. "I think it is the best of all the attempts to represent the genius of Brecht and Weill on disks."[13]

Avakian's friendship with Lenya brought dividends for other musicians. In the middle of the *Mahagonny* project Avakian persuaded Louis Armstrong to record Weill's "Moritat" ("Mack the Knife"), which gave Armstrong a presence on even nonjazz-oriented jukeboxes across the country. Some years later Avakian would record Sonny Rollins on the same tune, and the result was a jazz classic.

No question, Avakian was overworked. To ease the load, earlier in the decade he'd arranged for Irving Townsend to come into pop A&R from advertising, and brought in Cal Lampley to help produce as well. Lampley had graduated from North Carolina State University and studied piano with Lillian Freundlich at the Peabody Conservatory in Baltimore, hoping to become a concert pianist. Finances forced him to take a job editing the Masterworks product and, with Howard Scott overseeing his work, related fare on labels pressed by Columbia. In fact Lampley made his concert debut at Carnegie Recital Hall in 1956, long after he had begun editing for Columbia.[14] Vin Liebler, who was still running engineering, was willing to permit Lampley to jump over to A&R as long as Avakian found someone to take Lampley's place.

Avakian came up with Teo Macero, a saxophonist and composer who'd come out of Juilliard with Bachelors and Masters degrees. Attilio Joseph Macero was born in Glen Falls, New York, in 1925, raised there, and spent four years in the navy before heading to the Juilliard in New York. He taught music in New Jersey and New York and played saxophone in various bands, notably with Charles Mingus on the 10" LP *Explorations*, issued on Debut Records in 1953. Macero was a disciple of Edgard Varèse and was particularly simpatico with some of the more difficult contemporary composers whose work would later come to be regarded as Third Stream (though Gunther Schuller hadn't yet conceived the phrase). Knowing that George Avakian had produced early recordings by John Cage and Alan Hovhaness, Macero asked him if he'd listen to some acetates of his compositions.[15]

Preceding Macero's arrival at the label, Avakian had the help of the young composer Bob Prince. In fact, Macero and Prince each contributed a twenty-minute side to the album *What's New?*, conceived by Avakian. Leonard Bernstein, impressed by Macero's piece, commissioned him to write a concerto for jazz sextet. The result was *Fusion*, which Bernstein and the Philharmonic performed in 1958. Jerome Robbins, who'd choreographed Bernstein's music for *Fancy Free* and its fully grown issue, *On the Town*, and would partner with him for *West Side Story*, was taken with Prince's composition. "Keep three of the moods," Robbins told Prince about his piece, "and add two more." Prince's expanded piece became Robbins's dance *N.Y. Export: Opus Jazz*, a benign variation on the Jets and Sharks turf wars, which also premiered in 1958.

● ● ●

Avakian had other responsibilities: Miles and Brubeck and Garner and Ray Conniff and the Newport Jazz Festival and Johnny Mathis's first album and many more artists than he could handle properly, though he did so anyway. By now Irving Townsend had taken over much of the Mahalia Jackson and Duke Ellington recording work; Teo Macero had begun his long professional relationship with Miles Davis; and Mitch Miller, with Helen Noga peering over his shoulder, had assumed control of Mathis's Columbia output. Avakian had been running two departments, neither of which paid him royalties beyond his contracted Columbia salary, each of which alone would have exhausted any one man. He had recently supervised his one and only original cast recording, of the David Martin–Langston Hughes show *Simply Heavenly* (based on Hughes's stories about Negro self-styled philosopher Jesse B. Simple), and Lieberson had denied him a producer's credit because the show had opened not in the theater district but on West 85th Street. At last Avakian's health broke. He didn't sleep for 48 hours, then finally went to sleep and couldn't wake up. Columbia's physician Jack Nelson examined Avakian and, diagnosing hepatitis and jaundice, prescribed bed rest. Avakian took his rest in

Bermuda where, joined by his wife and one of his daughters, he realized he had to make some changes.

When he returned to New York, he made arrangements to partner with Dick Bock at Bock's West Coast–based jazz label World Pacific. Producing from the East Coast, Avakian would be able to maneuver at his own pace, and without all the corporate manipulations he detested. He resigned from Columbia Records on his birthday, 1958. Gerry Mulligan tipped Avakian to office space in the Carnegie Hall building. Avakian, who had already put up money for this joint venture with Bock, prepared to move in. Three weeks later he went back to 799 Seventh Avenue to find that essential papers, including extensive correspondence with Armstrong and Ellington, and rare test pressings had been stolen.[16]

The Bock-Avakian joint venture soon collapsed. Later that year Avakian went to work as a freelance producer for his old boss Jim Conkling, who had signed on to run the revived Warners label in Los Angeles. Conkling had already hired Columbia's revolutionizing sales maven Hal Cook, who had been with him at Capitol in the 1940s, though Cook remained in New York. Avakian did, too. He and Anahid had three children and a spacious apartment on Central Park West. There was jazz to be heard in town every night of the week. Avakian also maintained close ties to his family and their rug business, located for many years at 33rd Street and Fifth Avenue. Plentiful Hollywood sunshine and movie stars weren't enough to induce him to give all that up.

But movie stars were bread and butter to Warners. The combination of stereophonic sound and the studio's access to stars became Jim Conkling's foundation for the new record label. Warners' parent company had begun to produce a number of television shows under the imprimatur of William T. Orr, Jack Warner's son-in-law. Once a month Avakian and Cook would fly to the West Coast to meet with Conkling and several other executives at the Burbank offices. The idea was to audition actors under Orr's aegis to see if any of them could sing. As Fred Goodman recounted in his book *Mansion on the Hill*, an early experiment of Conkling's was to have his pal Jack Webb (*Pete Kelly's Blues, Dragnet*) recite lyrics to love songs in front of an orchestra.[17] Even with Billy May's orchestra behind him, Webb's monotonic baritone *Sprechstimme* made Rex Harrison sound as loose as Satchmo. But Webb regarded himself as hip to jazz, and the album, *You're My Girl: The Romantic Reflections of Jack Webb*, was recorded in stereo. After Avakian held a round of auditions over the next month or so, two candidates survived: Dorothy Provine, who appeared as a nightclub hostess in *The Roaring Twenties*, and Connie Stevens, who was part of the cast of *77 Sunset Strip*.[18] Edd "Kookie" Byrnes, that show's heartthrob with the doo-wop pompadour, couldn't sing a note; naturally, Avakian, Cook, and Conkling saw this as a wasted merchandising opportunity. Avakian ad-libbed eight syllables—"Kookie, Kookie, lend me your comb"—and got comedy writer Irving Taylor to write an entire song. The result had Connie Stevens singing and Edd Byrnes safely just talking. It was a smash hit.

Meanwhile Avakian got the opportunity to record Bob Prince's *N.Y. Export: Op. Jazz*.[19] Widely regarded as a kid brother to Leonard Bernstein's music for *West Side Story*, *N.Y. Export* sounds more like Elmer than Leonard, with drum-heavy echoes of *Man with the Golden Arm*. It was odd that Avakian and Prince, former Columbia colleagues who had done so much to strengthen the jazz and pop catalogs throughout the fifties, would have to get the piece recorded at another label altogether. But that was the way the music business blew.

Still, the numbers at Warners didn't stay up long enough to satisfy corporate director Herman Starr (who, like Avakian and Cook, was based in New York). Long distrustful of the record business, Starr had attained his power in the industry as a music publisher, building Music Publishers Holding Corporation, whose catalog included the work of Tin Pan Alley's leading lights, into a juggernaut. Starr rebuffed an attempt by Conkling and others to buy the record division and start again. Instead he slashed jobs and department budgets.

Within the next six months, though, on the recommendation of Chicago disk jockey Dan Sorkin, Avakian brought in Bob Newhart, an accountant who had not only never recorded but never performed before a live audience. After recording Newhart at a bottle club (you bring the bottle, they give you a membership card and mixers) in

Houston called the Tidelands, Avakian edited the tapes to what became *The Button-Down Mind of Bob Newhart*. Released in spring 1960, the album stayed at number one on the *Billboard* charts for 14 weeks and sat in the vicinity for another two years. In the 1960 Grammy Awards, it won Album of the Year and Best Comedy Performance, Spoken Word. Avakian received an override on his production chores—unlike his earnings at Columbia, this gave him a piece of the action—and he made more money from this comedy album than from all his jazz recordings combined.

That same year the Everly Brothers, who'd been recording on Cadence, became available. Avakian went to Nashville to sign them. The Everlys' "Cathy's Clown" topped the *Billboard* singles chart in 1960. At Warners—and later at RCA, where he went to work after Conkling retired—Avakian proved that his considerable gifts didn't depend on employment by Columbia Records.

●   ●   ●

Avakian's old supporter and colleague John Hammond hadn't yet returned to the label. But Hammond's long-ago discovery Billie Holiday, more aged and toxin-filled than most 42-year-olds, was back at Columbia by late 1957 and determined to record with the arranger-leader Ray Ellis. "It would be like Ella Fitzgerald saying she wanted to record with Ray Conniff," Irving Townsend said.[20] Ellis had been a Columbia Records salesman in Philadelphia, and was then just a few years out of playing bar mitzvahs and Jewish weddings.[21] An ace arranger, he went to his first conducting session and panicked. "The music is handed out," he told Joe Smith, "and Mitch Miller walks out and says, 'What are you waiting for?' You gotta understand, I never gave a dog a downbeat."[22] By the time Ellis began to make arrangements for Holiday, he was hardly an unknown quantity—he'd had hits with Bennett, Mathis, Sarah Vaughan, and Clyde McPhatter, among others—but it was his Columbia album *Ellis in Wonderland*, a particularly intelligent easy-listening compilation, that had caught Holiday's ear. One topsy-turvy aspect of a jazz musician backed by strings is that she must follow the music as written; those potentially exciting, curving avenues of improvisation are road-blocked. Despite this, few artists can resist the monument of such musical backing, whether it's *Charlie Parker with Strings* (on Verve) or Mahalia Jackson's *The Power and the Glory* (on Columbia, arranged and conducted by Percy Faith). The result of Holiday's and Ellis's collaboration was *Lady in Satin*, an LP consisting of 12 standards of a very high order, a release that effectively divided Holiday's fans into warring camps. It's a curious album, at once pleasant and troubling, for the vicissitudes of Holiday's life can be heard in almost every parched phrase. Townsend's liner notes suggest as much—"So a challenging idea in recording was undertaken because Lady wanted it so much"—and so do the muted color tones in Arnold Newman's cover photograph.[23]

After the sessions were in the can, Holiday and Ellis arrived separately at a midtown Manhattan party celebrating the album's completion. Later, Ellis feared that the strung-out Holiday wouldn't be able to get home on her own power, so, while he propped her up with one arm, he tried to hail them a cab with another. One available taxi after another cruised past, avoiding this mixed-race couple, a black woman and white man who appeared to be in an embrace and on their way home together.[24]

•   •   •

Through much of the first half of 1957 a striking young composer named Elizabeth Larsen was looking for a job. She'd studied composition at Bennington and Columbia, then gone to Hamburg on a Fulbright. In New York she went to see one of her Columbia mentors, the composer Otto Luening, to hear what he'd advise; Luening wanted her to teach. That wasn't what Larsen had in mind. Lotte Lenya, whom she'd gotten to know in Hamburg, gave Larsen a letter of introduction to the conductor Ernst Ansermet. Somehow Ansermet got her an interview at Columbia Records, the record company that had trailed RCA Victor in sales for many years but was gradually catching up. In May 1957 the personnel manager at Columbia Records hired Larsen—as a typist.[25]

Larsen went to work in the Data & Scheduling Department. Almost all of the company's printed material—payments, ad copy, record copy, editing sheets—crossed Larsen's desk and provided her with a quick education in how business was conducted at Columbia Records. Larsen was soon restless, though. She'd been dating David Jones, of the company's literary department, and Jones wanted her to write copy and liner notes. That wasn't quite what she wanted, either. Discreetly she interviewed at Westminster Records, the classical label whose long-playing disks had been pressed for many years by Columbia. While she waited for something to happen that summer she attended a party on the roof of 799, where she met Lieberson for the first time.

So she was surprised when she was called into the office of administrative vice president Albert Earl, who told Larsen, "We're thinking about moving you out of Scheduling." For a minute or so Earl kept using the first person plural, leaving Larsen to wonder who "we" meant. Then she turned around and saw Lieberson sitting behind her, studying her—he had been in the room the whole time. Lieberson told Larsen that he and Earl were considering whether to make her his secretary. Larsen, as headstrong as she was lovely, hadn't spent years studying piano and composition to become anybody's secretary. In fact she and Lieberson had each set James Joyce poems to music, though they didn't know they had this in common, and early on had set their sights on New York City. Larsen asked what would be expected of her. Lieberson couldn't say, apart from making coffee. Sensing she was being offered some kind of opportunity, Larsen agreed to become Lieberson's secretary.

The job, as it turned out, mostly required Larsen to keep people away from Lieberson while making them feel they had access to him. Perhaps because they were both musically accomplished, physically attractive, and in close proximity several hours of the day, people assumed (mistakenly) they were having an affair. The rumors reached Brigitta, who finally came into the office to meet the new secretary. "Ah! Goddard didn't tell me you were a redhead!" she said.

Larsen began to date Louis Lauer, who would eventually become her husband—making her Mrs. Lauer at the office. In the meantime she fiercely guarded the entryway to the president's office, even when Lieberson's own boss came knocking. CBS president Frank Stanton liked to call first thing in the morning, sometimes before Lieberson had arrived. Larsen was coached to always say, "I will have to go get him and have him call you back." But one morning Larsen forgot her instructions. "No, Dr. Stanton," she said guilelessly, "he hasn't come in yet." Each morning Lieberson ambled from his house on East 61st Street, between Second and Third Avenues, crosstown to 799 Seventh Avenue, at 52nd Street; it was his only regular exercise, and it often got him to the office as late as 9:45. On this morning Larsen reported what she'd said to Stanton. Lieberson, always mindful of how he was perceived by Stanton and CBS chairman William Paley, was upset that she hadn't somehow gotten word to him immediately. Larsen replied that Columbia Records made a substantial profit for CBS: *why should Dr. Stanton or anyone else care what time its president came in?*

Within a year Larsen learned that Mitch Miller's secretary was being paid $100 a week, $15 more than she was. Confronted with this discrepancy, Lieberson admitted it made no sense, raised Larsen to $110 a week and designated her his "assistant."

•   •   •

In the office one day Lieberson, notorious for his love of word and musical games, said to Larsen, "Let's each write down a piece of music we think the other won't recognize." So they each grabbed staff paper and a pencil. "You think George Marek does this in the office?" muttered Lieberson, referring to RCA Victor's recording chief, without glancing up. In 1928, seventeen years after Lieberson's birth and several years before Larsen entered the world, Aldous Huxley published his novel *Point Counter Point*. Referring to Beethoven's Quartet in A Minor, Huxley wrote:

> More than a hundred years before, Beethoven, stone deaf, had heard the imaginary music of stringed instruments expressing his inmost thoughts

and feelings. He had made signs in ink on ruled paper. A century later four Hungarians had reproduced from the printed reproduction of Beethoven's scribble that music which Beethoven had never heard except in his imagination. Spiral grooves on a surface of shellac remembered their playing.[26]

Lieberson and Larsen were, in effect, reversing that reproductive process in an office a few stories above Seventh Avenue. When Larsen showed her staff paper to Lieberson, he roared with laughter. "You thought I wouldn't know this?" he said. Larsen had written down the opening bars of Bartok's Third Piano Concerto. Lieberson explained that Gyorgy Sandor, the pianist who'd premiered the piece on February 8, 1946, with Eugene Ormandy and the Philadelphia Orchestra, had been a close friend since Lieberson first moved to New York in the late thirties.[27] A couple of months after the premiere, in fact, Sandor was staying at Lieberson's apartment on West 55th Street but had proved elusive, prompting a telegram from the head of Columbia Masterworks:

TRIED TO REACH YOU IN VAIN. WANT YOU TO GO TO PHILA TOMORROW, FRIDAY, TAKING SCORE AND PARTS OF BARTOK CONCERTO ON POSSIBILITY THAT YOU RECORD SAME WITH PHILA ORCHESTRA. YOU MUST BE THERE BY 4 P.M. GODDARD.[28]

Columbia had released the Ormandy-Sandor recording soon after that— one of the rare gaps in Larsen's knowledge of the label's catalog. It was hard to put one over on Lieberson.

•　　•　　•

In early 1954 RCA Victor, still feeling the sting of Columbia's secret development of the LP, made the leap into true stereo recording. Its engineers, using two-track tape and Ampex equipment, recorded Charles Munch and the Boston Symphony's reading of Berlioz's *The Damnation of Faust*.[29] Columbia's earliest stabs at stereo were cruder. The so-called binaural process, which was in more common use among FM radio stations, finally gave way to the much-improved stereo. The recording companies, embarrassingly, trailed behind the movie studios, particularly Twentieth Century Fox, in the development of stereo. When it arrived, stereo was both ballyhooed and raspberried. In Cole Porter's *Silk Stockings*, in 1955, the song "Stereophonic Sound" ribbed the movies' latest development—the promotion of it, anyway—comparing it with "glorious Technicolor" and "breathtaking Cinemascope."[30] Stereo wouldn't revolutionize the recording industry as the LP had, but it wasn't a gimmick. Stereo mattered because it made the recordings sound truer and better. "Not one musician of consequence believes that the monophonic system is better than the stereophonic for any kind of music," Remy Farkas of London Records told the *New York Times*. "If such a revolutionary change in recording were not an improvement, it would die—and deserve it."[31]

David Oppenheim, firmly in the stereo-is-better camp, needed help if he was going to record—and, in many cases, re-record—in stereo. Howard Scott was already up to his ears with Glenn Gould and other Masterworks artists. So Oppenheim brought John McClure up from the editing table.

McClure had joined Columbia Records in 1952. A record collector and amateur musician with a particular fondness for the harpsichord, McClure held various sound-related jobs in and around New York. In the Village for a while he tested amplifiers for the Electronic Workshop. The music critic Edward Tantall Canby hired him to produce music programs for WNYC. At the Carnegie Hall Recording Company he learned how to splice tape and edit music. Seymour Solomon of Vanguard Records sent McClure over to Columbia where he interviewed with Vin Liebler, by then the dean of record engineers.[32]

Now in A&R, McClure flew by the seat of his pants—literally. Handed a tape of the fourth and fifth movements of Mahler's Second Symphony, recorded in Carnegie Hall, McClure was told, "Edit this and take it out to Bruno Walter in Los Angeles." Walter had suffered his first major heart attack and moved west to be near his daughter and recuperate. McClure found the maestro eager to record in stereo—a privilege denied his rival Arturo Toscanini, who died before stereo took hold. McClure found a place to live and brought his family out. Walter prepared to record all nine Beethoven symphonies in stereo. Using the best musicians from the Hollywood studios, a West Coast version of the Columbia Symphony Orchestra was assembled. The contractor was Phil Kahgan, the LA Philharmonic's former first violist who also worked as contractor for the Paramount Pictures orchestra. The concertmaster was much-in-demand violinist Israel Baker (who, McClure recalled, casually chewed gum while playing Stravinsky's *Histoire du Soldat* for the first time).[33] For a recording studio McClure chose the old American Legion Hall, on Highland Avenue just south of the Hollywood Bowl, because, McClure said, "It had a wonderful, innocent bloom to it. But you could hear the ten-wheelers shifting as they lumbered up Cahuenga Pass." McClure and his team built sound locks and a control room. Through all this McClure got experience reading a score; after a while he always knew where the orchestra was.

From 1958 to 1960 McClure was based in Los Angeles, recording Bruno Walter as the great conductor neared the end of his life. McClure recorded Walter on 1/2" three-track tape and began to use a new number 37 Sony condenser microphone. To some ears, Walter's Mahler cycle overpowered even the Beethoven. These recordings are of the very highest level both in their interpretations and technical qualities. (Shortly after he returned to New York, McClure played the tapes for Leonard Bernstein. "Listen, and learn," he advised Bernstein.) Then again, Walter had long been one of Mahler's two or three greatest interpreters. In 1953, reviewing Walter's version of Mahler's Fourth Symphony, which had been broadcast from Carnegie Hall by CBS, Irving Kolodin wrote, "The ability to cast a spell, to hold the listener absorbed and unmindful of anything save the meaning and purpose of a piece of music, is certainly a prerequisite for any fine interpreter. Among present-day conductors it has one of its most powerful demonstrations when Bruno Walter conducts Mahler."[34] A decade later that remained true.

Apart from Walter, several Masterworks artists lived in the LA basin, Stravinsky perhaps the most prominent, and part of McClure's job was to keep track of them. He drove down to Palos Verdes to visit Columbia's longtime violin virtuoso Joseph Szigeti, who gave McClure a personal recital, though with a sadly wobbly pitch, and made him borscht. As for Walter, he was ready to record *Fidelio* with his Columbia Symphony Orchestra when he suffered the final heart attack.

While McClure was away from New York, Oppenheim left Masterworks. He had gone through some personal upheaval, including a divorce from Holliday and a new marriage to the soprano Ellen Adler, and was now taking a job in television—specifically on the series *Omnibus*.[35] (Over the next few years Oppenheim would move farther away from the music business and deeper into theatrical production.) Lieberson, declining to entrust Scott with running Masterworks, and sensing that McClure didn't care to grapple with the administrative end of the business, went looking for someone to direct the division. He found Schuyler Chapin on the isle of Eigg, in Scotland, to ask him to come see him when he returned to New York.

* * *

Chapin was a curious choice. Member of a Social Register family, Chapin was only 35 but had already enjoyed a rich career in music. He was not a musician per se—early on, Nadia Boulanger had pronounced him "without talent"—but knew music and handled plenty of musicians.[36] He had worked as a page and then an announcer for NBC's subsidiary Blue Network, until the government, citing antitrust laws, ordered NBC to divest its interest. The war would have interrupted him anyway. Chapin flew in the Troop Carrier Command in China and Burma and was awarded several medals before going back to work at NBC. In 1947 he married Betty Steinway, of the Steinway piano family, in the Church of the Epiphany.[37] After working as concert promoter for the New York Pops, Chapin was given a job at Columbia Artists Management International (CAMI) by its founder Arthur Judson. As Jascha Heifetz's tour manager he had to leave his wife and kids for months at a time and earned every penny of his salary. Heifetz refused praise as readily as he refused criticism and never, ever smiled, thereby discouraging an audience, in Chapin's words, from pouring out "its collective heart." At CAMI's offices, Chapin ran afoul of Judson's partner Ruth O'Neill, who would dock his pay for being late. O'Neill's antipathy might have had something to do with her romantic relationship with an aunt of Chapin's.[38] Whatever the cause of friction, Chapin went looking for a job. He briefly considered becoming first executive director of the new Music Center in Los Angeles, but finally thought the position was buried beneath by much higher-profile roles. So Chapin took his family to Eigg, in the Hebrides, for a much-needed vacation and to think about his options.

The call from Lieberson was a surprise. The village's sole telephone, so old that it had to be cranked to ring the operator, was owned by a Mrs. Rutherford. "I could hear clicks and voices from Mallaig to Fort William, Fort William to Edinburgh, Edinburgh to London, London to New York, and New York, it turned out, to the office of Goddard Lieberson. . . ." Lieberson hadn't met Chapin and asked him for a CV. On Chapin's end, several men sat around within earshot smoking pipes. That night Chapin went back to his family's quarters and, with only a gas lantern illuminating the page, wrote to Lieberson.[39]

By October, with Oppenheim's job vacant since July, Chapin joined Columbia Records as "executive coordinator" for Masterworks—a title that essentially split the directorship's responsibilities with McClure, who remained in charge of music. "McClure had already been given Oppenheim's office at 799 Seventh Avenue," Chapin recalled. "I had the smaller office but had it decorated with better furniture."[40] When Chapin asked Lieberson how he should proceed, Lieberson, characteristically, replied, "Use your imagination." By this time the Masterworks roster was unmatched: pianists Gould, Serkin, Eugene Istomin, and Philippe Entremont; violinists Stern and Francescatti; singers Eileen Farrell and Richard Tucker; Stravinsky; the Mormon Tabernacle Choir; the Philadelphia and Cleveland Orchestras; the New York Philharmonic; and Leonard Bernstein as an artist apart from the Philharmonic.

As Lieberson had surmised, Chapin's social skills and connections were considerable. Chapin figured out ways to bring in some new artists—the brilliant but gray-miened pianist Charles Rosen, for one, was placed on the Epic roster—and dealt with the old ones. Lieberson passed Chapin the sizzling baton of the elaborate Stravinsky project, with the composer conducting many of his works (sometimes with considerable involvement from his right-hand man Robert Craft) for Masterworks. After Stravinsky's recent recording of the Firebird did well for the Record Club, Chapin proudly sent the composer a royalty check for $25,000. A couple of weeks later Chapin was buzzed by his secretary Juanita. "Mistah Stravinsky is heah to see you," Juanita said in her Southern lilt, letting Chapin know that trouble was in the air. When Stravinsky appeared in Chapin's office, he removed the recent check from its envelope. "I have come here to thank you for my tip!" he said to Chapin. The check fluttered to the office floor. All the way down to the street, Chapin tried to smooth things over. But Stravinsky, who apparently regarded the check as parsimonious, stepped into a hired car and rode back to the Pierre where he was staying. Over the years Lieberson had had a bellyful of such behavior, though in this case it turned out to be little more than the composer's way of testing the new man.[41]

Glenn Gould was already there too. Gould had been produced mostly by Howard Scott. In fact the label had been apprised of his work when Sasha Schneider of the Budapest String Quartet heard him play in Washington in January 1955 and phoned Oppenheim. "You've got to sign this guy!" said Schneider.[42] Sure enough, Gould arrived in New York to play at Town Hall and soon signed with Columbia. Martin Mayer was then writing about music for Esquire when he got a call from Debbie Ishlon. "We've got this nut," Ishlon told him, "and everybody's talking about how marvelous he is, you never heard anything like this." Mayer went down to the 30th Street studio and saw Gould immerse his hands in scalding water until they were lobster red.[43] After Gould's Goldberg Variations—recorded at 30th Street on June 25, 1955, and produced by Scott—became a best seller, Life referred to him as the "Music World's

Wonder," making him out to be an eccentric young genius.[44] Gould's idiosyncrasies—the gloves and greatcoats, the collapsible chair replacing a standard piano bench, the weird rituals involving hygiene—put a lot of people off, including George Szell, who couldn't abide him. People who looked beyond the idiosyncrasies found Gould as amusing as he was dazzling. Scott, who once showed up with a gas mask for Gould to wear during a recording session (and Gould obligingly wore it), had been amused. Chapin was mostly amused. One day Gould happened to be in the office when Chapin was preparing to present an orchestral transcription of Richard Strauss's Enoch Arden to Claude Raines, who was booked to narrate over Eugene Ormandy and the Philadelphia Orchestra. Getting wind of the program, Gould began to hum the piece, his fingers flying across the desk. Mrs. Claude Raines walked in, took one look at the goofily grinning Gould and backed away as though he were diseased.[45] (The recording was subsequently made with Gould and Raines, and Joseph Scianni producing.)

●　●　●

Duke Ellington's eccentricities were of a more elegant cast. He slept in opulent hotel rooms around the world but wrote many of his more celebrated numbers riding as a passenger in the car of his saxophonist Harry Carney. Too vain to wear glasses, though he needed them, he would sometimes notice an unfamiliar manuscript on a piano and recognize it as his own composition, as Irving Townsend said, only by "feeling the music in his fingers." One evening at 30th Street Townsend was recording the Percy Faith Orchestra, starting at 7 P.M., with Ellington scheduled to record later, through the wee hours. Townsend was surprised when Ellington, who was rarely early or particularly interested in someone else's recording session, entered the control booth during Faith's session and settled in. When Faith finally came in to listen to a playback, he said, "Duke! What are you doing here?" "I want to learn how to write for strings," Ellington replied sincerely.[46]

Through the late fifties Ellington was enjoying the renewed attention he'd won at the 1956 Newport Festival. It helped that, as he reached 60, his creativity remained almost as fecund as it had been in the late 1930s and early '40s. But not every project soared as Ellington wanted it to. *A Drum Is a Woman* was recorded two months after that celebrated Newport appearance, but it sold poorly and was deleted from Columbia's catalog, over Ellington's objections, in 1960.[47] *Liberian Suite*, the Ellington album that had been so critical to the testing of the new long-playing record, was also cut out. Enamored of Elizabeth II—and she of him, apparently —Ellington composed *The Queen's Suite* for her, recording his lovely "Single Petal of a Rose" and two other tracks in April 1959. At the time the record went unreleased—a master was prepared, a gold disk issued privately to the Royal Family—according to an agreement between Ellington and Townsend, with Ellington retaining rights to release the entire *Suite* at a later date. Eventually Ellington reimbursed Columbia $2,500 in production costs to buy it back. Eighteen years later Norman Granz released *The Queen's Suite* on Pablo, leaving both Townsend's and Teo Macero's names off the credits. The album won a Grammy in 1977, three years after Ellington's death.[48]

There were other Ellington-related follies. A batch of songs recorded with, of all singers, Johnnie Ray went unreleased, due largely to conflicting publishing interests. The session took place at 30th Street in September 1958. As the lyricist Don George remembered it, Johnnie Ray was so disconcerted by Billy Strayhorn's characteristically free-flowing arrangement of one number that he stopped Ellington and his band midway through and said, "Gentleman, what the fuck is this, an LP?" The musicians cracked up.[49] On an album apparently conceived by Townsend, Ellington's distilled version of *The Nutcracker Suite* was paired with Suites 1 and 2 of *Peer Gynt* but received blistering reviews. Townsend, trading like a Major League general manager, permitted Ellington to make a Roulette album with Louis Armstrong in exchange for Roulette allowing Count Basie to make *First Time! The Count Meets the Duke* for Columbia.[50] The album sold well, but, like the *Nutcracker* project, was shrugged off by critics, who seemed to regard it as musical bombast.

(It wasn't. "For You" and "Until I Met You" are only two of several memorable tracks.)

For the Ellington soundtrack of *Anatomy of a Murder*, director Otto Preminger wanted Mitch Miller to supervise—but he also wanted reassurance that Columbia would give it priority handling. "You know that *Anatomy of a Murder* has been the Number One best seller all through 1958," Preminger wrote. "In April a paperback edition will come out and the first printing will be 1,250,000 copies. So, we have a big title—and let me know what you think you can do for it in exploitation and maybe we can draw up a contract and get together for once on a record on my film." Preminger mentioned the distinctive Saul Bass titles, which provided the record cover.[51] Beginning in late May 1959, Ellington recorded the soundtrack with prosecutorial speed because the picture was set to open July 1.

Townsend might have felt pushed to the side by the *Anatomy* recording. He fired off a letter to Ellington's representative acknowledging Duke's "belligerent" dissatisfaction with Columbia, particularly what Duke regarded as meager advertising except by the Record Club, and said his patience with Duke had run out.[52]

Ellington was only a fraction of Townsend's troubles. His oldest daughter Susie was afflicted with Schoenberg's Disease, a rare and crippling bone disease—sometimes referred to as marbles bones—whose victims tend not to live long. Susie was then seven, her vision extremely limited since birth, and Townsend learned of a new treatment she could receive at UCLA, under the care of Dr. Marshall Urist, an orthopedic surgeon there. This dovetailed with the carrot of a promotion to vice president—and to run Columbia A&R on the West Coast. Townsend was ambivalent: he didn't want to leave Connecticut—the Townsends occupied a house at the border of Weston and Wilton, on property owned by the socialite Alice DeLamar—but he wanted Susie to have the best care, and the promotion was contingent on his going west.[53] After Townsend made several forays to Los Angeles in '59, the family made the move. Townsend got his vice presidency. Because of Susie's condition, he never regretted the transfer. But over the course of the next 15 years his feelings about working for Columbia Records on the West Coast would become increasingly conflicted.

•   •   •

In March 1958, addressing the first annual disk jockey convention, held in Kansas City, Mitch Miller decried the high percentage of radio shows and records aimed at teenagers. He wanted the delegates to agree that "much of the juvenile stuff pumped over the air wave these days hardly qualifies as music."[54] Miller got an enthusiastic response from the DJs. But radio shows were already being heavily programmed by teen-conscious programmers.

The emergence of rock 'n' roll as the dominant force in popular music didn't occur in a vacuum. To adolescents, the adult world seemed remote, or petrified, or both, cut off from what the writer George W. S. Trow called "the mode of exploration, becoming, growth, and pain."[55] Rock 'n' roll, however musically crude trained musicians found it, reflected—was in fact propulsed by—adolescent agitation (Trow calls it "nervousness").

Mitch Miller didn't want to make agitating music, just music that pleased his adult constituency. Two months after the Kansas City address, he released the first album in what would become a major industry phenomenon—his sing-along series. The idea for the sing-alongs had come a few years earlier from Stan Kavan, then Columbia's national merchandising manager. Kavan suggested that he make some recordings of the songs servicemen sang together during the war, and maybe call them "Barracks Ballads" (with apologies to Kipling and his *Barrack-Room Ballads*).[56] Miller already had a kind of model—the Landt Trio, three men in a sing-along show on CBS radio—and, in the wake of Columbia Legacy's *The Confederacy*, had made the whoppingly successful recording in 1954 of "The Yellow Rose of Texas." Among Miller's other recordings for the label was the theme to *Bridge on the River Kwai*, otherwise known as "The Colonel Bogey March." The tune went back to before World War I but was used so effectively in the David Lean movie as a symbol of Allied

defiance that Miller knew immediately he wanted to record it with his
Gang, the singers who essentially made up his chorus. Hits like "Yellow
Rose" and "Colonel Bogey" gave Miller that much more confidence to
try a sing-along album. It was as though Miller had been waiting all
decade for Kavan's suggestion.

Hewing closely to nineteenth- and early twentieth-century Americana (as opposed to the more recent and far more sophisticated Great
American Songbook of standards), Miller made a list of songs, had his
old Rochester pal Jimmy "Jigsie" Carroll make most of the arrangements, and got his singers together. The all-male chorus, 25 strong, was
such a hoary idea that it seemed new again. Most of these men had sung
with Miller since 1948, at Golden Records, including the Four
Norsemen of Chicago and the Texaco Quartet—groups that Miller had
used behind Guy Mitchell and the Four Lads. Listening to the acetate
tapes of what became the first album, Sing Along with Mitch, Columbia
engineer Roy Friedman—"a tough guy," according to Miller—was so
moved he began to cry.[57] (Friedman dismissed Miller's story as "crap,"
though he acknowledged Miller's ingenious exploitation of old songs.)

When Sing Along with Mitch was released, it took a while to build. A
Minneapolis disk jockey named Howard Viking played "That Old Gang
of Mine" and many of the other tracks over and over.[58] Word of mouth,
the best advertising of all, took over. Miller, though he'd produced hundreds of other artists' recordings and played the oboe himself on dozens
of others (including the Charlie Parker with Strings records), was now a
recording star. By the beginning of 1961 Miller had made 11 Sing Along
albums, with 4.5 million units sold.[59] Profits for Columbia, as well as
for Miller and his Gang, proved substantial. Apart from Stan Kavan, who
would have thought there was money to be made in an all-male rendition of "The Sidewalks of New York"?

From 1953, Miller had had a CBS radio show, Sunday Night with Mitch
Miller, broadcast from Sardi's beginning at 7 P.M. Like Peter Goldmark, he
employed a publicist. And like most of his artists, he had an agent. It
wasn't unusual to see this bearded Svengali turn up in advertisements.
In 1956 you could open an issue of Life, for instance, and find Mitch

hawking Thom McAn shoes.[60] You could count on Mitch's testimonial because, after all, he probably produced one of your favorite recent records.

It wasn't surprising when Miller wanted to try television. Why not do the sing-alongs in front of the camera? The natural first choice was Columbia's parent company. For one reason or another, CBS president Mike Dann declined to put Miller on. *Captain Kangaroo*'s producer induced Canada Dry to sponsor the show and took the package to NBC, which aired a one-hour *Sing Along* special. Ratings were so strong that the network took an option on the show and broadcast a *Sing Along* every other Friday night. In January 1961 the demands of twin careers in recording and television prompted Miller, even with his Olympian constitution, to relinquish the directorship of pop records at Columbia.

Miller was allowed to keep an office and a secretary at 799 but was no longer paid by CBS (though, presumably, the secretary was). Naturally, rumors flew that Lieberson—or Frank Stanton or even Bill Paley—had canned Miller because he had been so vociferously against rock 'n' roll. "How could I prevent a company like Columbia from making rock 'n' roll records?" he asked Stephen Paley, with irritation to spare, during an interview forty years later.[61] Miller scoffed at the notion that he'd had that kind of authority, just as he'd scoffed at suggestions that he'd ruined Sinatra's career. He was right in both cases. He'd been outspoken against payola and decried as "unimaginative" the playlists of so many radio stations aimed at teenagers—morally correct but naive in the first case, merely naive in the second.

• • •

As Mitch Miller cut back on his A&R responsibilities, Columbia was swollen with profits and influence—internationally as well as domestically—due, in part, to Miller's own anachronistic recordings. Tony Bennett's art was still deepening. Doris Day, the world's number one female movie star, still sold well. Johnny Mathis was a one-man album factory. Ray Conniff had begun to give large-scaled demonstrations of stereo fidelity in live concerts, with walls of speakers, his distinctive mixed chorus separating reeds and brass to give an exaggerated stereo effect.[62] It was terrific marketing for Conniff's albums and Columbia's stereo releases in general.

Sales by these pop artists enabled the label to support jazz artists who might otherwise not have been signed. Joya Sherrill, known to everyone at Columbia because of her long association with Ellington, released an album arranged by one of the label's favorite music men, Luther Henderson. John Carisi came out of Woody Herman's band and his compositions were no less complex than Teo Macero's. The great trombonist J. J. Johnson never made a dime for the label but was treated with respect, at least for a few years, and was forever championed by Macero. Les Paul's most commercial years (at Capitol) were behind him, but he recorded for Columbia, with Mitch Miller's support, into the early sixties. The alarmingly erudite baritone saxophonist-composer Gerry Mulligan—Judy Holliday's companion since the run of *Bells Are Ringing*—was on the label, then off, then on again. Columbia released *Mingus Ah Um*, by the untamable bassist Charles Mingus, whose ballads "Goodbye Porkpie Hat" (for Lester Young) and "Self Portrait in Three Colors" (composed for John Cassavettes' movie *Shadows*, but not used) worked their way under your skin.[63] Dave Brubeck more than held his own. For the time being, both Benny Goodman and Erroll Garner were recording elsewhere, but their albums—especially Goodman's two Carnegie Hall concerts and Garner's *Concert by the Sea*—continued to outsell most jazz.[64] Then Miles Davis's *Kind of Blue*, recorded at 30th Street in 1959, was an almost instant classic. The original producer had been Townsend, who'd inherited Miles from Cal Lampley when Lampley went to RCA, but Townsend's transfer to the West Coast left Teo Macero to look after the project. The passing of the producer's baton led to a conflation of the tracks "All Blues" and "Flamenco Sketches" on thousands of copies of the first pressing, making them something of a collector's item.[65] Many critics and listeners will agree, despite credits to the contrary, that Bill Evans was the driving force behind at least two of the tracks, "Flamenco Sketches" and "Blue in Green." Whoever wrote what, though, the album touched many people at Columbia, including Stan Kavan, who gave it a tremendous push.

There was one jazz album, however, that caused some turmoil at 799. Richard Du Page was the originator of Columbia's reissue *Thesaurus of Classic Jazz*. Du Page had written close to 10,000 words about musicians whom he deemed essential to the history of jazz, all of them having recorded on Okeh in the 1920s and early '30s: Mildred Bailey, Bix, Bobby Davis, both Dorseys, Eddie Lang, Fred Livingston, Don Murray, Chelsea Quigley, Adrian Rollins, and Frankie Trumbauer. These musicians didn't just happen to be white—they represented a time and place (mostly the Midwest) that Du Page felt had been unjustly neglected. As preparations to release the album intensified, Columbia's Nat Shapiro blew a gasket:

> Speaking from the points of view of a part time jazz "expert" and collector and as a member of the A.&R. staff, I feel that issuing these records, as now made up, would be a serious and sad mistake—putting the company in a position to be criticized by nearly every responsible and knowledgeable person in the jazz field.

> As now constituted, the *Thesaurus of Classic Jazz* does not include a single Negro musician. . . . To have a thesaurus of classic jazz with three albums not including Armstrong, Bechet, Henderson, Dodds, Noone, Hines, Clarence Williams, Ellington, James P. Johnson and dozens of other superior musicians approaches the scandalous.[66]

Shapiro was indeed a part-time expert—he had written *Hear Me Talkin' to Ya* with Nat Hentoff, as well as several other volumes on jazz recordings—and, among the white men at Columbia, he had been as vociferous about civil rights as John Hammond had been. The album was held up for more than a year. When *Thesaurus* was finally released as a four-record set, it contained additional text by the jazz historian Frank Driggs. Critics did note the exclusive focus on white jazz musicians, but no one seemed offended.

●　　●　　●

Goddard Lieberson might not have been aware of the *Thesaurus of Classic Jazz* or the anxieties about its release. That didn't mean he was oblivious to all of Columbia's nonclassical product. He was well aware of Johnny Horton's "The Battle of New Orleans," which would eventually sell more than two and a half million copies, and couldn't ignore "The Battle Hymn of the Republic," a collaboration between those two Masterworks phenomena, The Mormon Tabernacle Choir and the Philadelphia Orchestra. Even Marty Robbins's "El Paso" was a hit that Lieberson appreciated. At the beginning of 1959, Lieberson had been Columbia Records's president for two and a half years; his five vice presidents were Herb Greenspon, Norman Adler, Albert Earl, Alfred Lorber, and Andy Schrade; the treasurer was William Wilkins.[67]

A glance at two weeks' worth of entries from Lieberson's 1959 appointment book gives a fair picture of his daily routine: *Visit to the CBS doctor [Jack Nelson]. Lunch at Dinty Moore's with Lehman Engel. Robert [restaurant] with Groucho. Board of Directors meeting. Singles [as in records] meeting. Lunch with [writing partner] Hugh Wheeler. Reception for Lenny Bernstein. Annual report from Debbie Ishlon. Norman Adler at 11:30, Nat Shapiro at noon. Dietz & Schwartz at 4, Stravinsky at 5. Fiorello! at 7:45. Sound of Music recording on Sunday. Party for Doris Day at "21." Friday night Van den Heuvel dance. Lunch with FS [Frank Stanton]. Backers' audition at Dore Schary's on East 70th. Kay Kendall Memorial. Joe Higgins lunch at Top of the Sixes.*

This last entry was a retirement party held in the top-floor restaurant at 666 Fifth Avenue, which boasted one of the best views of midtown. Joe Higgins had been with Columbia, off and on, since World War I, with an important break to work with Ted Wallerstein in Camden, and was widely credited with getting the CBS-owned Columbia off the ground by negotiating mechanical rates that were favorable to the label. With his wife Sadie next to him on the dais, Higgins was meant to be the man of the hour, but Lieberson and his staff used the lunch to present an only slightly travestied tutorial in how a record was made. Lieberson began by saying, "After seeing you all drink I want to say there'll be no expense reports or contracts honored which are dated this afternoon. . . . This drunk on my right is Joe Higgins. I should tell you, Joe, that from this point on we're recording this. As you know, there are certain rights involved and the legal department is prepared to deal with you on the contract. As usual with our contracts, it will not be necessary to show it to your lawyer. If you'll just sign it, I'm sure if there's anything wrong we can fix it up by friendly discussion. You can always speak to Al Lorber or myself in case you find that we have a franchise on all works produced by your grandchildren."[68]

Every now and then Lieberson would permit himself to laugh along with the audience. He called on Neil Fujita to describe—"in English, please"—the album cover they'd selected in preparing an album honoring Higgins. Alfred Lorber tossed out some double-talking legalese in which the artist ends up paying Columbia: "You, the Copyright Owner, will pay to us, the Record Company, the sum of eight cents per album." ("That's *all?*" said Lieberson.) Art Schwartz outlined the label's advertising plans: "Naturally, Joe, we're gonna go all out." Norman Adler said a few words about how the Columbia Record Club would promote the new Higgins album. Debbie Ishlon said she was going to get Higgins on the covers of *Time* and *Life*. Then, from the back of the room, head of sales Bill Gallagher stood up and gave his presentation. Since taking over from Hal Cook, Gallagher had made the department even more influential. In a recent presentation to his salesmen, Gallagher's punning catchphrase was *Your Future Is in the Line*—meaning the Columbia Records catalog. "Sales disagrees with the creative idea for the album," Gallagher began, and the guests laughed because, though he was making fun of himself, he had often expressed impatience with the A&R staff's views on what was salable. The sales department was ready to sell an album called *My Fair Sadie*—all for a man whose negotiating skills with song publishers in 1939 had enabled CBS-owned Columbia to become competitive with Victor and Decca. The sales department's proposed songs, with no apologies to Lerner & Loewe, included "The Rain in Spain Is Mainly in Public Domain"; "With a Little Bit of Luck It's a Penny and a Half Rate"; "Get Me to Chappell on Time"; "I'm an Ordinary Man but the Publishers Think I'm Hip"; "I Could Have Bargained All Night"; "Why Can't the English Learn to Publish for Free?"; and "Shouldn't It Be Royalties?"

Lieberson asked if Mitch Miller was still in the room. But Miller had had to run off to a television taping, his priorities evident to everyone. "I guess Mitch is singing along with someone else by now," Lieberson cracked. The lunch ended with the guests following the recording of Mitch and his Gang singing "When Irish Eyes Are Smiling" in honor of Higgins. It was corny, all right—and terribly moving.

Lieberson had begun the decade fending off public charges of communist sympathies and masking his irritation at being passed over for the Columbia Records presidency. Now, at the end of the decade, he was on top of the industry. Columbia laid claim to being the number one label in the world. "For fifty years the Victor record division of the Radio Corporation of America has been the undisputed leader in all phases of phonograph disc sales and production," the Times reported, but Lieberson insisted Columbia had finally overtaken Victor, capturing 21 percent of the market in 1959, because of the many custom labels whose records it pressed and because of Columbia Record Club sales.[69] The numbers were impressive but didn't show how thoroughly Columbia dominated recordings that originated just down the block, on and around the Great White Way.

13

Curtain Up

By common consent, *Oklahoma!* was the first major commercial original cast recording of a Broadway show. The album of 78s, released by Jack Kapp at Decca, sold well because it had been a groundbreaking show in the first place—the first collaboration of Richard Rodgers and Oscar Hammerstein, and by far the most successful integration of music and book up to that time—and because it was well packaged, with a photograph of the entire company from the show on the cover.[1]

Oklahoma! wasn't the first original cast album, however—not by a long shot. All through the century there'd been bits and pieces of Broadway shows recorded by members of the original cast. Brunswick released 78-rpm albums of *Blackbirds of 1928* (in 1932) and *Show Boat* (in 1933), though these were really reconstituted versions of the original shows. On *Blackbirds of 1928*, the orchestras of both Ellington and Don Redman were used; Bill Robinson and Adelaide Hall (later of *South Pacific*) of the original cast performed, with Ethel Waters, Cab Calloway, and the Mills Brothers—all Brunswick artists at the time—added to the mix. On *Show Boat*, Victor Young led the studio orchestra, and the cast included Helen Morgan of the original show, with Paul Robeson, who'd appeared in a later production, and several other prominent singers doing excerpts. That was how Broadway "albums" were compiled—as collections of excerpts.

Although its purchase of American Record would give Columbia ownership of the two Brunswick albums, the label was barely in the Broadway game through the 1940s. In 1938 composer Marc Blitzstein and the original cast of *The Cradle Will Rock* made a long album of 78s for Musicraft, "twice the length of Decca's *Oklahoma!*," according to Jack Raymond.[2]

But *Oklahoma!* gave Decca bragging rights to the original cast recording. Through Jack Kapp, Decca locked up most of the important shows on record throughout the 1940s, including *One Touch of Venus*, *Bloomer Girl*, *Carousel*, *Call Me Mister*, *Annie Get Your Gun*, *Call Me Madam*, and peaking but by no means ending with *Guys and Dolls* in 1950. RCA Victor released the 1947 original cast recording of Lerner & Loewe's *Brigadoon*, but RCA bowed out of the game for a while because it kept recording flops.

Then Goddard Lieberson stepped in. As a young producer, his first studio recording of a show was probably the Kurt Weill–Langston Hughes *Street Scene*, in early 1947.[3] The control booth, though, couldn't contain Lieberson's ambitions. Even as the LP was still being developed, he conceived of an enormous archive of musical theater on disk. His contacts with composers created a network that was helping to build the Modern American Music series, the glowing filament of the Master-works catalog, but also to lure the best Broadway writers to the label. Lieberson and Zorina made a glamorous, dynamic couple, and their presence was as coveted by Mr. and Mrs. Richard Rodgers as by Mr. and Mrs. Igor Stravinsky. A musical scholar as well as a composer in his own right, Lieberson researched older musicals to record, too. In the studio he could be a fearless producer, beefing up an orchestra while staying strictly within his budget, and was often forced to be ruthless because of money and time constraints. He appeared to have no qualms about sticking his name on most original cast recordings because, after all, he had produced them. And so the phrase *Produced for Records by Goddard Lieberson* became familiar to every connoisseur of original cast recordings. The name connoted class and the excitement of the musical theater.

The earliest pressings of Rodgers & Hammerstein's *South Pacific*, which helped launch the long-playing record, featured on its cover the prominent credit *Produced by Goddard Lieberson*. The show's producers, Josh Logan and Leland Hayward, called in a fit about the credit, and 30,000 LP covers that had been printed had to be scrapped.[4] Subsequent pressings didn't contain Lieberson's name at all, as though he were serving penance.

Lieberson had, in fact, handled the South Pacific recording—at the label's new 30th Street studio and not, as had been rumored, in Boston—with authority. It's unlikely, however, that Lieberson would have had the opportunity to build such a superior Broadway division without the groundwork laid by Manie Sacks. As head of popular A&R, Sacks was responsible for bringing original cast recordings to the label. His coup, triggered when he negotiated for Burton Lane and Yip Harburg's Finian's Rainbow (1947), was to offer the Broadway producer a cut of the record proceeds instead of the time-honored practice of making an album wholly separate from the show's producer.[5] After Finian's Rainbow (an Irish fantasia to Brigadoon's Scottish fantasia), Columbia captured recording rights to Cole Porter's Kiss Me, Kate by providing some of the financing. Then came South Pacific, Irving Berlin's Miss Liberty, and Gentleman Prefer Blondes, by the Hollywood veterans Jule Styne and Leo Robin.

And then Sacks was gone, leaving the field open to Lieberson. Sacks's replacement, Mitch Miller, was immediately assigned to produce the cast album of Porter's Out of this World (1950), the only original cast recording Miller ever did at Columbia. Lieberson didn't get the next Rodgers & Hammerstein show, The King and I—song for song, maybe the team's greatest show—and lost Two on the Aisle, by his old friends Comden & Green and Jule Styne. But he got the sweet Arthur Schwartz–Dorothy Fields show A Tree Grows in Brooklyn ("Refinement," "Make the Man Love Me," etc.). Clarifying his role, his album cover credit now read Produced for Records by Goddard Lieberson. And then he inaugurated the musical theater series with conductor Lehman Engel, building a new library of Broadway recordings.

•   •   •

In this series Lieberson, for all his Renaissance-man talents and interests, discovered his deepest musical passion. He spent an increasing amount of time researching older musicals, found out what was available and went to work, trying to get them on record and sometimes restoring songs that had been cut from either the show or an earlier version. The costs involved in re-creating these older works rather than doing original cast albums were considerably lower, largely because Actors Equity minimums weren't a factor, and arranger and copyist fees were negotiated at a much lower rate than Broadway fees.[6] Advancements made by tape and the still-new LP format made the whole process much easier. A show's original orchestrations were used whenever possible, though Lieberson wasn't averse to beefing up the orchestra to get a bigger sound on record.

The 1951 version of *Porgy and Bess*, always technically referred to as a "folk opera," wasn't the first recording of this ongoing Lehman Engel project, but it was the largest.[7] Based on a 559-page vocal score (nearly twice as long as most operas), the Gershwins' show, originally staged in 1935 to mixed notices, made for a wallop of a record package. (There wouldn't be another complete libretto included for a show until Columbia released Frank Loesser's *The Most Happy Fella* in 1956. And, though Loesser denied it about his own show, it can be argued that both *Porgy* and *Fella* are at least as operatic as they are Broadway. There was, and still is, a much stronger tradition in opera of including the libretto.)

Lieberson was in close touch with the prickly Ira Gershwin, whose cooperation he needed. Happily, Gershwin, in Beverly Hills, was ready to oblige. "Will start going through 'P&B' in day or two," Gershwin wrote on March 14, 1951, "for substitutes for that these-days-objectionable-six-letter-word-which-I-thought-was-too-freely-used-even-in-those-days."[8] A month later, after discussing the matter with his chief liner-note writer, Morris Hastings, Lieberson wrote to Gershwin, ""How would you feel about writing something for what we call (rather erotically) the fly-leaf of the album, giving perhaps the story of *Porgy and Bess*, how it was engendered, its history, first performance, etc."[9] The title parts were sung by Lawrence Winters and Camilla Williams; New York artist Lewis Daniel made the Covarrubias-tinged front cover that depicted Catfish Row, and the ever-reliable Fred Plaut, the label's chief engineer, took the photographs—of Lehman and Lieberson, as well as of the cast—on the back. The recording at 30th Street has Lieberson's signature: the muscular orchestra; the precise timing; even enhancing sounds—the rolling of the dice in act 1, the drums connoting the washtub-playing in act 2—that he would later cut back on. Lieberson decided against printing a separate booklet to accompany the three records after he was warned that the booklet could possibly scratch the vinyl during shipping. Instead he and the art department settled on printing the lengthy libretto in sections on the sleeves of the three records. And Lieberson ended up writing the notes. In any event, Lieberson was hooked on producing the series and would focus on it for the next few years.

* * *

By the end of 1952 Columbia, invariably with Lieberson producing and Engel usually conducting, had made 30th Street studio versions of *Anything Goes*, *Babes in Arms*, *The Bandwagon*, and *Girl Crazy*—all starring Mary Martin—and a *Pal Joey*, with Vivienne Segal and Harold Lang, that proved so attractive that Richard Rodgers was spurred to revive the show once more. *The Desert Song*, featuring Columbia's on-again off-again artist Nelson Eddy, was released on 10". There were new versions of *The Merry Widow*, with Dorothy Kirsten and Richard Rounseville, and *The Student Prince* using pretty much the same cast. The series would eventually make recording stars, quite apart from their stage appearances, of Jack Cassidy, Portia Nelson, and several other itinerant singers and dancers.

Engel also conducted new recordings of old musicals for RCA and the *Reader's Digest* series—he wasn't married to Columbia. But Lieberson was. And he still had to prove to Jim Conkling, who was technically his boss, and to the brass at CBS that he could record the best in theater, musical and straight, while keeping costs down.

Noel Coward's *Conversation Piece*, which the author-songwriter first starred in in London in 1934, made a strong vehicle for Lily Pons. If any single figure could be said to be a model for Lieberson, it was Coward, whose epigrammatic wit Lieberson aspired to. Lieberson had first conceived of recording *Conversation Piece* in 1947 and approached Coward, whom he had not known, through Andre Kostelanetz. The two men would become friends. When the recording was finally made in 1951, with Carroll Huxley orchestrating and Engel conducting, the cast included the young Richard Burton.

• • •

Even the disappointments could win Lieberson admiration at CBS. Lieberson's friendship with José Ferrer was briefly tested when Lieberson expressed an interest in recording Ferrer's version of *Cyrano de Bergerac*. The play had been revived in the fall of 1946 to great acclaim; after that, anyone who doubted Ferrer's talents was either deaf or foolish. Lieberson had recorded Ferrer in *Othello* and knew this version would play well on record, particularly since Paul Bowles had composed incidental music that would have enhanced the recording. But Ferrer's agents, knowing they had a new star on their hands—and a star soon to become the husband of Rosemary Clooney—made such unreasonable financial demands that Lieberson lost interest. The recording went to Capitol.[10]

Given the low returns on such projects, Lieberson's determination to record writers reading their own works can be seen as ambitious. The idea went back to the nineteenth century, when poets were often recorded reading their verse. In 1937 Columbia had recorded speeches from Maurice Evans's acclaimed version of *Richard II*, and the practice of recording the spoken word was accelerated during the Petrillo ban, when union musicians were enjoined from recording anyway. Lieberson instituted a spoken-word series that whispered class. Introduced by Hollywood producer Henry Blanke to the master of the macabre, John Collier, Lieberson made a characteristic approach to Collier on January 11, 1952: "I have so far Somerset Maugham, Sir Osbert Sitwell, Katherine Anne Porter, Truman Capote, Edith Sitwell. I have promises from John Steinbeck and Ernest Hemingway. I would like to add you to this list, just for a sinister note." Backed by Paul Weston, in Los Angeles, Collier read his short stories "Witch's Money" and "Back for Christmas," among others.

In the spring of 1952, a star-studded *Don Juan in Hell*—technically act 3 of Shaw's *Man and Superman*—played one night at Carnegie Hall, then moved into a Broadway theater for a substantial run. Charles Boyer, Charles Laughton, Agnes Moorehead, and Sir Cedric Hardwicke performed on a stage dressed with only four reading desks. Lieberson supervised the recording. Within weeks, Charles Boyer heard himself on record and dashed off a furious letter, threatening to withdraw from the project. Lieberson replied that Boyer had no contractual right of approval, and asked him to listen closely to the long-playing test pressings, which he was sending to Beverly Hills.[11] Despite a reputation for coddling his recording artists, Lieberson could be as tough as any field marshal. In fact the resulting two-disk LP is beautifully produced— except for Boyer's voice, which is fuzzy and often unintelligible.[12] John Briggs, writing in the *Times*, regretted that Columbia didn't follow Shaw's explicit instructions to include Mozart, specifically *Don Giovanni*, in the background.[13] (Accompanying the *Times* critique is a photograph of Laughton and Moorehead taken by Fred Plaut during the recording.)

In 1952 Lieberson was drawn into spoken word competition with the new label Caedmon. Its first release was Dylan Thomas reading his "A Child's Christmas in Wales" and five poems, one of which was "Do Not Go Gentle into That Good Night."[14] Soon Caedmon was *the* spoken word label to beat.

That's when Lieberson instituted his Literary Series. "The series was SL 190-E," said Peter Munves, with his knack of instantly recalling a catalog number from the Rolodex of his brain, "Lieberson's biggest folly, the recording of all these great authors reading from their own works. It was in a leather attaché case with a big booklet and I think there are ten or eleven or twelve records in there. It didn't sell. It was very expensive to begin with. I think it sold for over $75.00." The series included Katherine Anne Porter, Edna Ferber, Edith Sitwell, and Collier. "Somebody said, 'That's what [Goddard] gets for hanging around with the snooty set.'"[15] The Literary Series and Columbia's other spoken word records were well meaning, sometimes even effective, but they never quite developed the traction that the Caedmon recordings, supervised by Marianne Roney and Barbara Cohen, did from 1952 on.

● ● ●

Broadway cast recordings were a better bet. The Wright-Forrest show *Kismet* opened on December 3, 1953, in the middle of a New York newspaper strike, which might have saved the show from negative reviews that could have closed it early. The music was freely adapted from various Borodin compositions. The recording was made on Sunday, December 6, at 30th Street, with Lieberson supervising, an Al Hirschfeld cover ready to go on the finished product. Howard Scott and engineer Buddy Graham took the reels into the editing room at 799 and, working through the night, cut a lacquer; when Lieberson came in the next morning, Monday the 7th, Scott handed it to him for his approval. By Wednesday the record was selling out at Liberty Music in Manhattan.[16] The speed with which some of these albums could be released was breathtaking. Into the sixties *Kismet* would follow only three other Columbia Records shows—*My Fair Lady*, *West Side Story*, and *South Pacific*—as its Broadway best seller.

The Pajama Game (1954) was Columbia's next major original cast recording. The Richard Adler–Jerry Ross score became widely known from regular airplay. Since *Carousel* John Raitt had become an audience favorite, his tenor heroic and reassuring. His number "Hey There" was profitably covered by Rosie Clooney (and was said to be a favorite tune of Charlie Parker's, though he never got to record it). The ensemble song "Steam Heat" was as infectious as the work of the show's director-choreographer Bob Fosse, and "I'm Not at All in Love" proved to be an even bigger hit when Doris Day sang it on the Columbia soundtrack album. Columbia didn't get the team's next show, *Damn Yankees*—and then Jerry Ross was dead (of chronic bronchiectasis), ending the partnership that had been so fertile for no more than three years. The Harold

Arlen–Truman Capote show *House of Flowers* was and remains a difficult show to sit through, with a primitive book and nowhere near the depth the subject demands, but the score is still lovely, especially "Sleepin' Bee" and "I Never Has Seen Snow." (On this last song it's reputed that Arlen himself negotiated the final *like* in the song because Diahann Carroll couldn't.)[17]

●　　●　　●

As Lieberson moved into the president's office in June 1956, he nudged along a pet project that was almost entirely spoken word, with a few musical touches: a long-playing recording of *Waiting for Godot*. He regarded the play as a masterpiece and wanted the recording handled right. This meant close attention to every literary detail. On June 5 Lieberson received a memo from his chief note writer George Dale: "I'd appreciate it if you would let me know what you want for the notes on 'Waiting for Godot.' I think it is beyond me, and Charles Burr feels it is beyond him, too. Unless you would like to write the notes yourself, is there anyone you can suggest?"[18]

The nod went to William Saroyan, who had already read—or *tried* to read, for he kept digressing and throwing off asides—for the Literary Series and, hardly inconsequentially, had contributed a considerable sum to the Columbia coffer by dashing off the mad quasi-immigrant lyric to "Come on-a My House." In a June 20 telegram, Lieberson wrote:

YOUR PIECE SHOULD BE IN THE NATURE OF A PREFACE OR INTRO-
DUCTION AS IN BOOK WITH ANYTHING YOU CARE TO SAY ABOUT
THE PLAY AND ITS RELATIONSHIP TO THEATRE ALL BEST GODDARD.

Lieberson also sent to Saroyan, in Malibu, a 7 1/2" tape of a Godot performance to look at, with players E. G. Marshall, Bert Lahr, Kurt Kaznar, and Alvin Epstein. For a fee of $200, plus an assortment of new LPs, Saroyan had his essay back to Lieberson in a matter of days. "I do not mean this unkindly," Saroyan wrote at the end of his liner notes, "but it isn't likely in my opinion that Samuel Beckett will write a better play. I don't know how he wrote this one, but I'm glad he did. It's really quite bad, but that's beside the point. It also happens to be great." Lieberson was so pleased with the essay that he carried it with him and read it to the Stravinskys at lunch, then to Irene Selznick and Alan Jay Lerner who were dining at the same restaurant.[19]

Then came the more delicate task of dealing with Beckett. Several weeks into his new presidency, Lieberson wrote, "Dear Mr Beckett: Since I am sure my name is unknown to you, I shall have to tell you at the outset that it is I, who, for better or for worse, have instigated the recording of *Waiting for Godot*."[20] Because you don't send a boy to do a man's job, Lieberson proposed bringing the recording, with the Saroyan notes and the added musical sounds, to Beckett in Paris, where they would listen together. Lieberson and Fred Plaut had embellished the recording with electronic sounds—a sensitive decision, considering the play's allegorical style—and it was difficult to predict how the intensely private author would react. But Lieberson needn't have worried. Beckett heard the recording, gave his blessing, and remained Lieberson's friend for life.

• • •

The simple title came from the centuries-old English children's rhyme, traced to the Plague. Otherwise *My Fair Lady* had had complicated origins, with various producers, composers, and lyricists involved—including, early on, Lerner & Loewe, who gave up for a while because they couldn't crack it. By some accounts, when they took the project again they had an atomic weapon in director Moss Hart, who shaped the show and usually found that extra spin it needed. One example is "I've Grown Accustomed to Her Face," the closest thing to a love song sung by one of the principals, which bloomed right out of Shaw's *Pygmalion* dialogue. "Apart from its other singularities," Kenneth Tynan wrote, "*My Fair Lady* is the only romantic musical in which neither of the principals has a love song. The nearest Higgins gets to passion is to concede that he has grown accustomed to Eliza's face: a grudging tribute, surely."[21] In the play, Higgins says to Eliza, "I have grown accustomed to your voice and appearance. I like them, rather." The genius of Lerner & Loewe and Moss Hart was to turn the phrase ever so slightly.

Some commentators have singled out the friendship between William Paley and the show's lead producer, Herman Levin, as the way *My Fair Lady* got to Columbia Records. If so, it was still Lieberson who persuaded Paley to write the check for $400,000, giving CBS a majority stake in the show.[22]

My Fair Lady had no more than the usual share of tryout problems, with Rex Harrison alternately scared and bullying. The show opened at the Mark Hellinger Theater on March 15, 1956. On the Sunday after the opening, as was customary, Lieberson supervised the recording session, beginning at 10 A.M. at 30th Street. The record was quickly in the stores—100,000 shipped, according to Lerner & Loewe's biographer Gene Lees—with the great Al Hirschfeld cover depicting Shaw as a heavenly puppet master controlling the strings of marionette Rex Harrison, who in turn controls the strings of Julie Andrews.[23] Lieberson told Peter Munves to "go out and sell the show"—meaning, of course, the album. Munves gathered the raves and the thing sold itself. For fifteen weeks it was the number one best-selling album in the country, and remained on the charts for an unprecedented 480 weeks—slightly more than eight years.

•　•　•

After *My Fair Lady* in 1956, the year Lieberson became president, original cast recordings of *The Most Happy Fella, Li'l Abner, Bells Are Ringing,* and *Candide* were all released. Although Lieberson had previously told his *Esquire* profiler Martin Mayer that he was no longer supervising recordings, he couldn't stay out of the control booth. "I think that the president of any company should know how the product is made and be able to produce it himself on occasion," quoted the *Times.*[24] Lieberson had made it a point to stay friendly with Frank Loesser, whose *Guys and Dolls* remained one of the supreme achievements not only on Broadway but in Dave Kapp's original cast recording for Decca. In 1955 Columbia, gathered together a few of its major recording artists—Clooney, Stafford, Frankie Laine and Jerry Vale—added three songs that Loesser had written for the rather limp MGM movie version, and put out a 10" record. Through such apple-polishing, Columbia landed the original cast recording of *The Most Happy Fella*.[25] Despite the hit song "Standing on the Corner," the show leaned away from musical comedy and toward opera, and might have been Loesser's least popular show, yet it's only grown in stature since 1956, due in large part to that first version starring former Met star Robert Weede and Jo Sullivan, who became Mrs. Frank Loesser. (Columbia took the risky step of releasing two versions of the show, one including the entire libretto, the other excerpted.) *Li'l Abner* was recorded in binaural as well as stereo, but the awkward binaural process was shelved in favor of the simpler mono. *Bells Are Ringing* was the first original cast recording released in true stereo, and it's in this record that Lieberson's genius for making show records can be heard, particularly in the ringing telephone that kicks off the album like an alarm clock but doesn't appear in the show itself. (It introduces the listener to Sue's Answerphone.)[26] *Candide* had a Broadway run so brief that neither Columbia Records nor the original cast was obligated to make an album; but Lieberson, believing in the phonographic possibilities of the show, prevailed. Two versions—one in monaural, the other in stereo— were recorded; the stereo was scrapped because the format was too new, and it was decided that the show's limited run had already made selling the album difficult. Nobody at Columbia and no one who bought the show—certainly no Bernstein fans—regretted its being made. Few shows have arrived on Broadway with such literary cache—its collaborators had won Pulitzer Prizes in three separate fields—and those that do usually flop miserably. *Candide* flopped, but not miserably. The things most of us love about the show are given to us through Lieberson's album production and its female star Barbara Cook. Bits and pieces of the show were scattered throughout the culture; in the early 1970s Dick Cavett used *Candide's* scurrying overture as his theme song. Several years after the mono version had been released, Miles Kreuger, who'd started working at Columbia after an interval as Alan Jay Lerner's assistant, was going through the Columbia vaults and discovered the unedited two-track recordings. Tom Shepard, by then an old hand at these matters, edited the stereo tapes, even shifting dialogue—Max Adrian's lines as part of the introduction to "Best of all Possible Worlds," for instance— where he knew it would play better.[27]

For all the courage it took to record *Candide*, the show's abortive run might have made Lieberson leery of another Leonard Bernstein musical. "The story I heard was that Lieberson didn't want to sign *West Side Story*," Peter Munves said. "He heard it and he didn't like it. And Oppenheim, who was very close to Bernstein, probably prevailed on him to sign. Lieberson told me to go down and see it in tryouts in Philadelphia. The word on the street was that it was a very interesting show. So I went down to see it and I was *bowled over* by the first act! They were having a lot of problems with it. They were taking numbers in, they were throwing numbers out, they were writing new numbers. And I saw Lenny there and Lenny knew me, you know, because of the Philhar-monic and I looked at him and I said, 'Lenny, this is one of the most exciting shows I have ever seen! It's going to make Broadway history!' He gave me such a hug I thought the air was going to leave my body!"[28] *Candide*'s aborted run had so embarrassed Bernstein that he remained anxious about *West Side Story*. He even dissuaded Howard Scott from investing in the show.[29]

The original cast album of *West Side Story* was the number one album on the *Billboard* chart for 54 weeks, and paved the way for the inter-minable chart dominance of the soundtrack, which Columbia also released.[30]

Munves, meanwhile, was so taken with Bernstein's dance music for *West Side Story* that he persuaded Lieberson to go back into the studio and make a new recording of the Bernstein–Comden & Green show *On the Town*. The show had been first captured piecemeal on 78s by Decca in 1945 (there were three conductors for the recording), and the time seemed right to do it again. Munves said, "Only one man from the original cast, one of the three sailors, had died; everyone else was still around—Nancy Walker, Comden & Green, you know. So we had to get John Reardon to replace the guy who died. And Lennie conducted it. I went to the recording session and Lennie was playing the pennywhistle. He said, 'I wish I could compose this way today. When I was composing, this music poured out of me." The Columbia studio version of On the Town was released in 1960.[31]

•   •   •

Columbia lost The Music Man to Capitol, but there wasn't much else it wanted in those days that it didn't get. Meanwhile Lieberson stroked and cajoled the creators of musical comedy, but without obsequiousness— by now most of them needed him as much as he needed them. So he replied with unchecked irritation to a letter from Oscar Hammerstein questioning Lieberson's defense of country music in the Times. (Hammerstein said he was only trying to discourage more of "that unspeakable trash." In fact Lieberson had been writing rather neutrally about the phenomenon of country having turned into a $50-million-a-year business. He ended the article by quoting Minnie Pearl, who patted her mink stole and said, "Hillbilly gets to be country when you can buy one of these!")[32] Lieberson reassured Harold Arlen that if he didn't like the way RCA Victor was handling a new album, he'd be glad to reissue Arlen's 1954 show House of Flowers with a new cover. "All that means is that anything you write is good enough for me," he wrote.[33] He eagerly read and responded to Irving Berlin's merrily ethnic songs "Yiddle with a Fiddle" and "Ike Ike the Yiddisher Ball Player."

Lehman Engel was displeased to see that many of his old show albums that had been converted to stereo, from series ML to series CL, had omitted his name. Lieberson, going to bat for his old friend, wrote to David Oppenheim: "Can't understand this oversight. No reason to leave out Engel name, particularly when mine is included! Please put back!" The albums in question were among the essential show recordings Engel and Lieberson had made for Columbia: On Your Toes, Oklahoma!,

Girl Crazy, The Merry Widow, The Desert Song, The Boys from Syracuse, Roberta, Babes in Arms, The Student Prince, and, saddest of all, *Porgy and Bess.* The problem was rectified, but only because Lieberson had intervened.[34]

The conversion to stereo could be a headache, but it was usually worth it. At the beginning of 1959, Lieberson went to London to re-record *My Fair Lady* in stereo, with the original cast. The resulting album sold millions of copies all over again as listeners gradually converted their collections to stereo.

One of the label's more adventurous original cast recordings was of Tommy Wolf and Fran Landesman's *The Nervous Set,* a gentle spoof of Greenwich Village beatniks that might have been just too narrowly topical to succeed for long. Originally produced in St. Louis, the show's book was written by Jay Landesman, the lyricist's husband, and Theodore J. Flicker, who would make irreverent movies (e.g., *The President's Analyst*) in Hollywood during the sixties. Only musical comedy aficionados remember *The Nervous Set* anymore (one of its stars was Larry Hagman, several years before he starred in *I Dream of Jeannie* on television). But the show yielded two memorable songs, "Ballad of the Sad Young Men" and the impossibly lovely "Spring Can Really Hang You up the Most," each of which turns hipster cool inside out to discover a dejected weariness.[35]

Then came *Gypsy.* Early on, with David Merrick and Leland Hayward producing, Jule Styne was aboard to write the music; Comden & Green, then working on the screenplay for *Auntie Mame,* signed to write *Gypsy's* book and lyrics, which would be a reteaming of the hugely successful *Bells Are Ringing* collaboration.[36] Comden & Green didn't stay on the project, however. Stephen Sondheim and Arthur Laurents, still ablaze in *West Side Story* glory, were brought in to write lyrics and book respectively. Wide in scope, the book rolled out as tantalizingly as a striptease, and the show produced several hits. Singers all across the Columbia label covered "Small World," though no one did it better than Ethel Merman. "Everything's Coming up Roses" immediately took its place in the pantheon of great musical theater anthems (alongside, perhaps, Cole Porter's "Another Opening, Another Show" and Irving Berlin's "There's

No Business like Show Business"). Beyond the hits, though, few musicals played so thrillingly as narrative. Lieberson produced the recording, enlarging the orchestra from the smaller Broadway pit band. To save union minimums, Lieberson jettisoned some of the actors who had only one or two lines. On the recording, when the father of Mama Rose (Merman) says, "You ain't gettin' eighty-eight *cents* from me, Rose!" it's spoken not by Erv Harmon, who played the role on Broadway, but by Sondheim.[37] Sondheim spits out the line with such venom that you almost think he's expressing his fury at Ethel Merman for having insisted that Styne compose the score, rather than the relative neophyte Sondheim, as insurance.[38]

In the wake of *Gypsy*'s excellent original cast recording sales, Columbia took stock. Vice president Alfred Lorber pointed out how well Columbia did in the 1958–59 theater season, from *Goldilocks* and *Flower Drum Song* to *Gypsy*:

> In some cases Columbia got its shows despite Victor's exclusivity on performers (*Oh Captain; Flower Drum Song*) and despite other labels' offers of better financial terms. This is a wonderful compliment to several departments and individuals at Columbia who have achieved a reputation for such "superior performance" that we can accomplish this. But, in a way, we may have built a too-better mousetrap. Other companies are desperate over this fact, and their financial offers wax higher and more ridiculous. For example, Victor offered R&H any terms they wanted on the forthcoming *Sound of Music* show. That didn't work, and Victor now seems to be taking a course which is ever more difficult to fight.[39]

Lorber previewed the upcoming season, with the Harnick-Bock *Fiorello!* the most attractive prospect. Lorber suggested Columbia wouldn't get the show, however, because producer Hal Prince was getting offers from other labels of a 50-50 partnership—a huge percentage for the recording company to give away. (Lorber was right. *Fiorello!* went to Capitol.)

The same theater season also brought Columbia the original cast recording of *The Sound of Music*. It was the valedictory Rodgers & Hammerstein collaboration—Hammerstein lived nine months beyond the show's opening but was already gravely ill—and more polite critics regarded it as saccharine. Columbia's original cast recording occupied the number one position for 16 weeks and would remain on the charts for four years—as impressive as RCA's 1965 soundtrack version (which had much more rock 'n' roll to compete with). Like the movie, which spawned an industry of spoofs and sing-alongs, the show stuck to the roof of your mouth.

•　　•　　•

Elizabeth Larsen, Lieberson's assistant in 1959, made no secret of her desire to produce recordings. She got her shot when Lieberson was recording *The Ages of Man*, John Gielgud's spoken word take on Shakespeare, based largely on George Rylands's 1939 Shakespeare anthology. Lieberson was recording Gielgud in Studio A, on the seventh floor of 799 Seventh Avenue, when he received a phone call summoning him to CBS headquarters. From the control booth Lieberson flipped a switch and said to Gielgud, "John, I must go to CBS immediately. Miss Larsen will carry on." Ever the trouper, Gielgud completed the recording with Larsen in charge of the session. When the test pressings of *Ages* were ready, Lieberson sent them to Gielgud in England. At the time Columbia was still selling a surprisingly high number of LPs of the original cast recording of *Flower Drum Song*, as well as some Pat Suzuki singles from the show. Lieberson wrote to Gielgud in London: "I am sending you under separate cover—as they say—a 45 rpm record which I presume you can play on your phonograph. It is a song entitled 'I Enjoy Being a Girl.' Will you kindly play this recording at 33 1/3 rpm, and cable me the results."[40]

The Ages of Man would become Columbia's most successful spoken word album since Edward R. Murrow's *I Can Hear It Now*. (From Garson Kanin's novel *Where It's At*: "In the record shop downtown I find—of all things—an L.P. of Sir John Gielgud reading a collection of Shakespeare sonnets. My idea of music.")[41] Released almost concurrently by Columbia was Hal Holbrook's *Mark Twain Tonight*, the role the actor's been identified with ever since.

For a while Larsen resumed her duties as Lieberson's assistant. And Lieberson resumed his role as producer-in-chief of original cast recordings. Some shows confounded expectations. *Christine* was a vehicle for Maureen O'Hara. Before it opened on April 28, 1960, the show appeared to have everything going for it: a score by Sammy Fain and Paul Francis Webster; singles from the show recorded by Johnny Desmond, Jo Stafford, Leslie Uggams, and Vic Damone; a UNICEF "marching song"; and O'Hara, of course—an exquisite movie star for twenty years and lately more popular than ever due to her movies with John Wayne. *Christine* turned out to be a dud—perhaps audiences didn't want to follow the travails of a western woman in India—and the recording didn't even make the charts. The surprise—though, in hindsight, it shouldn't have been—was *Bye Bye Birdie*. The team of Charles Strouse (another Eastman graduate) and Lee Adams was known to theater people who produced and followed musical revues, but not to theatergoers; Chita Rivera, despite her successes in *Mr. Wonderful* and *West Side Story*, wasn't yet a Broadway cult figure; and Dick Van Dyke was still more than a year away from starring in the television comedy series that would make his name and those of several others. *Bye Bye Birdie* turned out to be a shockingly right fit for Columbia, which maintained a close link to *The Ed Sullivan Show* (a key plot point in the musical) and was still resisting rock 'n' roll like an *Our Gang* kid clamping his mouth to a force-fed spoonful of castor oil. Among the show's fine songs was "A Lot of Livin' to Do," which Louis Armstrong promptly took possession of. *Bye Bye Birdie* spent a year and two months on the charts—deservedly so. Columbia had a sizable stake in the show, but the soundtrack was released three years later by RCA.

By far the most anticipated show of the 1960 season was the next Lerner & Loewe musical. *My Fair Lady* had proved so durable that when Ella Fitzgerald recorded Rodgers & Hart's "Manhattan" she substituted the show for Hart's original lyric, which referred to the record-breaking run of *Abie's Irish Rose*. *My Fair Lady* was well into its fourth year on Broadway when *Camelot* got underway. The new show wasn't quite *My Fair Lady Redux*, but almost. Lerner & Loewe had also conquered Hollywood with their score for *Gigi*, which won most major Hollywood awards for 1958. Once again Columbia Records, through parent CBS, bankrolled the musical to the tune of $400,000, but this time payouts on *Camelot* were structured to favor Lerner & Loewe and Moss Hart a bit more. As producers of record, the three men would divide 60 percent of the profits, with CBS taking the remainder.[42] The large, musical-friendly Winter Garden was booked. There was such anticipation that, after the producers ran an ad in a March Sunday edition of the *Times*, $400,000 worth of tickets were sold, causing a migraine when the show ended up at the Majestic instead.[43] Most theatrical projects should have such headaches. The show was press-agented by the legendary, highly literate Richard Maney, and preparations were made to do the album in the large scope of its phenomenal predecessor. Columbia's in-house publication *Insight* focused on it as the label's album of the year; November cover stories in *Cue* and *Time* (with a cover painting of Lerner & Loewe) stirred up anticipation.[44] And it seemed like every major artist on the label—Bennett, Mathis, Previn, Faith—grabbed a song from the show to record.

The show was impressive, yielding some wonderful songs: Burton's *Sprechstimme*, gusty rendition of "I Wonder What the King Is Doing Tonight"; the list-making of "If Ever I Would Leave You"; and the sweet title song. The original cast recording—made at 30th Street on December 11, 1960, eight days after the show's opening—did well, subsequently launched into Broadway heaven by the Kennedys' identification with it. The album contains the song "Fie on Goodness," which was cut from the show shortly after the opening to pare down the running time. Most original cast albums are edited versions of their shows, but the *Camelot* album gave the listener a bit more, not less.

Still, *Camelot* becomes hard to listen to repeatedly, and it may be for the same reason that the show itself feels less than great: the plot sculpted from the romantic mass of the Arthurian legend. Of the three major characters, one man is a cuckold, the other a blowhard, and the queen shared by them comes to seem shallow by association. "C'est moi!" sings Lancelot (Robert Goulet, who would soon become a major Columbia recording artist), and though the declaration is right for the character as Lerner has written him, you can't help think, What a jerk! The triangle is discomfiting to audiences and listeners, and the discomfort is neither deep nor stimulating. Although Lerner & Loewe's patented style is evident in most of the score, it doesn't move toward the inevitable change and love in *My Fair Lady*.

Oddly, the show corseted Julie Andrews, the object of so much passion by the two male characters, with her songs of maidenhood and wordless adoration. In 1957 Columbia had released Rodgers & Hammerstein's *Cinderella*, with Andrews abloom in the title role, and her comic abilities are undeniable in *Julie and Carol at Carnegie Hall*, the 1962 show she did with Carol Burnett, the recording produced for Columbia Records by Jim Fogelsong.[45] In Camelot, Andrews's ripeness and humor were barely evident.

• • •

Lieberson was enthusiastic about the next Wright-Forrest show, *Kean*, with a book by Peter Stone. Why wouldn't he be? He had the team that had made *Kismet*; he had Alfred Drake again; and he had a great theatrical subject. The show was recorded at 30th Street on Sunday, November 12, 1961, and stayed on the charts for 12 weeks. Although Lieberson praised his staff the following week—"I just want to compliment all those who had a hand in making the *Kean* album, which I think is by far one of the best we have ever done from the point of view of sound, production, etc."—little about it is memorable except Drake's powerful, magnetic voice, one of the great instruments in musical comedy history.[46] There was a potentially interesting Yip Harburg interpretation of Offenbach in *The Happiest Girl in the World*, an adaptation of *Lysistrata*, with Cyril Ritchard as Pluto and Janice Rule as Diana. The album did well enough, but perhaps it took Rodgers & Hart to adapt the ancient Greeks for Broadway. It seemed as though there'd been so much original cast activity at 30th Street, with one studio session after another booked shortly after Broadway openings, that the numbers are surprising: *Subways Are for Sleeping*, recorded on January 7, 1962, was only the forty-fifth original cast recording issued by Columbia; the label was so dominant in the field that one imagines hundreds of shows being recorded by that date.[47]

Columbia didn't get Stephen Sondheim's first composer-lyricist Broadway show, *A Funny Thing Happened on the Way to the Forum*. It also missed out on *No Strings*, Richard Rodgers's first show as lyricist as well as composer, that featured Richard Kiley and the exquisite Diahann Carroll. (Considered adventurous at the time for its depiction of an interracial romance, the musical sounds as fresh as ever in the twenty-first century.) It did get *All American*, the Strouse-Adams musical that yielded "Once Upon a Time" for Tony Bennett and several lesser singers. Columbia badly wanted Harold Rome's *I Can Get It for You Wholesale*. As an inducement to Rome, Lieberson offered to record the twenty-fifth anniversary version of his International Ladies' Garment Workers' Union show *Pins and Needles*. Liz Larsen had heard Rome play piano and sing his own songs on a 1956 record titled *Rome-antics*, and knew he could easily lead this new version. Larsen and Charlie Burr produced the record. The revelation on *Wholesale* was the 20-year-old performer Barbra Streisand, playing Miss Marmelstein, and she was hardly less impressive in *Pins and Needles*.[48] Larsen assisted Lieberson on Irving Berlin's *Mr. President*, the last Columbia original cast recording of 1962.

Meredith Willson's 1963 *Here's Love* was nowhere near as successful as his *The Music Man*, but then nothing Willson wrote after that approached *Music Man*. Columbia Records' old bandleader Elliot Lawrence was the music director. More insightful theatergoers might have considered "Here's love" to be the concentrated theme of Edward Albee's *Who's Afraid of Virginia Woolf?*, though you wouldn't know it from the publicity that swirled around the play—you had to see it, read it, or listen to Columbia's three-record set. The recording turned out to be one of Lieberson's finest moments, not because the play was "better" than any musical he had produced for records (there is no comparing them, really) but because he courageously stood by a spoken text that included so many profane and emotionally wrenching moments.[49]

Excelling at spoken word recordings, Columbia went for *Dylan*, a recording of the play about the poet Dylan Thomas, the sessions made in early February 1964, with music by Teo Macero and Laurence Rosenthal. In April Columbia bankrolled a *Hamlet*, "done in the manner of a polished rehearsal," with Sir John Gielgud directing Richard Burton and Alfred Drake, among many others. Columbia added sound effects: recorder music, bells, drums, cannon, etc.

What Makes Sammy Run? was a creditable stab at adapting Budd Schulberg's Hollywood novel for Broadway, with Lehman Engel conducting and Steve Lawrence as Sammy Glick. Lawrence's first Columbia single was probably "Poinciana"; since the single's release, he and his wife Eydie Gorme, guided by their manager Ken Greengrass, had been important Columbia artists. The show, composed by Ervin Drake ("It Was a Very Good Year"), managed to hit the charts but closed after a brief run. Sondheim's *Anyone Can Whistle*, fascinating but almost too cynical for Broadway audiences to bear, was another labor of love for Lieberson, whose sensibility wasn't all that far from the composer's. ("I hate the profane rabble and keep them far from me.") Lieberson recorded the show the day after it closed, after 21 performances—like *Candide*, an instance where everyone's devotion superseded the label's and the performers' contractual obligations.[50]

Meanwhile, in the tumultuous period following the Kennedy assassination, Columbia had lost *Hello, Dolly!* and *Fiddler on the Roof* to RCA. William Paley turned down the opportunity to invest in *Fiddler* because he wanted no part of poverty and pogroms.[51]

Columbia did get a musical trifle by *Fiddler*'s songwriters Jerry Bock and Sheldon Harnick. *To Broadway with Love* was a one-act salute to Broadway, harking all the way back to the 1866 extravaganza *The Black Crook*, performed three times a day at the Texas Pavilion at the 1964 World's Fair, in Queens.[52]

•　•　•

Columbia lost *Funny Girl* because Capitol, taking its cue from Columbia's profitable bankrolling of Broadway productions, had positioned itself as a major investor in the Broadway show. This turned out to be a major blow. By then Streisand was a Columbia recording artist through and through, appearing on the original cast recordings of the two Harold Rome shows, and had already made a couple of Columbia albums on her own. Lieberson had been apprised of what would become *Funny Girl* as far back as 1950 when he'd been in close touch with Fanny Brice. She wrote to him then about selling "the picture without doing the book. Ray [Stark, Brice's son-in-law] will be going to New York the end of this week, I think, and I'll have him call you and he can explain everything."[53] Almost a year later, Brice wrote that she had rejected Jerome Weidman, the novelist on whose stories *I Can Get It for You Wholesale* would be based, as librettist or screenwriter.[54] When the show appeared nearly ready, Ray Stark brought in Capitol, which capitalized nearly a third of the show's $800,000 cost.[55]

Despite his protests, Lieberson couldn't stay out of the 30th Street studio. In a life awash with excitement, he was never more excited than supervising an original cast recording there. The results were permanent and, to a great extent, his. In the 1965–66 period he was on a roll. Given its provenance, everyone had high expectations for the Rodgers-Sondheim musical *Do I Hear a Waltz?*, based on Arthur Laurents's play *The Time of the Cuckoo*, but Sondheim came to loathe the show. "The reason Waltz flopped was that it had no real energy—no excitement whatsoever," Sondheim said. Still, it pleased legions of fans of both composers.[56] "Someone Woke Up" stirred audiences because it reflected the heroine's complicated emotional response to Venice, and the title tune almost became a contemporary standard. But nobody could quite figure out what, if anything, was at stake. For Columbia in the 1965–66 theatrical season, the Cy Coleman–Dorothy Fields *Sweet Charity* was profitable, Jerry Herman's *Mame* even more so (66 weeks on the charts) and *Cabaret* refreshingly dark.[57] These shows had narrative weight, fed by well-known sources: *Sweet Charity* was adapted from *Nights of Cabiria*, maybe Fellini's greatest film; *Mame* was based on the Patrick Dennis novella

Auntie Mame, which, slight as it was, turned the title character into a type; and *Cabaret* was stitched together from Christopher Isherwood's *Berlin Stories* and John Van Druten's subsequent adaptation *I Am a Camera*. That Columbia Records would release these three cast recordings in the same season only reaffirmed the label's dominance of Broadway material. By now, two decades into the practice, Lieberson had a method of recording shows and a cogent philosophy built around that method:

> I'd usually be with the show since its inception, I'd go out of town two or three times, and by the time it came for the recording session, I'd know it pretty well. I sometimes changed the arrangements and tempos for the record—not always pleasing the arranger—[and for] the sound you need on an album. I don't believe in monkeying around electronically—I hate that—and it's a trap that a lot of record makers fall into. Another thing I did away with was dialogue lead-ins for songs unless they were absolutely necessary. I would have to explain patiently to the librettist that you could listen to a song on a record forty times, but to hear some banal, spoken introduction to the song drives you nuts after the third time.[58]

Lieberson worked in this manner right through his last show, *A Chorus Line*.

• • •

But there was a crack in Shubert Alley—a fissure in the wall of musical comedy as theatergoers had known it. The invading roots began with television, which supplied visual and cheap entertainment at home; dug deeper with rock 'n' roll, its dance rhythms infusing the culture and, in the process, frequently rendering lyrics inconsequential if not also indecipherable; and sprouted everywhere with American involvement in Vietnam and the revolution it wrought. Everything was *too real, too immediate*. It left the old guard at sea. Yip Harburg pored over Bob Dylan's lyrics to see what people were responding to, and what he was missing. The lyricist of *Finian's Rainbow*, the songs from the movie *The*

Wizard of Oz, and the songs "April in Paris" and "Brother, Can You Spare a Dime?" finally concluded he wasn't missing anything. In a poem titled "Music on the Rocks," he suggested that the latest hits were aimed at listeners for all ages—between five and ten, that is.[59] (Harburg was unaware that Dylan deeply admired the music of Harburg's frequent collaborator Harold Arlen. "In Harold's songs, I could hear rural blues and folk music," Dylan wrote. "There was an emotional kinship there.")[60]

In early 1968, some months after he became president, Clive Davis invited Richard Rodgers, who was waiting to go to lunch with Lieberson, into his office to listen to new Janis Joplin tapes. Davis put on Joplin's version of "Summertime"; when that got no response from Rodgers, he put on "Piece of My Heart." Rodgers asked Davis to stop the tape. "If this means I have to change my writing," he said to a disappointed Davis, "or that the only way to write a Broadway musical is to write rock songs, *then my career is over.*"[61] In a cultural climate where younger audiences were choosing the Fillmore East over the Winter Garden every time, only the most foolish or hardiest Broadway souls could mount a show. The ones that accommodated changing tastes in pop music were almost invariably *not* on Columbia: *Your Own Thing, Pippin, Godspell* and, most of all, *Hair.* The Bacharach-David show *Promises, Promises,* based on Billy Wilder's movie *The Apartment,* infused a cynical old story with pop songs written in the team's contemporary, complicated style. Lieberson, sending some Masterworks albums to the *Times's* eminent former theater critic Brooks Atkinson, wrote, "Isn't the music for *Promises, Promises* worthless or am I just an old grouch?"[62]

Columbia continued to record old-fashioned musicals, whether newly produced or revived: *Jacques Brel Is Alive and Well and Living in Paris; No No, Nanette; George M!; Dames at Sea;* the surprisingly successful *1776;* Jerry Herman's *Dear World;* the Harnick-Bock *The Rothschilds;* the Rodgers-Charnin *Two by Two* (a major Columbia Records investment, given a publicity boost when Danny Kaye appeared onstage on crutches because he'd broken his leg); and the Kander & Ebb show *70, Girls, 70.*[63] Rodgers, Berlin, Arlen, Wright & Forrest—they kept on working, but they looked on from the upper reaches of Park Avenue and Connecticut with perplexity.

Stephen Sondheim, at least a generation younger than the others (two generations younger than Berlin), had been trained in the same tradition, with Oscar Hammerstein II as his primary mentor, but had been doing his own thing for some time. For this reason and several others, Thomas Z. Shepard, born in 1936, was probably the right producer for Stephen Sondheim who, more than any Broadway composer before him, integrated the libretto into each song.

• • •

The Shepard family name was second generation; his grandparents had been named Shapiro. Tom Shepard grew up in East Orange, New Jersey, playing piano since early childhood and listening to Gilbert & Sullivan shows on record. He attended Juilliard Preparatory, then Oberlin where he was majoring in philosophy. He couldn't help noticing, though, that the music students were having a much better time than he was. In graduate school at Yale he went back to the piano.[64] Shepard left school before taking a degree and taught at the renowned Elisabeth Irwin High School in Manhattan; the songwriter Earl Robinson ("Joe Hill," "Ballad for Americans"), still feeling the effects of the blacklist, was also teaching there at the time. Leading into the summer of 1959, Shepard joined a road company of Li'l *Abner*. (Shepard met his wife Irene in the company.) When the tour was over, Shepard went looking for a job.

He stopped at Columbia Records and was quickly interviewed. Asked what his skills were, Shepard told his interviewer that he could play piano very well, read a score, compose, and conduct—though this last wasn't true. "Well, that's what our artists do," the interviewer said. "Thanks for stopping by." As Shepard made his way toward the elevator, however, a spectacled woman called out, "Young man?" and sent the puzzled but delighted Shepard, a pixieish kid with a Cary Grant–like cleft chin and Zachary for a middle name, up to Cliff Benfield, the head of personnel. Benfield, trained as a psychologist, believed he read people very well. He made Shepard a trainee in the Masterworks division.

For his first couple of years at Columbia, Shepard studied Howard

Scott, John McClure, and Teo Macero (though Macero wasn't officially part of Masterworks) in action. Scott was incurably brash. One day Shepard saw him pick up the phone and call the usually forbidding George Szell. "George, you old goat," said Scott. "How are ya?" Such casual intimacy! Maybe one day, Shepard thought, he too could address the likes of Szell as an old goat. Shepard absorbed Scott's brashness. To some it made Shepard seem egotistical—"An ego that wouldn't quit," said Schuyler Chapin, who was head of Masterworks at the time—but it was a way to get things done in an atmosphere of clashing personalities and musicianship.[65] When producer Joe Chianni left the label, Chapin reassigned Shepard to the open slot and had him work with John McClure before more permanent arrangements could be made. Shepard was all of 25.

About a year after Shepard had started with Columbia, an opportunity arose that tugged him away from purely classical recording. The Columbia Record Club wanted a series of Broadway shows with "dream casts"—that is, new recordings of famous shows, much like Lieberson's and Engel's earlier collaborations, but with more celebrated show people in them. Chapin asked Jim Fogelsong, who had made a beautiful new *Anything Goes* (released on Epic in 1962), to handle the series. "Behind the hick accent there was a very sophisticated musical mind," Shepard said of Fogelsong. Shepard asked Chapin if he could participate; Chapin gave his assent. In 1962 Shepard worked on a new *Annie Get Your Gun*, with the label's mainstays Doris Day and Robert Goulet, and Franz Allers (*My Fair Lady*) conducting, though Shepard wouldn't receive a producer's credit until the material was released on CD. Day, at the peak of her movie career, declined to come to New York to make the record. Instead, under Irving Townsend's supervision, she went into a Los Angeles studio and recorded her tracks with a Columbia staff arranger playing piano in the next booth. The tapes were sent to New York, where orchestrator Philip Lang wrote arrangements around Day's vocal tracks—an inside-out variation on the usual process. Shepard recorded Goulet and the other singers using Lang's arrangements, tailor-made around the Day vocal tracks.

In the same series there was a *Show Boat*, with John Raitt and Barbara

Cook, also released in 1962. Fogelsong moved to Nashville. Shepard went on to do an *Oklahoma!* with Raitt, Florence Henderson, and Phyllis Newman (Mrs. Adolph Green), and a *King and I* with Cook and Theodore Bikel—both albums in 1964. On his own, Shepard produced the 1964 *Bajour* (Chita Rivera and Herschel Bernardi, based on *New Yorker* articles by Joseph Mitchell about modern-day gypsies) and clearly knew his way around the recording studio. The following year Fogelsong returned to town and permitted the now-experienced Shepard to co-produce the latest Lehman Engel project, the Weill-Gershwin *Lady in the Dark*, which had been originally done in 1941 with Gertrude Lawrence.

For Shepard, all these were in preparation for Stephen Sondheim's *Company*. The show and its original cast recording have become something of a legend for several interlocking reasons. One was that the show defied unwritten Broadway rules by being mostly about a guy (Bobby) who can't commit. Another was that wallop of a score—Sondheim's first solo effort to reach Broadway in six years. Apart from "Ladies Who Lunch," the show lacked probable hits, but Sondheim's lyrics had taken on a new maturity, especially in "Ladies," "Sorry/Grateful," and the unspoken anguish in "Barcelona." (Sondheim was 40 when the show was produced.) The songs were orchestrated by Jonathan Tunick, the best in the business. The show, based on related stories written by the actor-writer George Furth, got at some very contemporary fears—commitment in general, marriage in particular—that other shows didn't go anywhere near.[66] For the recording, Shepard wanted to capture, he said, the "in your face" quality of the show.

Happily, the making of the cast album was filmed by D. A. Pennebaker. The film was meant to be the first in a series about original cast recordings, with Daniel Melnick as executive producer of the series. As it turned out, no other show recording was ever filmed. This one proved to be an extraordinary document, capturing small, telling moments among Shepard, the cast, orchestra, and Sondheim, while they recorded the album on eight-track tape at 30 IPS.

• • •

The entire film takes place on May 3 and 4, 1970, at the 30th Street studio. As the film opens, Shepard, constrained by a budget as always, is irritated by the number of percussion instruments, and he takes his irritation out on Fred Plaut. By this time Plaut, Columbia's longtime chief engineer as well as its amateur house photographer, has been at his craft for more than two decades, and he seems to shrug off Shepard's tension. Conductor Hal Hastings, who worked on several Sondheim shows, is seen going over the score with the cast. Half the members of the cast appear to be smoking even when they're singing. Shepard, too. Sondheim, wincing at the songbird chirping in "You Can Drive a Person Crazy," takes the (Gentile) Pamela Myers aside and tries to get her to pronounce "Bubby" like "Goody." Beth Howland sings "Getting Married Today" as though she's behind only by a neck in the Belmont Stakes. (Years later, as it happens, Howland would marry costar Charles Kimbrough, who had been a classical records advisor at the Columbia Record Club before returning to the stage.) During a rare break from performing, Susan Browning points out that a performer is looser onstage, dancing and moving before an audience, than in the studio—yet it's the studio version, the original cast recording, that becomes definitive. The sound effects recorded on "Personal Relationships," most of them footfalls and the impact made by bodies bouncing off one another, are Shepard's trademark touches—moments that Lieberson probably would have jettisoned.

Then comes the film's climax, the frustrating attempts to capture Elaine Stritch singing "Ladies Who Lunch" on record. What's not apparent in the film was that Stritch was sloshed, having guzzled champagne throughout the day. Sondheim complains privately to Shepard about Stritch's performance. "Well, what the hell do you want me to do?" pleads Shepard. In that moment they appear to be the oldest of colleagues, though they had never before worked together. After one more exasperated conference, Sondheim tells Stritch, sotto voce, that the orchestra will take the number down a half tone to make it easier to negotiate. But the change doesn't help; Stritch is simply too drunk to get the number right. Meanwhile, each failed attempt at "Ladies" becomes a comment on Stritch's condition, because the number is, in fact, about drinking and dining to ward off the inevitable, death. Deep into the postmidnight hours Shepard finally dismisses the few remaining cast members, including Stritch, and records Hal Hastings's orchestra sans vocal track.

And then a miracle occurs. Stritch, refreshed, comes back the next day and sings the number to the taped backing of the orchestra. She nails "Ladies Who Lunch" so true that the recording makes everyone—Stritch, Sondheim, Shepard, even the orchestra musicians who are long gone—come off as heroic. Shepard emerges from the control booth and, beaming, shouts, "Wonderful!" And there the documentary ends.

The original cast recording was quickly edited; ten days later the LP was in stores. In early November, Larry Kert, who had replaced lead Dean Jones (Bobby) just three weeks into the run—Jones was going through a difficult divorce and needed to get home to California—recorded separate vocal tracks at the behest of Company's publisher Tommy Valando. Shepard laid Kert's vocals into the previously recorded material. The Dean Jones version won a Grammy for Shepard as the best Broadway musical on disk—one of three he won for 1970, the other two in different categories (children's, classical). More than two decades later he got a crack at remixing the tapes for compact disc. The results revealed that the 1970 show remained as fresh as when it opened.

Shepard became Sondheim's main record producer. *Pacific Overtures, Sweeney Todd, Sunday in the Park with George*, and, perhaps most lasting of all, *Follies*—all these were recorded by Shepard. They bore the mark of a man who, unlike Lieberson, was introduced at an early age to the stereophonic process and knew how to exploit it. (Like the footfalls and floorboard jumps in *Company*'s "Personal Relationships," you can hear the brilliant use of stereo in, say, the horizontal laundry chute in *Sweeney Todd*.) But none of these midperiod Sondheim recordings were done at Columbia.

Shepard was so inventive as an original cast recordings producer—and received acclaim for that inventiveness relatively early—that he could comfortably admit when he'd been wrong. In early 1973 he had seen Sondheim's *A Little Night Music*, loosely based on Ingmar Bergman's film *Smiles of a Summer Night*, and didn't imagine it would do well. Shepard suggested to Clive Davis that they pass on it. But Brigitta Lieberson saw it and encouraged her husband to see it. Lieberson, entranced, was determined to record it and, in one of the rare cases where he overruled Davis, produce it himself.

In the control booth Lieberson's more acidic side sometimes emerged. The conductor on *A Little Night Music* was once again Hal Hastings, "a wealthy man," according to Tom Shepard, "who didn't have to conduct for a living but did so anyway." Trying to get the "Night Waltz" right, Hastings insisted that he and the orchestra be allowed to play it all the way through. When the complete run-through was over, Hastings turned proudly to Lieberson to ask him what he thought. "It's shit, Hal," Lieberson said into his microphone, devastating the conductor.[67]

"I respected [Lieberson's] musicianship," the conductor Jay Blackton said, "I just couldn't stand his Park Avenueship, so to speak. Very friendly, but in a way that was holier-than-thou. But I must say he knew his business. He would use that phone to speak to us from his control room; he'd make all these public statements—of praise, or minor suggestions— and, let's face it, a lot of Broadway people who came to a recording studio were in a strange element; they were a little bit in awe of things. And Lieberson took advantage of that."[68]

●   ●   ●

With Shepard eventually decamping to RCA Victor and Clive Davis having cut way back on original cast recordings (not that there was a lot to record), Columbia added little to its Broadway catalog after *Company*. After Davis was fired in May 1973, original cast recordings were hardly on the minds of Irwin Segelstein, who'd been charged with reviving the label's credibility as its new president, or of Lieberson, who'd resumed his position as chairman. Two years later, on Friday, May 16, 1975, Lieberson officially retired from Columbia Records. At 64 he had been with Columbia Records for 36 years. The following day Lieberson made plans to produce *A Chorus Line* for records. "I'd call that episode 'The Quickest Retirement,' wouldn't you?" crowed Joyce Haber, the *Los Angeles Times*' Hollywood columnist.[69]

As the show's lyricist, Ed Kleban was being talked about as the "new Stephen Sondheim," although their lyrics weren't all that similar. Kleban favored a dewy-eyed confessional tone that might have nauseated Sondheim had he found it in himself. On Broadway, folks knew how crucial Michael Bennett, who conceived, directed, and choreographed *A Chorus Line*, was to the musical; elsewhere Marvin Hamlisch, who composed the music, got most of the ink, largely because of his musical achievements in so many areas—film, television, even accompanying Groucho Marx in concert—and was already better known. Kleban, a relative of Norman Adler's, had been in A&R at Columbia. A native Long Islander, he had lived for years in Los Angeles before moving to New York in 1966 to get into musical theater. "Ed Kleban was gifted, though not necessarily as a record producer," Tom Shepard said. "He spoke like André Previn and was very well defended."[70] Those defenses crumbled in London, where he had gone to produce a recording of *Man of La Mancha*, starring Keith Michell, for Decca in 1968. The crackup took a lot out of him. Eventually Kleban pulled himself together, went to work for Columbia, and joined Lehman Engel's Musical Theater Workshop. It was there that he transformed himself from a middling musician into a clever lyricist.

Chorus Line would prove to be the last large-scaled Broadway musical in an older, pre–Lloyd Webber tradition, where characters mattered—in this case, dancers in a chorus line—and the music was still more important than stage spectacle. Lieberson made the recording on Sunday, June 2, which happened to be Marvin Hamlisch's thirty-first birthday, with Teo Macero and Larry Morton coproducing. Frank Laico and John Guerriere were the engineers. As happens with most musical comedy recordings, the piano had to be tuned three times, at twenty bucks a pop. (The piano tuner was Robert Belanoff, a frequent visitor to 30th Street.)[71] Later, Morton did much of the tape editing.

The record didn't amass the otherworldly sales of *My Fair Lady* or *South Pacific*—it was, after all, a different time in American culture, and original cast recordings were no longer must-have albums. On the charts for nearly a year, the album never rose higher than a 98—meaning the ninety-eighth best-selling album of the week.[72] A dozen years earlier, Columbia's original cast recordings accounted for 20 percent of its total sales; now even a successful Broadway album like *A Chorus Line* was an afterthought. But the show kept running—and running. John S. Wilson of the *Times*, meanwhile, took a shot at the recording in a Sunday Arts & Leisure essay, "Musicals to Be Seen and Not Heard." Wilson was irritated that the recording omitted the monologue of Sammy Williams describing his experiences as a gay man in a drag show.[73] Lieberson, irritated in turn, composed a letter in Santa Fe to the Arts & Leisure editor, including a plug for Columbia alum Kleban: "What is poignant and moving in the theatre to Mr Wilson (and, God knows, to me as well), when removed from that context and put down on a record and played over and over, deteriorates in its emotional appeal and can become an embarrassment. . . ." Lieberson, beyond even the twilight of his long career, was reinvoking the central thesis of years of his musical theater recordings. "And, finally, a gerontological note," his letter continued: "While it is true that I have retired as an executive of a recording company, I still hope to totter to a studio from time to time, particularly if a show or anything else as fascinating as *A Chorus Line* comes along."[74]

In the year following *A Chorus Line*'s opening and the release of the album, old friends and relatives of Kleban's were coming out of the woodwork, writing to ask for house seats or simply to congratulate him. They wrote about him, too. Screenwriter-columnist Burt Prelutsky wrote that it was tough "to be civil to an old friend who has had the bad form to make it big. This profound and universal truth came home to me recently when I saw Ed Kleban for the first time in more than 10 years. When last we had played tennis, he had a good job at Columbia producing records. Then I lost track of him. I assumed he had run off and joined the French Foreign Legion in order to forget Percy Faith or some such thing."[75] Prelutsky had reason to be envious. On May 3, 1976, Kleban shared the Pulitzer Prize in Drama with Michael Bennett, Marvin Hamlisch, and librettists James Kirkwood and Nicholas Dante.

Chorus Line was only the fifth musical to win the Pulitzer, after Of Thee I Sing, South Pacific, Fiorello!, and How to Succeed in Business without Really Trying.

There would be a handful more original cast albums that did well by and for Columbia, notably Annie (1977). These were of a thinner, more utilitarian design, aimed squarely at a specific audience. Occasionally an original cast album like Ballroom (1978) or Barnum (1980) harked back to more Broadway-friendly days. But after A Chorus Line the Broadway musical as we knew it began to lean heavily on marketing—of plots recycled from movies and television, of inadequately trained celebrities who worked on Broadway because it was positive public relations—and Lieberson was no longer around anyway to guide the label through its recordings. Over at RCA, Tom Shepard was handling a lot of Sondheim's later work, and more than once was forced to stand up to David Merrick, as despotic a producer as Broadway had seen in the twentieth century. But the Great White Way belonged to Andrew Lloyd Webber, whose recordings were done by Decca, then MCA and Polydor. Profitable as they were, it's unlikely Lieberson would have gone anywhere near them.

14

Just Before the Revolution

The widely praised musical *Kicks & Co*, which was showcased on a no less popular program than NBC's *Today Show*, never made it to Broadway. Its creator—composer, lyricist, and librettist rolled into one satanically entertaining, politically astute dynamo—was the young Chicagoan Oscar Brown Jr., who signed with Columbia Records in 1960. Through the sixties, show business commentators often cited Sammy Davis Jr. as the greatest all-around entertainer. Oscar Brown didn't dance—not on stage, anyway—but he wrote and performed songs that will be only more valued well into this current century. Also unlike Davis, he was at the forefront of the civil rights movement from the beginning of his recording career.

Brown had been a teenage radio personality on the "Negro Newsfront" program in Chicago. He spent a few years working for his father, a local real estate attorney who managed the Ida B. Wells Housing Project, Chicago's first Negro public housing works, and was president of the NAACP's Chicago chapter during World War II.[1] The younger Brown, born in 1926, spent two years in the army before turning to music. The songs Brown was writing—alternately angry, tender, and funny, and sometimes all three at once—were derived from his observations of the big city and from black folklore. They caught the attention of Robert Nemiroff, who was in town with *A Raisin in the Sun*, written by his wife Lorraine Hansberry. Nemiroff's enthusiasm for Brown infected Columbia's pop A&R department, particularly producer Al Ham. When Columbia released the album *Sin and Soul* in 1960, nobody at the label, let alone the record-buying public, had heard anything like it. It was jazzy, occasionally dirgelike, and never less than brilliant. Many of the songs were completed with music by other musicians—"Dat Dere" (Bobby Timmons), "The Work Song" (Nat Adderley), and "Afro Blue" (Mongo Santamaria), to name only three—but they were stamped with Brown's unique passion and playfulness. *Between Heaven and Hell, In a New Mood* (these two produced by Bob Morgan), and *Oscar Brown Jr. Tells It Like It Is* followed on Columbia. The albums contained fully worked out playlets like "Brown Baby," "Signifying Monkey," "Mr. Kicks" (which the Rolling Stones must have heard before writing "Sympathy for the Devil"), the punctured self-inflation of "But I Was Cool," and the chilling slave auctioneer's recitative "Bid 'Em In." Whatever its genesis, the album *In a New Mood* sounds like an anomaly—Brown singing standards, many of them associated with the label's shows. During Brown's four-album tenure at Columbia, Al Ham appeared to have left the A&R staff to manage Brown's career full-time.

Shortly after Brown departed, too, he made what might be his most interesting album of all, the live *Oscar Brown Jr. Goes to Washington*, on Fontana (a subsidiary rather than a partner of Philips), with his hopeful blues "Brother, Where Are You?" and a metropolitan medley that evokes a mid-century version of the symphony of the city.[2] There's a direct line from his comic-mordant songs to those of Gil Scott-Heron's and then Kurtis Blow's, but Brown is rarely acknowledged as the influence he must have been.

In the late sixties Brown's music finally made it to Broadway in *Buck White*, his adaptation of Joseph Dolan Tuotti's play *Big Time Buck White*. The musical was notable for starring, after much negotiating, Muhammad Ali—formerly Cassius Clay—who wanted two weeks off from the run of the musical in case his promoters got him a fight with heavyweight champ Joe Frazier—although, Ali reminded reporters, he needed only one week to train for "that bum" Frazier.[3]

It also took some negotiating to have Cassius Clay record for Columbia in 1962. Dave Kapralik, the nervy head of A&R at the time, had been delighted by Clay's off-the-cuff witticisms. He contacted

Clay's agent Jerry Brandt (William Morris), visited Clay in Louisville, and a deal was struck to record the young boxer reciting his poems. (The album's release was timed to promote Clay's championship match against Sonny Liston in 1964.) Kapralik assigned Mike Berniker to produce. To come up with a good chunk of material, Kapralik hired comedy writer Gary Belkin. Belkin suggested they bring in members of Chicago's famed Second City troupe to improvise behind Clay. A journeyman joke writer whose résumé included *New Yorker* captions and long stints with Sid Caesar and Carol Burnett, Belkin later insisted to have written every line declaimed by Clay on the album. Sportswriters dismissed Belkin's claim, citing the champ's well-known improvisatory skills.[4]

* * *

As a boxer Muhammad Ali was sublime. Whether or not Ali or Gary Belkin was the primary author of the album's material, Columbia Records was smart to exploit his charisma. In later years Ali would become the single most significant athlete in the world—less for his considerable boxing skills than for his brave antiwar stance, his willingness to give up his crown and go to jail for it, his outspokenness about American policy in Vietnam. Gary Belkin didn't write those heartfelt pacificistic words for him. Early and late, Muhammad Ali was one of a kind.

So was Aretha Franklin, even though, the general wisdom goes, Columbia Records didn't know quite what to do with her. She recorded her first Columbia sides in the summer of 1960, when she was barely 18, Aretha playing piano when she felt like it; otherwise it was Ray Bryant, with strong trombone support from Tyree Glenn; Bill Lee (Spike's dad) or Milt Hinton played bass. All the sides were made as singles. Six tunes were by Johnny MacFarland, and "Today I Sing the Blues" was by Curtis Lewis, which is the number that John Hammond first heard her sing on.

Hammond had been back at Columbia Records for about a year.

Pushing 50, his life on the surface seemed different than when he'd departed in 1946 under Ted Wallerstein's thundercloud. He was now married to the beautiful Esme Sarnoff, who'd been divorced from Robert Sarnoff, son of RCA's longtime chairman, and had settled into the life of a town and country gentleman: Manhattan during the week, Westport house on weekends. Hammond still possessed those amazing ears. In a letter to the jazz critic Leonard Feather, who'd recently moved west, Hammond wrote, "We are horribly busy here at Columbia, and I'm happy to say that Aretha Franklin looks as if she were going to become a very big star. The first record made the charts this week and the next one coming up is a real gasser. It's called 'Won't Be Long' and it will be released towards the end of December."[5] "Won't Be Long" was indeed a strong single in 1961. For all her power and evident woman-liness, though, Aretha was still only 18, already a mother of two chil-dren and buffeted among family members and protectors. Her manager Jo King was based on the Upper East Side of Manhattan, her legal guardian, Hobart Taylor Jr., in Detroit. Something had to give. Her early Columbia recordings were more theatrical than gospel; their charts could have been made for, say, Steve Lawrence. But they were extremely effective and made Aretha's name. Aretha and Jo King complained about Hammond's direction—or, more likely, his reluctance to direct—to Dave Kapralik. Soon Hammond was on the defensive. On March 22, 1962, he wrote to Aretha: "I did not understand your telegram dismissing me as your recording agent since, of course, I have never been an agent of yours in any way, shape, or manner. I am employed by Columbia Records as a producer and I can assure you that Columbia intends to enforce all the provisions of its contract with you. . . . We do hope to hear from you soon so that we can make more recordings without me as your producer."[6] Kapralik turned Aretha's recording sessions over to Al Kasha, and Hammond stepped back. Soon he would be excited about another young musician who had little in common with Aretha. At Columbia Aretha was assigned to other producers, including Clyde Otis and Robert Mersey, and made a lot of tape covering Dinah Washington, Billie Holiday, and Nina Simone.[7] In another couple of years, before

Aretha moved over to Atlantic Records where Jerry Wexler "put her back in church" and deferred to her own musical judgments, there was a break with Jo King as well. In early 1965 King sued her former client in New York Supreme Court.[8] Aretha would reach out again to Hammond, but by then she was comfortably under Wexler's protection.

As it was happening Hammond recounted a lot of this to Leonard Feather. And he also liked the idea that Feather was spending time with his friends the Townsends who, like Feather, had recently become Angelenos.

•　　•　　•

Irving Townsend was a Massachusetts Yankee. He described himself as "the most recent member of a long line of Townsends who for generations have refused to leave New England," whose idea of the West was the Berkshires.[9] He attended Hotchkiss, which bonded him forever to Columbia's other Hotchkiss alumnus John Hammond (who was a decade older), then Princeton. At Princeton, where the Columbia liner-note writer Charles Burr was a classmate, Townsend played the clarinet. Serving in the Pacific, he left the navy as a lieutenant and returned to New York. He worked briefly at an advertising agency, went to RCA, and to Keynote to join Hammond there. He arrived at Columbia as a copy-writer. George Avakian, recognizing not only his writing ability but his gentle way with artists, brought him into A&R as a producer, along with Cal Lampley, who had been editing tape.

As Avakian sensed, Townsend could write and handle some tough customers. Duke Ellington was alternately sweet and cranky, and Townsend let him have his way. After Avakian left the label, the magnificent Mahalia Jackson, who claimed to have had no formal training— she just listened to phonograph records, she said, particularly Bessie Smith—relied on Townsend to get her through each session. Townsend produced the original cast recording of Abe Burrows's *First Impressions*— he'd inherited the assignment because Lieberson hated the musical and, afraid to reveal this to his friend Burrows, fled to California—and managed to calm down Polly Bergen, a valued Columbia artist in her own right, after she lost her voice. A strong producer can save a recording session by improvising. Townsend had Bergen sing to just a harpsichord backing, which apparently did the trick.[10]

Sentence for sentence, Townsend might have been the most vivid prose writer still at the label. Avakian had a deeper knowledge of jazz; George Dale knew a lot about show music; and Charlie Burr knew a little about everything, literary as well as musical. But Townsend had a gift for the snapshot, for capturing a resonant moment involving an artist. In his notes for *The Memorable Claude Thornhill*, Townsend wrote that in 1943 he'd been an ensign at Admiral Chester Nimitz's Makalapa headquarters overlooking Pearl Harbor; he missed New York terribly, but suddenly hearing Thornhill's "Snowfall" turned out to be "better than a letter from home." Writing about Lionel Hampton's album *Golden Vibes*, Townsend pointed out that Hampton "has been heard at greater distances than any jazzman alive. I can remember hearing him at the drums when Benny Goodman was playing in the Empire Room of the Waldorf Astoria in New York City and I was walking by on Park Avenue." But *Golden Vibes*, Townsend added with his trademark delicate touch, "is an album you have to bend a little to hear." When Jimmy Rushing, Mr. Five by Five, needed a place to record again, John Hammond, who'd recorded him years earlier with Basie, welcomed him to Vanguard. But Hammond knew that Vanguard didn't have the promotional force of a larger company, namely Columbia, so he sent him over to Townsend, who signed him. Rushing turned out to be so in awe of Duke Ellington that he would accompany Townsend to Duke's 30th Street studio sessions and hang back shyly, watching and listening. "The Rushing-Basie association hung like an invisible curtain between Duke and Jimmy," Townsend wrote.[11] Rushing and Townsend became mutually admiring correspondents, with Rushing sending letter after letter from Europe in 1959. Writing about Ellington five years after his death, Townsend recalled walking with him one midnight into a Broadway record store, "a narrow stall lit by islands of white fluorescent tubes and filled with record bins. It was about to close, and there were no more than half a dozen insomniacs browsing through the ranks of the albums. As we walked down the center aisle, a young woman approached Ellington, hesitated until he noticed her, and then said, 'Mr Ellington, I never met George Gershwin, but I think you and he are the greatest composers in America.'" Duke was struck speechless, Townsend reported, but his eyes shone.[12]

Townsend was sensitive and funny and, to so many observers, seemed either perpetually nervous or to be suffering from alcoholic tremors. In fact he had a lifelong neurological disorder that had plagued his father, too; the disorder made him shake, as though he had Parkinson's, and was exacerbated by anger.[13] The anger was all the more corrosive for being banked. In Connecticut Townsend's marriage had been in trouble. His glamorous wife Winifred Harriet Thompson, more commonly known as Freddie and sister of the pulp writer Jim Thompson, longed to be in the city rather than the suburbs. Freddie had come into the marriage with a daughter, Randi, from a previous union, and she and Townsend had three more daughters: the chronically ailing Susie, Nicole, and Jeremy. When it came time to pack up and move to Los Angeles, to get Susie into the UCLA program and assume his responsibilities at Columbia's LA offices on Sunset Boulevard, Townsend turned the Connecticut house over to Dave Brubeck and his family, who were moving east from the San Francisco Bay Area.

The Townsends' first Los Angeles residence was in Brentwood. Freddie was pleased for a time because Brentwood wasn't far from UCLA or Hollywood. Townsend tended to be an indifferent, not to say negligent, husband, and for a while he immersed himself in the label's West Coast operations. Mahalia Jackson, for one, was so enamored of Townsend's studio demeanor that she moved her recording sessions to Los Angeles to continue working with him.[14]

But neither of the adult Townsends was particularly happy. Irv was disenchanted with Los Angeles. Settling in its concrete verdancy, Townsend wondered, "Where was the West I had watched on television back East?"[15] Freddie, longing for a view of the ocean, persuaded Townsend to move the family a couple of miles west to Pacific Palisades.

Townsend agreed to the move because he worked long days and evenings in Hollywood; placating his wife was the least he could do.

Into the sixties Townsend's work schedule rarely let up. He recorded André Previn with strings, the Hi-Lo's, the saxophonist John Handy and the pianist John Williams, a former Columbia staff arranger and not yet the one-man film-scoring industry he would become. Taking an opposite tack from Mitch Miller's, Townsend was particularly effective coaxing strong performances from female singers by being gentle and patient rather than authoritative. Because there was so much television scoring to be done in Southern California, the caliber of local musicians was higher than ever. In December 1962, in a declaration that it took the West Coast seriously, Columbia Records broke ground on a new record plant in Santa Maria, 150 miles north of Los Angeles, where operations were overseen by longtime vice president Andy Schrade. Townsend found himself in the thick of all this record-making activity. On the West Coast it was a high time.

Still, he found the business increasingly ugly. When youngest daughter Jeremy asked him what he actually did each day, he replied, "You don't want to know."

Susie's illness kept the Townsends together for a while. In April 1964 Columbia Records and Whittier College cosponsored a benefit concert for the Susan Townsend Scholarship Fund, with André Previn and Mahalia Jackson leading a bill that included the label's old spoken word master Norman Corwin and its number one singing star at the time, Andy Williams.[16] Townsend encouraged Susie's poetry and piano-playing, though long stays in the Metabolic Unit at UCLA Medical Center precluded the latter. Meanwhile he fell in love with the Santa Ynez Valley, less than an hour north of Santa Barbara but almost a three-hour drive to Los Angeles, and bought a ranch. In the coming years he would keep animals there, including a horse called Chestnut and a colt called Mattei, named after the nineteenth-century tavern in nearby Los Olivos. Freddie, a city girl, didn't share Townsend's love of the Santa Ynez Valley. She stayed married to him, though, mostly for the sake of the kids.

•   •   •

Townsend was mercifully far away from the downfall of Debbie Ishlon, who ran Columbia Records' Creative Services Department—advertising, art, literary, and publicity—as though it was her own Seventh Avenue duchy. Word was that throughout the 1950s, when she had real executive power, Columbia Records annually paid the highest unemployment bill in New York because she fired staffers so frequently.[17] On Ishlon's orders, building services administrator Hazel Rudis would have the dismissed employee's desk removed by lunchtime.[18] But Ishlon sometimes fired an employee herself, then retreated to her office facing Seventh Avenue, expecting her wounded victim to be gone by the end of the day. Bright and utterly devoted to Lieberson, Ishlon often rubbed people the wrong way. Stan Kavan claimed not to have had much trouble dealing with her, but there's evidence in the files that Ishlon badmouthed Kavan and Masterworks director Howard Scott and just about anyone else who didn't agree with her.[19] "She tried to make trouble for Bob Cato," art director John Berg recalled. "She would tell stories about him to Goddard and other people, trying to get him killed." Although Ishlon was Cato's boss, Cato didn't hide the contempt he felt in return for her. "He would talk behind her back so she could hear it," Berg said, "and call her a bitch and every possible thing."[20]

By the time Ishlon was made vice president in May 1960, she answered to no one but Lieberson.[21] "She was no feminist," said Maida Glancy, who started at Columbia Records fresh out of Hunter College working as a proofreader in the literary department. "This was before women's lib. Most men were terrified of her." Ishlon's memorandums were distinctively initialed: a lowercase d and an even smaller i that suggested, in their deliberate diminution, how much power she had. "When she didn't like somebody she deliberately misspelled his name," Peter Munves said.[22]

Yet Ishlon did her job very well. Her pull helped land Dave Brubeck on the cover of *Time*, the second jazz musician to be so honored, on November 8, 1954, shortly after he arrived at the label, and helped again two years later to arrange for Duke Ellington's *Time* cover. She is widely credited with conceiving Columbia's "I Like Jazz" campaign, generating publicity for its jazz artists through the 1950s. She looked after the more demanding Masterworks artists as well. After she had worked to arrange a documentary about the premiere of *Le Sacre du Printemps*, Stravinsky came up to the seventh floor at 799, where he was introduced to the Creative Services staff. "Ishlon?" said Stravinsky. "Is that a Russian name?" "No, Maestro, I'm Jewish," replied Ishlon. "Ah, I admire so much the Jews," Stravinsky said. "So clever with their fingers."[23] Ishlon was thick-skinned; garden variety anti-Semitism didn't faze her. Most important to Columbia Records, she anticipated what Lieberson wanted without being told. When chastised by her, irritated subordinates wondered why Lieberson was so attached to her—this plain, aggressive woman of limited social skills—and latched onto an unkillable rumor that placed Ishlon in a communist cell with Lieberson, Nat Shapiro, and Mitch Miller. The rumor still seems extravagant. Miller was an active Democrat, openly campaigning for Adlai Stevenson in both presidential elections in the fifties, as was Lieberson, who had already publicly defended himself from Red-baiting. "Miss Debbie Ishlon, our publicity gal," is how Lieberson referred to her in a letter to an old Seattle friend, the neutral phrase masking his dependence on her.[24] In the midfifties she persuaded Lieberson to appear in short films promoting Masterworks. Lieberson, as much of a ham in front of a camera lens as he was with a microphone at his chin, adored her for it.

Ishlon was an instinctive press agent. Born in 1926, she attended Penn State and the University of Chicago, then went to work as a secretary in the Columbia Records press department. In 1951 she was promoted to director of the department. For the next few years she worked closely with Lieberson, even when Jim Conkling was officially running the label.

For all her manipulativeness, she could ingratiate herself when she wanted to. Elizabeth Larsen Lauer, the classically trained pianist and composer who began at Columbia in the Data and Scheduling Department in 1957, remembered being warned about Ishlon. Stay clear of her, everyone told her. After Lauer went to work as Lieberson's assistant that December, she saw how Ishlon worshipped the boss. Ishlon wore big, perched eyeglasses and funny hats. (Photographs make her look like Andrea Martin's impression of Pauline Kael.) When Lauer returned to New York from a trip to Mexico and presented Ishlon with a new hat, she recalled, "You would have thought I'd brought her a Rolls Royce!"[25]

Doubleday's Ken McCormick needed Columbia Records to nudge Igor Stravinsky toward cooperating on a book project, so Lieberson put Ishlon on the case. "You have a love in that Debbie Ishlon," McCormick wrote to Lieberson on September 15, 1958. "She certainly has been a tower of strength to help us with the illustrations for Stravinsky's book [probably *Conversations with Igor Stravinsky*], and to help us a second time when he got capricious and cancelled out some illustrations and wanted some which are hanging on the walls of his closed house in California!"[26] In Ishlon, Lieberson had the closest he would come to having a protégée—not a musician but a loyal, can-do foot soldier.

In Ishlon he also had a strong writer. In the month following the Stravinsky intervention, Ishlon began to send sections of a novel to McCormick. "Your Debbie Ishlon is coming along with a charming novel," McCormick wrote to Lieberson.[27] A year and a half later the novel was in bookstores, where most of the copies sat—and sat. *Girl Singer: A Two Part Invention* (Doubleday) remains a fascinating piece of work, however. Whether Ishlon would have published it had Mitch Miller not had one foot out the door is debatable. More certain is that the models for the novel's central Trilby-Svengali relationship are Miller and the Columbia pop singer Jill Corey.

●　●　●

When *Girl Singer* opens, young Anna Lou Schreckengost, a lost western Pennsylvania girl with a big voice, is home when she gets a call from Sid Harper, head of A&R at Blackwood Records in New York and a very successful record producer. (Columbia's publishing arm was April-Blackwood.) Sid talks fast and calls her "Honey." He has heard a tape of her singing and wants her to come to New York to sing for him in person.

"Every minute was so different I never had time to think about New

York," Anna Lou says, "and did I want to go there, like I always waited for it to be Saturday night."[28]

Anna Lou goes to New York. Through her still-scaly eyes, in what is the novel's most hackneyed sequence, we see Manhattan as the majestic-scary place it's been to newcomers for centuries. Sid records her and makes her over, giving her the stage name Beth Adams. Married and an excellent musician in his own right, the prolix Sid is nagged by a conscience, usually in the voice of his old conservatory mentor Amos. "Why such anxious frenzy to listen to probable mediocrity, Sidney?" Because Sid makes a lot of money for Blackwood, that's why. Sid arranges for the pretty Beth to be photographed by *Eye* magazine and, after television personalities vie to claim her as their discovery, shoves her in the direction of morning TV host Dave Barry.

In 1953 Mitch Miller took under his wing the doe-eyed, comely Jill Corey, from Avonmore, Pennsylvania, coal mining country. (Corey was born Norma Jean Speranza and sang in her church choir and with a local dance band.) Miller had been sent a recording of the 17-year-old's voice and asked her to fly to New York. After Corey signed with Columbia Records, Arthur Godfrey and Dave Garroway vied to introduce her to a national audience; Corey, probably on Miller's counsel, went with Garroway (even though Godfrey had a strong link to Columbia). Garroway told the press he'd picked the name Jill Corey out of the phone book for her. The November 9, 1953, cover of *Life* teased, "Small-town girl gets a new name and a new career," and inside was a sweet photo spread of Corey shot by Gordon Parks. In *Girl Singer* the Svengali-like Sid doesn't overtly come on to Beth, but there's considerable sexual tension in the way he manipulates her, reminding her that the power belongs to *him*, not to her. The untutored Beth has an untrained voice that only he can lift to a listenable level. He even breaks up a brief romance Beth has with an actor. (Corey had dated Eddie Fisher before marrying the baseball player Don Hoak.) Ishlon conveys all this without resorting to a single purplish line; whatever went on between Miller and Corey outside the recording studio in the midfifties, it's only murmured here by Ishlon.

Girl Singer isn't a great novel; it may not even be a good one. It begins too slowly, and with a touch of condescension for its small-town German-American characters—the "little people" steeped in their churchgoing and cooking. Once Anna Lou/Beth's ascent to stardom is established, the narrative doesn't build. Instead it becomes an insider's view of the record business—a world where innocence is quickly snuffed out in the service of making a profit.

Yet Ishlon's novel is shot through with a vitality lacking in so much fiction about pop music. The novel is very American in its attempt to tell a jazzy story while observing differences in class, education, and income. Despite the book's deficiencies, Ishlon reaches further in it than Lieberson did in his 3 for *Bedroom C*. Ishlon, like Lieberson, published her only novel when she was 34; but hers is the more ambitious, even more mature, work. *Bedroom C* is professionally constructed, clever, and populated by types who disappear as soon as you turn the page; *Girl Singer* is messy, more quietly witty, and driven by character. *Bedroom C*'s central (and chaste) romance, musical references, and epigrams are finally all about Lieberson; in *Girl Singer* the conception of Sid Harper molding, then breaking, this poor girl is so strong that you forget it was composed by a record executive.

●　●　●

Right around the time *Girl Singer* was published, Ishlon moved from Greenwich Village to West 56th Street, just a roll out of bed and into the office. It was as though her devotion to Lieberson and Columbia Records demanded the closest proximity. The move to midtown did little to soften her, however. "She was difficult because she was so emotional," said Morris Baumstein, a Creative Services executive under Ishlon. "But she had an enormous awareness of art and literature."[29] In the course of eighteen months or so, Ishlon fired Baumstein five or six times and each time seemed to forget about it within hours. On vacation in Jamaica he got a phone call from Ishlon terminating him; when he returned to New York and went into the office to collect his things, she spoke to him as though the call had never taken place. So he went back to work.

In late 1961 Baumstein and Bob Cato accompanied Ishlon to Los Angeles to see designers there about creating a new look for Columbia's album jackets. They checked into the Beverly Hills Hotel. Ishlon, controlling her employees' mobility, rented an expense-account car for herself but not for them. Late one evening, long past Ishlon's bedtime, Baumstein hankered for an ice cream, so he grabbed Cato and together they went into the hotel garage to get the car, intending to drive to Wil Wright's in Beverly Hills. The parking valet, citing "strict orders" from Ishlon, refused them the keys. That was so much like Ishlon that Cato and Baumstein had to laugh. Determined to get ice cream anyway, the two men set out on foot. A cop stopped them and, because walking in Beverly Hills was then and is still an activity that invites suspicion, suggested they return to the hotel and go into town only when they had a car.

●   ●   ●

When the ax fell, it was swift. By early 1962 it was rumored that Norman Adler and Harvey Schein, two Columbia attorneys who each took an ear of Lieberson's, wanted Ishlon gone. Complaints about her, they argued, particularly her penchant for firing people and running up the company's unemployment obligations, had outrun her achievements. Lieberson was already beginning to turn away from his oft-repeated thesis that musicians make good businessmen; lawyers, he seemed to feel now, made *better* businessmen. (Lawyers also didn't threaten Lieberson's position as the preeminent musician-executive in the industry.) Finally worn down by the argument that Ishlon was a liability, Lieberson acquiesced to her termination. Arranging to be out of town on the black day, he left for Tokyo. Cliff Benfield, who was running Personnel, was dispatched to Ishlon's 56th Street apartment to fire her.[30] She had worked at Columbia for 16 years.

Most of Ishlon's colleagues weren't sorry to see her go. But Liz Lauer, who had begun to produce recordings for Columbia, was livid. When Lieberson returned to the office, she insisted he call Ishlon personally.

Mensch that Lieberson could be, he did so, and reported to Lauer that Ishlon seemed fine.[31]

Word piped through the music community. Eugene Ormandy, whose Philadelphia Orchestra had been ably served by Ishlon's publicity campaigns, checked in with Lieberson: "For quite some time I have been hearing rumors about Debbie Ishlon's leaving Columbia Records, and last week I heard that she had left. Not being a believer in rumors, I thought I would write you directly. If the report is true, I know you will miss her very much because she was certainly loyal to you."[32] Lieberson, perhaps with genuine optimism, replied, "When I see you, I will tell you more extensively about the position of Debbie Ishlon, who, by the way, I hope will stay on for some special work for us."[33]

It wasn't to be; Columbia's first female vice president was gone for good. Only 36 when she left, she went on to hold several more positions in advertising and publicity, including director of special projects for National Educational Television. At one point, searching for a job, she showed up at the Manhattan employment agency run by Tom Shepard's mother-in-law Toby Clark.[34] In her sixties Ishlon made what seems like a bizarre political leap by becoming corporate relations director for Pierre Rinfret, the conservative economist whom the GOP selected as its sacrificial lamb in the New York gubernatorial race against Mario Cuomo. Then again, maybe she was just making a living. She died of lymphoma in May 1994.[35]

Ishlon's position was vacant for a while. Lieberson finally promoted Schuyler Chapin from Masterworks director into the Creative Services slot, offering him a vice presidency in the bargain. Though Chapin now had a fancier title, with say-so over both classical and pop, he regarded Creative Services as a strangely remote continent, a department encompassing advertising, art and design, literary (i.e., liner notes), and promotion. Restless to go back to work with classical artists and their repertoires, Chapin stayed less than a year before accepting William Schuman's invitation to join Lincoln Center.

• • •

More than four decades after the fact, John Hammond's "discovery" of an enigmatic, cherub-faced kid who called himself Bob Dylan has passed into legend. By most accounts, it went back to Hammond's failure to sign Joan Baez. Accompanied by her manager Albert Grossman, Baez had visited the Columbia offices at 799 and had listened while Hammond talked about what the label could do for her. Up to this day, most recording artists want to know precisely that. But Baez was irritated that Hammond didn't suggest what she might be able to do for the label. As David Hadju described it, "the air conditioning gave her a chill, and the gold records on the walls seemed to glare like royal plunder."[36] Baez signed instead with Vanguard.

Dave Kapralik, who had idolized Hammond for his civil rights work and had celebrated Hammond's return to the label before becoming his boss, was displeased. So Columbia signed the folk singer Carolyn Hester. It was a consolation prize at best. Married to Richard Fariña, who would later become Baez's brother-in-law, Hester was no less beautiful than Baez and owned a powerful voice, but something was missing—an awareness, perhaps, of subtext in some of the songs she sang, as though she'd learned them by rote.

Bob Dylan admired Hester—she was from Austin and had played with Buddy Holly there—and agreed to play harmonica behind her on that first Columbia record. Hammond went to Hester's apartment to get a feel for the songs she intended to sing, and that's when he first heard Dylan. "Have you ever recorded for anybody?" Hammond asked Dylan, who simply shook his head no. When Dylan appeared second on the bill to the Greenbrier Boys at Gerde's Folk City, Robert Shelton's prescient review in the Times gave all the ink to Dylan. [37] The next day, at Hester's recording session, Hammond told Dylan he wanted to record him for Columbia Records. Dylan wasn't about to say no. The folk labels (Vanguard, for one) had declined to record him. And Columbia Records had recently signed Pete Seeger, one of Dylan's heroes, even though Seeger was still blacklisted by parent company CBS. "Where do I sign?" said the kid. Hammond showed him where and sent him home with two not-yet-released Columbia records, one of them reissues by a blues singer he'd never heard of, Robert Johnson, drawn from the pre-CBS vaults.[38] Listening to those 25-year-old recordings in his West 4th Street apartment, Dylan was mesmerized, then galvanized. Johnson's songs spoke to him directly without wasting a line.

Dylan knew the Queens girl Carla Rotolo because she was the personal assistant of the ethnomusicologist Alan Lomax, and through her met her sister Suze.[39] While Dylan was experiencing the hyperreal intensity of signing with Columbia Records—even for such an apparently insouciant kid it was a life-changing event—Suze turned him on to the poetry of Arthur Rimbaud. Robert Johnson's song forms and Rimbaud's visionary derangement of the senses were only two of Dylan's many influences, but they were the ones coursing through his blood as he worked out new material, even if some of that new material wouldn't appear on record for years.

Before recording his first album, Dylan provided Billy James, the young, button-down head of publicity, with a romanticized biography, claiming his parents were working-class folks from Illinois, his dad an electrician and his mom a housewife; that he'd been kicked out of their house when very young; had since worked construction and finally come to New York riding a freight car, hobo-style. James took it all down.[40] (The following year James would move out to the West Coast and become Columbia's point man on the Sunset Strip. By 1965, no longer button-down, he was promoting the Byrds, who successfully covered several Dylan songs.)[41]

Bob Dylan was recorded in Studio A at 799 Seventh Avenue, in just a few hours over two days in late November 1961. Most of the material wasn't original Dylan, though he made every song his own. Kapralik had his doubts about the album and contemplated leaving it on the shelf. Hammond fought hard for it. The album was finally released in March 1962. By then Columbia (in the notes signed by Stacey Williams) had straightened out much of Dylan's biography and reprinted about half of Shelton's *Times* article on the back cover.[42] The folk music boom was then at its loudest but, as Kapralik's instincts had warned him, the album didn't sell well.

But people who heard the album knew there would be more from Dylan. One of these people was Baez's manager, Albert Grossman, who officially became Dylan's manager and promptly tried to maneuver him out of the publishing and recording contracts he'd signed. Meanwhile Dylan was recording his second album, *The Freewheelin' Bob Dylan*, which was almost *all* Dylan originals.[43] This album took more than a few hours, though—it wouldn't be released until a year after its first recording session. During that time Dylan wrote to Hammond, on Grossman's direction, stating that the Columbia contract he'd signed was null and void because he'd been a minor at the time and he wanted back all the material he'd recorded thus far. "I got Bob Dylan into my office," Hammond wrote to Kapralik, "and had him sign a letter repudiating the previous one and reaffirming his original contract. His lawyer Dave Braun, who had prepared the previous letter, was actually Al Grossman's lawyer and not Bob's. . . ."[44]

It was all straightened out, but not before Columbia's young general counsel Clive Davis got involved. Like so many of the label's attorneys preceding him, and like Walter Yetnikoff after him, Davis had been with Rosenman & Colin before being lured to Columbia Records. A contract more favorable to Dylan was drawn up and signed by both parties.

But Hammond was on the way out—not of Dylan's life, just his recording career.

Through Dylan's next two acoustic albums, *The Times They Are A-Changin'* and *Another Side of Bob Dylan*, Hammond's support didn't waver.[45] Nobody else was writing songs at once so tough and poetic as "A Hard Rain's A-Gonna Fall," its wise, St. Matthew imagery rushing by like film through a Movieola. Journalists pressed him about why he wasn't overtly political, as though a song like "Masters of War" wasn't already more powerful than a picket sign or an appearance on the steps of the Capitol. Impresarios often introduced him to audiences as "yours," as though (unlike, say, Elvis) he belonged to the "people." The more his admirers spoke of him in proprietary terms, the more he bridled. Dylan didn't belong to anyone. In the next two years, a streak of cruelty emerged in his songs, leading toward that electric rail yard where he'd turn early folk fans into detractors while making some of the most durable, beautiful rock 'n' roll ever recorded.

* * *

Dylan had a major supporter in Johnny Cash, a Columbia Records artist since 1958. Recording mostly in Nashville under the supervision of Don Law, Cash borrowed well—from Tex Ritter, the Carter family, and Jack Elliot among them—and that bourbon-dark baritone made everything he sang his own. It shouldn't be surprising that Cash maintained a mutually admiring professional relationship with Lieberson, who'd asked him to come up with something for his Legacy project *The Badmen* (1963). Cash wrote "Hardin Wouldn't Run," about the desperado turned jailhouse lawyer John Wesley Hardin, though not in time for the Legacy record. (Dylan would also write about Hardin, whose autobiography was published in 1896, the year after he was killed in a saloon.) When Cash saw a 1964 *Look* magazine piece about three-dimensional photographs, the Man in Black proposed a 3-D album cover, though he acknowledged how expensive it would be. Typically, Lieberson wrote back assuring Cash that Bob Cato had reported they were at least two years away from turning out 3-D in mass production, but if they could make it work, the first 3-D cover would belong to Cash.[46] This was the period when Cash was hammering his music on an anvil, "Ring of Fire" released to great acclaim and his early "I Walk the Line" re-released with success. Jack Elliot had expanded on a song called "The Ballad of Charles Guiteau," about the man who shot President Garfield—and whose trial, incidentally, had been covered by the nation's top stenographer of the day, Edward D. Easton. Cash recorded "Mister Garfield," closing a Columbia Records circle that contained its first president and, half a century later, its most consistently popular Southern recording artist.

15

Silver Anniversary

Since Dave Brubeck's dissatisfaction with what he regarded as Columbia's myopic response to *Time Out*, things weren't the same. He and his wife, Iola, had worked for a long time on their show *The Real Ambassadors*.[1] An ambitious work, it was said to have been neglected because it was all about jazz. In fact the show is built around archetypes if not just plain types. In its first major public performance, at the Monterey Jazz Festival, September 23, 1962, Louis Armstrong played the Hero; Carmen McRae sang the Girl; and Lambert, Hendricks, and Bavan served as the Chorus. The show was written expressly for Armstrong, "having him participate in the performance in the unself-conscious manner peculiar to him."[2] The show's theme was the discovery of jazz by the State Department. The Hero's imagination is spurred by a revolution in the tiny kingdom of Talgalla. But first there's groundwork to be laid at home. "Forget Moscow," growls the Hero, "when do we play New Orleans!" Although Columbia recorded the show, it has remained largely in the shadows, save for "Summer Song," the wistful memory ballad Armstrong popularized.

* * *

Brubeck was still being handled by Teo Macero, who was producing so many recording sessions he made Columbia refugee George Avakian seem like a slacker by comparison. Each month brought a new demand from Miles Davis, who drew oxygen from the turmoil he created at the company. Macero was first in line to field these demands, and then he had other headaches. Could Columbia put up $1,000 to help bail Jon Hendricks, of Lambert, Hendricks & Ross, out of jail in Cleveland? The grand would be treated as an advance against unearned royalties. Could Columbia somehow get into the 30th Street apartment of Annie Ross, who was spending most of her time in England, to recover a phonograph the company had loaned her? Macero championed Mimi Perrin's Double Six of Paris; did what he could do to get vibraphonist Gary Burton, who was unhappy at RCA, to the label; and pleaded with Dave Kapralik and Lieberson not to drop that fine but consistently money-losing trombonist J. J. Johnson. (In a memo to Kapralik, Macero rightly called Johnson one of the "great jazz people on Columbia." The memo was returned with a note in the margin scribbled by Lieberson: "We've got to drop someone—is there another instead?—it becomes a matter of choice.")[3] Macero attended the funeral of Terry Snyder, who was briefly the label's resident jazz-in-stereo mavin before he'd died of a ruptured ileostomy, and the strain was evident when Macero wrote to Irving Townsend in Los Angeles about Snyder's unreleased new album, "I am so glad you are going to handle everything from out there."[4]

Overextended as Macero was, it was probably right that he be the one to look out for Thelonious Monk, an original among musicians, jazz or otherwise. They had even played together once on television—on *The Steve Allen Show*, on the night of June 10, 1955, with Macero on saxophone.[5]

Although Monk wouldn't receive mainstream national publicity until his widely publicized stint at the Five Spot in 1957, long after everyone in the jazz world knew who he was, Columbia had had its eye on him. In late September 1961, after the label had made its first approach to Monk, Riverside claimed that he still hadn't fulfilled his contract with them. Walter Dean sent a memo to Macero suggesting he keep in touch with Monk's manager, Harry Colomby, "and to push him for as early a signing as seems feasible under the circumstances."[6] Columbia was not a label that poached (or so it liked to claim), but Monk, who'd recorded for Blue Note and Prestige as well as Riverside, was probably ready to make the move again. Monk had a reputation for being difficult—not antagonistic, but absent, spacey, very much in his own world. Columbia had experienced one of Monk's no-shows back in December 1957, when the jazz critic Whitney Balliett had put together the show "The Sound of Jazz," part of CBS's *Seven Lively Arts* television series, and an all-star album, including a touchingly broken Billie Holiday, would be made from the show. When Monk failed to show up at the 30th Street studio for the taping (directed by Jack Smight), Irving Townsend called Mal Waldron at the last minute to play piano. So Columbia had reason to be wary. Monk finally signed a contract that called for three albums a year.

Macero was a sympathetic producer, mostly because his own compositions, like Monk's, were considered difficult, even avant-garde, unless of course you knew the vocabulary. The first Columbia album was *Monk's Dream*, recorded at 30th Street in the week between Halloween and November 6, 1962, and released a few months later.[7] *Criss Cross* came next. Many of Monk's tunes had been composed years earlier—his most famous, "'Round Midnight," was written during World War II—but he was constantly taking them apart and reassembling them. The Monk recordings released by Columbia aren't inferior to the earlier ones, exactly—there was never anything inferior about Monk's work—but they're orthodox rather than reform. Some of the Riversides—*Brilliant Corners*, for example—are like nothing that had come before. Most of Monk's Columbia albums, by contrast, seem indifferently annotated, with personnel rarely listed, and overly familiar.

Still, recycled Monk curved deeper than just about any other musician's original work. If Columbia didn't necessarily lift Monk's career to a higher plane, it probably lifted his tax bracket, and it did so through several blown recording sessions and the mental illness that began to enshroud him later in the decade.

•   •   •

In 1961 Columbia got another gift—another pianist who, on one hand, might be considered the far end of the Monk clusters, but on the other used to listen to Art Tatum whenever he could.[8] At the time, Vladimir Horowitz was widely considered to be one of the three or four greatest classical pianists in the world. Horowitz was recording for RCA, with his producer, Jack Pfeiffer, timing him with a stopwatch around his neck.[9] He was terribly disenchanted by the way RCA was marketing him. When someone at RCA pushed for him to record Gershwin, he balked. "I said to myself, 'These people don't really want me.'"[10] Horowitz remained at the label but, accompanied at most times by his wife Wanda, the daughter of Arturo Toscanini, took little pleasure in recording. Then Gary Graffman signed with Columbia. Liking the way he was being treated, Graffman suggested to Horowitz that he join the label, even though it would be major competition for him. Looking out for the maestro, Graffman called Schuyler Chapin, who was thrilled to bring Horowitz aboard. Chapin negotiated the Columbia contract and assigned the young Vienna native Tom Frost to serve as Horowitz's producer.[11]

"The first record I made [for Columbia] sold 120,000 copies!" Horowitz told the Times in 1975. "RCA couldn't sell 5000! It was Goddard Lieberson who did that."[12]

Partly Lieberson, anyway. Tom Frost had been, in fact, an excellent choice. His family had come to the United States after the Anschluss in 1938. Having studied violin as a boy, Frost studied composition at Yale with Paul Hindemith. Frost joined Columbia Masterworks as an associate producer, editing recordings that John McClure, who was still mostly in Los Angeles with Bruno Walter, didn't have time for. He was quickly assigned to edit Rudolf Serkin tapes and proved himself tuned to ultra-high and -low frequencies.[13] Horowitz couldn't have asked for a more sensitive producer than Frost, nor a more ardent champion than Chapin, even though Chapin wouldn't be at the label much longer. Before Chapin departed for Lincoln Center, he promised that if Horowitz ever returned to the concert hall, he would serve as the virtuoso's valet. With Chapin gone to greener—but perhaps duller—pastures, Horowitz would inherit Ken Glancy, whose rapport with his artists was, with the exception of Lieberson, incomparable among major label executives.

●　　●　　●

Around 1950 or so, Glancy had been a Yeats scholar going for his PhD at the University of Michigan. Square-jawed, with a face that reminded some people of William Holden's, he was married with a young daughter and went to work as a record salesman in Ann Arbor. Eventually he joined the Columbia sales force in New York.[14] Although Glancy wasn't a musician, he had vast musical knowledge (is there a more musical poet in English than Yeats?) and by the early sixties had moved into A&R. Among the artists he signed were Joe Mooney, the blind singer-organist with the peerless inner clock; Woody Herman, who hadn't recorded for the label for nearly two decades; and Mel Torme, whose album *That's All*, produced by the endlessly inventive Robert Mersey, is among the lushest collection of songs ever recorded—not a clinker among them.[15] (The album evokes a Manhattan even dreamier than does Torme's album *Sunday in New York*, on Atlantic.) Glancy had impeccable taste in music—and in liquor, which flowed freely at Columbia Records in those relatively unchaperoned years, when the label was still housed apart from CBS.

Then Bill Gallagher took over all of A&R so that Glancy had to answer to him. Columbia had had only a few heads of sales, and most of them displayed discrimination as well as authority. Paul Southard, who ran sales during the birth of the long-playing record, had seemed indispensable until an indiscretion with a female colleague proved otherwise; even then, Southard stayed close to the label through a major distributorship. Paul Wexler left Columbia and subsequently organized his own recording company, Orpheum Productions. (Later in the sixties, having been widowed young, Wexler would marry Jacqueline Grennan, the nun who'd served as president of Webster and Hunter Colleges before being laicized and running the Conference on Christians and Jews.)[16] Hal Cook and Jack Loetz had transformed the label's entire sales network from one dependent on outside distributors to a wholly owned network.

Yet, within Columbia Records, none of these men could boast of the power wielded by Gallagher. As pop records had become increasingly dominant over classical and jazz, Gallagher had adroitly maneuvered himself into heading up all of A&R.

But Gallagher lacked Glancy's breadth of musical knowledge. Although they had some things in common—they were each hard-drinking, affable Irishmen, excellent raconteurs and team leaders—they were unable to work together. As head of the international division, Harvey Schein arranged for Glancy to be transferred to England and oversee Columbia's operations there. Although the British office badly needed to be restructured, it was an open secret that Glancy was being exiled so he wouldn't threaten Gallagher.

On the eve of Glancy's transfer, he and first wife Peggy were part of an evening's entertainment at which Lieberson presided. Lieberson got one of the biggest laughs of the evening when he introduced him from the dais: "If I have anything against Ken Glancy tonight, it's that he's not as funny-looking as [Atlantic Records chief] Ahmet Ertegun. But then Ken Glancy is not Turkish, if you haven't guessed, but of Irish back-ground. Ken is that rare combination, a practically unknown combina-tion, I would say. A charming, cultured, witty man. An astute businessman. And a Gentile."[17]

* * *

Glancy was something of an anomaly in a business that had been pre-dominantly Jewish going back to music publishing in the nineteenth century, when law and medicine and even most journalism jobs were closed to Jews. Sacred Jewish music has been recorded in manuscript since the sixteenth century, and Jews' deep involvement with it has been represented by writers as unlikely as George Eliot, who was raised an Evangelical Christian but put five years of study of Jewish music into her 1876 novel *Daniel Deronda*. Joseph Dash, head of Masterworks during the 1980s, suggested that the "cantorial tradition" is what sends Jews into music, including the recording business.[18] Jews sing at every service, every ceremony, marrying, dying to music.

Columbia Records was predominantly Jewish—Lieberson, Mitch Miller, Percy Faith, Norman Adler, most of the Masterworks people among them—and perhaps a trifle more than other record labels. At RCA Victor, producer-attorney Axel Meyer-Woldin once chided records head Rudy Gassner, "How can you run a successful record company without Jews? You need more Jews!"[19] Lieberson was not an observant Jew but didn't hide his roots, unlike his boss William Paley, who preferred to distance himself from them. At Joe Higgins's retirement lunch in 1959, Lieberson acknowledged Bill Gallagher's remarks by saying, "[Gallagher] never comes in on Yom Kippur," and the guests roared at the quip because few executives in the industry were as decidedly Gentile as Gallagher.

One day in 1961 Columbia's literary utility man Charlie Burr found himself at a midtown restaurant dining and drinking with A&R man Nat Shapiro, Masterworks director Howard Scott, who had changed his name from Shapiro in 1949, and the young Tom Shepard, whose grandparents had changed the family name from Shapiro. After the bill was paid Burr stepped out onto the sidewalk and said to his companions, "Hey, I just had lunch with three Shapiros!" (When Elizabeth Lauer told the story, the exclamatory Gentile wasn't Charlie Burr but Michel Legrand. Paul Myers told another version, in which Leonard Bernstein was conducting a symphony by Harold Shapero; when the piece was over, Bernstein greeted the composer, as well as Scott and Shepard. "Here I am with three Shapiros!" said Bernstein. Tom Shepard pointed to the Charlie Burr version as the correct one. "I was there!" he said.)

•   •   •

From the dais during that good-bye dinner, Lieberson completed his introduction by pointing out "a darling girl, Mrs Ken Glancy; a darling boy, Perry Como."[20] The audience loved Goddard, as usual, and applauded the departing Glancys.

In London Glancy turned things around quickly. The Columbia office became a significant presence there, feared by both RCA and EMI. But Glancy's marriage finally unraveled. Maida Schwartz had already unhitched herself from a marriage and, by 1967, she and Ken were free to be together. Maida went to see Lieberson in his office and told him she was resigning from Columbia Records to be with Ken in London. Taken by surprise—office-born romances are often apparent to one's peers but not to the president of the company—Lieberson wished her well. Next morning in London, Ken Glancy reached into the overnight Columbia Records pouch from New York and found an advance copy of Leo Rosten's *The Joys of Yiddish*, courtesy of his boss.[21]

● ● ●

Most popular American singers weren't Jewish, though there were a few. At Columbia Records there was Dinah Shore. Steve Lawrence (né Sidney Leibowitz) and Eydie Gormé arrived at the label (separately, though they were already married to each other) in 1963. Gormé, who grew up in a Ladino-speaking household, scored with the single "Blame It on the Bossa Nova," Lawrence with "Go Away, Little Girl." Bob Dylan was Jewish, though for a while it appeared to be immaterial to his songs. Then along came a Brooklyn girl whose Jewishness was inseparable from her stage and recording persona.

Barbara Joan Streisand wanted to be a star for as long as she could remember. In Philadelphia to appear in tryouts for Harold Rome's *I Can Get It for You Wholesale*, Streisand confided to Liz Lauer that she was using her singing to eventually write, produce, and direct her own pictures. She'd already dropped an *a* in Barbara; her intention, as she became more successful, was to gradually drop every letter until there was nothing left but B, by which she'd be known throughout the world.

During the recording of *Wholesale* at 30th Street, Streisand stopped in the middle of her song "Miss Marmelstein" because she didn't like the orchestration. Lieberson, who produced the session, stepped out of the control booth, took her aside, and quietly but firmly got her to sing the song as written.[22] Streisand was becoming a star, no question, even if words like "homely" were pinned to her. She was, in fact, beautiful— uniquely so for being slightly cross-eyed. Her first major nightclub engagement was at the Bon Soir, on 8th Street in the Village, where Tiger Haynes served as master of risqué ceremonies and occasional accompanist. The engagement was a hit, particularly among the club's gay clientele.[23] Streisand took a railroad flat in the East Sixties while her tirelessly supportive Jewish mother remained in Brooklyn. She was all of 19. In May 1962, preparing to return to the Bon Soir for a two-week engagement, Streisand played up her lack of pretension for the New Yorker. She loved thrift shops, she said, TV dinners, and shawls that doubled as coverlets; she had a desire to sightsee in her hometown, probably because she hadn't ventured from Brooklyn into Manhattan until she was 14, and acknowledged that, yeah, she was going to be a star.[24] For the most part, she knew the musical effects she wanted and how to achieve them. There was surprising wisdom, for example, in her decision to slow down the confetti tempo of "Happy Days Are Here Again," imbuing it with romantic irony, and it became her signature song before she'd recorded a note for Columbia.

That was proving harder than it should have. Though he admired Streisand's talent, Lieberson remained resistant to signing her as a recording artist. Arthur Laurents tried to persuade him to reconsider. "He listened to her sing," Laurents wrote, "and sent me a note saying: 'Barbra Streisand is indeed very talented but I'm afraid she's too special for records.'"[25] One problem for Lieberson was that Streisand's singing was overpowering compared with the lighter voices and more delicate phrasing of his friends Doris Day, Jo Stafford, and Rosemary Clooney. Theirs were voices for the microphone; Streisand's seemed to be closer to the grander opera and cabaret singers who annoyed him.

It was probably Dave Kapralik's enthusiasm that turned the key to Lieberson's change of heart. Kapralik had been watching Mike Wallace's TV interview show P.M. East when Streisand came on; even on the tiny screen her power came through. Lieberson agreed to hear Streisand sing at the Blue Angel, on East 55th, where her singing knocked him to the canvas. "It takes a big man to admit a mistake," Lieberson said to her manager, Marty Erlichman, "and I made a mistake. I would like to record Barbra."[26]

Streisand was signed to Columbia Records in October 1962, agreeing to make two albums a year but with full creative control. It's not clear if anyone at the label, except perhaps Kapralik and Streisand's first producer Mike Berniker, realized how valuable she'd be to Columbia—and what a royal pain in the ass she'd be, too. In the pop field, Mitch Miller and George Avakian had served as authority figures, with Miller notoriously controlling and Avakian deferential but firm. But Miller and Avakian had both departed. And it's likely that Streisand would have insisted on control of her own recording career no matter who was running A&R at the time. In November the young producer Mike Berniker took a skeleton crew down to the Bon Soir to record Barbra Streisand, accompanied by Peter Daniels, the house pianist with whom she had a great rapport. Columbia scrapped the album, though everyone was paid under the terms of the contract.[27]

Over the course of three days in January 1963, Streisand laid down 11 tracks that went into The Barbra Streisand Album, which was released on February 25. Berniker, who proposed the title and had a budget of $18,000 (relatively low for an artist requiring arrangements and an orchestra, even by 1963 standards), ran interference with the label but otherwise tried to stay out of Streisand's way. Streisand rehearsed with arranger Peter Matz at his Upper West Side apartment. Like Sinatra and Ella Fitzgerald, Streisand couldn't read music but instinctively understood the arrangements. Matz, though possessed of a fine musical mind—he would work with Streisand, off and on, for several years— gave all of that early credit to Streisand's musical instincts and to Peter Daniels. Despite lavish critical praise, the first album didn't sell very well. For The Second Barbra Streisand Album, Streisand mined the endlessly fertile Harold Arlen canon, making each Arlen number new all over again.[28] The veteran Frank Laico was the engineer, and he got testy when Streisand and her manager Marty Erlichman hemmed him in at the control board.

●　●　●

Berniker produced again. He'd do the Third Album and then, on the trail of Streisand's supernova turn in Funny Girl, not quite half of the album People, which Mersey took over, with Peter Daniels still at the piano and Peter Matz and Ray Ellis doing the arrangements.[29] Streisand's albums charted higher and higher, peaking with People until The Way We Were was released the next decade. Those first few albums drew from the best of Broadway, the artist's choices impeccable (she even resurrected the neglected Rodgers & Hart "I'll Tell the Man in the Street"), even though they excluded her former benefactor Harold Rome. As for Berniker, his arrival at Columbia followed an almost classic pattern: young New Yorker growing up close to music—jazz and the clarinet in Berniker's case—and wandering a bit before finding his way to 799 Seventh Avenue. Berniker, who lost his mother when he was still a toddler, grew up mostly in Brooklyn and Scarsdale.[30] His father played clarinet and flute. In the cellar in Scarsdale, Berniker would play his dad's Brunswick and Columbia 78s—a lot of John Kirby, Albert Ammons, Goodman, and Duke. He started college at Bucknell. During freshman orientation a rangy New Jersey kid named Bruce Lundvall, who played the saxophone, heard Berniker whistling "A Night in Tunisia."[31] Berniker and Lundvall became friends and remained so even after Berniker transferred to Columbia, where he majored in philosophy and played a lot of basketball.

Berniker was drafted in 1958 and sent to the missile training center at Ft. Bliss, Texas. (Lundvall served his hitch closer to home, at Ft. Dix.) By now Berniker realized he didn't have the chops to be a professional clarinet player, and an aptitude test suggested he should stay away from the law as well. But he'd done all right in music, having sold records for Decca out of Queens and been told by the discriminating Milt Gabler that he had good ears. So Berniker DJ'd his own radio show out of El Paso—there were worse ways to get through the army—and wrote a music column for the local paper. When he got out in 1960, he went job hunting. Richard Avedon, a second cousin, recommended Berniker to Goddard Lieberson, who sent him into Columbia's A&R training program. Eager to share his good fortune, Berniker called his old pal Lundvall and had him come over to meet Cliff Benfield, head of personnel. Lundvall read music, but not quickly. "Can you keep up with a score if Bernstein is conducting?" he was asked. Lundvall admitted he probably couldn't, so he was sent into sales training.

Berniker got his feet wet reissuing jazz on Epic, mostly under Jim Fogelsong's direction. After several albums in just over two years, Berniker was assigned to record Lieberson's close friend Tammy Grimes. The self-titled album featured arrangements by Luther Henderson and came off well. When Streisand was ready to record at the Bon Soir, Lieberson and Dave Kapralik, pleased with the results of the Grimes sessions, assigned him the task.

One evening in early October 1963, you might have turned on the TV to watch *The Judy Garland Show*, expecting to find another Berniker artist, George Maharis, as her guest. If so, you got a surprise. For reasons known only to a few network executives, CBS substituted a more recently taped show featuring Streisand and the Smothers Brothers. The high point of that show, maybe the high point of the entire television season, was Garland countersinging "Get Happy" to Streisand's "Happy Days Are Here Again." Not quite twice as old as Streisand, Garland was passing the torch.

Berniker won a Grammy for *The Barbra Streisand Album*. Although Bruce Lundvall had wanted to go into A&R, too, things didn't work out badly for him, either. In those early years, before he ascended to the presidency of the label, Lundvall learned how to market recordings and to do so aggressively, though aggression didn't come naturally to him. In 1963, having prevailed upon Jerry Vale to agree to tie in his albums *Bravo Giovanni* and *Arrivederci Roma!* with a Ruffino chianti ad campaign, Lundvall went to work on no less a personage than Noel Coward. *The Girl Who Came to Supper*, Coward's musical set during the Coronation of George V in 1911, was scheduled to be recorded at 30th Street on December 15, 1963. With five days to go, Lundvall noticed that "When Foreign Princes Come to Visit Us," a song from the show, contained a reference to Bolinger. But Columbia had a deal with Moët, its chief competitor in champagne. (The proposed marketing campaign went something like

"Moët: The World's Bestselling Champagne! Columbia: The World's Best-selling Label!") Lundvall asked Teo Macero if the reference could be changed to Moët or Dom Pérignon (a Moët product); if Coward would agree, they'd send him "a supply of their products, including Teacher's Scotch and Hennessy."[32] Coward stuck with a reference to Cordon Bleu Châteauneuf du Pape. But Lundvall, trained by Bill Gallagher and the Barnum-like Peter Munves, was thinking like a first-class marketer.

• • •

The Girl Who Came to Supper recording session took place in the chilling aftermath of the nation's fourth presidential assassination. On that lack November day in Dallas, Tom Shepard was having lunch with Charlie Burr when their waitress told them that the president was in the hospital and not expected to live. John Berg and Maida Glancy (then Maida Schwartz) came out of the House of Chan on Seventh Avenue to find Mike Berniker running down the sidewalk. "Kennedy's been shot!" he said. The trio repaired to 799 and, finding a television in somebody's office, turned on CBS News.

Not a week went by when there wasn't some agitation on the street. February 7, 1964, was the day the Beatles arrived on Seventh Avenue. Maida Glancy remembered Scott Muni of WABC broadcasting from the roof of 799, with crowds gathered in front of the nearby Equitable Building and the Taft Hotel. The Beatles weren't recording for Columbia, but nobody at the label could deny that, like it or not, the rock revolution was coming. It would be another two years before Columbia had a small but reputable lineup of rock 'n' roll artists. By then some of the label's collegiality would be gone, smothered not by the music so much as its new headquarters on Sixth Avenue.

• • •

After Bruno Walter died in 1962, George Szell and the Cleveland Orchestra were pulled back to Columbia Records from Epic. The label was still holding on to the New York Philharmonic and the Philadelphia Orchestra, and still had Bernstein as a towering figure who often stood apart from his orchestra. But the sales department knew it could sell Szell because, by many lights, no individual knew more about music, period. With Szell's return to Columbia, the sales department began to pressure him.

Szell was austere, refined, and usually knew how his bread was buttered. After the Galimir recording of Lieberson's String Quartet was released in 1963, Lieberson sent it out to many of his friends and artists for their reaction. Many people responded enthusiastically to the quartet and let Lieberson know it. Szell did so with a single diplomatic sentence worthy of Lieberson himself: "If you had not become so eminently important and successful in your life I would say it is a pity that you gave up composing, but it is a good thing for all of us that a man in your position knows what music looks like from the inside."[33]

One day in New York, Dr. Szell was taken to lunch by Jane Friedmann and Peter Munves. Friedmann was one of several fine Masterworks producers—Howard Scott, David Oppenheim, Charlie Schicke, Paul Myers, and Andy Kazdin were among the others—who had recorded the Cleveland Orchestra over the years. Munves had already proved to be the most outlandish and, as often as not, most effective classical record salesman in the industry. Szell had just had a wisdom tooth pulled and was recovering from the aftereffects of Novocain.[34]

Munves kibitzed through lunch until the time felt right, then made his pitch. Telling Szell that Columbia Records needed him to record more popular works, Munves first proposed Ravel's *Bolero*.

"*Scheisse!*" spat Szell. "What else?"

"How about *The Overture of 1812?*"

"Double *scheisse!*"

Munves had done his homework, aware of what Szell hadn't yet put on record. "How about *Scheherazade?*"

"Not on your life!" said Szell. "This is really *scheisdreck!*" Szell had developed a constitutional aversion to such Saturday-night pieces. He'd long refused to record *The William Tell Overture* because, when he'd played it in the concert hall, during a rest some bozo in the balcony had yelled out "Heigh-o, Silver!" Szell didn't know what this bizarre ejaculation had to do with *The William Tell Overture*.

Munves tried again. "You could record *Capriccio Italien* and *Capriccio Español*."

"That's as low as I go!"

Munves was at a loss. Szell got a second wind and mounted an offensive attack for one of the most unsalable pieces imaginable.

"With a twinkle in his eye—and I knew I was in for it," Munves recalled, "he reminded me that the following year would be Richard Strauss's centenary." Szell, thirty-five years younger than Strauss, had apprenticed with him in Vienna. To celebrate the centenary, he promised to record the most magnificent version of Strauss's *Symphonie Domestica* ever heard.

"Come on," Munves protested. "Even Fritz Reiner and the Chicago Symphony Orchestra can't sell it."

"Who?!" replied Szell.

Munves held fast. "It's just not first-rate Strauss."

"It'll be a revelation!" cried Szell. Becoming more rhapsodic with each sentence, Szell made his case, fully aware that Columbia didn't have the piece in its catalog. As he slowed to a halt, he praised the label's superb technicians, including engineer Buddy Graham, whose name he pronounced *Boo-day*.

"I'm very sorry, Maestro," Munves said. "You cannot record that fugue for us!"

"And why not?"

"Because," said Munves, gloating—and he was sure he had Szell cornered—"do you know what the final three chords of that fugue are? They belong to our archrival, NBC." Indeed, for years the G-E-C chimes had accompanied the electronic bloom of the NBC peacock, one of the omnipresent logos in American culture. "Do you think William Paley is going to let you record those three chords on a Columbia record?"

As Szell got up to leave he glowered at Munves, who knew he was in for it.

"Mr. Munves," he said in his Otto Preminger–like voice, "you have an amazing memory—for shit!"

The maestro prevailed. About a year and a half later, Szell and the Cleveland's recording of *Domestica*, produced by Paul Myers, was chosen as the best recording of the Strauss centenary in several polls. Although it lost the Grammy as Best Classical Performance of 1964 to Erich Leinsdorf conducting the BSO in Mahler's Fifth, it was, as Szell had promised, a revelation. There was little further resistance from CBS or Columbia because, as Myers pointed out, "How would the listener know [about the last three chords, co-opted by NBC] until he got the record home?"[35]

· · · ·

Paul Myers was then a 32-year-old producer at Columbia. Born in London, Myers attended the University of London and spent the first half of his twenties in public service in what was then Rhodesia (now Zimbabwe), promoting a biracial coalition. That coalition failed, and Myers went to New York to find radio work. Largely self-taught in piano and clarinet, Myers knew something about music, something about broadcasting, and a lot about writing. In 1959 he found work at Kapp Records as an annotator and producer, then was hired at Columbia three years later by Schuyler Chapin. From 1962 to 1980 Myers would have a major influence on the way classical music sounded at the label.

Myers took over George Szell's production chores from Tom Frost, who had his hands full with Eugene Ormandy and the Philadelphia Orchestra. Because Leonard Bernstein had enjoyed such popularity when he spoke on recordings, explaining and analyzing musical pieces, Columbia decided to try something similar with Szell by adding bonus records of the maestro speaking, with patches of music as reference points. (Paul Myers referred to these as "talking dog" records.) The Szell commentaries are fascinating, though their hypercritical, lecturing tone generally made them less inviting than Bernstein's.

Szell's brilliance and austerity combined to make him one of the more feared figures in classical music. Yet he could be surprisingly easygoing, even naive. Shortly after Paul Myers arrived at Columbia, Szell complained that he didn't like the overall sound of his own recordings. He never did care for the 30th Street studio—"I can't hear anything in this barn!" he'd huff during a recording session there—and was sour about some of the Cleveland recordings that came back to him, requesting a remix more than once.[36] Myers suspected a systemic problem that had nothing to do with the recordings and asked Szell if Columbia engineers might take a look at his home hi-fi. The engineers went to his house to find an ancient, valve-operated unit still wheezing despite three dead tubes; it was amazing that he got any sound at all out of it. When Szell asked the engineers what he should do with the antiquated equipment, Frank Bruno, Buddy Graham's assistant, said, "Burn it!" Szell went into town the same day and purchased a new stereo system for $5,000. After that the recordings sounded just fine.[37]

A couple of years later Szell was awarded an Order of the British Empire—the honor was primarily for his services with the Scottish National Orchestra in the 1930s—by Elizabeth II. The announcement was made while Myers and his Columbia crew were in Cleveland to record Szell and the orchestra doing *Pictures at an Exhibition*. After the sessions Szell came through the control room to say good-bye. He turned to Buddy Graham and, with his heavy-handed joviality, said, "Well, Buddy, I suppose you're going to take these tapes home and, as usual, fuck up the sound!" Graham looked him in the eye and said, "Oh, no, Maestro, not since you got the OBE."[38]

In April 1968 Szell and Serkin re-recorded the Brahms First Symphony. The two men, both from the Austro-Hungarian Empire, had known each other since Serkin was 12. They had recorded the Brahms First at Cleveland's Severance Hall on November 30, 1952, for Columbia.[39] Four months after Myers produced the 1968 version, he moved to London to work for CBS Records there. Before Myers left (according to Peter Munves), he provided test pressings for his artists. Szell responded that there was too much piano, Serkin too much orchestra. Myers, figuring the soloist was the key figure here, emphasized the piano in his mix. Szell, hearing Myers's final mix, told *Billboard* that Columbia would be recalling the new recording of the Brahms. The recall never occurred, but Szell, still displeased, asked Myers's Cleveland Orchestra successor Andy Kazdin to re-mix with a few minor adjustments. Hearing his orchestra sound stronger—or thinking he heard it, anyway—Szell pronounced himself pleased.[40]

Myers had been director of international A&R since 1966, based in New York, a city he regarded as provincial when it came to European recordings. "Once you get off the island of Manhattan you realize it's a very insular place," he said.[41] Now, as classical recording—opera in particular—proved prohibitively expensive in the United States, much of the work was transferred to England. Myers went with it. From New York, John Hammond wrote to a British correspondent that his friend Paul Myers would be arriving in London on October 8 to take charge of classical recording. "You will find that he is extremely knowledgeable in many other forms of music apart from classical, and I think he is one of the finest producers we've ever had in America."[42]

•　•　•

In 1964, while Columbia Records awaited the completion of the Eero Saarinen skyscraper that would become CBS headquarters and dubbed Black Rock, it hired the Harvard Business School to analyze the organization. What could be done to improve it? This was a curious move on Lieberson's part because he'd long espoused the benefits of a broad liberal arts education, particularly in philosophy and literature, and liked to tell interviewers that it was easier to turn a musician into a businessman than a businessman into a musician. "This nonsense about fuzzy-minded artists not knowing the value of anything just isn't true," Lieberson told an interviewer as late as 1966. "On the contrary, they understand the value of notes and there's a close connection between music and mathematics. When you deal with artists, you learn that the best artists are good businessmen—and for very simple reasons. They know their own value and they know what they are trading for—and with."[43] Lieberson had already been advised that this was the time to expand. So Columbia had purchased Fender Guitars and Creative Play-things. When Harvard reported its findings, the primary suggestion was for the label to combine A&R and Marketing, essentially concentrating power in one man under Lieberson. Awkwardly, Norman Adler made it clear he wanted that newly proposed position. Adler had been the label's general counsel, the first president of the Record Club, and now the vice president closest to Lieberson, who had always been essentially an A&R man. Everyone knew Adler was brilliant—but could he handle A&R, which required a feeling for music of various kinds, an ability to find and nurture artists, and a sense of what was happening on the street, musically and otherwise?[44] Lieberson doubted it but, for better or worse, had never been the most confrontational executive in the industry. He let the matter hang for a while. It was his twenty-fifth year at Columbia Records; he'd been the label's primary producer of original cast recordings for 17 years and president for eight. He had enough on his mind.

In late July Columbia Records held its annual convention in Las Vegas. The open secret of the convention was that the label was honoring Lieberson's twenty-fifth anniversary there. Norman Adler spoke for a few minutes, although, inevitably, his presentation to Lieberson came off as flat when compared with the way Lieberson himself might have done it. Adler read a letter from Groucho to Lieberson, intercepted by Lieberson's secretary, telling him that one of Goddard's "false friends," Irving Townsend, had contacted him about appearing at the celebration; with every intention of making it to Las Vegas, Groucho then phoned Lieberson—the call was intercepted, too—to say he couldn't make it after all because he had to fly to New York to appear on the *Tonight* show. Oddly, the celebration was propelled by a repeated gag involving the song "Hello, Dolly!" from the Jerry Herman show that Columbia didn't get. (How many times can you hear "Hello, Goddard"?) Adler, on behalf of everyone at Columbia Records, presented Lieberson with a "bottom-less" bathing suit—something that looked flimsy and elastic, surely a spoof of Rudy Gernreich's recently introduced monokini, otherwise known as the "topless" bathing suit. No man was less of a prude than

Lieberson, and he accepted the present with good humor. Others, including Mitch Miller (who sounded as though he were still running pop A&R at the label), gave brief encomiums. Then Lieberson was given a wristwatch. The Columbia employees applauded long and loud but, as with so many testimonial events that aren't especially funny, you had to have been there to appreciate it.[45]

Far more lasting, perhaps, were the letters and drawings that came in to honor Lieberson. These had been solicited mostly by Charlie Burr on the East Coast and Irving Townsend on the West Coast, with Bob Cato and Morris Baumstein assembling two large scrapbooks of tributes. From Sherman Oaks, Jim Conkling sent a funny limerick. Artur Rubinstein, who was an RCA Victor artist, sent a note that went like this: *Famous pianist dies and tries to get into heaven. St. Peter asks sternly, "What company did you make records for?" "RCA Victor," he answers. "To hell with him," shouts St. Peter. Another pianist dies and tries to get in. Same question. "Capitol," he answers proudly. "To hell with him!" A third virtuoso shyly tries to sneak in. "And you?" asks St. Peter. "I always worked for Columbia." "Come into my arms, my son, you have suffered enough."* Replying to Charlie Burr, the playwright-screenwriter Harry Kurnitz wrote from Paris: "You have chosen an awkward moment to ask me for a tribute to Goddard Lieberson. I have had no free records in quite some long time and the last batch, if memory serves, consisted almost entirely of items like "The Yellow Rose of Texas," *The Girl Who Came to Supper* and Goddard Lieberson's First String Quartet. And for this I had to pay French customs!"[46]

Kurnitz adored Lieberson. So did Al Hirschfeld, whose caricature of Lieberson adorned the covers of the scrapbooks. Hirschfeld had drawn the covers for two of Columbia's huge sellers, *Kismet* and *My Fair Lady*. The bearded genius who made his caricatures while sitting in a barber's chair was only one of dozens of artists whose work had been critical to the success of Columbia Records.

16

Art for the Label's Sake

Before there were album covers, records were sold as a minor part of the appliance department—"white goods" relegated to the back of the store, with nothing to display except what they were—disks encased in sleeves. When the 23-year-old Alex Steinweiss arrived at Columbia Records in 1939 to take over as art director, the importance of an album cover in marketing was still arguable.

There weren't even record albums—two or more disks bound inside larger cardboard covers—until the mid-1930s, so there wasn't much to illustrate beyond the tiny circular disk label. As early as 1926 Victor released an illustrated cover of a Mother's Day record. In 1934 the two-month-old Decca placed single-disk nursery rhymes into brightly colored paper wraps. Five years later, when Victor released Bruno Walter's version of the Brahms First Symphony with an illustrated cover, sales jumped 40 percent. After Columbia reissued a newly illustrated Beethoven's Ninth, sales increased almost 900 percent. The profit in dressing up recordings for sale was hard to ignore.[1]

RCA Victor, well financed, was already regularly employing commercial artists. When Steinweiss joined Columbia, he was supposed to go into advertising but was aware that the label's cover art tended toward dark monochromes. "Some folks who are proud of their collections," the *Times* said, "have suggested to record companies that they bind their albums in varied colors instead of the usual formal black. After all, they ask, what would a library of black books look like? Columbia, at least, has taken the hint, and has gone so far as to engage an 'art director' to give expert attention to the matter."[2]

Steinweiss, like so many of the artists who followed him at Columbia, came out of a rich tradition of Western European graphic art. Born in March 1917, Steinweiss attended Abraham Lincoln High School in Brooklyn in the depths of the Depression. At Lincoln High he studied with Leon Friend, whose 1936 book *Graphic Design* was one of the first comprehensive books on the subject published in America. Steinweiss's richly colored artwork won him a three-year scholarship to Parsons. He worked as an assistant to the Viennese poster artist Joseph Binder, who had fled Hitler and was becoming just as prominent in the States as he'd been in Europe.[3] Then he went to work for Dr. Robert Leslie, a physician whose loss of an eye sent him back to his first love, typography. Dr. Leslie was co-owner of the Composing Room, which did advertising and graphic work for other companies, including the new Columbia Recording Corporation. At parent company CBS the art and design chief was Bill Golden. When it became apparent that Columbia needed some new blood in art, Dr. Leslie got Steinweiss an interview with Golden. Golden looked at Steinweiss's work and sent him to Bridgeport to meet with Columbia's advertising director, Pat Dolan, an imposing Irishman who was concerned about Steinweiss's youth but gave him some space at 1473 Barnum.[4]

At the time, letterpress printing from engraved plates—the process by which album covers were made—was limited to three or four flat colors, with halftones in one or two plates. There was also only one local high-quality engraver.[5] Consequently, most 78-rpm collections were simply bound in kraft-paper sleeves between pasteboard covers. There wasn't a lot to work with. Initially, under Pat Dolan's supervision, Steinweiss was to design only Columbia's advertising. Shortly after he arrived, though, he took a crack at jazzing up the cover of the 78-rpm album *Smash Song Hits* by Rodgers & Hart. Dolan and Ted Wallerstein realized Steinweiss, with his Gauguin-like colors and love of classical music, was more valuable to them designing album covers—"painting music," in Steinweiss's phrase. Columbia announced that Steinweiss had taken the "newly created post of art director" for the label.[6] In short order he began making the arresting covers for Arthur Murray's *Tango* album, with a bandoneón springing at the viewer, and for the earliest albums in George Avakian's Hot Jazz Classics series.

Steinweiss could paint jazz, obviously, but he was really a classical guy. To bring in some help, as well as another sensibility, Pat Dolan hired a young Buckeye named Jim Flora. "[Steinweiss] was a classical music lover," Flora said. "I think that was one of the reasons I was hired, because I was the jazz man. Eventually I did both."[7] Actually, Flora was three years older than Steinweiss, but he seemed younger because he'd recently come out of the Art Academy of Cincinnati and been illustrating for the small, quirky publisher, the Little Man Press, near there. (Recollections of the two men differ. Flora said that Pat Dolan hired him in 1940, paying him $50 a week. Steinweiss said that Dolan had given him a copy of Little Man Press; Steinweiss, impressed with Flora's artwork, summoned him to Bridgeport in July 1942 and put him to work.)[8] Steinweiss's style was creamy, favoring French-scented pastels and a subtle wit; Flora's style was jagged, his figures appearing to have been zapped by an electric current, his humor more overt. Of the two, Steinweiss's was the more beautiful, Flora's the more distinctive—a postnuclear Miro you could spot anywhere. They got along all right. During their respective educations, both men had admired A. M. Cassandre, probably the leading art deco poster artist, a Ukrainian who opened a Paris art school in 1934. Steinweiss was more confident. "Alex had an ego—boundless," Flora said. "He knew he was God's gift to art. It takes an ego to break through things like he did. He also had a heart of gold."[9]

As America went into the Second World War, these arresting album covers sold more records. At the same time the government needed metal that had previously gone into making the "white goods"—refrigerators, stoves, and other appliances—prodding store managers to move record albums to the front of drug and department stores. Now you could quickly thumb through racks of albums of 78s without having to pick up every disk to investigate the label. Steinweiss had a close rapport with Moses Smith, who selected the Masterworks lineup each season with Wallerstein. Every two weeks Steinweiss would travel from Bridgeport to Manhattan to learn what was in the pipeline; then he'd go back to Bridgeport and get started on the various designs.[10]

In the middle of the war, Pat Dolan joined the OSS,[11] so Steinweiss ran Columbia's advertising department for a while. Classified I-A in 1943, Steinweiss was drafted. In his absence Paul Southard, vice president in charge of sales, assumed the ad reins as well.[12] Steinweiss served in the navy, based in Manhattan, where he taught art to sailors under a program supervised by the illustrator Lt. Ed Millman. (Long before combat footage entered Americans' living rooms via television, Millman drew scenes that rendered the horrors of war with vivid immediacy.) The program, the Training Aids Development Center, had much more equipment to work with than Columbia's Bridgeport facility. Millman also got Steinweiss an apartment that he and his expanding family could use until V-J Day. Still working for Columbia when he could, Steinweiss mailed his sketches to Bridgeport, where Flora was supposed to execute them. Flora, born too early to be drafted, had been promoted to art director and was illustrating Columbia's new-release monthly *Coda*. Changes at Columbia, meanwhile, would have a future impact on Steinweiss. The major one was Goddard Lieberson's promotion to director of Masterworks, replacing Steinweiss's friend Moe Smith.

Inevitably, the combination of the war and the Petrillo recording ban slowed things down through the end of 1944. Still, some of the album covers from the war years are breathtaking. From Steinweiss there was the red, pink, and black *Porgy and Bess* (Fritz Reiner conducting the Pittsburgh Symphony Orchestra, 1943), and the deep-green ferns set off by whitewater and a dove on the cover of Villa-Lobos's *Seréstas* (the composer conducting, with mezzo-soprano Jennie Tourel, 1944). From Flora there was the cowboy/train motif on Burl Ives's *The Wayfaring Stranger* (1944).[13]

The following year Flora was promoted to advertising manager and the illustrator Bob Jones was brought in to take his place as art director. With the war over, Flora was as much executive as artist, joining the ranks of ad guys like Ken McAllister, Albert Earl, and Mefford Runyon.

Wallerstein had always been plugged into advertising and marketing—his undergraduate degree, after all, was in economics—and he liked having a brain trust of sorts with him in Bridgeport. Steinweiss stayed in New York, hung out his shingle on Riverside Drive, and announced he was accepting freelance commissions.[14] He continued to paint music for Columbia albums and also supplied artwork for the Container Corporation of America and Schenley Distillers, among others, and for Time-Life. (Practically every New York–based graphic artist of note contributed artwork to Time-Life's business magazine *Fortune*.) Pat Dolan came home from the war but couldn't get his old job back. (Why Wallerstein denied him his former position isn't clear.) Dolan promptly went to England and became one of the dominant forces in British advertising.[15]

●   ●   ●

In the late 1940s the majors of the recording industry—Victor, Decca, and Columbia—were centered in Manhattan, with satellites in Connecticut and New Jersey. Measured by geography or personnel, it was a narrow world. Advertising, even after the growth spurt of postwar marketing, was only slightly bigger. In both industries everyone knew almost everyone else. Artists and executives moved back and forth, recommending each other for jobs when they weren't competing for them—and sometimes when they were. The American artist Ben Shahn and the Dutch artist Leo Lionni, each possessed of singular drafting styles, knew each other well and knew CBS art director Bill Golden, who threw work their way at both CBS and Columbia Records. Golden was married to Cipe Pineles, *Seventeen*'s adventurous art director, and the couple shared an enormous record collection. Valuing that collection, Golden was predisposed to send only the best people to the record subsidiary.[16]

Steinweiss, an irascible maverick, was still around. In the spring of 1948, he knew something was up when Wallerstein asked him to lunch. Later, in his office, Wallerstein played for Steinweiss a new Kostelanetz recording. After several minutes Steinweiss said, "Don't you have to change the record?" Wallerstein put his fingers to his lips; the recording continued. The disk ran an astounding fifteen minutes. Wallerstein asked Steinweiss to come up with an idea for new packaging. With professional alacrity, Steinweiss developed the LP jacket—thin cardboard, one foot square, that could snugly hold the record, with front and back covers that could accommodate a larger image and a fairly long text without resorting to an insert. Most important, its size meant that the front cover could be reproduced on offset presses rather than the old letterpress.

In preparing for its first hundred or so releases on LP, Columbia had been using what came to be called the Tombstone cover, which featured a slightly angled, voluted cornice on a block that looked like a gothic headstone. Though Steinweiss had been charged with redesigning the jacket, the Tombstone cover wasn't immediately killed; in fact it would serve for hundreds of LPs in the next two to three years because there was only so much original artwork that could be made. (The Tombstone cover had the advantage of being a boilerplate: fill in the credits, write the liner notes and send it to the distributor.) But with the advent of the LP, there was suddenly a lot more artwork to get done. In some cases the album covers went half and half, using big type and LP stenciled in a circle, with a small illustration in the corner. For *Nelson Eddy in Songs of Stephen Foster*, Steinweiss papered a brown-and-yellow montage of figures representing Foster songs ("De Camptown Races," etc.)—a cover within a cover.[17]

Columbia began hiring more graphic artists from outside. Lewis Daniel did the renowned *Porgy and Bess* cover in 1951. A New Yorker, Daniel had a deliberately primitive style and, whether he was illustrating Walt Whitman or the Gershwins, what you can't help looking at are the mouths of his figures: they take over the landscapes. Several artists came from Monogram, the art studio founded by Art Schlosser. Among them was Rudolph de Harak, whose deceptively simple covers—the argyle pattern against an aqua blue backdrop, for example, for the Budapest String Quartet's interpretations of the Ravel and Debussy quartets—

showed what could be done on an album cover with a few lines and colors.[18] Steinweiss still worked sporadically for Columbia. He was still in touch with Wallerstein, who was sitting out the five years he had contractually agreed to in his resignation from the label. Steinweiss didn't have much contact with Jim Conkling, but it was natural for him to remain in touch with Goddard Lieberson because Lieberson had to keep the graphics artists apprised of the Masterworks lineup.

With Wallerstein gone, Lieberson took Steinweiss to lunch. Lieberson said to him, "Who's going to protect you now?" At first Steinweiss didn't know what he was talking about. As Lieberson elaborated, it dawned on Steinweiss that Lieberson was insinuating Wallerstein had slipped him extra dough under the table. Whatever evidence Lieberson might have had, Steinweiss felt humiliated. "Goddard Lieberson was a tricky guy who maneuvered himself into the job," Steinweiss said, with long-nursed bitterness, some fifty years after he last painted for Columbia. "He had very sharp stilettoes." In the early 1950s Steinweiss still blamed the dismissal of his friend Moe Smith on Lieberson, but he took Columbia work when it was offered. Then, in 1954, Neil Fujita was brought in as art director. Steinweiss said, "Lieberson gave Neil Fujita orders to push me out. Fujita was a shmuck who didn't know his ass from his elbow. He grudgingly gave me one or two assignments, then I had to go out and get other jobs."[19]

Fujita, for his part, said that Steinweiss was very helpful to him. Like Steinweiss, Fujita had arrived at the label through the offices of Bill Golden, who had conceived the CBS Eye (sometimes referred as "Cyclops") in 1951 while doodling on his desk. Fujita quickly got close to Lieberson. But first he had to spend several months in Bridgeport to learn how records were made.

●　　●　　●

Born in Hawaii of a Japanese family, Neil Fujita was interned for a while during the Second World War. Later, released from internment, he fought with a Japanese-American regiment in Italy, France, and Okinawa. After the war he returned to school at Chouinard Art Institute in Los Angeles. (The costume designer Edith Head was among Chouinard's graduates.) He married and moved east, working as a graphic artist for a while at N. W. Ayer Advertising in Philadelphia and teaching at the Philadelphia Art Museum. Fujita already possessed an identifiable style, a blending of colors and geometric forms. It was only a matter of time before his East Coast contacts landed him an art directorship.[20]

At Columbia, Fujita built a self-sufficient graphic design department. He saw no need for the label to keep paying retainers to two New York design houses and soon cut them out. (Fujita declined to name the design houses, though one of them was surely Monogram.) Early in his tenure there, Fujita took a good long look at Bill Golden's CBS Eye and reworked it so that it looked like a cartoon version of a decibel, a bug regurgitated in hi-fi. With two legs added, it also looked like a TV antenna turned upside down; the lines that stood out showed a C and an R, mashed together, that stood for Columbia Records. The figure was dubbed the Walking Eye and would become as ubiquitous in the recording industry as Columbia's patented LP trademark.

As Columbia's output increased in the mid-fifties, Fujita's art department was putting together some eight hundred record packages a year. His wide circle of contacts included Milton Glaser, who made several covers for the label. (Glaser's poster of Bob Dylan's shadowed profile, his hair aflame in psychedelic colors, would become a collector's item.) And Fujita knew a great many photographers. Under Fujita's auspices, the art department routinely placed an album's credit information in type near the top of the cover. This was less for an arresting design—in fact it narrowed design possibilities—than to make it easier to riffle through stacks of albums in a bin. Seeing the credits near the top gave you a lot of information quickly.

For three years Fujita stayed at Columbia, and not unhappily. He got along with Lieberson, who teased him about his pidgin Hawaiian-inflected English. Fujita, in turn, knew how to flatter Lieberson with layouts that depicted him as the dapper executive in command of his company.

But Fujita got restless. In 1957 he went to Lieberson, who had become president the previous year, and told him he wanted to design on his own. Lieberson gave his blessing and asked for a recommendation to fill his spot. Fujita recommended Art Kane, who was then art director of *Seventeen* and the photographer who would soon make the famous photograph of jazz musicians that provided the basis for the film documentary *A Great Day in Harlem*. (Kane's lovely photograph of the Carmel coastline had adorned Erroll Garner's *Concert by the Sea*, on Columbia.) Kane said yes to Columbia's offer, and Fujita prepared to open a design firm with his friend Ernie Sokolov.

Then Kane backed out. Feeling bad about it, Kane recommended the artist Roy Kuhlman, another Chouinard graduate who'd been designing book covers for Barney Rosset at Grove Press and often drew for *Esquire*. Kuhlman's year at Columbia turned out to be a nightmare—for the label if not also for him. He wasn't used to taking direction from recording artists who demanded that their images be rendered just so, or getting suggestions from salespeople who thought they knew what was commercial and what wasn't. No one was happy. Going over the heads of both Lieberson and Bill Golden, Kuhlman sent a letter of complaint to Frank Stanton. Fifteen years earlier, when the Columbia Recording Corporation was still a relatively small operation, this might have been tolerated; in an expanded corporate atmosphere, however, such an end-run was verboten. The numbers at the time showed that the CBS Television Network, Columbia's big daddy, boasted the highest gross of any advertising medium in 1957, with $210 million in sales, followed at some distance by NBC Television ($170 million) and then *Life* ($130 million), and no other entity taking in more than $100 million.[21] Lieberson, mindful of Columbia Records pulling its own weight, asked Fujita to come back.

For Fujita it was a two-way defeat: his man Art Kane had strung Columbia along and finally declined the job; and some people in art and advertising were under the impression that Fujita wanted his old job back and had engineered Kuhlman's dismissal. (In fact Kuhlman claimed that Lieberson said the reason he was being fired was because Fujita wanted to return.) Fujita agreed to return as art director, stipulating that Columbia employ his partner, Ernie Sokolov. Oddly, this brief period turned out to be the one Fujita is remembered for, at least by jazz lovers. Fujita liked Charles Mingus's music but didn't know Mingus; his painting for the cover of Mingus Ah Um (1959) mirrored the angular, revival-meeting blues of most of the tracks, as well as those unutterably quiet ballads, "Goodbye, Porkpie Hat" and "Self Portrait in Three Colors." His painting for the cover of Dave Brubeck's Time Out (1960), done in casein, became one of the most reproduced album covers in recording history. After Brubeck returned from a trip to Asia, Fujita went to a party celebrating the new album and took the Time Out painting, which he presented to Brubeck. Fujita's amoebalike shapes always seemed to be liquefied, stretching this way and that, trapped in a two-dimensional lava lamp.

Once again Fujita hired the best graphic artists he knew. Among them was Thomas Allen, who painted the haunting cover of Rushing Lullaby, Jimmy Rushing's first Columbia album after leaving the Basie band. (Fujita bought the Allen painting, then loaned it for a touring show and never got it back.)

• • •

After two decades Alex Steinweiss was still in the game. Although he remained passionate about classical music and often painted for Decca and Victor, he had no illusions about spending his entire professional career working for a recording company. But in early 1958, he got a call from Harry Belock, an electronics inventor and manufacturer of radar equipment based in Queens. To woo Steinweiss, the surprisingly rough-necked Belock bought him lunch and outlined his plan for a new record label. Steinweiss was openly skeptical. Belock said, "You make one step out that door and I'll plug you."

So Steinweiss heard Belock out and agreed to give the new company a try. Belock would run the new label from his company's headquarters in College Point, New York. He'd obtained rights to several recordings and, uneducated about how long it can take to get a new album out to the public, gave Steinweiss one week to design ten covers. Steinweiss squawked. Belock realized he needed an administrator, a career record man who knew how to compete with established companies like Columbia. Steinweiss experienced a descent of doves and recommended his old boss Ted Wallerstein, who was now more than five years gone from CBS's employ and permitted to work once more in the recording industry. (In the interim Wallerstein had been a paid consultant to Kapp Records but was contractually prohibited by the agreement with CBS from holding an executive position.) Steinweiss introduced the 66-year-old Wallerstein to Belock. The wedding was on.

It proved to be a troubled union. Wallerstein insisted on a Manhattan office, which he got, and on hiring son-in-law Charlie Schicke as his main A&R man, which he also got. More than a year after Belock announced the opening of a recording subsidiary, to be called Everest Records, Wallerstein was laboriously planning the new label's catalog. Instead of selecting the artists he wanted and weighing the costs, however, Wallerstein set out to build a catalog the old-fashioned way, by running through the alphabet of classical composers—first the A guys like Albeniz, followed by Bach, and so on. Steinweiss thought, *Oy gevalt*, I made a big mistake recommending this old-timer. To make matters almost farcical, Belock had built a recording studio in Bayside, Queens, but it was no good—it was too close to a train station. Steinweiss lost his temper with his old boss when his wife, Blanche, responsible for the literary side of the label, telephoned some executives to get notes; Wallerstein chided Steinweiss for "allowing Blanche to talk to my guys." That ingenious composer and bandleader Raymond Scott, who'd recorded for years for Columbia ("The Toy Trumpet," "Powerhouse," etc.), was in charge of pop recording for Everest but had virtually no management skills. Wallerstein left. The Steinweisses stayed on for another year. Although Everest recordings would eventually win admiration for their engineering, Harry Belock lost a fortune on his new label.[22]

●　　●　　●

Like the other major labels, Columbia Records began to use photographs of its artists for its covers. One of the reasons for this was technical: it was much easier to capture photographic detail in that large format. The more obvious reason, though, was commercial: what better way to sell Tony Bennett than to put Tony's proud mug right on the cover? As television took over American households and the weeklies Life and Look, with their emphasis on photographs, became the nation's best-selling magazines, people were winning fame in new ways. The image was paramount. Even in the world of phonography, the absence of an artist's image wasn't always negative, but it was almost never positive. Record labels began to routinely employ the best photographers in town. And no one in New York, at Columbia Records or anywhere else, was better than Don Hunstein.

Hunstein was raised in St. Louis, of religious parents. His father was German Lutheran, his mother a devout member of the Church of Jesus Christ Latter Day Saints, which became his church throughout childhood. After attending Washington University in St. Louis, Hunstein knew he'd be drafted. To avoid Korea he joined the air force and was sent to England, where he taught himself what he could about photography. The Cold War had begun. In the spring of 1951, Hunstein was stationed at Fairford, in Gloucestershire. There he fell in love with a nearby fifteenth-century church, which he wanted to photograph, so his mother sent him his old camera from home. Like many other college graduates, Hunstein volunteered to be a typist—anything to avoid being an air guard. He had weekend passes to London, took pictures wherever he could, and developed his photographs through the PX (post exchange). Then his camera from home was stolen.[23]

It didn't matter that much. The PX was like a candy store, with laughably inexpensive Leicas on display. Hunstein bought a Leica and a couple of lenses and took the new rig into London. Meanwhile the Army Corps of Engineers was converting the old RAF runways to handle B-52s. Hunstein petitioned a sympathetic commanding officer to be transferred to South Ruislip, a western suburb of London where an RAF headquarters had been taken over by the U.S. Army. The transfer was approved.

Hunstein was now snug against his favorite city, staying not in a barracks but in Hampden Court Palace, within walking distance of Waterloo
Station. Hunstein began to take more and more street pictures, working
on various elements of his photography. Then, during a three-day pass
to Paris, thunder struck. Walking along the Boulevard St. Germain, he
came across a first edition of Cartier-Bresson's *Images à la Sauvette*, which
hadn't yet been published anywhere but France and would be translated
in America as *The Decisive Moment*. The Cartier-Bresson book laid out much
of what Hunstein was trying to accomplish.

Before his hitch was up, Hunstein was permitted to take rooms above
an antiques shop near the center of Notting Hill Gate. He now had a
reverse commute to South Ruislip, going from London to the suburbs
each day and taking pictures whenever he could. He joined a camera
club on Manchester Square and began to process his own pictures, following darkroom instructions from a book. At the same time he became
interested in typography, the design field that has proved an essential
part of so many artists' educations. Hunstein took evening classes at
what was then the Central School of Arts and Crafts, in Holburn. The
only thing more valuable than one's portfolio was a rationed carton of
good cigarettes. In England the war was, in one sense, still on.

His hitch over, Hunstein returned to the States. Despite, or maybe
because of, pressure from his mother to come home to St. Louis, he was
determined to live in New York. In the spring of 1954, he stayed with a
friend and went looking for a job. He took a flunky position at Pagano,
a Third Avenue design house, and earned practically nothing while he
learned how to set up lights and load large cameras in seconds. It was
worth the miserable pay.

Hunstein moved a step closer to Columbia Records after a writer-
photographer friend linked him up with Gene Cook. Formerly the
entertainment editor for *Life*, Cook was an opera buff who occasionally
photographed for Columbia Masterworks. Cook had been assigned to
photograph the Boston tryouts of a Broadway musical (probably *Fanny*,
the recording of which subsequently went to RCA Victor; Hunstein
remembered it as a Harold Rome show) and took Hunstein with him as

an assistant. When they returned to New York, Cook hired him full time
to work in his studio adjacent to Carnegie Hall. The Cook job brought
Hunstein to the attention of Debbie Ishlon. On January 23, 1956, Ishlon
hired Hunstein to work in the picture files with picture editor Eleanor
Morrison.

Columbia's New York office had gone from a staff of sixteen in 1940
to ten times that many by 1956. In less than six months' time, Jim Conkling would leave, Goddard Lieberson would become president of the
label, and *My Fair Lady* would prove to cynics that its primary backer,
Columbia Records, was the equal of big bad RCA. But Columbia's art
department was still tiny. There were two staff photographers, Dan
Weiner and Dennis Stock, with chief engineer Fred Plaut (though he
considered himself an amateur) photographing many of the original
cast recording sessions. That was about it. RCA had had an in-house
studio for years and money to burn. Columbia was still watching every
penny.

Cataloguing was a tryout for Hunstein. Each day he went through the
files, plucking other photographers' work for consideration. At the same
time he continued to photograph on the street. Some time during Hunstein's first year at the label, Ishlon split off the photographers and
housed them in a studio at 250 West 57th, at Eighth Avenue. By this
point Neil Fujita had departed for the first time; Bob Cato was running
the art department, though chafing under Ishlon's authority. Hunstein
began to get assignments, photographing musicians at the 30th Street
studio and on the street. He had his black-and-white film developed at
Modern Age, on East 44th, which was then a kind of photographer's
row. When he used Kodachrome—"great film," Hunstein said—it was
processed at a Kodak lab in New Jersey. K&L, on East 46th, handled color
film other than Kodak.

Now Hunstein was on staff. He remembered being sent to Philadelphia
to photograph the tryouts for *I Can Get It for You Wholesale*, another Harold
Rome musical (which would bring Barbra Streisand to the edge of stardom).
Also on staff was Hank Parker, who eventually ran the West 57th Street
studio for a while and took great covers, including the Grammy-winning

cover of Streisand's album *People*. Sandy Speiser was an assistant at the time and a fine photographer. Freelancers like Vernon Smith, W. Eugene Smith, and Lieberson's close friend Richard Avedon came and went. Meanwhile Hunstein was photographing most of the artists at the label, from Cassius Clay and Tony Bennett to Leonard Bernstein.

If there is a single iconic photograph taken by Don Hunstein, it might be either one of the two Dylan covers he did. For the first one, released as *Bob Dylan*, Hunstein was told by Debbie Ishlon that they needed a cover photo immediately. Dylan had just recorded his first sessions right there at 799. On a quiet Saturday morning Hunstein took Dylan into Ishlon's unoccupied office and stood him next to a window that overlooked Seventh Avenue. Dylan was in his street clothes, including the fake suede coat that looked like he wore it to bed. Hunstein used a Hasselblad to photograph Dylan in natural daylight. The result is "true" in the way Dylan's memoir is true, even when it's deliberately elliptical, because it's faithful to who Dylan is—whoever he is. The subject looks at once sincere and insincere, earnest and mocking, an old soul inside a boy's skin, his blue eyes penetrating the lens but also seeing far beyond the room. (In *The Decisive Moment* Cartier-Bresson wrote, "The profession depends so much upon the relations the photographer establishes with the people he's photographing, that a false relationship, a wrong word or attitude, can ruin everything. When the subject is in any way uneasy, the personality goes away where the camera can't reach it.")[24] The room itself appears to be neither inside nor outside but an artificial space that happens to have been created by natural light—and by Hunstein's sensitivity to his subject. Is there a deeper photograph of Bob Dylan?

Hunstein's cover for *The Freewheelin' Bob Dylan*, with Dylan and girlfriend Suze Rotolo huddled against the cold, was taken on Great Jones Street, not the 4th Street of Dylan's later song. The street has a coverlet of snow, the setting sun glints off the fire escapes, and the blue VW bus parked along the street could stand for the entire whacked-out, tumultuous sixties caravan, starting from Greenwich Village up to Cambridge, with stops at Ann Arbor and Madison, Wisconsin, before putt-putting through Berkeley and down the coast to Southern California.

Hunstein didn't park the VW on Great Jones Street; he only captured it in a moment. For the next two decades Hunstein was all over the place. When Hank Parker left Columbia Records, the 57th Street studio was closed. Bob Cato subsequently asked Hunstein to run the new studio, which was housed in a three-story black brick building ancillary to Black Rock, with a loading dock on West 52nd and a darkroom. (According to Hunstein, Sandy Speiser resented being passed over for a job he'd waited patiently for.) Hunstein did that for a while but never stopped photographing the label's artists. In a week's time he might go to Detroit to photograph Aretha Franklin, to Philly to shoot Harold Melvin & the Blue Notes, and up to Toronto to take pictures of Glenn Gould. Forty years after *The Freewheelin' Bob Dylan*, when Dylan was ready to publish his memoir *Chronicles, Volume One*, he asked Hunstein for a photograph for the dust jacket. Hunstein's black-and-white photograph of a rain-wet Times Square, circa 1960, is a symphony-of-the-city image that sings no less melodically than anything by Gershwin or Rodgers.

●   ●   ●

Back at Columbia, Neil Fujita left a second time. The top art job went to Bob Cato, who'd been first recommended to Lieberson back in 1949 by Mitch Miller. Cato was of Cuban heritage, perhaps American Indian as well, and carried curriculum vitae that went in and out of focus. Sometimes he said he was from New Orleans, other times from Florida. He claimed to have been a student at the Art Institute of Chicago and to have studied with the great graphics designer Alexey Brodovitch. He claimed to have been, among other things, a chef at the Palmer House in Chicago and personal chef to the architect I. M. Pei. The designer Paula Scher described him as "phenomenally social and charming. His demeanor was one of a tall, elegant hipster, sophisticated and chic." He was talented and, by many accounts, lazy—more interested in women, though he had a family, than in work. He also struggled with a stutter. His successor, John Berg, referred to him as "C-c-cato." [25]

At *Harper's Bazaar* Cato had worked as an assistant to Alexander

Liberman, Hearst's legendary creative director, then became art director himself at *Glamour*. Reading and painting since boyhood—his mother, Ysabel, he would claim many years later, read all of *Ulysses* to him when he was eight—Cato liked to think of himself as a photographer, too.[26] After Neil Fujita left Columbia for the second time, Lieberson offered the job to Cato.

When Bill Golden died suddenly in 1959, the CBS art department went through some retooling. Golden's former assistant Lou Dorfsman, though he would not be officially named director of design for CBS, Inc. until 1964, would become Columbia's go-to guy.

Unlike parent company CBS, Columbia Records had usually hired outside ad agencies for much of their advertising work—their copy, anyway. In 1960 there was not yet any separation of advertising and packaging (album covers, etc.). But Cato figured he could handle a whole in-house operation. He called in his friend Morris Baumstein, who had been general manager of Irving Serwer Advertising, which specialized in high fashion. Baumstein had been doing all right, but he was particularly excited about the prestige of CBS, which had employed one of his father's heroes, Edward R. Murrow. Red Baumstein, called "Rojo" by Cato, took on one freelance project as a test. The project turned out fine, and Baumstein joined Cato in Creative Services, which was still overseen by Debbie Ishlon.[27]

Cato was responsible for all artwork that came out of the label. Baumstein, running advertising interference, hired Les Wunderman's agency, Wunderman, Ricotta & Kline, for Columbia's media-buying. By now Wunderman was a close friend of Lieberson's and knew the record business about as well as any advertising man could. Baumstein also became valuable to Lieberson, as much for his heritage as his ad acumen. Lieberson called Baumstein "Moishe," Yiddish for Morris. (Lieberson's brother Maurice, pronounced like Morris in the English tradition, was also known as Moishe.) The consummately Irish Bill Gallagher heard the sobriquet so often that he too began to call Baumstein "Moishe." In the early months of negotiations with Barbra Streisand's manager, Marty Erlichman, Lieberson would phone Erlichman at his mother's house; but since Erlichman's mother spoke only Yiddish, Lieberson would call in Baumstein to do the talking.[28]

With Baumstein handling most of the administration and the Wunderman agency doing direct mail, Cato was free to build up the art department. To help out, Cato hired the young graphics artist John Berg.

* * *

"Well, that's a funny story," John Berg said, remembering how he got to Columbia Records forty-five years earlier. "I had a career of my own going in New York. My wife was pregnant with our first child, and I was freelancing for a photography duo that met each other at my engagement party."[29] The duo was Steve Horn and Norman Griner, their shop known as Horn/Griner.

Berg was a Brooklyn boy, educated at Erasmus High. He majored in graphic design at Cooper Union, where he came under the sway of designer Henry Wolf, who used photography, typography, and illustration to tell a story. After graduation he took several agency jobs in New York and Atlanta. Magazine work included *Esquire*, the sister publications *Horizon* and *American Heritage*, and then *Escapade*, a girly magazine that won his work several awards. In 1960, hunting for a new job, Berg went to 799 Seventh Avenue. "I dropped my portfolio off with Bob Cato's secretary and he came running out of the office and spotted me. Now how the hell he knew who I was, to this day I don't know. But he hired me on the spot."

Berg's first album cover was for Andy Williams's *Moon River*. "That was a big head shot. It was really a boilerplate album cover except that I brought a little different sensibility to it since I was basically an editorial art director. I was punching type through pictures, and stuff like that wasn't really going on. Even Roy Kuhlman, who was a terrific designer, wasn't doing that. He was still sort of the old-fashioned way of doing record coverage. I was more of a point of sale kind of person."

Berg had done a fair amount of promotion and knew what got attention. He also knew he could attract the best photographers and designers by giving them credit. Cato didn't withhold credit, exactly, but the Columbia way since the advent of the LP cover had been to permit the artist or photographer to sign his work, the signature or printed credit in small type. Berg, feeding the hungry egos of the artists who worked at the label, would list photographers, designers, art directors, even the occasional artist relative who might have had a hand in a cover. (On the 1965 My Name Is Barbra, Streisand is cocredited with Berg as designer, her brother Sheldon with providing the picture of the five-year-old Barbra.)[30]

Gruff and prone to crankiness, Berg also drank. "The word was, don't talk to him after lunch," said Don Hunstein, who worked amicably with Berg for many years.[31] In the Seventh Avenue days, lunch was frequently at the House of Chan across the street, or at a smaller Chinese bar on the ground floor of 799. Berg drank there occasionally with the drummer Olatunji. In the all too brief but explosive period when Janis Joplin was with the label, she would call ahead in her throaty whisper—Berg often thought Miles Davis was on the line—to put in a request for Tom Collins mix and gin. "She would specify what kind of gin and two BLTs down with mayo. She would appear around one o'clock and we would have our sandwiches and we would drink the entire bottle of gin watered down with Tom Collins mix."

●   ●   ●

In 1964 Cato hired Berg's old colleague Arnold Levine. Like Alex Steinweiss much earlier, Levine had attended Lincoln High in Brooklyn; like Berg, he had spent several years at Esquire working under its art director Robert Benton (before Benton became a film director) and venerated the work of Henry Wolf.[32] Under Cato, Levine did a lot of the advertising artwork, while Les Wunderman's agency continued to produce the ad copy. After a while Levine wondered why Wunderman was controlling advertising from outside the company; why not keep advertising strictly in-house? Levine knew this was treacherous ground because Wunderman had long been close to Lieberson. Clive Davis went to Lieberson to test the water. He came back to Levine and said, "Do what you have to do." Gradually, some of the copy work shifted in-house to Columbia, giving Levine a bit more control.

Meanwhile Cato evaluated the album cover art, directed by Berg, and the advertising art, directed by Levine. "You never knew whether he was going to love you or hate you," Levine said. Every year, sometimes twice a year, Cato would sequester himself for weeks at a time to prepare slide-show presentations of the label's upcoming product. All along he shmoozed, cooked, made cocktails, and kept his hand in the artwork. He was attractive to, and attracted by, women. Occasionally he rolled up his sleeves and made a design. And he still thought of himself as a photographer. One of his most famous pictures happens to be one of his worst: the Christmas-motif cover for Simon & Garfunkel's *Parsley, Sage, Rosemary and Thyme*.[33] Needing a gimmick, Cato wanted to dress the guys in Victoriana. At a Catholic goods store across from St. Patrick's Cathedral, Berg found a puffy-sleeved white shirt for Paul Simon and slapped the purchase on a Columbia credit card. The 23-year-old Simon, according to Berg, was amazed that the label would pay for a shirt. Cato's resulting image is blurry and it's hard to grasp what the cover intends; it's also hard to forget because the two artists (Simon in particular) would never again seem so innocent. In 1969 Cato illustrated Moby Grape's *Wow*—part Dali, part Canaletto—which showed how strong a designer he could be when he put his mind to it.

Through the sixties John Berg's covers, and those of his contributors, would help sell a lot of albums and draw considerable attention within the graphics industry. Among his contributors were the artists Edward Sorel, Milton Glaser, Tomi Ungerer, Paul Davis, Ron Coro, Virginia Team, and Bob Weaver. Phil Hays was prized for his bright, idealized Bessie Smith portraits. Former Columbia staffer and Broadway musicals maven Miles Kreuger produced several albums (Dick Powell, Paul Whiteman, etc.) in Columbia's Hall of Fame series and usually had a strong voice in their designs. By the late sixties Tony Lane was handling a lot of the art on the West Coast. In New York, Berg relied a lot on designer Henrietta Condak, who often brought in her freelancing husband Clifford to work with her. Now and then Berg got a birthday present of an artist's services, like the time John Hammond came around with his friend Romare Bearden, who promptly painted a cover for an album of Billie Holiday reissues. Album covers in general, with their head-turning artwork and extended liner notes, had come a long way from the Dennison labels George Avakian had used to annotate the jazz 78s in Marshall Stearns's closet.

Given a budget for the year, Berg went his merry way. Commuting between Manhattan and New Canaan, Connecticut, he would work on the train. "First you get your seat and you go through the big envelope full of bills, sign off on them or write notes on them or what the hell is this for, blah blah blah. I kept track of where the money was going. Then I had the rest of the train ride to get out my little sketchpad or a blank piece of paper or something and write the titles down and then start to torture it to see what would come out of it." For the most part, Berg knew how far he could go, or let his artists go, on a cover. The one that received the most ire within the company was one he played only a minor role in: Big Brother and the Holding Company's 1967 *Cheap Thrills*, which was largely a collaboration between Janis Joplin and R. Crumb. Clive Davis and Bob Cato loathed Crumb's drawing. "It was too new," Berg said, "too crazy, too this, too that. Janis was the big promoter of it and Crumb adored Janis." If an album cover could ever be said to be folk art, certainly *Cheap Thrills* qualifies. Crumb's patented characters, whether considered goofy hippies or just plain misfits, invite you to put the sweaty electric blues recording on the phonograph and get comfortable.

Berg was always under budget. A Streisand or a Leonard Bernstein cover could get expensive, but most of the pop albums didn't cost much. This enabled Berg to use the best photographers he could find. Some of them were already on staff: Parker, Speiser, Hunstein. Berg also had money to spend for the services of W. Eugene Smith, Avedon, Kane, and Jerry Schatzberg (who took the cover photo of *Blonde on Blonde*, with Dylan's mop of hair and checkered scarf and everything else out of focus). When Berg turned to his former boss Norman Griner, the results could be electrifying. The cover of *The Underground Monk* makes Thelonious out to be the vantage point of a sort of hyperreal vision; and there's something similar going on in *Switched-On Bach*, the powder-wigged Bach stand-in appearing to have arrived by carriage from the pages of *Mad* or the *National Lampoon*. Berg said he doped that one out on the train home, then gave the concept to Horn/Griner; the photography agency built the set, hired the actors, costumed them, and made them up before Norman Griner took the shot. *Switched-On Bach* would become the best-selling classical album of all time.

It's not surprising that Berg and his Columbia colleagues were largely immune to the influence of psychedelic art. "Psychedelic art just absolutely missed the East Coast," said Berg. "It never went anywhere that I can think of. I thought it was decoration and it didn't tell stories and it was hard to read, and it was passé by the time it got over the Rocky Mountains." Berg didn't go out of his way to reject LSD-inspired artists, but they rarely shared his sensibilities. Nevertheless, surfacing from the psychedelic sea were several arresting Columbia covers executed far from Berg and his staff, like George Hunter's Maxfield Parrish–like painting for *It's a Beautiful Day* (1969) and Mati Klarwein's for Santana's *Abraxas* (1970).[34] By then, with or without the enhancement of drugs, consumers often prized albums for the covers themselves rather than the data contained on the disks behind them. Some marketing genius at Restoration Hardware subsequently came up with the idea of selling 12" by 12" frames to go around those album covers. Even if you couldn't bear to hear "White Bird" ever again, you could hang *It's a Beautiful Day* on the wall. "For the highest praise of album art," Evan Eisenberg wrote, "is that it finally renders the record unnecessary, as a perfect idol displaces the god it represents."[35]

●　　●　　●

After a decade at Columbia, Bob Cato was made a vice president. For years he had seemed indifferent to getting a promotion. Then he was apprised of the benefit to the people in his department. "All of us stepped up a notch," Berg said. "We redid his office, made it a third bigger. Then suddenly he's up and quitting, going to *McCall's*." Cato took Henrietta Condak with him.

Paula Scher, who went to work at CBS Records in 1971, had another take on Cato's departure. "Cato hated [Clive] Davis. To Cato, Davis was 'pure sleaze' and unworthy of Lieberson's position. Apparently the feeling was mutual. Almost from the day he became president, Davis began meddling with Cato's ads. Cato quit." [36]

In any case, Cato's new position didn't last long. He left *McCall's* for Revlon, and the employment door would keep revolving for the rest of his career. By then in his fifties, Cato exhibited work in art shows all over town, collaborated on a cookbook, and worked on the designs of several books and magazines. Although never terribly innovative, he'd proven himself a strong leader in the art department, a master chef commanding an insanely busy kitchen throughout the 1960s.

Morris Baumstein had left the label in 1966 to manage a new ad agency, but when a major account went into Chapter 11, he found himself back on the street. Recently divorced, he had two children to support. He ran into Les Wunderman, who invited him to work on the CBS account and make him a vice president. So Baumstein ran between the Wunderman office on Madison Avenue and the CBS office at Black Rock. Needing help with CBS, Baumstein hired a willowy young Californian named Linda Barton. Eventually the two married. Wunderman's agency was bought by Young & Rubicam. Baumstein wanted to continue to work with CBS as a consultant. Warned that he'd never make vice president at Y&R if he consulted on his own, Baumstein opened his own firm to do what he called "cross-promotion." Soon he was combining Dr. Pepper and CBS Records in ad campaigns. Linda Barton would rise to head of media advertising, and would eventually become vice president of Creative Services—only the third female vice president in CBS Records' history. [37] The first, of course, had been Debbie Ishlon. Had Ishlon still been at Columbia Records, she wouldn't have recognized the bloated corporate structure of the small but influential department she'd ruled for a decade.

• • •

Henrietta Condak returned to Columbia Records, and to Berg. Clive Davis's regime was then at its most powerful. In the wake of Cato's sudden departure, Berg and Arnold Levine pulled their respective departments even farther away from each other—according to Paula Scher, Berg didn't want to be responsible for anything involving advertising—and were each made vice presidents. Each reported to Creative Services head Bill Farr, who had come out of Bill Gallagher's marketing team, and Farr reported only to Clive Davis. Berg and Levine were supposed to be equals. But it was tricky. For most designers, packaging was always considered more desirable than advertising because it was glamorous, it put you in frequent touch with the artists, and the work you did often lasted—the album cover went home with the record buyer—rather than the more ephemeral ad work. When Paula Scher first went to work there, Levine was her immediate boss. "I was there for two and a half years," she wrote, "and never had any idea that promotion and packaging had ever been one department. The two departments were on the same floor at Black Rock. Both sides were filled with designers, but an icy wall existed between the two. The packaging department was the glory department, and the promotion department was the cootie department. Clive Davis rewrote almost every ad."[38]

If any one design during this period could be said to have led the way that an artist was marketed, it would probably be Berg's and Nick Fasciano's design for the band Chicago. The band's first Columbia album was released under the name Chicago Transit Authority. Reaching back to his roots in Henry Wolf typographical storytelling, Berg made the big embracing C of *Chicago* as familiar as the Coca-Cola logo, at once paying tribute to it and parodying it. Berg got close to Chicago's producer James Guercio, so there were fewer problems walking the tightrope between artists' demands and the label's. Through the midseventies, Chicago's albums made a fortune. This meant Berg had a large budget for them, but he didn't need it. The cover of *Chicago IV* was simply white raised lettering; for *Chicago XI* the map Berg used cost 75 cents; for *Chicago XVI* Berg used a thumbprint from Jim Rollins, one of his colleagues on the tenth floor of Black Rock, and spent about a hundred bucks to make the lettering clear inside it. The money Berg saved on the Chicago franchise paid for the occasional Avedon or Irving Penn photograph.

●　　●　　●

Champing at the bit, Paula Scher left CBS Records for more creative freedom in 1973. After a year designing covers for Atlantic Records, she returned to CBS to work on the packaging (cover) side of Creative Services. "The creative director of advertising saw himself as the leader of an organization in service to corporate management. He wanted to build personal relationships with label heads, sought them out socially, and didn't want to provoke, challenge, or offend them. He protected the status quo." On the other hand, Scher wrote, "The creative director of the cover division saw himself as an art director and designer. He wanted to be well-respected in the design community, win design awards, and make his service to the company a by-product of the excellence of the department."[39] These are Scher's perceptions of Levine (advertising) and of Berg (packaging). Another way to read them is that Levine was loyal to Clive Davis, liking the man as well as admiring him—grateful, even, for the micro-management that irritated so many others; Berg, meanwhile, just wanted to be left alone. "I admired Clive in a lot of ways," Berg said. "I admired his business acumen, his toughness. I didn't care about the money. If he wants to steal from the company, it's his company, he can steal from it. What do I give a shit? I'm not going to see any of it anyway. But the stealing of the credit that blatantly—it was very grating. It grated on almost everybody."[40]

Before Davis left the label, the product manager began to emerge as a key position, acting as liaison between the recording artist and the company—a middleman to take some of the heat off the staff artists. Unfortunately, this also had the effect of further separating the artist from Columbia Records. Meanwhile, according to Scher, the company "grew layered and fat. Departments got restructured and restructured again. Berg got older while the rest of the company got younger." Creative Services became a division of something called Central Core Marketing.[41]

It was almost a given that the label's art directors preferred to illustrate jazz albums over rock albums. Far fewer people would take note of the average jazz album because the whole category had been marginalized by then, but it didn't matter. Scher wrote that jazz musicians "felt at ease with wit, abstraction, fantasy, and surrealism," and that it was tougher to illustrate for rock bands because there were so many opinions about every single image, with looking cool being of vital importance.[42] Berg liked working with the Chicago pianist Ramsey Lewis more than practically any other artist, with the possible exception of Taj Mahal. These artists were open to whatever ideas Berg tossed at them. Then again, with these artists the stakes were lower because they weren't expected to hit the charts every time. Paula Scher once designed the cover for the jazz guitarist Eric Gale's Ginseng Woman; Scher's favorite illustrator from the period, David Wilcox, executed the illustration. Her design—a kimono, a tatami mat, a sandal, and the cord to Gale's electric guitar entwined with a woman's ankles—was meant to honor Gale's love for his Asian wife. The day after the cover was nominated for a Grammy in 1978, CBS Records received a letter from the National Organization of Women (NOW) protesting violence to women in album cover art. Scher wrote to NOW explaining the "violence" was in the mind of the beholder—and also asking the organization's help in being on parity with all the male art directors who earned more money. NOW never replied to Scher.[43]

Oddly, Scher's Boston album cover, with its sci-fi comic-book motif that had little to do with anything but adolescent thrills, would become so prominent in the years since the album was released in 1976. The cover—a benign heavy-metal image that could take on all sorts of meaning with just a little pharmaceutical nudge—played directly to Boston's fans. Yet Scher seemed embarrassed by it. "Recently I was being considered for the design of a large packaging program for a major technology company," Scher wrote. "When I was interviewed about my branding expertise, I was asked what previous experience I had with technology companies. I had no experience whatsoever with technology brands, so I mentioned that I was the art director of the first

Boston cover. I felt a rush of reverence permeate the room. I was given the assignment."[44]

Less benign than the *Boston* cover but perhaps no less effective was Gene Greif's cover for the Clash's *Give 'Em Enough Rope*, which showed other artists what could be done in the punk milieu. Greif (born in 1954) was on staff at CBS Records from 1977 to 1980.

By 1982 the label was hit particularly hard. The sales force was pared way down. After 26 years on staff, Don Hunstein was let go. Paula Scher left again. A couple of years later, after CBS president Thomas Wyman had slashed at almost every CBS division and unloaded the least profitable ones, CBS Records was in somewhat better shape; but Ted Turner was making a run for the whole CBS network, and Wyman was cornered into a billion-dollar debt to buy back nearly a quarter of the company's stock.[45] John Berg was fired. Paul Smith, who had been a key figure in Columbia's distribution system many years earlier and was now Arnold Levine's immediate boss, fired Levine. "When I left, Holland McDonald took my place [as East Coast art director]," Levine said, "but the more significant move was making Linda Barton Baumstein, who at the time had been head of media, in charge of Creative Services. This proved to be a bad idea. Due to her lack of any creative background the labels became increasingly displeased with the creative group efforts."[46] Packaging and promotion were fused back together under merchandising. McDonald had every designer working on every aspect of the united department, from cover art down to the smallest print ad. Linda Barton, surely overwhelmed by antagonism in a swollen department, resigned. Other people quit. Berg and Levine each freelanced, still doing plenty of work for CBS Records but no longer on staff. Al Teller, then running Columbia Records, finally lured Arnold Levine back and, removing Creative Services out from under merchandising again, made him head of the department. Holland McDonald (in Scher's telling) quit because he didn't want to work under Levine, who made the art department strong again.[47]

Through the 1980s and into the end of CBS ownership of the label, Christopher Austopchuk appears to have been the premiere designer-director. Stacy Drummond also did many of the high-profile covers.

But the glory days of record album art were over. The CD shrank the canvas to practically nothing; the Internet gobbled up data about recording artists and their music, with images no longer even secondary. Don Hunstein worked for CBS Corporate Design for four years. In the hand-sized dimensions of the compact disc, the notion of hiring a world-class photographer became almost laughable—a luxury that only the top-selling artists could afford. Neil Fujita was long gone from Columbia but kept designing; among his notable book covers was the Putnam hardback edition of Mario Puzo's *The Godfather*. Bob Cato had thrived as an artist in the corporate world but closed his career as a designer for hire before fighting a protracted battle with Alzheimer's, spending his last days in a midtown hospice. Alex Steinweiss moved with his wife Blanche to Florida where, in his tenth decade, he was still "painting music" that you can practically hear as you look at it.

17

High Above Manhattan

In late February 1963, RCA Victor announced the introduction of its "Dynagroove" recording system. In recent years RCA Victor had made one technological advance after another, particularly with what came to be known as its Shaded Dog series—beautifully engineered albums that put almost all other labels to shame. Columbia, though, was feeling its oats. Goddard Lieberson pronounced the Dynagroove system a step backward because it wasn't a faithful reproduction of the artist: "In an attempt to limit what is sometimes called distortion in recording, the electronic system introduces limitations upon artistic expression."[1] In 1964 RCA, taking on not only the Columbia Record Club but the Longines Symphonette Society, began to offer low-priced classical recordings through *Reader's Digest*.

If Columbia was worried, it didn't show it. It brought the classical guitarist John Williams (whose namesake was working in television by then) into Masterworks. It made plans to start its Odyssey line of LPs that undercut even the *Reader's Digest* offerings. Masterworks remained sturdy, even if it was continually being propped up by the pop division. By October 1964, the top 100 best sellers in the Masterworks catalog provided striking evidence of Eugene Ormandy's dominance, with 30 titles in the top hundred. Leonard Bernstein had fewer (26), though with five of the top ten, including the catalog's best seller, his recording of *Rhapsody in Blue*. The list is filled out with a lot of Mormon Tabernacle Choir, whose recordings cost Columbia practically nothing up front because their tapes were expertly made in Salt Lake City, then sent to New York ready to be pressed, packaged, and marketed. Then there were those three wacky piano players—Horowitz, Serkin, and Gould—a smattering of Bruno Walter, and odds and ends like Phillippe Entremont, André Previn, and E. Power Biggs.[2] Catalog sales never tell the whole story, but they do indicate which recordings listeners want to go back to. The sound of the Philadelphia Orchestra—whether captured and shaped over the years by Howard Scott, John McClure, or Tom Frost—remained a perennial favorite of record-buyers.

Lieberson had every reason to feel good. Moving into his midfifties, he had little left to prove. In the eyes of many colleagues, he still aspired to Noel Coward's elegance and his ability to toss off bon mots without noticeable effort. The sad thing is that Lieberson had all this and more, including the responsibility of overseeing one of the more influential media companies in America. But he regarded himself as a failure, in part because he'd stopped composing serious music. So exalted was Lieberson's reputation in New York's cultural circles in the midsixties that a widely read essay in the Sunday Times pronounced him a member of the In Crowd, a shifting but undeniably attention-getting set that, unlike the Social Register, required achievement, usually in politics or the arts, and some wealth to show for it.[3] (Jacqueline Onassis and Leonard Bernstein were the two prime models of the set.) For all his alleged elitism, Lieberson would exchange pleasantries with the elevator man and the mop-wielding janitor as readily as he did with, say, Kitty Carlisle Hart. Maida Glancy remembered taking taxis in the mornings from her East 62nd Street apartment to 799 Seventh Avenue. "On many occasions I would see Goddard loping through the streets to work, and sometimes offered him a ride, which he never accepted, saying that he wanted the exercise."[4] Noel Coward wouldn't have been caught dead taking such a healthy walk; the walk itself would have killed him, especially if no one recognized him. And though Lieberson, whose emotional chambers were rarely left ajar, may have felt lonely at times, he had, unlike Coward, a supportive and loving family.

Of the Lieberson family, Lincoln Kirstein once made the devastating remark that "the parents are without talent but they created two masterpieces—their sons."[5] If Lieberson was not, after all, a gifted composer who had squandered a potentially brilliant musical career to become a well-paid executive, he still ran his company with more verve than anyone else did. The annual Columbia Records convention was Lieberson's home court, the arena where he was in peak form. Many of the conventions were held in Miami, at the Diplomat or the Americana, and Columbia Records employees arrived to play, with Lieberson as a combination of toastmaster and tummler. "It seemed that Lieberson was at heart a performer," observed Joan Simpson Burns, who worked (as Joan Meyers) as Legacy's book editor in the midsixties before interviewing him for her own book, *The Awkward Embrace*. Burns watched Lieberson at one of the Miami conventions in the late sixties. "The air was charged, and when I ran across Lieberson in the lobby, his face was flushed and his eyes were glittering with excitement. He was to go on stage and introduce a Columbia Records recording star to the assembled convention, and this he did with witty brilliance and evident enjoyment. The salesman loved their own. Then, retreating to the side, he sat on the floor behind the curtain, his feet sticking out under it, and by tapping them in time to the music managed to upstage the performer."[6]

At another convention he took the stage. The opening strains of "It's Not for Me to Say" came over the sound system as Lieberson prepared to lip-synch Johnny Mathis. "Sing it, Goddard!" someone called out from the audience. "Don't you worry," Lieberson replied in his radio announcer's voice, delighting the minions as well as himself.[7]

When the recording of Lieberson's String Quartet was released by the label in 1963, his friends praised it, sometimes lavishly. But there was a sense that the world was not poorer for his decision to become a record executive. "Tell me what kind of guy keeps photographs of the celebrities he's known on his office wall?" said Peter Munves. "Goddard basked in their reflected glory."[8] Though Lieberson was reputed to have treated everyone the same, his elitism could blow through a room like a draft. One evening Howard Scott was dining with his first wife Elsa at Chateaubriand, on East 58th Street, when Lieberson walked in with the poet Robert Lowell. Scott stood up to be introduced to Lowell. "What do you wanna meet him for?" said Lieberson, pulling Lowell away, leaving Scott with his hand in mid-air.[9]

Yet Lieberson could be kind and unutterably charming to people from whom he wanted nothing. As Lieberson turned 54, Columbia Records was girding to move into Black Rock. Liz Lauer, remembering her former boss's birthday, baked him a chocolate cake with mocha icing and, with her two-year-old daughter Amy, took it up to 799. Lieberson hovered over the cake's icing. "Do you know what this is?" he said with a mischievous gleam to Amy. "It's pâté!" said Amy. "Pâté! How is this child being raised?!" Lieberson slid his finger across the top of the mocha frosting and then put his finger in his mouth. Amy got the idea.[10]

The move into the Saarinen building was, according to many Columbia Records alumni, the beginning of a new and metallic corporate tone. The move had nothing to do with Columbia Records and everything to do with CBS's desperate need for a change. Frank Stanton had been the instigator. He'd convinced Bill Paley of the necessity of getting out of 485 Madison Avenue where, as one CBS employee carped, "the urinals stank, the toilets hardly ever flushed, and there was no air conditioning." Various sites were considered before the Sixth Avenue and 52nd Street lot was bought. Stanton and Paley—and, for that matter, most business executives in New York—knew all about Eero Saarinen, if only by the TWA terminal, with its undulating, come-fly-with-me sensuality, that he'd designed for what was then called Idlewild. (At Yale Architecture School, Saarinen's roommate for a while had been, of all people, Harold Rome.)[11] When Saarinen died of a heart attack in Ann Arbor in 1961, Paley considered bringing in a new architectural firm; Stanton reminded him that the CBS headquarters would be Saarinen's only skyscraper, which was enough to persuade Paley to stay with Saarinen's firm. While the CBS building was under construction, the site was blocked off by Plexiglas so pedestrians could watch its progress without having to peer through knotholes. Lou Dorfsman designed a passageway of panels as part of the site, which welcomed rather than repelled the curious. Completed near the end of 1964, the building

reached 491 feet above the Manhattan sidewalk, intimidating, even forbidding, in its granite immensity.

Columbia Records was finally moved one long avenue east into the
new building at 51 West 52nd on May 3, 1965. The sales operation was
awarded the zippy new telephone number 765-4321.[12]

*   *   *

Black Rock had been erected largely on proceeds from television entertainment. Columbia Records' contribution was less substantial than the
network's advertising revenue, but it was still considerable, and almost
all of it came from its pop division. Pop music itself, though, was
changing drastically, moving away from the rich jazz tradition it had
mined under Avakian and more toward rock 'n' roll. That was happening
at every major label, in fact, but it was a more painful process at
Columbia, where Mitch Miller, with Lieberson's approval, had bolted the
rock 'n' roll door shut for so many years.

Meanwhile the Masterworks lineup was as impressive as it had been
in the fifties. Isaac Stern was the kind of artist you could invite to the
White House—virtuosic, diplomatic, and uncontroversial—even
though, when he played there for the visiting dignitary Indira Gandhi,
his 1740 Guarnerius chin-guard bit him in the cheek, forcing him to
wear a bandage while he played.[13] Stern recorded for Masterworks with
various symphonies and with the trio whose other musicians, cellist
Leonard Rose and pianist Eugene Istomin, also had individual contracts
with Columbia. Istomin was no less fussy than any other artist. Tom
Shepard recalled the time Istomin was recording the Schubert Trio in B
flat, opus 99, and hit a piano key that made him stop playing. Shepard
had been warned that Istomin would do this, no matter how many
times the piano was tuned. "I cannot record on this piano," Istomin
declared. Weary of deferring to such prima donna behavior, Shepard said,
"Then I'm going home." Istomin sputtered that Shepard couldn't go
home—his job was to produce the session. Once he realized that
Shepard was sincere about leaving—and at what would have been at

great cost to Columbia Records for the blown session—Istomin sat down and played through the piece.[14]

The dual piano team of Arthur Gold and Robert Fizdale had been with Columbia for a while and recorded with only the very best, from Bernstein to Brubeck. Partners in life, residing on Central Park West, they also played together and wrote together—cookbooks and biographies would be among their extensive list of publications—and were probably at their peak in the midsixties.[15] Gary Graffman was still playing. Andre Watts, born in Nuremberg in 1945, the son of an American soldier, had been Leonard Bernstein's protégé and had made a splash ever since he'd substituted for Glenn Gould on a Philharmonic program. Rudolf Serkin, barely losing a step and wiser than ever, was still a Masterworks artist setting an absurdly high standard for every pianist who dared to sit at the keyboard.

Then there was Horowitz. He didn't carry the extreme eccentricities worn like an overcoat by Glenn Gould. He didn't sand the legs off his piano chairs or soak his hands in scalding water. He didn't repel civilians in the room by being sweatily overdressed, or by doing mediocre impressions of musical personalities. Always beautifully attired, Horowitz didn't show up in drag or wearing a gas mask. He was the stillest of pianists, athletically the anti–Keith Jarrett, moving only his arms, hands, and those practically prehensile fingers across the keyboard to produce high-voltage interpretations. He didn't sing or grunt along with his playing.

But Horowitz had his quirks. He stayed up late, slept late, and, compared to other virtuosi, practiced relatively few hours each day. He possessed a loud horselaugh that whinnied at the most peculiar times—i.e., when nothing discernibly funny was at hand. He preferred to record only on alternate days, starting at 4 P.M., at the 30th Street Studio, where a Steinway awaited his touch. Taking an occasional break to lie down on a couch provided for him by Columbia, Horowitz would record till 6 P.M.—an intense, compressed workday that yielded astonishing results.[16]

Horowitz and Glenn Gould had something else in common: although neither would cease recording, both of them had stopped giving concerts—Horowitz temporarily, Gould permanently—though for different reasons. Horowitz buckled under the demands of grueling travel and audience expectations, weary of playing "Stars and Stripes Forever" for concertgoers who'd already heard him play it a dozen times. "Most pianists would have given anything for his kind of pianistic control," Howard Klein wrote in the Times, "his supervirtuosity, his power of reducing an audience to the level of screaming bobby-soxers. But Horowitz was secretly ashamed of it, like a pretty girl who wants to be loved for her brains."[17] Gould eliminated live performances because they were imperfect, and because they subjected him to the Daniel-in-the-lion's-den vulnerability of the concert hall. Particularly after the advent of stereo, Gould felt he could do everything he wanted to in the studio. Recorded music, he insisted, was pure—unsullied by the concert hall's unpredictability. This proved to be a boon to Columbia Masterworks, which recorded him extensively in New York and, after train schedules were cut back and limited his travel options, near his home in Toronto.

• • • •

At 61, after 12 years in retirement from live performances, Horowitz was finally ready to return to the concert hall. In this case the concert hall was Carnegie Hall, on the afternoon of May 9, 1965. Schuyler Chapin, though gone from Columbia Records for nearly three years, was in Spain when he received a cable about the planned concert. He returned to New York to make good on the promise he'd made years earlier—to serve as Horowitz's valet if and when he returned to the stage. Fifteen hundred Horowitz admirers waited all night on West 57th Street for the box office to open at noon the next day, April 26. "Is this a Beatles thing?" a pedestrian asked a cop.[18] Tickets were sold out by 2 P.M.; hundreds had to be turned away after the long wait, which had been made more comfortable only because Mrs. Horowitz had coffee sent to the people in line.

But the concert was a smashing success. Horowitz played what was, for him, a not atypical repertoire of Bach-Busoni, Schumann, Scriabin, and Chopin, with Debussy and Moszkowski thrown in for the encores. Don Hunstein and Hank Parker took photographs for the Columbia album. Three weeks later a Talk of the Town piece on the concert, "The Return," appeared in the New Yorker, May 29, 1965. The squib is noteworthy because, eight days after the triumphant concert, sitting in the Horowitzes' town house on East 94th Street, it's Lieberson who's the nervous one as the unusually calm Horowitz listens to the Columbia test pressing of the album in production. Delighted by the publicity, Leonard Burkat sent out copies to all CBS division head and officers.

A member of the Carnegie Hall audience surreptitiously recorded Horowitz, and later compared his recording with Columbia's product.[19] But the secret that was supposed to be revealed—that some sounds in a highly anticipated recording were edited out, while others were enhanced—proved to be a nonissue with record buyers. In a blur of production and marketing speed, Columbia managed to get the two-disk set out a mere month after the concert. At the Grammys the following winter the Columbia recording of the concert, the two-disk Historic Return, produced and indeed closely edited by Tom Frost, was named best classical album of 1965; Horowitz's the best solo instrumental performance; and Fred Plaut's engineering the best of any classical recording.[20]

Horowitz continued to record with Frost until 1968, when Frost declined to use videotape rather than film for a CBS special. Paul Myers was brought in to handle Horowitz and make the recording.[21]

●   ●   ●

Almost 40 years after it was recorded in 1965 at Studio A at 799 Seventh Avenue—shortly before Columbia's move to Black Rock—"Like a Rolling Stone" was named by Rolling Stone as the greatest rock 'n' roll song of all time. Like so much of Dylan's most impressive work, it sounds based on dark, all too human emotions, especially vindictiveness. Drummer Bobby

Gregg's opening drum beat, in Fred Goodman's words, "resounded like a rifle shot from radios across the country."[22] Shaun Considine, coordinator of new releases at the time, remembered that Gallagher's sales force at Columbia wanted to cut the six-minute song in half to sell it as a single, and that it was designated an "unassigned release" as sales and the other record divisions packed up and, during the summer of 1965, moved over to 51 West 52nd Street. It wasn't until Considine, a partner in the new discotheque Arthur, got the song played there that it caught the attention of some important disk jockeys, who wanted to know why Columbia hadn't released the single. Gallagher's team finally did put out the single—at three minutes per side, effectively cutting the song in half. According to Considine, irked disk jockeys recorded the two sides together as one and played their taped version. Columbia finally caught on and released the single in all its six-minute glory.[23]

Assuming that Considine's version is accurate, it's safe to say that before the end of that summer Columbia Records knew what it had, particularly when it came to *Highway 61 Revisited*, the album that contained "Like a Rolling Stone." It was Dylan's second electric album. He had already ruffled feathers with *Bringing It All Back Home* and his notoriously brief appearance at the Newport Folk Festival—one of several places where he'd been booed for daring to sustain an electric set and labeled a sell-out.[24] Sell out to what? Commercial rock 'n' roll?

Columbia Records, just about the last kid on the block to get into rock, stood by Dylan. At the beginning of September merchandising vice president Stan Kavan sent out a memo about *Highway 61 Revisited*:

Dylan!

With all the things going for Bob Dylan—a big hit single, soldout concerts, a fantastic press, and industry acknowledgment that he is today's leader of the pack—*Highway 61 Revisited*, that long awaited release, *has got to be a Number One album.*

And just to rocket the album to an even faster start, we are going to include in the package, for a limited time, the unique Dylan portrait enclosed. This will be packed under the skin wrap on the liner side, and a sticker on the cover will herald the portrait's inclusion. The portrait will be included in all copies of your initial shipment as well as in your reorders for the next few weeks, or as long as the supply lasts.

Wail.[25]

The first pressing of Highway 61 Revisited quickly became a collectible because it included an alternate take of "From a Buick 6." There was also a bonus black-and-white drawing of Dylan, signed by an artist named Lambert, that was packed under the back skin wrap, sent out to one region of the country as a test. For subsequent pressings the drawing and the alternate take were put on the shelf. In this case the artwork may not have mattered much. "Like a Rolling Stone" reached number two on the charts—somebody was listening to that traitor!—and Highway 61 hit number three and stayed on the charts for 47 weeks. Electrically powered rock 'n' roll had been around for more than 15 years, but it took Dylan's 1965 plugging in to yank his followers—implicitly left-wing and equating "pure" acoustic folk music with the proper political stance—into the pop world of the present, never mind the future. The cruelty that was only hinted at in the early acoustic years now peppered half his new songs, its nastiness positively bracing.

Blonde on Blonde, recorded in Nashville with some of the best musicians in the land, would come next.[26] In the meantime John Hammond was standing by, nodding with approval. "I certainly was not surprised to see [Dylan] become the founder of folk rock," Hammond wrote, "and I must confess that I like his performance on Highway 61 Revisited better than on either of the albums that I produced. I think he is an important poet and I am not disappointed that he has sought a wider audience with his 'electric sound.' I will not be able to predict that the present Dylan is the final Dylan, but I can remember Pete Seeger saying three years ago that Dylan will be the most important folk singer in America if he doesn't burn himself out first."[27]

At the beginning of autumn 1966, weeks after the announcement of Dylan's mysterious motorcycle accident, there was further discussion among Columbia Records executives and Albert Grossman's attorneys about keeping Dylan happy. No one knew how extensive his injuries were; no one knew when he would record again. Hammond asked Lieberson to come into the negotiations.[28] Whether or not that did the trick, Dylan stayed put for a while. While Dylan recuperated, electric music was moving into bohemia, its neglected old buildings cheaper and roomier to produce a concert in. Midtown discotheques like Arthur, where "Like a Rolling Stone" first got serious DJ attention, and the Peppermint Lounge were quickly becoming passé. Bill Graham's Fillmore East soon opened on Second Avenue. The critic Gene Santoro wrote, "The no-man's land between the Lower East Side, the Village, and Gramercy Park, a Ukrainian neighborhood where Beats like Allen Ginsberg and artists like Larry Rivers had moved during the 1950s to avoid the Village's overpriced rents and tourists, filled with teenyboppers and hippies and was renamed the East Village."[29] A midtown nightclub couldn't contain all those kids clamoring to hear live electric anymore; it couldn't contain the music itself. British bands had been playing to large stadium crowds since the beginning of the sixties; Dylan's electric albums made it respectable—and, in many cases, profitable—for American bands to blast rock 'n' roll not just to dozens but to thousands.

When Dylan finally recorded again, it was with the Band, his recent backup musicians, but the recordings weren't official and weren't for Columbia. (Bootlegged, they emerged as the so-called *Basement Tapes*.) The familiar folklore of *John Wesley Harding* (1968) suggested that Dylan had mellowed, though he had always been so deliberately contrary that he might have been simply thumbing his nose at the prevailing psychedelia. The album was lovely, though, and yielded "All Along the Watchtower," which Jimi Hendrix plucked for his own signature in the brief time he had left. *Nashville Skyline* (1969) was pleasant enough, with Dylan's avuncular pal Johnny Cash joining him on "Girl from the North Country." *Self Portrait* was praised as guileless and knocked as self-indulgent. *New Morning* was contemplative rather than vituperative, with the residue of pine left over from his time in the Catskills. Dylan would leave Columbia only briefly, to go to David Geffen's Asylum Records, where in 1974 he made *Planet Waves* and *Before the Flood*, their apocalyptic titles perhaps more poetic than the songs they contained. At 33 Dylan could have been considered a rock 'n' roll eminence, but the honorific, no matter how well-meaning, would have made him wince.

•   •   •

A score of folksingers had been likened to Dylan; some of them he'd come up with in the Village. But Dylan was unique. The only other musician who combined a gift for original lyrics, song after song, with deceptively simple melodies was Paul Simon. And, curiously, Simon and his longtime partner Art Garfunkel were really more like the Everly Bros. than they were, say, Peter, Paul & Mary.

In the spring of 1964 staff producer Tom Wilson bought Paul Simon's song "He Was My Brother" for the Pilgrims.[30] Soon Wilson had Simon & Garfunkel signed to the label and assigned them to record with engineer Roy Halee. The Halee connection would prove central to the duo's success—more so than either Wilson, who produced *Wednesday Morning 3 A.M.* and subsequently made them electric, and Bob Johnston, who got the producer's credit on *Sounds of Silence* and *Parsley, Sage, Rosemary and Thyme* but seemed to have little input.

Simon and Garfunkel were born weeks apart in the autumn of 1941; had each attended P.S. 164 in Queens, though they barely knew each other before adolescence; and had appeared as Tom & Jerry on *American Bandstand*, Thanksgiving Day 1957, when they were 15. (A dozen years later, giving his blessing as he sends him off to Mexico to appear in the movie version of *Catch-22*, Simon refers to Garfunkel as Tom in "The Only Livin' Boy in New York.") They were obviously talented, and also more openly Jewish than recording artists like Steve & Eydie, whose names didn't announce it. (It was Lieberson, according to Columbia legend, who persuaded the boys to record under their own names.) Simon moved to London for a while—a period that would inform his songwriting ("Fakin' It," etc.) for years to come. Back in the United States, Columbia released the boys' album *Wednesday Morning 3 A.M.* The album appeared to be buried amid weightier records in the folk-rock genre, including Dylan's first two electric albums. But one track, "Sounds of Silence," was played so often by a Florida disk jockey that Tom Wilson in New York took notice. Wilson listened to the track again and overdubbed it with electric instruments.[31]

As the new single was being retooled for release, Mort Lewis, who had managed Dave Brubeck at Columbia and was still managing the Brothers Four, got a call from Gene Weiss. Part of Bill Gallagher's crackerjack sales team, Weiss wanted Lewis to hear Simon & Garfunkel. "*Wednesday Morning* has stiffed," Weiss said, "but radio stations keep playing 'Sounds of Silence,' so something's going on. They're signed with William Morris but they can't get a job."[32] In fact Lewis was aware of "Sounds of Silence" because he'd been to Columbia's July 1965 convention in Miami. While he stood at the bar with Irving Townsend, Mort Lewis had heard Mort Weiner, head of the local sales branch, talking about all the airplay the song was getting.

Lewis listened to Tom Wilson's embellished (drums, electric bass) recording of "Sounds of Silence." By midautumn this second version had proved even bigger. Listeners were responding, it seemed, to lyrics that described an alienated sensibility, informed by drugs and now revolted by America's recently enlarged role in Vietnam. Apart from Bob Dylan, whom Simon would parody with affection in "A Simple Desultory Philippic," few songwriters could employ images as concrete and tactile as Simon could. After a decade as a manager, Lewis knew how to negotiate and worked easily with the Columbia executives, most of whom had been around since Lewis's Brubeck years. Lewis met Simon & Garfunkel at the Hole in the Wall Deli, on First Avenue near 57th Street, where he agreed to manage them, all three parties signing the back of a napkin.[33]

Protective of his new clients, Lewis objected to their participating in the film of the 1967 documentary *Monterey Pop* because, though their stars had risen dramatically, they were getting only scale from the event's producer Lou Adler. It was at that 1967 Monterey festival that Clive Davis began to run with rock acts, finding his groove, while the older guard felt the ground shift beneath them. Lewis remembered standing at the bar of the hotel in Monterey with Lieberson and Gallagher. As electric guitars screeched in the distance, one of them said, "What's the world coming to?" and the others shook their heads in despairing agreement.

After *Parsley, Sage* there was a brief quiet interval. Although it had as many tracks electric as acoustic, that album had been embraced by many of the folkies who'd scorned Dylan a couple of years earlier, primarily because of its ingenious, deeply moving version of "Silent Night," with the audio broadcast about Vietnam war casualties in the background. Its headlining song, "Scarborough Fair," was interstitched with the hymnlike "Canticle." At the time there wasn't much pop music that folded lacy harmonies into such political fury.

With *Bookends*, Simon & Garfunkel, ably supported again by Roy Halee, managed to keep a grip on the production of what seemed like the ultimate concept album. (It's deceptive because the concept isn't quite articulated.) Still, there are few albums with not only so many memorable songs but so much subtle emotion, from the sepia-toned self-castigation in "Fakin' It" to the conversational mythologizing of "America," and then the poignancy of "Old Friends" and the playfulness of "Punky's Dilemma" and "At the Zoo." *Bookends* was released in June 1968, and it shared one song, "Mrs. Robinson," with the soundtrack of *The Graduate*, released that same month. The Mike Nichols movie was talked and written about everywhere and made a star of Dustin Hoffman. For many record buyers, in the aftershock of two cataclysmic assassinations and the open-wound presidential race, not to mention Americans landing in Khe Sanh and on the moon, it was a summer of bold type, a Simon & Garfunkel summer. Soon *The Graduate* was the number one album on the charts, trailed closely by *Bookends*, and, though it had been released two years earlier, *Parsley, Sage* at number three.[34]

Bridge over Troubled Waters came at the end of the partnership and, despite good work on "Baby Driver," "The Boxer," and "The Only Livin' Boy in New York," it was bloated with treacly orchestrations and more commercial success than the boys knew what to do with. Simon fell in love with Peggy Harper, who had been married to Mort Lewis. Their marriage would inspire some of Simon's more agreeable work yet, particularly on *There Goes Rhymin' Simon*. Columbia Records had Simon through the Clive Davis years and briefly into the tenure of Walter Yetnikoff, their mutual antipathy ticking away like a hand grenade. Art Garfunkel also recorded solo for Columbia, his trilling high tenor as sweet as ever, though, without Simon's strong writing, no longer so special.

• • •

That Tony Bennett never recorded a Paul Simon song isn't unusual. Simon's lyrics often lack the love interest or the general wistfulness so endemic to the saloon ballad Bennett specialized in. Through the sixties, though, Bennett remained the quintessential Columbia Records artist: dependable, profitable, often taking musical risks.

"I Left My Heart in San Francisco" was originally written in 1954 by George Cory and Douglas Cross, aspiring songwriters living in New York in the mid-fifties. They routinely gave pianist Ralph Sharon, who became Bennett's prime accompanist in 1957, their songs. One of the Cory-Cross songs Sharon had put in a drawer was "I Left My Heart in San Francisco." Sharon remembered it and showed it to Bennett while they were on tour. When they got to San Francisco, Bennett finally sang the song, to enthusiastic response. In New York Marty Manning, whose arrangements were considered square but who knew Bennett's abilities inside and out, recast the song for a record. The recording was made at 30th Street on January 23, 1962. "I Left My Heart in San Francisco" appeared as the B side of "Once Upon a Time," which Bennett recorded at Columbia's behest because the label was putting out the original cast recording of the show it was from, *All American*. (The "Once Upon a Time" rendition is trademark Bennett, with the song getting away from him more than once, like a plastic bag taken by the wind, but the elegiac tone so close to Bennett's sensibility that it works.) "San Francisco" got all the attention, though, and subsequently won Bennett his first

Grammy. Goddard Lieberson called him and said, "You're never going to stop hearing about 'San Francisco' for the rest of your life."[35]

Lieberson was right. Bennett virtually owned the song—who else could sing it without it sounding like a parody?—while Cory and Cross actually owned it, the song's royalties enabling them to build a house for themselves in Clearlake, in the Sacramento Valley. Columbia, thrilled by profits generated by the single and the album, gave Bennett a major push, with Ernie Altschuler, who produced "San Francisco" and won his second Grammy for it, watching over his recordings. In one 15-month period between 1962 and '63, Bennett followed up the I Left My Heart in San Francisco album with Tony Bennett at Carnegie Hall, This Is All I Ask, and I Wanna Be Around. The Carnegie Hall concert (June 9, 1962) was particularly significant for Bennett: growing up in Astoria he'd been aware that Carnegie Hall was where a musical artist arrived. Bennett had arrived. He usually had Ralph Sharon accompanying him, and Altschuler delivered, in addition to Marty Manning, the best arrangers and conductors in the business: Don Costa, Dick Hyman, Frank DeVol, Ralph Burns, Marion Evans, Neal Hefti. Bennett's favorite engineer Frank Laico, who first got a job as a clerk at a recording studio after delivering groceries before World War II, recorded most of these albums. During this period Bennett took on a whole new folio of signature songs, including Alec Wilder's "I'll Be Around," Sacha Distel's "The Good Life," and Johnny Mercer's "I Wanna Be Around." (In a 1971 appearance at New York's 92nd Street Y, Mercer told the story of Sadie Vimmerstedt, of Youngstown, Ohio, the non-pro who sent him the title and the first two lines. After the song was recorded to acclaim, Vimmerstedt found herself making radio and television appearances. Drained by newfound celebrity, she wrote to the lyricist, "Mr Mercer, I'm tired. I've gotta get out of show business!")[36] In contrast to Sinatra's readings of ballads like these, which tended to plumb them for their wee-small-hours anguish, Bennett's interpretations usually let a few sun rays slant through. The Bennett narrator could be crushed but remained hopeful.

By 1965 Bennett had accepted his first movie role—as sidekick to an ruthlessly ambitious actor (played by Stephen Boyd) in the movie The

Oscar. The resulting movie, released in early 1966, is so dreary and obvious that it isn't even fun the way atrocious movies can be fun. But Bennett isn't bad in it. More important, he wanted Columbia to push his version of the movie's theme song, "Maybe September," written by his old musical cohort Percy Faith. Frustrated by the label's lack of a specific marketing plan, Bennett claimed that Frank Sinatra wanted him on his label Reprise, and Bennett was weighing the offer (even though, inevitably, his albums wouldn't be promoted the way Sinatra's would). "If I see fantastic action on Tony Bennett then you'll have a happy cat on your hands," he was quoted as saying to West Coast–based executive Billy James. "Columbia has a habit of laying on heavy promotion as you're leaving the label, to convince you to stay . . . but I need it now, it'll help the movie if they see I am a major recording artist. . . ." Nobody at Columbia, of course, or at any other label doubted that Bennett was a major recording artist. "Tony likes to push the panic button every once in a while," James reassured his colleagues in New York.[37] "Maybe September" was part of the lineup of Bennett's *The Movie Song Album*, a smartly designed potpourri of film themes, with several arrangers contributing, and probably Bennett's favorite of all his albums.[38]

Around 1967 Altschuler left Columbia to accept a vice presidency at RCA Victor. Before he departed, though, he oversaw *The Many Moods of Tony*, which included the lovely song by Jack Segal and Bob Wells, "When Joanna Loved Me." (Joanna would become the name of one of Bennett's daughters, Antonia the other.)[39] Altschuler also produced "Georgia Rose," a recording that Columbia Records tried to shelve. Bennett thought at first that the NAACP had complained about its patronizing lyrics (e.g., "Don't be blue because you're black"), then later gathered that the label didn't want to alienate record buyers in the Deep South.[40] Bennett, who'd worked to promote civil rights throughout his career, could be accused of misjudgment but not of paternalism.

Even before Clive Davis had been named president in the afterburn of the Monterey Pop Festival in the summer of 1967, the label's priorities were changing, due to a large extent to Davis's influence and to that of Bill Gallagher, who didn't care for rock but was finding it much easier to market. The staff meetings that used to be about Mathis, Conniff, and Bennett were now about the Byrds and Paul Revere and the Raiders. Bennett felt neglected.

With Altschuler gone, Bennett was assigned to producer Howard Roberts. Their first record together, *Tony Makes It Happen*, displayed Bennett's uncanny ability to swing while remaining utterly sincere (e.g., "That Old Devil Moon").[41] In fact he was incapable of insincerity—an asset that in pop circles would come to be viewed as a liability. Bennett also had the knack of picking up strays and bringing them home, like Robert Farnon's gorgeous "The Country Girl." Job sheets on the next album produced by Roberts provide some evidence of the expenses that a 1968 Tony Bennett recording session entailed. The session, held at 30th Street on February 26, began at 8 P.M. (it was a Monday, when outside gigs wouldn't interfere) and ran to 11 P.M. Forty-five musicians were paid $65 each, with extra pay to the arranger and music copyist, plus rental, cartage and piano-tuning fees. The session cost $4,745—all for three hours' worth of recording.[42] With Clive Davis toting up numbers and openly favoring rock-oriented groups that didn't require forty-five musicians per session, it's no wonder such recordings would soon vanish—even at Columbia.

In 1971 Bennett was guaranteed $50,000 a year by the label. It wasn't perceived as a lot of money anymore, but it was still a risky chunk for a company with a direction that largely precluded jazz singers. Over the course of two decades Bennett had undeniably enriched the label—but he was at heart a jazz singer and sensed he was being increasingly marginalized. On July 8, 1971, Bennett appeared on *The Merv Griffin Show* along with Peggy Lee. While Columbia had promoted Bennett's recent album *Love Story*, with the movie title song its centerpiece, Peggy Lee had more comfortably handled Lieber & Stoller's "Is That All There Is?" and a cover of Bread's "Make It with You." "Capitol Records is going all out with promotion, advertising, etc., for Peggy and we should do likewise for Tony," Teo Macero implored his colleagues. "He is on the verge of leaving the label and I think our action regarding the above will help cement relations. After all, he is a great artist and should be treated as such."[43]

Irving Townsend and Duke Ellington. *Courtesy of Jeremy Townsend.*

Peter Munves in a gag photo to promote an Anna Russell album, 1955. *Photo by Fred Plaut. Courtesy of Fred Plaut Papers, Yale.*

Thelonious Monk. *Wood engraving by James Todd.*
Courtesy of James Todd.

The Dylan drawing was included inside the skinwrap in a testing pressing of
Highway 61 Revisited, September 1965. *Illustration by Lambert. Courtesy of the author.*

Listening to playback of *Harold Sings Arlen* (with Friend). Left to right: Tom Shepard, Harold Arlen, Barbra Streisand, Jonathan Schwartz, Edward Jablonski, and Peter Matz, November 1965. *Courtesy of Tom Shepard.*

Roy Halee and Laura Nyro, Studio B at 49 East 52nd Street, New York City, 1969.
Photo by Stephen Paley. Courtesy of Stephen Paley.

Producer Harold Prince and Elaine Stritch during recording of *Company*.
Courtesy of Tom Shepard.

Left to right: Irving Townsend, Esme Sarnoff Hammond, and John Hammond.
Courtesy of Jeremy Townsend.

Recording session of *The King and I*, 30th Street studio, 1964. Left to right: Fred Plaut, Tom Shepard, Lehman Engel, Barbara Cook, Philip Lang, Theodore Bikel. *Courtesy of Tom Shepard..*

Bob Dylan at Madison Square Garden, 1971. *Photo by Stephen Paley. Courtesy of Stephen Paley.*

At the Americana Hotel's Royal Box to hear Engelbert Humperdinck. Left to right: Stephen Paley, Dave Wynshaw, Clive Davis's cousin Jo, Janet Davis, and Clive Davis. *Courtesy of Stephen Paley.*

Clive Davis and Sly Stone, Beverly Hills, 1971. *Photo by Stephen Paley. Courtesy of Stephen Paley.*

Stephen Paley and Sly Stone, backstage at Sly's wedding, Madison Square Garden, 1974.
Courtesy of Stephen Paley.

Left to right: Joseph Dash, Dick Asher, Isaac Stern, and Tom Wyman.
Photo by Don Hunstein. Courtesy of Joseph Dash.

David Kapralik in Los Angeles, 2004. Photo by Stephen Paley. Courtesy of Stephen Paley.

Before Davis's six-year run as president was over, however, Bennett was out the door—first to MGM/Verve, then starting his own label, Improv. During this period the singer Annie Ross, herself a decade gone from Columbia, suggested to Bennett that he record with pianist Bill Evans. A superb Bennett-Evans album on Fantasy followed, supervised by Evans's longtime producer, Helen Keane, with enough material for at least one more album.[44] Evans tended to only imply notes that other pianists felt the need to state, and it gave Bennett space—enough so that you could hear what the critic Kirk Silsbee called the "slightly roughened veneer" the singer was acquiring.[45] After much personal turmoil, including tax problems and a divorce, Bennett would return to Columbia—but not until he'd been gone for 14 years.

18

Music from A to Z

Tony Bennett's halcyon days at Columbia began to darken in the period bracketing 1965–67. He was still making one remarkable album after another but, like a weathervane spun around by the wind, the label's energies were pointing in a new direction. In the fall of 1965, when Goddard Lieberson went to Los Angeles largely to see Stravinsky, Billy James acted as his guide along the Sunset Strip, where country-inflected rock music was blooming right out of the desert-hot sidewalk. Lieberson, who had put great faith in Mitch Miller's disdain of rock 'n' roll and had himself once declared it to be music about postadolescent problems for preadolescents, was apparently intrigued.[1] Columbia Records still hadn't embraced rock 'n' roll as ardently as other labels had. Before they'd been signed to Columbia, the British drama students Chad & Jeremy had had a hit with "Yesterday's Gone." This was a period when Andy Williams and Percy Faith were outselling just about everyone else on the label, and Chad & Jeremy seemed positively hard by comparison. Billy James had promoted the Byrds, which had its first Columbia hit in June 1965 with Dylan's "Mr. Tambourine Man." The label saw the Byrds as "out there," psychically as well as geographically. Paul Revere and the Raiders were also on the West Coast, having relocated from Portland, Oregon, to Los Angeles and, with and without singer-saxophonist Mark Lindsay, were gearing up for several hit singles. And then, practically around the block from Black Rock, Simon & Garfunkel were moving away from the folk tunes they'd first recorded and turning no less inventive or electric than Bob Dylan, who had ignited rock 'n' roll's insurrection in the first place (at least in America). By the beginning of 1966, with Lieberson having another year and a half to go in the president's office, the label was waving its arms out of the warm, easy-listening surf that had once been so inviting—Faith, Conniff, Weston, etc.—and had since turned to riptides. Apart from Faith's compositions, the guys who made this music were essentially trained as arrangers; they didn't write their own songs, weren't compelled to say much about politics or society, and, most condemning of all, kids didn't want to dance to their records. Most of them were now in their fifties and, to the ears of the largest record-buying demographic, sounded out of touch.

The label flailed for a while. Many of their A&R men could appreciate rhythm and blues and rock 'n' roll, but there was still nobody on the East Coast charged expressly with finding new rock acts.

Teo Macero became enchanted with a quartet of comely young women who called themselves the What Four. They were led by China Girard, their statuesque rhythm guitarist, but they got press because their bassist, Diane Hartford, was married to the A&P heir Huntington Hartford. To provide them with better material, Macero connected them with the songwriter Rick Shorter. He even arranged for Girard to sublet the Greenwich Village apartment of his friend Anna Sokolow, the choreographer for whom Macero had composed dance music. Out of Columbia's support of the group came the single "Baby, I Dig Love." But the What Four proved to be more about mod clothes than about rock 'n' roll.

Macero also handled Ed Sullivan, a Columbia-Harmony "artist" throughout the sixties, a man who was known for neither musicianship nor charm but could sell records because he remained television's premiere impresario. (Elvis *and* the Beatles? No other TV host had come close to that.) So Columbia, determined to merchandise Sullivan to the hilt, arranged for him to put out Irish folk song compilations, Jewish folk song compilations, and Broadway score compilations, often with the services of a cobbled-together chorus called the Ed Sullivan Singers and sometimes with Macero adding music himself. For a little licensing income, Columbia had a dance created called the Sully Gully, an imitation of Sullivan in nine steps:

1) Pull shoulders up

2) Insert tongue under lip

3) Shake head from side to side

4) Fold arms

5) Hold chin with one hand

6) Hold tie knot

7) Place hands on small of back

8) Clasp hands together and point fingers

9) Clap hands three times, then, by waving arms above head, beckon audience to applaud

Considering that Macero put himself out for stylish girl groups, handled the Ed Sullivan line of products, and continued to produce Brubeck, Miles Davis, and Thelonious Monk, as well as less illustrious but admired jazz artists like guitarist Charlie Byrd, it's a wonder he had time to eat and sleep, let alone compose his own music. In fact Macero had an even bigger responsibility at the time—producing the recordings of Andre Kostelanetz. Against the odds Kostelanetz, then in his midsixties, was still trying to stay current—and, for a while, succeeding.

•   •   •

In December 1979, CBS Records attorney Walter Dean wrote to Kostelanetz, at his home at 10 Gracie Square in Manhattan, overlooking the East River. The parties were going to have to renegotiate the terms of the maestro's new contract because, Dean wrote, "the last two albums sold less than 15,000 units through normal retail channels in the United States and resulted in an out-of-pocket loss to us."[2] Kostelanetz had been with the label for forty years, since shortly after it was bought by CBS. Goddard Lieberson, his longtime protector and, briefly, neighbor at Gracie Square, had died two and half years earlier. For Columbia, Kostelanetz had made well over a hundred albums, ranging from opera to light classics to transcriptions of nursery rhymes to what he called melodeclamation (music with the spoken word). His name had become

synonymous with a certain type of recorded music. He had first made
that name on radio at a time when radio concerts reached millions of
listeners each week. Now CBS, as was its right, wanted to pay him a
much lower rate than he was used to commanding. The renegotiations
that Walter Dean had proposed were not yet completed when Kostelanetz died one month later, in Port-au-Prince.

That final stay at Port-au-Prince was the fade of a career-long pattern
of completing an album, then jetting off with his wife at the time—first
the soprano Lily Pons, later Sara Gene—to a place of sun and pampered
living. Kostelanetz had just turned 79 and worked like a demon right up
to the end. If anyone had earned a bit of fun now and then, it was the
conductor affectionately called Kosty by his musicians and recording
colleagues.

No other Columbia artist was as crucial to the label for recording, and
consistently selling, music of so many styles. It may also be argued that
no other single musician, American or otherwise, did as much to open
up the idea of conducting an orchestra in the confines of a studio.

Kostelanetz was a toddler in Russia when John Philip Sousa's marches
were recorded acoustically, with a crude horn capturing and funneling
the sound, by the U.S. Marine Band. As a teenager Kostelanetz studied at
the St. Petersburg Academy of Music and served as assistant conductor
for a year at the Petrograd Grand Opera. He had been playing piano
since early childhood and, by the time he came to the United States, in
1922, he was intrigued by the complexities of orchestration. He loved
the Russians, particularly Tchaikovsky, but was in thrall to Debussy and
Ravel and their swirling, pastel colors. Joining much of his family in
New York, Kostelanetz went to work as a pianist and arranger. Arthur
Judson, who founded Columbia Artists Management and had been a
driving force in CBS's forerunner United Independent Broadcasters,
encouraged the diminutive Russian to go into radio. Kostelanetz apprenticed with Howard Barlow, the workhorse musical director of the CBS
Network in general and of March of Time (1931) in particular. As a peripatetic radio conductor in New York, Kostelanetz began a series of studio
experiments, to quote Dick O'Connor, "to determine how the physical

placement of instruments, the arrangement of microphones, the control of acoustical reverberation, and the manipulation of sound technology might be employed to enhance the performance of orchestral music. In 1933 he devised the format and planned the style that would make his name a household word. Despite the many triumphs and honors of later years his success rests squarely on his 1934 to 1944 radio achievements."[3]

Kostelanetz quickly embraced American music—that is, the show music and songs that were to become part of the standard repertoire. These were suited to radio broadcast because they were done in a song form—two to four minutes, tops—and were usually made with lyrics whose meaning Kostelanetz would take care to bring out, even when there was no singer. By the time he'd been speaking English for a dozen years, he was as attuned to the lyrics of Larry Hart, Oscar Hammerstein II, Ira Gershwin, Cole Porter, Irving Berlin, and the young Johnny Mercer as he was to any melody in the classical repertoire.

In 1934 Kostelanetz signed to make records with RCA Victor. Victor's president at the time, Ted Wallerstein, had already supervised some serious experiments involving the long-playing record. Although those possibilities wouldn't be fully realized for another 13 years, Wallerstein never wavered in his support of Kosty. But the conductor was then recording, while giving so many hours to radio, at a much slower pace than he would later. The 1936 Victor catalog lists only three Kostelanetz sides; in years to come, Kosty would knock off three sides in a few hours at Columbia's 30th Street studio.[4]

Kostelanetz broadcast his Coca-Cola-sponsored radio program from 1938 to 1943, from Liederkranz Hall, on East 58th Street. Liederkranz, which had been used for years as headquarters for the German Singing Society because of its pleasing acoustics, served Kosty's purposes well. It was mostly at Liederkranz that he taught himself how the orchestra sounded on the air. "I realized," he wrote, "that equally important with the seating of the musicians and with carefully marking scores for bowings and other subtleties of interpretations was the placement of the microphone. Some instruments were virtually lost; others came through several sizes too big, so to speak. One of the first corrections was to hang the mike above the whole group of musicians, not favoring any section."[5]

The Chesterfield Hour was a CBS tentpole that combined music, talk, and, in summer, baseball scores. Broadcast three times a week on CBS radio, the show gobbled up as much music as Kostelanetz and his arrangers could prepare, all of it played by fifty-five men—half CBS staff musicians, half freelancers. One of the show's themes was "A Cigarette, Sweet Music and You." Kosty was only one of several conductors, but perhaps the most dependable because he was the most demanding. (He and Eugene Ormandy each liked to practice conducting in front of a mirror. Conducting is, after all, a facet of show business.) An early radio variety show, *Chesterfield* needed new guests each week. One of those guests was the soprano Lily Pons. She would become the first Mrs. Andre Kostelanetz.

*   *   *

Pons, born in Cannes in 1904 (some sources say as early as 1898), was a piano student before she began to seriously study opera, relatively late, in 1923. She made her Met debut on January 3, 1931, in Donizetti's *Lucia di Lammermoor*. In the midthirties she appeared in several movies, notably RKO's *That Girl from Paris* (1936), and was in demand almost as much for her looks as for the voice. So popular was Pons that Lilypons, Maryland, is named after her. The story goes that the previously unnamed town's chief industry was the culture of lilies. The managers applied to the post office to be listed as Lily Ponds, Maryland. Learning there was already an incorporated Lily Ponds, Maryland, some wag suggested the town name itself after the opera singer. Well, why not? The eponymous movie-opera star was flattered, while RKO was grateful for the extra publicity.[6]

After her 1937 appearance on *The Chesterfield Hour*, Pons and Kostelanetz fell in love. They married the following year. For the next two decades, theirs was among the most admired musical-conjugal partnerships, recording and traveling together throughout the world.

Meanwhile Kostelanetz, with Pons clutching his hand, had followed Ted Wallerstein to Columbia Records. Under Wallerstein's aegis Kostelanetz picked up his pace of recording, turning out many sides on 78s each year. The radio work enhanced Kosty's stature as a recording artist, and vice versa. He treated his musicians with respect, addressing them in a slightly fractured English that had its own unassailable logic. Mitch Miller, who played oboe for him for years, once heard him say, "In this passage I want the penultimate of schmaltz."[7] The music was fine, the recordings—even those made at Liederkranz Hall—not always so fine. Convinced that Wallerstein was officially with the OSS, Kostelanetz believed him when he told him that Kosty's disks of "Clair de Lune" had been used "to send messages to American prisoners of war. The device was simple and played on the fact that the quality of recordings in those days was not all it should have been: a Morse code message would be scratched onto a disk, which would then be sent to a Red Cross station, where it was played on the air. The prisoners would know that it contained a coded message and listen for it, but to anyone else it seemed like just another record with bad surface noise."[8]

Rewarding Kostelanetz for his productivity in those days, Columbia didn't stint on promotion. July 1946 was proclaimed "Kostelanetz Month" in record stores. The following month the label sponsored a Lily Pons Window Display Contest.[9] It was a crude but ultimately effective bit of marketing—having record buyers compete to arrange Pons photographs—and no less clever than Tom Sawyer getting his friends to paint a fence for him.

For his Columbia popular recordings, Kostelanetz depended on some of the most interesting arrangers in New York. A classical piece usually came fully orchestrated, with every part noted, but a pop song was usually notated as just a piano lead sheet and an appropriate arrangement had to be made. Carroll Huxley arranged most of the semiclassical fare. Nathan Van Cleave handled a lot of the pop stuff, along with George Bassman, who'd been a staff writer for Irving Mills. Bassman, according to Kostelanetz, had "little knowledge of harmony but great imagination and fresh ideas."[10] At John Hammond's East 91st Street house one night in 1934 or '35, Bassman worked out a melody for hours, a repeated figure that made Hammond cringe; by morning, though, he'd completed what would bloom, after Ned Washington had added lyrics, into "I'm Getting Sentimental over You." Although it became Tommy Dorsey's theme song, Bassman wouldn't receive royalties on it for another twenty-eight years because Mills took ownership of anything Bassman wrote at the time.[11] Bassman would do some work for Benny Goodman before heading west to score motion pictures. Van Cleave also went west, orchestrating Copland's Academy Award–winning score for *The Heiress* (1949). Another Kostelanetz pianist, Walter Gross, wrote the lovely standard "Tenderly." Claude Thornhill was on call in the 1930s, and then, into the 1950s and '60s, came Hugo Montenegro, who had served as Columbia's music director for a while, plus Eddie Sauter, Johnny Richards, Luther Henderson, the saxophonist and occasional *Tonight Show* bandleader Tommy Newsom, Al Capps, Torrie Zito, and even Macero, who handled every imaginable musical chore for the maestro.

• • •

For many years Kostelanetz was produced by Howard Scott, who was there at the birth of the LP. In fact the LP provided Kostelanetz with a wider spectrum of color because the pieces he tackled could be longer and more complex than ever. The LP also gave him more cover text to work with. In his *La Bohème for Orchestra*, made for Columbia around 1955, Kosty had Fannie Hurst, queen of warm-blooded, often musically informed American melodramas (*Humoresque, Back Street*, and *Imitation of Life*), write the synopsis of each of *La Bohème*'s four acts. Fourteen years later, when Kosty recorded *La Bohème* in stereo, he insisted on retaining Hurst's liner notes for the resulting album.[12]

Like Mitch Miller, Kostelanetz was highly educated and astute without disdaining what was popular. On one hand he could turn out perfectly crystallized renditions of large classical works; on the other he could rip off ("embellish" was the official word) Tchaikovsky to offer the popular songs "Moon Love" (from the Fifth Symphony) and "On the Isle of May" (from the String Quartet). Kostelanetz's appeal was said to be middlebrow; but if the highbrow, as Russell Lynes pointed out in his famous 1949 essay "Highbrow, Lowbrow, Middlebrow," "is often more interested in where the arts have been, and where they are going, than in the objects themselves," the erudite, hyper-aware Kosty qualified as highbrow as well.[13] There were other excellent conductors in the field who crossed fluidly between light classical and pop: Mantovani, of course; Morton Gould; Camerata; and, later, Percy Faith. But Kostelanetz was the most consistently rigorous among them, and his interpretation of a given piece often became the standard. His 1958 recording of Harold Arlen's *Blues Opera* was orchestrated by Carroll Huxley, produced by Howard Scott, and executed to perfection; although it sold poorly, it has never been surpassed.[14]

*   *   *

By the late forties, Kostelanetz records were everywhere. They were teaching the swelling American postwar middle class about classical music. People who owned a phonograph but not all that many records usually had at least *one* Kostelanetz record, though sometimes they owned everything listed in the catalog under Kosty's name. Inevitably, the music we own tells a lot about us. In *Kafka Was the Rage*, his memoir of Greenwich Village after the Second World War, Anatole Broyard describes meeting "the best female dancer" at the Park Plaza, a Cuban named Carmen. Broyard believes that Carmen has (in the phrase of his friend Dwight Macdonald) "drums in her belly, that her life was a strong rhythm" and that she could "direct her sexuality wherever she pleased." When Carmen goes home with him, however, she confesses to hating Afro-Cuban music. What kind of music do you like? he asks. "Andre Kostelanetz, Morton Gould," she tells him.[15]

In Philip Roth's *Goodbye, Columbus*, narrator Neil Klugman spends time in the home of new girlfriend Brenda, whose brother Ron boasts, "I got all the Andre Kostelanetz records ever made." If the story had been set only four or five years later, Ron is of the age and temperament where he'd be listening mostly to rock 'n' roll. But Kostelanetz was then still the main current of American music, at the front of the "popular" record bin, and in Ron's mind he runs neck and neck with Mantovani for best record-making honors. When Ron retreats to his bedroom, Neil observes, "From across the hall I heard Andre Kostelanetz let several thousand singing violins loose on 'Night and Day.'"[16]

By the end of the 1950s Kostelanetz commanded a sterling annual income from Columbia—a guarantee of $100,000, a veritable fortune by the standards of the day. The label's executives, in and out of Master-works, argued the finer points over whether the maestro, who had been advertised on his album covers as "Music's Leading Man," was worth it. "Mr Kostelanetz has been using his own contractor," complained Columbia's lead attorney Harvey Schein to Messrs. Chapin, McClure, Scott, and Townsend, on October 29, 1959, "and has agreed to pay bonuses to some of the musicians on his sessions held under his new contract with us, thus running up the costs we have to pay." Kosty had his favorites, of course, and preferred to have, say, harpist Myor Rosen available to him at all times. "I might point out," Schein continued in that same memo, "that when we were negotiating the new contract with Kostelanetz, we had inserted a provision which would have required him to pay the costs of each album in excess of a certain amount. The provision was removed when Kostelanetz promised that he would not run up the costs of his albums."[17]

In fact the costs of Kostelanetz albums, despite the large number of musicians routinely employed, were relatively low. This was due in part to the watchful eyes and ears of producers Scott and Macero.

●　　●　　●

Kostelanetz had his favorite contemporary composers. He loved Aaron Copland, whose 13-minute *A Lincoln Portrait* he commissioned, with narration by Carl Sandburg. The commission was one of three—Jerome Kern and Virgil Thomson were the other two composers—made by Kostelanetz "to represent a musical portrait gallery of three great

Americans. . . ." Kostelanetz premiered *A Lincoln Portrait* with the Cincinnati Symphony Orchestra on May 14, 1942.[18] Lieberson, still second in command at Masterworks, got in two Columbia artist plugs at once when he reviewed the premiere for the New York *Herald Tribune* the next day: "Mr Kostelanetz was able to get from the composers what he wanted, music for large masses of people. And, in the vernacular, he hit the jackpot. . . ." At 41 Kostelanetz, through his radio conducting and his increasingly prolific Columbia output, had acquired enough influence to commission such works. He recorded Kern's musical portrait, *Mark Twain*, for Columbia in mid-June 1942 (though the album wasn't released until 1946). Kostelanetz was fond, too, of the work of Paul Creston, premiering *Frontiers* with the Toronto Symphony Orchestra on October 14, 1943.[19]

Perhaps no contemporary's music was closer to his heart, though, than that of Alan Hovhaness. With bass-baritone Simon Estes, Kosty recorded Hovhaness's beautiful *The Floating World* in 1965. (The piece is dedicated to Kostelanetz.) Hovhaness was one of three composers, along with Henry Cowell and Paul Creston, to contribute music to the curious Eastern Airlines promotional record *Images in Flight*. The project was representative of the marriage of industry and popular music, an attempt to promote a product (in this case an airline) through high culture. The *Images in Flight* idea appears to have been cooked up by someone close to Eastern's president, Floyd Hall, and Eastern's ad agency, Young & Rubicam.[20] At Columbia the imaginative special projects man Al Shulman coordinated the label's part of the marketing, which pretty much meant advertising Kostelanetz. Each composer had no more than six weeks to complete his piece. Kosty wanted them arranged for recording by the reliable Hugo Montenegro; but Montenegro was delayed because he had a more lucrative deadline scoring an episode of the Shirley Booth TV series *Hazel* on the West Coast. Conducting members of the New York Philharmonic, Kostelanetz recorded the three pieces in March 1965.

Three years later Kostelanetz wanted to record a Hovhaness piece for his one hundredth Columbia album, igniting a spirited exchange between the protective Macero and Masterworks director John McClure. Concerned about what seemed to him a musical collocation, McClure wrote to Macero, "You are mad to couple Rachmaninoff and Hovhaness! Please convince AK to couple Rachmaninoff & Rimsky & Moussorgsky/Tchaik [sic], Kabalevsky and Hovhaness for a new coupling." Macero replied, "You are right—we are mad. This is the reason we are doing so well for the [Record] Club, especially for the Masterworks division. We are not changing our position regarding the coupling of [Rachmaninoff's] *Aleko* and Hovhaness. I don't have time for nonsense." The album featured a Golden Edge static preventative, one of the newer vinyl "improvements" Kosty was only too happy to play guinea pig for. But he wasn't happy about Columbia's marketing plans for the album, whose selections continued to puzzle most of the executives. Writing to Bill Farr, head of Creative Services, Macero conveyed the maestro's dismay that the label had no plans to advertise the album. "To celebrate a 100th recording and not advertise it anywhere," Macero wrote with characteristic bristle, "is redundant and ridiculous."[21]

One particularly lovely Kostelanetz-Hovhaness collaboration was the 1972 album *And God Created Whales*, recorded two years earlier, which included the composer's eleven-and-a-half-minute title track. Kostelanetz had become intrigued by the work of Dr. Roger Payne, a young research scientist from Rockefeller University, who studied the sounds that whales make. For the album the Lamont-Daugherty Labs supplied the taped sounds.[22] (The singer Judy Collins had heard some of the same whale "melodies" recorded by Dr. Payne and made her own album using them.)

•   •   •

While Kostelanetz was alive, New York was brimming with musicians educated before the rock era. "There was a pool of several hundred people in New York who did almost all the pop recording," Dick Hyman said. "We did what could be called 'the music in between,' with big orchestras like Kostelanetz and Percy Faith."[23] For most of these recording sessions, Kosty depended on orchestra contractor Morris Stronzek, a cellist who seemed to be connected to just about every musician in town. In preparation for each new album, Kostelanetz would hold a meeting at 10 Gracie Square to discuss the finer points of the music. Teo Macero was invariably there. So was Frank Laico, Kosty's preferred engineer. If the album's arrangers were in town (Montenegro was usually in Los Angeles), they too were expected for the meeting. If you couldn't make it, you were expected to phone—BUtterfield 8-9552—and explain why. (Forty-four years after he stopped producing Kostelanetz for Columbia, Howard Scott barked out the number as though he'd dialed it that morning.)

A surprisingly high number of the projects discussed at 10 Gracie Square were melodeclamation recordings, in which Kosty and his orchestra backed narration by various personalities. In 1961 Kosty recorded Grofe's *Grand Canyon Suite*, which was paired with Johnny Cash narrating "A Day in the Grand Canyon" in front of Kostelanetz's orchestra. (Kostelanetz and Cash would have made one of the great mismatched pairs of the notorious Braniff Airlines ads, conceived in the late sixties by the art director George Lois.) The *Grand Canyon* album wasn't released until a decade later. Much the same happened with another 1961 recording, *The Nutcracker Suite*, with Peter Ustinov reading a narration written by the poet Ogden Nash. Over the years the Ustinov piece was dropped from the Columbia catalog. Meanwhile Nash had become a favorite collaborator of Kosty's, if not a close friend.

Ten years after the *Nutcracker* recording, Nash wrote—and narrated—something called *Carnival of Marriage*. The idea was to release a Kostelanetz album pairing *Carnival* with a new synthesizer piece by Dick Hyman. As was already the case, everybody had youth on the brain. Masterworks director Tom Frost suggested ditching Nash as narrator because "he holds absolutely no appeal for the young people who might be buying this piece"—meaning the Hyman composition.[24]

In the meantime the 30th Street studio underwent two months of renovation as 16-track recording machines were installed. Unlike conductors who'd emerged from an older classical tradition, Kosty embraced each new technology. His postrecording notes to Macero, who was usually in Manhattan editing closely, were models of precision, all rendered in flowing hand. For his much earlier album *Stereo Wonderland of Sound—Broadway's Greatest Hits*, Kosty listened to the acetate tapes that Macero had sent him, made his notes, and wrote back, "II. RAIN IN SPAIN—BASS CLARINET B—3–4 TOO SOFT! AFTER LAST CHORD— ECHO PECULIAR—BUILD UP LAST BAR. . . ."[25] These critiques—most of them were about engineering, but many were about deficiencies in his musicians' performances and in his own—were often composed and mailed from far corners of the world. Whether he was in Antigua or Tel Aviv, Kosty would listen and respond. "'Lady Madonna,'" he wrote to Macero about one of his pop compilations: "In the Db-major section in the middle of the record, trombones have the melody. Should be brought up. Ending is very abrupt. Was there more to the ending? If not I suggest a CRESC. in the last 4–6 bars."

As for the *Carnival of Marriage* album, Nash never made it to the renovated 30th Street to record. In March, warned that Nash would soon have to go into the hospital, Macero and engineer Buddy Graham went to Baltimore to record Nash's narration. Nash died May 19, 1971, at 68, following abdominal surgery. The great light versifier was gone, but Macero and Kostelanetz made an album out of his last poems.

After Nash died, Kostelanetz's favorite narrator was probably Douglas Fairbanks Jr. Like David Niven and Goddard Lieberson, Fairbanks owned a magnificent speaking voice that came through on records. On several of these, Kostelanetz used the singer Linda November to give the recordings, whether of Cole Porter or Alan Hovhaness, some vocal heft.

The 1972 Cole Porter album, *Andre Kostelanetz Plays Cole Porter*, was rife with problems. It was a two-disk set and, for the first time in 14 years, Columbia had to pay overtime for a Kosty session. Upon hearing the edited recording that Macero sent him, Kostelanetz fired a letter back to New York to say it all sounded "bad, really bad," and he wanted its release held up until it was reedited.[26] The album was all too typical of the problems he was having with the direction of his career—or, more bluntly, the label's problems. Clive Davis wanted to respect

Kostelanetz's eminent position at Columbia Records, but he'd been finding it increasingly difficult to approve Kostelanetz's penchant for movie scores.

As a younger Columbia artist had predicted a few years back, the times they were a-changin'. In an undated (probably 1968) memo to Macero, Clive Davis wrote, "Because Kosty has been around so long, I really question the wisdom of his recording old standards. It either dates the album or looks like a repackaging job. In other words, I think the album would have been much stronger with contemporary standards along the lines you went with in 'Scarborough Fair' and 'Love Is Blue.' The quality of the album is excellent and you should be proud. The above comments are just 'sales' considerations." Davis was referring to the album *Andre Kostelanetz Plays Scarborough Fair (and Other Great Movie Hits)*, though of course "Scarborough Fair" was only exploited by *The Graduate*, not written for it.[27]

But Kostelanetz knew what he wanted to do, however much it went against the new Columbia grain. "After this memo," Clive Davis wrote, "I learned of the *Funny Girl*—*Star*—and *Finian's Rainbow* project which couldn't be stopped. I questioned that strongly but time prevented a cancellation. Now, as though nothing previous had been discussed, comes this, his umpteenth movie album."[28]

Kostelanetz had a tough time obeying these new edicts. His longtime champion Lieberson had been moved upstairs, removed from day-to-day operations of the label. It was Clive's label now. Couldn't Kosty record music composed by Columbia Records artists? Kostelanetz did have a sincere admiration for Paul Simon. But he couldn't find a way to pay homage that seemed less than laughable. On his 1973 album *Andre Kostelanetz Plays the World's Greatest Love Songs*, he included Simon's "Sounds of Silence." (It's a compelling song—but a *love* song?) There was also an autumn 1971 tribute to the music of the Columbia group Chicago, with Kosty and orchestra covering "Color My World," "Make Me Smile," "Beginnings," and "Does Anybody Really Know What Time It Is?" These smoothed-out instrumental versions of pop hits would become standard Muzak fare, piped through supermarkets and elevators.

• • •

Ever since the Johnny Mathis test, every major recording artist has had to have a Greatest Hits album eventually. Kosty, who was used to making such compilations of other people's music, prepared one for his own recordings in late 1968, when he was 67. Macero's assistant Corinne Chertok sent Kosty the proposed cover. Early the next morning Kosty telephoned Chertok in a rage, complaining that he had already rejected that particular cover, which prominently showed the bald or balding heads of his musicians and his own hands looking strange. "He insists that this picture be destroyed," Chertok wrote to art director John Berg in a January 14, 1969, memo, "because he never wants it used for anything, never, never. Lots of luck!!!"

That same month Kostelanetz attended the Super Bowl between the New York Jets and the Baltimore Colts. Prior to the game, Joe Namath had guaranteed a Jets victory over the heavily favored Colts—a gesture of bravado that recalled Babe Ruth at the plate pointing over the right field wall. The maestro, whose knowledge of football was cursory at best, was no less enthusiastic about Namath's quarterbacking the Jets to victory than any other New York fan—except that he had the means to sponsor a musical response. With Columbia's backing, Kosty commissioned Dick Hyman to write music celebrating Namath's life (Namath was then all of 26), with sportswriter Dick Schaap drafting a narration. As it evolved, the idea was for Namath himself to narrate, in effect creating a musical autobiography, with musicians from the New York Philharmonic participating. Namath subsequently dropped out of the project—football players aren't known for their musical commitments any more than world-class conductors are for their enthusiasm for football—and the completed Hyman-Schaap musical work celebrated instead a National Hockey League player in Winnipeg, where Kostelanetz conducted the work's only performance.[29]

Through the 1970s Kostelanetz pushed for recording projects he wanted, notably with his friends Hovhaness and Fairbanks. But the times and the label had less use for him. In the early seventies A&R head Don

Ellis tried to quietly release Kostelanetz from his contract, sending him out to graze in the pastures of Carl Schurz Park and the Upper East Side; but when Lieberson got wind of it, he sent down word that Kostelanetz was "unfirable."[30] What would Columbia Records have been without him? As Oscar Levant said of Kostelanetz, "Here's one conductor who knows his music from A to Z." It's a great pun, but it would have been true even if the maestro's name had ended in B.[31]

19

Spinning Wheels

Kostelanetz's 1966 album *I Wish You Love* sold a sorry 4,000 albums through the Columbia Record Club. Those 4,000 were all in monaural, however. The club sold another 142,000 copies of the album in stereo—a confident sign that mono could soon be phased out without losing too many customers, and that the Record Club, after a decade in business, was doing its job.

In the mail-order field the Record Club had become only more dominant. It had inspired something similar with the RCA Music Service, but Columbia still ruled the market, particularly after it renamed itself Columbia House. Its first president, Norman Adler, had left to devote his energies to Columbia Records—alumni of the label at the time said Adler had more authority than anyone there except Lieberson—and turned the reins over to the Harvard-trained attorney Neal Keating. Bill Bell, who had worked at Columbia under Doug Duer in the 1950s, was the club's A&R director. Right under Bell was Ralph Colin Jr., son of the CBS lawyer and Paley confidante. After college and three years as an air force pilot, Colin had gone to work on Wall Street. Weary of investment banking after a few years, Colin wanted to work in the music business but didn't want to use his father's influence to do so. He did, however, talk with CBS's Dick Salant, who had been at his father's firm, and out of that came an interview with Lieberson, who said he'd try to find a place for him. When Colin was assigned to a training program for the Columbia Record Club, his initial reaction was to feel shuffled off, far from the action. As it turned out, he would work at the Record Club for 31 years, 15 of them running its A&R.[1]

After a year at Black Rock, Goddard Lieberson was only 55, but a change was in the air and he would soon make way for it. To do so, the most musically savvy of all record label chiefs was going with the lawyers. "I have a penchant for lawyers," he told the writer Joan Simpson Burns, "because they think logically and clearly, most of them, and I think the training they've had gives them some cultural background, in addition to a very clear way of thinking that's not—oh—not too frequently messed up with emotionalism or other things."[2] The law firm of Rosenman Colin had served as a kind of Columbia Records University, turning over its graduates—Norman Adler, Harvey Schein, Clive Davis, and Walter Yetnikoff—to become powerhouses at the label, there to advise Lieberson and handle the complex international business as well. According to Yetnikoff, Davis had shed his Brooklyn accent at Harvard but retained a New Yorker's street sense. "He was a go-getter who burned with ambition," Yetnikoff wrote. "I saw him as someone I could learn from."[3] A couple of years after Yetnikoff arrived at the label, following Davis almost step for step, he observed that Lieberson was usually out of the office by five, while Davis was still in the office past eight. "Goddard had arrived. Clive was trying to get there. Goddard was riding the crest of a glorious past. Clive was looking for the wave of the future."[4]

In the year or so before Clive Davis was named president, a more corporate tone, exemplified by the move to the monolithic Black Rock skyscraper, was hard to miss. Nonclassical artists who didn't sell records were quietly let go. The freelance jazz producer Frank Driggs had been trying, with John Hammond's encouragement, to record older musicians who'd released records decades earlier on Vocalion and Okeh. Driggs's artist Henry "Red" Allen, the great New Orleans trumpeter, was dropped after only one new record, and Driggs was livid.[5] "What the [jazz] reissue program really needs," John Hammond wrote to the jazz critic Ralph Gleason, "is sound merchandising and I am trying to borrow Peter Munves from Masterworks who has done a magnificent repackaging job on Beethoven and Brahms symphonies, etc., etc. to revitalize what was dead merchandising."[6] Outside of Masterworks, though, it was frustrating to try to sign an artist past a certain age. It was a far cry from the days when Ted Wallerstein had given George Avakian carte blanche to go into the vault and see what he could find. And then that artist usually had no more than one or two albums to prove he or she could sell.

The Columbia Record Club couldn't get interested in a new recording made by Ella Fitzgerald and Duke Ellington. The club's jazz membership had shrunk, according to A&R head Bill Bell, and Bill Gallagher felt that there was just too much Ella and Duke product on the market to warrant another release. That smart, inventive keyboard player Clare Fischer, who had been briefly musical director of the Hi-Lo's, put out the Columbia album *Songs for a Rainy Day* to ecstatic reviews and atrocious sales. In the jazz community Fischer was highly valued for his lovely, often exotic-sounding compositions ("Pensativa"), but he wasn't a star and the label couldn't justify putting much sales muscle behind him. Apart from a smattering of big-city commercial stations and a few dozen smaller university stations sprinkled throughout the country, jazz wasn't played much on the radio anymore.

Hammond's latest discovery, George Benson, arrived at the label too late—or perhaps too soon. Around the New Year 1966, Hammond had taken his wife, Esme, to Harlem to hear Bo Diddley, Muddy Waters, and T-Bone Walker at the Apollo. Walking to the theatre, Hammond saw a sign at the Palm Cafe advertising the George Benson Quartet. Later that night Hammond and Esme stopped in to listen, expecting to stay only a few minutes. Hammond said that he and Esme and were "absolutely flabbergasted" by what they'd heard. Hammond soon had Benson signed to Columbia. But when Benson wanted to borrow a few thousand dollars from the label, he was turned down because his sales for the previous six months had amounted to only $600. (The megahits "On Broadway" and "Masquerade" were several years into Benson's future—and at another label.) Six months later, in a maneuver all too familiar to Hammond, Benson was taken away from him and reassigned to Howard Roberts, who was now handling Tony Bennett, too. [7]

As a producer and talent scout, though, nobody had Hammond's track record. In the months before the 1967 Monterey Pop Festival and Davis's ascension to the presidency, Hammond's most recent discovery was probably the Canadian poet-songwriter Leonard Cohen. The previous year Hammond had seen a documentary film, *Ladies and Gentlemen ... Mr. Leonard Cohen* and, impressed, asked him to come to New York and play for him. Cohen recorded his first Columbia album, which included "Suzanne," on May 19, 1967, at the 30th Street studio, with Eric Weissberg on guitar and Felix Pappalardi on Fender bass. There was a tremendous push by the legal department to have Cohen sign with its publishing unit April-Blackwood because, of course, the songs would be more expensive if the album became a hit. With memos from Dick Asher and Walter Dean flying back and forth, Cohen and his producer Hammond felt the pressure. Fortunately, Cohen responded positively to incoming publishing chief Neil Anderson, and the deal was made. Cohen's career was an illustration of the move away from Tin Pan Alley, in which songwriters sold their wares to publishing companies, who connected the songs to singers, or "artists." At Columbia, Cohen wasn't the first songwriter to record his own music the way he wanted to. Oscar Brown Jr. was probably the progenitor of the practice, Bob Dylan the prime mover, and Paul Simon no less an original than Dylan. Cohen's style, however, was unique—his druggy, susurrant *parlando* backed by guitar and voices—and appealed to record buyers who surrounded themselves with books of poetry, incense, and macramé. In Dylan and Simon, as with so many novelists, their content was said to be their style; in Cohen, his style was the content. This was true even after Hammond, extending the old pattern, was pulled away from producing Cohen—apparently at Cohen's request—and young Columbia producer John Simon brought in to provide a more elaborate, cathedral-like sound.[8]

Cohen fit snugly into the roster of artists after Clive Davis became president. Davis's promotion was said to have been in the works for a time, but there's little doubt that Davis covered the grounds of the Monterey Pop Festival as if by divining rod. The festival was organized primarily by Lou Adler and John Phillips of the Mamas and the Papas and held on June 16–18, 1967, and seemed to be a revelation even for the younger listeners familiar with the acts who appeared. Simon & Garfunkel and the Byrds were representing Columbia Records, but what proved to be the more important act for the label was Big Brother & the Holding Company, whose lead singer, Janis Joplin, possessed such a wrenching blues style that even the most blasé listener couldn't fail to respond. The connection between Joplin and Davis was quickly fused, its fusion insinuating that everyone else at the label had been sleeping on the job. It's as though Davis were saying, *This is how you do it now.* Before summer's end, Davis was president of Columbia Records and Lieberson president of the CBS-Columbia Group, making Lieberson nominally still Davis's boss but no longer officially involved in the day-to-day operations of Columbia Records and its subsidiaries.

For all the credit Davis received for turning the label toward rock music in the wake of Monterey, it's not quite accurate to say that Lieberson was uninterested in rock. Bruce Lundvall recalled a July 1966 convention, a year before Monterey, at the Diplomat in Miami. To promote its few rock acts, Columbia held a battle of the bands in a high school gymnasium near the hotel. The kids who attended, Lundvall said, went nuts. And across the floor everyone could see Lieberson, snug in his safari jacket, moving to the music.[9]

But that wasn't what was publicized. Even Davis's detractors admitted that he had fantastic ears, particularly attuned to sixties pop, and he continued to negotiate with an aggressiveness tempered by lawyerly caution. "After I became head of Columbia Records," Davis said years later, "I watched and waited for about a year or a year and a half and then realized that tremendous changes were coming about in music. No longer were Broadway shows or classical music or middle-of-the-road predominating. I realized that since these were the foundations upon which Columbia Records had been built for so many years that I would have to not look within the company because its people had all grown up in music which was quite alien to what was going on in the rock world."[10]

• • •

During the next year, Davis may have watched and waited, but he was hardly slow to exploit the so-called Youth Movement, with its daring, colorful fashions and its more personalized songs. Advertising a new Columbia album with the badly punning title *The Medium Is the Massage*, by the sociologist Marshall McLuhan, who was then at the peak of his influence, Davis approved its marketing, which entailed miniskirted young women parading placards up and down the block. Though based in New York, Davis knew the new sounds were coming mostly from the West Coast—"the Coast," in sixties terminology. Irv Townsend was still the head music man in Los Angeles, but Davis appeared to pay little heed to his judgment. A year earlier, Billy James had bolted for Elektra and a Los Angeles band called the Doors. But Dave Rubinson, who had produced the San Francisco–based rock group Moby Grape when he was still a teenager, was now 24 and considered by Davis to be in touch with the street. Davis, who had watched Dave Kapralik reach outside the label for new material earlier in the decade, also relied on independent producers who watched over stables of songwriters. Charles Koppleman, of the New York team Koppelman & Rubin, was called on to provide material long before he too joined the Columbia staff.[11] (More than three decades later, Koppelman would play a key role in running the empire of tastemaker Martha Stewart.)

By the time Davis held the next summer's convention in Puerto Rico, he could boast the Chambers Brothers, Big Brother & the Holding Company, and a new group called Blood, Sweat & Tears as proud additions to the pop roster. As president, Davis stuck his hand into every aspect of record making except for the actual recording.

• • •

Davis never claimed to be a classical music guy, and it was inevitable that Masterworks would be affected by his ascension. In 1966 Paul Myers had been made international director of classical A&R. Although

McClure, Frost, and Shepard were still producing records for Columbia, a lot of the artists, whether they were European or not, were being recorded in Europe. Columbia still had a slighter opera lineup than half a dozen other labels. "Lieberson didn't like opera," Myers said. "He used to say that operagoers don't really like the music, they like singers."[12] "Goddard thought opera singers were a pain in the ass,"[13] Tom Shepard said. Lieberson had had more than his share of headaches keeping many of them, from Lotte Lehman to Eleanor Steber, happy. (An October 4, 1944, telegram from Rise Stevens reads: DEAR GODDARD DO NOT LIKE UNCONDITIONAL SURRENDER TERMS OF COLUMBIA CON-TRACT COME ON YOU CAN DO BETTER THAN THAT LOVE AND KISSES=RISE)[14] "To build a great opera catalog," Peter Munves said in his tommy-gun delivery, "you need a big divo, which is a big tenor, or a big soprano. You have to have one or the other because, if they become hot, no matter how many copies these opera buffs have, they're gonna buy it for the new one. So in the fifties it was Callas and in the sixties it was Sutherland. A Callas they went mad for. And before Sutherland it was Tebaldi. I remember in the sixties London [Records] had Tebaldi and Sutherland. That was big! They owned the opera market! They had the big singers. And if Columbia had stayed with EMI, they would have had Callas! They would have been in the opera business!"[15] Eileen Farrell, who lacked glamour and a taste for Wagner—one or the other, that is, if not both—didn't qualify as a *big* soprano, though that didn't seem to bother her. An earthy woman who lived on Staten Island and was married to a New York City cop, Farrell was one of the few opera singers who could record popular material (with Luther Henderson, Percy Faith, and André Previn) for Columbia without sounding formal. But she didn't tour much—a requirement for most divas—and appeared to be just as comfortable singing blues-inflected standards as she did singing *Medea*. Richard Tucker (né Reuben Ticker) had recorded across the spectrum, from Puccini to the *Kol Nidre* service, on Columbia since before the birth of the LP. But Tucker was an American rather than inter-national opera star. He could thrill New York audiences by holding a B flat for what seemed like eons, but few tenors after Caruso have inspired the fanatical following that the glamorous sopranos did, and Tucker wasn't one of them. He felt privileged to be at the label under Lieberson, and he referred to Tom Shepard, his last producer at the label, as "a nice kid." But as Clive Davis paid increasingly close scrutiny to the Masterworks numbers, he let Tucker go, with counsel Walter Dean playing executioner.[16]

Ken Glancy was still in London with second wife Maida, and he and Paul Myers still attracted artists like Pierre Boulez (influenced, perhaps, by Brigitta Lieberson, who was a friend of Boulez) and the pianist Raymond Lewenthal. Pressure was increased on everyone when Eugene Ormandy and the Philadelphia Orchestra left for RCA in November 1967, after twenty-four years with the label, leaving six albums' worth of unreleased material. Ormandy apparently felt hogtied by Davis's dictates about repertoire. Davis was unapologetic.

In New York, Leonard Bernstein was still the Masterworks honcho. Hipper classical music lovers were onto his Mahler cycle. When you went to Philharmonic Hall to *see* Bernstein conduct Mahler, there was no better theater in the city. "He had such independence of parts of his body," Peter Munves said of Bernstein. "He was doing that eerie scherzo to the Mahler Second Symphony and the hips were going like a hula—de, de, de, de, de, de, de—and the shoulders are doing another rhythm completely. It was incredible to see him! He was like a Whirling Dervish!" Listening to the recordings, however, you could hear—whether or not you were stoned, mind you—how Mahler disassembled European Romantic music, then rebuilt it as sumptuous Technicolor music, full of cinematic character and emotion. Younger listeners who couldn't sit through Bach or Beethoven often responded to Mahler, whose music was hardly shallow.

Peter Munves was always investigating why conductors favored one composer over another. So one evening he went backstage at Philharmonic Hall to find Bernstein sitting in his dressing room holding a glass of Scotch and a cigarette—his usual post-concert pleasures—and he brought up the age-old issue of Mahler versus Bruckner.

"The difference between Mahler and Bruckner," Munves said, "was that Mahler all his life was searching for God, and Bruckner had found God."

"Bullshit," Bernstein said.

"What do you mean, bullshit?"

"Look, there are no real orgasms in Bruckner's music," Bernstein said. "He doesn't reach a climax. He's always gonna be, but it never happens. He takes so long to make his points. He's very loquacious. No matter what you say about Mahler, he made his points."[17]

• • •

Masterworks began to aim squarely at the same youth market that bought albums by the Byrds. "America Listens While the Establishment Burns" went one of the Masterworks marketing phrases. "Charles Ives Sold Insurance, But His Real Gig Was the New Music." "Hector Berlioz Took Dope, and His Trips Exploded into Out-of-Sight Sounds."[18] Peter Munves began to package classical compilations with more than a touch of irreverence (*Beethoven for Breakfast*) so that younger record buyers, especially those who had never attended an orchestral concert before, were intrigued. John Berg brought in Milton Glaser to illustrate, and suddenly the three Bs were cool. Lieberson, profane and no less irreverent in private, was dismayed that the music he loved most couldn't be sold with less bombast. But he liked the numbers, relatively high for Masterworks reissues, coming in. So did Clive Davis.

In the autumn of 1968, in a season when every week seemed to bring a new turn of political and cultural revolution, Paul Myers gave Munves a tape and said, "Tell me what you think." Munves listened to the tape: some guy playing some Bach and Leroy Anderson's "Waltzing Cat" on superimposed tracks on the Moog synthesizer. Munves pronounced it dynamite. The keyboard artist was Walter Carlos, before he became Wendy Carlos. Munves wanted all Bach, and he and Myers chose the music. When the record was completed, Columbia had to market what was essentially a new sound. "So we were having a sales meeting," Munves said.

For the title I suggested *Turned-on Bach*. Somebody looked over and said, "No, too drug related," because it was turned on, tuned out, drop out, turned off. So Bill King said, "What about *Switched-on Bach?*" and I said, "Perfect."

I didn't have the idea for the cover but they must have shown me the cover because I loved the idea with [the Bach character] mugging a bit. That got under Lieberson's skin. He said, "This time Munves went too far." You see, he was subtle and I was not subtle. He was an elitist and I was a populist.

But I proved my point. You couldn't just put out classical music and hope it was going to sell. You really had to do something for it. So this was probably one of the granddaddies of crossover albums. I said, "Look what's going on! The synthesizer is a popular instrument in rock bands! This is an audience that doesn't know diddlysquat about Bach so we'll do Bach on the synthesizer and we'll get 'em by the balls!"[19]

Art director John Berg brought in his old pals from Horn/Griner. Norman Griner conceived of an illustration of a kind of seventeenth-century drawing room, opulent and baroque, except that there's a synthesizer in the middle of the room and wires are coming out of it as though the instrument itself has freaked out. In the first *Switched-on Bach* pressings the Bach figure is sitting down and mugging. Munves pushed for—and got—an inner sleeve, produced at two and a half cents more than the usual sleeve, that showed all the Columbia synthesizer records on one side and all the Bachs on the other. When *Switched-on Bach* was released, sales were high for a classical recording but still disappointing to Munves and Myers. The merchandising power of television can't be underestimated, however. In February 1969 Walter Carlos played Bach on the *Today* show, hosted at the time by Hugh Downs, and sales suddenly skyrocketed. On the later pressings Bach was standing, wearing a somewhat more sober smirk.

Munves's marketing technique still made Lieberson wince. The Greatest Hits idea, which had exploded with Johnny Mathis in the mid-fifties, was getting a workout. Bruce Lundvall, who had Stan Kavan's old job of running merchandising, and Fred Salem came up with the idea of a genre's greatest hits as budget LPs: *Rock's Greatest Hits* (all Columbia tracks, of course, like Gary Puckett and the Union Gap's "Woman, Woman" and Paul Revere and the Raiders' "Louie, Louie") and *Country's Greatest Hits* (ditto, including Johnny Horton's "North to Alaska" and Johnny Cash's "I Walk the Line"). The customer was supposed to feel he was getting a bargain—and he was, even if the pairings were sometimes on the strange side (e.g., Moby Grape and O. C. Smith) and seemed to feature the same flaxen-haired, high-cheekboned model on the covers. But the Greatest Hits packages were also aimed at the all-powerful rack jobbers, the guys who decided which albums out of the many they had to consider would go into the larger stores. Munves and his colleague Pierre Bourdain had come up with the Composers' Series, another variation on Greatest Hits aimed squarely at the rack jobbers. "We know that the racks haven't been handling the classics," sighed the opening article in a June 1969 edition of *Insight*, Columbia's merchandising publication. "We know that the reasons for this are that rack jobbers tend to 'cherry pick' just what they are absolutely certain will sell extremely well and that most of them are simply in the old habit of ignoring the classical field altogether. . . . Psychologically, dealer and rack accounts should now be perfectly primed for this mass-market LP series."[20] In short order there was *Bach's Greatest Hits, Strauss' Greatest Hits, Tchaikovsky's Greatest Hits, Chopin's Greatest Hits,* and *Mozart's Greatest Hits.* Not that the composers were being interpreted by shlockmeisters; instead these were compilations of recordings made by Ormandy, Szell, Bernstein, Gould, Casals, Entremont, Previn, and Kostelanetz. In other words, the best of the best. Meanwhile, most of these artists had their own Greatest Hits series. The enterprise turned circusy when *Bernstein's Greatest Hits* combined Tchaikovsky's "Waltz of the Flowers," Bernstein's "*Candide* Overture," and Grofe's "On the Trail" on the same album. (Listeners could get a buzz just from the juxtaposition.) Lieberson the elitist said, "For God's sake, tell Munves to stop putting out Greatest Hits packages because that's all we have on the charts."

Well aware that his compilations had the highest profit margin of any single line on the label—the Greatest Hits and Best Of compilations were usually of old recordings that only had to be repackaged—Munves asked Clive Davis for a vice presidency. "Everybody around me was being made vice president and people were making a lot more money than I was," Munves said. He knew his repackaged classical product was pure profit, and he wanted to be sure Davis knew it, too. Davis knew it, all right, but was apparently reluctant to invest any more than was necessary in Masterworks. He said no. Munves gave his notice. "Where are you gonna go?" said Davis. "When you find out it'll be too late," Munves said.

Munves went to RCA. He was gone throughout the 1970s—a decade of doldrums for Masterworks, with only a few bright spots, like Jean-Pierre Rampal and Claude Bolling's *Suite for Flute and Jazz Piano*, to lift sales.

•   •   •

In the early sixties, when Schuyler Chapin left the label for Lincoln Center, Leonard Burkat took over as director of Masterworks. Like the first Masterworks director, Moses Smith, Burkat came out of music criticism in Boston. Eventually Burkat, a fussy man with a formidable intellect, was promoted to vice president of Press and Publicity and, later, vice president of Information Services—divisions that Debbie Ishlon had controlled on her own. Accompanying Burkat each step of the way was Tina McCarthy, a Carolinian who'd graduated from Stetson University in Florida and arrived at Columbia Records in 1960 through a Manhattan employment agency. She began her career there as a Dictaphone transcriber in Central Files for $99 a week. As Burkat moved up, he named McCarthy head of the new Columbia Archives, an expanded variation on Central Files, with McCarthy and a staff of four filing recording data, lending LPs to producers, and even handling consumer correspondence. (McCarthy would run the Archives for nearly forty years, seeing it through at least three moves—Black Rock to the MGM Building on West 55th, then to the label's old 49 East 52nd Street facility and finally to Sony headquarters at 550 Madison—and inevitable computerization.)[21]

Burkat's Information Services vice presidency gave him official time to write liner notes and produce recordings. He did a lot of work on the Legacy project *Medicine, Mind & Music*, the twelfth or thirteenth in the series Lieberson had begun in 1953. One of the earlier titles for the project had been *Drugs, Doctors and Diseases*. The more melodic new title might have been borrowed, consciously or not, from Lieberson's old friend Dr. Gregory Zilboorg, who published *Mind, Medicine, and Man* in the 1940s. Emanuel Winternitz, Curator of Musical Instruments at the Metropolitan Museum of Art, had composed an essay, "Music, the Physician of the Soul," that became the linchpin of the project. The musicologist Nicolas Slonimsky was involved, with connective music by the composer Fred Karlin and Lieberson taking a crack at some of the text. The project wouldn't be completed until 1971.

The link between medicine and music was as intriguing as Lieberson's other ideas for the Legacy series. His ideas were never mundane, their investigation invariably a learning process for the creators. Lieberson can be accused, as he often was, of setting up a kind of vanity division in which he courted prestige among statesmen as well as famous artists. He asked Eamon de Valera, then the president of Ireland, to write an introduction to the Legacy book *The Irish Uprising*, which celebrated the fiftieth anniversary of the 1916 Easter Week Uprising. Lieberson probably would have preferred to execute the projects with little or no outside help, apart from his trusted literary man Charlie Burr.[22] The Legacy projects meant something, however, reaching for significance beyond what was charting that week, even though almost every single one lost money.

Clive Davis permitted Lieberson to play with his Legacy toy, then threatened, like a dad who knows what's good for his kid, to take it away. Writing from upstairs at Black Rock, Lieberson made a case for keeping the series alive:

> In regard to Legacy, I think we should remember that with our establishment of the department, supervised by, unfortunately, a series of poor managers, a burden was placed on these albums that never could be met. The history of Legacy is simple: it originated basically as a one-man job

with some help from one or two people. The art work was done by the art department (not by one person assigned to do all of Legacy, which has had, in my mind, a rather stifling effect). I can understand that the Legacy department should be closed out, particularly if it's operating at a loss, but I would not have the Legacy series handled by the regular A&R, in the sense that anyone who has an idea for Legacy could just go ahead and do it. Furthermore, I still think that the question of merchandising these products has not really truly been solved. I'm all for dropping the large department for Legacy, but I would like to discuss with you how Legacy projects can continue without large expenditures—and I think to Legacy's advantage.[23]

Lieberson was sincere. He would become passionate about a subject that wasn't on its face musical—the Civil War, medicine, JFK—and mount a recording project, usually with a text to show for it. (By the time Lieberson wrote the Davis memo, the list of Legacy projects included *The Confederacy, The Union, The Revolution, The Badmen, Mexico, The Irish Uprising/1916–1922, The Russian Revolution, The Bullfight, The American Musical Theater, The Generations of Israel, The Mormon Pioneers,* and *John Fitzgerald Kennedy . . . As We Remember Him.*) As the top executive at the label, Lieberson no longer had time to write long texts. Charlie Burr was always on hand to write at least parts of a project, though Burr had plenty of other responsibilities at the label, whether it was composing liner notes for the latest original cast recording or taking Alec Guinness to lunch in Lieberson's stead.

Between 1963 and 1965 Joan Simpson Burns (then Meyers) worked as the lone Columbia Records book editor during the Legacy project *John F. Kennedy . . . As We Remember Him.* "I felt [Lieberson] had no talent for the written word," Burns wrote, "but since he was a musician and a businessman, I didn't expect him to. He, however, thought that he did, and this occasioned some difficulties between us. All of his writing that I knew about was considerably reworked by others, including myself. He didn't think he needed protection, and he didn't so long as no one in the literary world took his writing seriously. His 'special projects' were a good example: since they existed to give a gloss of prestige, it was necessary that they have real substance. Trying to add it only made problems—for everyone." Burns believed that her work at CBS was intended to enhance Lieberson's prestige, with little thought about profit. After completing the Kennedy book, Burns took it to Atheneum where she had publishing contacts. The book sold well and, combined with the recording, won a Grammy. Explaining the bilious tone that runs through her chapter on Lieberson in her book The Awkward Embrace, Burns said, "I put together a best-selling book [about JFK] which [Lieberson] hardly even saw until there was a dummy to send to Jacqueline Kennedy and Robert Kennedy, [then] he took credit for it and refused to allow me to attend the awards ceremony and then fired me (I was supporting myself and two children at the time) so you can see why I felt a bit jaundiced about him. He was not generous at sharing kudos and I did some neat things for him to claim but I reckon my talking back to him got to be too much."[24]

Burns was replaced as Legacy book editor by Midge Decter, whose view of the job, if not of Lieberson, wasn't all that different from Burns's. Decter regarded the Legacy operation as "a kind of vanity press put together at the behest, and for the pleasure, of the company's president, Goddard Lieberson. We published books that were meant to be packaged with records. This was an impossible job, not because of Lieberson, who was charming, but because there was not a single member of our little enterprise who had the faintest idea about what he was doing or how to do it. It was strictly amateur night in Dixie."[25]

Some potentially interesting Legacy projects couldn't be completed for one reason or another—usually because they never quite came into focus. There was an abortive project about the NASA space program, another about ballet. Only hours before Martin Luther King's stunning "I've been to the mountaintop" speech and subsequent assassination, Dave Rubinson proposed a project that he called The Black Man in America. With Davis's blessing, a fair amount of work was done on it, with Leroy (Sam) Parkins acting as point man and John Hammond looking over the Legacy team's shoulder. The initial idea was to use material from the label's vault: Marion Williams (Epic), Mahalia Jackson, the Fisk Jubilee

Singers, the Abyssinian Baptist Choir, Reverend J. M. Gates, Reverend Oscar Micheaux (CBS radio), Robert Johnson, Son House, Screamin' Jay Hawkins (Epic), W. C. Handy, Bessie Smith, Mamie Smith, Clara Smith, Sara Martin, Fats Waller, Leadbelly, Leroy Carr, Big Bill Broonzy, Pete Johnson, Albert Ammons, Meade Lux Lewis, Aretha Franklin, Bert Williams, James Reese Europe, Ethel Waters, and many others. Looking over the tentative list, Burkat caught the flaw in the concept: "[It's] not yet what we need," he wrote to Lieberson. "Titles are more critical than artists' names. I've told Parkins and John Hammond repeatedly that what you want is not a history of the music but a *social history in music.*"

Rethought and reworked, the project could have been magnificent. But there wasn't enough time. Effective November 15, 1968, Davis pulled the plug on the small Legacy division and had Walter Dean reassign most of its staff members.[26] Because so much of *Medicine, Mind & Music* (which Lieberson had taken to calling *Blood, Sweat and Tears*) had been written and recorded, it remained in the pipeline. Otherwise the adventurous, erudite, but money-losing series that Lieberson had fed and nursed along for 15 years was put to sleep.

•   •   •

As Lieberson's influence waned, a quiet frustration set in. He was only in his midfifties, still physically fit and endlessly curious. But he was no longer the hands-on president of the most creative phonograph company since the beginning of recorded sound. "Goddard lost his dais," Peter Munves said of the boss he sometimes infuriated but always loved.[27] Lieberson continued to see friends from all over the world and from every avenue of accomplishment, from Groucho and the Kanins to Dorothy and Richard Rodgers and Marietta and Ronald Tree. And he could take comfort in having that extraordinary family.

When she'd married for the second time, Brigitta entered the University of Goddard, an older student carrying books across a quad crowded with accomplished classmates. She was as smart as she was beautiful, however, and, gradually, made her own artistic opinions matter to

Lieberson as much as his had to her. Her 1961 Santa Fe Opera appearance in Stravinsky's and Andre Gide's *Persephone*, written decades earlier for Ida Rubinstein and requiring dance as well as narration, was the event that took the Liebersons to Santa Fe in the first place, and there they would return, off and on, for the remainder of their lives.[28] In 1967 Brigitta made her directorial debut with a Santa Fe Opera production of *La Bohème*, proving herself knowledgeable and tough. Then she flew to New York to narrate Honegger's *Jeanne d'Arc Au Bucher* with Seiji Ozawa and the New York Philharmonic, before undertaking two New York City Opera projects.[29] A lesser man than her husband might have felt threatened by such activity; Lieberson, reveling in the role of Pygmalion to her Galatea, was proud of her.

He was no less proud of his sons. That's not to say filial relations were breezy. Peter, the older, often distanced himself from his father. Lieberson, declining to be a stage parent in any way, encouraged Peter's interest in music but didn't push it. When Lieberson asked him what he'd miss most if he were sent to a desert island, Peter said it would be his piano, a Baldwin spinet. (Lieberson owned a Steinway grand he'd bought in the late thirties.) Having been presented by both parents and their friends with the best musical examples in the world, Peter remained deeply involved with music, though he majored in English at New York University. In some ways younger son Jonathan had a closer rapport with his father, both of them intensely private and owning highly discriminating sensibilities. After S. N. Behrman, who regarded himself as a kind of uncle to the boys, had written Jonathan a letter of recommendation to Harvard, Jonathan repaid the favor with an unkind remark about him. Lieberson wrote to Jonathan in London, where he'd been turning out articles on pop music, to chide him: "I do hate to see you reward old friends who have been so sweet to you with such contempt!"[30] At Choate, and later at Columbia University, Jonathan wrote about movies. His early critical writing was so lofty that he often soared above Hollywood's essential vulgarity, unable to see anything fun down below. In a review of *The Professionals*, for instance, Jonathan referred to the fine actor Robert Ryan as an "eagerly forgotten fossil." Only a few years earlier Ryan had starred in Irving Berlin's *Mr. President*, which Lieberson had produced—happily, by all accounts—for records. In the years before he became a teacher, Jonathan seemed to be rooting around for a style that didn't owe so much to his hypercritical father.

Like Mark Twain, Peter Lieberson realized as he got older how much his father had known all along. "Dear Dad," he wrote to Lieberson in September 1968, "I was rereading your old letters to me and you said in one that you liked to hear from me, so despite the fact that I'm not at Deerfield anymore I thought I would renew our correspondence. Also, after many years of rebelliousness and other Oedipal fancies, I've decided that you have been a good dad, especially after reading [Alan Valentine's 1963 compilation] *Fathers to Sons: Advice without Consent*."[31] The letter went on to express Peter's trepidation about committing himself to music. His parents and their friends were lions patrolling a potentially treacherous path. Within the year, however, Peter had decided to take extension courses at Juilliard, to attend graduate school at Columbia, and to become a composer—a decision that Lieberson supported if not openly applauded.[32] Over the two final decades of the twentieth century, Peter Lieberson would distinguish himself as one of the more inventive and emotional contemporary composers, his work often played in concert by Rudolf Serkin's son Peter. The two fathers would have approved.

•　•　•

While Lieberson traveled and tried to find projects to occupy his still considerable energies, Clive Davis was trying to pull the label into a post–Summer of Love world, where the blue blazer and the pin-striped suit were being cast off for a tie-dyed shirt and love beads, and the war in Vietnam informed every aspect of American culture. The war suggested that there was no God, and if there's no God, then anything—sex, drugs, rock 'n' roll—was allowable. In the canyons of power like Wall Street and midtown Manhattan in 1967, the musician Al Kooper remembered, he felt searing hostility from businessmen who had contempt for his long hair and his loose clothing.[33] By the spring of the following year, many of those same businessmen took the daring step of letting their sideburns grow long. One of those businessmen, Clive Davis, took private dancing lessons at Black Rock so he could loosen up.[34] If Davis had been previously as uptight and conservative as any Ivy League–educated suit, he still had ears that picked up what was fresh and passionate.

Lauro Nyro was nothing if not passionate. A great many artists did well by her compositions—Blood, Sweat &Tears' version of "And When I Die," the Fifth Dimension's "Stoned Soul Picnic," and Streisand's "Stoney End," to name only three—and it's safe to say that there was no one like her. Nyro also made incomparable versions of other writers' soul hits on *Gonna Take a Miracle* and her influential rendition of the King-Goffin "Up on the Roof" on *Christmas and the Beads of Sweat*. No other pop artist has more vividly captured in music the street soulfulness of New York City.

In the spring of 1966, Nyro's father went to the office of music publisher Artie Mogull, then supervising Dylan's publishing company, Dwarf Music, to tune the piano. Like a good dad he talked up his 18-year-old daughter's songs. When Laura came in the next day to sing "Stoney End" for Mogull, he signed her. Soon she was making her first album, *More Than a New Discovery*—but for Verve. (Columbia subsequently re-released it as *First Songs*.)[35]

By most accounts her appearance at the 1967 Monterey Festival was a disaster. But David Geffen, then on the ground floor of his own career, couldn't get Nyro's "Wedding Bell Blues" out of his head and was determined to represent her.[36] He took her to meet with Clive Davis, who graciously permitted her to turn out all the lights in a Black Rock conference room while she sang "Eli's Comin'." Those amazingly plugged-in Columbia albums followed, though not rapidly: Nyro could take years to write, then months to record. She couldn't read or notate her own music but heard chords in colors, sometimes of very fine shadings, that she conveyed to her musicians. *Eli and the Thirteenth Confession* contained several songs that would become pop standards, even if their lyrics sometimes sounded deliberately coded, less logical than felt. *New York Tendaberry* took ten months to record—then she threw it all out and started over, with Roy Halee as co-producer and Jimmy Haskell as conductor-arranger. [37] The wasted cost was perceived as self-indulgent by old timers like Mitch Miller who, though away from the label for nearly a decade, was appalled by the stupefying deal April-Blackwood cut with Geffen for Nyro's publishing company, Tuna Fish Music. (The name came from Nyro's penchant for tuna fish.) Worth 75,000 shares of CBS stock, the deal made Geffen a media tycoon at the age of 27.[38] "Where's Laura Nyro today?" said Miller, while Nyro was alive but had stopped recording. "Ask [Clive Davis]."[39] But Nyro's body of work is unique: soulful, witty, a musical portrait of New York City from her earliest recordings. When it was finally released, *New York Tendaberry* would contain all of Nyro's vices as well as her virtues. If you responded to her, you put up with the frequent fingernails-on-blackboard screeching, the cacophonic tracks that made Times Square sound sylvan, and the occasionally perplexing lyrics, to get to the heart of those eccentric songs. Nyro remained with Columbia for the rest of her life.

• • •

Laura Nyro had a strong musical personality, but she depended a lot on Roy Halee and her producers to extract the music from her and get it right for records. Apart from Halee, the man she most wanted approval from was Miles Davis. Hearing the mixed tapes of *New York Tendaberry*, Miles said Nyro was doing just fine without his help. For all of his popinjay, belligerent behavior, Miles could be uncommonly generous to other musicians.

Most of the time, though, he was a pain in Columbia's ass. While Nyro was writing the songs that would make her name, Davis was recording steadily, prolifically, and often beautifully with a handful of musicians who stayed with him for a while. From *Seven Steps to Heaven* (1963) through *Nefertiti* (1968), the albums weren't groundbreaking so much as expertly put together. Teo Macero could be at once protective of and exasperated by Miles. Irving Townsend wrote to Teo: "Miles Davis's wife, Frances [Taylor], called me regarding fees due her for modeling for Columbia album covers. She said you were taking care of this, but so far she has received no check." Frances Taylor had charged $75 for modeling for the cover of Miles's *Someday My Prince Will Come*, and yes, it fell to Teo to take care of it.[40] *Miles Smiles*, thoroughly pleasing with its fine Wayne Shorter blues-based compositions, is punctuated by Miles calling out, in his glass-gargling voice, to Teo at the end of "Ginger Bread Boy." Completing the recording, Miles requested a $20,000 advance; the request was denied. Miles had loans outstanding, and CBS Records wasn't inclined to indulge him again.[41] The albums *Sorcerer* (with Miles's girlfriend, Cicely Tyson, on the cover) and *Nefertiti* were recorded weeks apart in late spring and early summer of 1967.[42] A year later George Benson, a proud and recent discovery of John Hammond's, contributed guitar work on *Miles in the Sky*, the first Miles album that, nearly a decade after Columbia began to record in stereo, wasn't released in a monaural version. In September, while Macero edited the tapes, he received a memo from Dick Asher informing him that, though the label had been giving Miles $10,000 upon the completion of each new album, his outstanding loans now totaled approximately $32,000, going back to 1964. Asher proposed speaking to Miles about withholding $2,500 from each additional advance. "Are you putting me on?" replied Macero.

It got more awkward. Miles had never needed a profitable album to speak his mind, and in late winter of 1969 he publicly railed at Columbia Records for not having more black promotion men and women. It was understandable: although Columbia had the valuable services of the Chicago-based Granville (Granny) White for many years and a few other black promotion men, most of the major labels, including Columbia, were overwhelmingly white even when the music was black. It was only partly a question of equal opportunity; the greater issue was getting music by black artists out to black radio stations and neighborhoods; the white promotion men were perceived to be out of touch. The *Washington Post* ran a story quoting an anonymous "New Wave official" as saying, "The trouble with a company like Columbia is that when they get a good black artist they don't promote him. And they spend very little money with the black media. But they manage to cash in on the black cat's money-making potential. . . ." Miles added, "First thing, the white man thinks all Negroes want to laugh."[43] His ire was sincere. Miles's usual stage manner, in which he turned his back on the (mostly white) audiences who'd paid to hear him, repudiated the notion of the black artist as minstrel. Miles was nobody's Mr. Bones. If Bert Williams had felt the same way, he'd handled the matter with somewhat more civility.

On the day the *Washington Post* story appeared, Teo Macero's longtime assistant Corinne Chertok returned a termination contract to CBS Records executive Marc Pressel. The termination was of the recording agreement with Betty Mabry—who happened to be married to Miles Davis at the time. "Teo will have no part of this action," Chertok wrote, "and suggests you get someone else to send them."[44]

In a Silent Way came next.[45] In his *New York Post* column Ralph Gleason gushed over the album, calling it "another milestone" and anticipating another Miles album to come that fall.[46] Every few years Miles had charted new musical territory, beginning in the late forties with *Birth of the Cool*, then the Gil Evans big band experiments in the midfifties, and *Kind of Blue* in 1959. As Gleason saw it, *In a Silent Way* was another outpost along Miles's pioneering trek. During the autumn, as Columbia awaited daily sales figures on *In a Silent Way*, it was Andy Williams's album *Happy Heart*, released April 23, 1969, that eclipsed everything on the label except *Johnny Cash at San Quentin*. (Cash's popularity had been cresting ever since he'd introduced Shel Silverstein's "A Boy Named Sue" on his summer replacement TV series in 1968.) Yet *In a Silent Way* was selling so well for a jazz album that it more than paid its own way. A few months after its release, Martin Williams wrote in the *Times* that the album was hampered by "horrendous" annotating and packaging, with tape editing that inadvertently repeats a portion of the music.[47] Williams wasn't wrong; one long section of *Silent Way* sounds like it's simply starting over again rather than being reprised by the musicians.

Months before Williams got around to expressing his distaste for In a Silent Way, Miles's next album, a more elaborate variation in a similar mode, had been recorded and edited. Once again Macero was in the hot seat, running interference for the label while trying to plead the artist's case. "We made payment to Miles recently of $10,000 for his new album which will be released in January," Macero wrote to Clive Davis. "However, this will be a 2-record set." Miles was requesting an extra $10K for the extra record but really wanted $20K. "Of course, Miles laughs at all of this. I am rather bewildered but he says a deal is a deal and he is requesting more money for the additional record."[48] In a handwritten response to Teo's perspiring note, Davis wrote, "Walter Dean will speak to you. I feel Miles has to be realistic about the loans. Also, we don't sell anymore if it's a 2-record set, perhaps less in view of the higher price. . . . We should be fair but Miles must be realistic." Walter Dean countered with an offer of an extra $5K. At that point Miles was in the hole for $90,000 in paid advances and outstanding loans—money that Columbia Records had little hope of recouping.

It's not clear whether Miles took the five thousand. In the next few weeks, though, excitement was building for the new album. Teo wrote to Irving Townsend, "Miles wants to call the new album Bitches Brew. Please advise."[49] The title was okayed. Ralph Gleason heard the tapes and wrote to Macero that the music was "beautiful, important and exhilarating."[50] Given Gleason's enthusiasm, Macero, on behalf of Columbia, asked him to write the liner notes. Gleason was pressured to deliver his copy in two weeks, which might have prompted him to gush ("this music will change the world like the cool and walkin' did") more than he usually did. Even Clive Davis came on board: "Teo Macero—I finally had a chance to hear [Bitches Brew]. It's really wild—and great!"[51] The album's release was held back for a bit so as not to blow past In a Silent Way. When Columbia finally released Bitches Brew in the spring, it charted higher and longer than any other Davis album—or, for that matter, any other jazz record of the period. The Mati Klarwein–John Berg cover, its voodoo themes rendered in bright arresting colors, seemed to be displayed in every record store you walked into.[52] Along the way Miles's sometime keyboard player Joe Zawinul got Miles to agree that Zawinul had composed both "In a Silent Way" from the previous album and "Pharaoh's Dance" from *Bitches Brew*. This had always been a tricky business—it took its most egregious form when Miles had failed to give credit to Bill Evans, the unmistakable author of at least two modal lines on *Kind of Blue*—but here Zawinul was assertive and Miles relented for a change.

Despite further demands for advances, Miles remained on Columbia even after Macero left and produced Miles on his own. For years it was a thrillingly combustible mix—a moody, frequently angry black man, capable of making music of great beauty and innovation, contemptuous of the soulless white company that recorded, promoted, and supported him.

●   ●   ●

Miles was still jazz and, like Peter Munves's "crossover" and Greatest Hits classical recordings, simply couldn't put up the astronomical numbers that pop records could. George Avakian was briefly back at the label with Charles Lloyd, then considered the hippest of jazz groups and featuring the young pianist Keith Jarrett, whom Avakian would produce for a while. The pianist Don Shirley was on the label, though his music was perceived as more cocktail piano than anything remotely innovative. Brubeck was still there, though the Quartet had disbanded in 1967. Jazz and cabaret artists were decrying Beatlemania. Tony Bennett was attempting to sing lyrics that must have embarrassed him. In the spring of 1969 Harry Colomby, perhaps hoping to keep his client Monk's Columbia patronage alive, proposed a concept album with Taj Mahal and Monk to "bring Monk into the current bag of soul / blues and Taj Mahal would have fabulous musical backing."[53] It was difficult, if not impossible, to get Monk into anyone else's bag. Apart from a witty Riverside album made with Clark Terry (*In Orbit*, 1958), Monk invariably dominated every project he was involved in. Columbia supposedly wanted Monk to do an album of Beatles songs with Blood, Sweat & Tears, but

Monk refused."[54] This might not have been as far-fetched as it sounds. Harry Colomby was an older brother of Blood, Sweat & Tears drummer Bobby Colomby.

Blood, Sweat & Tears had emerged like ectoplasm out of the New York–based Blues Project, which included the folk-oriented Steve Katz and the sixties' premiere utility man Al Kooper. Known for being in the right place at the right time, Kooper was an excellent keyboard player who could also play guitar. In 1965 he had been eager to play lead guitar on Dylan's *Highway 61 Revisited* sessions when Dylan suddenly walked in with Mike Bloomfield, a musical force of nature. Deferring to Bloomfield's superior skills, Kooper ended up playing organ on "Like a Rolling Stone" and "Ballad of a Thin Man." Bobby Colomby was a graduate student in psychology who wanted to play drums the way he had as a kid. As Blues Project disintegrated, Colomby and new friend Katz kicked around the idea of starting a band with a horn section. Kooper invited Colomby to play drums for him at a Cafe Au Go Go gig. Kooper had been impressed by bassist Jim Fielder at the Monterey Pop Festival. Now there were four musicians, all talking about forming a new band with horns. When a band dropped out of a Village Theater date, the promoter asked Kooper if he'd put his new band together. Kooper said yes. "Does it have a name yet?" asked the promoter. "Uh, yeah. Blood, Sweat & Tears," Kooper said, improvising as though he were already playing the date. The name stuck. Colomby brought in saxophonist Fred Lipsius, making Blood, Sweat & Tears a quintet. The promoter and the Village Theater audience were expecting a larger band with a lot of brass. "Al told the audience that the horn section got stuck in a car in a snow storm," Colomby recalled nearly a decade after that night. "That was very shocking to me that he told this audience that the horn players weren't coming. We played a half-hour. The audience kind of liked it. It wasn't very special. We did old Ray Charles tunes and a few of Al's stuff that was nice and I got $242. I said, $242 for thirty minutes? I want to do this around the clock!"[55] That was the end of Colomby's graduate studies in psychology.

Kooper's manager Aaron Schroder made a recording deal with Clive Davis, who had been primed to sign the band because Kooper, his own best publicist, had spread the word that BS&T was the most fantastic new band in the world. For the first album, Columbia staff producer John Simon (no relation to Paul) took over the technical chores, was given a budget, and came up with a weirdly compelling sonic punch.

But Kooper was too restless to stick around. Since BS&T was widely viewed as Kooper's band, word on the street was that it was finished. Experimenting with several singers, the band finally settled on the burly, moody Canadian David Clayton-Thomas, whose growling tenor could knock out your back teeth. Before Kooper departed, he had given Colomby a Buckinghams album produced by James William Guercio. The album made an impression. Guercio, who would be key to Columbia's long-awaited pop-rock profits, was brought in to do the second album. *Blood, Sweat & Tears* 2 may not be everyone's favorite album—many listeners prefer the subtler, more dialed-down Kooper-Katz aggregation—but it's the first of two that dominated the charts. "You've Made Me So Very Happy," "Spinning Wheel," "Smiling Faces," and "More and More" were originals; covers of "And When I Die" (Nyro) and "God Bless the Child" (Billie Holiday) proved just as popular.[56]

As producer, Guercio had a strong hand in the success of Columbia's other big band behemoth, Chicago Transit Authority, its name abbreviated to Chicago by its second album. That first album included "Does Anybody Really Know What Time It Is?" and "Beginnings," opening the way for another seven years, despite personnel changes, of chart-smashing records.

Perhaps there was something appropriate in the fact that, as the sixties became the seventies, Columbia's two major rock 'n' roll groups were horn-heavy bands—one from New York, the other from Chicago—that were only nominally rock. Clive Davis was hardly displeased with BS&T's and Chicago's sales, but Columbia Records was still lagging behind RCA, Warner Brothers, and even the formerly small folk outfit Elektra in producing and releasing new rock albums. Columbia did, in fact, boast some powerful rock acts—but most of these were on the subsidiary known as Epic, which had existed for less than two decades but had recently asserted itself as a major label in its own right.

20

Epic Out of Hell

Three years after the advent of the LP, Columbia's classical catalog had swollen to the bursting point. Goddard Lieberson had moved the label farther away from European-made recordings and was promoting music by American composers—Ives and Copland, to name two of the most important—that was recorded in America. The artists were beginning to get in each other's way, one resenting the attention Columbia paid to the next. "Yesterday Fritz Reiner was in my office," Lieberson wrote to Andre Kostelanetz, "when George Szell walked in and it was exactly like two old ladies meeting on Easter Sunday, wearing the same hats!"[1] In late 1952 the idea was floated to market the American-made classical product in Europe—and vice versa, for Columbia was about to terminate European distribution by the powerhouse EMI, the parent of English Columbia, and begin its long association with the Netherlands-based Philips. A new label was spun off to handle this classical product. Columbia Records and CBS executives decided to call the label Epic.

In 1953 Jim Conkling hired Jim Fogelsong, yet another Eastman School alumnus, to oversee all three of the new Epic divisions—classical, jazz, and pop. Fogelsong, a West Virginian with impeccable hillbilly credentials but a much wider musical range, had gone to Eastman on the G.I. Bill and emerged to sing backup for several bands. Soon he'd found his way to 799 Seventh Avenue and signed on at Columbia as a music assistant. In 1952 he took a leave of absence to sing with Fred Waring and the Pennsylvanians. During that first stint at Columbia, however, he'd so impressed Conkling that upon his return he was tapped to run Epic.

The shuffle of artists began. The Cleveland Orchestra, conducted by George Szell, was shoved from Columbia to Epic. Szell was widely considered to be one of the great conductors in America, perhaps the greatest of all, and his presence on the Columbia label was a bit intimidating to Eugene Ormandy, with whose wife Szell was said to have had a torrid affair. Epic also recorded the pianists Leon Fleischer (in the days when he had use of both hands) and Alicia de Larrocha. Besides Ormandy's Philadelphia Orchestra, Columbia had Bruno Walter, the New York Philharmonic before Leonard Bernstein was named music director, Bernstein himself as a separate entity, Isaac Stern, and such longtime artists as the Budapest String Quartet, Pablo Casals, and Rudolf Serkin—all with the label either prior to or shortly after CBS's acquisition of the label. The stern, brilliant Szell, who always pretended to be a Czech bumpkin with a poor command of English but was invariably more articulate than anyone else in the room, knew this was no demotion because he and his orchestra would get more attention this way.

Epic's was a skeletal staff. Joining Fogelsong was Charlie Schicke, Ted Wallerstein's highly capable son-in-law, to handle much of the classical material. Schicke was right for Epic's needs at the time because he'd been a trainee at Columbia, then had moved over to Urania, the budget label that imported European recordings.[2] Besides these guys and the occasional itinerant Artists & Repertoire man like Joe Sherman, Epic got by with a national sales manager, a part-time administrator, and a secretary; it did not yet have its own field personnel and relied on Columbia's elaborate branch organization—first put into place by Hal Cook; then expanded by Bill Gallagher—to distribute its product.

That product was mostly classical, with a smattering of jazz and pop. Epic's first two releases were Antal Dorati and the Hague Philharmonic's new recording of Dvorak's Symphony No. 5 in E Minor—seen as a can't-miss release, even though it was the thirteenth recording of that symphony committed to LP—and Hits from "Wonderful Town" on 45 rpm.[3] A batch of recordings from the Berlin Philharmonic, the Amsterdam

Concertgebouw, and the Vienna Symphony were released in the next few months—all through the new Philips pipeline.

New pop recordings, produced domestically almost by definition, took longer to make and release. There were singles that, despite bare-bones promotion, proved to be modest hits, like the Four Coins's "I Love You Madly" (1954). Along with 10" long-playing polka albums and dinner music albums, there were highly listenable piano records by Stan Fisher and Cy Walter, and 10" albums by the delightful pianist-singer Nellie Lutcher, who could sound like an orchestra all by herself. There were albums that got too little notice, like *Meet Betty Carter and Ray Bryant*, a May 1955 session that introduced the burly Philadelphia pianist and the unsurpassable singer from Flint, Michigan, whose hornlike vocals owed more to Louis Armstrong than to any other female singer.[4]

In the midfifties the industry's hits, whether or not they'd sold half a million dollars' worth of disks that qualified them as Gold, came from a pop tradition that hadn't yet accommodated rock 'n' roll. It wouldn't be until early 1956 that Elvis Presley was picked up by RCA and became a national star. Meanwhile the *Billboard* charts began to post hits by Little Richard, The Platters ("Only You" and "The Great Pretender"), Chuck Berry, James Brown and the Famous Flames, and the future Columbia artist Johnny Cash, then on Sun Records. Epic, still too green and unsure of itself, and still patronized by Columbia as its kid sister, was groping for an identity. At this point it could boast of two dependable attractions: the Szell-helmed Cleveland Orchestra; and its Radial Sound logo, a simple but ingenious reworking of CBS's "golden eye." But Epic wasn't yet equipped to compete for youth-oriented music. It was more comfortable handling easy listening and show music. Typical was Jay Blackton's 1957 compilation of Irving Berlin tunes, *Let Me Sing and I'm Happy*.[5] Berlin was pleased with the album and told Lieberson, who in turn was pleased that the album hadn't lost too much money.

As head of Epic pop music for two years, Joe Sherman did what he could. In 1958 the Jamies's "Summertime, Summertime" fell into his lap after Archie Bleyer at Cadence Records discarded the recording he'd financed. The song's cowriter, Sherm Feller, took the song across Seventh

Avenue to Sherman at Epic. Too late to capitalize on the anticipation of the season (as Epic would do later so brilliantly with Sly and the Family Stone's "Hot Fun in the Summertime"), Sherman released the 45 on July 18; it still sold over 200,000 copies in the next few weeks. Epic would release the record, more doo-wop than rock 'n' roll, three more times at two-year intervals, always making money.[6]

Even though rock 'n' roll could be profitable, Mitch Miller had such a pronounced distaste for it that the label reeked of a kind of three-chord pesticide, repelling and intimidating Miller's fellow producers and executives from picking up a rock act. One new Columbia hire in 1957 wasn't intimidated by Miller, although he was filled with admiration for him. That new hire, David Kapralik, wouldn't be specifically aligned with Epic for several more years, but his authority would be felt long before then.

● ● ● ●

"I had bupkus," Dave Kapralik said about his 1957 job search. Having just passed 30, this pint-sized kid from Plainfield, New Jersey, had been a radio actor, carnival barker, and shoe salesman. "I was working for my brother-in-law shlepping sample cases of shoes."[7] At Brentano's he picked up a book about careers, then wrote letters to five companies he thought he might like to work for. He had no music background but loved music. Hal Cook, Columbia's vice president in charge of sales, invited Kapralik to come in and talk. In preparation for the interview Kapralik walked into every uptown record store he could find, checking out Columbia's sales promotions. Cook, impressed by his ideas, hired him as a trainee.

Kapralik took a desk in a line of offices, on the third floor of 799 Seventh Avenue, that included Cook's, Bill Gallagher's, promotion head Dick Linke's, and a secretarial pool in the common area out front. Kapralik's first job was to write promotional blurbs for the singles that Mitch Miller produced. "Mitch would be racing through the hallways brimming with enthusiasm," Kapralik said. "He'd come halfway around the building and drag me back to his office so I could hear the new Tony Bennett and write the blurb." Miller's enthusiasm was infectious—few music men have been so tirelessly extroverted—and Kapralik, like just about everyone else at the label, wanted to please him. At Miller's weekly singles meetings, Kapralik overflowed with promotion ideas. He spoke fast, his dilated dark eyes appearing too wide for his elfin frame (Kapralik has been described by several friends and at least one writer as "sprightly"), and quickly shed the shyness that a new employee often feels at a large company. He spotted 16-year-old Leslie Uggams— adorable, smart, black, the daughter of a member of the Hall Johnson Choir and already a veteran trouper—on *Name That Tune*, the musical quiz show, and told Miller about her. (Miller would later take on Uggams as a management client and female singer on the otherwise all-male *Sing Along with Mitch*.) On a fast track, Kapralik was pulled off blurb-writing to edit *Insight*, the Columbia sales magazine, then made head of national promotion. Kapralik was plugged in.

As director of promotion, Kapralik held weekly conference calls. This is how he met pop impresarios Don Kirshner and Al Nevins. Among their clients was a New York teenager named Michael Anthony Orlando Cassavitis, a mouthful edited down to Tony Orlando. Mitch Miller, with one shoe already out the corporate door, wouldn't have anything to do with the kid—since his experience with Johnnie Ray, most of Miller's starmaking energies homed in on young women, not young men—so Kapralik got permission from Bill Gallagher to record Orlando on Epic. In early 1961 Orlando's "Bless You" and "Halfway to Paradise" hit the charts—if not the first rock 'n' roll hits under CBS's umbrella, surely the first rock hits by and aimed at teenagers.

Kapralik's stock went up. Gallagher, VP of Sales after Cook's departure, didn't know what to make of Kapralik who, as a nervy Jewish guy and closeted gay man, was hardly in the Gallagher mold. "Gallagher was called the Pope," Kapralik said. "The people who reported to him were team players." The men (and they were invariably men) in Columbia's sales department tended to be glad-handing, hail-fellow-well-met serious drinkers. That wasn't Kapralik.

Mitch Miller, made wealthy by the success of his *Sing Along with Mitch* albums for the label, was granted a year's leave of absence—a paid secretary and an office, but no salary for him. Miller's right-hand man, Percy Faith, had already gone west to try his hand at film scoring. So Lieberson appointed longtime producer Frank DeVol as head of A&R. Years before he became known to television audiences for his hurdy-gurdy theme to *My Three Sons* and his regular role as Happy Kyne on *Fernwood 2-Night*, DeVol was a widely respected orchestra leader with an outrageous sense of humor. (Bald and vaguely resembling a basset hound, DeVol once swore to John Doumanian, Columbia's man in Chicago, that he'd French-kissed his own mother.)[8] Kapralik, finding DeVol's musical taste "old-timey," repeatedly ran into problems. At the weekly singles meetings DeVol, who had played behind Tony Bennett at Columbia and Ella Fitzgerald at Verve, was put off by Kapralik's enthusiasms, particularly for the New Jersey group the Shirelles. Disagreeing with DeVol wasn't easy because he was so affable. To make matters more challenging for Kapralik, DeVol's administrative assistant was the widely adored Stan Kavan, who had been with Columbia since 1940, when he was a high school student, and had given Mitch Miller the idea for the sing-alongs. Kapralik found himself isolated by "Mitch's people," including producers Teo Macero and Ernie Altschuler.

With Miller gone, though, Lieberson figured it was time to overhaul pop A&R. In April 1961, Lieberson removed DeVol as head of A&R and appointed Kapralik to take his place. DeVol was spending more time in Los Angeles anyway. Adopting a "floating" concept of pop Artists & Repertoire, in which staffers would work on the music they were most drawn to—Macero to jazz, for instance, Don Law to country, Bob Morgan to middle-of-the-road vocalists—Lieberson also announced he would actively oversee the pop A&R department.[9] He sensed that an unchecked Kapralik—"a live wire, kinetic," according to Bob Morgan— would create more electricity than Columbia's insulated corporate atmosphere could bear.

Still, Lieberson gave Kapralik a lot of room. When it appeared that Mitch Miller was gone for good, Kapralik encouraged Don Law to introduce rock 'n' roll out of Nashville. He hired the respected musician Bob Mersey, a gruff, crusty guy who could build a gorgeous arrangement by scribbling on a piano top in a matter of minutes, to orchestrate for various artists. Mersey arranged Dion's "Ruby Baby," which announced to the recording industry that Columbia was finally in the rock 'n' roll business. When Kapralik brought Andy Williams to the label, Mersey got the arranging assignment—and the hits rolled in. "It was either stupidity or courage," Kapralik said of his own frenetic activity during this period running A&R. In fact he would demonstrate both at once when he took on the already legendary A&R man John Hammond.

•   •   •

For a while Epic was almost sustained by the dance music of Lester Lanin, the society bandleader who'd been with the label off and on since the pre-CBS days, and by Buddy Greco, the lounge singer–pianist whose style was surfacey but rhythmic and unpretentious.[10] Apart from the Cleveland Orchestra recordings, the label hadn't established a strong identity. The singer Roy Hamilton had had a hit in 1955 with an R&B version of "Unchained Melody," a close call with the 1958 "Crazy Feeling," and his 1961 "You Can Have Her" would become one of the first true rock 'n' roll singles on the label. With more than a dozen well-received albums behind him, Hamilton had been a major Epic artist. But no longer. The label itself wasn't major. It was a repository of musical oddities, like *Jack Lemmon Sings and Plays from Some Like It Hot*.

After Mike Berniker had served an apprenticeship under Cliff Benfield's aegis he was given producing assignments at Epic, as though that label were a safer place to fail. Goddard Lieberson, in fact, didn't allow anyone to fail—not if you wanted to stay at Columbia Records— but Epic was seen as more marginal, a farm team in a big-city market, the Newark Bears to the New York Yankees. "You graduated up from Epic," Berniker said. By early 1961 Epic had lost $400,000 on gross income of $700,000—paltry sales even by standards of the day. There was talk of closing Epic altogether. William Paley was so proud of

Epic's Radial Sound logo, however, that he was willing to keep it going for a while.[11]

Bill Gallagher liked what Len Levy was doing over at Coral Records, a subsidiary of Decca. Levy had gotten into the record business in Rochester, New York, a background that would endear him to Lieberson. With artists like the McGuire Sisters and Don Cornell, Levy had made Coral profitable. Gallagher figured Levy had a shot at achieving the same thing at Epic. Almost immediately Levy brought along his longtime lieutenant Vic Linn. "We were 27 or so," Linn said. "Epic was in the cellar. We couldn't make it any worse!" Jim Fogelsong was still in the building but working mostly on projects for Columbia (including Robert Goulet albums) and would soon decamp to Nashville.[12]

Levy got the go-ahead from Gallagher to hire four regional sales managers. Epic, if nowhere close to boasting Columbia's elaborate sales system, now at least had its own people in place. To run A&R for the label, Lieberson moved Bob Morgan over from Columbia.

•　•　•

Born in Buffalo, New York, of Canadian parents, Bob Morgan was raised in Larchmont and went to Yale intending to become a doctor. As a kid he'd played piano and vibraphone; at Yale he played string bass in Eli's Chosen Six, a Dixieland band, because the band needed a bass. George Avakian wanted to record two albums of college bands—one modern jazz, the other Dixieland—and selected Eli's Chosen Six for the Dixieland, not least because Avakian still had close ties to the school. Eli's Chosen Six included Roswell Rudd on trombone—Rudd would become one of the more important trombonists of the post-bop era—and future New Yorker artist Lee Lorenz on trumpet.[13] Avakian's brother Aram (known as Al), codirecting Jazz on a Summer's Day at the Newport Jazz Festival, inserted scenes of Eli's Chosen Six as a kind of musical comic relief—playing in a moving antique car, on a miniature train, and on the breakwater as if serenading the sea. Mitch Miller was overseeing the festival's radio broadcasts and invited Morgan to come to Columbia as a trainee. (So much for becoming a doctor.) Graduating in 1958, Morgan reported to the Columbia offices, spent two weeks in Manhattan, then two weeks in Bridgeport watching how records got made. At 799 Seventh Avenue Morgan was assigned to go through the slush pile, the songs that Mitch Miller couldn't get to each week. Soon Cal Lampley and Bob Prince followed their mentor George Avakian out the door, leaving two A&R slots open. Teo Macero got one of them; Morgan got the other.[14]

Mort Lewis, who had been managing Dave Brubeck for the previous five years or so, discovered a folk-singing group out of the University of Washington; they were called the Marksmen but soon changed their name to the Brothers Four. Morgan was assigned to produce them. Out came "Green Fields," a haunting folk tune that sounded as if it had been around for a century but had been written only a couple of years earlier. As a producer, Morgan was on his way.

● ● ●

From 1959 through the end of 1962, "The Twist" sold millions of 45s in various versions. Hank Ballard and the Midniters had the first hit, followed by Chubby Checker (né Ernest Evans), the Philadelphia poultry worker who renamed himself after Fats Domino. Lester Lanin grabbed a piece of the action and recorded "Twistin' in High Society," a dance band version that made some money for Epic.[15] So did Rolf Harris's "Tie Me Kangaroo Down, Sport." Harris, a musician-painter from Australia, had recorded the song for Columbia Britain in 1960; Epic released it the following year in the United States.

The label was hanging on—barely.

Then there was Bobby Vinton from Canonsburg, Pennsylvania. Vinton, the son of Pittsburgh-area bandleader Stan Vinton, came out of Duquesne with a musical degree and a facility with several instruments. Like his father, he fronted a big band and liked to sing. "Jim Fogelsong found me at Epic," Vinton said. "He wanted to bring back the big band sound, which had died."[16] Beginning when he was 26, Vinton made several singles for Epic, including "The Hip Swinging, High Stepping Drum Majorette," which amounted mostly to an artist-label courtship. Everyone knew Vinton was talented, but no one could figure out what to do with him. The following year he went into the studio with Bob Morgan, who by now was ensconced as head of A&R at Epic. They took several stabs at "Roses Are Red," written the previous year by Al Byron and Paul Evans; Morgan knew the sound he wanted but wasn't getting it.[17] On the third try Morgan pronounced it done. The "Roses Are Red" single sailed like a comet up through the charts, its tail hailing the long, lucrative union of Vinton and Epic. In 1963 Vinton recorded Burt Bacharach's "Blue on Blue," which led to the *Blue* album that included "Blue Velvet," recorded in Nashville. (Vinton had a knack for taking old Vaughn Monroe recordings like "Blue Velvet" and "There, I've Said It Again" and making them sound fresh.) Vinton could also write: "Mr. Lonely" was composed as a response to his army hitch at Ft. Dix. He was appearing at the Copacabana in New York when Morgan, standing at a urinal in the men's room, was approached by uber-manager Allen Klein to discuss Vinton's representation. "I'd be up in his office," Vinton said years later, "and the Beatles would come in, the Rolling Stones would come in. I'd joke with Allen. He'd say, 'Are we still friends?' I'd say, 'Sure. You've eliminated all my competition.' The English groups were so strong that only a few male performers were left alive."[18] Besides making so much money for the label, Vinton was one of the few big band holdovers to survive the British Invasion, right up through 1972's "Sealed with a Kiss."

Unlike so many pop stars who'd traveled in both directions on the career escalator, Vinton had a sense of humor about himself. After "Sealed with a Kiss" had done so well, the young Epic executive Gregg Geller began to compile ten or eleven songs for Vinton to consider. That's when he got a call from songwriter Irwin Levine, who said that he and partner Larry Brown had the perfect new song for Vinton. Levine and Brown arrived at Geller's office and played their new song on the piano. (Every A&R office at Black Rock had a piano.) "Tie a Yellow Ribbon 'Round the Ole Oak Tree" was based on a Pete Hamill story reprinted in

Reader's Digest. Geller, knowing these guys had a winner, added it to the compilation he was taping for Vinton. Vinton ignored the song, which went on to be a major hit for Tony Orlando and Dawn. Fully two years later Geller was watching television in a Memphis hotel room when Vinton appeared on an afternoon talk show and proclaimed himself "a dumb Polack" for passing up "Tie a Yellow Ribbon."[19]

•   •   •

When Len Levy took over Epic Records, it was kept alive due to the patronage of big brother Columbia and their parent, CBS. But it was also struggling to distinguish itself from the dozens of mom-and-pop labels that would put out a few 45s before vanishing into cultural history. One of the more respected small rhythm and blues labels was Baton Records, started by Sol Rabinowitz in the midfifties. Like Columbia's Stan Kavan, Rabinowitz had been a pilot in the European Theatre of Operations, folding his 6' 4" frame into the cockpit of a B-24, a jazz fan who wanted to get into the record business. Five hundred bucks was the startup cost because that was the price of recording the R&B group the Riveleers in the old WOR studios in New York. When the session turned out to produce the modest hit "A Thousand Stars," Rabinowitz had himself a record company. Over the next seven or eight years, Rabinowitz did all right with several records, notably Ann Cole singing the original version of "Got My Mojo Workin'" (later recorded by Muddy Waters and Jimmy Smith).[20] Baton's recordings, however, which tended to be R&B or on the fringes of jazz, were getting buried by Top 40 playlists; Rabinowitz couldn't get the records played on, say, *American Bandstand.* And then his distributors, answering more to movie companies like Warners and MGM that had ramped up their record divisions, stopped paying for the records. Sensing it was going to get worse before it got better, Rabinowitz pulled the plug and spent a few months selling records in Manhattan.[21]

One day in 1961, on the sidewalk right in front of 799 Seventh Avenue, Rabinowitz bumped into his old friend Dick Smith, who worked in sales at Columbia. "What are you doing these days?" asked Smith. Rabinowitz had been just about everything in the business—talent scout, producer, recording engineer, promotion man, bookkeeper; surely there was something he could do at Columbia Records. Smith arranged for Rabinowitz to see Bill Gallagher, who assigned him to Epic.

Sharing an office with Mike Berniker, Rabinowitz was charged with finding rock 'n' roll and black talent for the label. Both men were on the phone a lot. "Jazz guys would be coming in all the time to borrow money from Mike," Rabinowitz said, though Berniker himself was still very young, still in his Epic training phase and in no position to be a creditor. But Berniker had a job and his musician friends didn't.

Within weeks of Rabinowitz's arrival at Epic, Dave Kapralik took over A&R for both Columbia and Epic. Except that they were both Jewish and in their thirties, Kapralik and Rabinowitz couldn't have been more dissimilar: Kapralik was compact, filled with ambition and chutzpah, and spoke in a high-flowing, actorly idiom; Rabinowitz was towering, straight-talking and relatively modest, and resented the way Kapralik was installing his own staffers at the expense of previous hires. "He was a pain in the ass," Rabinowitz said. "He kept hiring other gay people and treating them with preference." Before tensions between them snapped, Rabinowitz was only too happy to follow his mandate to find black artists. In 1961 Rabinowitz became intrigued by Piano Red, who was presiding over his own R&B radio program, Dr. Feelgood, in Atlanta after more than a decade's worth of recordings. Piano Red, also known as Willy Perryman (younger brother of R&B artist Rufus), recorded several sides at Columbia's Nashville studio in May 1961, and the results were issued on the mostly inactive Okeh label. For a while Rabinowitz got to do what he did best—scouting black musical talent that could put Epic and Okeh on an equal footing with the hippest contemporary labels.

Okeh had a real shot when Kapralik and Len Levy (each claims credit) reactivated it as a full-fledged label in June 1962 by establishing an A&R office in Chicago and hiring record producer Carl Davis to run it. Okeh had been through so many iterations that its catalog was hard to keep track of. Shortly after the purchase of American Record Corporation in 1938, CBS had revived the jazz and blues label it had once owned by folding Vocalion into Okeh. After more than a decade Johnnie Ray probably had the first hit, "Cry," on this reconstituted label; but then Ray, as a money-making artist supervised by Mitch Miller, was pulled into the more mainstream sibling Columbia. Except for an occasional surprise, like Screamin' Jay Hawkins's "I Put a Spell on You," and sublime R&B groups who never sold especially well, like the Ravens, Okeh had gone quiet through most of the 1950s. Now Carl Davis brought in Curtis Mayfield, who was still a member of the Impressions but became Okeh's chief songwriter. This brief Okeh period produced the "Chicago Soul" sound—warm brass figures and rhythms that swayed more than rocked—in other words, Mayfield's distinctive style. The Okeh experiment came to an end after Kapralik departed and Levy had complete authority over the Chicago operation. Carl Davis had been producing for Vee Jay and Atco, among other labels, and Levy wouldn't abide the moonlighting, especially when it produced a hit record like Mary Wells's "Dear Lover."

.   .   .

While he was still Epic's sales manager, Levy saw the actor George Maharis, then cruising in the front seat of Route 66 stardom, appear as a guest on a talk show where Maharis agreed to sing. Levy, whose wife had attended the same high school in Queens as Maharis, brought him in through his manager, Mimi Weber, a close friend of Kapralik's. Although Route 66 was broadcast on CBS, the connection to Epic's parent company had nothing to do with Maharis's signing with the label. Signing a television star, however—one who could sing, anyway—was never a bad idea. At Columbia, good ol' boy Jimmy Dean wasn't hurt by his TV program, and Andy Williams, who had just come over to Columbia from Archie Bleyer's Cadence Records, would prove to be the best illustration of the interdependence of prime-time visibility and record sales. Warners had scored surprisingly well, courtesy in part of George

Avakian, with "Kookie, Kookie, Lend Me Your Comb," exploiting Edd ("Kookie") Byrnes's role on 77 Sunset Strip, and MGM was preparing to present Richard Chamberlain (Dr. Kildare) as a singer. Maharis, even with his pronounced Flushing accent, could easily hold his own against Chamberlain, whose singing was almost colorless, and against Byrnes, who really didn't sing at all. One of Len Levy's favorite songs was "Teach Me Tonight" (recorded years earlier by the DeCastro Sisters, among many others), so that became part of Maharis's first album, George Maharis Sings![22] Robert Mersey was brought in for the arrangements, Bob Morgan to produce. Morgan found Maharis easy to work with and private, almost reclusive. On tour to promote that first record, Maharis tooled around in a Corvette, the car that Buzz (Maharis) and Todd (Martin Milner) drove in Route 66. A television and recording star driving his own character's sports car? In the history of Epic Records, not to mention celebrity quirks in general, it would prove to be a terribly innocent time.

After Maharis recorded a couple of albums, Mike Berniker took over the producer's chores. But albums of standards, no matter how well executed, were being slowly pulled out of the mainstream.

• • •

Kapralik was all over the place. He was instrumental in reviving Okeh, made plans to open an A&R office in Nashville, and kept in touch with almost every established and aspiring pop producer on both coasts. First and foremost, he was a dealmaker. Courting the great alto saxophonist Cannonball Adderley—as a member of Miles Davis's Kind of Blue group, Adderley had already made history on Columbia Records—Kapralik was told by Adderley's manager that he could have the artist on Epic if he were willing to release some old Florida recordings of Adderley's. Kapralik assigned Sol Rabinowitz to handle the unreleased Adderley stuff. Rabinowitz listened and reported that the recordings were no good—certainly not worth releasing on Epic. For this perceived insubordination, Kapralik fired Rabinowitz.[23]

Rabinowitz went to Bill Gallagher, who had hired him in the first place. Gallagher sent Rabinowitz to Jack Loetz, who promptly made Rabinowitz Epic's new national promotion manager.

Levy, meanwhile, wanted as much authority over A&R as he had over sales and marketing. Lieberson was reluctant to give him that—at that point executives didn't cover both A&R and sales—so, as a compromise, he named Levy vice president and general manager of Epic Records. When it came to A&R, though, Levy still had to answer to Dave Kapralik.[24]

•   •   •

That hierarchy was shattered—for a few years, anyway—by Kapralik's over-the-cliff temerity. John Hammond was only 15 years Kapralik's senior, but he'd been in the record business since 1931, before Kapralik was in kindergarten. More than 30 years later, Kapralik and Hammond sat in a conference room at 799 and exchanged heated words. Kapralik had come to believe that Hammond—his career at Columbia entwined with Bessie Smith, Count Basie, Billie Holiday, his brother-in-law Benny Goodman, and Bob Dylan—was a dinosaur in a company that needed to change.

The cruel irony is that the two men had so much in common. Hammond's commitment to black jazz and racial integration was already widely respected when he returned to Columbia Records in the late fifties after nearly a decade at Vanguard and Mercury. And Kapralik's own background had made him an ideal cohort of Hammond's.

"I have found a thread," Kapralik said, "a seam that's run through my life since earliest childhood, that led me in my early twenties to found a non-profit organization with Jane White, the daughter of Walter White, one of the founders of the NAACP." The organization was called Torchlight Productions and was dedicated to the integration of actors, particularly radio and theater players, in days when black women's roles were mostly maids and black men were relegated to playing valets, porters, or boxers. Torchlight's board of directors included Eleanor

Roosevelt and Ralph Bunche.[25] Kapralik's belief in a fully integrated American culture, in and out of the arts, was genuine. But it wasn't until he arrived at Columbia that he could address the problem professionally.

As Kapralik was moving up through Columbia's promotion ranks, Hammond returned to producing at his old label. "After attending my first singles meeting," Kapralik remembered, "John invited me to his office—a cubbyhole, that's all—and we touched heart to heart in these realms." In early March 1960 Hammond produced Ray Bryant's dance tune "The Madison Time"; Kapralik, eager to show his older friend how much he believed in it, promoted the hell out of it. "The Madison Time," pre-figuring the Twist, first caught on in the Baltimore-Washington area and ended up charting at number thirty for 1960.[26] Once he shifted into A&R, Kapralik had no compunction about fighting for black acts, particularly several gospel choirs who were booked into the Sweet Chariot club on West 46th Street in Manhattan. When a contingent of black Baptist ministers threatened to picket Columbia Records for the sacrilege of sponsoring their choirs where liquor was sold—the club's waitresses were draped in white tunics with wings and served drinks on tambourines—Lieberson and Paley stood behind Kapralik and the choirs.[27] This was Hammond's arena, too. As a journalist he'd covered the Scottsboro trial in 1933 and 1935. He had become a member of the board of the NAACP in 1937, when he was only 26. And his two "From Spirituals to Swing" concerts, presented in 1938 and '39, would become the model for jazz and gospel concert hall recitals for the remainder of the century. Undoubtedly Hammond and Kapralik had a lot in common.

So it got sticky when Kapralik began to field complaints about Hammond as a producer. The complaints weren't new. For years Hammond had been seen as a marvelous talent scout but an indifferent producer, more interested in the periodicals spilling from his arm than in properly recording his musicians. (In fact Hammond made no secret of his tendency to let the artists do their thing, without interference from him.) Hammond could also frustrate the artists by insisting that they stay with the style he liked, i.e., as he first heard them.

Hammond had brought Aretha Franklin to Columbia Records in 1960 and planned to produce her. Next thing Kapralik knew, Franklin's manager, Jo King, and husband, Ted White, were complaining that Hammond wouldn't allow their artist to record as she wanted to be recorded. "John, bless him, was a purist," Kapralik said. "He'd heard Aretha right out of her father's church and he continued to want to record her as he'd first heard her." Kapralik permanently removed Hammond from Franklin's recording sessions and assigned Al Kasha to the production chores. When "Rockabye My Baby" became a hit in '61, there was no going back.

Then came the Dylan episodes. Hammond was in favor of Dylan singing "Talkin' John Birch Society Blues" on The Ed Sullivan Show, but CBS, which owned both Columbia Records and the television show, wouldn't allow it. Kapralik sided with the bosses, infuriating Hammond who, in the corporate structure, reported to Kapralik. Dylan seemed not to care that he had Hammond's support; the Sullivan show, powerful as its exposure could be, was no longer worth his time. Then Dylan's manager Albert Grossman came to see Kapralik. "We're off the label!" Grossman huffed. According to Kapralik's recollection, Grossman made Hammond's retrogressive sensibility the issue, though surely Grossman was playing several cards at once—A&R with Kapralik, contracts with attorney Clive Davis, etc. (In his memoir Davis doesn't mention either "Talkin' John Birch Society" or Grossman's displeasure with Hammond.) To address his side of the problem, Kapralik brought in Tom Wilson to complete Dylan's second album, The Freewheelin' Bob Dylan.[28] That Wilson was black may have preempted Hammond's possible objections.

"I don't think I did it as a conscious psychological ploy," Kapralik said. Whatever his motives—and they may have boiled down to the simple conviction that Wilson was the right man for the job—Kapralik introduced Wilson to Dylan. Hammond, pushed aside, suffered his first heart attack. Kapralik was sympathetic but unapologetic. He had a company to run—actually three companies, overseeing A&R for Columbia, Epic, and Okeh—and felt he was only acting in the best interests of CBS.

Recovering from the heart attack, Hammond returned to the office. Tensions reached a boiling point. At the close of their conference-room meeting at 799, Kapralik threw up his hands and fired Hammond.

On its face, the episode seemed to be a case of old Columbia vs. new. Hammond was then in his early fifties, his primary contacts in the music business of an older generation; younger musicians and writers continued to reach out to him, and no one doubted that he still had extraordinary musical antennae, but he was no longer on the street the way Kapralik was. Or so it seemed at the time. There also was a quieter source of tension: Hammond's remarks sometimes suggested a casual homophobia.[29]

"David, it's your department," Lieberson reminded the guilt-ridden Kapralik by way of support. "You've got to make the decisions." Lieberson, despite a friendship with Hammond that went back 25 years, appeared to be in Kapralik's corner. Just about when they were having that conversation, Hammond was driving out to Long Island to meet with Bill Paley. Paley had none of Hammond's left-wing activist credentials, of course, and his interest in CBS's record divisions was all about business and not at all about music, certainly not jazz; but Paley knew too that Columbia Records would be heckled mercilessly if word got out that John Hammond had been fired.[30] Paley made a call to Rosenman Colin, Columbia's venerable law firm. The matter was handled from there.

"Well, I was not terminated immediately," Kapralik remembered with a self-deprecating laugh. "I got sidelined to April-Blackwood." April-Blackwood was Columbia's music publishing firm. For just about anyone else in the record division, April-Blackwood would have been a plum assignment; for Kapralik it was a demotion.

Hammond was reinstated. In the next few months he would make peace with Bob Dylan and his handlers. He would be instrumental in getting several artists, including the Staple Singers, Little Richard, and Johnny "Guitar" Watson, signed at Okeh. And all this was several years before Hammond the dinosaur would discover Bruce Springsteen and bring him to Columbia, as well as Stevie Ray Vaughan. Meanwhile

Kapralik tackled his April-Blackwood assignment with energy. He hired Tom Catalano (who would later become Neil Diamond's manager-publisher) to handle the day-to-day management of the publishing company. Kapralik kept up his contacts. He still had Lieberson's support, though he was aware that Lieberson, as president of Columbia Records and a CBS board member, ultimately had to answer to Madison Avenue.

*   *   *

In 1963 Joe Sherman returned to Epic, where he'd been A&R director for two years in the late fifties, with a group often described not quite accurately as folk. The Village Stompers were, in fact, a collection of eight Dixieland players who'd gigged around New York City for a while.[31] In one recent incarnation they'd recorded as Frank Hubbell and the Hub-caps (Hubbell was their trumpeter-leader). Reorganized as the Village Stompers, they hit the charts in summer with Sherman's banjo-heavy arrangement of Bob Goldstein's "Washington Square." The single did very well for Epic, though it was somewhat eclipsed at the company by the New Christy Minstrels's "Green, Green."

In that same year, 1963, Sol Rabinowitz got a call from New York attorney Paul Marshall, who was representing EMI. After nearly three decades, EMI still had control of the Columbia name in Great Britain; its primary American distributor was Capitol Records, which had first refusal of its product. Marshall had concerns about Capitol's handling of the EMI recordings and asked Rabinowitz if Epic would agree to be next in line. One of the groups dangled before Epic was the Beatles, whose singles had been released in the United States on Vee Jay and Swan. Capitol was said to be lukewarm about the Beatles until New York–based executive Manny Kellem persuaded the Capitol Tower in Hollywood to sign them.[32]

So the Beatles got away. But out of that EMI connection—further cultivated by Levy, Linn, and Morgan—came Epic's U.S. releases of the Dave Clark Five, the Yardbirds, and two British artists who didn't quite translate to American tastes, Cliff Richard and Helen Shapiro. The latter, talented as she was, must have seemed tame to American listeners used to the tougher, dolled-up girl groups of the early sixties. Cliff Richard, though Britain's biggest pop star (voted British Top Male Artist in 1960 by *New Musical Express*) before the Beatles, shrugged off American record promotion. Richard was also busy making movies and soon immersed himself in Christian evangelism. But he did come to the United States for four recording sessions, two in New York and two in Nashville; Burt Bacharach and Neil Diamond each wrote songs for him, but Richard still didn't catch on in the States.[33] The Dave Clark Five packed a wallop with "Can't You See That She's Mine" and "Glad All Over" in 1964, and never topped the playful propulsiveness of "Catch Us If You Can" the following year. The Yardbirds proved to be influential far beyond their brief existence, hauling the stonework of American blues across the Atlantic to erect monuments of guitar-heavy electric R&B. In an 18-month period the Yardbirds would successively include Eric Clapton, Jeff Beck, and Jimmy Page—three of the most revered guitarists in rock 'n' roll history.

In early 1965 the people at Columbia and Epic were trying to catch the theatrically ethereal and elusive Scotsman Donovan. In August, John Hammond fired off a cranky memo to Clive Davis saying that Donovan had departed the States for the United Kingdom "and now that he is on the charts here it will be very tough to deal with Rose and Pye," his recording company.[34] Epic finally landed him—*Sunshine Superman* in 1966 was his first Epic release—when his producer Mickie Most moved Donovan to EMI. Then there was the pert Scotswoman Lulu, whose title track for *To Sir with Love* (1967) reached number one on the American charts though it was barely noticed in England, where the movie was filmed and the song recorded. By 1967, when Lulu also scored with her version of the Isley Brothers' "Shout," American record buyers were in thrall to British pop. Much of that product belonged to Epic.

To more effectively market the British Invasion material—and also to further distinguish itself from older sibling Columbia—Len Levy wanted a special art director. "Through the mid-sixties," Len Levy said, "I had the support of Morris Baumstein and Bob Cato. But Cato was so ingrained with Columbia that I thought it was time to have our own man." Sid Maurer was a young painter, influenced by Pollock and Kline, who'd already done a stint in the Columbia art department before going freelance and working for several record companies. Capitol's link to the Beatles notwithstanding, Maurer's artwork (particularly on Donovan's albums) defined Epic as the British Invasion label to beat.

As if to more deeply chisel that identity, after the death of Bruno Walter Columbia took back George Szell and the Cleveland Orchestra. Even with a solid, pop-heavy roster, however, Epic's financial picture was murky. Epic's books at the time were set up so that its sales figures were folded into Columbia's, diluting whatever profits it might have shown. It frustrated Levy. But one day Levy, walking through a corridor at 799, was buttonholed by vice president Norman Adler, who praised him for Epic's recent performance. The numbers, read closely, didn't escape Lieberson's notice either. When Levy and Vic Linn attended Columbia's annual convention in Las Vegas, Lieberson said to Levy, "It's time you guys [at Epic] had your own convention."

Epic, like most companies on the rise, became increasingly political. When he needed a national sales manager, Levy brought young Mort Hoffman over from Columbia. Hoffman was smart, aggressive, and well connected across the country; his presence in sales freed Levy to more easily handle A&R. Soon Hoffman's disparaging remarks about him were getting back to Levy.[35] By late 1965 Sol Rabinowitz, who thought Levy was being "bamboozled," was getting restless with the whole business. Before he arranged with Harvey Schein, president of CBS International, to begin an A&R department for that division, Rabinowitz lured from Chicago a young go-getting promoter named Ron Alexenburg. Within a few years Alexenburg would make his personality—charming, often unctuous, dead-eyed when necessary—felt at CBS Records—first at Columbia, later at Epic.

•   •   •

Everything at Epic was in flux in 1965. The CBS record divisions moved into Black Rock, so called because it was built with steel and charcoal-gray granite from a quarry in Quebec.[36] The interior was designed by Florence Knoll, who used movable steel walls that sat on rollers and could be reconfigured if necessary within minutes to signify a staff member's position in the company: a director would get so many square feet, a typist a third of that, etc. The move to Black Rock, for both Epic and Columbia employees, marked the end of the record division's collegial feeling. The labels were now in the same building as corporate headquarters—indeed, as was Paley himself, way up on the 35th floor—and being watched over. The change from 799 Seventh Avenue, Stan Kavan recalled, "was pretty dramatic. You know, we were all by ourselves and now we went into this corporate building. Very strict, very formal, very severe." "It was a dehumanizing thing," said Maida Glancy, who'd been with the Columbia literary department since 1960, "making it more of a business than a creative affair. People felt like they were coming into their cells each day. Nobody from 799 wanted to adhere to the rules. You could water only your own plants, and you couldn't touch the artwork." Stephen Paley wouldn't join Epic for several more years, but even then the offices were cold. Unable to bear the overhead fluorescent lights, Paley would unscrew them, only to come in next morning to find they'd been screwed back in. [37]

Apart from Black Rock's alienating corporate aura, 1965 was also the year Goddard Lieberson, responding to a Harvard Business School report delivered to the company the previous year, restructured the corporate hierarchy so that Clive Davis answered only to him. Meanwhile, as administrative vice president, Davis had immediate authority over Bill Gallagher, who ran A&R and Marketing at Columbia, and Len Levy at Epic.[38] This was particularly galling to Gallagher, who had come up through the Columbia sales ranks in the fifties, learned his trade from Hal Cook and bolstered the branch distribution system that Cook had set up. Gallagher went to Lieberson and asked for a leave of absence. "Of course, Bill," said Lieberson, "but what for?" "So I can go back to college and get a law degree," Gallagher said bitterly, "because that's the only way to get ahead in this company." Lieberson parried Gallagher's anger with lavish praise for his service to the label. After that, however, according to Levy, Gallagher was a lame duck.[39]

Levy had a less pressing problem with Davis's promotion. "[Levy and I] had been friends in the past," Davis wrote, "and my new appointment hadn't raised any overt signs of hostility."[40] But Davis, true to form, couldn't leave Epic alone. Levy, whose abrasiveness had alienated several colleagues—Bob Morgan would eventually leave, citing too many A&R differences with Levy and not enough rapport with Davis—was signing comedians like Godfrey Cambridge and Norm Crosby. Comedians on record were not exactly Davis's idea of profit.

In the summer of 1966 Davis was anointed vice president and general manager of CBS Records. This new title, his second promotion in less than eighteen months, removed any question about his authority. Epic's A&R man Ted Cooper, who had come to the label after great success handling the Flamingos and the Four Seasons, couldn't deal with Levy, "who insists," John Hammond wrote in a memo to Davis, "on making A&R decisions Cooper cannot live with. . . . What he told me at lunch confirms all our worst fears about what is happening on the 13th floor."[41] So Davis rehired Dave Kapralik to run Epic A&R and returned Levy to the marketing arena he was originally hired for. "Levy was not happy," Davis wrote, "but he did not contest the explanation that the move was not personal, but simply structural."[42] Levy could see the handwriting on the wall. Trying not to chafe under Kapralik's familiar aggressiveness in A&R, he stayed for another year. He signed Kris Kristofferson and Bobby Sherman to Epic, but neither quite worked out there. Kristofferson's single on Epic flopped, though a few years later he would sign with CBS's associated label Monument, based in Nashville. When Levy finally accepted an offer to run Metromedia's record division, he took Bobby Sherman with him.

Vic Linn departed soon thereafter to tend to a family-owned business. Once again Dave Kapralik was making most of the A&R decisions at Epic. It had been a relatively short road back. It would be a long road, shadowed by drugs and guns and—yes, there is such a thing—too much money, ahead.

• • •

After running April-Blackwood in the wake of the Hammond debacle, Kapralik went out as an independent record producer. With singer-song-writer Van McCoy, who was still a decade away from his disco hit "The Hustle," Kapralik formed Daedalus Productions. Kapralik always thought in grandly mythic terms, and the name Daedalus came up a lot in his career. Daedalus produced Peaches & Herb (originally Francine Barker and Herb Fame). The group recorded for Date Records (a new subsidiary of Columbia, overseen by Tommy Noonan), had a few catchy R&B hits including "Love Is Strange," and changed only slightly when the first Peaches took a leave of absence.[43] McCoy departed to make his own records, forfeiting his equity in the company. Kapralik changed the company's name to Magic Mirror. But soon he was summoned by Clive Davis back to the CBS family to take over Epic A&R.

A San Francisco promotion man named Chuck Gregory served as Kapralik's Bay Area tout. One day in early 1967, Gregory called Kapralik and suggested he come west immediately to hear a band fronted by local disk jockey Sly Stone. A native of Denton, Texas, Sylvester Stewart had moved with his family to the Bay Area in the 1950s. He'd studied music at Vallejo Junior College. (Years later Stephen Paley would recall seeing Sly carrying a copy of Walter Piston's *Principles of Harmonic Analysis* wherever he went.)[44] He'd worked on the air at stations KSOL and KDIA; in 1963, when he was still 19, he was playing Streisand's "Happy Days Are Here Again" to a largely black radio audience. Kapralik flew to San Francisco and, accompanied by Gregory, drove down to Redwood City to hear Sly and his group at the Winchester Cathedral, an after-hours club there. Enthralled—Sly and the Family Stone was an integrated group that made everybody dance!—Kapralik arranged to sign them right away.[45]

Kapralik had been waiting his whole life for Sly. At that point, in early 1967, American revulsion at its own military incursion in Vietnam was rising. The civil rights movement was seen to have crested with the SNCC freedom marches and demonstrations of a few years earlier, but in fact it had only taken on more violent expression in cities—Los Angeles (Watts), Detroit, and, soon enough, Newark. In Sly's current hometown of Oakland, the Black Panthers were, in Todd Gitlin's words, "impressing young ghetto toughs" by "carrying guns, following the police, refusing to be scared. . . . The movement's antiwar tone was shifting from sympathy for slaughtered Vietnamese to identification with powerful Vietnamese whose victory would surely come."[46] The leader of Sly and the Family Stone occasionally took on aspects of the most menacing Black Panther—the shades, the sullen expression, the defiant, closed stance—as well as that of a street pimp. But what he sang about was inclusive, sometimes even warm. First with six musicians, then seven—three of whom were related to Sly by blood—the band managed to combine a quasi-psychedelic vision with highly danceable rhythms and political commentary that was pithy without being threatening to whites—for a while, anyway.

"At my last Epic convention, Sly and the Family Stone tore the place apart," Len Levy remembered.[47] However irksome Kapralik's authority was at Epic in his last two years there, Levy had to credit him with going with his passion. The group's first album, *A Whole New Thing* (1967), didn't do well for Epic. But Kapralik's belief in its potential didn't flag. Sly, writing all the songs and producing the band, quickly delivered "Dance to the Music," "Everyday People," "Sing a Simple Song"—all hits for Epic—and then "Stand!," the cross-rhythmic "Hot Fun in the Summertime," and the irrepressible "Thank You (Falettinme Be Mice Elf Agin)."[48] At Woodstock in the summer of 1969, "I Want to Take You Higher" proved to be an anthemic performance. (Upon hearing "Higher"'s bottom-pumping rhythm—*boom locka locka locka*—middle-aged white men have been known to gyrate spastically. What is the number, after all, but an ingeniously updated version of the call-and-response songs of the black South?) Everybody wanted to get high and dance. And why not? They might as well have been—to paraphrase Sly—at the county fair in the country sun, where everything was cool.

To more closely handle this outsized talent, Kapralik left Epic and began "the dialogue with Sylvester Stewart, the struggle for Sly Stone."

Larry Cohn, arriving with a law degree and an impressive list of publications, took over Epic A&R, answering to Clive Davis. Epic desperadoes from the sixties were gone—Levy, Linn, and Morgan permanently, Rabinowitz sporadically. Kapralik took a house on Woodrow Wilson Drive, in Nichols Canyon in Los Angeles, commuting between there and New York every few weeks. He and Sly were engaged in a "dance between the shadow and the light." "I was Daedalus to Sly's Icarus, flying too close to the sun," said Kapralik. Locked together in midair, neither man would pull the ripcord. When Sly produced songs like "Don't Call Me Nigger, Whitey," Kapralik gave him a hug.

• • •

Epic Records was now a go-to label, not a place to record by default. Some unexpected dividends from Len Levy's tenure came in. Tammy Wynette's "Stand By Your Man," put together from a few simmering ideas of Wynette's and then boiled by her producer Billy Sherrill, became a hit in 1968. Only two years later, when "Stand By Your Man" was employed to such heartbreaking effect on the soundtrack of *Five Easy Pieces*, it already had the credentials of a classic country tune. And there was the unkillable Bobby Vinton, whose "I Love How You Love Me," the last raspy breath of a more innocent postwar era, went gold the year Richard Nixon was elected president of the United States.

By 1969 Epic had gotten itself into rock 'n' roll to stay. It picked up on the hottest locale in pop music—Los Angeles and its canyons. One of the more curious deals Epic (or any other label) made at the time involved the country-rock band Poco. The band's original name was Pogo, but Walt Kelly, who drew the ubiquitous comic strip, brought a lawsuit—hence Poco.[49] In addition to Richie Furay and Jim Messina, late of Buffalo Springfield, Poco was made up of LA-based musicians of the first order. Furay, however, was still signed to Atlantic. Ahmet Ertegun at Atlantic wanted Graham Nash, an original member of Epic's group the Hollies, for his new supergroup Crosby, Stills & Nash. Brokered by (who else?) David Geffen, Furay was traded to Epic for Nash (with Messina eventually available to Columbia for Loggins & Messina) like baseball players on the block.[50] Poco never broke through the stratosphere the way the Eagles did, but in fact their personnel crossed over, and the group ably represented Epic in its foray into LA-based country-rock.

Also in Los Angeles, the erratic but fascinating local band Spirit joined Epic. The band had put out three earlier albums on another label, and its musicians would eventually splinter in different directions. But Epic got their most compelling work in *Twelve Dreams of Dr. Sardonicus*.[51] The single "Nature's Way" received a lot of airplay in 1970.

Don Ellis took over Epic A&R from Larry Cohn. Clive Davis hired Stephen Paley, a young former actor (*Take Her, She's Mine* on Broadway) who had lately worked as a photographer, mostly of musicians. Paley had been under contract to photograph Atlantic's artists, and then, freelance, took widely circulated pictures of both Sly Stone and Laura Nyro. A few years earlier Paley had been an assistant to the film director George Roy Hill on *The World of Henry Orient*. For such a young man, Paley came with an impressive résumé, not to mention the impressive name. The oft-repeated rumor was that Stephen was Bill Paley's nephew. "Steve knew all these celebrities," Sam Lederman said. "He'd deny that he was a close relative of Paley's. But then you'd see Angela Lansbury visit him at his office, and you'd wonder."[52] In fact Stephen Paley was William Paley's first cousin twice removed—the CBS chairman was first cousin to Stephen's grandfather—and was 12 before he even met him. "I had the stigma of the name and none of the power or the money," Stephen Paley said. A couple of years after he was hired, the newspaper heiress Patty Hearst was kidnapped, and Paley, whose name was listed in Black Rock's lobby directory next to that of the chairman's, felt as vulnerable as Hearst simply by virtue of having such a prominent last name.

Paley brought in the group Looking Glass, whose single "Brandy" seemed to be everywhere in 1971. "Brandy" was a good example of Epic's focus on singles at the time—a focus that sometimes caused the label to mis-time the albums associated with the singles. Written and sung by Looking Glass's leader Elliot Lurie, "Brandy" had an undeniable hook that dared you to turn it off whenever it came on the radio. "The test of character," Geoffrey O'Brien wrote, "was whether I could avoid paying attention to every note—every glide and inflection and expressive rasp and melismatic slur, every self-conscious variation of pitch or idiosyncratic deformation of vowel sound—of Dave Loggins, or Melanie or Maria Muldaur or the lead singer of Looking Glass. 'Brandy' came on at first light with the clock radio, and the day was shot."[53] Looking Glass's self-titled album didn't do half as well as the single.

The reconstituted Hollies, sans Graham Nash and now composed of only two original members, scored with "Long Cool Woman."[54] The million-selling single was welcome, even if *Distant Light*, the album that contained it, didn't rack up the numbers that Crosby, Stills & Nash did for Atlantic. Clint Holmes's "Playground in My Mind" took off like a shot in Omaha, but only in Omaha—it took several weeks to climb to number one. Don Ellis persuaded Holmes to come to Los Angeles and record an entire album. By the time Epic released Holmes's album, the single was half-forgotten.

In the spring of 1973, Dave Loggins, cousin of singer-songwriter Kenny and CBS United Kingdom A&R man Dan, was a professional songwriter, with an album on Vanguard, who came to New York to audition in a conference room on Black Rock's eleventh floor. (That's where Clive Davis was; you went to Clive.) Sitting in on the audition were Davis, Don Ellis, Los Angeles–based A&R men Eddie Wenrick and Michael Sunday, and rock journalist turned A&R man Gregg Geller. "Loggins played several songs," Geller remembered. "The twelfth or so was 'Please Come to Boston.' Everyone knew immediately it was a hit; it had a hook you couldn't get out of your head." A record company is in constant flux, however. By the time the single came out, reaching number five, Clive Davis was gone. And by the time Dave Loggins could complete an entire album, the song's impressive run was over.[55]

• • •

Sly Stone and Kapralik, meanwhile, were still locked in an Olympian clinch. In the two-year peak of his popularity, Sly, wrote Timothy

Crouse, "managed to rack up the most erratic performance record since Judy Garland. According to his agent, he canceled twenty-six of the eighty engagements scheduled for him in 1970—twenty because his stomach was in convulsions and another six because of a clash with Kapralik. He was late for eight shows. This year [1971] Sly has canceled twelve shows out of forty—ten because of a legal battle with Kapralik and two because his drummer quit."[56] This mattered to Epic because Sly and the Family Stone's *Greatest Hits*, released in 1970, less than three years into his career at the label, sold more than 3.5 million copies. Since then Sly had begun to work increasingly alone—that is, still reliant on his band, the Family Stone, for concert appearances, but less inclined to allow his musicians so much as a contributory note. The hangers-on multiplied. So did the guns. Kapralik liked to say that Sylvester Stewart was "creative, rational, responsible . . . a poet," while Sly Stone was "the street cat, the hustler, the pimp, the conniver, sly as a fox and cold as stone," and it was the street cat, mostly, who'd commanded the enormous crowds at Woodstock.[57]

Kapralik was on the defensive. Here he'd been trying to save Sly from himself—or at least save Sylvester from Sly—and the hangers-on were advising the musician to get rid of him. Kapralik was "the whitey Jew manager" (his own description of the advisors' view of him) and Sylvester was being pressured to "align himself with the voices of despair and nihilism and parochialism and separatism, and I pulled with all my energy to keep him from becoming a spokesman for those things. And Sylvester stood shoulder to shoulder with me. That poor kid was torn apart."[58] In January 1971 Kapralik sued Sly Stone for a quarter million dollars in loans and back commissions. Some of that was a ruse to get Sly to pare away an entourage that had turned unwieldy and more than a bit menacing. At the same time Sly himself couldn't hold on to a residence in Los Angeles. He was kicked out of one, failed to meet mortgage payments on another. What no one was saying, but what everyone seemed to know, was that cocaine had done its insidious head trip on both Sly and Kapralik.

"I looked in the mirror and hated, absolutely hated, what I saw,"

Kapralik said many years later. The "exaltation of healing energy between blacks and whites" that Kapralik had heard in Sly—the very passion that had driven him since his days as a radio actor—had taken on an undercurrent of violence he wanted no part of. After eight months of heavy cocaine use, Kapralik could no longer abide the daily torment. He survived three suicide attempts (massive doses of Nembutal) surely because he wanted to live. Between attempts two and three, Kapralik spent $15,000 to throw a picnic in Central Park and have "om" written across the sky, the letters billowing and fading a few thousand feet above Manhattan.[59] One night at his Nichols Canyon house he found himself on his knees begging Sly to accept rock promoter Ken Roberts as his manager. Sly, still wearing the gold Star of David that Kapralik had given him years earlier, wasn't inclined to let Kapralik go that easily.[60]

Ken Roberts took over Sly's management. Kapralik, who had already investigated various disciplines at the Esalen Institute in Big Sur and in New York, began to spend an increasing amount of time on Maui. Sly moved most of his operations back to the Bay Area and began to compose on the Univox, an electronic rhythm machine that rendered other studio musicians superfluous. If there was a problem with the music that Sly composed on the Univox, it was that listeners found it undanceable. Sly's 1973 Epic album *Fresh* charted as high as number seven but was still considered a disappointment. In May 1974, Sly telephoned Stephen Paley, who had become his handler at Epic, to say that he was marrying Kathy Silva, the mother of his 11-month-old son. Paley made the facetious suggestion that Sly and Kathy marry in Madison Square Garden. "Yeah, I could be my own opening act," Sly said.[61]

The Garden wedding idea mushroomed into a happening supported by Epic, at first warily, then enthusiastically. Paley, running interference between Sly's camp and the label, persuaded CBS to give Sly a wedding reception at the Starlight Room of the Waldorf-Astoria. The $10,000 wedding-apparel bill was paid not by CBS but by Sly, to Halston. The fitting at Halston's was filmed by the local NBC affiliate, with Mary Alice Williams reporting. Sly's behavior alternated between indifference and superiority. When Halston's radio suddenly emitted the sounds of a

Sly-like bassline—a musical bridge that connected funk and disco—Paley said, "Someone's been listening to Sly." "Yeah, a lot of people," Sly said.[62] Mary Alice Williams's subsequent account of the fitting reflected her resentment at being dismissed by Sly.

Sly failed to show up for his own wedding rehearsals. After he expressed dissatisfaction with his recording of the wedding march, with only hours to go before the actual ceremony, Paley played the jack of spades and prevailed upon John Hammond to "produce" a new recording. When Paley arrived at Studio B at the 52nd Street facility, Hammond was there—and Sly was not. Paley, tightly strung on a good day, didn't know what to do. Hammond smiled at him with self-assurance and said, "Hi, Stephen. Do you want a Valium?"[63]

Sly Stone and Kathy Silva were married at Madison Square Garden by Bishop B. R. Stewart (no apparent relation to Sly) of San Francisco's Church of God in Christ. Dave Kapralik stayed away. After losing his entire investment in something called Africa USA, an animal theme park in the hills around Malibu Canyon, Kapralik decided to pay a final visit to the animals. A hallucinatory encounter there with a baby hippopotamus and a Yiddish-inflected fairy godmother led him, naturally enough, deeper into communication therapy. With a young Massachusetts psychology counselor, Jim Dellemonico, Kapralik began a musical act. "I traded in a Sly Me for a Hi Me," Kapralik said. "And so began the wonderful, real time musical adventure of HiMe and Ilili. The derivation of the name HiMe and Ilili was when I realized, in the mythopoetical interpretation of my life and times, in my 'magic mirror,' that Sylvester represented the light within myself and Sly my shadow. What prompted the act was the same 'humanistic manifesto' that has inspired and propelled me from early childhood. And since the message was no longer being expressed and articulated by Sylvester (Sly was into a whole different, darker, more parochial bag), I became determined to express it myself, despite the fact that my singing is out of tune, and I'm definitely off beat. I found myself performing as a singing, fancy dancin' minstrel along with a musician/psychologist, first in Massachusetts as part of a 'self esteem program' given through the elementary school system."[64]

In Hawaiian Ili-Ili is a pebble, a stone; Kapralik truncated the word to Ilili and, to this day, signs his correspondence that way. After HiMe & Ilili played for years at senior citizen centers, hospitals, even EST meetings, Dellemonico had to redirect his energies toward the more dependable wages of state-run mental health employment because he had a family to raise. On Maui, Kapralik began to cultivate the proteum flower, an orchidlike bloom that has over 1,500 varieties. The name, Kapralik told Al Aronowitz, "is from the god Proteus, who changed his face or his look at will in an infinite variety of ways."[65]

Closing in on Christmas 1981 Kapralik received a letter from one-time nemesis John Hammond saying that Hammond had produced an album with Allen Ginsberg "in which Bob Dylan is on some sides and the Clash on the others. This also was an album that I'd cut for CBS, but they would not release it because of the glorification of [Ginsberg's] particular life style which they thought might offend [William] Paley." From Maui, Kapralik wrote back: "It blows my mind (whatever remains of it—though my heart remains intact) when I think of you still vitally involved and in the middle of such controversy and turbulence whirling around the core issue of freedom of speech and not wishing to offend Paley."[66] The two ardent integrationists and civil libertarians had put their differences aside and continued to exchange affectionate letters up to Hammond's death. Kapralik's proteum hothouse was far removed from the New York–Los Angeles–Nashville hothouse of the record business. Walking among his flowers Kapralik could again believe, once in a while, that everybody is a star.

• • •

Sly and the Family Stone broke Epic wide open. The label that had suffered growing pains with popular white artists like Lester Lanin and Bobby Vinton was now hospitable to R&B without consigning it immediately to Okeh. In 1972 Johnny Nash, who'd been kicking around the music business since he was a teenager, briefly became a household name with the hopeful "I Can See Clearly Now," the first reggae-inspired smash hit in the United States. The Houston-born Nash had appeared frequently on Arthur Godfrey's television show when he was 16 and then in a few movies, notably *Take a Giant Step* (1959), with Ruby Dee and Beah Richards. Burt Lancaster, one of *Take a Giant Step*'s producers, championed Nash as a young Sidney Poitier—handsome, intelligent, and modest. In a series of records for ABC-Paramount, though, Nash seemed to be casting about for a style, sounding eerily like Johnny Mathis.[67] As he reached his twenties, after making several recordings for Warners, it still hadn't crystallized for him. Just as Mathis's first, jazz-inflected album on Columbia was all right but not quite distinctive enough, so Nash kept making thoroughly professional records that didn't stand out.

Then Nash went to Jamaica.

After a period absorbing the musical culture and recording at existing studios, Nash partnered with Danny Sims and found his Jamaican sound. Nash and Sims formed JAD (Johnny and Danny) Records.[68] They had major hits with "Hold Me Tight" and a reggae version of Sam Cooke's "Cupid." In the States in the late sixties, marijuana had acquired a countercultural currency far wider than the jazz/bohemian circles where it had been popular, and that currency opened up the gateway to the ganja-heavy reggae sound. Nash was on to something new—for his own career, anyway. Dick Asher, then running CBS UK, heard it and signed Nash. Epic released "I Can See Clearly Now" in the fall of 1972 and "Stir It Up," originally a Bob Marley song, in '73, though it had been released earlier, and with much success, in England. Before Marley's own music eclipsed Nash's, there was Jimmy Cliff, whose appearance in *The Harder They Come* in '73 dynamited the reggae scene up from underground. (The ubiquitous soundtrack featured the title track, "You Can Get It If You Really Want," and "Many Rivers to Cross." Epic wished it had it.) Nash remained with Epic for years—at least four albums followed—but never again reached the green hills of those sweet reggae numbers.

Reggae's various roots—calypso, African work songs, and rhythm and blues—had all been musical forces for decades, but it wasn't until 1968, in the depths of America's social madness, that the word *reggae* came into vogue. In the first three months of that year the Tet Offensive began to change the balance of power, or at least lifted the scrim of what was going on. *Why Are We in Vietnam?* asked the title of Norman Mailer's novella, published a few months earlier, and though the narrative was ostensibly about wealthy Texans on a bear hunt in Alaska, the question was on everyone's mind. There was the government fear that Martin Luther King, long seen to be nonviolent, could do an about-face and emerge as the leader of a more militant coalition. Then King was killed, and so was Bobby Kennedy. It was also the year that two books, Eldridge Cleaver's *Soul on Ice* and Carlos Castaneda's *The Teachings of Don Juan*, enjoyed a wide readership that would have been unthinkable only three or four years earlier; the former chronicled the politicizing of the Black Panther author who would soon flee to Cuba and then Algeria to avoid another prison term, the latter celebrated the supernatural properties of Mexican peyote. Meanwhile reggae thrived on the relatively benign high of marijuana as well as by more malevolent factions distributing it. Johnny Nash's version of reggae hardly reflected the darker side of Rasta culture, but it made Epic a lot of money.

•　•　•

One advantage to Epic's kid-sister relationship to Columbia was that it was another step removed from CBS. Even in the early seventies Paley and Frank Stanton wanted Columbia Records to reflect class, a tasteful, discreetly elite tone set by Lieberson, who now sat high up near them at Black Rock. Epic had more leeway.

Clive Davis had wanted to sign more black artists to CBS Records. He had noticed, he wrote in his memoir, that *Billboard* was listing more R&B-inflected albums each week. Motown had built an empire on black hits, but they were mostly singles; Diana Ross and the Supremes, the Temptations, and the Four Tops were not enjoying album sales to compete with their own singles. Columbia had barely touched this market. Epic had its run with Sly and the Family Stone, of course, but Sly's unpredictability, both as a composer and performer, didn't inspire confidence for the future. Although CBS Records had employed several black A&R men, notably Dylan's producer Tom Wilson and the jazz-savvy Esmond Edwards, their few black artists (Johnny Mathis and Mahalia Jackson, to name two) tended to be favored by whites and gave no more than a passing nod to rhythm and blues.[69] Even the great Nigerian drummer Olatunji, who had first signed with Columbia in the late fifties, appealed mostly to white record buyers. Clive Davis didn't spell this out, but what he was looking for was a hit-making team along the lines of Motown's Holland-Dozier-Holland, the trio responsible for writing 50 percent of its hits.

He found it in Kenny Gamble and Leon Huff. How Gamble and Huff got to Epic Records in 1972 is a matter of dispute. Even Gamble and Huff's first meeting is an open question: some sources insist they knew each other in high school; others say they met in an elevator after they'd each entered the music business. In any case, before they would marry their company Philadelphia International to Epic, each man had served a long apprenticeship. "I used to watch *American Bandstand* every day on television," Kenny Gamble told Joe Smith. "I went down there a couple of times trying to get black kids in. They wouldn't let too many black kids on *Bandstand*. The Philadelphia-based show carried authority in the pop music world; it could break a pop music act the way Johnny Carson could make a comedian's career. In the early sixties Gamble was working by day in cancer research and moonlighted with the Philly-based Romeos, which covered Motown hits. Huff worked in the same hospital; keyboard player Thom Bell, who would become a major musical influence in his own right, worked in a fish store.[70] Huff moved to New York to become a session pianist. Eventually Gamble and Huff formed at least three record companies. They produced the Soul Survivors' "Expressway to Your Heart," which remains underrated despite its formidable position on the charts in '67—and an anomaly on the producers' résumé because the Soul Survivors was a white band.

Gamble and Huff, according to Davis, called to say they wanted CBS Records' merchandising and promotion capabilities. Whether the songwriter-producers approached CBS or the other way around, they contracted to have the Philadelphia International product distributed by Epic. Philadelphia International's offices, housed on South Broad Street, were literally a music factory.

And its music, fertilized by Thom Bell, Bobby Martin, and the house band known as MFSB (Mother Father Sister Brother), flowered abundantly. For Epic the blooms came early. In one week in October 1972, Harold Melvin and the Blue Notes' "If You Don't Know Me by Now" and the O'Jays's "Backstabbers" were each in the Top Ten on the charts. The O'Jays's "Love Train" would do just as well. Later that fall came Billy Paul's "Me and Mrs. Jones." Paul, slightly older than Gamble and Huff and from North Philly—he was a childhood friend of Bill Cosby's—had a weirdly mercurial style that could overpower Philly International's lush orchestrations. In fact "Me and Mrs. Jones" was far and away Paul's biggest hit. Staying with Gamble and Huff, his singles charted as R&B hits but never crossed over again.[71]

Gamble and Huff did well by other artists, and Epic reaped the rewards. Philadelphia International had dug into a pop-soul market that was being gradually vacated by Motown. Diana Ross was long gone from the Supremes. Gladys Knight and the Pips's biggest hits were yet to come, on Buddah. The Jackson Five would stay with Motown until 1976, and then its new incarnation would find a home in a familiar Sixth Avenue skyscraper. As the (preponderantly white) Epic executives got more comfortable in this almost exclusively black music world, other artists were brought in. Gregg Geller signed Labelle, the trio that had backed Laura Nyro in 1971 on *Gonna Take a Miracle* and had since garnered a wide gay following.[72] Labelle was made up of Nona Hendryx, who wrote a lot of their material, Sarah Dash, and Patti Labelle. The trio had gone from a hard-edged soul group to campy glitter, appearing at downtown clubs as well as the Metropolitan Opera. Walter Yetnikoff, who would become CBS Records president in 1975 and enjoyed an affair with Dash, described seeing them for the first time at Madison Square Garden: "They flew onstage, Martians in metal, silver-winged, G-stringed, titanium bras, glitter-gold tushy tights, feather headdresses like wild Indians, voices like horny angels."[73] Labelle's "Lady Marmalade" (*voulez-vous coucher avec moi ce soir?*), produced by Allen Toussaint in New Orleans, sold a million copies.

Geller also signed Minnie Riperton. A Chicago-born opera student reputed to possess a five-octave range, Riperton had sung in the late sixties with Rotary Connection. In Florida, Riperton and her husband Dick Rudolph put together a demo that got to Geller. Riperton's first Epic album *Perfect Angel* (1974) was produced by Stevie Wonder and included their hit "Lovin' You." Riperton's almost inhumanly high coda bored into your brain like a canary trilling outside the bedroom window before dawn. (So distinctive was Riperton's soprano that, even when trailing half a beat behind Wonder on "Creepin'," from his album *Fulfillingness' First Finale*, she could take your breath away.) She died of breast cancer in 1979, two years after her last Epic album was released.

• • •

Clive Davis's May 1973 dismissal—an industry earthquake high on the Richter Scale—had as much of an effect on Epic Records as it did on big brother Columbia. Gamble and Huff each got snared in a related scandal. (A Newark-based payola investigation would indict Gamble, forcing him to repay $2,500, and clear Huff.) One change that came about quickly was through Ron Alexenburg, the ace promotion man who had become Epic's marketing chief, and with at least as much authority as any A&R man. Shortly before Davis was forced out, Alexenburg had attended a CBS Records meeting in Century City, in Los Angeles. A Columbia executive, jabbing a finger at Alexenburg, told him, "Big Red [Columbia] will always bury Little Yellow [Epic]." Mortified, Alexenburg went to CBS Records art director John Berg and said, "Design me a new logo."[74] Over time, Berg would come up with two. The first was an orange labeled, lowercase *e*, drawn in four not quite closed circles encased in a square box—a typographer's dream; the second was *Epic* drawn in a kind of baseball-uniform script and was really a variation on Berg's artwork for Columbia's band Chicago, which in turn had mocked the Coca-Cola cursive. Those were the logos that

Epic went with for several years in the 1970s. Jettisoned was the beautiful, durable Radial Sound logo that, more than a decade earlier, had bought the label more time.

•   •   •

Logos may or may not properly reflect *logos*. The Greek *logos* is the defining cosmic principle. In those same years Epic's *logos* emerged from arena rock—the deafeningly amplified sound of heavy metal bands. Edgar Winter, younger brother of Columbia artist Johnny, was a progenitor of this phenomenon, first recording for Epic in 1970. Steeped in Southwestern blues, Edgar played keyboards and saxophones through at least two seminal bands, White Trash and the Edgar Winter Group; but it was his successive lead guitarists—Ronnie Montrose, Jerry Weems, and Rick Derringer—who provided blues-based licks that ricocheted off the rafters and prompted teenage boys to play air guitar for days on end. Epic signed the Illinois band REO Speedwagon in 1971, and the band's sales would only build as the band toured the United States. Touring was an essential for arena rock bands. So was the new ubiquitous FM program format called AOR (Album Oriented Rock), which emphasized albums over singles.[75] Epic's expert A&R man Tom Werman, who had been the rhythm guitarist for a fine rock 'n' roll band called the Walkers when he was attending Columbia, produced many of these bands, from Jeff Beck and Jan Hammer to Molly Hatchet and Ted Nugent. Jeff Beck had been associated with the label since the Yardbirds.[76] Ted Nugent grabbed the coiffure and sartorial trappings of a Vietnam-era rebel—hair long enough to whip an innocent bystander, handlebar mustache, open vest and suspenders over bare chest, headbands and high-heeled boots—and donned them for a heavy metal makeover that was startlingly conservative. "Ted Nugent is most probably the only legit metal guitar showman America has spawned in the face of the British onslaught," gushed the liner notes, torturously and inaccurately, to the 1975 album *Ted Nugent*. Tom Werman liked to sit in on percussion on the Nugent albums. Nugent's 1976 *Free-for-All* also featured Nugent's fellow

Texan Marvin Lee Aday, better known as Meat Loaf, singing on several tracks.[77] Heavy metal enthusiasts took note. Whatever his limitations, Meat Loaf refused to be ignored. Built like an offensive lineman, possessed of a theatrical sensibility and a rather thin voice belied by his girth, he would become a highly profitable Epic artist within two years.

* * *

In 1975 Epic's sales rose from $20 million to $33 million.[78] Some of this was due to exceptional sales by the Silver Fox, Charlie Rich, originally a rockabilly pianist and songwriter on the Sun label, whose Epic album *Behind Closed Doors* would make him a superstar at 40. Between 1973 and 1976, Rich would compile seven albums for Epic. But most of Epic's profits were made on the backs of arena rock bands that hadn't even peaked yet. Stephen Paley, dismayed by the label's keen interest in heavy metal and disco, arranged to work at home for a year, then left altogether. (For a while he would meld his job experiences by working as music advisor for the feature film divisions of Warners and Orion Pictures.) Gregg Geller transferred to Epic's Los Angeles office, salted away in a corner of the local CBS sales branch at the corner of Sunset and Cahuenga, in the Jolly Roger restaurant building. (Columbia's West Coast A&R office was housed in the old KNX radio building, down the street. The two offices would eventually move together to Century City, on L.A.'s West Side.) As head of West Coast A&R, Geller ran a staff of five. At this point a scorecard might help. Don Ellis, the Epic A&R chief for a few years, moved over to Columbia's LA office to run A&R there. From Black Rock, Ron Alexenburg, who'd previously run Epic Marketing, now assumed overall control of both Marketing and A&R for Epic. (Some observers suggested that he'd behaved as though he'd controlled both for years.) Alexenburg appointed Steve Popovich to run A&R nationally, which meant that Geller directly answered to Popovich.[79]

Before that structure shifted again, Geller heard the first stirrings of punk rock. It had been around for years in pierced, misshapen form, emerging out of England in the mid-1970s, kicking and wailing against corporately manufactured and distributed rock—the very product that Epic, among other major labels, was now peddling. From Los Angeles, Geller was intrigued. "I didn't know what I was missing at CBGB's," he said of one of New York's more punk-hospitable venues. (The letters CBGB stand for Country, Bluegrass, Blues.) But he knew that the scene in New York—fueled by the New York Dolls, the Stooges, Patti Smith, and the Talking Heads—was exploding with an energy that made L.A. sound stuffy.

It would be another couple of years before CBS Records, at either Columbia or Epic, tried to grab that energy. Meanwhile Epic's New York office passed on some homemade tapes that had been sent over the transom by a Polaroid product designer named Tom Scholz. The tapes were recorded in Scholz's basement on School Street in Watertown on a Scully twelve-track machine.[80] Epic said no—their rate of accepting music sent over the transom was about the same as that of the New Yorker buying a short story from the slush pile—as did several other labels.

Over the next few months, however, Scholz's tapes were heard by Charlie McKenzie and his partner, promotion man turned manager Paul Ahern. Scholz became their first management client, represented by renowned entertainment attorney Brian Rohan. Ahern knew the producer John Boylan from the days when he was working for Asylum and promoting its supergroup the Eagles, whose musicians Boylan had put together in the first place. Listening to Scholz's tapes, Boylan said to Ahern, "If you let anyone but me do that record, we are not friends anymore." Boylan got the producing job.

Boylan grew up in Buffalo, learning accordion and guitar early, and attended the State University of New York at Buffalo, majoring in theater. He joined the air force reserves in 1962. Returning to college at Bard, he played in a band called the Disciples. At one time or another the Disciples included Boylan's brother Terence, Chevy Chase, and Donald Fagen and Walter Becker (later to turn themselves into Steely Dan). A staff writing stint sent him to the West Coast to work with Rick Nelson. For years Nelson had enjoyed a string of rockabilly hits, but after his parents' show The Adventures of Ozzie and Harriet went off the air in the spring of 1966, Nelson lost his best advertising—and his musical direction. Boylan showed up the following year and introduced him to the loose collection of West Coast musicians that became the Stone Canyon Band. A strange amalgamation of Boylan's accordion- and guitar-playing and theater experience had refined his ear for stripped-down, quasi-country songs. After helping to revive Nelson's career, Boylan would become involved with the Association, Epic's band Poco, the seminal (and now undeservedly obscure) electric bluegrass band the Dillards, Michael Murphey, and Pure Prairie League, among many others. Located smack in the middle of that CV, Boylan's work with Scholz seems to be an anomaly. There was nothing country about Boston, the name Scholz and his fellow Boston-area musicians would take on only during the re-recording process.

Scholz's demo tapes were really okay, Boylan felt; the guitars were well recorded, but the other instruments didn't sound quite right. The tapes, now attached to a package that included Boylan as producer, went back to Epic—namely, to new director of East Coast A&R Lennie Petze. Like Alexenburg and Popovich (whom he replaced when Popovich left the company), the affable, moon-faced Petze came out of promotion. Whatever his other achievements during his tenure there, Petze's most significant might have been allowing himself to be cornered by Ahern and agreeing to listen to the tapes that Epic had already turned down. Petze, persuaded and enthusiastic, signed Boston, which now had some work to do.

Backed by CBS Records's dime, Boylan checked into the Holiday Inn on Massachusetts Avenue in Boston. A recent NABET (National Association of Broadcast Employees and Technicians) deal, worked out with the major labels, demanded that all recording be done at a label's studio or use the label's technicians if the artist was within 250 miles.[81] To address the NABET restrictions, Boylan brought in a CBS-approved sound truck from Providence, Rhode Island, and sent a microphone into Scholz's basement for some re-recording, particularly of the drums. This was effective, as far as it went. But Scholz was never available during the day because he insisted on keeping his position at Polaroid, where he was working on the design of an instant movie camera. Boylan went to Los Angeles and, without Scholz but with the other musicians, recorded a few more tracks in Los Angeles. Brad Delp did the soaring, multitracked vocals. Subsequently, Scholz took a leave from Polaroid and joined Boylan there. Along with engineer Warren Dewey, who was actually on staff at nearby Capitol, they worked on the mix at Westlake Studios (Wilshire and Crescent Heights). Boylan took the remixed analog tapes to New York. Everyone listened again.

The Epic executives knew they had something big, though it wasn't quite like anything they'd put out before. Meanwhile, Ron Alexenburg took Boylan to lunch at "21" and told him that Gregg Geller wanted him on staff at Epic in Los Angeles. "I had never worked for a large company," Boylan wrote, "and I thought I'd like to find out if it gave me some security and more clout in the industry. I wanted to see if I could actually sign and produce acts and have a home for them automatically."[82] The maverick country-rock record-maker joined Epic as an A&R staff producer.

The album *Boston* would peak at number three and sell 6.5 million copies—by *Billboard*'s reckoning, the fastest-selling album ever—while the single "More Than a Feeling" peaked at number five. According to Boylan, the album cost $28,000 to produce.[83] Twenty-three years after its inception, Epic had distributed an album that could truly be called a monster.

• • •

Amid all this frenetic business and musical activity, what prompted national A&R head Steve Popovich to leave Epic Records was a complicated thing. Popovich had apprenticed under both Clive Davis and Ron Alexenburg. Popovich and Alexenburg were white Midwesterners who grew up with a special appreciation for black music without disdaining white artists. Both had become CBS Records vice presidents at 29. Both had spent time as itinerant promotion men, going from radio station to radio station pushing records they believed in. Referring to them as "two of the most dedicated men I've known in the music business," Davis wrote that "each gained a lot of weight from the constant snacking that tension and strange hours will induce. Steve's trademark after a while became a can of low-calorie Tab."[84] Popovich could be seen in the halls of CBS Records carrying a boom box so he could play tapes at a moment's notice. And with some of these bands, there wasn't a moment to lose.

For years Popovich and his wife Maureen lived in the Warwick Hotel, two blocks north of Black Rock on Sixth Avenue. It was convenient, not to say expensive. One day Alexenburg accompanied Popovich down to Freehold, New Jersey, and watched him buy a house on the spot. During the long daily commute to Manhattan, Popovich station-hopped, his car antenna picking up obscure channels, checking out the playlists.[85]

That arrangement didn't last long. Maureen disliked New Jersey. Popovich missed his mother, in Cleveland, and began to think about going home to be near her. Long worn out by the telephone and travel demands of a promotion man, he was now weary of the daily high dudgeon clashes at Black Rock. "Steve got tired of the shit," his future partner Stan Snyder said, "like Irving Azoff jumping on the desk screaming."[86] Then the example of Wild Cherry really turned his head.

In 1975 Wild Cherry, the reorganized white Pittsburgh rhythm and blues band named after the cough-drop flavor, began to play in local discos because the older R&B clubs had closed. The band was often exhorted to "Play that funky music"; the band's drummer added the self-deprecating tag "white boy." Cutting a record in New York without a record contract, Wild Cherry covered the Commodores's "I Feel Sanctified," with the B side containing their original "Play That Funky Music." Executives from several companies, including Epic, heard the record and shrugged. A few weeks later Popovich heard the same record and called the group's handlers, Belkin Productions, based in Cleveland, to sign them.[87]

"Play That Funky Music" hit the top of the *Billboard* charts the week of September 18, 1976. Its eminently danceable beat and cute lyric put it over on both AM and FM stations. Popovich was pleased for Epic and for the band, but he also couldn't help noticing how well the Belkins made out financially on the Wild Cherry record. If he went independent like the Belkins, Popovich reasoned, he'd be answering only to his own artists, not the corporation's, and he could do it from home.

So Cleveland International was born. Popovich built the company vaguely along the lines of Philadelphia International, the most prominent associated label at Epic. His partners were Stan Snyder (sales) and Sam Lederman (administration), each CBS Records veterans who would continue to be based in New York while Popovich headed the label from Ohio.

* * * *

Sam Lederman, the child of Holocaust survivors, grew up in New Jersey. In August 1970 he earned an MBA from New York University and almost immediately went to work at CBS Records as a financial analyst.[88] Learning the business, Lederman scurried between the Epic offices on the thirteenth floor of Black Rock to Columbia legal and A&R departments on the eleventh. John Hammond and attorney Walter Dean knew where every CBS Records body was buried—they'd buried some themselves—and were pleased to share what they knew. At some point in 1972, Lederman distributed an analysis he'd made showing CBS Records subsidizing Columbia Masterworks at a loss of $5 million per year. That drew a bristling lecture from Group president Goddard Lieberson, who had built Masterworks into the most respected record division in the world. Despite this political misstep, Lederman was promoted that year to A&R administration at Epic.

The following year Clive Davis was fired, and few people at CBS were happier about it than Stan Snyder.

Before becoming head of sales at Epic, Snyder had already logged tens of thousands of hours in the record business. A Fairfield County kid, he went to Yale, then joined the marines. A civilian again by 1963, Snyder went to work for a while at a custom pressing label. Then Bill Gallagher hired him at Columbia. Snyder spent two years in sales in the Boston area. When he returned to Yale for his five-year reunion, Snyder's class-mates were making lucrative careers at Wall Street brokerage houses and corporations like Proctor & Gamble; Snyder had to confess that he was selling records.[89] In 1968 Snyder was transferred to San Francisco. "It was like being on Mars," the ex-marine said of working there the year after the Summer of Love. Snyder got to know Don Ellis, then the man-ager of Discount Records in Berkeley; when CBS Records bought the entire Discount chain, Snyder recommended Ellis to Clive Davis. (Ellis would expand—and often not get credit for—pop A&R for both Epic and Columbia, and on both coasts, through the midseventies.) At the San Francisco office Snyder was assisted by two secretaries who had no self-consciousness about getting high at the office. "By 9:15, 9:30 in the morning, they were whacked out of their minds," Snyder said. Snyder gave them each thirty days' notice. One of them accepted the termina-tion because she couldn't get by without smoking weed. The other—Snyder remembers her name as Janelle—promised to drop acid "only on Friday nights" and get her work done, even, if necessary, straight. Janelle kept imploring Snyder to come see the band her boyfriend man-aged, which turned out to be led by Carlos Santana. Atlantic Records' Ahmet Ertegun was already sniffing around. To help her boss woo San-tana, Janelle threw a dinner party in which the featured course was pot-laced spaghetti. After a false start or two, Santana signed with Columbia Records.

Snyder was brought back to New York and, replacing outgoing sales head Don Englund, given an office at Epic. The micromanaging Clive Davis barely let him operate, though. The two men mixed poorly, and it probably had little to do with Davis being Harvard and Snyder being Yale. Davis did have a law degree, a strong sense of entitlement, and complete confidence in his own pop-attuned sensibility; Snyder was a former marine and streetwise salesman who loved Horace Silver and played a little jazz piano himself, and didn't care for the self-glorifica-tion of so many media executives. Whatever the sources of their antag-onism, Davis soon brought Jack Craigo in over Snyder and, for reasons known only to Davis, left Snyder out of any bonuses that were being handed out. "The day Clive Davis was fired was one of the happiest days of my life," Snyder said with a laugh at the extravagance of his own statement. The night after Irwin Segelstein was named to replace Davis as president of CBS Records, he and Snyder ran into each other at a midtown bar and talked for four hours. Several weeks later Segelstein handed Snyder a bonus check that made up for some of the empty paydays under Davis.

Still, if Snyder hadn't quite left his heart in San Francisco, it was no longer at Black Rock, either. Like Sam Lederman, he was intrigued by the possibilities presented by Popovich and Cleveland International. So both men were in. Snyder and Lederman took an office at 538 Madison Avenue.[90] Popovich, comfortably home again in Cleveland, did what he did best: listened, pursued the artists he responded to, and promoted the hell out of the finished product.

The first major Cleveland International act was Ronnie Spector. Her single, "Say Goodbye to Hollywood," was written by Billy Joel after he'd seen Martin Scorsese's Mean Streets and been knocked out by its period soundtrack, which kicked off with the Ronettes doing "Be My Baby." Ronnie Spector was backed by most of Bruce Springsteen's E Street Band. It was a daring beginning, if not a profitable one. This was the middle of 1977. Walter Yetnikoff's wildman reign as Group president had just begun. Epic Records had not yet reached its twenty-fifth anniversary. Its deal with Cleveland International wasn't the first time it had gone into business with its own refugees—Dave Kapralik, among others, had made similar deals with Epic—but it would prove to be the most surprising.

* * *

By 1977 The Rocky Horror Picture Show, released two years earlier, was becoming a cult classic. Meat Loaf's appearance in it as the sweaty, trolllike Eddie had thousands of moviegoers shouting back at him at each screening. His was a recording career waiting to explode. The explosion came at a time when disco, as Stephen Paley had predicted several years earlier, had become the national musical currency. If disco's shake-and-spin rhythms weren't for you, or you couldn't relate to what was essentially a black dance culture commodified by whites—or, just as crucially, if the serrated blade of punk rock didn't draw blood—well, Meat Loaf might be your man.

Born September 27, 1947, in Dallas, Meat Loaf was the son of Orvis Wesley Aday, a Dallas policeman who knew Jack Ruby.[91] According to Meat Loaf, the surname is probably a corruption of O'Day. By the late sixties the burly son was calling himself Meat Loaf and fronting bands in and around Los Angeles. After he'd gone to the Aquarius Theater in Hollywood to check out a parking lot job, he lucked into a (clothed) role in *Hair* at the Aquarius Theater. That led to an appearance in co-librettist Jim Rado's next show, *Rainbow*, in New York. Meat Loaf auditioned for Jim Steinman, who was looking for a singer to carry his show *More Than You Deserve*. (Much of this activity took place in and around Joseph Papp's New York Shakespeare Festival Public Theater.)[92] If it wasn't quite Burt Bacharach finding his Dionne Warwick, it was still a match. Steinman's songs were highly styled, self-involved narratives that were fuel-injected without really being danceable. Meat Loaf's strong suit wasn't his rhythm anyway, but his low-center-of-gravity baying. He looked like a former Longhorn lineman but sounded like a choirboy on uppers.

This pop music version of Oscar Madison and Felix Unger attacked the songs Steinman had written for his *Peter Pan*–inspired musical *Never Land*. Much of the material that became *Bat Out of Hell* grew out of this show. Todd Rundgren, based in New York like Meat Loaf and Steinman and at the peak of his musical influence, became interested in the *Bat* project. Initially, Rundgren was under the impression, fertilized by Meat Loaf and Steinman, that the pair was signed to RCA Victor.[93] Rundgren took the Steinman–Meat Loaf tapes to Bearsville, New York, and began to fiddle with them. Like Stevie Wonder, Rundgren had taught himself to play practically every instrument in the studio and knew his way around the control panel.[94] He added his own distinctive, stinging guitar solo on the song "Bat Out of Hell" in just one take and, in general, made the

Bat Out of Hell numbers only more compelling. So he was surprised to learn that RCA had no involvement with the material. Jimmy Iovine remixed some numbers and brought in John Jansen to help remix "Bat Out of Hell" and "Paradise on the Dashboard Light." Steinman had conceived "Paradise," which recounts a nocturnal, stop-time teenage seduction in a car, as being narrated by a play-by-play announcer. The natural choice for the announcer was the Yankees' Phil Rizzuto, whose narration added some much-needed humor. Rizzuto's agent Art Shamsky conveyed his client's concern that people would have to get stoned to listen to the record.[95] Well, yes and no.

Meanwhile Albert Grossman, who owned Rundgren's label Bearsville, deemed the record too costly to produce. At Warner Brothers, music president Mo Ostin said yes, but his authoritative A&R chief Lenny Waronker was repulsed by the band's in-office performance, which included Meat Loaf ostentatiously making out with singer Ellen Foley during the long "Paradise" number.[96]

Warners wasn't the only label to say no to the finished tapes. Lennie Petze at Epic simply didn't get it. Other labels passed. With ingredients from Steinman, Rundgren, and Meat Loaf, *Bat Out of Hell* was a curious concoction. Meat and Steinman's manager, David Sonenberg—"Harvard Law," said Sam Lederman, "a sharp, good-looking kid"—got Steve Van Zandt (of the E Street Band) to call Steve Popovich at Cleveland International. Van Zandt told Popovich that "You Took the Words Right Out of My Mouth," one of the more bombastic songs in the *Bat Out of Hell* cycle, had "the best intro in the history of pop music."[97] For what worked on the airwaves, Popovich may have owned the most sensitive feelers in the business. Steinman and Meat Loaf signed with Cleveland International, now an associated label of Epic Records. Lennie Petze had already rejected the tapes, but Ron Alexenburg overrode him.

That's when Arnold Levine went to work on *Bat*. Years earlier, after observing his immediate boss Bob Cato assemble slide presentations, Levine proposed using film to advertise Columbia artists. "All right, *you* do it," Clive Davis told him. Levine was trained as an artist, not a filmmaker. He picked up a movie camera and, through trial and error, taught himself how to shoot film. Around 1970 Levine made a 16mm film showing Bob Dylan; Earth, Wind & Fire; and other CBS Records artists lip-synching to their own music. The sales department's enthusiastic reaction to this first film convinced Clive Davis this could be a viable sales tool. For subsequent films Levine needed help, so he hired Stephen Verona, who would eventually become a feature film director (*The Lords of Flatbush*). These short films ended up as clips in a Fairchild machine, with a cartridge that configured the films into a loop, to be played over and over again in record stores. (Columbia retained rights to the clips and cartridges.)

Under Davis's patronage, Levine kept experimenting. The pre-MTV, let's-give-it-a-shot relationship culminated in late spring 1973 during a week at the Ahmanson Theater in Los Angeles. Filming 21 CBS Records artists over seven nights—three acts per night—Levine persuaded Davis to allow him to shoot it for television broadcast. Davis was already working on a narration that would glue the segments together when he was summoned back to New York. By May 29, the Tuesday after Memorial Day, Davis was out.

"I went a little crazy without Clive," Levine said. "Clive was the only one who knew what we were doing." Levine finished shooting and went back to New York with his footage. Davis, demonized for questionable business expenses and now the object of long pent-up scorn from many colleagues, was edited right out of the Ahmanson films. Levine said that the CBS Records executives "wanted the films to show *their* interests, not Clive's. The compiled films had no narration, just music. And they never aired."

Four years later Levine filmed Meat Loaf, in a Chelsea studio and in a graveyard in upstate New York, for *Bat Out of Hell*. They were creating some of the earliest examples of music videos. Given his advertising background, Levine wondered if a product (the video), sold as a separate entity and with its own artistic slant, could sell another product (the record). A television commercial, no matter how ingenious it might be, was created and then aired specifically to sell its sponsor's product; who knew what impact a music video would have? The show *Popclips*, conceived by Michael Nesmith and hosted by Howie Mandel, was still three years into the future, the advent of MTV another year after that.[98] Levine had made four *Bat* videos for $28,000.

• • •

Bat Out of Hell still had a long way to go to succeed. Jim Steinman had written all the songs in his peculiar style and saw himself, naturally, as Meat Loaf's full partner in the album. Concerned how the cover would look, Steinman even wanted something along the lines of *Heavy Metal*, a magazine he was inordinately fond of. Meat Loaf and David Sonenberg, who managed Steinman as well as Meat Loaf, had a different view. The cover would make it Meat Loaf's album, with a tag at the bottom: *With Songs by Jim Steinman*. "I thought it was going to be Meat Loaf and Jim Steinman," the songwriter said plaintively to Sonenberg.[99] According to Meat Loaf's memoir, it was Cleveland International's "marketing" division, whatever that was, that dictated the title *Meat Loaf, Bat Out of Hell*.[100]

The album was released by Epic in the fall of 1977, within a week of Columbia's release of Billy Joel's *The Stranger*.[101] At first it seemed to be a case of stolen thunder. Joel's album included the songs "Movin' Out," "Just the Way You Are," "Only the Good Die Young," and "She's Always a Woman." With that lineup it practically promoted itself. Produced by Phil Ramone, *The Stranger*, first charting the week of October 8, sold more records more quickly than any CBS Records album up till then. The Columbia guys loved it. On the other hand, a number of Epic executives, including those in the now critical areas of sales and promotion, simply couldn't stand *Bat Out of Hell*.

A tour was a must. Ellen Foley, whose vocals on the album were essential to its sound (and who would become a Cleveland International recording artist on her own), was deemed, for one reason or another, not right for the tour and replaced by Karla DeVito. Meat Loaf was assigned by Epic to open in Chicago for Cheap Trick, whose fans tried to boo him off the stage.[102] To keep an eye on the numbers, Stan Snyder traveled with the tour. "In Tulsa, KMOD claimed to be pounding the album. Meat Loaf opened there for the Epic band Crawler. Something like forty-seven people showed up. I called Popovich and said, 'Nobody came. We're done.'" The dismal turnout would have been familiar to any artist and his handlers, but this was particularly wounding because Epic's sales people were already so skeptical. Backstage after the show, Snyder came across Meat Loaf with his arm around Steinman, going on about how it was just the two of them against the world, it always would be, and you could never trust the record company to come through. Snyder, exhausted by the road and missing his family, finally lost his temper. "Come on outside, you fat fuck," baited Snyder, taller than Meat Loaf but half as wide, "and we'll settle this thing right now!" Meat Loaf, according to Snyder, claimed he was misunderstood, and apologized.[103]

Relationships are strengthened in their repair. Meat Loaf continued to promote the record on the road, and Snyder stayed close by. Bat was selling well in New York, Epic's hometown, and in Cleveland, the associated label's hometown and, by common consent, an unbeatable rock 'n' roll city. But that's about all. Never mind comparison to Billy Joel's The Stranger, the Meat Loaf–Steinman–Rundgren record was in the doldrums.

Then the wind came up. Popovich (who only incidentally carried the same chunky, sweaty, longhaired mien as his artist) couldn't get Arnold Levine's videos played on Top of the Pops, the premiere music show on British television, but landed them on The Old Grey Whistle Stop, an underground variation. The response was instantaneous. Bat Out of Hell began to sell in the UK, in Canada, and especially in Australia, where it outsold local stars the Bee Gees even in their Saturday Night Fever phase.[104] Then, throughout Europe, at halftime of an important soccer match played in the Netherlands (Holland would subsequently lose the World Cup to Argentina), television viewers changed the channel and found Levine's Bat videos roaring before them. Even diehard soccer fans were reluctant to turn them off.[105]

The 1978 CBS Records convention was held in New Orleans in January. Walter Yetnikoff, as Group president, ran the show, which included label artists Billy Joel, Elvis Costello, Cheap Trick, Mother's Finest, and

Ted Nugent. Ron Alexenburg told Meat Loaf he'd be performing, too, even though *Bat Out of Hell* was still considered a disappointment. Sitting with Snyder in the back of the auditorium while another band performed for the CBS people, Meat Loaf turned to him and said, "Tomorrow night I'm gonna destroy this place." Next night Meat Loaf sang Steinman's "Crying Out Loud." When it was over, the place was silent for a few seconds—an eternity, in Meat Loaf's memory. Then the place erupted. Meat Loaf followed it up with "Johnny B. Goode." The same CBS sales people who'd sneered at him were now, according to him, dancing on the tables. Only Janis Joplin, Meat Loaf was told later, had caused such a ruckus at a CBS Records convention.[106]

By September 1978 *Bat* had gone double platinum. Epic claimed that royalties couldn't be paid yet, to Cleveland International or to Meat Loaf and Steinman, because the record was still in the hole. *Cross-collateralization* was the obfuscating industry term meaning that all recording costs, including the costs of the *Bat* national tour, had to be recouped before the first dime was paid. The relationship between Meat Loaf and Steinman, under pressure for more than a year, finally boiled over. Cocaine only made Meat Loaf's temperature hotter.

Epic finally knew what it had, though. Unlike Columbia, it had been financially manacled by its shallow catalog; now it had several albums that could serve as annuities. Although CBS Records and Cleveland International would go head to head in the coming years over the conjoined issues of logos and royalties, the parent company was willing to renegotiate terms. At Black Rock, Sam Lederman sat down with Yetnikoff. In one of his more sober, lawyerly moments, Yetnikoff warned Lederman, who knew most CBS Records contracts as he knew his own handwriting, that there were three artists he couldn't refer to. "You can't aspire to these three deals," Yetnikoff said, because the publishing and album royalty terms of these artists were considered unique. The first was Barbra Streisand, who had been a CBS Records artist for more than fifteen years, had always seemed to know what she wanted, no matter who the producer was, and always made money. Fair enough, Lederman thought. The second was Paul McCartney, less because he was a Beatle and among the most famous people in the world than because he was represented by his brother-in-law John Eastman, the son of Columbia's first attorney, Lee Eastman. Lederman didn't think much of this prohibition but went along with it. The third was the deal negotiated for Philadelphia International—hugely successful for Epic and CBS, Lederman admitted, but nowhere near its earning power of 1972–74. "Why? Because they're black?" said Lederman, referring to Philadelphia's principals, Kenny Gamble and Leon Huff. Yetnikoff nodded. Lederman knew this was Yetnikoff's way of short-circuiting an exorbitant leap in royalty terms, and Yetnikoff knew that Lederman knew.

In the midst of renegotiating Cleveland International's deal, Lederman was pacing the halls of Black Rock when he bumped into Dick Asher, then running CBS International and an old hand at the peculiar art of signing artists. "What's wrong?" said Asher. Lederman recounted his renegotiation headaches, all of them predicated on Meat Loaf's success with Bat Out of Hell, emphasizing how well the album had done all over the world for Epic. Asher listened for a few minutes, then leaned down and said, "You guys think you're hot shit? Ever hear of a guy named Julio Iglesias?"[107] He laughed. A CBS International artist, Iglesias flew below the radar of most American record producers and executives, but he outsold practically everybody, year after year, in over a hundred countries. Lederman, humbled, laughed too.

●   ●   ●

Epic had had a lot to prove. And, from the roses-are-red serenading of Bobby Vinton to the more self-referential priapism of Meat Loaf, it proved it. How far, it must have seemed, pop music had come in a quarter century. How far Epic Records had come! But nature, including human nature, moves from the unspoiled to the spoiled, from innocence to corruption, not the other way around. Hearing bad boys of the seventies like Meat Loaf from the distance of three decades, they too now sound innocent. Staying on the charts for an extraordinary eighty-two weeks, Bat Out of Hell brought Epic into a jowly, spoiled middle age.

In that same period, Epic had another strange, nocturnal creature on its hands—less a bat out of hell than one trapped in a farmhouse after dawn. When the slick, abundantly confident Ron Alexenburg brought the Jacksons to the label in 1976, their adolescent star-child Michael exhibited an almost rabid energy. In the next few years he would transform himself, gradually but inexorably, into something of a vampire, ravishing various musical styles faster than he could digest them. "Michael's got a lot to learn from Stevie Wonder," observed the New England Conservatory professor Ran Blake, "and Stevie's got a lot to learn from Al Green, who's got a lot to learn from Robert Johnson."[108] Blake made the remark in March 1983, three months after Epic released Michael Jackson's *Thriller*, which would become the best-selling album in history.

21
Explosions and Elegies

By the beginning of the 1970s, Columbia's international division also became more critical to worldwide sales. Goddard Lieberson had set this in motion shortly after the advent of the LP, when the importing and exporting of records became more feasible (lightweight disks, air shipping, etc.) as well as desirable. For years Lieberson and Harvey Schein had placed Columbia's representatives in various nations, preferring nationals who knew the culture as well as the language, but not averse to using men who were already with the company. Ettore Stratta, who had been an adroit musicals producer for Columbia Records (including the Yiddish version of *Fiddler on the Roof*), was a key roving A&R man in its international operations. Sol Rabinowitz, who had been assigned to international A&R in New York though it was really a sales position, would depart the label and then return, at the behest of Dick Asher, to set up shop in Athens. Rabinowitz took a three-week Berlitz course in Greek and went out searching for talent. One of his early international finds was Joe Dassin, a French folksinger and son of the blacklisted American film director Jules Dassin. But he found himself spending just as much time placating the Greeks, who feared and resented CBS's international power and often spoke of Rabinowitz as if he were a CIA field agent. Nevertheless, during that period Columbia and its labels had a particularly strong international roster of artists and projects: the great Brazilian guitarist Bola Sete; Tommy Makem and the Clancy Brothers, from Ireland; the Theodorakis soundtrack from Z., from Greece; the pretty Veronese singer Gigliola Cinquetti; and Momoe Yamaguchi, who'd been discovered in her native Japan in a talent contest when she was 13. Bombay-born Asha Puthli grew up hearing jazz on the *Voice of America*. In New York, where she had a scholarship to dance with Martha Graham, she introduced herself to the *New Yorker* writer Ved Mehta, who sent her to John Hammond. On that first album, *Asha Puthli*, she worked with Elton John's producer Del Newman. Teo Macero produced her second CBS album, which proved to be especially popular in Germany.[1] These were all international artists who sold at least as many records internationally as domestically.

In September 1970, though, a bomb was lobbed from overseas that had the effect of a terrorist attack on Black Rock. From his apartment in London's Park Lane, Ken Glancy called CBS International president Harvey Schein to say he was resigning to take over the reins at RCA in London.[2] Glancy had been working without a contract, which enabled him to jump over to RCA immediately—though not before waiting for Schein himself to appear in London to learn how Glancy's operation there had worked. Overnight, the balance of power in the UK's record industry shifted. Glancy had built Columbia Records's UK operation from a fallow patch of dirt into a blooming garden. Joined by Maida Schwartz after each had broken free from their first marriages, Glancy had gracefully accepted his exile five years earlier and immersed himself in London's cultural life. "Ken Glancy was a giant in the business," Tom Shepard said, "a man's man, a rainmaker who could attract composers and producers. People trusted Goddard and they also trusted Ken." In back of their second home in the South of France, Maida once found Ken sitting on a chaise with a scotch in his hand, a cigar in his mouth, and a Count Basie tape coming through the headphones. "You're in heaven, aren't you?" she said to him.[3] Glancy was neither a musician nor a record producer, but in his quiet way he loved musical artists and was loved by them in turn. It would be only a matter of time before Horowitz, now disgruntled by his treatment at Columbia, would return to RCA, due almost entirely to Glancy's presence there. Other artists would follow. If it wasn't quite like Jack Kapp leaving Brunswick for Decca 35 years earlier, it was still a devastating defection for Columbia.

• • •

Glancy left the company during a period when every week seemed to show a brand new dent in the old culture—a collision of forces that had been revved up years earlier. Throughout America the changes were evident each night on news broadcasts when cameras went right into the jungles and villages of Vietnam. In New York, fashions were more daring than ever. Pornography was not only out in the open but routinely advertised in most of the major metropolitan newspapers.

One day in January 1971, jazz critic Martin Williams called Teo Macero to tell him that a skin flick playing at the Orleans Theater in New York was using Miles Davis music on the soundtrack. "I personally have not seen the film entitled *History of the Blue Movie*," Macero wrote to Walter Dean. "Do you think we should check this out? Please advise."[4] Even a porno movie had to obtain rights from the copyright owner to use no more than a few seconds of Miles's music. Suddenly half the executives at the label were volunteering to monitor the movie—all for the company's benefit, of course. CBS Records counsel Herb Trossman was dispatched to see it and concluded there were no contemporary CBS pieces in it. "I'm curious. What was Herb's reaction?" some wag at the label wrote, then circled *curious* and wrote, "Yellow or blue?"[5]

In the sixties, as Vietnam and rock 'n' roll threatened to put Ray Conniff's music out to pasture, he had remade himself by giving live amplified stereo concerts, his singing group carefully arranged for maximum stereo effect, and by putting out one album after another featuring reliably blond cover girls. By 1970 Conniff's Columbia albums had become so indispensable to retro-inclined, middle-of-the-road record buyers that he turned out to be a favorite even of Richard Nixon. In January 1972 Conniff and his Singers were invited to the White House to sing for the President, the First Lady, and the honored guests, Mr. and Mrs. DeWitt Wallace, founders of *Reader's Digest*. A recently hired Conniff Singer named Carol Feraci, a 30-year-old Canadian whose wholesome looks could have placed her in Atlantic City in front of Bert Parks, stepped forward to hold up a sign that read *Stop the Killing!* Looking directly at Nixon, who was seated only twenty feet away, she asked him how he could go on bombing humans, animals, and vegetation. Conniff, overwhelmed by cries of "Throw her out!," quietly told her it would be best for her to leave. Escorted out of the White House, Feraci bravely declined to apologize and referred to herself as "an oobie-doobie girl," her vocals for Conniff evoking the pre-rock, pre-Vietnam era.[6] The episode recalled Eartha Kitt's antiwar outspokenness at the White House four years earlier, when Mr. and Mrs. Lyndon Johnson were still in residence. Thirty years later, with another (but perhaps not so different) war at hand, Columbia Records's the Dixie Chicks were said to have betrayed their largely conservative constituency with equal antiwar fervor. Kitt and the Dixie Chicks answered only to themselves, however (if not also to their respective record labels), while Feraci answered to Conniff. Her courageous outburst was an embarrassment to Conniff, who was not conservative so much as Establishment, a musical representative of a culture that was beginning to look downright imperialistic.

●　●　●

Though little of it could be still called Establishment, pop music was more profitable than ever. Wherever they came from, Clive Davis wanted hits. Some of these, like Andy Williams's rendition of the "Theme from *Love Story*" (released February 1971), came from artists who'd been with the label for many years. But most of the hits came from the artists who'd been recently signed—some of them poached from other companies, earning Davis a fair amount of scorn. In the 1950s and early 60s, the label was proud of the fact that it didn't aggressively court artists who had contracts at other labels. But part of Davis's plan was to plunder when he needed to, so he embarked, he wrote, "on the heaviest talent-raiding campaign ever conducted in the history of the music business."[7]

Meanwhile there were several profitable artists already in place. Blood, Sweat & Tears and Chicago continued their streak. Ray Price's third Columbia album, *For the Good Times*, charted as high as number twenty-three, the title song written by Kris Kristofferson and the album produced by Don Law, who was still part of the Columbia family after nearly forty years. (Law had recorded Robert Johnson in 1936.) Simon & Garfunkel's *Bridge over Troubled Waters* was the number one album in the country for ten weeks and would practically sweep the Grammys—by any reckoning, an extraordinary way to end a partnership. At Columbia Records, Paul Revere and the Raiders went back just as far as Simon & Garfunkel, and though their single "Indian Reservation" and the album of the same name didn't approach *Bridge*'s numbers, it was a good showing for the label's earliest rock 'n' roll band.

Out of Nashville, Lynn Anderson's "I Never Promised You a Rose Garden" single and the *Rose Garden* album were both enormous successes in 1971; Joe South, who'd played on Dylan's *Blonde on Blonde* and recorded for Capitol, wrote the song. Anderson was married to Glenn Sutton, a veteran songwriter who took over as Tammy Wynette's producer from Billy Sherrill. Mining Nashville as much as possible, in 1971 CBS acquired the rights to distribute Monument Records, its catalog including Roy Orbison. (Monument would soon break from CBS, then come back, then go out of business altogether in the mid-1980s.) Mac Davis scored with "Baby, Don't Get Hooked on Me," another single whose annoying self-regard belied its craft. It was tempting to dismiss Davis's songwriting because of the cowboy poses and high-wattage smile, but he'd written "In the Ghetto" and "Don't Cry Daddy," both recorded by Elvis Presley, and never seemed to lack confidence in his own work.

Loggins & Messina were formed in 1971, a duo very much in the family: Kenny Loggins's brother Danny was a valued member of Columbia Records UK, while Jim Messina had played with the Epic group Poco. For the next five years Loggins & Messina would release several albums that were as warm and breezy as a day at the beach. Boz Scaggs, a singer with roots in the Southwest, was already well known as a former member of the Steve Miller Band when he moved over from Atlantic Records and made *My Time*. It was the first of half a dozen stylish albums that showcased Scaggs's unique mixture of soul and cabaret. Jon Mark and Johnny Almond brought their jazz-inflected rock to the label in 1972. The semiannual Blood, Sweat & Tears and Chicago entries kept selling steadily. By the middle of 1972, Chicago was viewed by competitors as such a powerful franchise, with a brand name no less commercial than McDonald's or Taco Bell, that Warners released an artists' sampler titled Burbank, the cover spoofing the Berg-Fasciano typeface for Chicago.

In England the young actor-singer David Essex, who played Jesus Christ in the musical Godspell to almost hysterical adolescent acclaim, was already being courted by Columbia, though his hit "Rock On" wouldn't be released for another eighteen months. In the summer of 1971 Columbia released Ten Years After's A Space in Time, the British band's most popular album. Danny Loggins signed Mott the Hoople to CBS Records, and soon the band's "All the Young Dudes" encapsulated the strutting, insouciant, London music scene, with David Bowie as its current avatar. The band wasn't quite a precursor to the punk bands that were just beginning to stir—it was too theatrical, too dependent on money—but it was openly derisive about music that had no grit, even if the music was distributed by its own label. On their first Columbia-sponsored tour, in Rhode Island, Mott the Hoople opened for Columbia artist John McLaughlin, whose spiritual life so informed his guitar-playing that the concert hall was usually transformed into a temple. Though many critics regarded McLaughlin as one of the best guitarists in contemporary pop music, Mott's lead singer Ian Hunter was unimpressed, instead likening McLaughlin to a zombie, his music tuneless and formless. "The songs start in the middle and end in the middle," Hunter wrote, "but the kids loved it."[8] In England Mott the Hoople got strong support from Dick Asher, then running CBS Records UK. Hunter's thorough disgust with Columbia's career-building did prefigure the punks', however, and comes through loudly:

> O.K., so you've recorded, mixed and cut. Next stop the processing department of the record company you work for. An average working guy who doesn't even know you doctors up the final master disc and sticks it into the press. This master is the gear that makes the ruts in the record and a bit of shit or some other technical hassle can fuck up some

5,000 albums before you even know it. All the group press is geared to a certain date line. Adverts in the musical papers, interviews, radio plugs, TV appearances, etc. So the company has to let these 5,000 shitty copies into the shops.[9]

Back in New York, Columbia Records still went all out for Taj Mahal (birth name: Henry St. Clair Fredericks), who'd been with the label since 1968 and would have received more attention for his *Sounder* soundtrack if the film had drawn a larger audience. In 1972 Earth, Wind & Fire came over from Warners for a series of beautifully crafted albums that the label knew how to handle.

• • •

So CBS Records appeared to be in decent shape. Clive Davis had done what he'd set out to do—to transform the label's more traditional tone and drag it into the world of contemporary pop music. "Clive Davis still doesn't get credit for everything he did," Ron Alexenburg said.[10] In a few months a brand-new payola scandal would surface at the label, with outside and in-house investigations launched, and the very meaning of payola—what kind of gift and how much cash constitutes payola and, even if you can prove it, what's the big deal?—debated all over again. Before the payola questions came to a head, however, Black Rock was rife with old-fashioned palace intrigue. Davis was king, Lieberson having been bloodlessly deposed and exiled to a castle up north. Financially, of course, Lieberson wasn't hurting. In 1972 he owned 42,794 shares of CBS common stock, worth just under $2 million; his basic salary was $130,000, with $120,000 in bonuses.[11] He was also deeply involved in preliminary negotiations regarding Kawai instruments, with Sony as its partner, and he was cautious: "The whole question of Kawai bothers me until all the facts and figures are in," he wrote in May 1972. "So far, no musical instrument man with manufacturing expertise or indeed no one with what I call musical knowledge (perhaps excepting Ohga) or music instrument market feeling has visited Kawai and made a survey of its inventories."[12] (The Kawai deal, including Sony as partner, went through the following year.) For those who knew how Lieberson had revolutionized the recording industry, however, how he had delighted employees and dining companions with his epigrammatic wit and how he was capable of lending support to the lowliest employee, his occasional supplicatory tone toward Davis could be cringe-inducing. In a June 1972 memo to Clive Davis, after Richard Rodgers's secretary had returned two tickets to attend Leonard Bernstein's Mass, Lieberson wrote, "Enclosed is a self-explanatory letter from Richard Rodgers. As you perhaps know, Mrs Rodgers has been very ill and he is not going out much except during the day. If you don't mind I would like to keep the two tickets he sent in since I can use them. I assume this is OK with you." (Davis returned the memo after writing in the margin "Certainly. Clive.")[13]

At the 1972 Columbia Records convention, in London, Davis cut Lieberson, whose position as unofficial toastmaster had gone unchallenged for two decades, right out of the ceremonies. Lieberson wasn't pleased. Much of the Columbia Records staff had been overhauled since his presidency, however, and many of the label's newer employees weren't aware of Lieberson's unmatched legacy.

Lieberson tended to keep his fires banked, but executive changes at CBS probably inflamed them. Near the top of Black Rock, as of 1971, Dr. Stanton was out, replaced first by Charles Ireland, who had been a vice president and chief financial officer at International Telephone & Telegraph. After eight months on the job, Ireland suffered a fatal heart attack, and Paley brought in 37-year-old Arthur Taylor.[14] On July 12, 1972, only five days after agreeing to take the job, Taylor was elected president and a director of CBS, and assumed his responsibilities at the end of that month. Before he'd worked at International Paper, Taylor had spent nine years at First Boston. Paley liked his credentials: honors at Brown, Phi Beta Kappa, member of the Council on Foreign Relations, a solid WASP family man.

As head of the international record division, Walter Yetnikoff humored Taylor, whom he claimed to like. But Clive Davis was openly hostile to him. In five years Clive had managed not only to elbow Lieberson aside but often to get more press than the label's artists, and now he had to answer to this interloper, resenting Taylor's presumption that he knew anything at all about the record business. It probably didn't help that Taylor was slightly younger, projected an image that Paley likened (however delusionally) to his younger self, played a decent game of tennis, and, perhaps most galling to of all to Davis, was fluent in Hebrew.[15]

In October Davis gave his son a bar mitzvah at the Plaza Hotel. Skitch Henderson's orchestra played. Davis's lieutenant Dave Wynshaw was one of Henderson's closest friends, and it's likely that Wynshaw made the arrangements. A preponderant number of lavish bar mitzvahs are less for the child's coming of age—the commencement of religious and ethical responsibilities—than for his or her parents and parents' friends. The Davis bar mitzvah was no different, just on a grander scale. The guest list included many executives from the recording industry. It's possible, maybe even likely, that William Paley and CBS, Inc. would have picked up the tab if the ceremony had been posed as a business expense.

In the winter of 1972, CBS Records people began to be asked, quietly and surreptitiously, about Davis. One afternoon John Berg was called into Lieberson's office. "We were chitting and chatting," Berg said, "and I wondered where the hell this was going. No subject came up. Finally a subject came up. What do I think of Clive? I said, 'You want to hear what I really think of Clive? Because I'll put my job on the line by telling you.' He said, 'Yes, don't worry about it.' So I told him everything I could deal with. Basically, most of what I told him was about the credit that Clive would take for other people's work. For Goddard's work. For taking the staff, the top guys, out to Monterey. It was Goddard that did that."[16]

●　●　●

In the spring of 1973, Clive Davis appeared to have 12 or 13 fingers, each one poised over a different deal. Two years earlier he had made a deal with Neil Diamond that wasn't to go into effect until 1973—and then it would bear out Davis's faith in Diamond. The deal that was the most immediately critical to him involved the pianist-singer-songwriter Billy Joel, a Long Island boy who, though still in his early twenties, had been around for a while in both New York and Los Angeles. Joel had already made four albums (one of them, in fact, with his short-lived band Attila for Epic) when Columbia executives heard him at the Mary Sol Festival in Puerto Rico in the spring of 1972. They'd gone to monitor Columbia artists Dave Brubeck and the Mahavishnu Orchestra (John McLaughlin) when they heard this kid doing impressions of several singers, the wildest of which was Joe Cocker's spastic attack on "Mad Dogs and Englishmen."[17] Becky Shargo, who had heard Joel play in Kansas City—Shargo would become a key figure for Epic in the 1970s before moving to Los Angeles—also told her boss Kip Cohen about Joel. Joel's producer, Artie Ripp, was then negotiating a deal with Atlantic, widely regarded as the hippest label going; but Joel wanted to be with Dylan's label. After Cohen and Ripp opened negotiations, Cohen arranged for Joel's manager Irwin Mazur to meet Clive Davis in the lobby of the Beverly Hills Hotel. That was the deal Davis was most interested in making when he was called back to Black Rock.

Joel didn't disappoint. His early hit "Piano Man," the title song from his first Columbia album, was a comically self-pitying condensation of his tenure playing at the Executive Lounge, on Roscoe Boulevard in Panorama City.[18] *Piano Man* and *Street Life Serenade* were recorded in North Hollywood. "New York State of Mind" was written when he and his family moved back to New York, specifically Highland Falls, from Los Angeles, but *Turnstiles*, the album that included it, sold only moderately. (Streisand made a profitable version of the song for Columbia, though the best version—the most New York, that is—surely is by Ben Sidran.) *The Stranger* was recorded under the aegis of fabled New York–based producer Phil Ramone, and the album flew across the land like a scientifically engineered Frisbee. "Only the Good Die Young," "Movin' Out," "She's Always a Woman," "My Life," and "Just the Way You Are" were all cut into those grooves.[19]

Before Billy Joel's star rose so high, though, the Clive Davis drama was being played out, beginning Tuesday, May 29, 1973, the day after the Memorial Day Weekend.

"I'll never forget that day as long as I live," Sam Lederman said. Davis's longtime assistant Octavia Bennett called around. "There's no meeting today," she told the executives. Ron Alexenburg knew something was up because Davis was supposed to be in Los Angeles, and here he was in the building on 52nd Street. When the call came summoning him to the thirty-fifth floor, Alexenburg ran across the street to the Hotel Americana to buy himself a necktie. "Kip Cohen was one of the people called up there," Lederman recalled, referring to the young vice president of pop A&R. "He had to borrow my jacket." In the thirty-fifth floor conference room Alexenburg sat between the two Walters, Yetnikoff and Dean, and whispered that he thought Clive was about to be fired.

In fact he already had been. Arthur Taylor introduced Irwin Segelstein as the new president of CBS Records. Segelstein, the television network's number two programmer, had gotten the call the previous night while he was sitting at "21" drinking with CBS vice president Oscar Katz.[20] CBS, already bloodied from the slings and arrows of the Newark investigation, was trying to stanch the bleeding by bringing in Segelstein immediately. It was a good choice, too, because, although Segelstein knew next to nothing about the record business, he was ethically unassailable.

Davis, meanwhile, twisted in the wind. In the memoir he published a year later, he recounted the humiliation and loneliness of his termination day. Lieberson, having suffered Davis's condescension, wasn't inclined to come to his rescue. Lieberson said to friends, "The trouble with Clive Davis was that he thought he was me."[21]

On May 29, just an hour or two before Davis saw the TV news report of his own dismissal, CBS sent out a memo and press release, signed by Paley, to Officers and Department Heads of CBS, Groups, Divisions and Subsidiaries. The press release was carefully crafted to show that CBS was taking care of its own:

Columbia Broadcasting System, Inc. has discharged Clive J. Davis, President of the CBS/Records Group since July 1971, and has commenced action in Supreme Court, New York County, charging Davis with improper use of company funds.

The appointment of Goddard Lieberson, a CBS director and Senior Vice President, as President of the CBS/Records Group is announced today by William S. Paley, Chairman of the Board of the Corporation. Simultaneously, Mr Paley announces that Irwin Segelstein, a Vice President of the CBS Television Network, has been appointed President of the CBS Records Division, one of the Group's two divisions; the other is the CBS Records International Division, headed by Walter Yetnikoff.[22]

Yetnikoff had been named president of International in 1971, a decade after joining the record label. Segelstein had begun his career in 1947 at Benton & Bowles and risen to vice president in charge of programming there before moving to CBS. The memo closed with surgically worded encouragement: "To this let me add a further note in behalf of Arthur Taylor, our President, as well as myself: We have every expectation that the great momentum our records business has been experiencing will not only continue but will gather force in the months ahead."

The reasons for Davis's dismissal were confusing because there were so many factors in play, including Taylor's zealousness regarding expenditures that Frank Stanton probably would have shrugged off.

Davis . . . was specifically charged in the presentment submitted to the Supreme Court of the State of New York, County of New York, with the following complaints: that he had used, acting through his agent David Wynshaw, recently discharged by Columbia, company funds for extensive renovations of his Central Park West residence, in the amount of $53,729.20; that the funds were procured through the submission of false invoices or statements for work purportedly done for CBS by contractors; that he had misused company funds to cover all of the expenses incurred by him at a Bar Mitzvah held in October 1972 at the Plaza Hotel in New York City; that he had used company funds to obtain reimbursement for rental of a house in Beverly Hills at a total rental in excess of $13,000; that a $20,000 false invoice was issued to the Century Plaza Hotel in Los Angeles and that through the diversion of funds from that invoice to the defendant himself, his agent Wynshaw gave 65 or more hundred dollar bills to Davis; and that further, other substantial funds were diverted for various other goods and services for his own personal benefit. CBS seeks an accounting of all monies and property which may have been wrongfully obtained by Davis and to be paid all such monies.[23]

The rumor was that the FBI had sealed Wynshaw's office. But Bob Altschuler, the master of damage control at the record division, said it was CBS itself that had sealed the office as part of an in-house investigation.

At a May 31 press conference, Lieberson, bristling at the notion that Davis had single-handedly transformed the Columbia Records from an MOR and Broadway show label into rock, reminded the press that it "it was he, not Davis, who had signed such contemporary giants as Bob Dylan and the Byrds."[24] Lieberson was willing—maybe even secretly delighted—to put off his long-planned Santa Fe retirement. At 62 he was back in harness.

As Lieberson resumed control of the label, with Segelstein and Yetnikoff answering to him, his delegatory style was in marked contrast to Davis's. At Columbia Davis had been the supreme micromanager, permitting almost no autonomy among his executives and, like a one-man Army Corps of Engineers, diverting all currents to flow directly back to him. "When Clive left," said Gregg Geller, "we were all summoned to a meeting with Goddard, who was horrified by just how little we all did."[25] Lieberson wanted to know if anyone in the room had produced a record or edited a recording session. Apart from signing artists to make singles on Epic, nobody had been allowed to do much of anything without approval from Clive.

It was open season on Clive Davis. Sometimes the attacks were gleefully direct, other times oblique to make a larger point. "Akio Morita, president of the Sony Corp.," the Los Angeles Times reported, "says too many American businessmen have been spoiled by the big domestic market in the United States, think only in short range plans, and 'assume that their philosophy is always right anyplace in the world.'"[26] Morita's comments appeared to be directed at Davis.

Opening the CBS Records sales convention at the Cow Palace in San Francisco, Lieberson cracked, "A funny thing happened on the way to my retirement."[27] CBS Records employees were split on the calamitous events of the spring: some regarded Davis's creative accounting as a non-issue and suggested that he was being pilloried for charging the parent company for what should have been legitimate expenses—i.e., the bar mitzvah guests at the Plaza were mostly from the recording industry and there to do business as they might as at any industry function; some remained furious with Davis and Dave Wynshaw for tarring the entire record division, even if their actions were no big deal. As recounted in Hit Men, Bruce Lundvall told Frederic Dannen that a Cleveland branch manager named Jim Scully was accepting an award at the Cow Palace and broke down onstage because media coverage had made his kids think he was part of a Mafia organization. At that same convention a California state trooper warned Arthur Taylor there'd been an anonymous threat that he'd be shot if he went onstage to speak; Lieberson, apprised of the threat, took Taylor's arm and never left his side throughout the speech.[28]

While Lieberson and Segelstein tried to cool things down at the label, Stephen Paley introduced Clive Davis to the legendary literary agent Helen Merrill (not to be confused with the jazz singer).[29] At lunch in midtown Davis met Merrill's client James Willwerth. Plans were soon underway for Willwerth to write Davis's memoir of his tenure at Columbia Records, striking while the iron still burned to the touch.

•   •   •

Throughout the late spring and early summer of 1973, Columbia in New York had been at the eye of the storm. The West Coast offices felt the turmoil as well, but there was something else going on: because there was hardly any Masterworks activity in Los Angeles anymore, the product was almost exclusively about youth. Paul Weston was gone from the label. The veterans moaned that the label had gone from being A&R- and music-based to attorney-heavy and contract-based, even after Davis's dismissal. In June, Davis's former lieutenant, Ted Feigin, went west to oversee the administration there. John Hammond sent Feigin a note congratulating him on his promotion and suggesting he get together with his old friend Irv Townsend.[30]

For Townsend it was a time of unutterable sadness. Columbia wasn't recording his kind of music anymore—not Michel Legrand nor much of André Previn, never mind Goodman or Claude Thornhill or the sublime Mahalia. He had become especially active in the National Academy of Recording Arts and Sciences (NARAS), heading it from 1969 to 1971, and had capped his tenure by producing the 1971 Grammys live for the first time; but now that was over.[31] And then came the blow that was no less powerful for being so long anticipated: daughter Susie, not quite 21, succumbed to marble bones disease.

With Susie's battle over, all the fight went out of the Townsends, too. Townsend spent an increasing amount of time in the Santa Ynez Valley as a gentleman rancher and writer. He published several pieces about the valley, its schoolhouses and churches that recalled an earlier time (and were closer to Townsend's previous conceptions of the West), and wrote with almost quivering sensitivity about animals. In his much anthologized essay "The Once Again Prince," three sentences spoke to some readers far beyond their Hallmark card tone: "We who choose to surround ourselves with lives even more temporary than our own live within a fragile circle, easily and often breached, unable to accept its awful gaps. We still would live no other way. We cherish memory as the only certain immortality, never fully understanding the necessary plan."[32] Without minimizing Townsend's devotion to his animals, it's possible to read the incantation as an expression of grief over Susie's death.

Like his Princeton schoolmate Charlie Burr, Townsend occasionally dabbled in songwriting. In Susie's memory he wrote a lyric titled "Today Girl," and he was thrilled when Gordon Jenkins (composer of *Manhattan*

Tower and a longtime arranger of Sinatra's) set it to music. Jeremy Townsend remembered her father arriving home in Pacific Palisades after a productive session with Jenkins, pleasantly if dangerously smashed to the gills because the song now had a possibility of being recorded.[33]

It never was. Freddie Townsend, feeling neglected for years and unable to communicate with her intensely private husband, met another man in Las Vegas. For all intents and purposes the Townsends' marriage was over. At Columbia's LA offices Townsend dutifully went in now and then—and hated it. He wrote to Hammond that Ted Feigen was "thoroughly detested by everyone out here," but that Lieberson couldn't be bothered to do anything about it. "Jeremy and I are back for the week. I can't commute twice a week any more because of the gas shortage, but I'm rather aware that nobody cares."[34]

Whether anybody cared is hard to say. "I am the all-time ineligible bachelor now," he wrote to Hammond, playing the "utility man at Montecito parties . . . [daughters Nicole and Jeremy] visit and call me and are a continuing source of pride to me. . . . All animals are at the moment fine, altho [sic] we've had horses with lame legs, dogs with various problems, etc. I have a woodpile filled with kittens, six fat cows I can't find a home for, and a collie who greets everybody by knocking them down. But I feel fine, am thankful for every day here and not for a moment sorry to have left the music biz. I wish Freddie had been willing to try it. She might have been surprised." Townsend reported that his last Columbia convention, held in Toronto earlier that summer, was dreadful: "Not one note of jazz was performed, either on stage or in the presentations."[35]

Townsend resigned from Columbia after almost 30 years and moved permanently to his beloved valley. The man who'd made a living recording Duke's oceanic orchestra now spent an inordinate amount of time in relative solitude, the animals keeping him company. For a while he and daughter Jeremy had a standing Saturday night date at Mattei's Tavern. He would joke with Jeremy that, whenever she wasn't in residence, he could die on the ranch and not be found for days.

Alone in the valley for weeks at a time, Townsend worked on a novel titled *The Piano Player*. In its opening chapters narrator Jonas recounts a series of tragedies—the death of a grown daughter, a marriage unraveling—that bear an unmistakable resemblance to recent events in the author's life. Like Shep, the protagonist of Budd Schulberg's *The Disenchanted*, who accompanies a Scott Fitzgerald–like novelist back to Webster College (read: Dartmouth), Jonas goes east for the thirty-fifth reunion of his prep school Cambria. There he's reunited with the daughter of his late classmate Joe Springer, the title character. Townsend gets some musical opinions off his chest. There's a long disquisition on Bix Beiderbecke's "In the Mist" and a plausible theory about why younger jazz players grabbed hold of bebop. And there's an ambivalence about his alma mater. Townsend's parents were middle-class Yankees but somehow got up the money to send him to Hotchkiss; his classmates were, for the most part, from wealthier families. If he'd matriculated ten years earlier, John Hammond would have been one of those classmates.

Hammond called on him to help write his autobiography, the book that became *John Hammond on Record*. Hammond, time-pressured by his publisher, pressured Townsend in turn. Townsend spent four tense months transcribing tapes from Hammond, from Willis Conover and other recorded material; wrote, edited, and made suggestions. Worn out, he finally bridled at the pace. "You have to live with the book a long time, as I in a lesser way do," he wrote to Hammond, "and there simply is no sense to this kind of freeway speed."[36] The book was published in 1977. The reviews were mixed—some reviewers felt the anecdotes were self-serving, and there was no index for material that cried out for one—but it has remained an invaluable history to twentieth century left-wing politics as well as jazz in America.

●　　●　　●

The post-Davis era, with Townsend finally retiring and Hammond still associated with the label, was largely about recovering credibility and about the CBS-Sony partnership that officially began in 1967.

"CBS/Sony has started its 7th fiscal year on Feb. 21," Tatsu Nozaki wrote to Messrs. Lieberson, Segelstein, and Yetnikoff from Tokyo. "I am very pleased that I enclose herewith 'ooiribukuro,' which was given to all the employees here at CBS/Sony from Mr Ohga in the hope that our new business will be successful [sic] than ever in the new fiscal year."[37] (An ooiribukuro is a gift bag—"swag," in contemporary American terminology—presented to the attendees of a rakugo, or formal comic play.) Meanwhile, Irwin Segelstein had brought his toolkit down to CBS Records, working away to repair its image in every cornice. But he had to learn on the job. "I could walk into [Lieberson's] office and say, 'Here's what's happening, what do I do now?' But he did not get into the nitty-gritty. Goddard was usually on the phone talking to the great and near-great."[38]

So Segelstein turned to Yetnikoff to answer his daily queries. Like so many other executives, Yetnikoff had been reviewing his own expenses to see if he was vulnerable to the kind of charges that pulled down Davis. "Everyone was scared shitless," he wrote. "The code of the music business, especially in promotion, was loose. If you hired a hooker for a company party, you buried the charge among the flowers and wine."[39]

When Segelstein had completed his task of restoring CBS Records's credibility, he went back to broadcasting. For Yetnikoff, his good humor and apple-polishing paid off: Arthur Taylor named him president of Columbia Records. It was a good choice, if only because no one knew more about the workings of the record business. Observers wondered if Yetnikoff's style was at once too aggressive and too loose to sustain a presidency. The irony is that Taylor was fired the following year—John Backe was named CBS president in October 1976—while Yetnikoff would be the head man at the label for another decade and a half.

Born in 1933, Yetnikoff attended Brooklyn Tech High and the Brooklyn College before getting into Columbia Law School, where he made Law Review.[40] When his first wife June, a Pratt-trained painter, first took him down to Greenwich Village, it was as though they needed a visa, it was all so foreign to him. Yetnikoff followed Clive Davis to the Columbia Records legal department. At 799 Seventh Avenue, he was dazzled by all the pretty women, the sightings of music celebrities like Jerry Vale and Mitch Miller, and, best of all, by a desk phone with three buttons.

In 1965, after Lieberson promoted Davis to administrative vice president, Yetnikoff became Columbia's general counsel. He was named executive vice-president of CBS International in 1969. It was during this period—post-Monterey, with Flower Power blossoming on both coasts—that Yetnikoff got his first taste of marijuana. In Paul Mazursky's 1969 comedy I Love You Alice B. Toklas, Peter Sellers plays Harold Fine, a schlumpy Los Angeles personal injury attorney whose brief transformation into a happy hippie turns his world inside out. Young Jewish attorneys like Davis and Yetnikoff were undergoing similar transformations, albeit on a more affluent level, with all the accoutrements of the period: rock 'n' roll, recreational drugs, paisley patterns, jet travel, and women who unapologetically sought sex without marriage. "If we were square businessmen watching the sexual revolution play out in the music we sold," Yetnikoff wrote, "we sure as hell wanted free and easy sex for ourselves. Some execs were growing long hair, smoking pot and sporting love beads, but most were just Old School Horny."[41] This horny, self-aware man with the Russian cast to his eyes would revel for a while in sex and drugs, all the while determined to distinguish himself from his two predecessors, Lieberson and Davis, both criminally tough acts to follow.

●　　●　　●

Neil Diamond, one of Davis's proudest signings, had finally begun to record for the label in 1973, after Davis was gone. Jonathan Livingston Seagull was the first album in what would turn into a nearly annual event, each new one charting no lower than number ten. During negotiations in 1971, Davis's readiness to match Diamond's astronomical MCA terms were derided, but it turned out to be justified. In December 1978, "You Don't Bring Me Flowers Anymore," his duet with Barbra Streisand—two Jewish New Yorkers of relatively advanced rock 'n' roll age—was the number one single in the country. (Nearly 30 years later a Los Angeles executive held a karaoke party for his sales staff and, cajoled to go to the microphone, sang "You Don't Bring Me Flowers" with one of his saleswomen. The executive began to mangle lyrics, and suddenly he realized why. "I'm used to singing the Barbra part!" he explained to his audience.)[42]

Barbra Streisand was a movie queen now. Even more than Doris Day's had, Streisand's movie roles informed and helped market her Columbia recordings. *The Way We Were* went gold in February 1974, and then came "Evergreen" and the *A Star Is Born* album two years later. In *A Star Is Born* Streisand played the film role that Judy Garland, with whom she'd sung on TV a decade earlier, appeared to have locked down in the greatly superior George Cukor version. It'd be tempting to say that Streisand had become the closest thing to Garland in the hearts of Garland's fans, but Liza Minnelli was now on Columbia and had her own adoring followers.

On the other side of the pop music spectrum, Bob Dylan was back from his apocalyptic holiday at Asylum Records. *Blood on the Tracks* suggested a new maturity, hard-won through loss and regret, undeniable in deceptively simple songs like "Tangled Up in Blue" and "You're a Big Girl Now."[43] "Dylan is now looking at the quarrel of the self," wrote Pete Hamill in the liner notes. You could argue that Dylan had always been looking; but since those early Columbia records he'd acquired a wife, children, familial responsibilities, and the anguish and joy that came with them. He remained elliptical but maybe all the more compelling for the ellipses. "*I can change, I swear,*" Dylan sang of himself, and though he'd never been less than truthful, this time he might have been sincere.

Bruce Lundvall signed Willie Nelson to Columbia in 1975. Within three weeks Nelson released the spare, idiosyncratic *Red Headed Stranger*, which the label saw not as a commercial record but as a special album that would sell consistently as part of its catalog. Nelson was 42. After many years writing songs picked up by others (Patsy Cline's version of "Crazy" probably the most popular) and making his own records in Nashville in a relatively slick style, Nelson had gone home to Austin and sounded at last as though he was making precisely the music he wanted to. Two million *Red Headed Stranger* copies later, Columbia could be confident that Nelson would stay as long as the label didn't get in his way. It didn't, though. RCA, with traditional and perfectly legitimate competitiveness, kept countering each new Columbia release with reissues of recordings Nelson had made in the sixties. In 1978 Nelson released *Stardust*, his album of American standards, produced by Booker T. Jones, almost every track done in Nelson's plaintive croak. For the next decade there was at least one Nelson album a year, sometimes two a year, frequently with old friends like Waylon Jennings, Kris Kristofferson, and the longtime Columbia artist Ray Price. Profits from Nelson's "On the Road Again," from *Honeysuckle Rose* (1980), and "Always on My Mind" (1982, the platinum album had the same title) could have built a whole new recording complex in Austin.

A few weeks after *Red Headed Stranger* was released, Columbia realized it had on its hands a breakout album by one of its younger artists. Bruce Springsteen was only the latest "discovery" of John Hammond's. His first two albums, *Greetings from Asbury Park* and *The Wild, the Innocent & the E Street Shuffle*, had been recorded in a small studio in Nyack—not well, to Hammond's ears. The rock critic Jon Landau had famously referred to Springsteen as "the future of rock 'n' roll," a phrase that probably went a long way toward his becoming Springsteen's producer. Their collaboration, *Born to Run*, hit the charts in September 1975, peaked as the number three album in the nation, and launched an entire Springsteen movement that probably culminated in *Born in the U.S.A.* (1984). If some of us were less enthusiastic about Springsteen's later solemn, fist-in-the-air workingman anthems than the comic, rollicking narratives of his first few records, it was still easy to understand why he had become a new rock 'n' roll hero. He connected with the audience, left them gasping if no longer laughing, and didn't seem to ask for much in return.

•   •   •

It's not fair to say that no one had time for Masterworks. Clive Davis gave it little attention; Walter Yetnikoff would give it practically none. But that's why Columbia hired some fine musical minds to handle the division. John McClure had departed after twenty years with the label, deliberately shunning a retirement wristwatch. Tom Frost was still there and, until 1975, so was Tom Shepard. Pierre Bourdain was involved in many recordings of the decade. Paul Myers continued to bring in new artists, among them the lovely soprano Frederica Von Stade, who grew up in New Jersey and recorded extensively for CBS and Philips in the 1970s. Leonard Bernstein, that Peter Pan of American classical music, had a company called Amberson (*amber stone* in German) Enterprises, which had been managed for years by Schuyler Chapin. In 1971 Chapin moved on, and Bernstein's friend Harry Kraut assumed control of Amberson. Taking an accounting of Bernstein's Masterworks royalties going back some 15 years, Kraut didn't believe the numbers added up—and Bernstein was soon out of there, ensconced at Deutsche Grammophon, where he would become even more of an international star. The Masterworks lineup now included the pianist Murray Perahia, composer-conductor Pierre Boulez, and violinists Isaac Stern and Pinchas Zuckerman. The great crossover hit of the era was Jean-Pierre Rampal's *Suite for Flute and Jazz Piano* (with Claude Bolling), released in 1975 and making the *Billboard* charts in January 1976. Before the end of the decade, Masterworks would be home to the cellist Yo-Yo Ma.

It was still home to Glenn Gould, who would complete the circle of his Masterworks recordings in 1981 when he revisited *The Goldberg Variations* after a quarter of a century. In the early 1970s, though, he was still prolific if not necessarily healthy. At that point Gould's most frequent producer was Andrew Kazdin. Even in Toronto, where he lived and preferred to work, nobody recorded quite like Gould, who was, as a major solo artist, used to dictating the performance schedule. Kazdin told the story of Gould recording Schoenberg lieder in the late sixties with the soprano Helen Vanni and the baritone Cornelis Opthof; when the exhausted Opthof asked for a minute's rest, Gould said, "Why, of course!" and Kazdin, who was there in the auditorium, "became aware of the silent ticking of Gould's eternal clock." After exactly sixty seconds, Gould called out, "Good! Now let's continue with the passage at the top of page three!"[44]

It was Boulez and the New York Philharmonic who recorded, in 1972, the first quadraphonic Masterworks LP: Stravinsky's *Petrushka*. Quadrophonic was a great idea that proved impractical, hardly worth the effort. Quadraphonic meant more furniture. By the mid-seventies the industry product was a messy affair. Besides stereophonic 45s and LPs, you could buy recordings on quadraphonic vinyl; on eight-track cartridges; on cassettes; and on reel-to-reel tapes. There was something touching about all those choices. There was no more "breakage," the common term for what routinely happened with shellac 78s. But eight-track cartridges often cracked, and a cheap player would often move onto the next track before the previous one was finished. Tapes stretched out. The sonic horn o' plenty was served internationally, which meant politically as well.

CBS International was already feared and loathed for its westernizing influences. A January 1974 issue of *Television Digest* reported that a boycott of Sony products, particularly four-channel audio equipment and disks produced in Japan by CBS/Sony Records, had been launched in Syria & Kuwait. "An Arab League spokesman said total boycott of Sony products by 18 member countries would be started next June if Sony doesn't sever ties with CBS."[45]

         •   •   •

Lieberson retired from Columbia, once and for all, in 1975, at 64. "Did you know," Charlie Burr wrote to Ed Kleban, "that the goodbye film for GL, which was shown only at the Toronto sales convention this year, began and ended with 'What I Did for Love' as the theme song? It was the only music in the 15 minute film other than the little song Groucho did with Marvin [Hamlisch] at the piano. GL retired to that song of yours, and it worked so well it got him a standing ovation. Oh sure, he might have gotten it anyway, but that's hindsight or second-guessing."[46]

A year later Charlie Burr was dead, at 54. He had spent most of his adult career reading, writing, and listening for Columbia Records, working nights and weekends to get into the theater as a lyricist, and drinking. Having served in the China-Burma-India Theater during World War II, he'd contracted tuberculosis. Like a later version of a Hemingway hero, he was nursed back to health by the woman who became his first wife. "After he recovered, he could no longer relate to her as anything but nurse-patient," Tom Shepard, who met Burr in 1960, recalled.[47] Burr began a new family with Helen Blumstein, who became his second wife, and they set up house in what Shepard described as a rambling, meagerly furnished old apartment on Riverside Drive. Although Burr kept moving up the Columbia ladder he didn't, perhaps couldn't, hold on to money. Through the 1950s and much of the 1960s he had been a liner-note writer at large, able to knock out a few hundred words about a classical piece or a Broadway show with equal facility. He wrote songs with several people, Shepard among them. "Our first collaboration was a comedy song that was commissioned by Jim Fogelsong for Fay deWitt," Shepard said. "I still have the LP, of course."[48]

Burr had theater in his blood. His mother had appeared in at least one of Jerome Kern's Princess Theater shows a decade before he was born.[49] Burr entered Lehman Engel's BMI musical workshop and soon submitted a musical version of Terence Rattigan's *Separate Tables*. "It had some very beautiful songs in it," Shepard said.

Lieberson liked Burr within easy reach. When screenplays were being submitted to Lieberson for Cinema Center and then later to Columbia Records for financing, Burr was pressed into service as a story analyst. His evaluations, whether of musicals for recording purposes or of material to adapt for the screen, tended to be pithy and concise. About a screenplay titled *Long Time Comin'*, which had been submitted to Columbia probably because of its searching-for-Robert-Johnson theme, Burr reported that the screenplay made its points on "little cat feet," thereby tiring the reader. "It reads like a novel that might make a good movie. It ought to read like a good movie taken from a fine novel."[50] Getting an early look at the script for the Kander-Ebb musical *Chicago*, Burr praised it as fast and funny and filled with razzle-dazzle. "All totally superficial and played for maximum entertainment values," Burr wrote. "It is not meant to stick to the ribs or be in any way thoughtful. It is as hollow as a tambourine. I feel that, with Fosse direction, an investment would be safe. I wish I felt as sanguine about the recording merits. Discounting the audition's effectiveness, I reluctantly propose that we pass." The original cast recording went to Arista.[51]

Burr's polymathic qualities were invaluable to Lieberson, who made him associate editor of the Legacy series. Some people saw the relationship between the two men as more complicated. Joan Simpson Burns, admittedly bitter about Lieberson's refusal to credit her work on *John F. Kennedy: As We Remember Him*, saw Burr as Lieberson's general editor, mixologist, and factotum rolled into one. She remembered accompanying Burr to lunch one day with Alec Guinness and sitting by in horror as Burr cruelly dismissed the great British actor. (It was a period when Guinness was looking for a recording project, something along the lines of his idol John Gielgud's *Ages of Man*.) In Burns's view, Burr was like a bartender who, having served the guests, wasn't permitted to fix one for himself.

Alcohol consumption among Columbia Records employees—the sales department even more than A&R—had been considerable, and Burr's was conspicuous even among such champion drinkers. He remained loyal to Lieberson even beyond Lieberson's retirement. And, miraculously, he made time to work on *Home Sweet Homer*, a musical version of *The Odyssey*, with Mitch Leigh of *Man of La Mancha* success composing. The show opened just after the New Year 1976, with Alfred Marre (also part of the *La Mancha* collaboration) directing, Yul Brynner as Odysseus, and Joan Diener as Penelope. The siren song faded early, though; the show was received respectfully but not enthusiastically.[52] Burr also completed a lot of work on a stage version of *The Umbrellas of Cherbourg*, writing new lyrics to Michel Legrand's pastel music; but the project ran into all kinds of trouble—from its original filmmaker, Jacques Demy, who was livid about Andrei Serban's staging of it, and from earlier lyricist Norman Gimbel—and would reemerge only years later with extensively revised lyrics by Sheldon Harnick. "Burr's just wasn't a singing translation," Harnick said.[53] The man had composed some of the most literate liner notes in Columbia Records history, served as ongoing editor of the label's prestige line of book and record packages, co-produced an important original cast recording (Harold Rome's *Pins and Needles*), written some beautiful shows of his own, set lyrics to the music of others, played decent piano, and translated French with some facility. He had always been, according to Tom Shepard, a little consumptive-looking, and vast quantities of booze couldn't have helped. If he couldn't make the entire career sing, it was the price he paid for being so interested in so much: women, musical theater, alcohol, family, and the written word—though perhaps not in that order. In the fall of 1976 Burr suffered a massive stroke. He died at Lenox Hill Hospital.

• • •

Lieberson, meanwhile, kept moving around: New York to Santa Fe, Santa Fe to Los Angeles, Los Angeles to Oslo, then back to New York. His wit was still celebrated in Manhattan circles, literary as well as musical. Expressing his concern in a letter about the domestic partnership of his old friend Groucho, Lieberson referred to Groucho's young girlfriend Erin Fleming as Phlegming.[54] At a party hosted by financier Charles Engelhard, presumably held at Engelhard's New Jersey estate, Lieberson was seating the Duchess of Windsor when he pointed across the table to the Duke and said, "That man didn't give up enough for you." The line, according to novelist Paul Horgan, threw the Duchess "into gales of laughter across the room."[55]

Lieberson wasn't in great shape, however. His health appeared fine, but he was depressed—devastated that Columbia Records was no longer his. After 36 years he had retired to celebrations of tears and laughter, including a party for him at Paley's Fifth Avenue apartment and a valedictory smash hit with the *A Chorus Line* album. But then nothing quite worked out. Peter Lieberson remembered several abortive television projects. Although Goddard had written dramatically before—several plays remained unproduced, and there had been at least one collaboration with Hugh Wheeler, called *The Bird Cage*—television wasn't his medium.[56] He'd comported himself beautifully on David Susskind's TV show *Open End*, on *Cavett* and *The Bell Telephone Hour*; but in these he was either host or guest, not the author of a narrative meant to have mass appeal.

By now both Peter and Jonathan were long out of the house. Feeling the emptiness of the rooms and wanting to consolidate, the Liebersons sold the East 61st Street brownstone and moved into 10 Gracie Square, where their old pal Kosty was their neighbor. There was no thought of dying at Gracie Square; in fact they were spending more time than ever in Santa Fe. Lieberson had an itch to compose again. With the draining days of the corporate world behind him, he could decompress in Santa Fe, sit down at the keyboard with nothing but music on his mind.[57] And Brigitta was more in demand than ever, her late-blooming concert-hall career peaking when the National Opera Company of Norway asked her to become its director. Lieberson accompanied her to Oslo in one of the more triumphant journeys they'd taken in three decades of world travel.

Then, upon his return to New York, he was diagnosed with liver cancer.

Lieberson took the diagnosis with equanimity. "Don't worry, Bruce," he told Bruce Lundvall. "Las Vegas is giving me pretty good odds." Lieberson had always been irreverent about many things, including medicine. When company physician Jack Nelson tried to make it less embarrassing for Columbia employees to provide mandatory stool samples by arranging to have them mailed directly to the lab, Lieberson said, "We're used to it, Doc. We send shit through the mail every day."[58] Lieberson continued to make the requisite jokes, allowing few people besides Brigitta to see inside those well-guarded chambers. Alone one day with Avedon, perhaps the only man who really knew him, Lieberson said, "I have one more thing to teach my boys: how to die."[59]

As Lieberson's health deteriorated, he carried himself with great dignity. In his presence or in their correspondence his friends kept things light. Jacob Javits, aware of the Liebersons' frequent travels to Scandinavia, wrote that he'd recommended to Secretary of State Cyrus Vance that Lieberson be named Ambassador to Norway.[60] It was probably a joke. Nevertheless, Joseph Dash said, "Norway would have been lucky to have him there. Goddard would have made a great ambassador."[61]

In his midforties Lieberson had learned to speak Italian in three months so he could know the language during a trip to Rome. In his early fifties he was still composing pieces like *Piano Pieces for Advanced Children or Retarded Adults*, with André Previn recording them for Columbia. In his midfifties Lieberson had taught himself about the Irish Rebellion so he could assemble the text and recordings for his Irish Uprising Legacy recording. He analyzed material with what his son Peter called "that excessive critical eye," then had it reworked—or tried to rework it himself—so that its meanings were clear and the world might be a better place. If socialist/communist impulses had once quickened his blood, it was art of the highest order—in music, books, and drama—that sustained him, even in the last stages of his illness.

Lieberson died on May 29, 1977, at home at Gracie Square. Brigitta, Peter, and Jonathan were at his bedside.[62] After cremation a memorial service was held at Temple Emanuel, on Fifth Avenue. The famous synagogue throbbed with mourners—his friends, including the celebrated and the everyday colleagues, and the merely curious. "All of the major vice presidents attended the funeral," the art director Paula Scher remembered, "but the majority of the people who then worked for CBS Records were unmoved. Most had been hired after 1968 and had no idea who Goddard Lieberson was."[63] Still, dozens of articles memorialized him, and when Roland Gelatt wrote in the *Saturday Review* that Lieberson had been the most important figure in the recording industry for the past 30 years, the encomium didn't seem extravagant.[64] Other record label chiefs had been as astute as Lieberson, but they hadn't insisted on recording the likes of Ives and Webern, knowing they were loss leaders, and hadn't recorded even unsuccessful Broadway musicals that were subsequently beloved *because* of the recordings. That Lieberson could be so private as to be practically unknowable, even by his family, didn't detract from his considerable magnetism nor from—more lasting—his achievements in recorded sound.

22

Expansion and Bombast

Less than 24 hours after Lieberson's death, saxophonist Paul Desmond died. (The official cause was lung cancer, which had been diagnosed a year earlier.) Only 52, Desmond had also been gone from the label since the Dave Brubeck Quartet had officially disbanded in 1967. Desmond had spent the last decade as a Manhattan bon vivant, his horn silent after several recordings for RCA Victor, many of them under George Avakian's stewardship.

At the 1977 Columbia Records convention that summer, held at the Hilton Hotel in London, one would have expected an elegiac tone to the proceedings. It wasn't quite like that. The label assembled a memorial film in tribute to Lieberson, using the exhilarating number "One," from *A Chorus Line*, as its closing theme. It was a fine, if too brief, tribute. But the conventioneers had business to conduct.

On his thirtieth birthday Gregg Geller emerged from the convention accompanied by publicist Hope Antman, who would become his second wife; Walter Yetnikoff; and rock journalist Lisa Robinson. (In his memoir Yetnikoff mentions only Robinson.) Next to a sandwich-board sign that said *Elvis Costello and Stiff Records Welcome CBS Records to London*, Costello played an electric guitar hooked up to a pignose amp and sang his songs "Welcome to the Working Week" and "I'm Not Angry." A few minutes later two bobbies arrested Costello for public busking. But Geller made arrangements to sign Costello.

Geller went to see Costello's manager Jake Riviera, who shared his London flat with the singer-songwriter Nick Lowe. As Geller walked in,

Riviera was on the telephone with Clive Davis, who wanted to sign Costello for his label Arista. "Here's Gregg Geller now," Riviera said into the phone. Davis apparently replied, "Gregg Geller?! At CBS I hired him to work in the mailroom!" Geller had gone from staff writer at *Record World* directly into A&R at Epic, of course, and Davis's condescending lie had the opposite of the intended effect: Riviera and Costello were thrilled to be signing a contract with an executive who'd worked his way up from the mailroom.[1]

Nick Lowe produced Costello's first Columbia album.[2] Costello's loud jackets, skinny neckties, and horn-rimmed glasses gave him the appearance of an uber-geek, as though Buddy Holly had been disinterred and injected with a punkish sensibility, and he cultivated the look to great effect. "My Aim Is True," he sang, and you didn't doubt him. In those early years at Columbia his behavior was unpredictable at best, if also genuine. The most notorious incident occurred in 1979 in Dayton, Ohio, during a tour to promote his third album *Armed Forces*. One night after a performance Costello found himself in a hotel bar arguing with Stephen Stills and Bonnie Bramlett about Ray Charles's talent and employing racially charged words to make his points. The incident was picked up by rock journalists. Geller was forced to hold a press conference to amplify what happened and protect the label's artist—from himself as well as from the press.

Meanwhile Nick Lowe was making his own album. Geller, hearing "I Love the Sound of Breaking Glass," signed him for Columbia as well. Eventually Lowe went to Sweden to record himself, and told Geller, only half-facetiously, that he was going there "in search of the Abba sound." (To Geller's ears, *Armed Forces* was largely Lowe grafting the Abba sound onto Costello.)

For a while Abba too was part of the Columbia Records operation— that is, Columbia International. (In the United States their albums were released by Atlantic.) But the Columbia family in New York didn't seem to know what to make of Abba. The Zombies' former lead guitarist Paul Atkinson was on the A&R staff, and he couldn't seem to interest anyone else in Abba's "Waterloo." But there's something about synchronized voices carrying deceptively simple songs, from Mitch Miller & His Gang to Ray Conniff to Abba, that turns off critics but invites obsessively repeated listenings.

* * *

Jazz at Columbia in the 1970s was in a precarious state. It was a tough time for jazz in general, with so much marketing muscle and so many live venues deferring to the more ubiquitous and profitable rock 'n' roll. Columbia still wanted to release jazz records, of course, but too often the executives who weren't specifically behind an artist found what they heard either old-fashioned or too tough to market.

In some ways the beginning of the decade was worse for jazz. Hearing tape of journeymen guitarists George Barnes and Bucky Pizzarelli playing together, Kip Cohen wrote, "I find these two men to be brilliantly superior players, with a deliciously delicate touch. I intend to catch them next week when they do *Arthur Godfrey* and *Mike Douglas*. But hearing these discs strikes me as being analogous to hearing the Boston Pops play Leroy Anderson. The performance level is very high, but the musical mentality that would choose the Leroy Anderson, like the mentality that chose these selections, I find questionable. At best it seems like no better than Phi Beta Kappa cocktail music. . . . As well performed as this music is, these men do not live in the present for me and I simply cannot develop any enthusiasm for them."[3] Were there jazz players who "lived in the present"? Kip Cohen, who came to Columbia Records from Bill Graham's organization, had taste almost beyond reproach, but perhaps he knew that he simply couldn't market Barnes and Pizzarelli—not at that moment, anyway. The Barnes-Pizzarelli album *Guitars—Pure and Honest* went to another label.

Trumpeter Don Ellis was, on the surface, another story, but victim to many of the same marketing considerations. Ellis (unrelated to the label's A&R man of the same period) was a Columbia artist, based in North Hollywood, who'd finally gained wide recognition with his propulsive score for *The French Connection*. Fronting a 20-piece band,

Ellis composed pieces in quirky, jagged time signatures for at least four trumpets, sometimes five. But even when he covered pop songs by Carole King and Gilbert O'Sullivan, notably on his album *Connection* (exploiting the movie title), his interpretations sounded too difficult for airplay. Kip Cohen decried, "All in all, it's a very good Don Ellis album, but I see no way to exploit a single. . . . A few of the cuts could make it R&B if Don was [sic] a black artist. *French Connection* is too passé as a film to support the theme at this date."[4] Teo Macero produced Ellis, who was notorious for paranoid outbursts and some ultra-conservative views that didn't endear him to either his musicians or the Columbia executives. Gifted as he was, he soon left the label.

That other paranoid trumpeter Miles Davis was still releasing albums with Columbia, though by 1975 his producer, Macero, was preparing to depart and work freelance. Unfortunately, Miles's album *Aghartha*, recorded in Osaka on February 1, 1975, appeared to be a new low for both of them. Only after a year had passed, after much editing and the usual artwork questions, did Columbia finally release it. *Aghartha* is the Sanskrit name of Utopia in Oriental legend, but no amount of mythology or etymology could salvage it from the savage responses it got. In the *Village Voice* Gary Giddins panned the record. "*Aghartha* isn't just a bad record, it's a sad one," Giddins wrote. Miles was on the verge of 50 and falling in and out of hospitals for drug-related ailments. (Macero, as entwined as he'd been with Miles's career for the past seventeen years, had neither the influence on his artists that Avakian had had nor the desire to deny Miles—for two decades the label's premiere jazz artist—his wishes about recording.) Apart from the performance of Davis's saxophonist Sonny Fortune, whose playing he praised lavishly, Giddins appeared to have been disgusted with Davis's self-conscious despondency and hipster posing on *Aghartha*, where "his sound is blanched, his ideas unfocused, his melodic pattern gnarled and sometimes ugly."[5] It would be pleasing to insist that Miles came back from this disaster, but it would be false. Although the 1981 Columbia release *The Man with the Horn* sold as well as *In a Silent Way* had, Miles's increasingly frequent illnesses and hospital stays had taken their toll. He would soon give way to Wynton Marsalis as the most widely admired trumpeter in American music—and, of course, at the label.

Throughout the decade CBS Records continued to put out reissues, many of them as fine as any recordings on the market. Teo Macero, Frank Driggs, Chris Albertson, Michael Brooks, and Sam Parkins all had strong hands in these reissues. But there was so much resentment and in-fighting that you wondered how any jazz got released, let alone material that went back decades. In a not unfamiliar contretemps in 1973, Chris Albertson wrote a blistering letter to *Stereo Review* to say that John Hammond was claiming credit and receiving royalties for work Albertson had done on the latest Bessie Smith reissues. (Some jazz themes are reprised not over minutes but decades.) Albertson complained—correctly, but with more force than necessary—that the album had nothing whatsoever to do with John Hammond, though it was presented as part of the "John Hammond Collection."

Hammond responded in kind. "I could have sued and enjoined the book from coming out since it is a cold black lie that I received any royalties from the Bessie Smith series," he wrote to the critic Leonard Feather. "I have purposely waived any producer's incentive or royalties from our reissue series so that they can be put out at the minimum price of $5.98 per 2-record album. Chris' assumption that I was getting anything is totally in error."[6] Frank Driggs, a freelancer who was often on the label's payroll for jazz projects, didn't want Macero anywhere near the jazz archives.[7] These erudite men, with so much jazz history at stake—and, alas, so little money to work with—just couldn't get along.

Perhaps they would have bickered less if Bruce Lundvall had already had the top job under Yetnikoff. Few recording company presidents have been as passionate about jazz as Lundvall. When Lundvall became Columbia president in the late seventies, it suggested good things to come for jazz fans. The jazz that sold, however—or, perhaps more accurately, the jazz that the Columbia sales personnel were prepared to sell—was mostly of the then fashionable fusion variety (a rock 'n' roll beat with more complex chords), where amplification wasn't just desirable but essential. Released from the Columbia jazz division were, among others, albums by Weather Report (fronted by Miles Davis's former key-board player Joe Zawinul and his former sax player and composer Wayne Shorter), guitarist Al DiMeola, and the veteran trumpeter Maynard Ferguson. A star soloist with Stan Kenton in 1950, Ferguson was one of the few jazz musicians who came of age in the swing era and remade himself into a commercial recording artist. A native of Quebec, Ferguson, who was often referred to by his pleasing initials "M.F.," moved his family to Ojai, California, in the early 1970s and proceeded to release several fusion albums on Columbia showcasing his horn. Ferguson was often accused of trying to re-create the glory days with Kenton, and of having only one tempo—breakneck—and one volume—fortissimo. As a self-described jazz player, however, he paid his own way.

Ferguson's recordings weren't necessarily to Lundvall's taste. He preferred the playing of, say, saxophonist Dexter Gordon, whom Lundvall signed nearly a decade before Gordon appeared as the down-and-out musician in Round Midnight. Gordon's album Homecoming sold well as jazz albums went, but it was a fluke—the result of Lundvall's passion to get it out there, and at great cost to his in-house support. When George Avakian was overseeing pop records in the 1950s, jazz was still considered to be in the mainstream, and could be sold in the manner that most pop records were—with extensive advertising and radio promotion. That was no longer true in the seventies, when jazz had been pushed way out of the mainstream and needed special handling—i.e., sales-people who knew how to get the recordings to the fans.

To complicate matters, jazz artists spent a lot of energy second-guessing public taste. The numbers on Bitches Brew had turned the heads of most young men who owned a horn and had a record contract. But it was Miles Davis's cool demeanor, lately more intimidating than appealing, that too many jazz artists began to affect. A year after Bitches Brew's release, Philip Larkin wrote of wandering into a record store where racks of album covers depicted more or less the same thing: "a bunch of young people, mostly male, with clothes and faces appropriate to criminal vagrancy, stood scowling at me in attitudes eloquent of 'We're gonna do you, Dad.'" Decrying how a once-renowned jazz magazine readers' poll had elected Jimi Hendrix to its pantheon instead of Johnny Hodges, Larkin formulated the following painful truths: "1) No jazz today is popular; 2) The least unpopular jazz is reissues; 3) Hence, the only jazz issues from the big companies today are reissues, few and far between; 4) Current jazz comes on obscure, imported, highly expensive labels, and the ordinary public never sees or hears it."[8] Even given Larkin's simplifications and his distaste for almost everything that came after swing, including Charlie Parker and Miles Davis, it was hard to argue with his assessment.

•   •   •

Four years after leaving Columbia and presiding over Arista, Clive Davis reflected on his humiliating and highly public termination for NARAS president Bill Huie:

> I care just to say that when I left Columbia there was a tremendous amount of speculation raised as to whether there was any impropriety that was done, whether there was a personality conflict between me and a fairly new president of CBS that had just been there for six months; whether it was politics or envy; whether it was subterfuge or a coverup of payola or drugs or all sorts of wrongdoing that had occurred or other improprieties that had occurred in the company when I was president. People speculated about the separation since I had taken a company that was grossing 97 million and was then about 1/2 billion dollars. It was a difficult period. It was a painful period, one of speculation, when the investigations were conducted. But it has led to a very happy result for me because not only was there never any impropriety uncovered at Columbia Records. There was never any payola discovered at that company. There were never any drugs or improprieties participated in by myself or anybody at the company. It boiled down to a case involving taxes owed for the year 1972, $2700 that I had paid taxes on in that year on—well, it was public—$340,000 of income. The judge, in his decision, which was a very happy day for me, excoriated the press and the government itself

for really taking liberties as they did by speculation, by innuendo, by association and to the point of enormous damage and pain. Fortunately for me, people within the industry, and artists and friends that I had been associated with, never changed in their attitudes toward me.[9]

A few months after giving the interview above, Davis appeared at the convention of the National Association for Recording Merchandisers (NARM) and vented considerably more resentment at his former employers.[10] The Columbia Records that Clive Davis had been fired from in 1973 retained a lot of his tone. Lawyers and promotion men were still far more visible in the executive ranks than musicians had been. "When Goddard Lieberson and all the great people left," Teo Macero, several years gone from the label, told the English jazz writer Max Jones, "it was the end of an era and they've changed the company drastically. There are very few independent producers left up there. In order to do a project now you have to get fifteen signatures and the approval of the attorneys."[11]

For Columbia the rock 'n' roll revolution, dating from Clive Davis's coup at the 1967 Monterey Festival, was now a decade old. That revolution had opened the gates for more far-reaching expansion. In the summer of 1977 CBS added Lyon & Healy, the venerable harp manufacturer, to its Musical Instruments division, which now included Steinway pianos, Fender guitars, Gulbransen organs, Rhodes electronic pianos, Rogers drums, Gemeinhardt flutes and piccolos, Leslie Speakers, and V. C. Squier guitar strings. Besides Musical Instruments, the company had three affiliated divisions: Columbia House (the record and book clubs); CBS Retail Stores (Pacific Stereo, to name one); and CBS Toys (Creative Playthings and Wonder Products).[12] The CBS/Columbia Group was conducting business bigger than ever.

* * *

In the midseventies the former Chicago promoter Ron Alexenburg had an unusual amount of influence over pop A&R. Walter Yetnikoff was handling so much, internationally as well as in New York, that he could rarely make time, unlike Davis, to listen to new artists and chase them down. Alexenburg had moved into A&R through the promotion department. By common consent, there was nobody better at getting a record played on the radio. His abilities made him, up to that time, the youngest vice president CBS Records had had.

Alexenburg grew up in Chicago, the son of a South Side butcher who also owned a bowling alley. The bowling alley was home to a Seeburg jukebox that stored a hundred 45s at a time. After a 45 was worn out, Alexenburg, who played the trumpet, would take it home with him. During Alexenburg's teen years in the 1950s, the Windy City blew hot with some of the most interesting pop music in the country. Radio stations WLS (World's Largest Store), WGN (World's Greatest Network), and WVON (Voice of Negroes) rippled across the Midwest. Chess Records was part of Alexenburg's early education, and so were the clubs Mr. Kelly's and London House.

Only three years out of high school Alexenburg was working full-time in promotion. It was a period of major change in radio, when the old Storz playlists were being exploited in increasingly sophisticated ways. The Drake-Chenault Group handled the RKO stations, including the mighty KHJ (Kindness, Happiness and Joy) in Los Angeles. The Drake format was defined by smooth disk jockeys and spare jingles.[13] Alexenburg drove back and forth across the country effectively hawking R&B songs and records by Bobby Goldsboro and Gene Pitney to these stations.

Hired at Columbia Records, Alexenburg promoted its releases and those of its associated label Date Records, which was being run by Tom Noonan. The travel required of promotion men included abysmal fast-food habits, and Alexenburg attained an increasingly blocky physique. But he rarely failed to get the label's records played on the air, whether it meant supplying seats on the 50-yard line for a football-loving program director or waiting eight hours in the outer office of another program director who'd refused to see him.

Through the early seventies, while Davis was still president, Alexenburg maintained contacts that paid off at Columbia and Epic. He was close to Johnny and Edgar Winter, hung out with the Isley Brothers, championed Gamble and Huff's Philadelphia International label, and he knew how to delegate. With the equally hard-driving Midwesterner Steve Popovich reporting to him, Alexenburg kept CBS Records' pop division on top even after Davis's dismissal and industry-wide predictions that the label would collapse.

Suddenly the Jackson Five were in play. Alexenburg wanted the group, who'd been making hits at Motown since the late sixties. But it required some tiptoeing. Alexenburg sensed that the group wasn't being taken care of. There was no way for outsiders to measure the Jackson Five's sales because Motown, refusing to join the Recording Industry Association of America (RIAA), had kept its books closed. Who really knew how many records they sold? Only Berry Gordy and his accountants. Alexenburg had a sense that Michael Jackson in particular was worth pursuing. In 1972 the song "Ben," written for the sequel to the movie *Willard*, had been a surprise hit. When asked by puzzled colleagues why he was so interested in Jackson, Alexenburg had a standard line: "Anybody who can have a number one song singing about a rat is the guy I want to sign."

He got his chance in the summer of 1975 when the Jackson Five came to the New York metropolitan area to give concerts in New Jersey and on Long Island. During a publicity session in front of the Warwick Hotel, a block from Black Rock, kids screamed for the Jackson Five while Alexenburg casually tossed quarters with disk jockey Cousin Brucie Morrow. He kept an eye on the Jackson family. When he figured he knew enough to get in the game, he called Joe Jackson (the patriarch) and Ron Ahrens (the manager) and said, "Would you be interested in leaving Motown?"

They were. Alexenburg stepped up his campaign. In June he got Yetnikoff aboard by taking him to see the Jackson Five at the Nanuet Theater. Yetnikoff was impressed by their musicianship, yet surprised that the Jackson Five appeared so disheveled on stage—another strike against Motown. Alexenburg called Gamble and Huff in Philadelphia and said,

"How would you like to produce the Jackson Five?" Gamble and Huff didn't need the Jackson Five, but the brush that had painted Clive Davis right out of the picture had tainted them as well, and a pop group of such a wide fan base would go a long way toward restoring the prestige they'd enjoyed for years as producers. Sure, they said, who wouldn't?

Then Alexenburg invited the Jackson Five out to his place in Woodbury—not far from the Westbury Music Fair, where they were scheduled to play in their Las Vegas Revue the last week of August. "I've met your family," he said to them, "now I'd like you to meet mine." Alexenburg had begun a family early, and he was proud of his kids. The Jackson Five arrived by limousine—all except Jermaine, who was married to Berry Gordy's daughter and wouldn't (or couldn't) entertain the notion of leaving Motown. Alexenburg had arranged with neighbors to use their tennis court, and everybody seemed to be having a fine old time. His one misstep was the food: too late he realized that the Jacksons were vegetarians, so he scrambled and found a local deli to send over some salads.

It might sound precious, but it did the trick. The Jackson Five signed with Epic in the winter of 1976. The Jackson Five name belonged to Motown; Berry Gordy wasn't about to allow them to take it with them. Within CBS Records Alexenburg still faced doubters. The most troubling of these was Jim Tyrell, a former bassist for James Brown and now an expert marketing executive, because Alexenburg had always put great stock in Tyrell's opinion. The Jacksons were believed by many in the company to be over the hill.

As promised by Alexenburg, Gamble and Huff did their stuff, first producing The Jacksons and Goin' Places, before the Jacksons began to write and produce themselves. With the Jacksons' third Epic album, Destiny, Michael Jackson emerged as an incomparable entertainer. The single "Shake Your Body (Down to the Ground)" was only a taste of what he'd deliver as a solo artist, beginning with the 1979 Off the Wall.

Alexenburg, meanwhile, accepted an offer from MCA, with a mandate from its new Infinity Records label to sign artists at least as big as, if not bigger than, Michael Jackson. Who was bigger than Michael Jackson? Before the decade was over, Alexenburg had signed Pope John

Paul II to a recording contract. Though the signing was widely referred to as Ron's Folly and came to naught, it didn't surprise anybody who knew him. It was, after all, just two pontiffs making a deal.

• • •

In 1977 James Taylor was lured reluctantly to the label by Walter Yetnikoff and Al Teller. Taylor felt guilty about it all the way. Yetnikoff had been impatient with Taylor's guilt, but the impatience paid off: Taylor's first hit on Columbia was "Handy Man."[14] J.T., the Columbia album that contained it as well as "Your Smiling Face," was released in July 1977 and sold very well. At the time Taylor had been recording for less than a decade, but already he seemed to be a journeyman in midcareer.

About 18 months later Yetnikoff's inability to come to terms with Paul Simon on a new contract prompted Simon's defection to Warners, a kind of tit-for-tat move engineered largely by Warners chief Mo Ostin. The enmity between Simon and Yetnikoff was like a rank wind blowing from Manhattan all the way to Burbank. At Warners, Simon's screenplay about a musician recently signed to a major record label was greenlighted. A few months later the bilious and almost humorless One Trick Pony was released, with Rip Torn impersonating Yetnikoff as the growling sleaze Walter Fox. Perhaps to get back at Yetnikoff, Simon's character goes to bed with Mrs. Walter Fox (played by Joan Hackett). Surely it was one of the costliest fictional cuckoldings on celluloid.

By decade's end Yetnikoff had thoroughly marked out his own CBS Group presidency as distinct from his predecessors—the debonair, musical Lieberson and the micromanaging, hit-attuned Davis—by transforming himself into a madman. In the hopes of taming him, CBS named Dick Asher, then the chief of CBS Records International, as deputy president and chief operating officer.[15] Asher's sobriety was meant to check Yetnikoff's intemperance. It also set the stage for a power struggle, just beneath Yetnikoff's level, between Asher and Bruce Lundvall. Through it all, Yetnikoff was known to have his eyes on the movie business. Eventually that would lead to an even closer connection to Sony.

23

Tokyo Calling

In 1980 Joseph Dash, a New Yorker who had begun at CBS Records in 1969 and worked his way through business development at the label, became Masterworks' general manager. The venerable division, despite that stupefyingly powerful catalog that Lieberson and a few others had built up, had been ailing. For a while in the 1970s, you couldn't *give* away classical recordings. At the end of the decade Walter Yetnikoff installed Simon Schmidt, who had owned and operated a record company in Israel, as head of Masterworks. Schmidt's brief tenure was, by most accounts, disastrous. Within a few months he was dismissed and Dash was promoted. (Coincidentally, Dash's wife and Schmidt were distantly related.)[1]

In the late sixties, when Leonard Bernstein, Glenn Gould, and Isaac Stern were considered the major living Masterworks artists, Dash—holding graduate degrees from the University of Texas and Rutgers, with a PhD from CUNY still in his future—was running international marketing and research for Celanese Plastics. After Dash had hired Art Rivel at Celanese, Rivel was lured away by Clive Davis at Columbia. Rivel, in turn, hired Dash. Dash went to work in CBS Records Planning, eventually moving into Diversification and Business Development. From the small operation Columbia Records had been in 1939, with a Bridgeport factory and less than a score of Manhattan-based employees, the company had ballooned into an international goliath, with a presence all over the world.

In Dash's first position he reported to Stan Kavan, who was still with the company after some 30 years, with a break for World War II. In the meantime Dash couldn't help but be impressed by Clive Davis, even though Davis had only a passing interest in classical music, which was Dash's first love. In Business Development, Dash reported to Bruce Lundvall.

After the Simon Schmidt interval, Dash was named vice president and general manager of CBS Masterworks. The division was in deep trouble. If Dash seemed to be yet another embodiment of the takeover of the industry by attorneys and businessmen, he had been deeply immersed in classical music since childhood, when his mother took him to see *La Traviata*. Before he'd assumed the general managership, Dash had attended a Masterworks presentation that was booed by field people. "It was imprinted on my soul," he said of that moment, "because they were booing the music that I loved." At that point even the sterling Masterworks catalog, built brick by brick and session by session by Lieberson and a handful of others, was no longer profitable. Nobody could sell that nonpareil music anymore.

Or so it seemed.

Around that time news of a newly created digital disk was leaking out. Sony and Philips, two companies long linked to Columbia Records, had jointly developed the compact disc (CD) and had now come up with a prototype of the player.[2] The compact disc contained no grooves but was coded with numbers that were converted to sound signals by laser light. The development was attractive to industry forecasters because the compact disc was even sturdier than the LP, lighter and smaller, and held half again as much music as the LP. So, as Sony and Philips perfected the disc, it was also a bit terrifying to Columbia.

Dash knew the disc was coming. Meanwhile he still had the Masterworks division to run. He asked CBS art director Lou Dorfsman to come up with a new Masterworks logo. Dorfsman had an artist produce a circular logo containing a violin bisecting flutes and a French horn, with a banner underneath—two wide blue bands squeezing a red band, giving it the appearance of a ribbon. (Farsighted eyes might have confused it with London Records's emblem of the British flag.)

Dash had his new logo. He was aware that the division's records that sold best in recent years were considered "crossover," the hybridized genre that had often proved profitable since Paul Myers and Peter Munves put together the *Switched-on Bach* project with Walter Carlos back in 1968. Trying to get Masterworks up and running, Dash signed Placido Domingo, Claudio Abbado, Philip Glass, and Claude Bolling, among others. He also insisted on the division's recordings being released worldwide under the CBS Masterworks banner, rather than the more haphazard way records were released in foreign countries, most but not all of them on the CBS Records label.

In corporate America the most formidable pressure often comes from the next office. Dash had inherited Christine Reed as Masterworks A&R director from Simon Schmidt. There was some question about Reed's knowledge of classical music. But Dash and several Masterworks people, along with Yetnikoff, felt they were under intense scrutiny because Reed was especially close to CBS's most recent chairman, Thomas Wyman.[3] Reed was otherwise well connected—she had been recommended in the first place by Zubin Mehta who, as New York Philharmonic conductor, carried considerable weight at Masterworks—and Dash found himself treading lightly.

In his new capacity as general manager Dash went to Covent Gardens, in 1981, expecting—what? He wasn't sure. As fortune would have it, he found himself sitting next to longtime producer and manager Milt Okun, whom he'd never met. Okun pulled out a demo tape by his client John Denver singing "Perhaps Love." It's not clear whether Okun or Dash articulated the idea, but one of them suggested the song would make a great duet between Denver and Placido Domingo—from any angle, at least an interesting pairing. Denver was exclusive to RCA, so Dash negotiated with RCA head Bob Summer (who would later take over CBS International), and Denver was permitted to make the record with Domingo for Masterworks. "Perhaps Love" went gold all over the world.[4] Perhaps George Szell and Bruno Walter wouldn't have approved. But Dash's mandate was to make Masterworks profitable again.

The line of "Mastersound" audiophile records helped, too. As the digital age waited in the green room of American culture, another step had to be taken. For classical music at the time, the revered label was Telarc. Dash went to work with CBS Labs, which had introduced quadraphonic sound more than a decade earlier, to get as good a fidelity as the label deserved.

The compact disc and player finally came on the market in March 1983. The primary problem was finding consumers willing to make the switch. It had been easier during the introduction of the LP, because the technology required only some tweaking; the digital compact disc and player were components from a whole other system, and, as with almost any new electronic equipment, prohibitively expensive. The second problem was having the product—the music—to sell on the technology. In the month the CD was first marketed, CBS Records had only 16 titles available—a fraction of the number of LPs that Wallerstein and his team, including Bachman and Scott, had prepared for their new format. But Dash and other Columbia executives knew this could lift not only the label but the entire industry from another long-term slump. Listeners would want to duplicate, if not replace, the music they loved on vinyl. And something like an old Bruno Walter recording would simply sound better on compact disc. "It will be like hearing the tapes that Walter's recording engineer heard, without the limitations and distortions of the old pressing process," Andy Kazdin told the *Times*.[5]

If the compact disc was seen as a panacea for the industry, it wasn't universally hailed. Many people missed the LPs large format, its square cover that served as canvas for some of the more arresting pieces of art since 1940, and the space for all those notes. More critically, many people missed the LP's sound. To be simplistic, analog sounded warm, digital cold—initially, anyway. No artist was more vociferously cranky about the issue than Neil Young. "Digital is a huge ripoff," he said. "This is the darkest age of musical sound. . . . Did you ever go in a shower and turn it on and have it come out tiny little ice cubes? That's the difference between CDs and the real thing—water and ice."[6]

But CBS Records, like most of the other major labels, was going with the new technology, and Masterworks plunged into the process. The label digitally recorded Yo-Yo Ma, Michael Tilson Thomas, and the underappreciated Murray Perahia. Later in the decade that list would include conductor Esa-Pekka Salonen, the violinist Midori, pianist Emanuel Ax, the pianist Vladimir Feltsman, and Taiwanese violinist Cho-Liang Lin, known to Americans as "Jimmy."

One of Dash's more interesting signings was the trumpeter Wynton Marsalis. Seventeen at the time, Marsalis was already with CBS Records as a pop musician—that is, as its premiere young jazz trumpeter. George Butler, vice president of jazz A&R, gave Dash a scratch tape of Marsalis playing the Haydn Trumpet Concerto. Knocked out, Dash signed Marsalis to Masterworks. For a while Marsalis covered the waterfront, going from Haydn to Duke Ellington and back again. Eventually it proved to be too much, particularly after Marsalis got involved in running the Lincoln Center Jazz Orchestra—but not before winning Grammys for both classical and jazz albums in 1983 and '84.

Masterworks named three Artist Laureates—a kind of emeritus designation that served several purposes: Isaac Stern, a Masterworks artist for his entire career; Leonard Bernstein, though he'd been contractually tied to Deutsche Grammophon in recent years; and Rudolf Serkin, whom Tom Frost now recorded in Serkin's Vermont barn, picking up the maestro's most vagrant piano wanderings. It's neither false nor cynical to suggest that even the greatest artists must be marketed somehow, and an important-sounding designation usually helps more than it hurts.

●　●　●

In the early 1980s there were signs that a Columbia era was already ending. The 30th Street studio was sold in 1981. There wasn't much need for it now. Classical recordings were made in the concert hall or overseas. Rock recordings were made in Los Angeles or in a given band's hometown. It no longer paid to have a rock 'n' roll band come to New York just to have use of a fantastic recording studio like 30th Street, where its nuances were beside the point.

Irv Townsend had left 30th Street sessions behind him two decades earlier; now he was gone from the West Coast office, too. At 61, his long marriage over, he had turned himself into a prolific freelance writer and gentleman rancher, spending weeks at a time at his Santa Ynez ranch with only his beloved horses and dogs to keep him company. He had reflected that he could die there and no one would know. One day in mid-December 1981, in fact, Townsend's neighbor noticed that he hadn't made his daily appearance at the local dump. This wasn't like Townsend. At his ranch he was found lying lifelessly in the leaves, a metal rake nearby, having suffered a heart attack; he'd probably been dead for two days, the animals he'd loved and written of wandering about the property, their master's own sweet thunder silenced.[7] Hearing about his old friend's death, John Hammond wrote to Townsend's daughter Jeremy. "It was criminal that he had been stepped on for so many years after Goddard Lieberson gave up the reins at CBS Records. Irving had integrity that could never have been understood by Clive Davis and most of the lawyers involved in the CBS Records operation."[8] Townsend was buried next to his daughter Susie in a churchyard in nearby Ballard.

● ● ●

Townsend wouldn't have recognized the pop songs that CBS Records could boast in 1983 as hits—or vice versa. Maybe Yetnikoff, who grew up on swing music, couldn't either, but he wasn't complaining. He'd been CBS Group president since 1975 and was startled himself by the numbers. The slump in previous years was blamed on home taping, enabling consumers to tape two entire albums and paying only for the cost of the cassette, rather than on bad or uninteresting records. Prices were cut, which helped stimulate sales. CBS Records was doing particularly well in the spring of 1983 with Men at Work's *Business as Usual* and, of course, Michael Jackson's *Thriller*, whose sales figures were still only suggesting the mind-boggling numbers to come.

Thriller was the high point of Michael Jackson's art. But in a media-choked era when it's tempting to ascribe artistic achievement to a lone "genius," to the outpouring of a single mind, *Thriller* belonged almost as much to producer Quincy Jones and songwriter Rod Temperton. Jones had been part of the Columbia Records family as far back as the late fifties, when he worked on *Meet Betty Carter and Ray Bryant*. In 1960 he brought Mimi Perrin's vocal group the Double Six of Paris to record at the label.[9] In the years before he became an entertainment impresario, producing movies and shows as well as recordings, Jones was among the busiest arrangers. On his Columbia résumé was Tony Bennett's *The Movie Song Album* (1966), which Bennett regarded as a favorite. In those days Jones was represented by Peter Faith, Percy's son and a successful music agent in Hollywood. Jones had a hand in Paul Simon's *There Goes Rhymin' Simon*, the second Columbia album sans Garfunkel, and initially worked with Jackson on *The Wiz*. Jackson's handlers perceived Jones as a jazz man and all wrong for their client, who was exploiting the disco era for all it was worth. But Jackson wanted Jones, maybe even needed him, and the result was *Off the Wall* (1979). Jackson had unhitched his diesel engine from the family train and, after *Off the Wall*, there was no going back.

Thriller did not come easily. Rod Temperton cowrote several songs. After two months of constant work, Jackson and Jones had 28 minutes of releasable music on each side, which would have necessitated tiny grooves and resulted in a certain tinniness.[10] Jackson always had a big fat sound, so it meant going back to work. Jackson and Jones reworked most of the songs and reduced each side to under nineteen minutes.

While they were working on *Thriller*, a cross-media hurricane blew through the project. Jackson and Jones were persuaded to contribute to Warners's E.T. *Storybook Album* soundtrack. Even dynamos like Jackson and Jones can work only so many hours in a week, and Thriller's completion was inevitably delayed. Yetnikoff, running hot in the coolest of times, blew a gasket and got an injunction against Universal (Warners's partner on the project) for failing to secure permission to employ Jackson, who was signed exclusively to Epic. Yetnikoff's Brooklyn street toughness, shaped and hammered as he followed two legendary company presidents in the position, was in sharp contrast to the coolly hip demeanor of

Universal's LA executives. To clear Jackson's participation, Yetnikoff got a half-million-dollar payout to CBS Records—and not a dime, Jones pointed out, went to the artists.

Not that they desperately needed the money. Both already wealthy men, Jackson and Jones would reap almost unimaginable rewards in 1983. Their E.T. Storybook Album won the 1983 Grammy for Best Record for Children. That was Warners's, of course. In the same year, however, Jackson's "Beat It" won Record of the Year; "Billie Jean" won for Instrumental Version; and "Pretty Young Thing" won Best New R&B Song. All of these were from Epic's Thriller, which won Album of the Year and sold some 50 million copies in vinyl. More than any artist before him, Jackson toyed musically with the components of microgroove recording—not just the grooves themselves but the notion of the phonograph needle as its own downbeat, the danger of its rumbling and sliding, or of sticking at times. The headache of needle-stick—the needle stuck in a groove of a "broken" record, its inadvertent effects apparent at the beginning of the century—became an appealing rhythm unto itself. Starting with the ABCs of R&B, Jackson—and, to some extent, Quincy Jones—infused the recording process with a technical subversiveness that made everybody shake.

The CBS/83 Annual Report to the Shareholders featured a theatrically snarling, red-jacketed Michael Jackson on its cover—only the second time in CBS history that an individual appeared on the annual report cover. (The first time was the previous year, when new retiree William Paley was its cover boy.)[11] In 1983 Thriller was way out ahead of the pack, with over 27 million albums sold. Columbia could also boast of Billy Joel's "Tell Her about It," Culture Club (Boy George was the lead singer), and its homegrown artist Bonnie Tyler, who was signed by CBS Records in the UK and recorded "Total Eclipse of the Heart," a ballad whose sales built slowly but steadily in America through MTV exposure. There was also the heavy metal debut of Quiet Riot, and the first American album by Julio Iglesias. Over the next couple of years, the Beastie Boys and Cyndi Lauper would begin to roll out hits. Yetnikoff presided over these like a proud but chronically angry papa, chiding his artists when he wasn't suing other companies for copyright infringement or antitrust violations.

The struggle between the perennially inebriated Yetnikoff and the sober Asher came to a head in 1983. Asher was widely seen to have over-powered Bruce Lundvall, who departed for Elektra before going on to run the premiere jazz label Blue Note for the rest of the century. But Asher couldn't overpower Yetnikoff, who canned him. Asher had been a linebacker at Tufts before earning a law degree at Cornell.[12] He'd been an entertainment lawyer since the 1950s because the pay was better. He was not soft. So he dusted himself off, went to Warners for a year, then jumped to Polygram, which by then was Philips's American partner, as its president. During the disco craze of the late seventies Polygram had been a major player, but by 1980 the label had imploded from defecting artists like Donna Summer, disbanded groups like the Bee Gees, and Andes-sized mountains of debt.[13] Even the considerable skill with Euro-pean artists Asher had demonstrated at CBS wasn't going to make a Poly-gram turnaround easy. Yetnikoff, meanwhile, wrote Asher out of his autobiography.

•   •   •

John Hammond had cast off once again from Columbia and begun his own company. There were several investors, some of them apparently brought in by Columbia's San Francisco–based promotion man Chuck Gregory. The new label, Hammond Music Enterprises, was to be pressed and distributed by CBS Records. HME, as it was called, was based in and around Columbia Circle and then nearby on 57th Street; in either case it was just a short walk to Black Rock.

But the label was short-lived. Hammond had his reputation, and he had the tireless help of Mikie Harris, who was devoted to him and could practically parrot the boss's voice in prose. But times in the industry were tougher than ever. Hammond was guiding the late stages of the career of singer Alberta Hunter and, along with Jerry Wexler, the "blue-eyed soul singer" and songwriter Steve Bassett. It wasn't enough to keep a mini-label going, not even one run by John Hammond. Responding as encouragingly as she could to a Massachusetts-based manager who had sent a demo tape for HME's consideration, Mikie Harris wrote, "The business is now in a complex state, in that master purchases are (in my opinion) outweighing actual signings and development of artists as was done in the past. High percentages and very little money are the deals being cut . . . and in many cases a licensing situation with distribution is all that can be gotten."[14] Hammond and Harris packed up and moved back to Black Rock. In most large American companies the average worker is ignorant of, or at best indifferent to, his company's history: give me the paycheck on Friday and let me clock out. By the mid-eighties CBS Records wasn't much different. Fewer and fewer employees were aware who John Hammond was.

But in Texas there was a blazing blues guitarist who wouldn't make a move without Hammond.

Gregg Geller, who'd been heading A&R back at Epic since 1981, would go to lunch several times a year with Columbia attorney and executive vice president Walter Dean. Except for Hammond, Dean probably knew more about the label's history and inner workings than anyone alive. Dean liked to dine at the Hotel Dorset, on 54th Street off Sixth Avenue, because it afforded privacy—the large old-fashioned dining room didn't attract too many music types. Dean said to Geller, "You really should call John. He's got a young artist he very much wants to record."[15]

Stevie Ray Vaughan signed with Epic, according to Hammond's recollection, primarily because Hammond thought Geller was the right A&R man for his material. Geller was soon fired by Don Dempsey and moved over to RCA.[16] In any case, Vaughan proved to be Hammond's final great discovery—a white Southwestern bluesman descended from Charlie Christian as much as from Jimi Hendrix. Vaughan was 29. His Texas manager, Chesley Millikin, had sent a Vaughan demo to Hammond Music Enterprises, on 57th Street; but Hammond Music Enterprises was about to close up shop once more and couldn't handle Vaughan. Still, several people told Vaughan that Hammond was the man to produce him; one of them was John Hammond Jr., who hadn't been especially encouraged by his old man and had no reason to campaign for him.[17] That's when Hammond took Vaughan to Epic. After his first Epic album, *Texas Flood*, was released, Vaughan played lead guitar on David Bowie's *Let's Dance* (EMI) and went on tour with him. But Vaughan felt so underpaid that he left the tour and made a second album, *Couldn't Stand the Weather*, under Hammond's supervision.

Hammond had another heart attack after returning from the Grammys in Los Angeles, where he'd supervised overdubbing of Stevie Ray Vaughan's new album. "Incidentally, I survived and as far as I can tell, I'll never supervise overdubbing for anybody again!"[18]

On March 26, 1985, Hammond wrote to Marvin Cohn: "I've been back in the building since January . . . and, as Rodney Dangerfield would say, 'I still don't get no respect.'" Hammond asked that Mikie Harris, a good producer in her own right, finally get paid and be allowed into the building without having to sign in every day. "As you know, I have some very good and close friends in the record division. I have a wonderful relationship with Walter Yetnikoff (at least I think I do), and yet my fifty-four years experience with Columbia Records, the old American Record Company and Epic is not being appreciated and costing me money to work here. This is not fair, and I am extremely frustrated. What I would like, in addition to my payment of $35,000.00 a year that I receive as a consultant, is an expense account, and I want to be made to feel appreciated and valued as I think my connection to CBS entitles me to after all these years. . . ." Hammond went on to mention all the artists he'd signed for CBS, wanting $100,000 a year at least, and reminding Cohn that he was responsible for bringing Goddard Lieberson to the label two months after Hammond himself was hired by Wallerstein.[19] It was a rough time for "the ardent swing fan," as the *Times* had described Hammond more than forty years earlier. At 75 he was working harder than ever, still aided by Mikie Harris but constantly worried about his two sons and, most of all, about his wife Esme. Once impossibly glamorous, she had been ailing for years, undergoing two mastectomies. When she died in 1986, at 66, it was the end of a torturous, protracted period of medical treatments.

•   •   •

Paul Myers, not unhappily turned loose from the revamped Masterworks and serving as Decca International's classical general manager in London, decided to try his hand at fiction. "I figured if they can write junk," Myers said, "I can write junk." Myers hadn't written novels before; he'd composed many short stories, all of them unpublished, and written a long piece about Glenn Gould that appeared in *Gramophone*. In quick succession Myers cranked out four thrillers, the Deadly series filled with allusions to classical music. The central figure in these is conductor Konstantin Steigel, though the hero—that is, the character who deals with most of the thrilling stuff—is Steigel's young manager Mark Holland. *Deadly Variations*, the first in the series, was published in 1985 and is set in Vienna. At first Steigel, handsome and Teutonic, appears to be based on Herbert Von Karajan—never a Columbia artist, though some of his EMI recordings were distributed by Epic in the midfifties. Myers said it was more George Szell who, despite his reputation for autocratic severity, had been paternal, even affectionate toward Myers. "You can't give good taste to people who don't have any," Szell cautioned Myers, and the credo reflects Steigel's elitist character. The opening of *Deadly Cadenza* (1986) provides a snapshot of the first moments of a classical recording session for Magnum Records:

> The record producer pushed a button marked "Talkback" on the desk in front of him and leaned toward the small microphone.
>
> "Why don't we try a take? Stand by, please."
>
> For a moment, there was silence. Then the loudspeaker at the other end of the room erupted with the random cacophony of an orchestra tuning up.[20]

Deadly Aria and *Deadly Sonata* followed in 1987. At that point Myers appeared to have gotten the "junk" out of his system. A decade later, several years after his subject had died, Myers published an incisive biography of Leonard Bernstein, threaded by the argument that Bernstein was driven by Jekyll and Hyde forces. On the one hand, Bernstein's arrogance made him snap at worshippers who gushed over *West Side Story*, as though that achievement had been insignificant, and would airily dismiss composers, like Elgar, whose work he regarded as unworthy of his conducting talents. On the other hand, Bernstein's emotions tended to stay close to the surface, and he was inebriated with self-recrimination. After a fifty-fifth birthday celebration in Edinburgh, Bernstein wept on Myers's shoulder and "complained bitterly that he was only two years younger than Beethoven at the time of his death, and had still not created a lasting musical work by which to be remembered."[21]

Joseph Dash, who'd made do without Myers's services through the 1980s, was given a lot of leeway under Yetnikoff, who was usually busy fighting other wars, personal as well as professional. Dash found Yetnikoff crude. He once brought James Wolfensohn, then the chairman of Carnegie Hall and also a member of the CBS board, to Yetnikoff's office. Wolfensohn was then trying to persuade CBS Masterworks to sign his good friend Daniel Barenboim, the pianist-conductor and widower of Jacqueline du Pre. Yetnikoff had a three-foot salami hanging on his office wall; he proceeded to yank it off the wall and wave it around. Dash was embarrassed.

Sony's Norio Ohga, longtime second in command, had been a champion of Daniel Barenboim's, as well as a loyal supporter of what Dash was doing at Masterworks. Ohga had studied as a baritone in Vienna where he'd been a classmate of Claudio Abbado and Zubin Mehta, and he had remained a great lover of classical music. Ohga had some authority at Masterworks even before the official Sony purchase, according to Dash, because Yetnikoff wanted the use of a private Sony jet in exchange for Ohga's input in the classical division. As the 1980s were more than halfway over, Ohga told Dash, "There is only one natural successor to Von Karajan: Daniel Barenboim." Ohga wanted Dash to sign Barenboim so he could record all the Bruckner symphonies. Dash knew this was the kiss of death because Barenboim would be expensive though his name, Dash felt, just didn't sell records. Dash quietly declined to sign Barenboim, and the matter was never brought up again.

But he eventually paid for his tacit insubordination. When the Sony deal went through, Dash was soon relieved of his day-to-day Masterworks responsibilities and replaced by Günther Breest, who'd run Deutsche Grammophon. Given a senior vice presidency, Breest presided over the name change from Masterworks to Sony Classical and moved its headquarters to Hamburg, to stay close to the cluster of radio and publishing concerns there. In 1990, at 58, Dash accepted a retirement package from his Sony employers and started his own consulting firm. Ironically—again, this is how these things develop—one of Dash's major clients was Columbia House, which he served for nine years as one of its resident classical experts.

• • •

In 1986, while Sony began its long, frequently befuddled courtship of CBS Records, Columbia instituted its Legacy series. In the previous three years compact discs had begun to dominate the market—industry insiders were already speaking of the LP as obsolete—and Columbia needed a division for its older material. Someone had come up with the name Heritage; but RCA Victor already had a Heritage line, so Legacy, though hardly original, was the next best thing. It had nothing whatsoever to do with Lieberson's prestige line of record-and-book packages that began with The Confederacy.

The first Legacy CD producer was Jerry Shulman. Out came the old recordings as Shulman and his small team scoured the vaults. Mike Berniker, who had begun with the label as a trainee a quarter century earlier, and Michael Brooks handled a mountain of jazz, and Nedra Olds-Neal mostly gospel. Columbia music from decades earlier was given new life through the series. Audiophiles and everyday consumers were either replacing their old records or getting into this music for the first time.

In 1979 CBS had confiscated the 100-plus album catalog of CTI Records, the jazz label founded and operated by Creed Taylor, which had defaulted on a sizable CBS loan. The catalog was folded into Epic. Eight years later, compact disc reissues of the CTI product began to appear on the market, to healthy profit for CBS.[22]

*   *   *

Sony's full-court press to acquire CBS Records began in mid-1986. Sony's cofounder Akio Morita wanted the record label to be part of the great Japanese electronics firm, and Sony's initial offer, $1.25 billion, reflected how badly he wanted it. But William Paley was ambivalent. Larry Tisch, CBS's first Jewish president after Paley, wanted to make the deal. Tisch was appalled by, maybe even a bit afraid of, Yetnikoff, whose wild and unpredictable temperament kept Tisch in a sweat. Where Yetnikoff was free-spending, Tisch was tight-fisted; where Yetnikoff was provocative, Tisch was conservative. In a series of apparently petty confrontations that widened the gulf between them, according to Yetnikoff, the most egregious involved Yetnikoff being chastised by Tisch for ordering a bagel at the Beverly Hills Hotel. "Do you know what they charge for a bagel in this hotel?" said Tisch. Yetnikoff skipped the bagel.[23] Tisch would prevail in the sale to Sony, not because he was listening closely to Yetnikoff but because he was reorganizing CBS's cash flow by selling various divisions and managing its stock price. At the same time Sony wanted to own the software (the records) to go with its hardware (the compact disc player and other components). As the writer Peter J. Boyer put it, "Stock management on one side, company management on the other."[24]

Larry Tisch was already a major CBS stockholder when he became president. The record division was hugely profitable again, thanks in large part to Michael Jackson. More recently, it had sold close to 2 million copies of the Top Gun soundtrack—not the first time the label scored so well with a soundtrack (e.g., *West Side Story* and *The Graduate*), nor the last (*Titanic* in the late nineties).[25] When it came to its reputation, however, CBS Records was taking it on the chin. By the mideighties a series of inquiries into the expanding power of independent promoters—what would become the central theme of Frederic Dannen's *Hit Men* a few years later—made the label appear that it had something to hide. Promoters like Los Angeles–based Joe Isgro and New Jersey–based Fred DiSipio were viewed as wielding enormous influence over what records got played on the air. Some labels affected outrage; others, like CBS, shrugged.[26] It didn't look great for either CBS or Yetnikoff. When Yetnikoff heard from a friend at Drexel Burnham Lambert that CBS was suddenly in play, he went ballistic. In what was threatening to become a contact sport, Yetnikoff confronted Tisch for the umpteenth time. Tisch explained that Yetnikoff was free to make his own deal for the record label.

A few weeks later Yetnikoff called Mickey Schulhof, Sony's vice chairman of American operations, and told him the CBS board was meeting in two days. The price was still $1.25 billion, "plus a side deal," as Boyer put it in his *Times* chronicle of the sale, "that would keep Yetnikoff and his management team in place." Yetnikoff wanted $50 million for himself and his *mishpocheh*. This wasn't so far-fetched because, as a young CBS Records attorney twenty years earlier, Yetnikoff had drafted the deal that became CBS/Sony, the profitable, Tokyo-based joint venture that Lieberson and Harvey Schein had begun to chisel out even earlier.

But the first round collapsed because the CBS board, apparently stunned that the record division was in play, overruled Tisch. Sony president and CEO Norio Ohga was perplexed by the way CBS was negotiating—if, in fact, it was negotiating at all. If the head of a company says they have a deal, they have a deal—don't they?

Technically, Paley and Tisch were running the same company—Paley as CBS chairman and Tisch as CEO and president—but they couldn't communicate. Schulhof eventually recognized that, in a conflict, Tisch would prevail. As Paley became increasingly open to at least expanding the old partnership with Sony, Tisch went for broke, offering the record division for $2 billion. As the two companies circled around the new, considerably higher figure, Schulhof flew to Tokyo and, though it was a Japanese holiday, found Morita and Ohga waiting to talk to him. Yetnikoff, already in town to watch over Michael Jackson's performances there, stopped by as a kind of friend of both sides of the court. (If he played his cards right, Yetnikoff would be in good shape with Sony.) Morita, according to Peter Boyer's account, sensed that the $2 billion price was locked in, and he finally gave his assent. Feeling at once victorious and empathetic, Morita phoned Paley in New York and offered him an honorary chairmanship. The deal seemed to be done.

It wasn't. The CBS board was still chewing it over, and had even contemplated hiring a consulting firm to project where the record business was going. The deal was finally concluded after the stock market crash of October 19, 1987. (Black Monday was the term used on the street and in the papers, recalling the crash of fifty-eight years earlier.)[27] The crash gave Tisch the leverage he needed to persuade Paley and the board, once and for all, to sell Columbia Records. And, despite the crash, Sony and Morita were no less interested in the $2 billion price tag. Even adjusting for a half century of inflation, Paley's original 1938 investment had returned nearly 3,000 times its price.

• • •

In April 1988 CBS Records Division, the U.S. record company of CBS Records, Inc., a subsidiary of Sony Corp. of Tokyo, named Tommy Mottola president, replacing Al Teller.[28] Mottola had run a management company of thirty employees rather than the seven hundred then at CBS Records.[29] More than a year after the Sony deal went through, CBS Records picked up the jewel of Nashville's music publishers, Tree International, for more than $30 million. Tree's catalog included "Heartbreak Hotel" and songs by Merle Haggard, Buck Owens, and Roger Miller, among many others.[30] Columbia and Epic had kept a strong presence in Nashville since the early sixties, but the purchase of Tree was significant for two reasons: Tree was probably the last of the major independently owned and operated Nashville companies, its business decisions made right there, and now it too was going international; and Tree was also meant to help rebuild CBS's song catalog after the sale, three years earlier, of CBS Songs to Stephen Swid, Martin Bandier, and Charles Koppelman, who'd renamed the publishing company SBK Entertainment.

But CBS Records was said to be in trouble. Honest to a fault, the naturally overheated Yetnikoff didn't deny it. Data compiled by its closest competitor, Warners, suggested that, from May 1988 to May 1989, Warners had outsold CBS two to one. Despite Sony's brand-new ownership, the label was perceived to be over the hill. Springsteen was about to turn 40; Billy Joel and James Taylor were getting close to it; Streisand and Dylan were well past it. Irving Azoff of MCA told the *Times* that CBS had failed to break in younger, less expensive artists who'd remain for a while at the label. Yetnikoff dismissed most of the criticism, insisting that the label needed to return to its Artists & Repertoire emphasis to sign and produce new talent.

Buffeted by the press and by his masters in Japan, Yetnikoff resigned on September 4, 1990. He was 57. Until a new president was named, CBS Records was to be run by Mottola, by Bob Summer of CBS International, and by Neal Keating, who was still president of the Record Club after three decades—and all of them reporting to Norio Ohga.[31] Everybody had a theory. Some said Yetnikoff's two-year contract, by definition, undermined his ability to maintain close relationships with his artists. Some said that Frederic Dannen's *Hit Men*, his exposé about promotion excesses under Yetnikoff's long tenure—excesses that amounted to graft and payola—had eviscerated his authority. Those who knew him well clucked that Yetnikoff, who was notorious for abusing his body— this was the man, after all, who'd explained to Mick Jagger that he hadn't returned his calls because his liver was about to blow—was still on a path to self-destruction. But Yetnikoff had taken the label into its final CBS chapter with a roar. As Sony assumed control of the label, the Columbia/CBS years under Yetnikoff would be evaluated not as innovative (as they were under Lieberson) or pop-musically dominant (under Davis), but as flexible with changing media and technology. On top of that, Yetnikoff made sure those years weren't dull.

ALTERNATE TAKE:

After CBS

24
Walk Down 30th Street

Columbia Records and its subsidiaries belonged to Sony. Although CBS/Columbia had already been a powerful international media company, it now became global—a brand known worldwide, though not necessarily for recordings. Sony would soon add Columbia Pictures to its holdings, not because of its name but because the deal, nurtured partly by Walter Yetnikoff, was the right movie studio deal for it to make (even if Sony notoriously overpaid for the services of Peter Guber and Jon Peters). Sony made one far-seeing business move when it bought back international rights to the Columbia name from EMI.

The 1990s at Sony were overseen by Tommy Mottola, whose protégé Mariah Carey proved to be one of the great stars for Columbia Records during the Clinton years in America. But it was so different as to be another record label altogether. Apart from the women and men who handled the Legacy reissues, Columbia under Sony ownership was a new company, only nominally connected at all to the oldest operating record label in the world. Even the venerable classical division, overseen by Peter Gelb, was kept afloat not so much by world-class artists like Isaac Stern and Yo Yo Ma but by the soundtrack to *Titanic*. In the wake of its oceanic success, the label leaned more heavily on its Music Soundtrax division, run from the West Coast by Glen Brunman.

Columbia Records's greatest years, when innovation combined with excellence to make it the most consistently imaginative record label, were probably right after the Second World War and through 1960. This is the period when the LP was developed; when the Record Club began;

when Goddard Lieberson built Masterworks into the greatest classical archive available to us, and also put the best of American musical theater on record; when George Avakian patiently made the label into a hospitable place for jazz players; and when Mitch Miller turned out pop hits that supported the entire company through experimentation and less profitable times. That same period also happened to be a glittering time in New York City, where Columbia Records was headquartered. Housing and transportation weren't yet the struggle they would become; the streets were relatively clean, people dressed in fine clothes to go to work and strolled down the sidewalk looking at the city, and at each other, rather than at their cell phones.

Goddard Lieberson made that New York his own. And he adhered to the principle articulated by the philosopher Don Gifford when, with a nod to Aristotle, he wrote that "we can choose to see or not to see. We can turn our heads or close our eyes. But we cannot as easily choose not to hear. The ear is always in touch."[1]

"The age of recording," Geoffrey O'Brien wrote, "is necessarily an age of nostalgia—when was the past so hauntingly accessible?—but its bitterest insight is in the incapacity of even the most perfectly captured sound to restore the moment of its first inscribing. That world is no longer there."[2]

But is it gone forever? And is the third or fifth or fiftieth hearing of a recording less significant than the first? Since the late nineteenth century the miracle of phonography is that, at least potentially, each new hearing can evoke responses that have nothing to do with nostalgia. In what remains the most resonant poem about phonograpy, Howard Nemerov wrote:

Deep in a time that cannot come again
Bach thought it through, this lonely and immense
Reflexion wherein our sorrows learn to dance.
And deep in the time that cannot come again
Casals recorded it. Playing it back,
And bending now over the instrument,

I watch the circling stillness of the disc,
The tracking inward of the tone-arm, enact
A mystery wherein the music shares:
How time, that comes and goes and vanishes
Never to come again, can come again.[3]

Edward Easton, Edward Wallerstein, Goddard Lieberson: all of them knew that recorded music and the spoken word, played once or a thousand times, would—will—allow our sorrows to dance.

"I walk down 30th Street between Second and Third Avenue," Peter Munves said, "and with each step I say the name of a Columbia person who recorded there. Johnny Mathis. I take a step. Barbra Streisand. I take a step. Kostelanetz. Another step. Horowitz, Glenn Gould, Andy Williams. I say each one."[4] The former Greek Orthodox Church that housed the 30th Street studio is gone—razed to make room for an apartment building. Also gone is Trinacria, the Third Avenue food importer where Mitch Miller bought sandwiches for his artists and staff during recording sessions. Long after the apartment building has been demolished and Americans are importing food from Venus, long after all those magnificent Columbia artists and you and I and our descendants are dead and the label itself barely a footnote in the history of great media companies, those recordings will be in the air somewhere.

ACKNOWLEDGMENTS

Like so many book projects, *The Label* began as one thing and turned into another—a history that required considerably more primary source material and secondary detective work than the original idea would have. Many people contributed time and leads to more information, as well as books, photographs, and office correspondence. Some were willing to talk or write over the course of several months; others were able to give no more than a few minutes but were no less appreciated. Without their help, *The Label* would have amounted to little more than a few lists and broad generalizations that would be hardly worth a reader's time. Please forgive my antipathy to making distinctions in print among the contributors; each person knows what he or she was able to contribute. Their contributions have given the book whatever value it might have; its mistakes, however, are mine. My heartfelt thanks to the people listed below—and to those whom I have regretfully, inadvertently omitted.

From the Irving S. Gilmore Music Library at Yale University: Suzanne Eggleston Lovejoy and her expert staff there; Richard Warren; and Susan Hawkshaw of the Oral History Department.

From the New York Public Library for the Performing Arts, Astor, Lenox, and Tilden Foundations, George Boziwick, Chief of the Music Division; from the Sound Archives there, Don McCormick; and the curators of the Rodgers & Hammerstein Archives and Music Division.

From the Astor-Lenox branch of the New York Public Library: Wayne Furman and David Smith.

From the Columbia/Epic/CBS Records family: Arnold Kim, Tina McCarthy, Harry Palmer, Mike Berniker, Tom Shepard, Howard Scott, Stan Kavan, George Avakian, David Kapralik, Peter Munves, Didier Deutsch, John Jackson, Seth Rothstein, Mitch Miller, John McClure, Neal Keating, Arnold Levine, John Berg, John Doumanian, Paul Myers, Maida Glancy, Sol Rabinowitz, Leonard Levy, Victor Linn, Bob Morgan, Gregg Geller, Sam Lederman, Stan Snyder, Don Hunstein, Schuyler Chapin, Mikie Harris, Bruce Lundvall, John Boylan, Elizabeth Larsen Lauer, Joe Sherman, Linda Barton, Morris Baumstein, Ron Alexenburg, Joseph Dash, Stephen Paley, Mort Lewis, Tom Noonan, Neil Fujita, and Ralph Colin Jr.

Also: Scott Moyers, Jeremy Townsend, Jane Schicke, Helen Burr, Joan Simpson Burns, Dick Hyman, Sheldon Harnick, Mimi Perrin, Kirk Silsbee, Chuck Wilson, Claire Stern, Joseph DeBragga, Tamara Conniff, Rich Conaty, Mary Bryden, and Peter Lieberson.

Anne Townsend of the Harley Alumni Association; Harley School alumni Ruth Bennett and Arthur Lowenthal.

Also: Sue Bernstein (my mom), Joe Bernstein (her husband), Dan Segal and Susan Kitzen, Judy Tobey, and Arnie Berger. From the Susan Golomb Literary Agency, Kim Goldstein. And from Thunder's Mouth Press: Anita Diggs, Michele Martin, Lynn Mazur, Lukas Volger, John Oakes, Peter Jacoby, Amy Scott, Diane Burke, and Jofie Ferrari-Adler.

For permission to quote from "Lines and Circularities," Margaret Nemerov. And for permission to quote from the Goddard Lieberson Papers at the Irving S. Gilmore Music Library of Yale University, once again Peter Lieberson.

NOTES

Endnote Key:
AI=Author Interview
NYT=New York Times
LAT=Los Angeles Times
WSJ=Wall Street Journal
ISG=Irving S. Gilmore Music Library, Yale University
NYPL=New York Public Library
TM Collection=Teo Macero Collection, Music Division, the New York Public Library for the Per-
      forming Arts, Astor, Lenox, and Tilden Foundations
GL Papers=Goddard Lieberson Papers, Irving S. Gilmore Library
JH Papers=John Hammond Papers, Irving S. Gilmore Library
Other periodicals are identified by their full name; every attempt has been made to obtain page
      numbers. For verification purposes, a catalog number for a recording is provided only
      when the recording—whether on disk, tape, or compact disk—is in the author's posses-
      sion; other catalog numbers can be usually obtained on the Internet.

Liner Notes: One Boy's Columbia Records
   1. John Hammond on Record, p. 349.
   2. Frank Sinatra, "You Go to My Head" and "I Don't Know Why" C 112-1 & 2, 36918, 78 rpm.
   3. Deborah Solomon, "Lincoln Center's Culture Gap," NYT, 10/05/2003, p. SM24.
   4. Clive Davis, Clive: Inside the Music Business, p. 5.
   5. John Hammond on Record, pp. 211–12.

Side A: Some Pre-CBS History

1: My mother was a Phonograph
   1. NYT, 01/24/1908, p. 1. Tim Brooks, "High Drama in the Record Industry: Columbia
      Records, 1901–1934," ARSC Journal 33, no. 1 (Spring 2002): 34.
   2. NYT, 10/27/1907, p. 3.
   3. Brooks, "High Drama," p. 34.
   4. Some material following comes from Columbia Records's in-house history, "History of
      Columbia Records and Related Companies," prepared by Florence Gilbert for Clive J. Davis,
      General Attorney, 10/03/1962; and from Charles Schicke, Revolution in Sound: A Biography of the
      Recording Industry.

5. Alfred O. Tate, *Edison's Open Door: The Life Story of Thomas A. Edison, a Great Individualist*, p. 139.
6. Schicke, *Revolution in Sound*, p. 17.
7. Ibid., p. 18.
8. Raymond R. Wile, "The North American Phonograph Company: Part I (1888–1892)," *ARSC Journal* 35, no. 1 (Spring 2004): 4.
9. George C. Waldo, *History of Bridgeport and Vicinity*, vol. 1, p. 153.
10. Allen Koenigsberg, introduction to *Columbia Phonograph Companion*, by Howard Hazelcorn.
11. James R. Smart, "Emile Berliner and Nineteenth-Century Disc Recordings," in *Wonderful Inventions*, p. 348.
12. Peter Martland, *Since Records Began: EMI: The First 100 Year*, p. 14.
13. *Boyd's District of Columbia Directory 1890*.
14. Brooks, "High Drama," p. 22.
15. Schicke, *Revolution in Sound*, pp. 26–27.
16. Ibid., pp. 20–21.
17. Wile, "North American Phonograph Company," pp. 8–9.
18. Schicke, *Revolution in Sound*, pp. 21–22.
19. Wile, "North American Phonograph Company," p. 13.
20. "Fate of a Scientific Fad," NYT, 09/11/1894, p. 1.
21. Tate, *Edison's Open Door*, p. 175.
22. Wile, "North American Phonograph Company," p. 23.
23. "The Graphophone Company: Why It Suspended Business and Why It Is Going to Renew It," NYT, 01/16/1891, p. 5.
24. NYT, 08/20/1886, p. 5.
25. Wile, "North American Phonograph Company," p. 18.
26. "Business Troubles," NYT, 05/10/1894, p. 6.
27. Wile, "North American Phonograph Company," p. 23.
28. "Obituary Record," NYT, 04/20/1894, p. 2. "An Inventor with a Business Head," NYT, 09/13/1894, p. 2.
29. Schicke, *Revolution in Sound*, pp. 34–35. "History of Columbia Records," p. 5.
30. Martland, *Since Records Began*, pp. 92–93. NYT, 06/15/1940, p. 15.
31. "History of Columbia Records," p. 4.
32. Evan Eisenberg, *The Recording Angel*, p. 90.
33. Smart, "Emile Berliner," p. 347.
34. Many sources say Len Spencer was the son of Platt Rogers Spencer. Since the elder Spencer died two and a half years before Len's birth, in the days before frozen sperm, it's unlikely.
35. Quoted in Tim Brooks, *Lost Sounds: Blacks and the Birth of the Recording Industry, 1890–1919*, p. 28. Some material surrounding the quote is also drawn from Brooks.
36. NYT, 12/21/1899, p. 5.
37. NYT, 10/13/1899, p. 7.
38. Brooks, *Lost Sounds*, pp. 54–56.
39. Edward Marks, *They All Sang: From Tony Pastor to Rudy Vallee*, p. 104.
40. Tim Brooks, *The Columbia Master Book Discography*, vol. 1, p. 38.
41. Paul E. Bierley, *John Philip Sousa: American Phenomenon*, p. 51.
42. NYT, 06/29/1901, p. 9.

2: Litigation vs. Innovation

1. "History of Columbia Records," p. 6.
2. Michael W. Sherman and Kurt R. Nauck III, *Note the Notes*, p. 12. *John Hammond on Record*, p. 212.
3. Brooks, "High Drama," p. 26.
4. "History of Columbia Records," p. 6.
5. Ibid.

6. Marc Kirkeby, notes to Sony CD compilation *Soundtrack for a Century*.
7. Sherman and Nauck, *Note the Notes*, p. 5.
8. Ibid.
9. Ibid., p. 14.
10. William Faulkner, *As I Lay Dying*, p. 225.
11. Brooks, "High Drama," p. 26.
12. "History of Columbia Records," p. 7.
13. Brooks, "High Drama," pp. 26–27.
14. John M. Picker, *Victorian Soundscapes*, p. 142.
15. Schicke, *Revolution in Sound*, p. 58.
16. Archeophone Records has collected on CD many of Burr's recordings, dating from 1903.
17. Pekka Gronow, "Ethnic Recordings: An Introduction," *Ethnic Recordings in America*, p. 16.
18. "History of Columbia Records," p. 7.
19. Bierley, *John Philip Sousa*, p. 351.
20. John Philip Sousa, "The Menace of Mechanical Music," *Appleton's Magazine*, September 1906, cited by Bierley, *John Philip Sousa*, p. 71.
21. Editorial, NYT, 12/13/1907, p. 10.
22. "Theatrical Gossip," NYT, 10/20/1898, p. 12.
23. *Bert Williams: The Early Years, 1901–1909* (Archeophone Records 5004, CD). Notes by Allen G. Debus and Richard Martin. Some of the material following is drawn from their notes.
24. Ad quoted in Eric Ledell Smith, *Bert Williams: A Biography of the Black Comedian*, p. 91.
25. Allan H. Spear, preface to *Black Manhattan*, by James Weldon Johnson.
26. George W. Walker, "The Real 'Coon' on the American Stage," *The Theatre Magazine*, August 1906, p. 224, quoted by Debus and Martin in the liner notes for *Bert Williams: The Early Years, 1901–1909*.
27. Caryl Phillips, *Dancing in the Dark*, p. 173. Phillips spoke extensively about Williams on Leonard Lopate's radio show, WNYC-FM (New York), 01/16/2006.
28. Robert Sobel, *RCA*, p. 21.
29. "History of Columbia Records," p. 7. Sherman and Nauck, *Note the Notes*, p. 24.
30. NYT, 09/12/1906, p. 9.
31. Sherman and Nauck, *Note the Notes*, p. 24.
32. *Graphonotes* 1, no. 1 (April 1907): 2.
33. Ibid., p. 11.
34. *Graphonotes* 1, no. 2 (July 1907), p. 7.
35. Brooks, "High Drama," p. 66. NYT, 10/14/1908, p. 5.
36. Sherman and Nauck, *Note the Notes*, p. 26.
37. Brooks, "High Drama," p. 35.
38. 1908 *Sears Catalog*, pp. 199–200.
39. Hazelcorn, *Columbia Phonograph Companion*, p. 10.
40. Martland, *Since Records Began*, p. 103.
41. "Sir Louis Sterling, Industrialist Born on Lower East Side, Dead," NYT, 06/03/1958, p. 31. Martland, *Since Records Began*, p. 104.
42. NYT, 06/03/1958, p. 31.
43. *Saturday Evening Post*, 06/13/1914, pp. 38–39.
44. Garden's earliest recordings, made in 1911 and 1912, were rereleased by Columbia's subsidiary Odyssey on *Legendary Performances: The Great Mary Garden* (32 16 0079, vinyl).
45. Gracyk, *Popular American Recording Pioneers: 1895–1925*, pp. 65–73.
46. Sigmund Spaeth, *Read 'Em and Weep: The Somgs You Forgot to Remember*, p. 63.
47. Douglas Gilbert, *Lost Chords: The Diverting Story of American Popular Songs*, pp. 244–45.

3: Foxtrotting In and Out of War
1. Brooks, "High Drama," p. 40.
2. These quotes are taken from "A Proposal Made in 1911 to Consolidate Edison and Columbia," text written by Tim Gracyk, who credits Peter Fraser with copying Dyer's original memo at the Edison National Historic Site. www.garlic.com/columbia.htm.
3. "History of Columbia Records," p. 8.
4. "Castle House Is Opened," NYT, 12/16/1913, p. 11.
5. Gracyk, Popular American Recording Pioneers, p. 277.
6. "The Beginnngs of Mr Castle," NYT, 07/23/1916, p. X7.
7. Irene Castle, My Husband, p. 65.
8. Schicke, Revolution in Sound, p. 76.
9. Joseph Murrell, Million-Selling Records 1903–1980, p. 15.
10. Joe Hayman, "The Biography of Sam Cohen," Cohen on the Radio, p. 5.
11. W. C. Handy, Father of the Blues, pp. 178–79.
12. David Levering Lewis, When Harlem Was in Vogue, pp. 158–59.
13. Brooks, Lost Sounds, p. 93.
14. Brooks, "High Drama," p. 44.
15. NYT, 08/21/1915, p. 8. NYT, 08/24/1915, p. 7.
16. Maureen Howard', excerpt from Bridgeport Bus, anthologized in How We Live, p. 61.
17. Brooks, "High Drama," p. 44.
18. NYT, 12/15/1897, p. 3. NYT, 05/05/1909, p. 11.
19. NYT, 07/14/1915, p. 3.
20. Sherman and Nauck, Note the Notes, p. 52.
21. Hammond, Hammond on Record, pp. 213–14.
22. Olin Downes, The Lure of Music, unpaged.
23. Brooks, "High Drama," p. 44.
24. Trow's General Directory of the Boroughs of Manhattan and Bronx, City of New York 1861-1935.
25. The Peptimist, vol. 1, no. 3, May 1917, p. 2.
26. The Grafanola in the Classroom: Graded Catalog of Educational Records.
27. Henry Sapoznik, Klezmer! Jewish Music from Old World to Our World, p. 93.
28. Cantor David Roitman, "Hayom Teamtzenu" b/w "Vachol Beeay Oilom" (Columbia Graphophone E 5266, 78 rpm). Cantor Josef Rosenblatt, "Haben Jakir Li" b/w "Melech al Kol Hoolom" (Columbia Graphophone E 5148, 78 rpm).
29. Waldo, History of Bridgeport, p. 166.
30. NYT, 07/26/1918, p. 7.
31. Sherman and Nauck, Note the Notes, p. 55.
32. Rosa Ponselle and James A. Drake, Ponselle: A Singer's Life, p. 63.
33. Sherman and Nauck, Note the Notes, p. 40.
34. Sophie Tucker with Dorothy Giles, Some of These Days: The Autobiography of Sophie Tucker, p. 99.
35. NYT, 08/30/1919, p. 3. Brooks, "High Drama," p. 44.
36. Hazel Meyer, The Gold in Tin Pan Alley, p. 70.
37. NYT, 02/11/1919, p. 1. NYT, 10/06/1919, p. 10.
38. Picker, Victorian Soundscapes, p. 140.
39. "Business Men Vote for Mellon Plan," NYT, 11/21/1923, p. 4.

4: Acoustic Prohibition to Electric Depression
1. Martland, Since Records Began, p. 104.
2. "History of Columbia Records," p. 9.
3. Bob Thomas, King Cohn: The Life and Times of Harry Cohn, p. 34.
4. "Women to Hold a Radio Revel," NYT, 05/11/1925, p. 17. "Alfred H. Grebe, 40, Radio Pioneer Dies," NYT, 10/25/1935, p. 21. "History of Columbia Records," p. 9. The in-house

history says that the station itself was WABC, but ABC appear to be the initials of the holding company.

5. Schicke, *Revolution in Sound*, pp. 81–82.
6. Rich Conaty, Author Interview, 03/16/2005. Sherman and Nauck, *Note the Notes*, p. 48.
7. NYT, 03/07/1925, p. 20.
8. *New York City Directory 1925*.
9. "History of Columbia Records," p. 10.
10. Sobel, *RCA*, p. 82.
11. *Columbia Records Catalog 1928*, pp. 273–74. This particular model dispensed with the radio itself but installed the Kolster "Power Cone Speaker" for "the finest and latest development in amplification."
12. *Delius Orchestral Works*, Vol. 2 (Columbia L 2087, CD). *George Gershwin* (Columbia AL 39, 10" vinyl).
13. Paul Oliver, *Bessie Smith*, p. 15.
14. Chris Albertson, *Bessie Smith: Empress of the Blues*, p. 7. Some material following comes from Albertson.
15. David Levering Lewis, *When Harlem Was in Vogue*, p. 173. Thirty-three essential Smith selections, recorded between 1923 and 1933 and including the later John Hammond–produced sessions, can be heard on *Bessie Smith: The World's Greatest Blues Singer* (Columbia CG 33, vinyl). The notes are by Chris Albertson.
16. Ben Selvin, interview by Rich Conaty, "The Big Broadcast," WVUF-New York, 12/12/1976.
17. Oliver, *Bessie Smith*, p. 44.
18. Ethel Waters with Charles Samuels, *His Eye Is on the Sparrow*, p. 135.
19. Jimmy Durante and Jack Kafoed, *Night Clubs*, p. 190.
20. *His Eye Is on the Sparrow*, p. 173.
21. Ben Selvin, interview by Rich Conaty.
22. John Hammond and Frank Driggs, memo to Bill Gallagher, JH Papers, ISG, 4/27/66.
23. Ben Selvin, interview by Rich Conaty.
24. NYT, 03/07/1925, p. 20.
25. Charles E. Mack, *Two Black Crows in the A.E.F.*, p. 24.
26. Jean Pierre Lion, *Bix*, p. 336.
27. Ralph Ellison, *Invisible Man*, p. 11.
28. "Profit for Columbia Phonograph," NYT, 05/12/1927, p. 45.
29. Martland, *Since Records Began*, p. 130.
30. "History of Columbia Records," p. 11.
31. Sally Bedell Smith, *In All His Glory*. pp. 56–59. Some of the material following is drawn from this biography.
32. "Victor Control Passes," *WSJ*, 12/08/1926 p. 18.
33. "And All Because They're Smart," *Fortune* June 1935, pp. 80-86. The unsigned article said that Major White also made the first commercial broadcast of a sports event—the Dempsey-Carpentier fight on July 2, 1921, held in Jersey City—and then went to work for Westinghouse.
34. "New Chain of Stations Will Exploit Movies," NYT, 06/23/1927, p. 22. "Plan Radio Chain East of Rockies," NYT, 07/02/1927, p. 20.
35. "'King's Henchman' Led by Taylor over Radio," NYT, 09/19/1927, p. 32.
36. Ralph Colin Jr., AI, 01/03/2006. E-mail to author, 06/20/2006. *Who's Who in American Jewry*, p. 190.
37. *Columbia Records Catalog 1928*, p. 77.
38. "Columbia Company in Deal with Pathé," NYT, 10/10/1928, p. 41.
39. In her squib on *À Nous la Liberté*, directed by René Clair, in *Kiss Kiss Bang Bang*, Pauline Kael quoted Charles Pathé as saying, "Only the armaments industry made profits like ours."

40. Martland, *Since Records Began*, p. 125.

41. NYT, 03/27/1930, p. 30.

42. Edward Marks, *They All Sang*, p. 217.

43. Durante and Kafoed, *Night Clubs*, p. 36.

44. Clayton, Jackson & Durante, "Can Broadway Do Without Me?" (Columbia 1860, 78 rpm).

45. "History of Columbia Records," p. 12.

46. "Graphophone Deal Talked," NYT, 09/11/1929, p. 42.

47. *Time Capsule* 1929, p. 152.

48. Samuel Brylawski, "Cartoons for the Record: The Jack Kapp Collection," in *Wonderful Inventions*, p. 361.

49. "History of Columbia Records," p. 13.

50. Schicke, *Revolution in Sound*, p. 97.

51. Chris Albertson says as much in *Bessie Smith: Empress of the Blues*, p. 17.

52. "Radio's Gramophone Merger Interest 30%," *WSJ*, 03/20/1931, p. 1.

53. "Grigsby-Grunow to Buy Columbia," *WSJ*, 12/25/1931, p. 1.

54. NYT, 04/19/1912, p. 13.

55. Philip Mauro, *The Wonders of Bible Chronology*, p. 2.

56. Philip Mauro, *The Hope of Israel? What Is It?* p. 11.

57. Advertisement, NYT, 03/26/1933, p. BR19.

5: Cheap but Often Unforgettable

1. *John Hammond on Record*, p. 215.

2. Edmund Wilson, *The Thirties*, p.163.

3. *John Hammond on Record*, p. 9.

4. E. J. Kahn, "Young Man with a Viola," *New Yorker*, 07/29/1939, p. 21.

5. *John Hammond on Record*, p. 68.

6. Ibid., pp. 64–65.

7. Eve Brown, *Champagne Cholly: The Life and Times of Maury Paul*, p. 56.

8. Kahn, "Young Man with a Viola," p. 19.

9. John Hammond, letter to Arthur Bronstein, 03/02/1981. JH Papers, ISG.

10. *John Hammond on Record*, p. 87.

11. Kahn, "Young Man with a Viola," p. 24.

12. The location is suggested in *Bix*, p. 337, and clearly stated by Hammond's notes for his article "From Jazz to Swing." "Honeysuckle Rose" and "Underneath the Harlem Moon" were recorded on 12/09/1932 and can be heard on Col. 2732-D, CD.

13. John Hammond, letter to Arthur Bronstein, 03/02/1981. JH Papers, ISG.

14. Schicke, *Revolution in Sound*, p. 102.

15. Brian Priestley, *Jazz on Record: A History*, p. 80.

16. "Grigsby-Grunow Gets Receivers," NYT, 11/25/1933, p. 5.

17. *John Hammond on Record*, pp. 215–16.

18. "History of Columbia Records," p. 14.

19. Gary Giddins, *Bing Crosby: A Pocketful of Dreams*, p. 371.

20. Schicke, *Revolution in Sound*, p. 98. Hammond, *Hammond on Record*, p. 216. "History of Columbia Records," p. 14.

21. NYT, 02/27/1935, p. 33.

22. NYT, 03/28/1937, p. 31.

23. *New Masses*, 04/20/1937, p. 36.

24. *John Hammond on Record*, p. 190. *New Masses*, p. 05/25/1937.

25. Gene Autry with Mickey Herskowitz, *Back in the Saddle*, p. 15.

26. Edwin Schallert, "Soria, Here on Survey, Plans Studio in Mexico," *LAT*, 09/25/1941, p. A10.

27. Leroy Carr, *Blues Before Sunrise* (C 30496, vinyl). All sixteen tracks include Carr's frequent guitarist Scrapper Blackwell; three tracks include Josh White.

28. Peter Guralnick, *Searching for Robert Johnson*, pp. 32–33. Much of the material following is drawn from Guralnick.

29. *Robert Johnson: King of the Delta Blues Singers Vol. 2* (C 30034, vinyl). The release was produced by Frank Driggs, the accompanying essay written by Pete Welding. Driggs wrote the liner notes to the first volume when it was released in 1962.

30. Paul Oliver, *Blues Fell This Morning*, p. 255.

31. *New Masses*, 03/03/1937, p. 29.

32. Guralnick, *Searching for Robert Johnson*, p. 52.

33. NYT, 05/30/1958, p. 21.

34. Alec Wilder, *Letters I Never Mailed*, p. 70. Hammond, *Hammond on Record*, p. 219.

35. George T. Simon, *The Big Bands*, pp. 51–53.

36. NYT, 04/23/1985, p. D27.

37. Henry Johnson [John Hammond], *New Masses*, 07/07/1936, p. 29.

38. *Hammond on Record*, p. 126.

39. "History of Columbia Records," p. 15.

40. Agate, *The Later Ego*, p. 560.

41. Irving Mills, interview by Stephen Lesser, 04/09/1975, for the American Jewish Committee's Oral History, New York Public Library, pp. 32–33 of transcript.

42. "Sir Louis Sterling Resigns 'E.M.I.' Post," NYT, 05/13/1939, p. 5.

43. Quoted by Martland, *Since Records Began*, p. 104.

44. "Swing: The Hottest and Best Kind of Jazz Records Reaches Its Golden Age," *Life*, 08/08/1938, p. 60. Many of these recordings were rereleased on *Swing Street* (Epic JSN 6042, vinyl).

45. "History of Columbia Records," p. 15.

46. Smith, *In All His Glory*, p. 148. Hammond, *Hammond on Record*, pp. 216–17.

47. Jane Schicke, letter to author, 06/24/2005.

48. Some sources say CBS's purchase price was $750,000.

Side B: The CBS Years

CHAPTER 6: Sign 'Em Up

1. "To Head American Record," NYT, 01/05/1939, p. 41.

2. "C.B.S. Expansion Program," NYT, 04/11/1939, p. 36.

3. *Hammond on Record*, p. 218.

4. Ibid., p. 210.

5. Ibid., p. 220.

6. John Hammond, letter to Clay Felker, undated but probably 1973, JH Papers, ISG.

7. Granville Hicks, *John Reed: The Making of a Revolutionary*, pp. 339–40.

8. Jane Schicke, letter to author, 06/24/2005. Some biographical material comes from this letter and earlier phone conversations.

9. Peter Munves, AI, 02/11/2005.

10. Not, apparently, the same Jimmy Long as the North Carolina–based talent scout who directed John Hammond to Blind Boy Fuller and Mitchell's Christian Singers in 1938.

11. Stan Kavan, AI, 01/24/2005.

12. Ted Fox, *In the Groove*, p. 6. Szigeti's recording of Bach's *Praeludium* from *Partitia No. 3 in E Major*, for Unaccompanied Violin, made in 1908 when he was 16, is astonishingly clear, not to also say gorgeous. It can be heard on *The Art of Joseph Szigeti* (Columbia M6X 31513, vinyl).

13. Peter Munves, AI, 04/29/2005. Philip Hart, "The Budapest String Quartet Recordings (Part II)," *ARSC Journal* 29, no. 1 (Spring 1998): 86.
14. "History of Columbia Records," p. 16. *Hammond on Record* gives the date as one year earlier.
15. Howard Taubman, "Columbia Adds New Group of Singers to Its Roster—Recent Releases," NYT, 03/30/1941, p. X6.
16. "Notes Here and Afield," NYT, 11/09/1941, p. X6.
17. *John Hammond on Record*, p. 165.
18. Gama Gilbert, "Records: Studio News," NYT, 02/11/1940, p. 134.
19. The second "From Spirituals to Swing" concert was staged by Joseph Losey, the American who subsequently moved to England and became a major film director (*The Servant*, *The Go-Between*, etc.) there.
20. The Golden Gate Quartet, *Swing Down, Chariot* (Columbia 47131, CD).
21. *Negro Spirituals/Gospel Songs 1926–1942* (Fremeaux & Assoc. S.A. 008, CD).
22. Ralph Ellison, "The Charlie Christian Story," *Shadow & Act*, pp. 229–30.
23. Benny Goodman and His Orchestra, "Solo Flight" (CO 36684, 78 rpm). Charlie Christian with the Benny Goodman Sextet & Orchestra (CL 652, vinyl).
24. JH Papers, ISG.
25. *John Hammond on Record*, p. 236.
26. George Avakian, AI, 11/23/2005.
27. Some of this material comes from George Avakian, interview by Sarah Fishko, New York's WNYC-FM, 12/24/2003, as well as George Avakian, AI, 01/18/2005.
28. George Avakian, AI, 01/18/2005.
29. George Avakian, AI, 06/28/2006.

CHAPTER 7: Battlegrounds

1. *John Hammond on Record*, p. 220.
2. Simon, *Big Bands*, p. 222.
3. "Mrs Duckworth Wed to Benny Goodman," NYT, 03/21/1942, p. 20.
4. *Echoes: Memoirs of Andre Kostelanetz*, p. 84.
5. Jane Schicke, AI, 05/18/2005.
6. "Defense News," *WSJ*, 04/15/1942, p. 2. Schicke, *Revolution in Sound*, p. 107.
7. "Broadcasters War on 'Song Monopoly,'" NYT, 09/16/1939, p. 24.
8. Brylawski, "Cartoons for the Record," p. 362.
9. "Record Makers 'to Do the Best We Can' in the Face of Ban Set by Petrillo," NYT, 08/02/1942, p. 1.
10. Howard Taubman, "Records: 1943 Outlook," NYT, 12/27/1942, p. X6.
11. Ibid.
12. Joseph Murrells, *Million-Selling Records 1903–1980*, p. 37.
13. E. J. Kahn, "Just a Kid from Hoboken," *New Yorker*, 11/09/1946. Some of the material preceding and following is drawn from this article, and from Kahn's earlier sections of the three-part profile, dated 10/26/1946 and 11/02/1946.
14. "Sinatra Backs Boogie Against Rodzinski Slur," *The Sun*, 01/22/1944, p. 1.
15. "Ormandy Records Again," NYT, 11/20/1944, p. 26.
16. George Avakian, AI, 11/23/2005.
17. Jack Gould, "Ban on Records Off As Petrillo Wins; RCA, CBS to Pay Fees," NYT, 11/12/1944, p. 1. Some material leading up to the quote comes from Gould's article.
18. Bill West, *Remington Arms & History*, chap. 9, p. 1.
19. John Hammond, letter to Clay Felker, undated but probably 1973. JH Papers, ISG.
20. GL Papers, ISG.
21. George Avakian, AI, 01/05/2005.
22. Bill C. Malone, *Country Music U.S.A.*, p. 199.

23. Some of this material comes from *Columbia Promotion News*, published in-house in Bridgeport between 1946 and 1950.

24. Rosemary Clooney with Joan Barthel, *Girl Singer: An Autobiography*, p. 50.

25. *The Voice of Frank Sinatra* (set C-112, 78 rpm; Columbia Legacy CK6100 CD).

26. *Frank Sinatra Conducts the Music of Alec Wilder* (Columbia Masterworks M-637, 78 rpm).

27. Dorothy Baker, letter to Goddard Lieberson, undated, GL Papers, ISG.

28. Stan Kavan, AI, 01/29/2005.

29. George Avakian, AI, 03/14/2005.

30. George Avakian, AI, 01/18/2005.

31. George Avakian, e-mail to author, 06/01/2005.

32. *John Hammond on Record*, p. 272.

33. John Hammond, letter to Joseph Bevana Bush, 03/06/1975. JH Papers, ISG.

34. Leroy Friedman, AI, 04/27/06 and 05/05/06.

35. *Columbia Promotion News*, March 1947.

36. Arthur Godfrey, "Too Fat Polka" b/w "For Me and My Gal" (Columbia 37921, 78 rpm.).

37. Dorothy Shay, "The Old Apple Tree" b/w "Grandpa's Gettin' Younger Ev'ry Day" (Columbia 38309, 78 rpm). The orchestra backing Shay was conducted by Mitchell Ayres, who was briefly in charge of Columbia pop A&R in the late forties.

38. Edward Wallerstein, interview by Ward Botsford, April 1969.

39. "Columbia Records Changes Top Officers," NYT, 12/29/1947, p. 29.

40. Moses Smith, *Koussevitsky: The Life and Times of a Great Conductor*.

41. "Moses Smith, Music Critic, Dies; Biographer of Koussevitsky, 63," NYT, 07/29/1964, p. 33.

CHAPTER 8: Bedroom, Boardroom

1. George Avakian, e-mail to author, 05/03/2005.

2. Soundtrack to *"Goddard Lieberson: A Tribute,"* memorial film narrated by Charles Kuralt, July 1977.

3. Joan Simpson Burns, *The Awkward Embrace*, p. 201. Peter Lieberson, e-mail to author, 10/29/2006. Some sources, including Burns's book, say Goddard Lieberson's father was named Davis. (Lieberson himself appears to be the source for this.) Peter Lieberson gave his grandfather's name as Abraham.

4. Martin Mayer, "Goddard Lieberson: Renaissance Man Behind the Recording Booth," *Esquire*, July 1956, p. 105.

5. Rudolph Ganz, letter to Goddard Lieberson, undated, GL Papers, ISG.

6. Malcolm Muggeridge, *The Thirties 1930–1940 in Great Britain*, p. 117.

7. Mayer, "Goddard Lieberson."

8. Thomas Z. Shepard, AI, 01/15/2006. Burns, *Awkward Embrace*, p. 205.

9. The Harley Information Bulletin of the academic year lists Lieberson as one of five "Teachers of the Arts" and includes a mention of his composition study with George McKay at the University of Washington.

10. Arthur Lowenthal, AI, 05/12/2006.

11. The Harley School Comet, 1936. *Rochester Democrat & Chronicle*, 10/20/1935, 10/30/1935, 11/07/1935, and 12/15/1935.

12. Ruth Bennett, AI, 05/14/2006. Ruth Bennett, letter to Anne Townsend, 05/08/2006.

13. GL Papers, ISG.

14. Galimir Quartet, Goddard Lieberson *String Quartet* (Columbia ML 5841, vinyl).

15. Mitch Miller, AI, 03/30/2006.

16. "Men of Fashion," *Time*, 09/23/1929, p. 14.

17. Goddard Lieberson, letter to Margaret Callahan, 12/18/1956, GL Papers, ISG.

18. Thomson, *Virgil Thomson*, p. 279.

19. Howard Scott, AI, 04/01/2006.

20. NYT, 03/14/1938, p. 17.

21. NYT, 11/06/1938, p. 180.

22. Desmond Stone, *Alec Wilder in Spite of Himself: A Life of the Composer*, p. 69.

23. Soundtrack, *"Goddard Lieberson: A Tribute."*

24. Goddard Lieberson, letter to Minna Lederman, 03/16/1939, GL Papers, ISG.

25. Howard Scott, AI, 01/28/2005.

26. Some Wilder libretti can be found in GL Papers, ISG.

27. "Essex House Adds Ten New Tenants," NYT, 08/27/1942, p. 32.

28. Goddard Lieberson, letter to George Kalenin, 06/30/1942, GL Papers, ISG.

29. NYT, 01/23/1943, p. 14.

30. NYT, 05/22/1938, p. 151.

31. NYT, 04/12/2003, p. A14.

32. Ibid.

33. F. Scott Fitzgerald, "Teamed with Genius," *The Pat Hobby Stories*, p. 30.

34. Goddard Lieberson, letter to Samuel Goldwyn, 10/28/1955, GL Papers, ISG.

35. *Zorina*, p. 285.

36. Ibid., p. 293.

37. José Ferrer, letter to Goddard Lieberson, 09/27/1944, GL Papers, ISG.

38. Goddard Lieberson, letter to Andre Kostelanetz, 02/10/1944, GL Papers, ISG.

39. GL Papers, ISG.

40. Stephen Lehmann and Marion Faber, *Rudolf Serkin: A Life*. p. 125.

41. Goddard Lieberson, letter to Peggy Rea, 11/30/1943, GL Papers, ISG.

42. Garson Kanin, letters to Goddard Lieberson, 07/24/1943 and 01/08/1943, GL Papers, ISG.

43. Goddard Lieberson, telegram to Vladmir Bazykin, 11/09/1945, GL Papers, ISG.

44. Howard Scott, AI, 01/28/2005.

45. Goddard Lieberson, letter to Gregory Zilboorg, 11/17/1944, GL Papers, ISG.

46. Cheryl Crawford, letter to Goddard Lieberson, 1945, GL Papers, ISG.

47. *3 for Bedroom C*, p. 15.

48. Ibid., p. 70.

49. Jane Schicke, AI, 05/18/05.

50. Morton Gould, letter to Goddard Lieberson, 11/11/1946, GL Papers, ISG.

51. Nancy Ladd, "Guests of Mr Thrumm," NYT, 02/02/1947, p. BR18.

52. *Variety*, 09/08/1949.

53. Goddard Lieberson, letter to Andre Kostelanetz and Lily Pons, 08/23/1949, GL Papers, ISG.

54. Milton Bren, letter to Goddard Lieberson, 09/08/1949, GL Papers, ISG.

55. Alexander Steinweiss, AI, 05/20/2005.

56. Paul S. Nathan, "Books into Films," *Publishers Weekly*, 07/14/1951, p. 126.

57. Goddard Lieberson, letter to Mary Bard Jensen, 10/02/1952, GL Papers, ISG.

58. Soundtrack, *"Goddard Lieberson: A Tribute."*

59. Arthur Lowenthal, AI, 05/12/2006.

60. *Time*, 11/14/1949, p. 82.

61. Charles Seaton, letter to Goddard Lieberson, 10/02/1949, GL Papers, ISG.

62. Goddard Lieberson, letter to Igor Stravinsky, 06/15/1948, GL Papers, ISG.

63. Goddard Lieberson, letter to Artur Rodzinski, 03/31/1947, GL Papers, ISG.

64. Goddard Lieberson, letter to Leopold Stokowski, 06/07/1949, GL Papers, ISG.

CHAPTER 9: Creation of the LP

1. Peter Goldmark, *Maverick Inventor*, p. 141.

2. Jon Pareles, "What Albums Join Together, Everyone Tears Asunder," NYT, 07/20/2003, p. WK3.

3. Edward Wallerstein interview on tape by Ward Bostford, April 1969. R&H Archives, NYPL. Some of the material following comes from this interview.

4. *Victor Artists' Party* (D L 5-A, 33 1/3 rpm Victorlac, November 1931).

5. Goldmark, *Maverick Inventor*, p. 126.
6. "The Birth of the Long-Playing Record," *Audiophile*, no. 14 (June 1998). Avakian and Howard Scott were interviewed by Michael Hobson.
7. Goldmark, *Maverick Inventor*, p. 130.
8. Ibid., pp. 131–32.
9. Ibid., p. 133.
10. Ibid., p. 135.
11. Ibid., p. 136.
12. John Hammond, letter to Clay Felker, undated but probably 1973, JH Papers, ISG.
13. "Birth of the Long-Playing Record," p. 5.
14. Martin Mayer, "Rocking the Boat," NYT, 03/16/1958, p. XX2. Some of the material following comes from this article.
15. John Hammond, letter to Clay Felker, undated but probably 1973, JH Papers, ISG.
16. Wallerstein, interview by Bostford.
17. George Avakian, AI, 01/18/2005.
18. John Hammond, letter to Clay Felker, undated but probably 1973, JH Papers, ISG.
19. Joe DeBragga, AI, 11/14/2005. DeBragga worked for close to fifty years in the CBS International division and named Leo Murray as the man who handled Goldmark's publicity.
20. Duke Ellington, *Liberian Suite*, recorded 12/24/1947 (CL 6073, 10" vinyl, and 469409 2, CD).
21. Mayer, "Rocking the Boat."
22. Isaac P. Rodman, Patent No. 2,426,241, 08/26/1947. *Index of Patents 1947*.
23. "Birth of the Long-Playing Record," p. 3.
24. Howard Scott, "The Beginnings of LP," *Gramophone*, July 1998, p. 112.
25. Howard Scott, letter to author, 05/03/2005.
26. Goldmark, *Maverick Inventor*, p. 140.
27. Scott, "Beginnings of LP," p. 113.
28. Howard Scott, e-mail to author, 05/01/2005.
29. Peter Munves, AI, 04/29/2005.
30. Howard Scott, e-mail to author, 05/01/2005.
31. Goldmark and Wallerstein each remembered a meeting at a CBS boardroom. As Kevin Cooney pointed out in a *New York Times* review (08/17/1975, p. 210) of CBS, by Robert Metz, not everyone shared that memory. CBS executive Howard Meighan said that Paley and his minions went to RCA's labs in Princeton to demonstrate the LP. And Frank Stanton claimed to have told General Sarnoff about the development of the LP over lunch.
32. Goldmark, *Maverick Inventor*, p. 142.
33. Smith, *In All His Glory*, p. 282.
34. Wallerstein, interview by Bostford.
35. "I don't know when [the special typewriter key] was instituted, but I can say it was already being used when I came to Columbia in 1960." Tina McCarthy, e-mail to author, 03/18/2005.
36. Scott, "Beginnings of LP," p. 113.
37. "Develops Long Playing Phonograph Record," *Life*, 07/26/1948, p. 39.
38. Howard Scott, e-mail to author, 05/01/2005.
39. George Avakian, AI, 11/23/2005.
40. Goddard Lieberson, letter to John Kirkpatrick, 02/04/1946, Kirkpatrick Papers, ISG.
41. Charles O'Connell, *The Other Side of the Record*, pp. 20–23.
42. Howard Scott, AI, 11/30/2005.
43. "Birth of the Long-Playing Record," p. 6. The 1954 *Radio Annual* lists 207 East 30th Street as WLIB's address for that year.
44. *Kiss Me, Kate* (ML 4140, vinyl).
45. *Promotion News*, February 1949.

46. *Finian's Rainbow* (OL 4062, vinyl).
47. *South Pacific* (MM-850, 78 rpm; OL 4180, vinyl).
48. Robert Slater, *This . . . Is CBS: A Chronicle of 60 Years*, p. 133.
49. Wallerstein, interview by Bostford.
50. *Promotion News*, March 1949.
51. Charles L. Granata, "The Battle for the Vinyl Frontier," in *45 RPM: A Visual History of the Seven-Inch Record*, ed. Spencer Drate, p. 8.
52. Howard Taubman, "Records: Rivals," NYT, 01/16/1949, p. X6.
53. Wallerstein, interview by Bostford. "Mutual Broadcasting Names New Officers," NYT, 04/09/1949, p. 21.
54. "New Record Aimed to Bolster Sales," NYT, 06/21/1948, p. 29.
55. Howard Taubman, "Records: New Type," NYT, 08/08/1948, p. X5.
56. Peter Munves, AI, 02/11/2005.
57. Goldmark, *Maverick Inventor*, pp. 143–44.
58. "RCA Victor Plans 33 1/3 RPM Disks," NYT, 01/04/1950, p. 30.
59. *The People's Chronology*, p. 921.
60. Philip Larkin, introduction to *All That Jazz*, from *Required Writing*, pp. 286–88.
61. John Hammond, letter to Ben Bauer, 10/01/1973, JH Papers, ISG.
62. *The Columbia Record*, February 1955.
63. Bill Bachman, memo to Goddard Lieberson, 11/10/1958, GL Papers, ISG.
64. "Birth of the Long-Playing Record," p. 3.
65. Joe DeBragga, AI, 11/14/2005.
66. Victor K. McElheny, "Crash Kills Dr Peter Goldmark," NYT, 12/08/1977, p. 57.

CHAPTER 10: Midcentury

1. Stan Kavan, AI, 09/01/2005.
2. Martin Mayer, "Portrait of the Artist as a V.P.," *Esquire*, July 1956, p. 106.
3. Howard Rushmore, "CBS Disc Exec Wrote for Reds," *Journal-American*, 12/22/1950, p 3.
4. Goddard Lieberson, letter to New York *Journal-American*, 12/22/1950, GL Papers, ISG.
5. Malcolm Muggeridge, *The Thirties 1930–1940 in Great Britain*, p. 296. Muggeridge wrote of Joachim von Rippentrop, the Cliveden Set's "alleged mainstay," that his "position was a difficult one. He wanted to be a social success in London, and at the same time ambition necessitated that he should be considered an ardent Nazi in Berlin; the former aim led him, for instance, to enter his son at an English public school rather than at one of the establishments in Germany which inculcate National Socialist views and behaviour, the latter, to give the Nazi salute when he was received by the King." Rippentrop, whose first name isn't mentioned by Muggeridge, eventually returned to Germany to become Foreign Minister under Hitler. After the war the Nuremberg Tribunal sentenced him to death.
6. Goddard Lieberson, "Invitation from Lady Astor," *New Masses*, 06/07/1938. A quick review of some of the poem's references: Lord Rothermere was a press tycoon whose papers made Hearst's (one of which was the *Journal-American*), by comparison, read like hard news, and he was briefly a supporter of the British Union of Fascists; Nancy Astor was an American who became the first female Member of Parliament; Lord Lothian had been Lloyd George's private secretary and would become England's ambassador to the United States; Lord Halifax had held the position of British Foreign Secretary, among many other posts, and infamously accompanied Prime Minister Chamberlain ("Neville" above) to Germany in 1937 to talk appeasement with Goering and Hitler.
7. Howard Scott, AI, 02/26/2006. The lesser-known members of the Revuers were John Frank and Alvin Hammer.
8. Groucho Marx, letter to Dinorah Press, 10/08/1953, GL Papers, ISG.
9. Burns, *Awkward Embrace*, p. 210.

10. Lieberson memo quoted by Mayer, "Portrait of the Artist," p. 106.
11. Biographical material on Miller is drawn in part from Stephen Paley's 2002 interview with Miller at Miller's Manhattan apartment; and Miller, interview by Martin Bookspan, 04/06/1978, for the American Jewish Committee's Oral History, Jewish Division of the New York Public Library.
12. Desmond Stone, *Alec Wilder in Spite of Himself*, p. 54.
13. Wilder, *Letters I Never Mailed*, p. 61.
14. Ibid., p. 55.
15. Ibid., p. 60.
16. Bernard Herrmann, letter to Goddard Lieberson, 06/23/1945, GL Papers, ISG.
17. *Off the Record*, pp. 42–43.
18. Frankie Laine and Joseph F. Laredo, *That Lucky Old Son*, p. 89.
19. Jay Blackton, AI, 12/15/1989.
20. Some listeners swear it's not Williams playing trumpet but Buck Clayton.
21. Laine and Laredo, *That Lucky Old Son*, pp. 95, 100.
22. Gene Lees, *Inventing Champagne*, p. 90.
23. Fox, *In the Groove*, p. 43.
24. Miller, interview by Bookspan, p. 50.
25. "I Believe," *Popular Favorites, Vol. 7* (CL 6256, 10" vinyl).
26. Laine and Laredo, *That Lucky Old Son*, p. 155.
27. Ibid., p. 112.
28. Ibid., p. 140.
29. *Love Me or Leave Me*, orchestra conducted by Percy Faith (CL 710, vinyl).
30. Tony Bennett, *The Good Life*, p. 89. Some of the material following comes from this autobiography.
31. JH Papers, ISG.
32. John Doumanian, AI, 01/15/2005.
33. Stan Kavan, AI, 01/22/2005.
34. Bennett, *The Good Life*, p. 109.
35. Mitch Miller, interview by Paley.
36. Bennett, *The Good Life*, p. 112.
37. Ibid., p. 124.
38. Ibid., pp. 124–25.
39. Darden Asbury Pyron, *Liberace: An American Boy*, p. 140.
40. George Avakian, e-mail to author, 01/05/2005.
41. Pyron, *Liberace*, p. 157.
42. *Suddenly It's the Hi-Lo's* (CL 952, vinyl).
43. Clooney, *Girl Singer*. Some material preceding and following comes from this memoir.
44. Frank Loesser, letter to Goddard Lieberson, undated, in response to Lieberson's letter, 05/24/1950, GL Papers, ISG.
45. Malone, *Country Music U.S.A.*, pp. 145, 225.
46. *Saturday Evening Post*, 01/01/1955, p. 40.
47. Rosemary Clooney, *Jazz Singer* (CK 86883, CD).
48. Fox, *In the Groove*, p. 51.
49. The *Studio One* episode can be seen at the Museum of Television & Radio in New York City.
50. Meyer, *Gold in Tin Pan Alley*, p. 144.

CHAPTER 11: Changing Horses in Midstream

1. Arthur Honneger, *Jeanne d'Arc Au Bucher*, starring Vera Zorina and Raymond Gerome, music by Eugene Ormandy and the Philadelphia Orchestra (Columbia Masterworks 178, vinyl). Hear also Columbia Masterworks of Music Commentary, James Fassett interviewing Zorina (Program #301, LP 14268, 10" vinyl).

2. Howard Scott, AI, 11/29/2005.

3. NYT, 02/15/1953, p. X9. NYT, 12/08/1955, p. 45. NYT, 03/18/1956, p. 352.

4. Hart, "The Budapest String Recordings.". The Budapest String Quartet, *Beethoven: Quartet No. 9 in C Major, Quartet No. 11 in F Major* (MS 6187, vinyl). The excellent notes are by David Johnson.

5. Howard Scott, AI, 12/25/2005. Hear also *The Louisville Orchestra featuring works by Paul Creston, Jacques Ibert, and Henry Cowell* (Columbia KL 5039, vinyl).

6. Dinu Lipatti, *piano* (Columbia ML 4633, vinyl). The LP contains what may be the definitive interpretation of Bach's *Jesu, Joy of Man's Desiring.*

7. Joseph Dash, AI, 03/01/2005.

8. Peter Munves, AI, 02/11/2005.

9. *The People's Chronology*, p. 599.

10. George Avakian, AI, 01/18/2005.

11. Didier Deutsch, AI, 11/28/2005.

12. David Patmore, "Sir Thomas Beecham: the Contract Negotiations with RCA Victor, Columbia Records and EMI, 1941–1959," ARSC Journal 33, no. 2, Fall 2002, pp. 188–89.

13. *Columbia Retailer, Vol.* 1, *No.* 2, 1955 (vinyl).

14. *Bach: Toccata in D Minor* (ML 5032, vinyl). *Hear It Now* on L.P., narrated by Walter Cronkite (LZR 17751, vinyl).

15. Howard Scott, AI, 04/24/2006.

16. *Anna Russell Sings! Again?* (ML 4733, vinyl).

17. *Richard Rodgers Conducting the Philharmonic-Symphony Orchestra of New York* (CL 810, vinyl).

18. *Columbia Retailer, Vol.* 1, *No.* 4, 1955 (vinyl).

19. Jonny Whiteside, *Cry: The Johnnie Ray Story*, p. 78.

20. *The Columbia Record*, February 1954, p. 2.

21. Goddard Lieberson, telegram to Noel Coward, 08/09/1955, GL Papers, ISG. *Noel Coward at Las Vegas* (ML 5053, vinyl).

22. Some biographical material comes from the TV documentary *Rediscovering Dave Brubeck*, Image Entertainment, Hedrick Smith, executive producer and correspondent.

23. Ted Gioia, *West Coast Jazz*, p. 94.

24. *The Audiophile*, Issue 10, 1997.

25. Mort Lewis, AI, 04/11/2005.

26. George Avakian, "The First Jazz Reissue Program," *Jazztimes*, October 2000, p. 44.

27. *Satch Plays Fats* (CK 64927, CD). *Satchmo the Great* (CK 62170, CD). *Ambassador Satch* (CK 64926, CD). *Louis Armstrong Plays W.C. Handy* (CL 591, vinyl). George Avakian email to author, 06/05/2006.

28. *I Like Jazz* (JZ 1, vinyl).

29. Harold Schonberg, "Music: Jazz Comes of Age at Newport," NYT, 07/18/1955, p. 17.

30. George Wein with Nate Chinen, *Myself Among Others: A Life in Music*, p. 151.

31. *Music Is My Mistress*, p. 241. *Ellington at Newport* (CL 933 and CL 934, vinyl; C2K 64932, CD).

32. Columbia Record Club magazine, Vol. 5, 1960, p. 19. George Avakian, AI, 12/07/2005.

33. Mitch Miller, interviewed by Paley.

34. Tamara Conniff, e-mail to author, 04/14/2005.

35. *Johnny's Greatest Hits* (CL 1133, vinyl). *More Johnny's Greatest Hits* (CL 1344, vinyl).

36. Goddard Lieberson, telegram to Sol Hurok, 08/17/1955, GL Papers, ISG.

37. Martin Mayer, *Madison Avenue U.S.A.*, pp. 39–40.

38. Ralph Colin Jr., AI, 01/03/2006. Neal Keating, AI, 05/25/2005.

39. Stan Kavan, e-mail to author, 09/01/2005.

40. Howard Taubman, "The Philharmonic—What's Wrong with It and Why," NYT, 04/29/1956, p. 139.

41. Burns, *Awkward Embrace*, p. 210. Val Adams, "Van Volkenburg to Quit C.B.S.-TV," NYT, 11/02/1956, p. 54.

42. CBS press release, 06/04/1956. GL Papers, ISG.

43. Howard Scott, AI, 12/25/2005.

44. Peter Lieberson, AI, 05/15/2005.

45. J. D. Salinger, *The Catcher in the Rye*, p. 162.

CHAPTER 12: Catching Up to Victor

1. *Columbia Retailer Vol. 1, No. 2*, April 1955 (vinyl).

2. George Avakian, AI, 01/18/2005.

3. Goddard Lieberson, letter to Sammy Davis Jr., 10/01/1956, GL Papers, ISG.

4. "Share Earnings of C.B.S. Rise 28%," NYT, 04/18/1957, p. 41. "2 Will Get Music Honors," NYT, 05/05/1957, p. 74.

5. "Miles Davis Talking," *Crescendo International* 8, No. 5, December 1969, interviewed by Les Tompkins.

6. Stephanie Stein Crease, *Gil Evans: Out of the Cool*, p. 199.

7. John Szwed, *So What: The Life of Miles Davis*, p. 213.

8. Goddard Lieberson, letter to Ken McCormick, 05/19/1952, GL Papers, ISG.

9. George Avakian, AI, 01/18/2005.

10. Radio City Music Hall program, 03/16/1950.

11. Nick Clarke, *Alistair Cooke: A Biography*, pp. 293–94.

12. Didier Deutsch, AI, 11/28/2005.

13. Eric Bentley, letter to Goddard Lieberson, 05/12/1958, GL Papers, ISG. The *Mahagonny* album (Columbia K3L 243, vinyl) included a 32-page booklet, designed by Fujita, in German and English.

14. George Avakian, e-mail to author, 04/20/2006.

15. *The Best of Teo Macero* (Stash Records 527, CD). Notes are by George Avakian and Bill Coss. *The New Encyclopedia of Jazz*, p. 318.

16. George Avakian, e-mail to author, 01/23/2005.

17. Fred Goodman, *The Mansion on the Hill*, p. 46.

18. George Avakian, e-mail to author, 07/21/2005. Much of the material following comes from this letter.

19. *N.Y. Export: Op. Jazz, from Ballets U.S.A. and Ballet Music from Leonard Bernstein's West Side Story*, Robert Prince conducting (Warner Bros. B 1240, vinyl).

20. Donald Clarke, *Wishing on the Moon*, p. 413.

21. *Columbia Retailer*, Fall 1957 (XLP 41875, vinyl).

22. *Off the Record*, p. 64.

23. *Lady in Satin* (CL 1157, vinyl).

24. Clarke, *Wishing on the Moon*, pp. 414–15.

25. Elizabeth Larsen Lauer, AI, 01/14/2005. Some of the material following comes from this interview.

26. Aldous Huxley, *Point Counter Point*, pp. 427–28.

27. Nicolas Slonimsky, *Music Since 1900*, p. 570. According to Slonimsky, the Third Concerto's final 17 measures were only sketched out in shorthand, because Bartok was then near death. He had scrawled in pencil the Hungarian word vege—the end—on the last bar of his sketch copy "as though he were desperately trying to reach it."

28. Goddard Lieberson, telegram to Gyorgy Sandor, 04/18/1946, GL Papers, ISG.

29. "The History of Living Stereo," *Copland, Gould: Composers Conduct*. Reissue produced by John Pfeiffer, essay unsigned (RCA Victor 09026-61505-2, CD).

30. *The Complete Lyrics of Cole Porter*, p. 312.

31. Joseph Michalak, "The A&R Job Has Not Changed Very Much," NYT, 03/15/1959, p. M3.

32. John McClure, AI, 03/26/2005. Much of the material following comes from this interview.

33. John McClure, e-mail to author, 09/10/2006.

34. Irving Kolodin, "Music to My Ears," *Saturday Review*, 01/17/1953, p. 31.
35. Val Adams, "TV to Tell Story of Photographer," NYT, 07/30/1959, p. 55.
36. Schuyler Chapin, *Musical Chairs: A Life in the Arts*, p. 33.
37. *All Souls Quarterly Review*, Vol. VII, No. 4, Fall 2002.
38. Schuyler Chapin, AI, 12/17/2004.
39. Chapin, *Musical Chairs*, pp. 129–30.
40. Schuyler Chapin, AI, 12/17/2004.
41. Ibid.
42. Peter Munves, AI, 04/29/2005.
43. Otto Friedrich, *Glenn Gould: A Life and Variations*, p. 50.
44. "Music World's Wonder," *Life*, 03/12/1956. The Gould recording was re-channeled for stereo by Andrew Kazdin and Ray Moore in late 1967 (MS 7096, vinyl).
45. Schuyler Chapin, AI, 12/17/2004.
46. Irving Townsend, "Duke's Sweet Thunder," *Horizon*, November 1979, p. 57.
47. Duke Ellington, *A Drum Is a Woman* (CL 951).
48. Norman Granz, letter to Teo Macero, 03/24/1977, TM Collection, NYPL.
49. George quoted by Whiteside in *Cry*, p. 250.
50. Walter Dean, memo to Goddard Lieberson, 06/13/1961, TM Collection, NYPL. *First Time! The Count Meets the Duke* (CS 8515, vinyl).
51. Otto Preminger, letter to Mitch Miller, 02/27/1959, TM Collection, NYPL. *Anatomy of a Murder* (CL 1360, vinyl).
52. Irving Townsend, letter to Sol Jaffe, 06/29/1959, TM Collection, NYPL.
53. Dave Brubeck, letter to author, 10/12/2004.
54. "Disk Jockeys Chided," NYT, 03/09/1958, p. 64.
55. George W. S. Trow, "Within That Context, One Style: Eclectic, Reminiscent, Amused, Fickle, Perverse (Ahmet Ertegun)," *Within the Context of No Context*, pp. 130-31.
56. Stan Kavan, AI, 01/22/2005. Fox, *In the Groove*, p. 68. Miller, interview by Bookspan, p. 62.
57. Miller, interview by Bookspan, p. 68.
58. *Sing Along with Mitch* (CL 1160, vinyl). *More Sing Along with Mitch* (CS 8099, vinyl). Miller, interview by Bookspan, p. 64.
59. John P. Shanley, "Mitch Makes Music," NYT, 01/29/1961, p. X13.
60. *Life*, 03/05/1956, p. 183.
61. Mitch Miller, interview by Paley.
62. Wally George, "Strictly Off the Record," LAT, 06/06/1959, p. C7. Mimi Clar, "Stereo Gives Bowl New Musical Scope," LAT, 09/20/1959, p. A8.
63. The J. J. Johnson Quintet, *Dial J.J. 5* (CL 1084, vinyl). *The Fabulous Les Paul & Mary Ford* (Harmony HS 11133, vinyl). The Gerry Mulligan Quartet, *What Is There to Say?* (CS 8116, vinyl). *Mingus Ah Um* (CS 8171, vinyl).
64. Erroll Garner, *Concert by the Sea* (CL 883, vinyl).
65. Ashley Kahn, *Kind of Blue*, p. 150. Miles Davis, *Kind of Blue* (PC 8163, vinyl).
66. Nat Shapiro memo to Messrs Townsend, Kavan, and Macero, 06/19/1959, TM Collection, NYPL.
67. *1959 Annual Reports to the Stockholders of Columbia Broadcasting System, Inc.*
68. "50 Golden Years in the Record Industry," banquet honoring Joe Higgins, 10/21/1959, Tape in author's possession.
69. Alfred R. Zipser, "Upset Claimed in Record Sales," NYT, 02/13/1960, p. 24.

CHAPTER 13: Curtain Up

1. *Oklahoma!* (Decca album no. 359, 23M Personality Series, 78 rpm).
2. Jack Raymond, *Show Music on Record*, p. 2.
3. Roland Gelatt, "The Cool Conscience of a Hot Industry," *Saturday Review*, 07/23/1977, p. 28. Raymond, *Show Music on Record*, p. 111.

4. George Avakian, AI, 01/18/2005. Howard Scott, AI, 05/02/2005.

5. Murray Shumach, "Theatre-on-disks Gaining Favor," NYT, p. X1. *Finian's Rainbow* (OL 4062).

6. Lehman Engel, *The American Musical Theater: A Consideration*, pp. 195–96.

7. *Porgy and Bess* (Sl-162, vinyl).

8. Ira Gershwin, letter to Goddard Lieberson, 03/14/1951, GL Papers, ISG.

9. Goddard Lieberson, letter to Ira Gershwin, 04/12/1951, GL Papers, ISG.

10. Goddard Lieberson, letter to Paul Bowles, 09/20/1951, GL Papers, ISG.

11. Goddard Lieberson, letter to Charles Boyer, 06/04/1952, GL Papers, ISG.

12. *Don Juan in Hell* (Columbia Masterworks, SL-166, vinyl).

13. John Briggs, "Records: G.B.S.," NYT, 09/21/1952, p. X10.

14. Dylan Thomas, *"A Child's Christmas in Wales" and Five Poems* (Caedmon TC-1002, vinyl).

15. Peter Munves, AI, 02/11/2005.

16. *Kismet* (OL 4850, vinyl). Howard Scott, "Birth of the Long-Playing Record."

17. *House of Flowers* (OL 4969).

18. George Dale, memo to Goddard Lieberson, 06/05/1956, GL Papers, ISG.

19. Goddard Lieberson, letter to William Saroyan, 06/27/1956, GL Papers, ISG.

20. Goddard Lieberson, letter to Samuel Beckett, 08/02/1956, GL Papers, ISG. *Waiting for Godot* (Columbia 02L-238, vinyl). In 1971 Caedmon re-released the 1956 recording, which had been cut out of Columbia's catalog.

21. Kenneth Tynan, *Tynan Left and Right*, p. 213.

22. According to Lewis J. Paper's *Empire*, p. 232, the $400,000 gave CBS only a 40 percent stake in the show.

23. Lees, *Inventing Champagne*, p. 138. *My Fair Lady* (OL 5090, vinyl).

24. Alfred R. Zipser, "Personality: Composer Turned Executive," NYT, 06/17/1956, p. 151.

25. *The Most Happy Fella* (OL 5118).

26. *Bells Are Ringing* (OS-2006, vinyl).

27. Thomas Z. Shepard, AI, 01/12/2006.

28. Peter Munves, AI, 02/11/2005.

29. Howard Scott, AI, 12/25/2005.

30. Goodman, *Mansion on the Hill*, p. xi.

31. *On the Town* (OS 2028, vinyl).

32. Goddard Lieberson, letter to Oscar Hammerstein II, 10/01/1957, GL Papers, ISG. Goddard Lieberson, "'Country' Sweeps the Country," NYT, 07/28/1957, p. 153.

33. Goddard Lieberson, telegram to Harold Arlen, 09/16/1957, GL Papers, ISG.

34. Lehman Engel, letter to Goddard Lieberson, 05/24/1958. Neil Fujita, memo to Goddard Lieberson, 05/27/1958. Goddard Lieberson, letter to David Oppenheim, 05/27/1958. GL Papers, ISG.

35. *The Nervous Set* (OS 2018, vinyl).

36. Arthur Gelb, "Play by Hughes Closed Uptown," NYT, 07/05/1957, p. 13.

37. Elizabeth Larsen Lauer, AI, 01/14/2005.

38. Didier Deutsch, AI, 11/28/2005. *Gypsy* (OL 5420).

39. Alfred Lorber, memo to several executives, 06/22/1959, TM Collection, NYPL.

40. Goddard Lieberson, letter to John Gielgud, 03/13/1959, GL Papers, ISG.

41. Garson Kanin, *Where It's At*, p. 38.

42. Sam Zolotow, "'Dear Liar' Plans to Open March 17," NYT, 02/09/1960, p. 27.

43. Arthur Gelb, "News and Gossip Gathered at the Rialto," NYT, 08/14/1960, p. X1.

44. *Cue*, 11/12/1960. *Time*, 11/14/1960.

45. *Julie and Carol at Carnegie Hall* (OS 2240, vinyl).

46. Goddard Lieberson, memo to several executives, 11/20/1961, GL Papers, ISG.

47. The figure comes from the TM Collection, NYPL.

48. Richard Warren, email to author, 12/07/2005. Elizabeth Larsen Lauer, AI, 01/14/2005. I

Can Get It for You Wholesale (KOS 2180, vinyl). Pins & Needles, 25th Anniversary Edition (AOS 2210, vinyl).

49. Who's Afraid of Virginia Woolf? (DOS 687, vinyl).

50. Craig Zadan, Sondheim & Co., p. 95.

51. Paper, Empire, p. 232.

52. Official Guide to the New York World's Fair 1964/1965, p. 236.

53. Fanny Brice, letter to Goddard Lieberson, 06/02/1950, GL Papers, ISG.

54. Fanny Brice, letter to Goddard Lieberson, 04/28/1951, GL Papers, ISG.

55. Sam Zolotow, "Price Rise is Set for 'Funny Girl,'" NYT, 05/31/1965, p. 9.

56. Stephen Sondheim quoted by Didier Deutsch in notes to Do I Hear a Waltz? (Sony Broadway SK 48206, CD).

57. Mame (KOS 3000, vinyl). Cabaret (KOS 3040, vinyl).

58. Zadan, Sondheim & Co., p. 173.

59. E. Y. Harburg, At This Point in Rhyme, p. 14.

60. Bob Dylan, Chronicles: Volume 1, p. 49.

61. Davis, Clive, pp. 36–37.

62. Goddard Lieberson, letter to Brooks Atkinson, December 1968, GL Papers, ISG. Promises, Promises (United Artists 9902).

63. Jacques Brel Is Alive and Well and Living in Paris (D2S 779 vinyl). Columbia's longtime A&R man Nat Shapiro is listed as "Consultant to the Producers."

64. Thomas Z. Shepard, AI, 11/11/2004 and 05/04/2005. Much of the material following is drawn from these interviews.

65. Schuyler Chapin, AI, 12/22/2004.

66. Company (SK 65283, CD).

67. Thomas Z. Shepard, AI, 05/05/2005. A Little Night Music (JS 32265, vinyl).

68. Jay Blackton, AI, 12/15/1989.

69. Joyce Haber, "Royal Treatment at King's Classic," LAT, 05/22/1975, p. G14.

70. Thomas Z. Shepard, AI, 05/04/2005.

71. TM Collection, NYPL.

72. Joel Whitburn, Top Pop Albums 1955–1985, p. 444.

73. John S. Wilson, "Musicals to Be Seen and Not Heard," NYT, 08/31/1975, p. 99.

74. Goddard Lieberson, letter to Times editor William H. Honan, undated and forwarded to Ed Kleban, Ed Kleban Papers, NYPL.

75. Burt Prelutsky, "When a Pal Strikes It Rich," LAT, 08/01/1976, p. 87.

CHAPTER 14: Just Before the Revolution

1. "W-G-N to Honor Dunbar Today on Citizens' Period," Chicago Tribune, 03/28/1943, p. SW5.

2. Oscar Brown Jr., Sin & Soul (CL 1577, vinyl). Between Heaven and Hell (CL 1774, vinyl). In a New Mood (CL 1873, vinyl). Mr Oscar Brown Jr. Goes to Washington (Fontana MGF 27540, vinyl).

3. Louis Calta, "Cassius Clay to Appear in a Broadway Musical," NYT, 10/15/1969. Peter Keepnews, "Oscar Brown Jr., Entertainer and Social Activist, Dies at 78," NYT, 05/31/2005.

4. Dave Kapralik, e-mail to author, 08/05/2005. Douglas Martin, "Gary Belkin, 79; Wrote Comedy for TV Variety Shows," NYT, 08/04/2005, p. A17.

5. John Hammond, letter to Leonard Feather, 11/23/1960, JH Papers, ISG.

6. John Hammond, letter to Aretha Franklin, 03/22/1962, JH Papers, ISG.

7. Aretha Franklin: The Early Years (CK 65068, CD).

8. NY Supreme Court Index No. 260/1963 Calendar No. 42599.

9. Irving Townsend, The Less Expensive Spread, p. 1.

10. Elizabeth Larsen Lauer, AI, 01/14/2005.

11. Lionel Hampton, Golden Vibes (CL 1304, vinyl). Jimmy Rushing, Mr Five by Five (C2 36419, vinyl).

12. Irving Townsend, "Duke's Sweet Thunder," *Horizon*, November 1979, p. 57.

13. Jeremy Townsend, AI, 10/28/2005. Some of the material following is drawn from this interview.

14. "He Wanted Live Look for Grammy," *LAT*, 12/21/1981, p. C8.

15. Townsend, *Less Expensive Spread*, p. 6.

16. Program for "Susan's Evening," presented by the Associated Students of Whittier College, 04/03/1964.

17. Stephen Paley, AI, 04/11/2005. Paley was repeating a story told to him by Miles Kreuger.

18. Maida Glancy, AI, 01/07/2005.

19. Stan Kavan, AI, 01/22/2005. GL Papers, ISG.

20. John Berg, AI, 02/07/2005.

21. Robert Alden, "Advertising: On Political Scene," NYT, 05/16/1960, p. 50.

22. Peter Munves, AI, 04/29/2005.

23. John McClure, AI, 03/26/2005.

24. Goddard Lieberson, letter to Margaret Callahan, 01/23/1957, GL Papers, ISG.

25. Elizabeth Larsen Lauer, AI, 01/14/2005.

26. Ken McCormick, letter to Goddard Lieberson, 09/15/1958, GL Papers, ISG.

27. Ken McCormick, letter to Goddard Lieberson, 04/09/1959, GL Papers, ISG.

28. Ishlon, *Girl Singer*, p. 92.

29. Morris Baumstein, AI, 03/28/2005.

30. Don Hunstein, AI, 12/21/2004.

31. Elizabeth Larsen Lauer, AI, 01/14/2005.

32. Eugene Ormandy, letter to Goddard Lieberson, 04/02/1962, GL Papers, ISG.

33. Goddard Lieberson, letter to Eugene Ormandy, 04/13/1962, GL Papers, ISG.

34. Thomas Z. Shepard, AI, 05/04/2005.

35. NYT, 05/12/1994, p. B14.

36. David Hadju, *Positively 4th Street*, p. 57.

37. Robert Shelton, "Bob Dylan: A Distinctive Folk-Song Stylist," NYT, 09/29/1961, p. 31.

38. Dylan, *Chronicles*, pp. 278–80.

39. Ibid., pp. 264–65.

40. Ibid., p. 7.

41. Goodman, *Mansion on the Hill*, pp. 54–56.

42. *Bob Dylan* (CS 8579 vinyl).

43. *The Freewheelin' Bob Dylan* (CS 8786, vinyl).

44. John Hammond, memo to David Kapralik, 10/09/1962, JH Papers, ISG.

45. *The Times They Are A-Changin'* (CS 8905, vinyl). *Another Side of Bob Dylan* (CK 8993, CD).

46. Johnny Cash, letter to Goddard Lieberson, 05/16/1964. Goddard Lieberson, letter to Johnny Cash., 06/05/1964. *Letters from God*, Sony collection of letters courtesy of Howard Scott.

CHAPTER 15: Silver Anniversary

1. Dave and Iola Brubeck, *The Real Ambassadors* (OS 2550, vinyl). Gilbert Milstein wrote the liner notes. The score was published in 1973 by Charles Hansen Music & Books.

2. *The Real Ambassadors* sheet music, p. 127.

3. Teo Macero, memo to Dave Kapralik, returned by Goddard Lieberson, 11/09/1962, TM Collection, NYPL. *Les Double Six* (BMG 74321643142, CD).

4. Teo Macero, memo to Frank DeVol, 02/07/1961. Teo Macero, letter to Annie Ross, June 1962. Teo Macero, memo to Irving Townsend, 03/19/1963. TM Collection, NYPL. Terry Snyder's new album was *America's Most Popular Stereo Orchestra: Terry Snyder's World of Sound*, recorded in four-track stereo September 1962. (CS 8744, vinyl).

5. Leslie Gourse, *Straight, No Chaser*, pp. 110–11.

6. Walter Dean, memo to Teo Macero, September 1961, TM Collection, NYPL.

7. *Monk's Dream* (CK 40786, CD).

8. Mitch Miller, interview by Bookspan, p. 70.

9. Chapin, *Musical Chairs*, p. 89.

10. John Gruen, "The Curse of Being Vladimir Horowitz," NYT, 11/23/1975, p. 390.

11. Harold Schonberg, *Horowitz: His Life and Music*, p. 202.

12. Gruen, "Curse of Being Vladimir Horowitz."

13. Lehmann and Faber, *Rudolf Serkin*, pp. 161–64.

14. Maida Glancy, AI, 01/07/2005. Some of the material following comes from this interview. Thomas Z. Shepard, AI, 01/12/2006.

15. Mel Torme, *That's All* (CS 9118).

16. "Educator, Ex-Nun, Will Resign and Wed," NYT, 3/04/1969, p. 20.

17. Soundtrack, "*Goddard Lieberson: A Tribute.*"

18. Joseph Dash, AI, 03/01/2005.

19. Thomas Z. Shepard, AI, 05/04/2005.

20. Soundtrack, "*Goddard Lieberson: A Tribute.*"

21. Maida Glancy, AI, 01/07/2005.

22. James Spada, *Streisand: Her Life*, p. 108.

23. During Streisand's May 1962 run at the Bon Soir, the comedian Dick Gautier, who later appeared as a regular on the TV series *Get Smart*, was on the bill.

24. "Coming Star," *New Yorker*, 05/19/1962, pp. 34–35.

25. *Original Story by Arthur Laurents*, p. 222.

26. Spada, *Streisand*, p. 110. Dave Kapralik, AI, 02/04/2005.

27. James Gavin, *Intimate Nights*, p. 251. On the bill with Streisand was the cabaret singer–pianist Jimmie Daniels, no relation to Peter Daniels.

28. Spada, *Streisand*, p. 118. *The Barbra Streisand Album* (CS 8807, vinyl). *The Second Barbra Streisand Album* (CS 8854, vinyl).

29. Barbra Streisand, *The Third Album* (CS 8954, vinyl). *People* (CL 2215, vinyl).

30. Mike Berniker, AI, 10/23/2004. Some of the material following comes from this interview.

31. Bruce Lundvall, AI, 11/10/2004.

32. Bruce Lundvall, memo to Teo Macero, 12/10/1963, TM Collection, NYPL. *The Girl Who Came to Supper* (SK 48210, CD).

33. George Szell, letter to Goddard Lieberson, 04/15/1963, GL Papers, ISG.

34. The story was told by Peter Munves in his address to the 2004 conference of the Association for Recorded Sound Collectors & Society for American Music, Cleveland, OH, March 10–14, 2004.

35. Paul Myers, e-mail to author, 12/14/2005.

36. Peter Munves, AI, 04/29/2005.

37. Paul Myers, e-mail to author, 12/12/2005.

38. Ibid.

39. Serkin/Szell/Cleveland Orchestra, *Brahms First Piano Concerto in D Minor* (ML 4829, vinyl).

40. Peter Munves address to the 2004 conference of the Association for Recorded Sound Collectors & Society for American Music, Cleveland, OH, March 10–14, 2004. Paul Myers, e-mail to author, 12/12/2005.

41. Paul Myers, AI, 04/16/2005.

42. John Hammond, letter to David Howells, 09/26/1968, JH Papers, ISG.

43. Vincent Marsilla, "Probe into the World of Ideas with Goddard Lieberson," *Columbia Journal of World Business* 1, no. 4 (Fall 1966): 138–39.

44. Davis, Clive, pp. 19–22.

45. *GL 25: Goddard Lieberson: A Tribute* (LP distributed to Columbia Records employees).

46. Artur Rubinstein, letter to Goddard Lieberson, undated but probably June 1964. Harry Kurnitz, letter to Charles Burr, 06/20/1964. GL Papers, ISG.

CHAPTER 16: Art for the Label's Sake

1. "Covers Up," Newsweek, 12/25/1944, p. 70.
2. Gama Gilbert, "Records: Studio News," NYT, 02/11/1940, p. 134.
3. Henry C. Pitz, "Alex Steinweiss, Advertising Designer," American Artist, April 1944, pp. 33–37.
4. Alex Steinweiss, AI, 05/20/2005. Jennifer McKnight-Trontz and Alex Steinweiss, For the Record: The Life and Work of Alex Steinweiss, p. 41.
5. Ibid., p. 2.
6. "Advertising News," NYT, 02/08/1940, p. 41.
7. Jim Flora, interview by Angelynn Grant, included in 'The Mischievous Art of Jim Flora, p. 46.
8. Ibid., pp. 9, 103–4.
9. Ibid., p. 46.
10. Alex Steinweiss, AI, 05/20/2005.
11. "Advertising News and Notes," NYT, 04/22/1943, p. 40.
12. "Advertising News and Notes," NYT, 01/13/1944, p. 25.
13. McKnight and Steinweiss, For the Record, pp. 67 and 97. Chusid, Mischievous Art of Jim Flora, p. 38.
14. "News and Notes in the Advertising Field," NYT, 01/30/1946, p. 36.
15. Alex Steinweiss, AI, 05/20/2005.
16. Leo Lionni, Between Worlds: The Autobiography of Leo Lionni, p. 209.
17. Nelson Eddy in Songs of Stephen Foster (ML 4099, vinyl).
18. Budapest String Quartet, Ravel, Debussy (ML 4668, vinyl).
19. Alex Steinweiss, AI, 05/20/2005.
20. Neil Fujita, AI, 01/28/2005. Much of the material following comes from this interview.
21. Mayer, Madison Avenue U.S.A., p. 142.
22. Alex Steinweiss, AI, 05/20/2005.
23. Don Hunstein, AI, 12/21/2004. Much of the material following comes from this interview.
24. Cartier-Bresson, The Decisive Moment, unpaged (unofficially p. 5 in 1952 edition).
25. Maida Glancy, AI, 01/07/2005. Make It Bigger, p. 261. John Berg, AI, 02/07/2005.
26. Bob Cato and Greg Vitiello, Joyce Images.
27. Morris Baumstein, AI, 01/22/2005.
28. Morris Baumstein & Linda Barton, AI, 03/28/2005.
29. John Berg, AI, 02/07/2005. Much of the material following comes from this interview.
30. My Name Is Barbra (CS~9126, vinyl).
31. Don Hunstein, AI, 12/21/2004.
32. Arnold Levine, AI, 04/28/2005. Much of the material following comes from this interview.
33. Simon & Garfunkel, Parsley, Sage, Rosemary and Thyme (CS 9363, vinyl).
34. Reproductions of these two covers, as well as many others, can be found in Storm Thorgerson and Aubrey Powell, 100 Best Album Covers: The Stories Behind the Sleeves.
35. Eisenberg, Recording Angel, p. 66.
36. Make It Bigger, p. 262.
37. Morris Baumstein & Linda Barton, AI, 03/28/2005. Bunny Freidus was the second female vice-president.
38. Make It Bigger, p. 262.
39. Ibid., p. 11.
40. John Berg, AI, 02/07/2005.
41. Make It Bigger, p. 262.
42. Ibid., p. 11.
43. Ibid., p. 19.
44. Ibid., p. 29.
45. John Berg, AI, 02/07/2005. Smith, In All His Glory, pp. 572–73.
46. Arnold Levine, e-mail to author, 11/27/2005.
47. Make It Bigger, p. 263.

CHAPTER 17: High Above Manhattan

1. Columbia Records press release, February 1963, GL Papers, ISG.
2. Chapin, *Musical Chairs*, p. 150. In-house list of catalog best-sellers, 1965.
3. Sherman L. Morrow, "The In Crowd and the Out Crowd," NYT, 07/18/1965, p. SM12.
4. Maida Glancy, e-mail to author, 01/09/2005.
5. Burns, *Awkward Embrace*, p. 205.
6. Ibid., p. 194.
7. Soundtrack, *"A Tribute to Goddard Lieberson."*
8. Peter Munves, AI, 02/11/2005.
9. Howard Scott, AI, 04/28/2006.
10. Elizabeth Larsen Lauer, AI, 01/14/2005.
11. Harold Rome, interview by Martin Bookspan, 11/22/1982, for the American Jewish Committee Oral History, NYPL, p. 18 of transcript.
12. Paper, *Empire*, pp. 247–48. Dick Hess and Marion Muller, *Dorfsman & CBS*, pp. 33–36. The height measurement of Black Rock comes from *Eero Saarinen*, p. 124. Stan Kavan memo to distributors and branch sales managers, 04/27/1965.
13. Nan Robertson, "Mrs Gandhi Is Guest at White House Dinner," NYT, 03/29/1966, p. 14.
14. Thomas Z. Shepard, e-mail to author, 07/31/2006.
15. Arthur Gold & Robert Fizdale, pianos, with members of the Juilliard String Quartet and Leonard Bernstein and the New York Philharmonic, all-Mozart program (SMK 60598, CD). Recorded 1966.
16. Schonberg, *Horowitz*, p. 203.
17. Howard Klein, "The Horowitz Method: 'Listen and Sing,'" NYT, 05/09/1965, p. 33.
18. Richard F. Shepard, "Horowitz Tickets Are Sold Out in 2 Hours," NYT, 04/27/1965, p. 39.
19. Fox, *In the Groove*, p. 6.
20. *An Historic Return: Horowitz at Carnegie Hall* (MZS 728, vinyl). Howard Klein, "'Taste of Honey' Disk of the Year," NYT, 03/16/1966, p. 49.
21. Schonberg, *Horowitz*, p. 223.
22. Goodman, *Mansion on the Hill*, p. 90.
23. Shaun Considine, "The Hit We Almost Missed," NYT, 12/03/2004, p. A29.
24. *Bringing It All Back Home* (KCS 9128, vinyl). *Highway 61 Revisited* (CL 2389, vinyl).
25. Stan Kavan, memo to distributors and branch sales managers, 09/01/1965.
26. *Blonde on Blonde* (C2S 841, vinyl).
27. John Hammond, letter to Michael Roddy, 01/21/1966, JH Papers, ISG.
28. John Hammond, memo to Goddard Lieberson, 09/26/1966, JH Papers, ISG.
29. Gene Santoro, "Electric Blues Revival," *Highway 61 Revisited*, p. 172.
30. Victoria Kingston, *Simon & Garfunkel: The Biography*, p. 24. Some of the material following comes from this book.
31. Stan Kavan, AI, 01/22/2005. Kingston, *Simon & Garfunkel*, p. 52.
32. Mort Lewis, AI, 04/11/2005.
33. Ibid.
34. Kingston, *Simon & Garfunkel*, p. 84. *Wednesday Morning 3 A.M.* (CS 9049, vinyl). *Sounds of Silence* (CK 9269, CD). *Bookends* (KCS 9529, vinyl).
35. Bennett, *The Good Life*, pp. 163–65.
36. *An Evening with Johnny Mercer* (DRG 5176, CD).
37. Billy James, memo to various Columbia colleagues, 08/17/1965, TM Collection, NYPL.
38. Tony Bennett, *The Movie Song Album* (CS 9272, vinyl). *I Left My Heart in San Francisco* (CS 8669, vinyl). *Tony Bennett at Carnegie Hall* (CS 8705, vinyl). *This Is All I Ask* (CS 8856, vinyl). *I Wanna Be Around* (CS 8800, vinyl).
39. *The Many Moods of Tony* (CL 2141, vinyl).
40. Bennett, *The Good Life*, pp. 183–84.

41. *Tony Makes It Happen* (CS 9453, vinyl).
42. The figures come from material on Bennett in the TM Collection, NYPL.
43. Teo Macero, memo to several Columbia executives, 06/30/1971, TM Collection, NYPL.
44. *The Tony Bennett/Bill Evans Album* (Fantasy F-9489, vinyl). *Tony Bennett & Bill Evans, Together Again* (Rhino R2 75837, CD).
45. Kirk Silsbee, "Bennett's Still the Best Singer in the Business," *Southern California Senior Life*, August 2003.

CHAPTER 18: Music from A tO Z

1. Goodman, *Mansion on the Hill*, p. 55.
2. Walter Dean, letter to Andre Kostelanetz, 12/11/1979, TM Collection, NYPL.
3. www.percyfaithpages.org.
4. *Catalog of Victor Records 1936*, unpaged. The catalog lists the sides "Chant of the Wind," "Revenge with Music," and "Rumba Fantasy."
5. Kostelanetz, *Echoes*, p. 70.
6. B. R. Crisler, "Two Virtuosi: Miss Pons and Miss Henie—a Chat with a Character Actor," NYT, 12/27/1936, p. X4.
7. Mitch Miller, interview by Bookspan.
8. Kostelanetz, *Echoes*, p. 84.
9. *Columbia Promotion News*, July 1946.
10. Kostelanetz, *Echoes*, p. 78.
11. *John Hammond on Record*, p. 126.
12. *La Bohème for Orchestra* (CL 797, vinyl).
13. Russell Lynes, "Highbrow, Lowbrow, Middlebrow," *Harper's Magazine Reader*, p. 97.
14. *Blues Opera* (CL 1099, vinyl). Sony Archives doesn't list the arrangers, but most of it sounds like the work of Carroll Huxley.
15. Anatole Broyard, *Kafka Was the Rage*, pp. 118–20.
16. Philip Roth, *Goodbye, Columbus*, pp. 64–65.
17. Harvey Schein, memo to several Columbia executives, 10/29/1959, GL Papers, ISG.
18. Aaron Copland and Vivian Perlis, *Copland/1900–1942*. p. 342.
19. Mention of both the Copland and Creston premieres can be found in *Music Since 1900*, pp. 519 & 535.
20. All the material on the Eastern Airlines project comes from the TM Collection, NYPL.
21. Teo Macero, memo to Bill Farr, 11/21/1968, TM Collection, NYPL.
22. *And God Created Whales* (M 30394, vinyl).
23. Dick Hyman, AI, 02/08/2005.
24. Tom Frost, memo to Teo Macero, 01/13/1971, TM Collection, NYPL.
25. TM Collection, NYPL.
26. *Andre Kostelanetz Plays Cole Porter* (KG 31491, vinyl). Andre Kostelanetz, letter to Teo Macero, 04/30/1972, TM Collection, NYPL.
27. *Andre Kostelanetz Plays Scarborough Fair (and Other Great Movie Hits)* (Col. CQ 1006, vinyl).
28. Clive Davis, letter to Jimmy Wisner, undated but probably August 1968, TM Collection, ISG.
29. Dick Hyman, AI, 02/08/2005.
30. Stephen Paley, AI, 04/11/2005.
31. In one of the more deftly composed musical jokes found on the Internet, a 2005 April Fool's posting, supposedly from the Associated Press, announced the upcoming Disney production of *Magnificent Maestro: The Andre Kostelanetz Story*, starring Tom Hanks as Kosty and Julia Roberts "slated for the part of Coloratura Soprano Lily Pons. . . . Shooting will begin this summer in New York's Central Park where Kosty, as he was known to his fans, often conducted the New York Philharmonic in its free summer park concerts." The posting closes with the news that poet-author Richard Kostelanetz, a nephew of the conductor, was writing the

screenplay, and that outgoing chairman Michael Eisner had "named himself as Executive-in-Charge of Production and said he will announce his choice for Director at a noontime news conference tomorrow at the Waldorf-Astoria Hotel in New York." www.imgag.com.

CHAPTER 19: Spinning Wheels

1. Ralph Colin Jr., AI, 01/03/2006.
2. Burns, *Awkward Embrace*, p. 207.
3. *Howling at the Moon*, p. 51.
4. Ibid., p. 58.
5. Frank Driggs, memo to Bill Gallagher, 04/05/1966, JH Papers, ISG.
6. John Hammond, letter to Ralph J. Gleason, 02/04/1966, JH Papers, ISG.
7. Jack Weidenmann, memos to John Hammond, 08/23/1967 and 09/15/1967, JH Papers, ISG.
8. Dunstan Prial, *The Producer*, p. 263.
9. Bruce Lundvall, AI, 11/10/2004.
10. Clive Davis, interview by Bill Huie, *NARAS Institute Journal* 1, no. 1 (1977), p. 20.
11. Donal Henahan, "Pop-Record Industry Turning to Young Producers," NYT, 09/13/1967, p. 40.
12. Paul Myers, AI, 04/16/2005.
13. Thomas Z. Shepard, AI, 05/04/2005.
14. Rise Stevens, telegram to Goddard Lieberson, 10/04/1944, GL Papers, ISG.
15. Peter Munves, AI, 02/11/2005.
16. Richard Tucker, interview by Janet Bookspan, 04/23, 06/05, 06/19, and 07/03/1973, for the American Jewish Committee Oral History, NYPL, p. 90 of transcript.
17. Peter Munves, AI, 02/11/2005.
18. Robert Shelton, "Rock Music Groups Going for Baroque in the New Eclectism," NYT, 09/06/1968, p. 37.
19. Peter Munves, AI, 02/11/2005.
20. *Insight*, 06/23/1969, p. 3.
21. Tina McCarthy, e-mail to author, 03/18/2005.
22. Eamon de Valera, letter to Goddard Lieberson, 03/10/1967, GL Papers, ISG.
23. Goddard Lieberson, memo to Clive Davis, 09/10/1968, GL Papers, ISG.
24. Joan Simpson Burns, e-mails to author, 01/14/2006 and 01/20/2006.
25. Midge Decter, *An Old Wife's Tale*, pp. 59–60.
26. Walter Dean, memo to Robert E. Kalaidjian, 11/01/1968, GL Papers, ISG.
27. Peter Munves, AI, 02/11/2005.
28. Peter Lieberson, AI, 05/05/2005.
29. Digby Diehl, "A Ballerina Steps into the New World of Directing," NYT, 07/02/1967, p. 51.
30. Goddard Lieberson, letter to Jonathan Lieberson, undated, GL Papers, ISG. Jonathan Lieberson clippings can be found among GL Papers.
31. Peter Lieberson, letter to Goddard Lieberson, 09/06/1968, GL Papers, ISG.
32. Goddard Lieberson, letter to Samuel Beckett, 08/19/1969, GL Papers, ISG.
33. Davis, *Clive*, p. 92.
34. *Howling at the Moon*, p. 66.
35. Laura Nyro, *More Than a New Discovery* (Verve Forecast, FTS 3020, vinyl). *First Songs* (KC 31410, vinyl).
36. Goodman, *Mansion on the Hill*, pp. 122–24.
37. Maggie Paley, "Funky Madonna of New York Soul," *Life*, 01/30/1970, pp. 44–47. *Eli and the Thirteenth Confession* (CS 9626, vinyl). *New York Tendaberry* (KCS 9737, vinyl).
38. *Howling at the Moon*, p. 63.
39. Fox, *In the Groove*, p. 70.
40. Irving Townsend, memo to Teo Macero, 08/30/1965, TM Collection, NYPL.

41. Morton M. Drosnes, Senior Attorney CBS Records Division, letter to Miles Davis, 07/28/1966, TM Collection, NYPL. *Miles Smiles* (CS 9401, vinyl).

42. *Sorcerer* (CS 9532, vinyl). *Nefertiti* (PC 9594, vinyl).

43. Hollie I. West, "Black Tune," *Washington Post*, 03/13/1969, p. L1, L9.

44. Corinne Chertok, memo to Marc Pressel, 03/13/1969, TM Collection, NYPL.

45. *In a Silent Way* (PC 9875).

46. Ralph Gleason, "Miles Davis' Impact on Jazz," *New York Post*, 09/17/1969, p. 76.

47. Martin Williams, "Jazz: Some Old Favorites Are Back," NYT, 01/18/1970, p. 112.

48. Teo Macero, memo to Clive Davis, 10/23/1969, TM Collection, NYPL.

49. TM Collection, NYPL.

50. Ralph J. Gleason, letter to Teo Macero, 12/05/1969, TM Collection, NYPL.

51. Clive Davis, letter to Teo Macero, 01/19/1970, TM Collection, NYPL.

52. *Bitches Brew* (GP 26, vinyl).

53. Harry Colomby, letter to Jimmy Wisner, 04/04/1969, TM Collection, NYPL.

54. Gourse, *Straight, No Chaser*, p. 268. Leslie Gourse was quoting Paul Jeffrey.

55. Bobby Colomby, interview by Al Steckler, "Interview with Bobby Columby," *NARAS Institute Journal* 1, no. 1 (1977): 43–44.

56. *Blood, Sweat & Tears* (CS 9720, vinyl).

CHAPTER 20: Epic Out of Hell

1. Goddard Lieberson, letter to Andre Kostelanetz, 05/27/1948, GL Papers, ISG.

2. Jane Schicke, AI, 05/18/2005.

3. Harold Schonberg, "New Label on the Market," NYT, 10/05/1953, p. X11. *Columbine* 2, no. 7 (April/May 1974), p. 10.

4. Stan Freeman & Cy Walter, *Manhattan* (Epic LG 1001, vinyl). *Meet Betty Carter and Ray Bryant* (Epic LN 3202, vinyl).

5. *Let Me Sing and I'm Happy* (Epic 3408, vinyl).

6. Joe Sherman, AI, 06/06/2005. www.onehitwondercentral.com. Sherm Feller, interview by Charles White, 1987.

7. David Kapralik, AI, 05/15/2005. Much of the material following comes from this interview.

8. John Doumanian, AI, 01/15/2005.

9. *Cash Box*, 04/29/1961.

10. Buddy Greco, *My Buddy* (LN 3660, vinyl) and *I Like It Swinging* (LN 3793, vinyl).

11. Mike Berniker, AI, 10/23/2004. Victor Linn, AI, 05/14/2005. Len Levy, AI, 05/16/2005.

12. Victor Linn, AI, 05/14/2005. Robert Goulet, *Two of Us* (CS 8626, vinyl).

13. George Avakian, e-mail to author, 06/01/2005.

14. Bob Morgan, AI, 05/26/2005.

15. Lester Lanin had the most durable society band in America. His brother Sam led the Ipana Troubadours and recorded widely for Columbia in the late 1920s. So did brother Howard. See *Columbia Record Catalog 1928*.

16. *Off the Record*, p. 194.

17. In 1959 Paul Evans and The Curls had a hit on the Guaranteed label with "Seven Little Girls."

18. Bob Morgan, AI, 05/18/2005. *Off the Record*, p. 195.

19. Gregg Geller, AI, 12/15/2005.

20. Arnold Shaw, *Honkers and Shouters*, pp. 470–71.

21. Sol Rabinowitz, AI, 04/30/2005.

22. *George Maharis Sings!* (Epic LN 24001, vinyl).

23. Sol Rabinowitz, AI, 04/30/2005.

24. Len Levy, AI, 04/30/2005.

25. David Kapralik, AI, 05/15/2005.

26. JH Papers, ISG.

27. Robert Shelton, "Cabarets Offer New Folk Talent," NYT, 04/29/1963, p. 26.

28. Hadju, *Positively 4th Street*, pp. 104–7.

29. Stephen Paley, AI, 05/10/2005.

30. According to Smith's *In All His Glory*, the CBS chairman was said to have "an appreciative ear" (p. 36). Frank Stanton insisted that Paley was "musical" (p. 399). Fundamentally, Paley thought of himself as bringing elite tastes to the public.

31. Joe Sherman, AI, 06/06/2005.

32. Len Levy, AI, 05/16/2005.

33. Bob Morgan, AI, 05/26/2005.

34. John Hammond, memo to Clive Davis, 08/10/1965, JH Papers, ISG.

35. Len Levy, e-mail to author, 06/14/2005.

36. Smith, *In All His Glory*, p. 444.

37. Stan Kavan, AI, 01/25/2005. Maida Glancy, AI, 01/07/2005. Stephen Paley, AI, 04/12/2005.

38. Davis, *Clive*, pp. 20–23.

39. Len Levy, AI, 05/16/2005.

40. Davis, *Clive*, p. 26.

41. John Hammond, memo to Clive Davis, 10/07/1966, JH Papers, ISG.

42. Davis, *Clive*, p. 29.

43. David Kapralik, e-mail to author, 02/24/2005.

44. Stephen Paley, AI, 05/10/2005.

45. David Kapralik, AI, 05/15/2005.

46. *The Sixties: Years of Hope, Days of Rage*, p. 249.

47. Len Levy, AI, 05/16/2005.

48. Sly and the Family Stone, *Greatest Hits* (Epic 30325, CD).

49. *The Rolling Stone Encyclopedia of Rock and Roll*, p. 433.

50. Gregg Geller, AI, 05/20/2005.

51. Spirit, *Twelve Dreams of Dr Sardonicus* (Epic 30267, vinyl).

52. Sam Lederman, AI, 04/21/2005.

53. Geoffrey O'Brien, *Sonata for Jukebox*, p. 258.

54. *The Hollies: Anthology from the Original Master Tapes* (Epic EKG 46161, CD). The Hollies had been with Epic since 1967. (Earlier hits like "Bus Stop" were on the Imperial label.) In the Nash days, "Carrie-Anne" reached number nine on the American charts. Curiously, the Hollies's 1972 single "Magic Woman Touch" seems to be aiming at Crosby, Stills & Nash harmonies and closely miked acoustic guitars.

55. Gregg Geller, AI, 06/01/2005.

56. Timothy Crouse, "The Struggle for Sly's Soul at the Garden," *Rolling Stone*, November 1971, p. 135.

57. Ibid., p. 136.

58. Ibid., p. 137.

59. Al Aronowitz, "The Pink Hippopotamus, the Fairy Godmother and Ilili," *The Blacklisted Journalist*, Column 15, 11/01/1996. Before having a widely read column in the *New York Post*, Aronowitz worked at CBS Records.

60. David Kapralik, AI, 05/15/2005.

61. George W. S. Trow, "The Biggest Event This Year," *New Yorker*, 08/26/1974, p. 30.

62. Ibid., p. 36.

63. Ibid., p. 37.

64. David Kapralik, e-mail to author, 05/19/2005.

65. Aronowitz, "The Pink Hippopotamus," p. 8.

66. John Hammond, letter to David Kapralik, 12/22/1981. David Kapralik, letter to John Hammond, 12/31/1981. JH Papers, ISG.

67. *Johnny Nash* (ABC 244, vinyl).

68. Gregg Geller, AI, 06/01/2005.

69. Davis, *Clive*, pp. 144–46.

70. *Off the Record*, p. 323.

71. *Billy Paul: Super Hits* (Epic/Legacy EK 86553, CD). *The O'Jays—Collectors' Items* (Philadelphia International Records ZGK, 35024, CD). *The Best of Harold Melvin & the Blue Notes* (Epic/Legacy ZK 66338, CD).

72. *Gonna Take a Miracle* (Columbia KC 30987, vinyl). Gamble and Huff were the producers.

73. *Howling at the Moon*, pp. 90–91.

74. Ron Alexenburg, AI, 05/31/2005.

75. Richard Neer, *FM: The Rise and Fall of Rock Radio*, p. 165 and Ken Tucker, "Hard Rock on the Rise," *Rock of Ages*, p. 484.

76. Gregg Geller, AI, 12/15/2005. *Jeff Beck with the Jan Hammer Group* (Epic 34433, vinyl).

77. *Ted Nugent* (Epic PE 33692, vinyl). *Free-for-All* (Epic PE 34121, vinyl).

78. Sam Lederman, AI, 04/21/2005.

79. Gregg Geller, e-mail to author, 08/03/2005.

80. John Boylan, AI, 07/18/2005. Much of the material following comes from this interview, and from an e-mail from Boylan to the author on 07/21/2005. The Scully, he wrote, "featured a waveform restoration circuit to help offset tape compression. It used standard one-inch tape, but that format never caught on until someone made a two-inch, 24-track version, which became the standard for a long time."

81. At other times the union radius was 300 miles.

82. John Boylan, e-mail to author, 07/21/2005.

83. John Boylan, AI, 07/18/2005.

84. Davis, *Clive*, p. 197.

85. Ibid., p. 195. Ron Alexenburg, AI, 05/31/2005.

86. Stan Snyder, AI, 04/28/2005.

87. Sam Lederman, e-mail to author, 07/22/2005.

88. Sam Lederman, AI, 04/21/2005. Much of the material following comes from this interview.

89. Stan Snyder, AI, 04/28/2005.

90. Sam Lederman, AI, 04/21/2005.

91. Meat Loaf and David Dalton, *To Hell and Back*. Some of the material following comes from this memoir.

92. Appearing in Papp's Shakespeare in the Park production of *As You Like It*, with Raul Julia, Marybeth Hurt, and Kathleen Widdoes, Meat Loaf was referred to as "Mr. Loaf" by *New York Times* critic Clive Barnes in his review, "'As You Like It,' Papp Opens season at Delacorte in Park," NYT, 06/29/1973, p. 16. In *Howling at the Moon* (p. 109), Walter Yetnikoff claimed that William Paley, upon introduction, asked the singer, "Do I call you 'Meat' or 'Mr. Loaf'?" Ron Alexenburg said (AI, 5/31/2005) that when Meat Loaf was about to make an appearance on a late-night talk show, he became enraged when addressed by the associate producer as "Mr. Loaf"—until he learned the associate producer was Alexenburg's daughter, and then he embraced her warmly. Since the hip-hop era, the novelty of a showbiz moniker that owes nothing to the Christian tradition has worn off.

93. Meat Loaf and Dalton, *To Hell and Back*, p. 164.

94. Rundgren's engineering gifts are no more evident than in his *A Wizard, A True Star* (Bearsville 2133, vinyl).

95. Meat Loaf and Dalton, *To Hell and Back*, p. 196.

96. Ibid., p. 171.

97. Ibid., p. 173.

98. *Rock of Ages*, p. 592.

99. Sam Lederman, AI, 06/02/2005.

100. Meat Loaf and Dalton, *To Hell and Back*, p. 170.

101. Billy Joel, *The Stranger* (Columbia 34987, vinyl).

102. Meat Loaf and Dalton, *To Hell and Back*, p. 181.

103. Stan Snyder, AI, 04/28/2005.

104. Sam Lederman, AI, 04/21/2005.

105. Stan Snyder, AI, 04/28/2005.

106. Meat Loaf and Dalton, *To Hell and Back*, pp. 184-85.

107. Sam Lederman, AI, 04/21/2005 and 06/02/2005.

108. Ran Blake, AI, 03/12/1983.

CHAPTER 21: Explosions and Elegies

1. Jon Pareles, "A Singer Embracing Countless Cultures," NYT, 08/12/2006, p. B7.

2. Rodney Burbeck, "CBS Shock—Glancy Quits to Become RCA's British Boss," *Music Business Weekly*, 09/19/1970, p. 1.

3. Maida Glancy, AI, 01/07/2005.

4. Teo Macero, memo to Walter Dean, 01/04/1971, TM Collection, NYPL.

5. TM Collection, NYPL.

6. Todd Gitlin, "Oobie Doobie," *Busy Being Born*, p. 39. "Peace Plea Disrupts White House Dinner," LAT, 01/29/1972, p. A1.

7. Davis, *Clive*, p. 135.

8. Ian Hunter, *Reflections of a Rock Star*, pp. 43–45.

9. Ibid., p. 78.

10. Ron Alexenburg, AI, 05/31/2005.

11. Burns, *Awkward Embrace*, p. 207. Burns got her figures from the CBS 1973 Annual Report to the Stockholders.

12. Goddard Lieberson, memo to Charles T. Ireland, 05/15/1972, GL Papers, ISG.

13. Goddard Lieberson, memo to Clive Davis, 06/16/1972, GL Papers, ISG.

14. Smith, *In All His Glory*, pp. 482–83.

15. *Howling at the Moon*, pp. 76–78. *Hit Men*, pp. 82–83.

16. John Berg, AI, 02/07/2005.

17. Hank Bordowitz, *Billy Joel: The Life and Times of an Angry Young Man*, p. 59.

18. Ibid., p. 68.

19. *The Stranger* (Columbia 34987, vinyl).

20. *Hit Men*, 97.

21. Tom Shepard, AI, 05/04/2005. *Howling at the Moon*, p. 79.

22. CBS press release, 05/29/1973.

23. Allen Levy, "Clive Davis Discharged by CBS," *Record World*, 06/09/1973, p. 3.

24. Ibid., p. 12.

25. Gregg Geller, AI, 12/15/2005.

26. Sam Jameson, "American Businessmen Spoiled—Sony's Chief," LAT, 06/18/1973, Business & Finance, p. 9.

27. *Hit Men*, p. 85.

28. Ibid., p. 100.

29. Stephen Paley, AI, 04/11/2005).

30. John Hammond, letter to Ted Feigen, 06/25/1973, JH Papers, Yale Music Library.

31. "He Wanted Live Look for Grammy."

32. Irving Townsend, "The Once Again Prince," *Separate Lifetimes*, p.167.

33. Jeremy Townsend, AI, 10/28/2005.

34. Irving Townsend, letter to John Hammond, 07/11, no year given but probably 1974, JH Papers, ISG.

35. Irving Townsend, letters to John Hammond, 07/28/1975 and 08/01/1975, JH Papers, ISG.

36. Irving Townsend, letter to John Hammond, 11/24/1976, JH Papers, ISG.

37. Tatsu Nozaki, memo to Lieberson, Segelstein, and Yetnikoff, 04/18/1974, GL Papers, ISG.

38. Hit Men, p. 113.

39. Howling at the Moon, p. 79.

40. Ibid., p. 45.

41. Ibid., p. 68.

42. Chuck Wilson, e-mail to author, 01/20/2006.

43. Bob Dylan, Blood on the Tracks (PC 33235, vinyl).

44. Andrew Kazdin, Creative Lying, p. 8.

45. Television Digest, 01/21/1974, p. 14.

46. Charles Burr, letter to Ed Kleban, 10/02/1975, Kleban Papers, NYPL.

47. Thomas Z. Shepard, e-mail to author, 01/25/2006.

48. Ibid.

49. Helen Burr, AI, 05/20/2005.

50. Charles Burr, memo to Clive Davis, 07/08/1971, GL Papers, ISG.

51. Charles Burr, memo with no addressee, 06/06/1974, JH Papers, ISG. Chicago (AL5-8076, vinyl).

52. Clive Barnes, "The Stage: Musical Odysseus in Port," NYT, 01/05/1976, p. 34.

53. Sheldon Harnick, AI, 04/26/2005.

54. Goddard Lieberson, letter to Dick Cavett, 04/04/1973, GL Papers, ISG.

55. Paul Horgan, letter to Goddard Lieberson, 10/11/1975, GL Papers, ISG. Horgan was writing to Lieberson to ask if he minded if he gave some anecdotes to E. J. Kahn for a profile of Engelhard in the New Yorker. The profile never ran in the magazine.

56. Sam Zolotow, "Shulman Plans Show from Book," NYT, 02/28/1958, p. 18.

57. Burns, Awkward Embrace, p. 199.

58. Bruce Lundvall, AI, 11/10/2004.

59. Peter Lieberson, AI, 05/15/2005.

60. Jacob K. Javits, letter to Goddard Lieberson, 02/11/1977, GL Papers, ISG.

61. Joseph Dash, AI, 03/01/2005.

62. John L. Hess, "Goddard Lieberson, Who Fostered LP's at Columbia Records, Dies," NYT, 05/30/1977, p. 1.

63. Make It Bigger, p. 262.

64. Roland Gelatt, "The Cool Conscience of a Hot Industry," Saturday Review, 07/23/1977, p. 28.

CHAPTER 22: Expasion and Bombast

1. Gregg Geller, AI, 12/15/2005.

2. My Aim Is True (Columbia 35037, vinyl).

3. Kip Cohen, memo to Bruce Lundvall, 11/05/1971, TM Collection, NYPL.

4. Kip Cohen, memo to Teo Macero, 09/23/1972, TM Collection, NYPL.

5. Gary Giddins, "Miles Davis Plays Dorian Gray," Village Voice, 3/18/1976, pp. 71–72.

6. John Hammond, letter to Leonard Feather, 02/03/1973, JH Papers, ISG.

7. Frank Driggs, memo to John Hammond, 05/23/1974, JH Papers, ISG.

8. Philip Larkin, "Minority Interest," 01/25/1971, reprinted in Required Writing.

9. Clive Davis, interview by Huie.

10. Hit Men, p. 119.

11. Teo Macero quoted by Max Jones, "The Return of Miles Davis," Melody Maker, 06/21/1980.

12. "CBS Acquires Lyon & Healy" CBS press release, 08/08/1977.

13. Richard Neer, FM, p. 54.

14. Timothy White, Long Ago and Far Away, p. 256. Howling at the Moon, p. 96.

15. Patrick Goldstein, "A&M Styx It to the Critix," LAT, 10/14/1979, p. 90.

CHAPTER 23: Tokyo Calling

1. Joseph Dash, AI, 03/01/2005. Much of the material following comes from this interview.
2. N. R. Kleinfeld, "Sony, Philips Present Digital Disk Players," NYT, 05/28/1981, p. D6.
3. Joseph Dash, AI, 03/01/2005.
4. *Perhaps Love* (CBS 37243, vinyl).
5. Bernard Holland, "Digital Compact Disks: Replacement for LP's?" NYT, 03/31/1983, p. C13.
6. Editorial, *Guitar Player*, May 1992, quoted in Jimmy McDonough, *Shakey: Neil Young's Biography*, pp. 567–68.
7. Jeremy Townsend, AI, 10/28/2005. John Hammond, letter to David Kapralik, 12/22/1981, JH Papers, ISG.
8. John Hammond, letter to Jeremy Townsend, 12/29/1981, JH Papers, ISG.
9. Mimi Perrin, e-mail to author, 02/02/2005. *The Double Six of Paris Meet Quincy Jones* (Columbia FPX 188, vinyl, BMG 74321643142, CD).
10. Quincy Jones, *Q: The Autobiography of Quincy Jones*, p. 238.
11. CBS/83 Annual Report to the Shareholders, p. 5.
12. *Hit Men*, p. 20.
13. Frederic Dannen, "A New Act Takes Over at Polygram," NYT, 03/29/1983, p. D6.
14. Mikie Harris, letter to Alan Sisitsky, undated but probably early 1984, JH Papers, ISG.
15. Gregg Geller, AI, 12/15/2005.
16. Fox, *In the Groove*, p. 10.
17. Jesse Kornbluth, "Blues Brothers," *New York Magazine*, 04/02/1984, pp. 64–65.
18. John Hammond, letter to Jesse Kornbluth, 03/27/1984, JH Papers, ISG.
19. John Hammond, letter to Marvin Cohn, 03/26/1985, JH Papers, ISG.
20. Paul Myers, *Deadly Cadenza*, p. 7.
21. Myers, *Leonard Bernstein*, p. 10.
22. Didier Deutsch, AI, 11/28/2005. Stephen Holden, "Edgy Wistfulnes from Fleetwood Mac," NYT, 05/13/1987, p. C20.
23. *Howling at the Moon*, p. 197.
24. Peter J. Boyer, "What a Romance!," NYT, 09/18/1988, p. SM35. Some of the material following is drawn from this article.
25. Stephen Holden, "Movie Soundtracks Score in Top 10," NYT, 08/06/1986, p. C19.
26. Michael Cieply, "A Few Promoters Dominate the Record Business," *WSJ*, 04/18/1986, p. 6.
27. Tom Herman, "Investors Rush to Buy Treasury Bills; Bond Prices End with Sharp Advances," *WSJ*, 10/20/1987, p. 59.
28. "Executives," NYT, 04/29/1988, p. D5.
29. Geraldine Fabrikant, "A Cold Spell for CBS Records," NYT, 05/17/1989, pp. D1–2.
30. Jon Pareles, "CBS Records to Buy Tree, Ending an Era in Nashville," NYT, 01/04/1989, p. D1.
31. Geraldine Fabrikant, "Yetnikoff Stepping Down as Chief of CBS Records," NYT, 09/05/1990, p. D1.

Alternate Take: After CBS

CHAPTER 24: Walk Down 30th Street

1. Don Gifford, *The Farther Shore*, p. 54.
2. O'Brien, *Sonata for Jukebox*, p. 16.
3. Howard Nemerov, "Lines & Circularities," *Collected Poems*, pp. 416–17. Peter Goldmark also quoted part of the poem in his memoir, *Maverick Inventor*.
4. Peter Munves, AI, 02/11/005.

BIBLIOGRAPHY

1908 Sears, Roebuck & Co. Catalog. Northfield, IL: DBI Books 1971.

Autry, Gene with Mickey Herskowitz, Back in the Saddle Again. Garden City, NY: Doubleday 1978.

Agate, James, The Later Ego. New York: Crown Publishers, Inc. 1951.

Balliett, Whitney, Alec Wilder and His Friends. Boston: Houghton Mifflin 1974.

Bennett, Tony, with Will Friedwald, The Good Life. New York: Pocket Books 1998.

Bordowitz, Hank, Billy Joel: The Life and Times of an Angry Young Man. New York: Billboard Books 2005.

Bridgeport: Industrial Capital of Connecticut. Bridgeport Chamber of Commerce 1929.

Briggs, John, Leonard Bernstein. New York: Popular Library 1961.

Brooks, Tim, The Columbia Master Book Discography Vol. 1. Westport, CT: Greenwood Press 1999.

_____, Lost Sounds: Blacks and the Birth of the Recording Industry, 1890-1919. Urbana & Chicago: University of Illinois Press 2004.

Broyard, Anatole, Kafka Was the Rage. New York: Carol Southern Books 1993.

Brubeck, Dave, The Real Ambassadors. New York: C. Hansen 1973.

Burns, Joan Simpson, The Awkward Embrace. New York: Alfred A. Knopf 1975.

Cartier-Bresson, Henri, Images à La Sauvette. New York: Simon & Schuster 1952.

Castle, Irene, My Husband. New York: Charles Scribner's Sons 1919.

Catalog of Victor Records. Camden, NJ: RCA Manufacturing 1936.

Cato, Bob and Greg Vitiello, Joyce Images. New York: Norton 1994.

Chapin, Schulyer, Musical Chairs: A Life in the Arts. New York: G.P. Putnam's Sons 1977.

Chusid, Irwin, The Mischievous Art of Jim Flora. Seattle: Fantagraphics Books 2004.

Clarke, Donald, Wishing on the Moon: The Life and Times of Billie Holiday. New York: Viking 1994.

Clarke, Nick, Alistair Cooke: A Biography. New York: Arcade Publishing 1999.

Clooney, Rosemary with Joan Barthel, Girl Singer: An Autobiography. New York: Doubleday 1999.

Coleman, Mark, Playback: From the Victrola to MP3, 100 Years of Music, Machines and Money. New York: Da Capo 2003.

Copland, Aaron and Vivian Perlis, Copland/1900-1942. New York: St. Martin's/Marek 1984.

Cornyn, Stan with Paul Scanlon, Exploding: The Highs, Hits, Hype, Heroes, and Hustlers of the Warner Music Group. New York: HarperCollins 2002.

Coward, Noel, The Complete Lyrics. Edited and annotated by Barry Day. Woodstock, NY: Overlook Press 1998.

Crease, Stephanie Stein, Gil Evans: Out of the Cool. Chicago: A Cappella 2002.

Dannen, Frederic, Hit Men. New York: Times Books/Random House 1992.

Davis, Clive with James Willwerth, Clive: Inside the Record Business. New York: William Morrow 1975.

Decter, Midge, An Old Wife's Tale: My Seven Decades in Love and War. New York: Regan Books 2001.

Derrida, Jacques, Acts of Literature. Edited by Derek Attridge. New York, London: Routledge 1992.

Downes, Olin, The Lure of Music. New York: Harper & Brothers 1917.

Drate, Spencer, 45 RPM: A Visual History of the Seven-Inch Record. New York: Princeton Architectural Press 2002.

Dylan, Bob, Chronicles, Volume One. New York: Simon & Schuster 2004.

Eisenberg, Evan, The Recording Angel: Explorations in Phonography. New York: McGraw-Hill 1987.

Ellington, Duke, Music Is My Mistress. New York: Da Capo 1985. (Originally published by Doubleday 1973.

Ellison, Ralph, Invisible Man. New York: Signet 1952.

_____, Shadow and Act. New York. Signet 1966.

Engel, Lehman, The American Musical Theater. New York: CBS Legacy/Macmillan 1967.

Ethnic Recordings in America. Washington DC: Library of Congress 1982.

Faulkner, William, As I Lay Dying. New York: Vintage 1964 (originally published by Random House 1930).

Feather, Leonard, The Encyclopedia of Jazz. New York: Bonanza Books 1955.

Fox, Ted, In the Groove: The People Behind the Music. New York: St. Martin's 1986.

Friedrich, Otto, Glenn Gould: A Life and Variations. New York: Random House 1989.

Friend, Leon, and Joseph Hefter, Graphic Design: A Library of Old and New Masters in the Graphic Arts. New York, London, Whittlesey House, McGraw-Hill, 1936.

Gammond, Peter, The Oxford Companion to Popular Music. New York: Oxford University Press 1991.

Gavin, James, Intimate Nights: The Golden Age of New York Cabaret. New York: Grove & Weidenfeld 1991.

Giddins, Gary, Bing Crosby: A Pocketful of Dreams. Boston: Little, Brown 2001.

Gifford, Don, The Farther Shore: A Natural History of Perception. New York: Atlantic Monthly Press 1990.

Gilbert, Douglas, Lost Chords: The Diverting Story of American Popular Songs. New York: Cooper Square Publishers 1942.

Gioia, Ted, West Coast Jazz: Modern Jazz in California 1945-1960. New York: Oxford University Press 1992.

Gitlin, Todd, Busy Being Born. San Francisco: Straight Arrow Books 1974.

_____, The Sixties: Years of Hope, Days of Rage. New York: Bantam Books 1987. Gold, Arthur and Robert Fizdale, Misia: The Life of Misia Sert. New York: Alfred A. Knopf 1980.

Goldmark, Peter C. with Lee Edson, Maverick Inventor: My Turbulent Years at CBS. New York: Saturday Review Press 1973.

Goodman, Fred, The Mansion on the Hill: Dylan, Young, Geffen, Springsteen, and the Head-on Collision of Rock and Commerce. New York: Times Books 1997.

Goodman, Peter W., Morton Gould: An American Salute. Portland, Oregon: Amadeus Press 2000.

Gourse, Leslie, Straight, No Chaser: The Life and Genius of Thelonious Monk. New York: Schirmer Books 1997.

Gracyk, Tim with Frank Hoffman, Popular American Recording Pioneers. New York: Haworth Press 2000.

Grafanola in the Classroom: Graded Catalog of Educational Records. New York: Columbia Graphopone Company (U.S.) ca. 1920.

Griffin, Nancy and Kim Masters, Hit and Run. New York: Touchstone Books 1997.

Guralnick, Peter, Searching for Robert Johnson. New York: Dutton 1989.

Hadju, David, Positively 4th Street. New York: Farrar Straus & Giroux 2001.

Halberstam, David, The Powers That Be. New York: Alfred A. Knopf 1979.

Hammond, John with Irving Townsend, John Hammond on Record. New York: Ridge Press 1977.

Handy, W.C., Father of the Blues. New York: Macmillan 1941.

Harburg, E.Y., At This Point in Rhyme. New York: Crown Publishers 1976.

Harper's Magazine Reader. New York: Bantam Books 1973.

Hayman, Joe, Cohen on the Radio. New York; Samuel French 1928.

_____, Twenty Different Adventures of Cohen on the Telephone. New York: George Sully & Company 1927.

Hazelcorn, Howard, Columbia Phonograph Companion. Woodland Hills, CA: Mulholland Press 1996.

Heller, Steven and Seymour Chwast, Graphic Style: From Victorian to Post-Modern. New York: H.N. Abrams 1988.

Hess, Dick and Marion Muller, *Dorfsman & CBS*. New York: American Showcase, Inc. 1987.

Hicock, Larry, *Castles Made of Sound*. Cambridge, MA: Da Capo 2002.

Hicks, Granville, *John Reed: The Making of a Revolutionary*. New York: Macmillan 1936.

Hills, Rust L. and Penny Chapin Hills, *How We Live*. New York: Macmillan 1968.

Hunter, Ian, *Reflections of a Rock Star*. New York: Flash Books 1976.

Huxley, Aldous, *Point Counter Point*. Normal, Illinois: Dalkey Archive Press 1996. (Originally published 1928.)

Irwin, Jane, *George Eliot's Daniel Deronda Notebooks*. Cambridge: Cambridge University Press 1996.

Ishlon, Deborah, *Girl Singer: a Two-Part Invention*. Garden City, NY: Doubleday 1960.

Johnson, James Weldon, *Black Manhattan*. New York: Atheneum 1969.

Jones, Quincy, *Q: The Autobiography of Quincy Jones*. New York: Random House 2001.

Kael, Pauline, *Kiss Kiss Bang Bang*. New York: Bantam Books 1969. Kanin, Garson, *Where It's At*. New York: Signet Books 1969.

Kahn, Ashley, *Kind of Blue*. New York: De Capo Press 2000.

Kazdin, Andrew, *Creative Lying: Glenn Gould at Work*. New York: E.P. Dutton 1989.

Kingston, Victoria, *Simon & Garfunkel: The Biography*. New York: Fromm International 1998.

Kluger, Richard, *The Paper: The Life and Death of the New York Herald Tribune*. New York: Vintage Books 1986.

Kort, Michele, *Soul Picnic*. New York: St. Martin's 2002.

Kostelanetz, Andre with Gloria Hammond, *Echoes: Memoirs of Andre Kostelanetz*. New York: Harcourt Brace Jovanovich 1981.

Laine, Frankie and Joseph F. Laredo, *That Lucky Old Son: The Autobiography of Frankie Laine*. Ventura, CA: Pathfinder Publishing 1993.

Larkin, Philip, *Required Writing: Miscellaneous Pieces 1955–1982*. London: Faber & Faber 1983.

Lasby, Clarence G., *Project Paperclip: German Scientists and the Cold War*. New York: Atheneum 1971.

Laurents, Arthur, *Original Story by Arthur Laurents: A Memoir of Broadway and Hollywood*. New York: Knopf 2000.

Lees, Gene, *Inventing Champagne: The Musical Worlds of Lerner & Loewe*. New York: St. Martin's Press 1990.

Lehmann, Stephen and Marion Faber, *Rudolf Serkin: A Life*. New York: Oxford University Press 2003.

Leighton, Isabel, *The Aspirin Age 1919-1941*. New York: Simon and Schuster 1949.

Lewis, David Levering, *When Harlem Was in Vogue*. New York: Oxford University Press 1981.

Lieberson, Goddard, *3 for Bedroom C*. New York: Doubleday 1947.

Lion, Jean Pierre, *Bix: The Definitive Biography of a Jazz Legend*. New York: Continuum 2005.

Lionni, Leo, *Between Worlds: The Autobiography of Leo Lionni*. New York: Alfred A. Knopf 1977.

Mack, Charles E. *Two Black Crows in the A.E.F.* Indianapolis: The Bobbs-Merrill Company 1928.

Malone, Bill C., *Country Music U.S.A.* Austin: University of Texas Press 1991.

Marks, Edward as told to Abbott J. Liebling, *They All Sang: from Tony Pastor to Rudy Vallee*. New York: The Viking Press 1934.

Mauro, Philip, *The Hope of Israel? What Is It?* Oak Hill, West Virginia: The Church Times ca. 1960 (originally published 1929).

Mayer, Martin, *Madison Avenue USA*. New York: Harper 1958.

McKnight-Trontz, Jennifer and Alex Steinweiss, *For the Record: The Life and Work of Alex Steinweiss*. New York: Princeton Architectural Press 2000.

Meat Loaf with David Dalton, *To Hell and Back: An Autobiography*. New York: Regan Books 1999.

Meyer, Hazel, *The Gold in Tin Pan Alley*. New York: Lippincott 1958.

Murrells, Joseph, *Million-Selling Records*. New York: Arco Publishing 1984.

Myers, Paul, *Deadly Cadenza*. New York: Vanguard Press 1986.

_____, *Deadly Sonata*. New York: Vanguard Press 1985.

_____, *Deadly Variations*. New York: Vanguard Press 1987.

_____, *Leonard Bernstein*. London: Phaidon Press Ltd. 1998.

Nemerov, Howard, *Collected Poems*. Chicago: University of Chicago Press 1977.

O'Connell, Charles, *The Other Side of the Record*. New York: Alfred A. Knopf 1947.

Official Guide to the New York World's Fair 1964/1965. New York: Time Incorporated 1964.

Oliver, Paul, *Bessie Smith*. Cranbury, NJ: Barnes 1961.

_____, *Blues Fell This Morning*. Cambridge: Cambridge University Press 1960.

Panassié, Hugues, *Hot Jazz: The Guide to Swing Music*. New York: M. Witmark & Son. 1936.

Paper, Lewis J., *Empire: William S. Paley and the Making of CBS*. New York: St. Martin's 1987.

Phillips, Caryl, *Dancing in the Dark*. New York: Alfred A. Knopf 2005.

Picker, John M., *Victorian Soundscapes*. New York: Oxford University Press 2003.

Ponselle, Rosa and James A. Drake, *Ponselle: A Singer's Life*. New York: Doubleday 1982.

Prial, Dunstan, *The Producer: John Hammond and the Soul of American Music*. New York: Farrar, Straus & Giroux 2006.

Priestley, Brian, *Jazz on Record: A History*. New York: Billboard Books 1991.

Pyron, Darden Asbury, *Liberace: An American Boy*. Chicago: Chicago University Press, 2000.

Ramsey, Frederic Jr., *A Guide to Longplay Jazz Records*. New York: Long Player Publications 1954.

Raymond, Jack, *Show Music on Record*. New York: Ungar Publishing 1982.

Roth, Philip, *Goodbye, Columbus*. Boston: Houghton Mifflin 1959.

Ryding, Erik and Rebecca Pechefsky, *Bruno Walter: A World Elsewhere*. New Haven: Yale University Press 2001.

Saarinen, Eero, *Eero Saarinen*. New York: Simon and Schuster 1971.

Santoro, Gene, *Highway 61 Revisited: The Tangled Roots of American Jazz, Blues, Rock & Country Music*. New York: Oxford University Press 2004.

Sapoznik, Henry, *Klezmer! Jewish Music from Old World to Our World*. New York: Schirmer Books 2000.

Scher, Paula, *Make It Bigger*. Princeton: Princeton Architectural Press 2002.

Schoenbrun, David, *On and Off the Air: An Informal History of CBS News*. New York: Dutton 1989.

Schonberg, Harold, *Horowitz: His Life and Music*. New York: Simon & Schuster 1992.

Shaw, Arnold, *Honkers and Shouters: The Golden Years of Rhythm & Blues*. New York: Macmillan 1978.

Sherman, Michael W. and Kurt Nauck III, *Note the Notes: An Illustrated History of the Columbia Record Label 1901–1958*. New Orleans: Monarch Record Enterprises 1998.

Shulman, Arthur and Roger Youman, *How Sweet It Was*. New York: Bonanza Books 1966.

Simon, George T., *The Big Bands*. New York: Macmillan 1967. Slater, Robert, *This ... Is CBS: A Chronicle of 60 Years*. Englewood Cliffs, NJ: Prentice-Hall 1988.

Slonimsky, Nicolas, *Music Since 1900*, Third Edition, New York: Coleman-Ross Company, Inc. 1949

Smith, Eric Ledell, *Bert Williams: A Biography of the Pioneer Black Comedian*. Jefferson, North Carolina: MacFarland 1992.

Smith, Joe, *Off the Record: An Oral History of Popular Music*. New York: Warner Books 1988.

Smith, Moses, *Koussevitsky: The Life and Times of a Great Conductor*. New York: Allen, Towne & Heath 1947.

Smith, Sally Bedell, *In All His Glory: The Life of William S. Paley*. New York: Simon & Schuster 1990.

Sobel, Robert, *RCA*. New York: Stein & Day 1986.

Spada, James, *Streisand: Her Life*. New York: Crown 1995.

Spaeth, Sigmund, *Read 'Em and Weep: The Songs You Forgot to Remember*. Garden City, NY: Doubleday, Page & Company 1927.

Stearns, Marshall, *The Story of Jazz*. New York: Oxford University Press 1958.

Stone, Desmond, *Alec Wilder in Spite of Himself*. New York: Oxford University Press 1996.

Szwed, John, *So What: The Life of Miles Davis*. New York: Simon & Schuster 2002.

Tate, Alfred O., *Edison's Open Door: The Life Story of Thomas Edison, a Great Individualist, by Alfred O. Tate, His Private Secretary*. New York: E.P. Dutton 1938.

Terrace, Vincent, *The Complete Encyclopedia of Television Programs 1947-1979*. Cranbury, NJ: A.S. Barnes 1979.

Thomas, Bob, *King Cohn*. New York: G. P. Putnam's Sons 1967.

Thomson, Virgil, *Virgil Thomson*. New York: Alfred A. Knopf 1966.

Thorgerson, Storm and Aubrey Powell, *100 Best Album Covers: The Stories Behind the Sleeves*. New York: DK Publishing 1999.

Time Capsule/1929. New York: Time Incorporated 1967.

Toohey, John L., *A History of the Pulitzer Prize Plays*. New York: Citadel Press 1967.

Townsend, Irving, *The Less Expensive Spread: The Delights and Dilemmas of a Weekend Cowboy*. New York: Dial 1971.

_____, *Separate Lifetimes*. Exeter, New Hampshire: J.N. Townsend Publishing 1986.

Trow, George W. S., *Within the Context of No Context*. Boston: Little, Brown 1981.

Trow's General Directory of the Boroughs of Manhattan and Bronx, City of New York 1861-1935.

Tucker, Sophie, written in collaboration with Dorothy Giles, *Some of These Days: The Autobiography of Sophie Tucker*. [No publisher listed] 1945.

Tynan, Kenneth, *Tynan Left and Right*. New York: Athenium 1967.

Vitiello, Greg and Bob Cato, *Joyce Images*. New York: Norton 1994.

Waldo, George C., editor, *History of Bridgeport and Vicinity*. New York-Chicago: The S.J. Clarke Publishing Company 1917.

Ward, Ed and Geoffrey Stokes and Ken Tucker, *Rock of Ages: The Rolling Stone History of Rock & Roll*. New York: Rolling Stone Press/Summit Books 1986.

Wein, George with Nate Chinen, *Myself Among Others: A Life in Music*. Cambridge, Massachusetts: Da Capo 2003. West, Bill, *Remington Arms & History*. Published by author, Azusa, CA. 1970.

Whitburn, Joel, *Top Pop Albums 1955-1985*. Menomonee Falls, Wisconsin: Record Research Inc. 1985.

White, Timothy, *Long Ago and Far Away: James Taylor: His Life and Music*. London, New York: Omnibus Press 2002.

Whiteside, Jonny, *Cry: The Johnnie Ray Story*. New York: Barricade Books 1994.

Who's Who in American Jewry. New York: Jewish Biographical Bureau 1938.

Wilder, Alec, *Letters I Never Mailed*. Boston: Little, Brown 1975.

Wilson, Edmund, *The Thirties*. New York: Farrar Straus & Giroux 1980.

Wonderful Inventions: Motion Pictures, Broadcasting, and Recorded Sound at the Library of Congress. Edited by Iris Newsom. Washington: Library of Congress 1985.

Yetnikoff, Walter, with David Ritz, *Howling at the Moon*. New York: Random House 2004.

Zadan, Craig, *Sondheim & Co*. New York: Macmillan 1974.

Zorina, Vera, *Zorina*. New York: Farrar Straus & Giroux 1986.

INDEX

Note: page numbers followed by "n" indicate endnotes